THE

FORDS

AN AMERICAN EPIC

Also by the authors

THE ROCKEFELLERS
An American Dynasty

THE KENNEDYS
An American Drama

DESTRUCTIVE GENERATION
Second Thoughts about the Sixties

THE

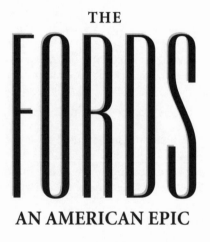

AN AMERICAN EPIC

PETER COLLIER
DAVID HOROWITZ

ENCOUNTER BOOKS
SAN FRANCISCO

Paperback published in 2002 by Encounter Books, an activity of Encounter for
Culture and Education, Inc., a nonprofit tax exempt corporation.

Encounter Books website address: www.encounterbooks.com

Manufactured in the United States and printed on acid-free paper.

The paper used in this publication meets the minimum requirements of
ANSI/NISO Z39.48-1992 (R 1997)(*Permanence of Paper*).

Library of Congress Cataloging-in-Publication Data

Collier, Peter.
    The Fords : an American epic / Peter Collier and David Horowitz.
    p. cm.
    Bibliography : p.
    Includes index.
    ISBN 1-893554-32-5 (alk. paper)
    1. Ford, Henry, 1863-1947—Family.   2. Ford Family.   3. Ford Motor
Company—History.   4. Automobile industry and trade—United States—History. I. Horowitz, David. II. Title.

    TL140.F6C65 1987
    338.7'6292'0922—dc19
    [B]87-18948

    10 9 8 7 6 5 4 3 2 1

CONTENTS

PROLOGUE:
DETROIT, JUNE 4, 1896

I T WAS AFTER MIDNIGHT when a light summer mist started to fall outside the backyard workshop and Henry Ford began putting the final touches on the peculiar-looking machine which had obsessed him, in one form or another, all his adult life. On most other evenings, Felix Julien, the old man who lived in the flat next door to the Fords and had cleared out his half of the shed to give the machine more space to grow, would have been there, too, sitting in a corner of the shed, watching the painstaking assembly in silent awe. In fact, Ford had often arrived home from his daytime job as chief mechanic at Detroit's Edison Illuminating Company to find Julien sitting alone in the shadows, staring at the odd contraption slowly taking shape, impatient for him to hurry through dinner and get to work. But now, on this night of nights, the old man had unaccountably decided to go to bed early and so he missed the last act of the great drama.

It was almost 2 A.M. when Henry and his friend Jim Bishop finished work. Although he was haggard from having gone two nights without sleep, Ford's recessed gray eyes flashed with excitement. His invention was finally ready for a test. But as he began to maneuver it toward the door there was a revelation of the myopia everyone who knew him accepted as a paradoxical part of his visionary nature: the machine was too big to fit through the doors of the shop. Without hesitating, Ford seized a maul and began to knock out an opening in the brick walls.

Henry rolled the vehicle he later referred to as "the baby carriage"—a light chassis on four bicycle wheels—out into the night. The metaphor came naturally: it was as if the womb of his creativity, gravid since boyhood, was finally opening. Ford would tell what happened next thousands of times in the coming years, never tiring of the repetition and always speaking in the tones of wonderment most men used to describe the birth of their firstborn. As it became worn smooth with frequent retelling, the story eventually came to have the understated simplicity of a Creation myth:

> It was raining. Mrs. Ford threw a cloak over her shoulders and came outside. Mr. Bishop had his bicycle ready to ride ahead and warn drivers of horse-drawn vehicles—if indeed any were to be met with at such an hour. I set the choke and

1

spun the flywheel. As the motor roared and sputtered to life, I climbed aboard and started off. The car bumped along the cobblestones of the alley, as Mr. Bishop rode ahead on the bicycle to warn any horse-drawn vehicles. We went down Grand River Avenue to Washington Boulevard. Then the car stopped. We discovered that one of the ignitors had failed. When we had repaired it, we started the car again and drove back home. Both Mr. Bishop and I went off to bed for a few winks of sleep. Then Mrs. Ford served us breakfast and off we went to work as usual.

The following day Henry took his wife for her first ride. Clara Ford had sacrificed, too, during the past few years, begging the neighborhood hardware store to increase its fifteen-dollar limit on credit purchases so that her husband could buy nuts and bolts, occasionally helping with his experiment on the gasoline engine, and worrying about his health as he worked in the freezing backyard shop night after night. Now she climbed up onto the narrow seat of the machine grimly clutching their two-year-old son, Edsel, her prim round face and heart-shaped mouth almost obscured by her bonnet and veil. By the time they had returned from the harrowing trip over the cobble-stone streets, their landlord, William Wreford, was standing in front of the Bagley Avenue house, indignant at the damage that had been done to the backyard shed the night before. But after Henry showed him the horseless carriage and breathlessly explained its wonders, Wreford was so completely won over that he not only rejected Ford's offer to repair the damaged brick but insisted that the opening be widened to allow the quadricycle easy entry and exit.

The rest of the week Ford drove all through Detroit. Jim Bishop bicycled ahead of him as a flagman, stopping at saloons and stores to tell people to come out and hold their horses. One day the little vehicle knocked a man down; by the time Ford had turned off the engine and climbed down, the victim lay on the ground, caught between the front and rear wheels. Ford leaned over and discussed the problem with him. Should he start the engine again and finish driving over him, or should he try to move the car? Finally another man appeared and helped Ford pick up the quadricycle and move it off the prostrate man, who stood up, dusted himself off, accepted Ford's apologies, and walked off, victim of the first recorded auto accident.

Seeing the strange little car coughing and wheezing along the narrow streets during the next few days, people would sometimes yell out the nickname his obsessive drive to build a horseless carriage had earned Ford—"Crazy Henry!" But whenever he stopped, crowds immediately surrounded his invention, examining it with such enthusiasm that he finally had to begin chaining it to lightposts for fear they would carry it off. "Yes, crazy," he sometimes said, tapping his temple with a forefinger. "Crazy like a fox."

On the first weekend after the birth of his car, Henry drove out to the family farmstead where he had been born, Clara sitting beside him holding Edsel, who still wore baby's dresses. The deep ruts worn into the road during the spring rains had not yet been filled in and the little car tilted, the wheels of one side sinking down in the tracks worn by wagon wheels, while those of the other side rode higher up on the center of the road. With several stops along the way to adjust the engine, the ten-mile trip took better than an hour. When they arrived, Clara and Edsel dismounted so that Henry could give rides to his family. One of his sisters, Margaret, always remembered "the great speed and the sense of bewilderment" she experienced while in his car, although after the ride was over she felt that this was just "another interesting toy" her clever brother had built.

The only one who refused a ride was Henry's father, William. His son's desertion of the farm had been a disheartening experience for him. Unlike his brothers, Henry seemed incapable of settling down, because of the obsession with the horseless carriage; at thirty-three, he was already on the edge of middle age, a failure by his father's definition and by anyone else's except his own. William Ford stood silently in the doorway watching the noisy vehicle kick up dust. Soon neighbors began crossing the fields to see what was causing all the commotion; eventually a dozen or so were standing there looking laconically at the car and then sympathetically at William Ford as if commiserating with him for Crazy Henry's strange behavior.

Finally Henry said to Clara, "Let's get out of here," and headed his invention back to Detroit.

Back home on Bagley Avenue, he was photographed atop the little quadricycle. Fragile and handmade, with a doorbell for a horn and a tiller for a steering mechanism, it looked like some new mutant species of machine. Wearing a derby and a mustache, Ford stared back ironically at the camera. Master of a new creation, an Adam filled with innocence although he had just created the original sin of the modern industrial world, he was about to step into and forever alter history.

For the next forty-five years, long after he had driven the automobile into the heart of American life, Ford would remain an enigma—to some a simple man erroneously assumed to be complex, to others a complex man whose genius was to project a misleading aura of simplicity. For a time he would be the archetypal optimist embodying the hope and commitment to human perfectibility which had been a motif of American life since the Transcendentalists; later he would become the quintessential crank, destroying those he loved best and reacting bitterly to the modern world he, perhaps more than any other man, had made. Whatever his outlook, however, he would always be a representative American, able to drive Presidents off the front pages of the nation's papers by his words and deeds until the day he died.

Henry Ford had finally built his first automobile. Still to come was the company which would be the lengthened shadow of this man—an institution which would long outlast him. The Ford Motor Company would enrich the members of his family, but would wound them, too. It would make them preeminent in the country's industrial aristocracy, but also divide them from themselves and one another and make the development of the Ford dynasty to come at once a comedy, a melodrama and a tragedy.

PART I

CRAZY HENRY

It will take a hundred years to tell whether he helped us or hurt us, but he certainly didn't leave us where he found us.

—Will Rogers

ONE

L ATER IN HIS LIFE, AFTER he had become the world's richest and most controversial man, Ford would hire genealogists to help him search for his origins. John D. Rockefeller and other of the great industrialists who had attained sudden riches and power in America also looked for their past, anxious to see if this New World success had been prefigured by a coat of arms on the Continent. But Ford wasn't interested in finding some noble ancestor. In fact, he was scornful of such motives; he wanted the answers to more profound questions: What was the heritage that had produced him? Did it somehow account for his accomplishment? Who was he?

The inquiry centered on Ireland. There, at the height of the potato famine of 1847, his grandparents John and Thomasina Ford were evicted from an Englishman's estate in County Cork called "Madame" where they had worked as tenant farmers. Their eldest son, William, who, at twenty-one, was almost on his own when the famine struck, convinced them that there was no future in Ireland, even if the Great Hunger should someday end. And so, early in the spring, they made the decision to emigrate. After urging them forward and helping them get ready, William packed his carpenter's tools onto the cart of a cousin, who drove him to Bandon Station, where he caught a train for Queenstown and joined his family in boarding a packet ship headed for the United States. He was of medium height, with a thewy strength, gray agate eyes and a serious demeanor. In the Irish manner he was called a "boy" because his father was still alive, but he was very much the leader of their party, which included not only his parents but also his brothers Henry and Samuel and his sisters Rebecca, Jane, Nancy and Mary.

Like other desperate Irish packed into the dread "coffin ships," the Fords suffered a tragedy when Thomasina became ill and died and was buried at sea. But they were different from most of the immigrants who would define the Irish experience in America. For one thing, they were Protestant, descendants of English from Somersetshire who had been settled in Ireland by Queen Elizabeth in the late sixteenth century as part of a program to pacify that trouble-some nation. Tradition had it that soon after arriving in County Cork these English yeomen—Ford ancestors among them—had put up a sign on the outskirts of Bandon with this message:

A Turk, a Jew or an Atheist
May live in this town but no Papist.

The fact that relations would never be good with the indigenous Irish was suggested by the rejoinder that was soon scrawled underneath that couplet:

He that wrote these lines did write them well
As the same is written on the gates of Hell.

Outsiders even in the homeland they were fleeing, people like the Fords would not maintain a sentimental attachment to the Old Country and its ways when they reached the New World. Their survival strategy was a fierce adaptability. Another thing that set William Ford and his family apart from the Catholic Irish packed beside them in their ship was that they were not merely fleeing tragedy. They were also traveling toward something, an ideal of prosperity and independence that made America more than a refuge from tragedy. They had experienced the promise of this new land vicariously in the letters of William's uncles Samuel and George, who had journeyed to the United States fifteen years earlier, letters which told of wild forests, individual rights and cheap land.

But the most important difference between the Fords and the masses of Irishmen fleeing the Old Country was that they did not stop at Boston or New York, falling into the wage slavery that went along with teeming tenement life and the sordid political machinery that seemed its only antidote. Instead they went by oxcart and then by boat down the Erie Canal, and finally on foot to Detroit, and from there to the small neighboring town of Dearborn, determined to buy a piece of the new land and achieve self-sufficiency and rugged individualism.

The legendary uncles Samuel and George Ford were there to greet them, well settled and land rich. When they had arrived in 1832, Dearborn was still a dense wilderness filled with deer, wolves and bear, as well as Indians who would appear as if by magic in clearings, sometimes walking curiously into the settlers' log houses, fingering their possessions for a moment and then disappearing as quickly as they had come. Even in 1847 Dearborn still had a frontier atmosphere, although the town was served by its own railroad and also by a plank road called Michigan Avenue which ultimately stretched to Chicago. By the time William arrived, there were dozens of Fords in the Dearborn area, Samuel and George having had large families in which the same names—an Old World device for binding a clan together—recurred so often that geography, location, appearance and paternity were used to distinguish one of them from another. As one member of the family said later on, "There was Big Sam, Little Sam, Uncle Sam, William's Sam, Henry's Sam; there was Red-Headed George, George on the Hill, Foxy George; there was Uncle Henry, Hank, Uncle Will, John's William, and so on." Newcomer William was dubbed William South because the eighty acres his father bought immediately upon their arrival was below the land of a Cousin William who became known as William North.

Soon after the family had established itself in Dearborn, William's younger brother Henry left, lured by the prospect of quick riches to the gold fields of California, where he laboriously scrawled out letters shuddering with memories of the one Michigan winter he had scarcely had time to experience: "i like the Climate in California so well on a Count of no Snow in the winter and Pleasant in the Summer." The romance and excitement of his brother's letters tugged at William, but as firstborn he had a duty to the family. He worked with his father to clear his land, and also helped pay off the $350 the eighty acres had cost by hiring himself out as a carpenter to the Michigan Central Railroad. Only after the family had sent roots down into the fertile soil of Dearborn did William begin to think of himself and begin looking for ways to make money to buy a plot of his own. By the late 1850s he was working as a handyman for his neighbor and countryman Patrick O'Hern.

Originally from Fairlane, County Cork, O'Hern had come to America about the same time as the first Fords, George and Samuel, although his route—joining the British Army, deserting in Quebec, and taking the ferry to Detroit—had been less direct. O'Hern and his wife, Margaret, were relatively well off in terms of land (their holdings were assessed at $1,000 as of 1850), but were impoverished in family, having been unable to have children of their own. Hearing of four children who were orphaned when their father, William Litogot, an immigrant from Belgium, died in a fall off a house he was roofing, they adopted one of them, three-year-old Mary, and raised her as their own.

A teenager by the time William Ford began working for her adoptive parents, Mary Litogot O'Hern soon blossomed into an attractive and accomplished young woman who had "brown hair and dark eyes," as her daughter Margaret later wrote, "and a manner and vivacity which were well remembered by all who knew her." These qualities made an impression on William, who, although fourteen years older, waited for Mary to graduate from the local Scotch Settlement School and then asked her to marry him. They posed for pictures soon after the wedding in 1861. She was young, her proud face conveying a sense of hidden strength and withheld emotions. William was lean and handsome, with curly brindle-colored hair and beard, and eyes so clear they looked as though they had been implanted by taxidermy.

William Ford got not only a wife from the marriage, but property as well. Patrick O'Hern sold him ninety-one of his prime acres at a low price with the understanding that he and his wife would live with the newlyweds. To make this easier, O'Hern also helped William raise a handsome two-story house. Mary planted evergreens in the front yard, a pear tree along one side and an apple orchard on the other. A large willow at the rear shaded the house from the noonday sun.

By the time they set up housekeeping, Dearborn was growing up. Its horizon was smudged with haze made by Detroit's factories and by the smokestacks of the freighters moving nonstop between Lake Huron and Lake Erie with copper ore from Michigan's upper peninsula and timber from its forest primeval—cargoes ultimately worth a billion dollars more than all the gold taken out of California by the Forty-Niners. There was a less visible but nonetheless keenly felt excitement in the air because of the war between the states. William's cousin Henry, son of Samuel Ford, played the fife in the Dearborn band, whose members wore Phil Sheridan mustaches or Abe Lincoln beards. Mary's two Litogot brothers, also grown up from orphanhood, joined the Union Army and fought side by side at the battle of Fredericksburg, where one of them was killed and the other was wounded when a bullet hit the stock of his rifle and took off two fingers at the first knuckle.

William Ford spent the war years at home developing his farm. He planted hay and wheat; raised pigs, cows and horses; grew his own vegetables and smoked his own meats; tapped maples for sugar and carpentered for pay. As a sign of his prosperity, he was the first Ford in Dearborn able to afford a buggy with a top on it. Entering middle age, he had become a churchwarden and justice of the peace, the sort of steady civic figure named to a committee that Detroiters sent to Cleveland to investigate how that city had made the transition from horse-drawn trolleys to electric streetcars.

He was also a father. Mary's first child, a boy, had died at birth early in 1862. Her next pregnancy, coming to term the following summer, was therefore a time of anxiety. On the night of July 30, 1863, William got up and rode out into the full moon to get the midwife, Granny Holmes, and a few hours later a son was born, named Henry after William's brother, who had long since given up prospecting for gold but continued to live in California. Other children followed for William—John, Margaret, Jane, William and Robert, the boys' names particularly linking them with the extended Ford family. But none of the others would give him the pride and heartache of his firstborn.

Henry Ford's earliest recollections involved his father:

> The first thing I remember in my life is my father taking my brother John and myself to see a bird's nest under a large oak…. John was so young he could not walk. Father carried him. I being two years older could run along with them…. I remember the nest with four eggs and also the bird and hearing its song…. The next thing I remember is having the ague the summer I was six in 1869. I would be all right in the forenoon and would have fever, chills and shakes in the afternoon. I remember seeing the red head woodpecker, swallow, blue birds and robins. My grandfather [O'Hern] told me the names of all the birds.

William Ford figured prominently in Henry's dreams and memories, and gave him a profound love of nature that would last throughout Henry's long and complex life. His father was the solid object Henry would repeatedly run into, defining himself by the collision. But his mother was in much sharper focus. Henry was struck by her tart, aphoristic reactions to life— always perceptive, always emphasizing responsibility and accomplishment. "You must earn the right to play," Mary Litogot Ford would say. "The best fun follows a duty done." Her lectures made such an impact on him that Henry carried them with him the rest of his life, often quoting them verbatim to people who asked what his mother had been like. ("Life will give you many unpleasant tasks to do," went one of her well-remembered maxims, "and your duty will be hard and disagreeable and painful to you at times, but you must do it. You may have pity on others, but you must not pity yourself.") Henry later said that Mary Ford was "of that rarest type, one who so loved her children that she did not care whether they loved her. What I mean by this is that she would do whatever she considered necessary for our welfare even if she thereby lost our good will."

She taught him to read long before he began trudging off each day to Dearborn's one-room Scotch Settlement School. But he was no prodigy. In fact, his attention wandered and he often got into trouble, as his best friend Edsel Ruddiman, who had the desk next to his, recalled in a letter written when they were both young adults: "Do you remember how we used to write notes to each other in school? And the alphabet we devised so that the teacher couldn't read it…. I remember distinctly one time Miss Proctor kept us there on the back seat in the corner and gave us a lecture on being better boys. I am afraid she labored in vain to reform two such hard cases as we are." The only aspect of his schooling that seemed to make an impact on Ford was the lessons in the McGuffey Reader, which taught through exercises promoting a sharp sense of duty so like his mother's, and through maxims which, like hers, stuck into the conscience like little pins.

Because of his mother's discipline, Henry became quiet and relentlessly inward. As he remembered it later on, his approach to life as a youngster was almost mystical, and he always tried to discover epiphanies of meaning about an experience. He remembered being taught to box, for instance, by a Canadian fighter who worked for his father as a laborer. The man made a head of rags which he put on a fencepost and painted with human features, then taught Henry and his brothers to punch for maximum effect on the temple just above the ear. Soon there was a chance to implement what Henry had learned. "A boy in school kicked my lunch over and when I kicked his foot he started chasing me," Henry later recalled. "A woman leaning out of her window having seen what had happened yelled, 'You lick that boy or I will.' At that I turned and hit the boy in the temple. He fell kicking to the ground. Never did I use that blow again."

Another thing he learned early was that he didn't like farm life. Doing his chores grudgingly, Henry gave in to the slightest distraction. Characteristically transforming this aversion into a "philosophy," he said precociously of the farm, "Considering the results there is altogether too much work." He was interested in other questions—what made things happen, what made things tick. Observing the teakettle boiling on the wood stove, he asked his father what would happen if the hole where the steam came out were to be plugged up. Not satisfied by William Ford's perfunctory response, he eventually got his answer when he plugged the kettle and it exploded, spewing scalding water onto the walls and sending out shrapnel that cut his cheek. He engaged in similar "experiments" at school which also led to disaster. In one traumatic case, he built a steam turbine and set it up alongside the school fence. It achieved a high RPM, but then the boiler blew up, a huge piece of it hitting one boy in the stomach and knocking him down; while he was being revived the school fence caught fire and burned, and William Ford had to replace it later on.

Less dangerous to the body than these experiments with steam energy but more hazardous to the soul was his fascination with watches, which he began taking apart and reassembling after a friend, on the way to church one Sunday, bet him he couldn't fix his timepiece. On that occasion Henry went home, took the watch apart, cleaned it and put it back together again. He won his bet but missed church.

William Ford approved of Henry's interest in mechanics to the degree that this discipline had practical application on the farm; but he disapproved of that which seemed to be "pure science," although he did let his son set up a workbench in the house. The other children in the family treated their brother's obsession with ridicule. When they got new toys, especially those with wind-up mechanisms, they wouldn't let him touch them because they knew he'd want to take them apart. A neighbor said, "Every clock in the Ford home shuddered when it saw him coming." Henry felt about machinery the way his brothers John and William felt about sports, often making the all-day walk to Detroit simply to visit the hardware stores and look over the watch-making tools. People called him a "queer duck." Only his mother seemed to understand and sympathize with him. Praising him as a "born mechanic," she let him have her darning needles to make into screwdrivers for his watch repairing, and corset stays to transform into tweezers.

When Henry was thirteen, William Ford went to the Centennial Exposition in Philadelphia, the first time he had been away from home since arriving in America more than twenty years earlier. Henry questioned him closely when he returned from this celebration of American ingenuity and innovation, which had galvanized amateur inventors and Horatio Alger types all over the country. His father told about seeing Machinery Hall with its steam engines, locomotives and power lathes. But he didn't mention the one thing that probably would have interested Henry most—a side exhibit of internal-combustion engines running on illuminating gas. One of these engines operated a demonstration printing press; another pumped the exhibit's aquarium.

This same year, Mary Ford became pregnant for the ninth time. Early the next spring she went into labor. It was the first time William had called in a doctor instead of the midwife Granny Holmes. The baby didn't make it through the long and troubled delivery. After it was buried, Mary herself became sick and feverish, and a few days later she, too, died.

William's sister Rebecca, now Rebecca Flaherty, came from Detroit to help out the bereaved family. But something had gone out of Henry's life. Using a metaphor embodying a depth of feeling that only someone familiar with his mechanical bent could have appreciated, he said that the Ford house was now "like a watch without a mainspring." Realizing just how different he was from the rest of them now that there was no one to tell him that this difference was a strength, he withdrew deeper into himself. He held his father responsible for his mother's death, conceiving a grudge he would hold throughout the alternating periods of conflict and truce that comprised the rest of their lives. ("You see that home?" he asked a Litogot cousin over sixty years later when he was showing him the Ford homestead. "That's my mother's home. My father just walked into that place. That belonged to my mother.") He was also repelled by the fondness for drink William Ford had brought with him from Ireland. He isolated himself from his father and his family. Without anyone to draw him out, he became wary and guarded, saying to one teenage friend who had remarked on these qualities, "It is not necessary to expose your inner self to anyone." He scarcely talked anymore, instead spending hours at his workbench after the rest of the family was asleep, fondling tools made from Mary Ford's sewing implements.

Not long after his mother's death, Henry was riding in silence with his father in the wagon on the way to Detroit when suddenly the horse reared as they came upon a strange and, for Henry at least, wonderful sight: a steam engine crawling along the road. Such devices were not uncommon on local farms, where they were used for threshing or for sawing logs, but the ones Henry had seen before were portable engines and boilers pulled from job to job by teams of horses. This one was moving under its own power, driven by a chain from the engine to the rear wheels of the cart on which it was mounted. As the engineer stopped the machine to keep from frightening William Ford's horses, Henry jumped out of the wagon and "fairly flew" to the steam engine, pouring out questions which the engineer, a kindred spirit, tried to answer. Even after he and his father had driven on, Henry later recalled, he couldn't get the sight out of his mind. At home he tried to make a replica of the engine, fashioning a body of wood and using a five-gallon oilcan as a boiler. It was an odd but characteristic way of trying to salve his desperate grief: looking to fill with a machine the void his mother's death had left in his life.

After this experience, Henry was only serving time on the farm—an exile waiting to find a home away from the place where he lived. William Ford found that invoking the memory of his dead wife by saying such things as "Your mother would have wanted you to do this" worked with all the children except Henry. He had little control over his oldest son and said sadly, "Henry is not much of a farmer, he's a tinkerer." Paying less and less attention to school, Henry spent his time taking watches apart, allowing himself to be drawn into their mechanical perfection, and dreaming of their works magnified in giant engines of locomotion and power. He wanted to go to Detroit where the machines were. In arguments designed to dissuade him from this ambition, William Ford would cite his own example—how he had gone from poor immigrant to prosperous farmer. ("The great miracle of America," his daughter Margaret later said, "seemed to him to be that here was a place where a man could own the land upon which he lived and worked.") He would contrast the cleanliness and morality of rural life with the filth and depravity of the city, a Jeffersonian vision of America as a nation of self-sufficient farmers whose existence was in dramatic opposition to that of the oppressed masses packed into the decaying metropolises of Europe. Henry internalized this dichotomy—eventually it would become the cornerstone of his own philosophy—but for the time being he wanted to exempt his own life from its logic.

He spent some time with his only close friend, Edsel Ruddiman, but for the most part when he wasn't tinkering he occupied himself by taking solitary walks through the stands of virgin forest still remaining on the banks of the Rouge River, which ran through Dearborn. One morning in 1880, not long after he had turned seventeen, he took a different kind of walk. After setting out for school with his brothers John and Will, he didn't turn off for the schoolhouse with them as usual, but this time kept going, eventually catching a ride in a farmer's wagon heading down Michigan Avenue to Detroit. In someone else it might have been a whim. But as his sister Margaret later said, "My feeling is that Henry planned this step very carefully, as he always had a motive and reason for his actions." He didn't come home for the rest of the week. Finally his father went looking for him and found that he was staying at his Aunt Rebecca's house. William tried to get him to return to the farm, but Henry told him that he had gotten a job at the Michigan Car Company, a manufacturer of railroad boxcars, and that he wanted to stay where he was. William had no choice but to yield: "All right, if that's the way you feel. But come home when you change your mind or when you feel like coming." He went back to the farm knowing that his family life had suffered another amputation.

THE MICHIGAN CAR COMPANY was large—nearly two thousand employees. Henry's starting wage, $1.10 a day, was fairly high, but he was fired after six days on the job when he quickly solved a problem in the construction process which a number of employees had worked all day trying to correct, thus embarrassing them and their foreman. The lesson reinforced the suspiciousness that had seeped into his personality after his mother's death. As he said later, "I learned then not to tell all you knew."

If the rest of the country was creeping toward the machine age, Detroit was entering it in one step. Skillful workers were highly regarded, and Henry had no difficulty finding another job, this time with James Flower and Brothers, a small machine shop. He worked as a roustabout, making valves on a small milling machine, and learned skills he had not yet mastered, such as reading blueprints.

But he was paid only $2.50 a week, and since room and meals at the boardinghouse he had moved into cost $3.50 he had to make up the deficit by moonlighting in a jewelry shop doing watch repair for fifty cents a night.

After a few months with Flower Brothers he moved on to Detroit Dry Dock Engine Works, the largest of the city's shipbuilding firms—an attractive prospect because it allowed him to work with motors. Sitting by himself at lunchtime, he read mechanics magazines. He had not stopped thinking about locomotion since the vision of the road machine five years earlier. Most of the engines he read about were also powered by steam, but one article that caught his eye described the wonders of a gasoline engine built by Dr. Friedrich Otto in Germany. Along with the author of the article, Henry thought it was simply a "curiosity," but he filed it away in his memory nonetheless.

Even though he had served no formal apprenticeship, his boyhood tinkering had made him an accomplished machinist. Someone with his know-how could have had his choice of the machine shops springing up all over the city. But, as he told his sister Margaret, who was the closest to a confidant he had, he intended to be a manager, not an employee. He wanted whatever he made to be done cheaply but well and in volume. For a time he thought of going into the watchmaking business, but changed his mind after calculating that he would have to sell 600,000 watches a year simply to break even. Instead he wrote away for catalogues of machinery and read Faraday's treatise on the steam engine. He wanted a source of power to use in his experiments, but Detroit was only partly electrified, so he built a miniature turbine and attached it to a water spigot in the backyard of his boardinghouse. Using water pressure, it developed one-half horsepower, enough to run a lathe. It was his first practical engine.

No enterprise offered him a focus for his ambition. In his indecision about what to do with his life, he gave in to his father's constant pressure to come back to the farm, returning in 1882 after two years on his own. However, he made it clear that returning to Dearborn did not mean that he would become a farmer as William Ford hoped. He was through with that forever and made clear his intention never again to pick up a shovel or milk a cow. Although living in his father's house, he continued his city interests by doing part-time work for the Westinghouse Engine Company as an expert in steam engines such as the one that had seized his imagination three years earlier. But instead of being an awestruck spectator, he was now an "engineer," driving these machines from farm to farm when someone rented them to help with the harvest. Still considering himself a future entrepreneur, Henry also enrolled in night courses at Goldsmith Business College in Detroit, going there twice a week to study shorthand, typing and accounting.

It was an atypical moment of glide in a life that up until that time had seemed filled with busy purpose. That others perceived a lack of commitment is suggested by a letter he received from a young woman named Mary Catherine Noble whom he had known during his time in the city. Inviting him to return to Detroit to hear the popular preacher Dwight L. Moody, she wrote:

Henry perhaps you will get helped there, as you may never be if you stay away.

> And just think how much better it will be for you to go to a little trouble to come in and do all you can to be led into the right way than to just let it go by and perhaps never come into the band of soldiers for Christ.... If you begin your studying as a Christian, then you will do your work with more satisfaction. I tell you Henry, an educated Christian is one of the grandest objects on the face of the earth.

He didn't act on this request, although he was beginning to realize that his single minded courtship of the machine had made his social life dreary. To improve his prospects he took dancing lessons, concentrating on the waltz and the polka. Then, late in 1884, he met a young woman named Clara Bryant from nearby Greenfield township at a harvest moon dance. Daughter of a prosperous farmer who had served in the state legislature, Clara had been a friend of his sister Margaret for some time, but Henry had been so self-absorbed that he hadn't noticed her. Now that he had come up for air from his romance with the machine, he saw her as if for the first time. He liked her looks—the intriguing combination of a "friendly" mouth and a determined, even stubborn jaw; the luxurious chestnut hair everyone agreed was the chief point of her beauty. But the earnestness of this proper young woman, her pragmatism and lack of frivolity, was for him her most outstanding feature.

One of their first meetings occurred at the Martindale House, a leading local hotel. Henry never forgot the play of soft light thrown by candles in the wall sconces on Clara's face, or the fact that she sat out two dances with him as he shyly showed her the unusual double-dialed watch he had made which told both railroad and "sun" time. Someone else might have humored him and then cruelly caricatured his self-absorption behind his back, but not Clara. Describing Henry to her mother after returning home that evening, she simply said, "He's different. He didn't just chatter about the music or talk about people. He's a serious-minded person." One who usually didn't make snap decisions, Henry was also impressed, telling his sister Margaret that he had realized after thirty seconds of conversation that Clara Bryant was the girl for him.

They danced only with each other a few weeks later on New Year's Eve. All during that winter Henry took Clara for chaperoned sleigh rides in the new green "cutter" he had bought and escorted her on ice-skating parties. The next summer they took buggy rides and went on picnics. They joined the Bayview Reading Circle, a group modeled on the Chautauqua Movement, although their true purpose was not so much edification as getting an opportunity to spend evenings together. The climactic event in their courtship came the following year when Henry took one of the Westinghouse steam engines out on a stump-removal project. Clara sat up on the driver's seat with him while he talked about what he believed was the coming machine revolution. She was the first person since his mother who had expressed unconditional confidence in him. Making her a disciple to his vision of the future, Henry began calling her "the Believer." The depth of his feelings were suggested by the rough-hewn card he sent the following Valentine's Day:

Dear Clara,

    I again take the pleasure of writing you a few lines. It seems like a year since i seen you. It don't seem mutch like cutter rideing to night does it but i guess we will have some more sleghing.... Clara Dear, you can not imagine what pleasure it gives me to think that i have at last found one so loveing kind and true as you are and i hope we will always have good success. Well i shall have to Close wishing you all the Joys of the year and kind Good Night.

        May Floweretts of love around you be twined
            And the Sunshine
        Of Peace Shed it joy's o'er your Minde
        From one that Dearly loves you

                        H.

When he saw that his son was in love William Ford tried one last time to set the hook that would make him a farmer, by offering him an eighty-acre parcel he had acquired a few years earlier which was still called "the Moir place" after its former owners. There was a little house and thick stands of harvestable hardwoods. Henry quickly moved in, set up a sawmill and began cutting and milling the black oak, maple and elm. To William Ford's dismay, however, he also immediately built a shop and resumed his tinkering, this time with gasoline engines as well as steam.

Early in the spring of 1887 Henry was returning from church with his sister Margaret, discussing the text of the sermon, "Hitch your wagon to a star," when he noted that the horse was having difficulty pulling the buggy over the rutted roads. "Hitch your wagon to a star: that's what I'm going to do," he said. It was a subtle pun, but Margaret immediately got his meaning: "This 'star' was going to be some sort of transportation which would let people get around easier." Until that time, although he had emotionally distanced himself from the farm, Henry had been thinking only of building some sort of vehicle that would help make the farmer's tasks easier; now he began considering some kind of motorized transportation that would replace the horse and allow people to move from the farm to the city.

When he saved enough money from his lumber operation he asked Clara to marry him. She immediately said she would. The ceremony took place at the Bryant house on April 11, 1888. Sitting for a portrait in a formal blue suit and high collar, his hair parted in the middle as if by calipers and wisping above his ears in little wings, Henry had a distant look in his recessed eyes and a quizzical smile on his thin mouth. Clara had piled her hair on her head and wore an antique brooch her mother had brought when she emigrated from England. She had made the elegant white wedding dress herself.

After they had said their vows before an Episcopalian minister the couple cut the cake with their initials "H.F. and C.B." entwined in frosting. They went into the bedroom to look at the gifts, among them a clock which William Ford had given, perhaps an ironic reference to his son's well-known fixation with timepieces. As they sat on the bed examining the presents, Henry and Clara suddenly slipped off the edge of the mattress, causing a loud crash as they landed on the floor. The guests came rushing in to see what had happened and found them buried in gifts and unable to stop laughing.

The newlyweds skipped a honeymoon and drove to the Moir place in a buggy, setting up housekeeping there while waiting to build their new home, whose lumber Henry cut, milled and seasoned himself. Because of his growing reputation as a mechanic, he was sometimes hired to go out of town to help farmers with his steam machine. If the work involved an overnight stay, he wrote morose letters home to his "dear little wife." ("I will never go so far from you again," he wrote in a typical phrase. "I'm *so* lonesome for you darling.") Often his jobs required a day trip to Detroit, where he could visit machine shops and listen to the shop talk, which sometimes involved the horseless carriages being built in Europe. About this time Ford himself built two small steam engines, one of which traveled some forty feet before stopping; the other didn't go at all.

Those who knew him well felt that Henry was happier than he had been at any time since his mother's death. But while he enjoyed the predictable pleasures of domestic life in the new house, where he and Clara were now living, he also felt that time was running out. The timber on the land his father had given him would someday be exhausted; when that happened he would have no choice but to begin removing the stumps and planting a farm. During one of his trips to Detroit in 1891 he saw something that intensified his struggle to escape this fate. It was a gasoline engine at a soda-bottling plant, and it struck his imagination with the same force that the steam thresher had exerted on him years earlier. He came back filled with excitement and waited for the right moment to make a proposal to Clara.

One evening when they were sitting in their parlor, she chording on the piano and he standing above her humming absently, he blurted it out. "I've been on the wrong track," he said. "What I would like to do is make an engine that will run by gasoline and have it do the work of a horse." As she looked up at him uncomprehendingly, he quickly snatched a piece of sheet music and sketched out a rough conception of an engine harnessed to wheels. "But I can't do it out here on the farm. I need money for tools and money to pay for other things."

She saw what he was driving at and, after a moment's hesitation, agreed that a move to the city might be necessary sometime in the future. Then he told her that he had already been offered a job at the Detroit Edison Company. In shock, she paused for a moment and then said that she would go with him to Detroit.

On September 25, 1888, they loaded the last of their furniture into a wagon and started off. Clara's Bryant relatives noticed that the tears in her eyes belied her frozen smile. William Ford watched sadly from the sidelines, aware that he had lost his son for good. Henry alone was happy, jabbering and waving his arms. He could point to no significant achievement in nearly a decade of tinkering: one experimental "road engine" that had gone a few feet, another that hadn't gone at all; motors that had never started; disassembled watches and clocks that hadn't been put back together. Yet he was cheerful. He was finally off to seek his fortune.

THEY MOVED INTO A HOUSE on John R Street a few blocks from the Detroit Edison substation, where Henry immediately began working a twelve-hour night shift beginning at six o'clock in the evening. Clara, lonely during the daytime when he slept, looked forward to the visits her father-in-law made every couple of weeks to check on the son he thought of now more than ever as wayward. When Henry's brother John stopped with produce after delivering milk to stores in Detroit, Clara would sometimes ask him to give her a ride back out to the farm, where she would stay until Henry walked out to get her after work.

If she felt like an immigrant in a strange land, Henry was perfectly happy in Detroit and at home at Edison with the dynamos and the steam generators. The company was the leading power producer in Detroit, serving 1,200 of the 1,650 residents of the city who had electricity in their homes. Ford rose rapidly, getting a transfer to the main powerhouse and raises from his starting salary of $45 a month which put him at $75 per month not long after taking the job. Because he was always reading articles in mechanics magazines and sketching out crude diagrams, his fellow workers soon discovered his private fixation with horseless carriages. Every night he went out with them for a short break at the horse-drawn lunchwagon that pulled up outside the plant. The others would sit around with their coffee and doughnuts kidding him about what he was making now: "Have you got a piece of an engine in your pocket, Henry?" Sometimes he would join in, giving back as good as he got. But more often than not he would stand there with an enigmatic smile one man remembered as resembling Mona Lisa's. A few of his co-workers said he was a "queer duck," the dread epithet of his childhood, but most regarded him as a "good fellow" whose taste for practical jokes often had a sharp edge—as on the occasion when he nailed onto the plank floor the street shoes of one of the other workers who always left them strewn on the floor of the plant after changing to his work boots.

To some he might be just another laborer; to others he was an adventurer sailing into new worlds. His cousin Clyde Ford, a teenager when Henry moved away from the farm, regarded him as an almost heroic figure who became the focus of the family's weekly Saturday trip to Detroit. They would leave their horses at Reynaud's store, a meeting place for the farmers of Dearborn, and from there take the horse-drawn trolley the rest of the way "downtown," stopping at the Edison plant. "Invariably my father would call at the 'Lightning plant' to have a visit with Henry, who would show him the engines, dynamos and all the switchboards…how smooth everything worked, how free of vibration. There was only one thing that could enter my mind at the time, and that was that Henry Ford was the man responsible for all this and somehow had created it all."

Henry was soon made chief engineer at $1,000 a year. He was on call even when he wasn't at the plant, and slept with his clothing laid out like a fireman's, in case of an emergency. His rising stature was confirmed when the Detroit YMCA asked him to teach a course for aspiring machinists. Yet he continued with his own work, taking advantage of the fact that he now had the right to use the Edison Company machine shop when he was off duty. The mechanics magazines he read made him feel a new sense of urgency. The machine revolution to which he had dedicated himself was beginning to unfold with gathering speed, especially in Europe.

Gottlieb Daimler had demonstrated a crude gas car on the streets of Paris in 1886, and the French firm of Panhard et Levasson, using his patents, had evolved a basic design for the automobile. (The French term had taken hold in America, despite xenophobes' preference for "motor carriage.") But if the auto was European by birth, it was about to become American by adoption. The United States had a larger self-contained population of potential users than France or Germany, and a longer tradition of innovation and experimentation in precision machinery by Eli Whitney, Elias Howe and others. There was an active industry for bicycles and carriages, devices which had laid important technological groundwork for the automobile. (Bicycles in particular had paved the way, not only by creating innovations such as the pneumatic tire, but also, in the way that a rider's legs moved up and down like pistons, suggesting a moving diagram for an engine.) Early in 1889 in Springfield, Massachusetts, Charles and Frank Duryea built and drove the first gasoline-operated vehicle in the country. America had taken its first tentative step toward automotive domination.

Henry continued his experiments, on the trailing edge of this ferment, but most of his attention was focused on Clara, who had become pregnant. On November 6, 1893, he summoned Dr. William McDonald, a "modern" young physician who made his rounds on bicycle instead of by horse and buggy. McDonald was impressed by how brave Clara was during the delivery and how stoical Henry was while waiting downstairs for news. When the doctor told him he had a boy, Ford said that he planned to name him Edsel after his old high-school friend Edsel Ruddiman.

Shortly after the child was born the Fords moved to Bagley Avenue, occupying one side of a two-family house. Henry began experimenting in a shed in the backyard because Alexander Dow, head of Edison Illuminating in Detroit, was fearful of gasoline being used in his shop. Occasionally Henry brought the engine he was developing into the kitchen so that Clara could help him. Once he propped it on the kitchen sink and asked her to feed in gasoline while he spun the flywheel. The engine roared into life with a horrible noise and a cloud of black smoke, and Clara was sure that the baby sleeping in the next room would be awakened and then asphyxiated.

What began to take shape in the backyard shed was unlike anything else produced, far lighter than the Duryea brothers' cumbersome vehicle, much more streamlined than their wagonlike contrivance. Ford and his friend Jim Bishop tried to give the vehicle a light and mobile look—a chain drive like the bicycle, and a bicycle seat which could be removed and replaced by a carriage seat holding two persons.

Clara worried about his being in the shop night after night. She was humiliated to have to beg credit, yet she was certain that Henry would succeed, and made wry jokes about their straitened circumstances by showing family members her "Irish apron," which she reversed when it became soiled on one side. After the baby was asleep for the night she often wrapped a shawl around her shoulders and went out to watch the work, joining their elderly neighbor Felix

Julien, who sat in a corner transfixed by what was taking shape out of the pile of tin and steel parts. She was as protective of the invention as if it were partly hers. Even when her favorite sister Kate visited, Clara refused to take her out to the shed lest she ridicule Henry's work. "Henry is making something," she said enigmatically, "and maybe someday I'll tell you about it."

TWO

A N ACQUAINTANCE RECALLED DRIVING with Ford in his little quadricycle when he was in one of his mischievous moods. A man who didn't get out of their way quickly enough was deliberately chased by Ford, who sounded the doorbell he used as a primitive horn and bumped the car aggressively over the cobblestones until the pedestrian had scrambled up onto the wood-plank sidewalk. Continuing on his way as the pedestrian glared at him, Ford saw that a couple of dozen curious bicyclists were following him. Quickly he drove around the block and let his passenger off in front of a stable with instructions to open the stable door as Ford drove off. When he came around the block again, he drove quickly into the stable and was locking the door when the bicyclists showed up.

"Mister, can you tell us where that horseless carriage went?" one of them asked.

"Yes, right up that alley," Ford said, pointing, and he chuckled as the cyclists took off on their wild-goose chase.

His car brought out strange qualities in Ford, qualities that made people grin and continue to refer to him as "Crazy Henry." George Holmes, grandson of the midwife who had delivered him, said, "Everyone thought Henry was crazier than heck with that darned car of his; they used to say, 'Here comes that crazy Henry Ford.' "

But while he was ridiculed on the streets of Detroit, he continued to be highly esteemed as a mechanic and supervisor at the Edison Company, where he now made $140 a month. In August 1896, a few weeks after his historic ride, his supervisor, Alexander Dow, invited Henry to accompany him to New York for the annual convention of the Association of Edison Illuminating Companies. It was the first time he had been away from home since his marriage. Clara took Edsel to visit her parents in Dearborn to escape Detroit's sweltering summer, writing her "darling husband" as soon as he got there:

> I suppose there is a letter waiting for me but Pa is going to the city tomorrow and I will get it. And I will be so glad. I was never so anxious to hear from you as I have been this week.... It is 3 pm now and the baby is having a glorious time on the lawn. They have been cutting the grass and he enjoys it. I can tell you I asked him if he would like to send Papa a kiss and he said, "Yes, paper him over

one." Just like one of his speeches, isn't it? I hope you have been well and enjoyed your trip. I suppose you have seen great sights.... I hope things at the station will be all right when you come back so you can come out, for I want you awful bad...

Henry had indeed seen great sights. But they had to do with a man, not a city. The climax of the convention was a banquet at Long Island's Oriental Hotel. There he saw the great Edison himself, surrounded by colleagues and sycophants who talked loudly and made dramatic gestures to penetrate his partial deafness. The talk turned to the use of storage batteries to run electric cars, an area in which Edison himself had experimented. Alexander Dow pointed at Ford and said with amusement, "This young fellow has made some sort of car he runs with gasoline." Cupping an ear, Edison asked to hear more about it. Henry came and sat beside him, taking out a pencil and making a sketch on the back of the menu as he explained how his invention ran. Suddenly Edison took his hand away from his ear and slapped Ford on the back.

"Young man, you have the right idea," he said. "Keep right at it." Then he turned to the skeptical Dow and said, "This car has an advantage over the electric car because it supplies its own power."

Coming from the sage of Menlo Park, this statement had the force of divine revelation. Henry said later, "That was the inspiration I needed." On his return home to the lonely Clara he said, "Well, you won't be seeing much of me for the next year." Then he sold his first automobile for two hundred dollars and began working on another one during his free time.

Detroit's Mayor William Maybury had become acquainted with Ford and interested in his work. He issued him a driver's license (an award in the pioneering days of automobiles, rather than a necessity), and also began gathering backers for a commercial venture. On August 5, 1899, the mayor and some friends put up $15,000 to form the Detroit Automobile Company, with Henry as "chief engineer" and partner. It was a development which sharpened Ford's conflict with his boss Alexander Dow. "Electricity, yes, there's the coming thing," Dow said, "but gas—no." He offered Ford a position as general superintendent of Edison on the condition that he give up his experiments with gasoline-driven vehicles and instead devote himself to "useful" work. This was an attitude that raised Henry's hackles, reminding him of his father's scorn for his experiments at an earlier time in his life. He quit his job at Edison on August 15, 1899, after nearly nine years. He was thirty-six years old now and stepping once again into the unknown.

A PROTOTYPE OF THE DETROIT Automobile Company's vehicle was ready on January 12, 1900—a "delivery wagon" eventually donated to the local postmaster for mail runs. But Henry seemed more interested in romancing curious members of the local press than in putting the car into production. There was a brief article in the *Detroit Journal* by a reporter who did not find anything especially revolutionary in the machine. "The body is built like any of the better class of its kind drawn about town by horses," he wrote, "and the whole thing is so constructed as to almost wholly conceal its motive power." The reporter for the rival *News Tribune*, on the other hand, was struck by exactly how new and different this machine was. In a long article he wrote breathlessly about a ride Henry gave him:

> There has always been at each decisive period in the world's history some voice, some note, that represents the prevailing power. There was a time when the supreme cry of authority was the lion's roar. Then came the voice of men.... The shriek of the steam whistle has for several generations been the compelling power of civilization. And now, finally, there was heard in the streets of Detroit the murmur of this newest and most perfect of forces, the automobile rushing along at the rate of 25 miles an hour. What kind of noise is it? It is not like any other sound in the world.... [It is] a long mellow gurgling sound, not harsh, not unrhythmical, a note that falls with pleasure on the ear.... And the sooner you hear its chuck! chuck! the sooner you will be in touch with civilization's newest voice.

Ford had no doubt that buyers would react with similar zeal. But the assembly process was painstakingly slow, with each car having to be put together by hand and requiring so many small adjustments to body and engine that it was virtually custom-made. Ford wasn't satisfied with this situation or with the fact that the backers of the company didn't give him room to experiment with and perfect the assembly process, but rather cared only about immediate sales. In November, a little more than nine months after beginning the business, he resigned and the company folded.

For most people it would have been a time of taking stock. It was nine years since Henry had uprooted Clara and moved to Detroit; it had taken him five years to build his first car and almost five more to build an improved version, which he failed to get into production. During this time the automobile had ceased to be a futuristic device people gawked at and dismissed as irrelevant to their lives. Aristocrats like the Whitneys, the Vanderbilts and the Belmonts had made the car a chic item by holding an "Automobile Festival" in Newport, Rhode Island, in the summer of 1899 at which cars garlanded with flowers were driven from one elegant home to another. Soon Theodore Roosevelt would be the first President to ride in a car, although he would be followed along the Hartford parade route by a horse-drawn carriage just in case there was trouble, and would be praised the next day by one newspaper editor for "the display of courage typical of him." Four thousand cars had already been manufactured in America. It was true that three fourths of them were steam and electric, and that New England, center of this new technology, was still dominant in the fledgling industry. But with the growing influence of the gasoline engine, the center of gravity was switching to the Midwest. Alexander Winton was building cars in Cleveland and setting speed records with them. Ransom Olds, who had begun his company the same year the

Detroit Automobile Company was started, was building a popular little car in Lansing and was about to move to Detroit. In 1901 he had gotten a local businessman named Roy Chapin to drive an Olds from Detroit to New York for an auto show there, and the following year he sold 750 cars in Manhattan alone.

Although Henry was without a company at the time of this great leap forward, he didn't quit or panic; he simply moved in another direction, deciding to make himself a household name, in Detroit at least, by building a racing car. Racing was the perfect metaphor: he was indeed involved in a race against others' innovations and against time itself.

He wasn't under any illusions about what he had to do. Racing might have excited other auto pioneers, but it offended the pragmatic aspect of Henry's character. He considered it an improper use of the automobile, as he did the attempt of the rich to make the car a toy. "I never really thought much of racing," he said later on, "but following the bicycle, manufacturers had the notion that winning a race on a track told the public something about the merits of an automobile—although I can hardly imagine any test that would tell less. But as others were doing it, I too had to do it…. If an automobile were going to be known for speed, then I was going to make an automobile that would be known wherever speed was known."

He also claimed in retrospect that he was "never happier" than in this period between building his first car and forming the Ford Motor Company. "I was learning something every day and what I was learning was of use to myself and everybody else." But in fact he went through some difficult times. To save money, he and Clara moved in with his father, who had come to live in Detroit when farming became too hard for him. But while he had succumbed to the city, William Ford was still skeptical of his son's ambition, saying of the automobile company, "You'll never make a go of it. They'll never sell."

That Henry had swallowed his pride to the extent of becoming dependent on his father again showed that this was a time of groping for him. His uncertainty had a spiritual as well as a professional dimension. Oliver Barthel, a mechanic who helped Ford build his racer during these difficult months, later recalled that they spent almost as much time talking philosophy as engineering. Both were shocked by McKinley's assassination; the day of his burial, work stopped for a moment and Barthel pulled out a book he had been reading called *A Short View of the Great Questions* which dealt with theology, reincarnation and similar subjects. Ford asked to see the book and began to read it intensely, pursuing the lines of print with a grimy index finger and trying to grasp unfamiliar words by silent movements of his lips. Barthel understood for the first time in their acquaintance that Ford had spiritual longings that remained for the most part inarticulate; that he was starving for ideas to go along with the blueprints he spent his waking hours studying.

He had escaped from the farm, but it remained his sole point of reference. He was an almanac of superstitions and prejudices. In the forefront of new technological ideas, he still worried when black cats crossed his path and about inadvertently passing under ladders. If he put a sock on inside out in the morning, he wouldn't change it. Whenever he saw a red-haired person he immediately looked for a white horse and vice versa, believing for some reason that the two went together. On Friday the thirteenth it was difficult to get him out of his house.

Yet he understood that he was limited, and that in his pellmell rush to establish himself and his car he had never taken time to develop his intellectual resources. At this time he began buying little notebooks by the gross, always carrying one in his pocket not only to sketch hasty designs of motors or axles, but also to try to transcend his seventh-grade education. He would take a word that he had heard and break it into syllables ("meta-physic," "meta-physical," "meta-physician"). He also wrote down little sayings—some of them commonplace thoughts, others self-conscious attempts to find the lucid depths of Emerson, whose "Self Reliance" and other essays Ford read over and over during this period of his life: "There is a gold mine in the sky." "Prayers are a disease of the will." "Wheat 6 ft. tall in China, what about it?" "You've got to keep going and keep doing."

His family was his one source of stability during this difficult time. Clara never stopped believing in him. Edsel was very much the beloved only child, and Henry was unusually close to him in defiance of Victorian notions that fathers should be remote and authoritarian figures. He joined Clara in dressing the boy up in various costumes for the camera. He was physically close to his son, nuzzling and kissing him in front of the photographer. When Clara took Edsel to visit relatives in Kentucky, Henry wrote to him:

> My dear little son,
>   I am well and I hope you are ok. Say do they carry whisky jugs in their blouse in Ky? Hope you are having a good time and will be back soon for i am lonesome.
>   Your loving Pa-Pa

The affection was reciprocal. Even when Henry was gone overnight Edsel wrote him lonely letters that showed how dependent he was on the triangular relationship that joined the two of them and Clara:

> Dear Papa,
>   I thought i would write a few lines. Did you get there alright. I think Mama is getting what I have got. Mama thinks I am getting the whooping cough. I went out only once tonight. A goodbye.
>   Your loveing little boy
>   Edsel Ford

Edsel had Clara's dark hair and eyes, but he looked like Henry and had his father's medium build and long-leggedness. A childhood friend later recalled him as being quiet and reserved, and somewhat bewildered by his parents' overprotection: "We had a peach tree, apple trees, a regular little orchard. I always liked to climb trees and I found that Edsel had never climbed one and I thought it was time he did. So I got him up in a tree and he fell down and broke his arm."

Henry decided that the boy had an artistic temperament. He went to a craftsman friend named Charles Beebe and said, "Charley, Edsel is interested in music, especially in the violin. I'd like to have him take lessons, but I can't afford the violin." The two of them struck a deal by which Beebe made a violin on credit. Edsel sawed away doggedly on the instrument for several months and then abandoned it.

A diary Clara kept around the time the three of them were forced to move in with William Ford captured the tone of their family life.

> Sat Jan 5, 1901—Took Henry his lunch every night.
>
> Jan 7—commenced to pack to move. Where?
>
> Jan 8—Went to depot this morning to meet Eva [one of her sisters] who came home from Kate's [another sister]. Then moved down to Grandpa Ford's. Got there just as men got there with furniture.
>
> Jan 9—worked all day getting settled. Very tired. Tonight Edsel found lots of his playthings he had not seen for quite some time. Decorated rocking horse with Xmas tree trimmings.
>
> Jan 11—Snowed all day. Edsel got soaking wet. He and Grandpa played checkers. Edsel cheated awful and beat every time. Went to bed so full of laughs he could not say his prayers.
>
> Jan 12—Went down town and got Edsel's shoes and leggings. Went into Shaffer's store to hear the music. After supper we tried to learn Grandpa to play cards. Henry got pattents [*sic*] of entire machine.
>
> Jan 15—Edsel and I went to Sunday School. Came home. Had dinner. Then Henry fixed Edsel's old sleigh to take him coasting. But Edsel said sleigh no good. He was sent upstairs for punishment for his pride. Said he was sorry.
>
> Jan 19—Henry bought Edsel a new coaster.
>
> Jan 20—Henry and Edsel went coasting on the boulevard...
>
> Jan 29—Met Henry at the street car. He had a bad headache. Put brown paper and vinegar on his head—mustard plaster on back of neck.

A few days later, Clara went with Edsel to Jasper to visit her sister Kate, who was about to have a baby, while Henry stayed behind in Detroit working on the racing car. Her February 8, 1901, letter shows that the love between her and Henry was still strong after ten years of marriage:

> Dear Husband
>
>   ...I have thought of you so much today. What are you doing? I suppose it seems strange for you to be staying there without us. Are you lonely? I am. I suppose I will have it bad if I have to stay two weeks...

She wrote again on February 13. Her letter makes it easy to imagine what Henry was writing to her:

...I cannot get home Saturday. Too bad isn't it sweetheart. You can't want me anymore than I want you. But it would be very selfish for both of us if I was to come. Kate is in bed helpless and until I get someone to help her I cannot leave here. Such is life...

Kate, to whom Clara had devoted all this attention, gave a thumbnail sketch of the little family: "Edsel is growing quite a little. Clara is awfully fleshy. But Henry is awfully thin—he's been working around the clock getting the machine ready."

The "machine" she referred to was the racing car. If Henry had worked and worried himself thin over the vehicle, it was because he knew that his future rested on its performance. Soon the big day was at hand—October 10, 1901. The race took place at the Detroit Fairgrounds. The prize was $1,000 and a beautiful crystal punch bowl which had been picked out, it was rumored, because auto pioneer and world speed record holder Alexander Winton felt that it would look good in the bay window of his living room.

The first race involved steam cars, the winning entry making a mile in 1:52. Next the electrics lumbered around the track, taking nearly four minutes to complete a mile. Finally it was time for the big moment—the twenty-five-mile race for the speedy gasoline-driven cars. By post time some of the contestants had been forced to pull out, notably William Vanderbilt, who had hoped to race the Red Devil, his French-built car which was said to have cost some $15,000. Winton and William Murray were still in the field along with Ford. But Murray's car developed an oil leak as it was being brought to the starting line and had to be withdrawn. It was Ford against Winton.

At the starting gun, Winton zoomed out quickly. Henry started slowly, swinging wide on the turns but pulling up on the straightaway. For better than half the race he trailed, with dirt from Winton's tires spraying his face and body. But then he began to pull up, finally passing Winton and roaring out ahead to cross the finish line first. Henry got out of the racer muttering to himself, "Boy, I'll never do that again! I was scared to death." But it had been exciting for Clara. She captured her experience in a letter she wrote to her brother Melvin:

> Henry has been covering himself with glory and dust.... I wish you could have seen him. Also heard the cheering when he passed Winton. The people went wild. One man threw his hat up and when it came down he stomped on it. Another man had to hit his wife on the head to keep her from going off at the handle.

But there was also a cautionary note in her euphoria: "The race has advertised him far and wide. The next thing will be to make some money out of it. I'm afraid it will be a hard struggle. You know rich men want it all."

Henry had no choice but to try these rich men again. And on November 30, 1901, a group of backers headed by William H. Murphy who had seen the race invested $30,000 in the Henry Ford Company. Given a few shares of stock in the company and the title "engineer," Henry hoped to improve the family's standard of living. Edsel for one was getting impatient, writing a letter on Christmas Eve 1901:

> Dear Santa Claus
>   I haven't had any Christmas tree in 4 years. And I have broken all my trimmings. And I want some more. I want a pair of rollar skates. And a book. I can't think of anything more. I want you to think of something.
>   Good by,
>   Edsel Ford

But the new company was doomed to a crib death. Feeling that he had not been given an adequate stake in the business, Henry held back. He began by ironically calling the owners "the millionaires" but was soon venomously referring to them as "parasites." Oliver Barthel, the old friend who had come into the company with him, later said: "He wanted another racing car built, but Mr. Murphy, spokesman for the five millionaires, put his foot down.... They wanted a car for production. Ford insisted on having a racing car, but Mr. Murphy instructed me not to lay one out. So, contrary to his instructions, Mr. Ford and I worked nights..." Annoyed by Ford's stubbornness, the investors brought in famed Detroit engineer and designer Henry Leland. It was a confrontation between an educated craftsman (Leland had built devices able to tool parts to within a tolerance of 1/100,000th of an inch) and an inspired trial-and-error mechanic. In March 1902 Henry resigned, declining to put himself "under orders" to Leland or anybody else. As part of the settlement, he got $900, the blueprints for his next racer and the agreement that the concern could no longer use his name. Leland took over the company and began to produce a car he called the Cadillac.

By 1903 most Americans had heard of the automobile but never seen one. In Detroit, however, the car was an idea whose time was rapidly coming. The atmosphere of the town was reminiscent of the Gold Rush, a fury of automotive wildcatting based on the certain knowledge that fortunes would be made and lost in the next few years. Detroit's old families tracing their descent back to the forefathers who came to America under the banner of Louis XIV watched in amazement as a new "gasoline aristocracy" emerged almost overnight.

In 1900 thirty-eight new companies began production, another forty-seven the following year, and fifty-seven more in 1903. But others were falling by the wayside. Twenty-seven companies failed in 1903, thirty-seven more in 1904. Already in the field were Franklin, Pierce, Locomobile, Packard, Stanley—names to conjure with in the future. In 1903 a former carriage maker named William Durant bought the Buick Company and made it the centerpiece in a grandiose plan to assemble the combine that would eventually become General Motors. Ransom Olds stole a march on all the producers with his vision of a cheap small car—the curved-dash, two-seater Oldsmobile cost-ing $650 "including mudguards," a friendly and familiar car of the sort that inspired popular songs.

At this historic moment, Henry continued to put his efforts into racing, hoping that a fast car would attract potential investors. He built the "999," a low and rakish vehicle named after the New York train that had made a record run to Chicago. Argued out of driving it by Clara, he hired a daredevil bicyclist named Barney Oldfield for the special five-mile Challenge Cup race. Once again the opponent was Alexander Winton. Oldfield had only a week to learn to drive.

Shortly before the race, Henry became worried about the risks and asked Oldfield to pull out, but the driver replied with the bravado he would carry with him into a brilliant racing career, "Well, this chariot may kill me, but they will say afterwards that I was going like hell when it took me over the bank." The car had to be towed to the track for fear that the formidable sound of its engine would frighten horses if it were driven through town.

As the race began, Oldfield sprinted out to an immediate lead. Winton tried to move up, but the 999 quickly pulled away. Oldfield's winning time for five miles was 5:28. (A few weeks later he would set a world's record for the mile in 1:01.) Winning the race had the desired effect of putting Ford back in business. The day after the victory a local reporter wrote: "Mr. Ford's name has hitherto been connected with his fast speed freaks, but he is preparing to put a 'family horse' on the market. He has it practically completed, and in con-nection with a well known Detroit businessman is now looking for a suitable location for a factory."

The businessman mentioned was Alexander Malcomson, the first backer Henry had found who believed without reservation in his genius. A restless, energetic Scot whose severe prelate's face was framed with mutton-chop whiskers, Malcomson was a self-made man who had become the dominant coal merchant in Detroit after buying out several competitors. He was not only a shrewd entrepreneur who had made a small fortune, but also a plunger who had lost a great deal of money in various schemes, including one involving the manufacture of iceboxes. Both sides of him, the business-man and the gambler, were attracted to Ford.

They set up a plant on Mack Avenue and placed an order for 650 engines, transmissions and axles at $250 each from John and Horace Dodge, brothers who had one of the best machine shops in the Midwest. Orders were also placed with a local carriage company for wooden bodies at $52 each and with the Hartford Rubber Company for tires at $40 a set. Then Malcomson set out to raise money to help him finance these purchases. One of the first people he approached was Charles Bennett of the successful Daisy Air Rifle Company. Bennett was enthusiastic about the new car and talked of assem-bling it at the Daisy plant in Plymouth, Michigan. (There was even some talk of calling it "the Daisy.") But his lawyers feared that a failure of the automo-bile company would jeopardize Daisy stockholders' equity in their own company, and so the deal fell through, although Bennett decided to invest personally. Next Malcomson solicited a banker friend named John Gray.

"Invest in a horseless carriage?" the influential Gray snorted. "Assinine folly."

Malcomson replied, "Put up some money and I'll guarantee it anytime within a year."

Gray agreed, joining Bennett in putting up $5,000. Horace Rackham and John Anderson, attorneys who worked for Malcomson collecting bad debts, put up the same amount. Anderson wrote his father a letter conveying his excitement about the opportunity to make an investment of such "high character":

> Mr. Ford, of this city, is recognized throughout the country as one of the best automobile mechanical experts in the United States. From the very beginning he has been interested in their construction and development. Years ago he constructed a racing machine which was a wonder.... I simply mention this to indicate his reputation as his name is widely known in automobile circles everywhere and is consequently a very valuable and favorable asset to any automobile company.... Horace is going to put in all he can raise and I too want to do the same if I can because I honestly believe it is a wonderful opportunity and a chance not likely to occur again.... [It is] one of the most promising and surest industrial investments that could be made. At a conservative estimate profits will be fifty percent . . .

Shortly after this letter, the Ford Motor Company was formed, Malcomson and Ford sharing 51 percent of the stock between them. Ten workmen were hired at $1.50 a day and put to work at the Mack Avenue plant. Henry Ford was in business with his Model A—a two-cylinder car developing 8 horsepower and going up to thirty miles an hour.

MALCOMSON WAS EXACTLY WHAT Ford needed at this point in his career—a solid businessman of good reputation able to attract capital and also to deal with suppliers like the Dodge brothers, who were not only tough bargainers but also hard-drinking men who had been known to pull pistols during Detroit barroom arguments. In the public estimation, the reliable businessman Malcomson made a good balance with the obsessed mechanic Ford, who already had two strikes against him because of the previous companies that had failed. But Malcomson and Ford couldn't have done it alone. At the beginning of the new enterprise, they hired two other individuals who made a difference.

One was engineer Childe Harold Wills, who always introduced himself as "C.H.," never volunteering what the initials stood for. It was hard for somebody to be Byronic in the hard world of machine shops, but Wills had that quality as well as the name. He was tall and elegant, with an intense personality and an inclination toward dissipation. He had started as an apprentice in the Detroit Laboratory Company, soon becoming a journeyman toolmaker. While working he took night courses in engineering, chemistry and metallurgy.

By the time Ford met him in 1902, Wills had made a name for himself in the infant auto industry as an engineer whose gifts far exceeded the ability of any company to utilize them. Ford had hired him first for the doomed Henry Ford Company and taken him along when he left that venture, realizing that Wills would be indispensable in designing a racer. They had worked nights in a room on the fourth floor above a Detroit machine shop, drawing blueprints for the car. When their fingers became too cold to hold pencils any longer, they had put on boxing gloves and flailed away at each other to get warm. After the 999, they worked in close harmony on the prototype for the Ford Motor Company's new Model A. Upon finishing that design they realized that the new car needed a logo. Imitating the distinctive capital "F" in Henry's signature, Wills wrote out "Ford" in script, and they decided to use it as the insignia on the radiator cap.

If Wills' abilities as a designer complemented Ford's intuitive flashes and embodied them in tangible form, James Couzens gave the business side of the new enterprise an equally solid and predictable structure. Couzens was Canadian, his father having decided as a young Londoner that England was "finished" and that the United States was the coming nation, although he never got past Ontario upon emigrating. Couzens was born there in 1872 with a caul, which in some places signified evil but in his town meant good luck. (His mother kept it in a little hand-sewn sack which she eventually gave to his wife when he married.) At the age of eighteen he got a job with the Michigan Central Railroad in Detroit as a car checker. Malcomson hired him in 1895 as a bookkeeper and clerk.

Squat and pug-faced, Couzens, whom enemies accused of having the personality as well as the features of a bulldog, had become Malcomson's general counselor by 1903 and was involved in the origins of the Ford Motor Company. At an early negotiating session over the price of car bodies, he had surprised John Dodge by blurting out in response to some proposal, "I won't stand for that!" Dodge snapped, "Who the hell are you?" Malcomson intervened, saying, "That's all right, Couzens is my adviser in this." Convinced from the outset that the new company would strike it rich, Couzens had been desperate to make an investment for himself. He got Malcomson to advance him $500 and take a note for $1,500 to go along with the $400 from his savings and $100 of his spinster sister's money, for a total of $2,500 in stock.

Others might be put off by Couzen's icy formality, but Ford shrewdly saw what an asset such a man could become. He insisted on personally driving him home from the first organizational meeting of the Ford Motor Company in his odd, tiller-steered runabout. In the middle of a laconic conversation about salary, he looked at Couzens and said, "What do you think we ought to ask from those fellows?" It was a hidden invitation to form an alliance that bypassed Malcomson and the other investors and to see the new enterprise as one which was comprised of a few "producers" like themselves whose interests might not always coincide with those of the "coupon clippers." There was a perfect chemistry between the severe Couzens and the more affable but equally withheld Ford, who remarked to him on that drive home, "It is a mistake to make or have too strong attachments, because it weakens your will and character."

THE ENGINES OF THE fiRST Ford cars were loaded onto a wagon at the Dodge brothers' machine shop and then pulled by a team of horses to the Mack Avenue plant of the Ford Motor Company. They were carried inside and placed on blocks, where they were greased and wired and then given spark plugs, dry cells and a spark coil. The cars were road-tested with used bodies and wheels, then were brought back, cleaned and furnished with new bodies and wheels to ready them for shipment.

The first advertisement Couzens wrote for a general audience stressed the Model A's prudent utility: "Our purpose is to construct an automobile specially designed for everyday wear and tear...an automobile which will attain to a sufficient speed to satisfy the average person without acquiring any of the breakneck velocities which are so universally condemned." The copy he wrote for *Motor World*, on the other hand, reminded readers of the Ford racer's high performance: "The most reliable machine in the world, a two-cylinder car of ample power for the steepest hills and the muddiest roads, built to stand the severest strains. The same genius which conceived the world's record maker—the '999'—has made possible the production of a thoroughly practical car at a moderate price."

Although the first Model A's sold for $850, demand was strong from the outset, and Ford, Couzens and Wills often had to join the workmen in helping crate the finished cars for shipment to dealers by rail. After six months of operation, the company was able to declare a 10 percent dividend and begin work on the following year's car, the Model C, which sold for $800. In addition, there were two other cars in the Ford line—the Model F touring car at $1,000 and the more luxurious Model B four-cylinder at $2,000. Ford himself was disturbed by the two expensive models: the per-unit profit on each of them was large, but fewer of them were sold. About the time they were being introduced, one of the employees at the Mack Avenue plant, with whom he was driving downtown, remarked to him that automobiles were surely the coming means of transportation. "That's right," Ford replied pointedly, "if the manufacturer does his part and makes the cars practically free of trouble and lowers the price so more people can buy them." He was disturbed that the company bearing his own name seemed to be doing quite the opposite.

His irritation was augmented by Malcomson's insistence that there had to be a publicity event to remind the public about Ford cars and to drum up enthusiasm for the more expensive models. Nonetheless, he reluctantly agreed to one more race—this time against the clock instead of another car. In the dead of winter, he readied the Arrow, twin of the 999, for a one-mile straightaway course on the frozen surface of Lake St. Clair. Barney Oldfield was not available this time; Ford had to do it himself. Clara was there on the day of the race, so still in the bitter cold that she looked like a statue; eleven-year-old Edsel was beside her, jumping up and down to keep his blood circulating. Harold Wills was present, languidly tinkering with the racer's engine and then standing back and shrugging at Ford when it was fine-tuned. Another Ford Motor Company employee, Ed "Spider" Huff, had been conscripted to ride as copilot.

Later on Ford called this run across the frozen lake the most frightening experience of his life:

> That ice was seamed with fissures which I knew were going to mean trouble the moment I got up speed. But there was nothing to do but to go through with the trial, and I let the old "Arrow" out. With every fissure the car leaped into the air. I never knew how it was coming down. When I wasn't up in the air, I was skidding, but somehow I stayed topside up and on the course, making a record that went all over the world.

Bringing the buffeting car to a stop, he was pale and shaken, but he had done a mile in thirty-six seconds. It was a world's record; it was also a rite of passage. Determined to own what he had just risked his life for, he would now fight all the harder to control the company. It would also make him more committed in his insistence that the future lay with a cheap and dependable car that could be sold in volume, an idea which had become his equivalent of an industrial Holy Grail. To celebrate the fact that he was still alive after the record run on Lake St. Clair, Ford took Wills and Spider Huff to the Hotel Chesterfield for a dinner of muskrats.

Malcomson was right: as a result of the publicity surrounding Ford's daring ride, the new models were well received. In June 1905 alone the company had $356,000 in sales. It was necessary to expand operations to a new and larger plant on Piquette Avenue. Wills was given an experimental workroom on the top of a little two-story brick building behind the plant where it was necessary to climb stairs and knock on a trapdoor to find him. The first floor of the three-story main building was Couzens' domain. As for Ford, he was everywhere, a dominating if somewhat enigmatic figure. He moved through the plant slapping workers on their backs, urging them on, and playing practical jokes to take the edge off the intensity of operations. He stood on the threshold of success greater than anything he had dreamed about.

Before he could step across the great dividing line of his life, however, his father died. If William Ford lost the vicarious pleasure he might have had in seeing the full measure of his son's accomplishment, Henry was cheated out of the spectacle of his own vindication. Years later, when he was an old man at the end of his own long life, Ford said to an acquaintance, "There's just one thing I regret. I wish my father could have lived to see what happened."

THE TENSION FORD HAD ONCE FELT with his father was now increasingly projected onto Malcomson, who, though not much older, had functioned as a paternal figure during their relationship—advising, channeling, restricting and, when necessary, overriding. The conflict between them over the direction of the company took the form of increasingly heated discussions. Would the Ford Motor Company produce large numbers of a small car such as the one Ford had been groping toward in Models A and C, or make a greater profit per car on larger ones such as the new six-cylinder Model K backed by Malcomson and the Dodge brothers? ("A car should not have any more cylinders than a cow has teats," Ford had groused about this model.) When Couzens tipped the balance by throwing his weight on Ford's side of the argument, Malcomson felt betrayed and tried to take his place as business manager; the move was repelled by the directors. Board meetings became stormy sessions with shouting and table pounding that carried through to the eavesdropping clerks in adjacent rooms. Ford could not be moved. His opinions had remained unchanged since 1903, when he had told attorney John Anderson, "The way to make automobiles is to make one automobile like another automobile, to make them all alike, to make them come through the factory just alike, just as one pin is like another pin when it comes from a pin factory."

This conflict, which threatened the company's sanity if not its existence, was finally resolved in July 1906, when Malcomson angrily agreed to sell his 255 shares, more than a quarter of the company, to Ford for $175,000, which he planned to use to finance a competing automobile with an air-cooled engine, called the Aerocar. Ford, finally in control of his own company, walked around the plant with a look of supreme contentment on his face. He said to one of the employees, "This is a great day. We're going to expand this company, and you will see it grow by leaps and bounds. The proper system, as I have it in mind, is to get the car to the people."

THREE

ALMOST OVERNIGHT HENRY FORD had become a rich man. In 1907 the board of directors raised his salary to $36,000 a year, but this sum was small in comparison to the dividends which now spewed out of the company as if from a broken slot machine. He and Clara finally built a house of their own, a project they had been talking about for years. It was a stately brick home with stone trim on Edison Street which cost nearly $300,000 and required a small staff of servants and gardeners. The ample garage contained, in addition to several Fords, Clara's "feminine" electric car and the Model N which fourteen-year-old Edsel had been given to drive to Detroit University School. Henry built for his son a shop of his own above the garage—a reprise on the workbench Ford himself had had on the farm. Almost immediately Edsel lost a fingertip while working at his lathe.

If some of her old friends felt that Clara was becoming rather "grand," Henry paid little attention to money. (Clara found a crumpled weeks-old check for $75,000 one day while turning out his pants pockets before having the pants laundered.) Ford understood that the long process of invention and experiment had reached a climactic moment and that the auto industrial age was at hand. The statistics seemed to bear him out. In 1902 there had been one car for every 1.5 million people in the country; two years later the ratio had shrunk to one car for every 65,000 people; and by 1909 it was one car for every 800 people. *The Nation* correctly diagnosed the situation: "As soon as a standard cheap car can be produced...that does not require mechanical aptitude in the operator and that can be run inexpensively, there will be no limit to the automobile market."

Ford had seen this, too. He knew that the opportunity was at hand to make the car a necessity rather than a plaything.

Working with Wills, he had done modified versions of the Model N called Models R and S. Continuing to work through the alphabet, the company sent out the first circulars on its new Model T on March 19, 1908. It was awkward-looking but conveyed a sense of toughness: the undercarriage riding high above the rough roadway; stout wheels and springs; a four-cylinder engine generating 20 horse-power, with a magneto built into the motor for spark. It was slight but strong because of the revolutionary steel with a

35

vanadium alloy developed by Wills. Objectively it was homely, yet its utilitarian virtues of lightness, simplicity and power made the Model T beautiful.

The first steps toward creating the car had been taken in the winter of 1906 on the third floor of the Piquette plant when Ford told an employee whom he knew he could trust to tell Malcomson to partition off a room just big enough for the car. "Get a good lock for the door," he said, "and when you're ready we'll have Joe Galamb [Ford's favorite draftsman] come in here." A few power tools were installed in the room, along with a blackboard so that his rough sketches could be better visualized. "Mr. Ford first sketched out his ideas of the design he wanted," Galamb later said. "He would come in at seven or eight o'clock at night to see how everyone was getting along.... They worked on the design for over a year until about ten or eleven at night. Mr. Ford followed the design very closely and was there practically all the time. There was a rocking chair in the room in which he used to sit for hours and hours at a time, discussing and following out the development of the design." Ford set up a firing range near the secret room so that he and his aides could relax by shooting at targets with a .22 rifle. Sometimes he would play a practical joke on the others by sneaking in on weekends and altering the sights on their guns.

The design had progressed in secrecy because of Ford's fears that Malcomson would try to kill the new model because of its cheapness and durability, but after he had bought Malcomson out he no longer had to hide his growing excitement. When he met one of the workers helping build the Model T he would give him a playful kick in the pants or a punch in the shoulder. "He was like a kid with a new toy," one of the men said. As the first of the new cars were being built Henry often went out into the shop to kid the workers and tell them stories, cajoling and urging them on. One of them said later on, "God, he could get anything out of us. He'd never say, 'I want this done.' He'd say, 'I wonder if we can do this? I wonder?' Well, the men would break their necks to see if they could do it." The day the first Model T came out of the shop he took it out by himself—traversing all the main streets of Detroit and vindictively driving back and forth past Malcomson's office several times.

The Model T was more than a car; it was a calling, the vehicle Ford believed would take the auto industry to the promised land of efficiency and utility. "I will build a motorcar for the multitude," he said in prophetic tones. "It will be large enough for the family but small enough for the individual to run and care for. It will be constructed of the best materials, by the best men to be hired, after the simplest designs that modern engineering can devise. But it will be so low in price that no man making a good salary will be unable to own one—and enjoy with his family the blessings of hours of pleasure in God's great open spaces."

The Model T was the first car to capture the national imagination. Writers outdid each other in trying to describe its virtues; one of them ransacked the animal kingdom for his metaphors, saying that the T had "some of the characteristics of a mule, the patience of a camel, the courage of a bull terrier, and, in bad situations, it could be very gallant, although there was latent in it a whimsical hostility to the human race." It was the first automobile to appeal to farmers. (A few years earlier, it had not been unusual for rural people to dig ditches or use logs as roadblocks against cars; in one case they had even ambushed and shot a driver as a protest against his vehicle.) Sophisticated buyers also liked it, and the T was featured at a black-tie "Ford Clinic" in New York in which tools were placed on surgical tables and spectators watched from an "operating theatre" as mechanics "vivisected" one of them and gave out remedies for sprained axles, rheumatic valves, fractured bearings, etc.

Adopted as a sort of national mascot with the nicknames "Tin Lizzie" and "flivver," the Model T succeeded in large part because it lent itself so well to promotion. In 1912 it defeated all comers in a scramble up southern California's Mount Wilson. One dealer ran a T up the steps of the YMCA in Columbus, Nebraska, and another placed one on a large teeter-totter five feet above the ground and drove it back and forth for several hours to demonstrate its control.

Lizzies were stripped down and used in games of auto polo which showed off the way the planetary transmission allowed a driver to shift from forward to reverse without stopping. In Las Vegas a dealer staged a "Model T Rodeo" in which a flivver stood outside a gate and when a bull was released the flivver shot forward so that the cowboy could leap from its running board and wrestle the animal to the ground.

Ford himself began using the Model T as a sort of calling card. He sent one to John Burroughs, telling the famed naturalist, whom he deeply admired, that he hoped it would moderate his "grudge against progress." He also sent one to his idol Thomas Edison, whose encouragement at the 1896 Long Island banquet had remained enshrined in Ford's memory as a sort of prestige moment. Edison had remained interested in automobiles, experimenting with electric vehicles driven by his alkaline battery. (In 1902 he had gone so far as to announce, "I have solved the automobile problem. I can make an automobile so fast that a man cannot sit in it. The speed of storage battery machines is unlimited.") Edison had long since forgotten the encounter that meant so much to Ford, however. When Ford wrote for an autographed picture shortly after beginning his company, Edison treated it the same as the dozens of similar requests he got every day, scrawling "No Ans" on the letter and handing it back to his secretary to dispose of. But as the Model T began to put the Ford Motor Company on America's industrial map, the sales manager of Edison's battery department remembered Ford's adulation and invited him to the West Orange laboratory. Ford not only brought a Model T for his idol but swarmed all over him in an attempt to consolidate a friendship, asking Edison to develop a battery, a starter motor and a generator for the car and loaning him over $1 million to help him through a difficult period. It was the beginning of a prophet-disciple relationship that would last for the next twenty years, during which time, as one writer said, Ford acted "like a planet that had adopted Edison for its sun."

FORD HAD NOW HIT THE MOTHER lode of the automobile Gold Rush. By July 1909, company dividends amounted to $1.7 million in cash. New stock worth $1.9 million was distributed among the tiny group of stockholders; a week later another cash dividend of $600,000 was declared. But there was an ominous shadow over this great El Dorado. Did Ford have the right to make automobiles at all? Back in 1903, when the Ford Motor Company was only a few weeks old,

Couzens had received a disquieting notice: "United States patent no. 549,160 granted to George B. Selden November 5, 1895, controls broadly all gasoline automobiles which are accepted as commercially practical. Licenses under this patent have been secured from the owner by the following named manufacturers...." The list of those who had capitulated to Selden's claim to have the patent on the automobile was long in 1903 and had grown over the intervening years; but the Ford Motor Company was not one of them. With the advent of the Model T, however, the simmering controversy came to a boil.

Although he earned a good living as a lawyer, George Selden, like Ford himself, had been from his boyhood a tinkerer and an inventor. In 1877 he had managed to put together a primitive internal-combustion engine, later applying for patents on the road vehicle he thought it might someday propel. Selden never bothered to build the car; he was content to have a broadly worded claim in the event that someone else did. It was a waiting game which he knew he was bound to win. In 1897 a group under the leadership of former Secretary of the Navy William C. Whitney found out about Selden's patent and bought the rights to it for $10,000 and one fifth of any royalties they might collect. Eventually the Whitney group and the automakers who had decided to collaborate rather than defend against a suit formed the Association of Licensed Automotive Manufacturers to exercise Selden's rights.

Ford had tried to join the association when he was first served with notice of the Selden patent in 1903. But, partly because of his two previous business failures, the group decided that he didn't meet their standards and refused him membership. It was either cease making cars or defy the association, and there was never any doubt about the path Ford would choose. After a particularly frustrating meeting with the association's representatives, Couzens had exploded, "Selden can take his patent and go to hell with it!" and Ford, who had been leaning back in his chair watching the outburst with a slight smile on his face, told them, "Well, Couzens has answered you." When his opponents threatened to put him out of business, Ford leaped to his feet and shouted defiantly, "Let them try it!" On July 28, 1903, he put a notice in the Detroit *News* directed at dealers who might be concerned about carrying the Model A: "We will protect you against any prosecution for alleged infringement of patents. The Selden patent does not cover any practicable machine, no practicable machine can be made from it, and never was so far as we can ascertain...." The association filed suit against Ford a few weeks later.

For six years, as the Ford Motor Company was growing up, it was only a war of words. Not until the Model T was beginning to take the auto world by storm did the trial finally get under way—in New York on May 28, 1909. All eyes were on Ford himself, the only man in the auto world willing to challenge the Selden monopoly. When he took the stand, the New York press got a chance to see him for the first time. At forty-six, he had graying hair but was still lean and youthful, with the immobile smile and deeply set eyes that gave him an ironic look. On the witness stand he unnerved the prosecution by his composure and calm certainty. When one of Selden's attorneys accused him of creating a "social problem," Ford responded immediately, "No, my friend, you're mistaken. I'm not creating a social problem at all. I'm going to democratize the automobile. When I'm through everybody will be able to afford one and about everyone will have one.... The automobile will be taken for granted and there won't be any problem."

He candidly assessed his achievement in the distinctive high-pitched voice which still had the flattened accents of the farm in it: "I invented nothing new. I simply assembled into a car the discoveries of other men behind whom were centuries of work.... Had I worked fifty or ten or even five years before, I would have failed. So it is with every new thing. Progress happens when all the factors that make for it are ready, and then it is inevitable. To teach that a comparatively few men are responsible for the greatest forward steps of mankind is the worst sort of nonsense."

Midway through Ford's testimony, the first transcontinental automobile race from New York to Seattle began. Established as part of the Alaska-Yukon-Pacific Exposition by mining magnate Robert Guggenheim, the course comprised 4100 miles, with thirty checkpoints along the way and no restrictions except for a prohibition against driving on railroad tracks. Five cars were on the starting line, two of them Model Ts, when Frederic Coudert, a member of the Ford defense team, walked to the window of the courtroom and watched Mayor George B. McClellan, son of the famed Civil War general, fire the starting pistol after President Taft had pressed a golden telegraph key in Washington. "Your Honor," Coudert said to the court with mock innocence, "there is something that puzzles me. I don't see a Selden car. I see a Ford car, two Ford cars, but I see no Selden car!"

When the defense called auto pioneer Charles E. Duryea to the stand, he went through the genealogy of the gasoline motor: how the first two-cycle engine was built in Paris in 1860 by Étienne Lenoir; how twelve years later American George Brayton had built his own version, which was exhibited at the Centennial Exposition in 1876; and how, that same year, the first fully internal-combustion engine, a four-cylinder version, was built by German inventor Nickolaus Otto. Duryea also went through auto history since then:

how he and his brother Frank drove their one-cylinder car—the first operational automobile—in Springfield in 1889; how Hiram P. Maxim, son of the inventor of the Maxim gun, put an engine on a "tricycle" in 1895 and ran it; and finally how Ford himself had operated his quadricycle in 1896, the same year that Arthur Winton and Ransom Olds first designed vehicles for production. Duryea's overview showed how much had been accomplished in little more than twenty-five years; it also showed that Henry Ford was in the direct line of descent of the great figures of automotive invention.

Ford felt confident enough about the outcome of the trial to go off to Seattle to see the end of the transcontinental race. It had been a harrowing experience for the drivers. Through most of Missouri there were no roads. The cars had worked their way painstakingly through the mud of Nebraska and the sleet of Wyoming. They sank in quicksand thirty-five miles east of Denver. The Italian-made Itala broke down in Cheyenne and quit the race. As the two Model Ts entered the homestretch, the large four-cylinder Shawmut was eleven hours behind, the powerful 60-horsepower Acme almost a week. The leading Ford, driven by Bill Scott, went off a bridge in the darkness and had to have its axle straightened by a railroad gang. Finally reaching the Snoqualmie Pass, Washington, Scott found snow some four feet deep. He rode the Model T on the icy crust almost to the summit and then broke through; again a railroad gang came to the rescue, by shoveling him out. Ford came out to meet the car and was, in Scott's words, "tickled to death to see we were first." After the Ford drivers had entered Seattle in triumph, Guggenheim presented a gold cup to them. His words at the ceremony captured exactly Ford's accomplishment: "[His] theory that a lightweight car, highly powered for its weight, can go places where heavier cars cannot go and can beat heavier cars costing five or six times as much on steep hills or bad roads has been proven. I believe Mr. Ford has the solution of the popular automobile."

But while Ford won the race, he lost his lawsuit. Hearing the judge's September 15 ruling that no gasoline car could be sold without infringing on the Selden patent, Ford was disconsolate. He even gave thought to selling out. The prospective buyer was the energetic William Crapo Durant, who was quickly establishing himself, along with Ford, as one of the mythic figures in the auto world. While still in his twenties, the rotund, cigar-chewing Durant had been a clerk in a smoke shop, a salesman for municipal waterworks, and finally one of the most successful carriage makers in the country. Having made millions, he retired at the age of forty to play the stock market. Then he heard of a car company begun by a Polish mechanic; he bought it and decided to keep the odd name—Buick. Not really an auto man in the sense that Ford was and Walter Chrysler would become, Durant was a conglomerator, a builder of businesses rather than mechanical structures.

Even before the Selden decision, Durant had approached Ford and Couzens about building the Ford Motor Company into a union with Buick and with Reo, Ransom Olds' new company. But Olds, proud of his role as an auto pioneer, had demanded a sum equal to the $3 million Ford had casually stated as his bottom line, and the deal had fallen through. But now, after Ford's defeat in court, Durant made another offer to buy the company for the combine he thought at this point in his career to call International Motors. (In the course of negotiations he pensively crossed out "International" and penciled in "General" on the sheet of paper he was covering with doodles.) Durant had already acquired Cadillac, Oldsmobile and other companies to go along with Buick, using John D. Rockefeller's technique of paying for acquisitions by offering stock in the larger conglomerate to their owners.

Couzens agreed to meet Durant in the Belmont Hotel while Ford was upstairs lying on the cool tile floor of his bathroom to soothe a backache. Couzens came into the room and reported on Durant's offer: $8 million for the Ford Motor Company and Ford's personal agreement not to launch any competing ventures.

"Tell him he can have it if the money's all cash," Ford shouted. "Tell him also I'll throw in my lumbago."

"You want to let it go for that?" Couzens asked.

"What do you think?"

"I'll say yes," Couzens said.

"If we can get the cash."

"Cash or the answer is no," Couzens agreed.

In late October, Couzens met secretly with Durant in Dearborn for a review of the company's inventory. The deal was on the edge of consummation. But at the last minute bankers, fearing that Durant had expanded too quickly, refused to loan the money and the agreement was called off. Durant, who had been awaiting the outcome of the Selden suit, signed up Buick with the association of Licensed Auto Manufacturers, leaving Ford the only major holdout.

Throughout 1910, while the Selden decision was on appeal, the association warned the public not to buy Ford products, while Ford and Couzens fought back, using newspaper advertisements to reassure potential buyers that they would be protected by bonds the company had posted. Finally, on January 9, 1911, the appellate judge handed down a dramatic decision which said that the basic technology of the gasoline automobile was a "social invention" that must be available to all producers equally.

It was the vindication Ford had prayed for. The night of January 12, 1911, he went to a banquet his opponents had set up in advance on their assumption that it would be a victory party. Making an exception to his hatred of tobacco, he puffed on a clay peace pipe that was solemnly passed around and assured them that he had no hard feelings. But it was hard for him to be gracious. The next night at a Ford Motor Company victory party, while guests lampooned the association, Selden and his lawyers in lyrics improvised to the melodies of popular songs, Ford sat on the sidelines with a triumphant smile, obviously thinking about something else. When a friend sat down beside him and started to comment on how wonderful the party was, Ford turned suddenly and interrupted so abruptly that it was clear he hadn't heard a word the man said. "Nobody can stop me now," Ford said. "From here on in the sky's the limit."

INDEED, ONCE THE SHADOW OF Selden had been lifted, there was no reason not to proceed with the swift expansion which had previously been held off on the advice of attorneys. The Piquette plant had served Ford well when he was getting started but was now too small for his growing dreams. He had bought a sixty-acre former racetrack in the Detroit suburb of Highland Park when the money first started rolling in. Now he hired noted industrial architect Albert Kahn to design a giant four-story plant there. As it began to go up, onlookers started referring to the structure as the "Crystal Palace" because of the more than fifty thousand square feet of glass in the roof and walls of the building which let the sunlight splash down onto the cavernous work space below. Kahn made the plant into a sort of industrial cathedral for the Model T, which was soon being produced there in a variety of forms—town car, touring car, delivery car—all of them sharing not only a single chassis but a single color as well once Ford had issued his famous dictum "A customer can have a car painted any color he wants so long as it is black."

Highland Park was a wonder of modern planning. An elevator took raw materials up to the fourth floor, where fenders, hoods and other large parts were finished and leather upholstery was completed. On the third floor, tires were placed on wheels, floorboards were built, and the bodies were painted black. On the second floor the cars were assembled and then driven down a ramp past the first-floor offices. There were fifteen thousand machines for the increasingly complex operations of production and assembly, each one spotlessly clean and identified by a number on a brass tag; most of the tags were affixed by young Edsel during his summer vacations. When the Ford Motor Company had first begun production a few years earlier, nearly every part was produced by a subcontractor on the outside. Highland Park was self-contained, with furnaces for cylinders and other castings, a cold-pressed-steel plant that stamped out body parts, and forges for steel axles and crank shafts. In 1910, the first year of production, Highland Park turned out 19,000 Model Ts; the following year, 34,500; the year after that, 78,440.

Highland Park was a peaceable kingdom, and Henry Ford was very much its benign monarch. He liked to "ramble" through the assembly area, stopping to watch and chat with his workers. Sometimes he would see a new man struggling and take over his machine to show him how it was done. Occasionally the worker would not know it was Ford who had helped him. As one foreman later noted: "After Mr. Ford had shown how the process should be done he'd say, 'Now go ahead and try it.' Then: 'No, that ain't the way.... That's what they make these machines for—to do the work. You don't want to work. When you go home you don't want to be tired. When you go home to your family you want to feel good.' He'd stand there and do a dozen articles and finally the man got the hang of it. Mr. Ford would say, 'That's the way, John. You'll learn.' After he had left the foreman would say, 'Do you know who that man was, John?' John would say he didn't. 'Why that was Henry Ford.'"

Yet Ford was also capable of inclement gusts of temper, as on one occasion when he was walking through the Pattern Department and noticed on a workman's bench a couple of patterns he could tell were inaccurate. Ford picked them up, handed one to the workman and took the other to the window, saying, "I'll bet I can throw this farther than you can," and then tossed it outside and stomped off. Phobic about paperwork, he went into the Accounting Department one day, picked up ledgers and other bookkeeping tools and threw them out into the street. When the accountants returned from lunch, he told them he saw no point at all in keeping books. "Just put all the money we take in in a big barrel and when a shipment of material comes in reach into the barrel and take out enough money to pay for it."

His employees learned that most of his crotchets could be safely ignored. But they also learned that it was truly dangerous to cross him about the Model T. In 1912 Henry and Clara went to England. While he was holding talks with Sir Percival Perry about forming an English company, she took Edsel to visit Warwick, the town where her mother had grown up. Afterward they all went to Ireland and saw the house where William Ford had been born, a crumbling structure with a caved-in sod roof and two barren rooms. While the Fords toured, Harold Wills and others decided to welcome Henry home with a present—a new and streamlined version of the Model T which one employee felt was "so much over the original it was like night and day." When Ford returned to Dearborn, he went immediately to Highland Park, saw the car and asked what it was.

"Well, Mr. Ford," said an employee, "that's the new car."

"Ford car?"

"Yes, sir."

"How long has it been standing there?" Ford asked.

"Well, about two weeks. They just finished it. It's just going into production."

"It's going into production?"

"Yes, sir." The employee didn't catch the signs of Ford's rising anger in the flattened irony of his responses. "It's all tooled up and the orders are placed for the new car."

Ford circled the car a couple of times with his hands in his pockets, then suddenly released them and sprang on it with a fury, opening the driver's door and ripping it off its hinges. He did the same for the passenger side. Then he jumped up on the hood to kick in the windshield, and, yelling all the time, climbed up onto the top of the car and began to stomp down on the roof.

As one observer said later on, "We got the message. As far as he was concerned, the Model T was God and we were to put away false images."

IT WAS A TIME WHEN MOST of Henry's energies went into the pellmell expansion, which required new people as well as new facilities. Chief among the new executives was Edsel Ford himself. He was different from the other employees. For them automobiles were a job; for him they were a destiny. He had come of age with the car, driving one of his father's original Model A's with easy confidence at the age of ten and owning a Model N of his own by the time he was fourteen. In the garage at the Edison Street house he had taken apart and reassembled foreign cars, shoehorning Ford engines into European bodies. As a teenager he had taken Ford products on cross-country road tests, keeping careful records of performance and mileage. A talented artist, he had amassed a portfolio of sketches of sleek roadsters, elegant European sedans, and cars of the future by the time he graduated from high school.

As A BOY, EDSEL HAD HAD a vulnerable, deerlike quality, looking as if he was about to bolt away from a conversation at any moment. Thin and frail, his face often broken out in angry patches of acne, he had been certain about only one thing: that his future would involve the Ford Motor Company. If Henry's earliest memories involved William Ford explaining the wonders of nature, Edsel's involved *his* father extolling the wonders of the automobile. He said later, "My first clear recollection has to do with the 999 that Barney Oldfield raced, and that was the start of our business...[which] was all the family talked about."

Edsel had come into the office every day after school to stamp letters and help with the administrative chores his father loathed. On arriving, he would put his books down on the desk of his father's secretary George Brown, say hello to him, and continue on into the experimental room, which was his father's domain. Henry looked forward to seeing him and would get anxious if he was late, coming out to ask the men in the outer office, "Have you seen Ed? Oh yes, he's here. I see his books." When he located the boy the two of them would go into the experimental room and begin poring over blueprints and chattering about cars. Henry was extremely proud of Edsel. "Yes, I have a fine son to carry on," he told one acquaintance. "If he keeps on as he is now this company will be in good hands someday." And Edsel, for his part, worshiped his father, imitating him in every regard, even to keeping a notebook as Ford did, with entries ranging from the mundane ("get turpin hydrate for cough") to the professional ("for 1911 car—color grey, white strip, footrail, radiator screen, chauffeur seat, clock claxon horn").

While in Detroit University School, Edsel had always assumed that he would go, along with most of his classmates, to some Ivy League university. But his father felt that his own experience proved that higher education was an affectation. He liked to illustrate its pitfalls with the story of a friend's son who had studied forestry at a West Coast college and then taken a job with a lumber company which sent a wagon to meet his train and take him up into the cutting area. The young graduate was bounced out of the wagon on a primitive mountain road, run over and killed, Ford would say, readying the moral of the story: "They forgot to teach that boy in college how to ride a wagon." His position was that Edsel could learn everything worth knowing in the Ford plant, which was itself a microcosm of human wisdom and industry.

Although disappointed, Edsel obeyed without question—not from fear but from loyalty. "My father is a great man," he solemnly told a newspaper reporter interviewing him about family matters. He had to behave like a great man's son. After graduating from high school, he came to work full time at Highland Park, taking an office adjoining his father's. Among the artifacts on his desk was the first gasoline motor Henry Ford had made in the backyard shop on Bagley Avenue—a dramatic reminder of the creativity he would have to compare himself to and the ego with which he would have to contend.

If Edsel was someone in the Ford Motor Company's future, one of those in its present was William S. Knudsen, a tall thin Dane with a lean face and a gunfighter's mustache drooping over the sides of his mouth. Energetic, almost driven, he had immigrated to America from Copenhagen in 1910 at the age of twenty. He had gone to work for Keim Mills of Buffalo, New York, the country's leading manufacturer of pressed steel, and had come to Ford when Henry bought them out. Wary of the infighting at the Dearborn headquarters, Knudsen asked for a job that would keep him away from the bureaucracy. This matched perfectly with the company's need for someone who could coordinate the string of branch assembly plants Henry had long wanted to build. Under Knudsen's direction, Ford Motor Company facilities began to appear in Long Island, Chicago, Memphis, Denver and on to the Pacific Coast. Over the next few years Knudsen would become chief outrider for the growing Ford empire.

There was also Charles E. Sorensen, another Dane. He had, in fact, been born within months of Knudsen and only a few miles away. Sorensen had come to the United States much earlier, however, arriving with his family at the age of four, and had gotten into automobile work as a pattern maker when the industry was still in its infancy. He had first met Ford in 1902, after the victorious race against Winton. At that time, Sorensen had applied for a job, and Ford had told him that he didn't yet have the money to hire him but would once he had begun a new company. True to his word, in 1905 Ford had brought Sorensen into the Mack Avenue plant, where he had immediately distinguished himself because of his blond hair and chiseled good looks and a temper that made him by turns a passionate and a melancholy Dane. One admirer called Sorensen "Adonis"; to Ford, however, he was always "Cast Iron Charlie" because of his preference in metals, although the nickname also fit his tough and at times impenetrable personality. Unlike his countryman Knudsen, Sorensen soon established himself as a vigorous and adroit practitioner of company politics, as well as something of a visionary when it came to production. It was Sorensen, in fact, who was primarily responsible for the advent of the classic Ford innovation of the assembly line.

The concept was very much in the cultural air by the time Sorensen came to work for Ford. Frederick W. Taylor, preeminent industrial "scientist" of the era and author of classic time and motion studies, had been saying for years that scrutiny of the smallest operations in a factory yielded data for dramatically increased efficiency. The Studebaker plant in Detroit had implemented some of Taylor's thinking; other auto companies had invited him to present his ideas to their executives. But because of Henry Ford's love of tinkering, the Ford Motor Company was especially receptive to the new and revolutionary ideas about production. As far back as 1908 Sorensen and some co-workers at the Piquette plant had gotten the idea of pulling a chassis by a rope past laborers at their work stations. But Highland Park was designed for a swifter and more sophisticated process which would meet the huge demand the Model T had created. And although Ford himself later claimed authorship of the assembly line that was installed there, saying that the concept first occurred to him when he went to a watch plant and saw a staged assembly process, it was actually the hard-driving Sorensen—archetype of the auto industry plant superintendent—who implemented this innovation.

He began with a belt conveyor which took radiator parts to assemblers and then carried their work to solderers to finish the product. After integrating other production processes, he soon had a continuously moving line fed by overhead conveyors. More than quantity production, the assembly line involved, in Ford's own words, "the focussing upon a manufacturing process of the principles of power, accuracy, economy, system, continuity, speed and repetition."

Soon the Highland Park plant was kinetic, with everything in constant synchronous motion. There was no more hand lifting, no stationary bins that workers had to walk to for material. The benefits were clear: in August 1913 it took an average of twelve and a half man hours to assemble a Model T; the following year, after Sorensen had installed assembly lines, it took only one and a half hours.

Henry never would have been interested in the assembly line if it had been simply a matter of technical advancement for its own sake. The concept was appealing in part because it was consistent with his philosophy. ("Time loves to be wasted," he said in one of the epigrams that would eventually establish him as Poor Richard come into the twentieth century. "From that waste there can be no salvage. It is the hardest of all waste to correct because it does not litter the floor.") But from the moment he saw the conveyors, he realized that the assembly line was a tool that would allow him to pursue his obsessive interest in increasing production by decreasing prices, thereby tapping a deeper strata of demand. When he cut the price of the 1913 Model T to $440, profits per car went down (to $93 from about $200 two years earlier); but sales went up (from 78,440 cars to 248,307), and so did net income.

As Ford said gleefully, "Every time I reduce the charge for our car by one dollar, I get a thousand new buyers." Only a system such as the one he and Sorensen put in place could have coped with the huge demand for the Model T, a demand he intensified by continuing to lower prices. In 1908 the Ford Motor Company had built less than 10 percent of the nation's cars; by 1914 it produced almost half of them.* Yet the real benefit of the assembly line, although it wasn't clear at the time, was not really numbers of cars made or wealth generated, but rather the creation of a womb in which the idea and practice of modern industry would take shape.

THE MODEL T CREATED UNPARALLELED riches, turning Henry into a sort of Midas figure. He hated questions about money, once saying "Oh shit" and turning his back on a reporter who asked how it felt to be a multimillionaire. But he couldn't keep Ford wealth from being a subject of discussion in publications like *The Nation*, one of whose editorialists wrote:

> Men now hardly past middle life were brought up with the idea that the Astor fortune represented the boundless possibilities of profit in real estate invest-ments, the Vanderbilt fortune the result of the control of transportational opportunities.... Now two or three decades later they were thrown into the shade by the names of Carnegie and Rockefeller. But even the Carnegie and Rocke-feller fortunes appear to have been piled up by a slow and lumbering process when one sees the great golden stream flowing into the coffers of a man who not long ago was a simple mechanic, who has no recourse to combination or manip-ulation or oppression or extortion, who has simply offered his wares to a public eager to buy them and distanced his competitors by no other art than that of turn-ing out his product by more perfect or more economical methods than they have been able to devise or execute....

Ford's wealth was indeed staggering, but, as it piled up, another issue was increasingly raised, both inside and outside the company. What of the work-ers? Would they share in this great bounty? For a time it seemed doubtful. Detroit was the open-shop capital of the country. Police were provocative, fre-quently allowing themselves to be used as strikebreakers; but the laborers in the auto companies, many of them timid Eastern European immigrants, ignored the message of organizers of the International Workers of the World who tried to lighten their misery.

If unrest and agitation had not yet become labor issues, demoralization and transience were. Employees saw themselves as robot laborers; those with skills found that they were of little use on the assembly line with its endlessly repetitious activities. Anyone who outproduced another worker had to wait for

---

* The Ford Motor Company, with some 13,000 employees, made 267,720 cars. The other American companies, with 66,000 employees, made 286,770 cars.

him to catch up; the only virtue was monotonous efficiency. That there was practically no identification with or loyalty to employers was shown by the help-wanted advertisements swelling the Sunday newspapers. So great was the alienation that in 1913 the Ford Motor company had to hire 963 workers for every 100 it wanted to remain permanently on the payroll. Accountants pointed out that it took $100 to train each one, and that the company was thus losing $3 million a year solely because of worker defections.

It was Couzens who insisted on dealing with the issue. As he later recalled, it came to him a few days before Christmas 1913, when he was home leafing through a magazine of "socialist tendencies." Temperamentally intolerant of emotional appeals, he might easily have ignored the journalistic rhetoric about the "plight" of the workingman, he later admitted, except for the fact that it was a bitter winter night and outside his warm house he could see men walking hunched into the cold. He began thinking about the hard-pressed Ford workers and the fact that he and the rest of the company's board of directors were recipients of dividends so large it was hard to dispose of them. In time his concern would grow to the point where he excoriated other industrialists in a typically truculent speech to the Detroit Board of Commerce: "You fellows sit back smug and complacent and don't give a damn what becomes of your workmen…. You kick them into the streets and that's all there is to it." But for the time being he thought only about Ford workers' salary—at that point about $2.50 a day. The next morning he made a stunning proposal to Ford: they should raise the salary at the Ford Motor Company to a flat five dollars a day.

Ford was also concerned. Not long before Couzens came to him Ford had been walking through the plant with his son when he noticed a worker glower at Edsel and then seize a mallet as if to smash his machine, holding it for a moment before setting it down again. After the incident Henry said to Couzens, "He was saying, 'Look at Henry Ford's boy! What has mine beside him?'" Yet when Couzens suggested the five-dollar-a-day wage, Ford countered with a figure of three dollars.

Couzens replied, "Each of us realizes that the division of our earnings between capital and labor is unequal and that we ought to do something in the way of relief that is suitable for others. You yourself have often said that is what we should do."

A day or so later Ford suggested $3.50.

"No, it's five or nothing," Couzens responded tenaciously, restating his position when Ford raised his ante to four dollars: "A straight five-dollar wage will be the greatest advertising any automobile concern ever had."

This last argument won Ford over, and he agreed to the five-dollar-a-day wage, taking the precaution of calling it "profit sharing" so that it could be withdrawn if the company suffered reverses.

Couzens was right. The announcement caused an overnight furor. Several thousand men showed up at Highland Park looking for work. While they stood outside in the bitter cold waiting for a chance to fill out applications, a riot broke out; police doused them with high-pressure hoses, the water freezing on their clothes as it hit them. Ford felt so personally besieged by job seekers that he began leaving his office through a window. The other automakers accused him of being a traitor to his class and said he would wreck the industry. The issue soon escaped the parochial confines of Detroit. A *New York Times* reporter who was present when publisher Adolph Ochs received the news heard him say of Ford, "He's crazy, isn't he? Don't you think he's crazy?" The *New York Globe* editorialized about the plan: "It has all the advantages and none of the disadvantages of socialism." But the *Wall Street Journal* called it blatantly immoral, a misapplication of "Biblical principles" in a field where "they don't belong."

The new system worked for the company, however. Absenteeism dropped from some 10 percent a day to less than one half of one percent. Ford workers suddenly became proud of their association with the company, wearing their identification badges on Sunday, their only day off, as tiepins—a badge of honor and also a signal of solvency to potential and past creditors. But the most significant aspect of the five-dollar wage, an aspect whose importance would become apparent only later on, was the fact that it created a whole new group of consumers for Ford Motor Company products. By increasing the workers' salaries, Ford was elevating them to the middle class and enabling them to buy that most middle-class of objects, the automobile.

Having seen his workers as if for the first time, Henry immediately went a step further. He felt that more money might lead them to depravity, so he decided to make the profit sharing contingent upon a workman's sobriety and industry, and to enforce these virtues through a force of company social workers.

He would be criticized by some for paternalism, but the Ford Sociological Department was a result of thinking he had been doing for years. All the time the company was growing, he had been trying to sort out his own ideas, trying to mold his thoughts into a coherent worldview. He had puzzled his way through Emerson and liked to quote Thoreau. As a friend said, "He was trying so hard to grow. He didn't want to be just another rich industrialist. He wanted to be a philosopher-inventor like his friend Edison. Most of all, he wanted to put his ideas about human nature into practice." If these ideas were based on the Transcendentalists' belief in man's perfectibility, they also drew heavily on William Ford's commitment to self-reliance and rugged individualism.

Even before the five-dollar wage was put into effect, Ford would often stop his car to pick up tramps and hitchhikers and offer them jobs at Highland Park so that they could "remake their lives." He hired convicts to give them another chance. When one young man was caught stealing from the plant, Ford refused to fire him, saying, "Give him a better job and see if that will make him a better man." One of the ex-cons he hired was Norval Hawkins, his future sales manager, who eventually built the best sales force the automobile world had yet seen.

The Sociological Department offered Ford a chance to implement these ideas about self-help on a grand scale, to turn out better men the way the assembly line allowed him to turn out better cars. One of the men Ford hired to get the Sociological Department started said later on, "Mr. Ford told me he wanted it known that his plan is for every family working for him [to have] a comfortable home, a bathtub in it, and a yard with a little garden, and ultimately that he wanted to see every employee of his owning an automobile."

The Sociological Department began sending investigators to employees' homes, each with a car and a driver who sometimes doubled as a translator. The "social workers" were required to be cordial, but they were the long arm of the company and had its presumptive right to obtain information about the way the workers lived. Because Ford wanted to make sure that his men were saving their money and not living in sin, bankbooks and marriage certificates had to be produced during the interviews. As one Sociological Department investigator said later, "If some young fellow [was] being loose in his living or wasting his time, we suggested that he pursue some line of study, night school or correspondence school.... If he wasn't saving any money we suggested that he should start. We had no percentage of savings set up. We were satisfied as long as he spent his profit sharing in a constructive way." Investigators handed out a pamphlet entitled "Rules of Living" which urged employees to use plenty of soap and water in the home; not to spit on the floor; to avoid purchasing on the installment plan; and to go to Ford-operated schools to learn English if they were foreign born. The wives of employees were counseled not to take in boarders, lest a sexual relationship develop while the husband was at work.

Samuel Marquis, former dean of St. Paul's Church in Detroit, whom Henry and Clara recruited to be head of the department, always remembered one of the first things Ford said to him: "Let me lay my hands by chance on the most shiftless and worthless fellow in the crowd and I'll bring him in here, give him a job and a wage that offers him some hope for his life and I'll guarantee that I'll make a man out of him.... I do not believe in charity, but I do believe in the regenerating power of work in men's lives." For Marquis the classic case showing the lengths to which Ford would go to promote self-reliance involved a seventy-year-old black worker who was no longer able to pull his weight at Highland Park. Sociological Department investigators assessing the situation found that the man had a nice home, a younger wife able to work, and a stepson who had a job in a box factory. They got the wife to agree to turn the home into a rooming house and fill it up with a "good class of boarder." They got the stepson a five-dollar-a-day job at Highland Park, and got the aging black man light part-time work as a janitor near his home. "When we got through, the income of the family was about double what it had been," Marquis said of this newly created utopia. "Everybody was at work, everybody was happy."

FOUR

B EFORE THE ANNOUNCEMENT of the five-dollar day, Henry Ford was just another Midwesterner who happened to have struck it rich in the automotive Eldorado, an individual who might have been big news in Detroit but was so little known nationally that he didn't even rate an entry in *Who's Who*. But the five-dollar wage made him a national figure overnight. In the midst of the furor he came to New York and was discovered by journalists. In a mob scene in the lobby of the Hotel Belmont they crushed plants and broke furniture to get close to the man who was being proclaimed as a new industrial messiah. With an adroit sense of public relations that was all the more effective for appearing wholly ingenuous, Henry fueled their curiosity by comments that were unique in their idealistic candor. He granted every request for an interview, watching with delight as the reporters' pencils raced over their notebooks trying to capture his words. A routine subject such as wages and prices could call forth the sort of comment no other American businessman had ever made: "The right price is not what the traffic will bear, and the right wage is not the lowest sum a man will work for. The right price is the lowest price an article can be steadily sold for. The right wage is the highest wage the purchaser can steadily pay." It was the perfect intersection of a man and his times: within a few months Ford was a household name.

He had burst onto the national stage at exactly the right moment. The year Selden began harassing the Ford Motor Company, Theodore Roosevelt was making trusts the subject of a national campaign, and muckraker Ida Tarbell was publishing her classic study, *A History of Standard Oil*. Not only did Ford escape the scrutiny of the radical journalists who had taken on the robber barons of a previous generation, but he also became something of an anomaly, an industrial Saint George who had slain the "automobile trust." He offered himself to an era hungry for heroes as a populist upholding the values dear to grass-roots America at a time when these values were under assault by the modern world. He stood for the Puritan ethic of hard work and also for commonsense suspicion of "experts" who he claimed were long on theory and short on practical insight. He let it be known that he was not just another rich man who would donate his wealth to colleges or other philanthropies. Money was a way of keeping score in the game of life—not to be

51

hoarded or given away, but invested so that it would benefit ever greater numbers of people.

The American public couldn't get enough of him. Within a year after first bustling into public view, Ford had become famed for his laconic pronouncements on life, which, anchored as they were in the phenomenal success of the car bearing his name, made him seem prophetic. To the skeptic he preached faith in the machine; to the conservative he urged tolerance for change. To this package he added the wrapping of social uplift that made him unique: "I do not consider the machines which bear my name simply as machines. If that was all there was to it I would simply do something else. I take them as concrete evidence of the working out of a theory of business which I hope is more than a theory of business—a theory towards making this world a better place to live."

At first Ford was taken aback by his sudden celebrity. He came into the office one day and said to his secretary, "You know, I think I ought to get a pair of whiskers. Everybody seems to spot me." He tried the false beard for a few days and then came in and tossed it onto the desk, muttering, "Well, it won't work. I guess they spot the car." Mobs of the curious gathered outside his Edison Street house, making it difficult for him to get to and from the office. Finally he had to get away. He had considered building a more secure residence on a choice fifty-five acres he had bought at Gaukler Pointe, an exclusive site on Lake St. Clair fourteen miles from Detroit. But he was put off by the people there, Detroit's self-proclaimed aristocracy, and decided instead to build on a 1500-acre tract he had painstakingly assembled in Dearborn along the shore of the Rouge River—the very woods he had walked in with his father looking for birds and animals when he was a boy.

Edsel suggested that he hire Frank Lloyd Wright as his architect, but Henry was horrified by Wright's daring contemporary design. Instead he chose a stern structure resembling a Norman castle, and had it built in limestone at a cost of some $2 million, calling it Fairlane after the little Irish town where his grandfather O'Hern had been born. Hoping to keep Edsel at home, Ford had the architect include an immense indoor swimming pool surrounded by heated marble benches; a $30,000 organ; a bowling alley; and a game room with a cypress mantel over the fireplace into which he had a woodworker carve Thoreau's words, "Chop your own wood and it will warm you twice." The garage housed his own five Fords, his Rolls-Royce, the electric car Clara drove around the estate and the Marmon, the Mercedes and other foreign cars that intrigued Edsel.

Henry insisted that the estate have its own source of power. About half a mile from the main house, and connected by an underground tunnel, he built a powerhouse with two giant generators, powered by the Rouge River, which required three men to operate. He was prouder of the powerhouse than of the main house itself, and always showed it to visitors first. The grounds of Fairlane also reflected his personality. He had a lagoon made so that he and Clara could ice-skate as they had done when courting, and a small house for changing into skates beside a fire. A concealed dock was cut into the banks of the Rouge for Clara's electric boat, the *Callie B*. Learning that some Dearbornites, especially immigrants working in his plant, were coming onto his property to shoot game, Ford hired a crew of groundskeepers and wardens. He would not allow deadfall to be cut into firewood, because he knew that the raccoons made their dens in the fallen logs. When Lord Percival Perry, head of Ford operations in England, sent him dozens of species of European birds, he had two hundred multistory "bird hotels" placed throughout the estate and hired a full-time worker to keep food and water at the feeding stations.

A huge place designed for only three people, Fairlane never became a place for the extended Ford family. Always the odd Ford out as a boy, Henry continued to be remote from his brothers and sisters now that he had attained fame and fortune. His brother William, who many people said was most like him, had tried to get involved in the company. After Henry began building tractors, he gave William a job selling implements. When they ran into each other in the hall, Henry always said, "Will, how's things going?" but with no particular feeling. Eventually William borrowed money and began a business of his own selling Ford tractors. Henry didn't tell him when he decided to shift the entire tractor operation to Ireland, and William went bankrupt. Henry also had a falling-out with his brother John. Taciturn and fiercely independent, John had turned out to be the most Irish of all the Ford boys, having farmed the family plot for a long time before buying his own land. Seeking to bridge the distance between them, Henry once sent his brother a Model T as a present; John told the man who tried to give him the key, "Take that danged thing back and tell him to keep it, because I don't want it."

Henry's Bryant in-laws visited Fairlane far more than his own relatives. Clara liked to see them, and Henry was tolerant. But at some point during their visits when no one was looking he usually ducked out, went down the tunnel to the powerhouse and tinkered in the small machine shop he maintained there, until everyone had left. Speaking of his own blood kin as well as his in-laws, Ford once told an employee, "Keep away from your damned relatives or they'll give you a hell of a lot of trouble."

The Ford family, as he construed it, was a triangle linking him, Clara and Edsel. When his son turned twenty-one, Henry took him to a Detroit bank and told one of the vice-presidents, "I have a million in gold deposited here. This is Edsel's birthday and I want him to have it." Edsel ran down to the vault to see the bullion and later said he made more errors on the job that day than ever before or again. His gratitude and admiration for his father were undying. By the time Fairlane was finished, he was twenty-three, a smoothly handsome and contemporary young man who occasionally banged on a drum set to entertain guests but otherwise spent little time at the estate.

Henry's unrealistic hope that his son would continue to live with him always was shattered when Edsel met Eleanor Clay. The lively young woman was the niece of department store owner J. L. Hudson, who had come to Detroit half a century earlier and parlayed a storefront selling fire-damaged clothes into one of the largest retail operations in the Midwest. Eleanor's father had been a manager in the business; after his early death, her uncle had taken in the widow and her children and raised them as his own. While he saw Eleanor as charming and amusing, Hudson thought that her sister Josephine had the toughness to be a top executive, and he raised her with the thought that she might play a role in the business. Both girls attended the prestigious Liggett School as well as Annie Ward Foster's dancing academy, a place where children of Detroit's better families learned social graces and waltz steps at the same time. When Edsel met her there, Eleanor was teaching dance to underprivileged children. The two spent hours on the dance floor together—a shy young man with darkly elegant good looks and a long-faced young woman with a fey manner who seemed always trying to draw him out. Edsel distressed his parents by telling them that he was Eleanor Clay's "devoted admirer."

FAIRLANE OFFERED FORD SOME privacy from the attention that had suddenly gathered him up, but it hardly signaled a withdrawal from the world of affairs into which the five-dollar-a-day wage had propelled him. On the contrary, he seemed to have discovered himself at the same time America discovered him. Gorging on a rich diet of publicity and adulation, he began to believe that he, the representative of the common man, had a responsibility to speak out on an ever-widening number of topics his Midwestern populism defined as important. By far the most controversial of his subjects was the coming war in Europe, a war in which he felt America had no stake. He feared that the United States would be drawn into the conflict by the "absentee owners and parasites" of Wall Street, chief among them the house of Morgan, which had recently negotiated a half-billion-dollar war loan to the Allies. In August 1915, not long after he attended the San Francisco Exposition with Thomas Edison and watched a replica of the Highland Park assembly line turn out twenty Model Ts a day, Ford issued a call to the common man to take events into his own hands and try to stop the conflict, pledging his own "life and fortune" to the cause of peace.

The statement came to the attention of Rosika Schwimmer, a Hungarian-American antiwar activist. Schwimmer contacted Ford and arranged an interview with him at Fairlane, joining an intense young pacifist named Louis Lochner who had already contacted him. Over lunch the short, bottom-heavy Schwimmer spoke about ending the war by the "continuous mediation" of a commission that would work unceasingly for peace. Lochner subscribed to the plan immediately, suggesting that a man of Ford's growing reputation might be able to ask for an interview to explain the idea to President Wilson. By the end of their lunch Ford had decided to go to New York and Washington, and he asked Lochner, whom he had decided to make his secretary for peace, to accompany him.

On the railroad trip east, Ford spent his time trying to create epigrammatic sayings worthy of the persona he had begun to establish in the press. When he hit one he thought was good ("Men sitting around a table, not men dying in a trench, will finally settle differences") he would say to Lochner, "Make a note of that; we'll give it to the boys in the papers when we get to New York." Immediately upon arriving, Ford began a series of conferences. At dinner with Jane Addams and others, the talk turned to Schwimmer's plan of sending an official mediating commission to Europe. Half joking, Lochner said, "Why not a special ship to take the delegates over?" Ford immediately seized on the idea. By evening he and Schwimmer had chartered the Scandinavian-American liner *Oskar II.*

The following day Ford and Lochner went to the White House to meet with Wilson. Ford slipped into an easy chair and dangled his left leg over its arm during a conversation which had the stilted improvisational qualities of a radio play.

"You are looking very well, Mr. President," Ford began. "Better than I've ever seen you before. What do you do to keep yourself in such good trim?"

"Well, I always make it a point to forget business after business hours," Wilson answered, "and I particularly try to enjoy a good joke."

Ford grew quite animated and said that he himself had recently made up a joke. "One day I was driving by a cemetery when I noticed that a large hole was being dug by the gravedigger. I wondered what this was for and said to him, 'What's the matter? Are you going to bury a family in one hole?' 'No,' he replied, 'this is for one man.' 'Then why so big a hole?' I demanded. The old gravedigger scratched his head, 'You see, it's this way: the man who is to be buried in this grave was a queer sort of fellow. He provided in his will that he must be buried in his Model T because he said it had thus far pulled him out of every hole and he was sure it would pull him out of the last.' "

The serious Wilson managed a terse chuckle at Ford's humor and tried to do his part by reciting a limerick. Then the talk finally turned to the war, continuous mediation and all the other things Ford had on his mind. Wilson listened but made no commitments. Suddenly Ford delivered an ultimatum: "Tomorrow at ten in New York, representatives of every big newspaper will come to my apartment for a story. I have today chartered a steamship. I offer it to you to send delegates to Europe. If you feel you can't act, I will. I will then tell the newspapermen that I will take a ship of American delegates to Europe."

When Wilson responded equivocally, Ford and Lochner thanked him and left. As they were walking across the White House lawn, Ford dismissed the President contemptuously: "He's a small man."

Continuing to act with the lightning speed that characterized all his enthusiasms, Ford announced his decision the next day, November 24. The *New York Times* was tolerant in its editorial, saying that Ford was likely to do "as little harm as good." But most of the comment was adverse, the *New*

York Herald, for instance, calling Ford's proposed crusade "one of the cruellest jokes of the century." Theodore Roosevelt spoke for most political leaders when he said, "Mr. Ford's visit abroad will not be mischievous only because it is ridiculous." Cartoonists exaggerated Ford's long face into the mournful countenance of a modern Don Quixote tilting at windmills from the driver's seat of a Tin Lizzie.

But Ford plunged ahead precipitously, naming December 4 as the departure date for his Peace Ship, which gave him only nine days to assemble the participants and plan the expedition. Schwimmer and Lochner handled the details; Ford handled the public relations. He telegraphed more than a hundred invitations to friends such as Edison and John Burroughs, also inviting national political figures including William Howard Taft, William Jennings Bryan, Hiram Johnson and David Starr Jordan, and journalists Ida Tarbell, Lincoln Steffens and others he thought to be sympathetic to the antiwar cause. At a rally at the Belasco Theatre on November 26, Lochner addressed the crowd when Ford was unable to summon the courage to appear on stage. But after cries of "We Want Ford!" he finally allowed himself to be pushed to the microphone, stammered, "Out of the trenches by Christmas, never to return!" and then ran for the wings.

Many of the luminaries Ford invited to accompany him appreciated what he was trying to do, but few of them wanted to risk becoming part of his entourage. Magazine publisher S. S. McClure and North Dakota Governor Louis Hanna signed up, but of the rest of the 120 people who boarded Ford's Peace Ship over half were journalists.

Antagonistic to the venture from the beginning and certain that the *Oskar II* would be sunk by German U-boats, Clara arrived from Detroit with Edsel in an eleventh-hour attempt to convince Henry not to go. But although she stayed up most of one night in his Bilt-more suite begging and crying, she could not move him. He told her he had made a will leaving everything to Edsel and suggested that she join him. She refused, saying that someone must be left to take care of their son if he happened to get killed. She convinced Henry to take along Samuel Marquis of the Sociological Department as a buffer between him and the rest of the voyagers, who she felt were all "after something."

As the Peace Ship was about to sail, some wag sent Ford a pair of caged squirrels "to live among the nuts." Edison, along with his wife and the grieving Clara, came aboard to see Ford off. Ford was said to have made the inventor a last-minute offer of $1 million to accompany him on his quest, but Edison's deafness, which he often used as a strategic asset, saved the day again as he kept complaining that he couldn't hear Ford above the din on the *Oskar II*.

Shortly before putting out to sea Ford suggested that the soldiers in the trenches ought to call a general strike. He repeated the sentiments he had announced before: "Do you want to know the cause of war? It is capitalism, greed, the dirty hunger for dollars. Take away the capitalist, and you will

sweep war from the earth." As the boat pulled away from anchor, a man calling himself "Mr. Zero" dived in after it. When he was pulled out by the crew
of a tugboat, he explained that he had planned to swim alongside the vessel to
ward off torpedoes.

Those who had accused Ford of having chartered a ship of fools seemed
vindicated by dispatches that were soon radiogrammed back by reporters.
Midway through the voyage, President Wilson delivered a message urging
preparedness, which caused an angry split in the delegation: those around
Madame Schwimmer were against the President, while Marquis rallied
another faction in support of Wilson. Ford managed to stay above the bitter
infighting, which at times threatened to swamp the *Oskar II*. To William C.
Bullitt, covering the expedition for the Philadelphia *Public Ledger*, Ford was
"the tenderest of the tender and the vaguest of the vague, a comic, charming
child." The only time he seemed truly happy on the voyage was when he
slipped away from the warring delegation and went below to inspect the
ship's engines. At one point he was doused by a wave and caught cold, retreat-
ing to his stateroom while the internecine struggle continued in the ship's
ballroom. But even in his quarters he was not safe from the press, as reporters
barged in at one point to check on his condition, one of them explaining
brusquely, "J. Pierpont Morgan was dead six hours before any newspaper
knew about it. We won't be scooped that way this time. So we've come to see
for ourselves whether you're still alive."

By the time the *Oskar II* docked in Norway, Ford had had enough.
"Guess I had better go home to Mother," he told a shocked Lochner. "You've
got this thing started and can get along without me." On December 23 he
slipped away from the hotel and booked passage on another ship headed back
to America, leaving the peace commission to talk to low-level government
officials in Scandinavia and the rest of Europe. Back in New York he insisted
that he had accomplished what he set out to do: "I believe the sentiment we
have aroused by making people think will shorten the war." Asked if the criticism had bothered him, he replied, "I was bothered only because my wife
didn't like some of the criticism. My son Edsel didn't mind and I am really
strong for it." Asked to explain this last statement, Ford said he believed that
criticism would actually help the antiwar effort because "the best fertilizer
in the world is weeds."

Schwimmer dropped out of the delegation, but Lochner and a few others stayed on in Europe, doggedly pushing for continuous mediation. At home
Ford pushed, too, in his own way, continuing to excoriate Wall Street and
arms makers for profiteering off the mass death in the trenches. But his antiwar passion cooled as the U.S. government got closer to involvement. When
Wilson severed ties with Germany, Ford took Lochner off the payroll and
told him to stop his work. Once the United States entered the war, he saw that
the Ford Motor Company got into the war effort. He got involved in a
contract for a submarine chaser called the Eagle boat, and also built Liberty
motors. He conceived of an armored version of the Model T to serve as a

battlefield tank, and of a one-man submarine which journalists derided as a "U-flivver" and which caused Franklin D. Roosevelt, then Assistant Secretary of the Navy, to say of Ford, "Until he saw a chance for publicity free of charge, he thought a submarine was something to eat."

But while his effort might be ridiculed by some intellectuals, for the mass of Americans—people who saw Ford as a genuine grass-roots hero—his reputation was enhanced. And if his idealism was bruised by all the criticism, the practical side of his character realized that it was all worthwhile. "I wanted to see peace," he said afterward. "At least I tried to bring it about. Most men did not even try." Later on, when someone noted that the total price tag for the Peace Ship was almost $500,000, Ford thought for a moment and then said, giving one of his Crazy Henry smiles, "If we had tried to break in cold into the European market, it would have cost us ten million dollars. The Peace Ship cost a twentieth of that and made Ford a household word all over the Continent."

THERE MIGHT BE DIFFERENT OPINIONS about Henry's antiwar activity, but as the war dragged to a conclusion there was no dispute about the importance of the Ford Motor Company itself. It had handled war work as well as auto production and was now being referred to as an archetypal American institution. Henry realized that the Ford Motor Company was the key to his growing influence as a national figure. He concentrated his efforts on possessing the company entirely.

The major roadblock was the formidable figure of Couzens. He and Ford had been co-conspirators at the beginning of the company and social friends for a while afterward. But they were too different for this closeness to survive success, and they had grown apart over the years. Ford would occasionally make light of Couzens' well-known irascibility, arriving at his office for meetings and inquiring archly of a secretary if the "Old Bear was in his den." Yet he had a healthy respect for Couzens, too. In the years of the company's sudden growth he had never challenged Couzens' influence, and he admitted to being frankly awed by some of his general manager's stratagems, such as depositing Ford money in certain banks with the understanding that this money would in turn be loaned to Ford dealers so that they could buy more cars at an interest rate which the bank would then split with the company. Ford knew that someone with this fiscal ability was important, and he appreciated the unquestioning loyalty Couzens had for the company, a loyalty which, in an extreme manifestation, had once led him to respond to an unfavorable article following the announcement of the five-dollar day by dashing off an angry letter to the editor: "Sir—I hereby forbid you ever again to mention the name of the Ford Motor Company in your publication. Jas Couzens, Gen Mgr."

They had worked a Mutt-and-Jeff routine over the years. Ford was the idealist overlooking human fallibility, Couzens the harsher figure enforcing rigorous standards. (He once wrote to a branch manager who had sent a blandishing note at bonus time: "I had put you down for $21,000 before I received your letter. Your letter has cost you $5,000 because it showed me you did not trust me to treat you fairly. I have now put you down for $16,000.") But as his reputation grew, Ford tired of the parity this act implied. He began to see Couzens as a thorn in his side, especially because his partner remembered the Henry Ford who had existed before his discovery by the national press, and showed him no more respect than he showed any other man, which meant, as one co-worker said, that he often "jumped on him with both feet." There were continual contests of will between the two men. Couzens criticized Ford for pushing his ideas at the expense of the company. Ford dismissed the things that the punctilious Couzens took so seriously. (Once he passed through the office and saw a clerk sitting disconsolately in front of a huge stack of correspondence. "I'll show you a good way to get rid of that," he said, picking up the unopened letters in both arms and dumping them into the wastebasket. "Now," he said, "you have a day free.")

Just before the war, Couzens had gone through a period of despondency because of the accidental death of his son Homer, who was killed when the Model T he had been given as a present went off a steep mountain road and sank in a lake below. Deep in a personal crisis, Couzens began to feel that the growing rift with his old friend was irreparable, especially once he discovered that Ford was having him watched and was telling people in the company that he had been at the plant only 184 days in the past year. Wondering if all the attention Ford had received had perhaps made him unstable, Couzens told close friends about the case of former Ford superintendent Walter Flanders. After Flanders quit and went to work for a competitor, Ford began to denounce him bitterly for "raiding" the company for workers.

"If you say the word I'll have his head knocked off," he had said to Couzens one day.

Couzens was taken aback. "What do you mean?"

"I have a couple of fellows who will beat him up."

"Oh no," Couzens had said, trying to dismiss the matter. "We will stand this without *that*." He knew that it might have been a whim on Ford's part or even a ruse to draw him out, but even so this comment confirmed his growing belief that Ford "was not one man but two men"—one sunny and mild, the other with hidden inclinations toward paranoia and ruthlessness.

The tension between Ford and Couzens had finally come to a head during the furor surrounding the Peace Ship. Ford had been freely giving his opinions about the war, and although this grated on Couzens' patriotism as well as his sense of reality, he withheld comment until the morning of November 11, 1915, when Charles Brownell, the Ford advertising manager, stepped into his office to get his approval for the next issue of the company magazine, the *Ford Times*. Couzens leafed through the proof quickly as usual and then suddenly stopped when he came upon an editorial by Ford opposing the war.

"You can't publish this," he said, his face swelling with anger.

"But Mr. Ford himself—" Brownell began.

"You can't publish this!" Couzens interrupted. "Hold it over." When Brownell started to stammer a response, Couzens added, "These are Mr. Ford's personal views, not the views of the company. This is a company paper. He can't use the *Ford Times* for his personal views."

The next morning Ford dropped by Couzens' office. After a few minutes of small talk, Couzens told him he had held back the article. Ford responded vehemently, "You can't stop anything here!"

"Well, then," Couzens replied, "I will quit."

"Better think it over."

"No, I have decided."

"All right, if you have decided."

Couzens left, some of his duties but none of his authority falling to a onetime bookkeeper named Frank Klingensmith. His departure marked an elemental break in the history of the company. Couzens had been the only person in the company Ford had ever respected, the only one who had ever wielded a power in any sense comparable to his own. They had stood shoulder to shoulder during the company's establishment and consolidation, fighting against Malcomson, Selden and other foes. Now it was over. When John Dodge bemoaned Couzens' departure, Ford disagreed, saying that it was "a very good thing for the company." His next target would be the remaining minority stockholders, the Dodge brothers chief among them, who stood between him and complete possession of the company that bore his name.

ONCE AGAIN FORD WAS DIVIDING the world into "we" and "they." He was the "producer"; *they* were the stockholders who had done nothing since making their initial investment except take out huge dividends. He had given them a taste of things to come in 1915 when he formed Henry Ford and Son, a company owned only by him and his family, to produce the tractor he had developed; in that enterprise, he had said ostentatiously, he would not have any stockholders at all, because they were "parasites."*

The Dodge brothers had long since stopped supplying parts for the Ford Motor Company. In fact, they had started their own car company in 1913, financing it with the immense dividends they received from Ford. In 1916 Ford dropped into John Dodge's office and gave him some shocking news:

---

* A success story, in its context as dramatic as that of the Model T, was that of the Fordson tractor. It played a central role in the technological revolution that catapulted American agriculture into the twentieth century. It allowed Ford to become a prophet of the fields in the same way he had already become a prophet of the highways. "Man minus the machine is a slave," he said of his tractor. "Man plus the machine is a free man."

Ford dividends, which had been some $60 million the previous year, would now be restricted to $1.2 million a year, with every cent above that going back into production. This meant that the Dodges' 10 percent of the company, which had previously been worth upward of $6 million a year, would now be worth no more than $120,000. Placing a value of $35 million on his holdings, John Dodge told Ford to buy him out. Henry ridiculed the idea, pointing out that with his controlling interest of 51 percent of the company he scarcely needed more stock.

It was not merely pique at others being enriched by his labor that led Ford to restrict dividends. He wanted to use company profits to finance a new dream plant beginning to take shape in his imagination. Highland Park, "maternity ward" of the Model T, had been modern when it opened, but was now outmoded. It was not just a matter of size and space. Ford had been struck by the way World War I had affected the company's supply of raw materials, and he wanted to make himself wholly self-sufficient through a new superplant the like of which had never been seen before in American industry. Using the assembly line as a sort of metaphor for a larger industrial process, Ford wanted to create a flow of raw materials—iron, coal, limestone, timber for auto bodies, silica for glass—and funnel them into a plant which would then transform them into the building blocks of automobiles. He had already gotten real estate agents to begin buying up land along the Rouge River where he could make his dream come true.

But the Dodge brothers vowed to fight to the end any attempt to divert dividends to Ford's giant construction projects, which they regarded simply as evidence of his growing megalomania. Directors' meetings became as bitter and recriminatory as they had been during Malcomson's last days with the company. The Dodge brothers rallied the minority stockholders; Henry casually defied them all.

In the middle of this business stalemate, a personal matter intruded. Edsel had proposed to Eleanor Clay. Henry and Clara were shocked, but the depth of their son's feelings for Eleanor had been clear to them in letters such as one he wrote home from Hot Springs, where he had gone with his friend Ernest Kanzler, fiancé of Eleanor's sister Josephine, after they met the two sisters for a chaperoned holiday in New York:

> We arrived yesterday morning after 9, got our room...and were out onto the golf course at 10. We played 18 holes. I made 101 which is quite good for the first time around this year.... We had a slick time in New York with Eleanor and Josephine. We went shopping with them two afternoons. We saw some beautiful gowns. Eleanor is buying a trousseau. Fancy that! We all went to shows every night and danced somewhere afterwards. The funny part of it was that with all the late hours and strenuousness, I felt great. Haven't had a pain or an ache since I left Detroit.

The match was oversimplified by the Detroit press as the union of wealth and society. While Eleanor did have a good name, she had not been a debutante and neither the Clays nor the Hudsons were part of the city's old French aristocracy. Nonetheless, Henry was disturbed by what he regarded as the "swank" prenuptial routine she established for Edsel—dinner at the "in" clubs of Detroit, followed by evenings at the theater or dancing at the Grosse Pointe Country Club among people he loathed as poseurs. He was concerned about the influence on Edsel of jazz and other suspicious pursuits that Eleanor enjoyed. (Chief among them was golf. Telling one writer that he believed young people "ought to play games so that they will be strong enough to protect themselves," Ford added, his voice trailing off, "But golf...") Yet he could not deny that Edsel was a good and loyal son, and he swallowed his doubts about the relationship.

The wedding took place on November 1, 1916, at the mansion of Eleanor's uncle, J. L. Hudson. It was the Detroit social event of the year, but, as with other galas involving the newly rich automakers, business provided the subtext for every conversation. At the reception, Henry ran into John Dodge, who was in attendance only because he happened to be an old friend of the Clay family and Eleanor had begged him to come. Midway through their conversation Dodge looked at him and said, "Henry, I don't envy you a damn thing except that boy of yours." Wondering about Dodge's avoidance of the large issue dividing the two of them, Ford nodded in agreement.

At midnight Edsel and Eleanor left the party. Upon leaving the Hudson mansion, their driver turned onto Michigan Avenue, where the young couple could see the huge Ford Motor Company sign above the Detroit Opera House: a Model T, its wheels turning, with a slogan in electric lights, "Watch the Fords Go By," and the number sold so far that year, 719,641. The next morning, newspaper headlines informed the city that the Dodge brothers had filed suit against the Ford Motor Company.

A week into the honeymoon, Edsel wrote to Clara from the Grand Canyon: "The ride out here was quite clear and by sleeping late the time passed quite quickly. Of course everyone had us spotted on the train but not in Chicago or out here.... We felt quite as important as you and father when we arrived. There was a big Pierce touring car to meet us and about six porters and bellhops." Next he and Eleanor went to Hollywood, where they visited several movie moguls and spent an afternoon with Douglas Fairbanks. But in his letters home Edsel was more interested in the outcome of the suit than in the movie stars he was meeting: "I have been buying Detroit papers in Los Angeles and am very anxious to hear how the Dodge suit comes out."

In fact, it seemed to be going quite well. In preliminary testimony, his father had proved an adroit witness, frustrating the Dodges' attorney Elliott G. Stevenson in exchanges such as this one, which Ford had begun by saying that he felt the company's profits had been "awful" the previous year:

> STEVENSON: Your conscience would not let you sell cars at a price that you did last year and make such awful profits? That is what you said, isn't it?
> FORD: I don't know that my conscience has got anything to do with the case.
> STEVENSON: Why did you say that it wasn't right to get such "awful" profits, if it wasn't your conscience?

FORD: It isn't good business.

STEVENSON:…You say you do not think it is right to make such profits? What is your policy about this business, Mr. Ford?

FORD: In what respect?

STEVENSON: You say you do not think it is right to make such profits? What is this business being continued for, and why is it being enlarged?

FORD: To do as much good as possible for everybody concerned.

STEVENSON: What do you mean by "doing as much good as possible"?

FORD: To make money and use it, give employment, and send out the car where people can use it…and incidentally to make money.

STEVENSON: Incidentally?

FORD: That's right. Business is a service, not a bonanza.

STEVENSON: Your controlling feature, then, is to employ a great army of men at high wages, to reduce the selling price of your car so that a lot of people can buy it at a cheap price, and give everybody a car that wants one?

FORD: If you give all that, the money will fall into your hands; you can't get out of it.

It was Ford at his ingenuous yet pragmatic best. Stevenson was unable to crack him, and Henry ended his preliminary testimony, and his lengthier appearance in the witness box a few weeks later, looking like a commonsensical humanitarian whose vision for the future was being blinkered by the ungrateful stockholders who had already received huge dividends for a paltry investment. Nonetheless the decision went in favor of the Dodge brothers, the court enjoining Ford from proceeding with the Rouge plant. As he appealed the decision, Henry jauntily wrote to Edsel, who was taking surfboard lessons in Hawaii on the last leg of his honeymoon: "Practically gained every point in Dodge suit…. Holding up annual meeting until you return."

Hurrying back to Dearborn, Edsel bought a postcard with a picture of his father on the back and wrote a playful message to Clara: "Seeing as how we live now in the big city, I thought I'd just drop you a short note. P.S. The picture on the other side is of one of my friends here in the city."

EVENTS WERE MOVING SWIFTLY for Henry. Involved in lawsuits, politics and national affairs as well as auto production, he was like a juggler with several balls in the air at once. Another man might have felt overpowered, but he thrived on the pressure and activity. Later he looked back on this period and said simply, "It was the time of my life."

On October 31, 1917, the Michigan State Circuit Court ruled on his appeal in the Dodge case, holding that the Ford Motor Company was guilty of "an abuse of discretion" in withholding dividends, and ordering it to pay $19 million immediately. The fact that he was having trouble controlling the company which bore his name was especially ironic in light of his growing power as a national figure, seen in a plea to him from Woodrow Wilson to run for the Senate in 1918 as the only electable Michigan personality who would stand up for Wilson's League of Nations. Ford reluctantly announced his candidacy as a nonpartisan independent, although he admitted that in thirty years he had voted only six times and then only because Clara had forced him to. He ran in both primaries, winning the Democratic nomination easily, but losing in the Republican primary to Truman Newberry, a career politician who had served in Theodore Roosevelt's Cabinet as Secretary of the Navy.

While Newberry began the general campaign by hiring hundreds of workers, Ford remained wholly inactive, telling supporters that if the people wanted him they would mark his name on election day. He was shocked by the brutality of politics, especially when the Newberry camp made Edsel's draft status a chief issue by pointing out that he had been deferred not because of the birth of a son, Henry Ford II, on September 4, 1917, but because of his alleged importance to the Ford Motor Company. The deferment had caused considerable invective at the time it was announced. One Michigan newspaper wrote: "All his life he will be singled out as a slacker and a coward." Congressman Nicholas Longworth, married to Theodore Roosevelt's daughter Alice, stated that there were seven men who got through the war unscathed—Kaiser Wilhelm's six sons and Edsel Ford. Now Newberry revived the issue with slogans such as "He kept his boy out of the trenches by Christmas." Ford did not defend Edsel, nor did he bother to counter an obviously false claim by Newberry that German spies were working in the Ford Motor Company and undermining its defense work. But despite his aloofness as a candidate, Ford lost the election by only a narrow margin, 212,000 votes to 217,000.

For the first time Ford saw the costs of being a public figure. If the lesson did not strike home as deeply as it might, it was only because running his company rather than running for office was paramount in his mind at this point in his life. Shortly after the election, Henry plunged the Dodge brothers and other stockholders into a panic by suddenly announcing that he was resigning as president of the company, effective December 30, 1918. He answered reporters' questions by stating mysteriously that he wished to be relieved of duties "to devote my time to building up other organizations with which I am connected." The directors had no choice but to comply with his request and, in accordance with his wishes, elected Edsel as his replacement.

Over the next few weeks there was constant speculation about Ford's intentions. Certainly he would devote more time to one of his pet projects, the Fordson tractor. Also he would be involved in the *Dearborn Independent*, a local newspaper he had bought with the notion of making it a national publication reflecting his views. But what else would he do? On March 15, 1919, came an announcement from California, where Henry and Clara were vacationing in seclusion: he would start a new business and make a cheaper, better car—a super Model T at half the price. Almost immediately, sales of Ford products slackened as people decided to wait for this dream car. When the

Dodges claimed that Henry was under contract to the company and should not be allowed to start a competing business, Ernest Liebold, recently hired as Ford's private secretary, told reporters, "The Ford Motor Company has no mortgage upon Mr. Ford's body, soul, or brains." Asked if the statement was not just a "club" being used against the stockholders, Liebold shook his head. "Mr. Ford never threatens," he said.

All this time, Ford, acting anonymously through brokerage agents, was feeling out the minority stockholders about selling their stock. Some of them suspected a ruse, but most believed that it was just possible he was serious about his new enterprise; if so, it meant an end to the high dividends they had just been awarded by court order.

THE QUESTIONS OF OWNERSHIP OF the Ford Motor Company and Henry's future as an auto manufacturer were still up in the air when Ford began another trial, this time a libel action he had initiated against the *Chicago Tribune*. Up until this time he had been remarkably successful with the press, having his way with reporters when it came to publicity for his cars and his causes. From the moment he appeared on the national stage he had been portrayed as a Saint George slaying the dragon of monopoly in the Selden suit, a native American genius with deeply sunk grass roots, an embattled entrepreneur righteously fighting for his own company in the action brought by the Dodge brothers. The Peace Ship extravaganza had qualified that support and opened him to questions; the defeat in the Michigan Senate race had shown him to be fallible. But now came an ordeal far more severe than anything he had yet faced, as he prepared to do battle with one of the most powerful newspapers in the country. This time the issue was not some abstract principle of business; the issue was Henry Ford himself.

On June 22, 1916, a *Tribune* reporter had called a Ford press agent for a comment about President Wilson's decision to call out the National Guard to deal with Pancho Villa's raids on the Texas border and had been told that company employees who bore arms for the National Guard would forfeit their positions. The next day the paper ran an editorial stating in part: "If Ford allows the rule of his shops to stand he will reveal himself not as merely an ignorant idealist but as an anarchistic enemy of the nation which protects him in his wealth. A man so ignorant as Henry Ford may not understand the fundamentals of the government under which he lives." On the basis of these words, Ford brought suit for $1 million in damages.

The trial finally took place in May 1919, after more than two years of legal maneuvering, as hundreds of reporters and onlookers jammed into the small town of Mount Clemens, Michigan, which had been chosen because of the impossibility of obtaining an impartial jury in Chicago or Detroit. Once again Ford's antagonist was lawyer Elliott Stevenson, who had come to the attention of *Tribune* publisher Colonel Robert R. McCormick because of his efforts to penetrate Henry's public persona during the Dodge suit. On his side, Ford brought eight attorneys as part of a sixty-three-man team coordinating research and publicity. Part circus and part media event, the *Tribune* trial also took on a metaphorical quality as one of the revealing legal moments of the era, like the Scopes trial to come.

It began the morning of May 15 with Ford, a youthful fifty-five, sitting with his chair tilted back against the wall, clasping a drawn-up knee with his thin pianist's fingers. The imperious McCormick, surrounded by a huge legal staff, was very different from the self-made industrialist. A classmate of Franklin Roosevelt's at Groton and a graduate of Yale, he had inherited the *Tribune* from his grandfather. While Ford had aligned himself with the forces of the future, the archconservative McCormick had been characterized as "the greatest mind of the fourteenth century." If Ford saw his suit as an opportunity to stop the rising chorus of questions being asked about his philosophy, McCormick saw it as a chance to attack someone whose patriotism he had questioned since the Peace Ship.

For the first two weeks of the trial Ford attorneys proved that the Ford Motor Company had in fact kept the jobs of National Guard volunteers open during the border action against Villa, and showed also that during their absence the Sociological Department had taken care of the families of the men who served. But Stevenson kept expanding the scope of the inquiry, making it an inquiry to Henry Ford's character rather than Ford workers' tenure. He managed to win a ruling from the judge that anything having to do with Ford's alleged anarchism, whether or not it bore directly on the *Tribune* editorial, was relevant.

The highlight of the proceedings came when it was Henry's turn to take the witness stand. His chief counsel, Alfred Lucking, had tried desperately to arm him for the ordeal, spending days of preparation in the local hotel in which he tried to tutor Ford on history and current events. But his student had refused to pay attention. One journalist who witnessed these sessions recounted that they would begin with Lucking lecturing,

> "Now don't forget this; remember the evacuation of Florida."
>
> But Ford would soon be away from his seat, looking out the window: "Say, that airplane is flying pretty low, isn't it?"
>
> Again the attorney would try to steer him back to the chair, but Ford would hop to the window with "Look at the bird there. Pretty little fellow, isn't it? Somebody around here must be feeding it, or it wouldn't come back so often."

He counted on his reputation as a homespun idealist to see him through, as it had in other courtroom appearances, but his old antagonist Stevenson was determined to persuade the court that there was another, less attractive Henry Ford than the one lionized by journalists.

"You call yourself an educator," the attorney began, after fencing with Ford over "educational" advertisements he had placed during the antiwar campaign. "Now I shall inquire whether you were a well-informed man, competent to educate people." After scathingly noting the remark Ford had made in a recent newspaper interview, "History is more or less bunk,"* Stevenson went on to test his historical knowledge: "Have there been any revolutions in this country?"

FORD: There was, I understand.
STEVENSON: When?
FORD: In 1812.
STEVENSON: When?
FORD: In 1812.
STEVENSON: In 1812, the Revolution?
FORD: Yes.
STEVENSON: Any other times?
FORD: I don't know.
STEVENSON: You don't know of any other?
FORD: No.
STEVENSON: Don't you know there wasn't any revolution in 1812?
FORD: I didn't know that. I didn't pay much attention to it.

This was just a prologue for a brutal tour Stevenson conducted during the next week of Ford's homemade philosophy and lack of formal education. Under his questioning, Ford defined "chili con carne" as "a large mobile army" and "ballyhoo" as "a blackguard or something of that nature." John Reed, fascinated by Ford, described him during his ordeal: "A slight boyish figure with thin, long sure hands unceasingly moving...the fine skin of his thin face browned by the sun; the mouth and nose of a simpleminded saint."

There were moments when Ford managed to puncture Stevenson's pomposity. Asked to explain "what the United States was originally," for instance, Ford affected hesitancy and then said innocently, "Land, I guess." But his palpable hits were few compared to his misses.

STEVENSON: Did you hear of Benedict Arnold?
FORD: I have heard the name.
STEVENSON: Who was he?
FORD: I have forgotten just who he was. A writer, I think.

Toward the end of his testimony Ford realized that he had been defeated, and he finally said, in response to one of Stevenson's questions, "I admit I am ignorant about most things."

---

* This statement was not far from one Ford might have read in one of the McGuffey Readers of his youth: "A great part of history is an account of men's crimes and wickedness." In making his statement Ford had really had in mind a distinction between history as it was written and history as it was lived. He had clarified his opinions in an interview with radical journalist John Reed in 1916: "I don't know anything about history and I wouldn't give a nickel for all the history in the world. The only history that is worthwhile is the history we make day by day."

As the trial was drawing to a close, Henry got some good news. The brokerage agents he had hired to buy out the minority stockholders in his company had gotten all the agreements. It was a huge settlement. James Couzens, now a U.S. senator from Michigan, got $30 million. His sister Rosetta, who had originally invested $100 in 1903, got $260,000. For initial investments of $5,000, each Dodge brother got $12.5 million, as did Horace Rackham and his law partner John Anderson, the man who had written a letter of desperate argument to his father thirteen years earlier to justify putting money into the new venture. The great loser was Alex Malcomson; his percentage of company stock, sold to Ford for $175,000 a few years earlier, would have been worth $64 million in the buyout formula.

In all it cost Ford $105 million to gain complete control of his company. Edsel, who, as a reward for playing his part in the charade of a competing Henry Ford enterprise, was given the 41 percent in minority stock his father had acquired, told the *New York Times*, "Of course there will be no need of a new company now." Henry was so happy when he was told the deal had been consummated that he danced a jig around the room.

While he won this one, however, Henry lost in Mount Clemens. He wasn't present to hear Stevenson begin his summation to the jury ("They forced us to open the mind of Henry Ford and expose it to you bare...to disclose the pitiable condition he had succeeded in keeping from the view of the public..."). But he could not deny the symbolism of the verdict that the jury reached after ten hours of deliberation: they found that he had been libeled, but awarded him only six cents in damages.

It was a painful and humiliating outcome, and it had profound consequences for Ford. He would never again be the sunny optimist who had captivated America a few years earlier. He now began to turn inward, not so much to the healing resources of an inner self as to his company. He was in a unique position: sole owner of Ford. John D. Rockefeller at the height of his involvement in Standard Oil had owned no more than 27 percent of that company's stock. By contrast, Henry owned all of the Ford Motor Company, which gave him a power no other American industrialist had ever possessed.

Now that he possessed it entirely, the company began to play a larger role in his emotional life than it had played previously. After the *Tribune* trial, he began to feel that it was the only thing he could count on absolutely, the only world he could regulate. The Rouge plant, on which he had continued to work during the years of his legal troubles, was now almost completed. The coke plant was finished late in 1919, the sawmill early in 1920. On May 17, 1920, there was the "blowing in" of the Rouge's Blast Furnace A, which was made into a dynastic ceremony to show the permanence of the Fords in the Ford Motor Company when Edsel's three-year-old son Henry II, cradled in his grandfather's arms, lit the pile of wood and coke placed in the furnace. There was a moment of difficulty ("The fun of playing with matches was almost too much for Henry II," the *Detroit News* noted the next day), but then the blaze started and the boy, along with his namesake, clapped his hands and shouted in glee.

Meanwhile the feature that would make the Rouge plant distinct from all others was completed as the Rouge River was deepened and widened to accommodate deep-water ships from the Great Lakes and beyond. Ford bought the Detroit, Toledo and Ironton Railroad and made it integral to the operation of the plant. In a few years its foundry would be casting ten thousand automobile blocks a day, fashioning all the iron, steel and bronze castings used by Ford products everywhere. There would be some 42,000 employees in this vastness and complexity, working from all sorts of conveyors—gravity, belt, bucket, spiral, overhead monorail, etc. Over ninety different buildings would have 229 acres of floor space, 330 acres of windows, 27 miles of conveyors, and 93 miles of railroad track. It would require a force of five thousand janitors merely to clean the Rouge. If it was the greatest edifice of its kind in the world, it was also a pyramid commemorating Henry Ford himself—the idealist murdered at Mount Clemens, and the crank born immediately afterward.

FIVE

T HE COMMON MAN WAS LESS likely to read about Ford's humiliation in the *Tribune* trial than about his annual summer camping trips with his friends Edison, John Burroughs and Harvey Firestone, which magazine photographs and newsreel footage made to look like an allegory of genius on vacation. Edison traveled with Ford in his Cadillac touring car, Burroughs followed in Firestone's Pierce Arrow, and a Ford truck specially outfitted as a traveling kitchen brought up the rear. Each camper had his own ten-by-ten-foot tent with a floor, electricity and fresh sheets. At their stops Edison would read or catnap, Burroughs would amble off to show Firestone the flora and fauna, and Ford would grab an ax and flail away at deadfall to get firewood for the evening's campfire.

The trips had become part of contemporary Americana. Ford liked to tell about the time the caravan stopped at a service station to replace a headlight on one of the vehicles. He claimed to have said to the attendant, "By the way, you might be interested to hear that the man who invented this lamp is sitting out there in my car."

"You don't mean Thomas Edison?" the man gasped.

"Yes, and, incidentally, my name is Henry Ford."

"Do tell! Good to meet you, Mr. Ford!"

Noting the brand of tire in the service station's racks, Ford added, "And one of the other men in the car makes those tires—Firestone."

The attendant's jaw dropped. Then he saw John Burroughs with his flowing beard, and his voice became skeptical: "Look here, mister, if you tell me that the old fellow with the whiskers out there is Santa Claus, I'm going to call the sheriff."

The story was probably apocryphal; Ford recognized that he had become the stuff of which folklore was made. Indeed, he was as dominant a figure in American cultural life as in American industry. A Ford for President movement simmered in the heartland of the country from 1916 until the mid-1920s. James Couzens, who had been appointed to the U.S. Senate to replace Truman Newberry (who had been unseated because of irregularities in his 1918 campaign against Ford), snorted, "How can a man over sixty years old who has done nothing but make motors, who has no training, no experience, aspire to such an office? It is most ridiculous." For Couzens, perhaps, but not for the American people. A 1923 *Collier's* poll showed Ford far and away the preferred candidate over Warren G. Harding, Herbert Hoover, Progressive Robert M. La Follette and other professional politicians.*

Henry Ford had become a representative American. He was a man of limited formal education, yet he inspired something like mass hypnosis in the American heartland. He stood for the populist values that grass-roots Americans believed in, values which were increasingly under assault in the modern world. Something like a Ford cult sprang up, its devotees seizing on his most offhanded comment as cabalistic wisdom. His myth grew larger and brighter. When, for instance, the *Detroit Times* published an item reporting that he had solved a rear-axle problem for the tractor he was building, the story grew larger as it traveled east. By the time it appeared in the *Baltimore Evening Sun* over two months later, it had developed into an epiphany with almost biblical overtones in which Ford was pictured standing on a rise in Dearborn with Edsel beside him, looking across the valley where he had been born and saying that he had been making cars for twelve years merely so that he could build a good tractor that would liberate farmers from their back-breaking toil.

In large part this mythic figure was Ford's own construct. In a series of autobiographical books written by his amanuensis and alter ego Samuel Crowther, Ford found his voice—commonsensical and pragmatic, yet able to dive to transcendental depths with a deft Emersonian epigram. It was the voice of the American dream, confident but also willing to be challenged. In fact, this voice was a lot like the Model T: useful and possessing many unsuspected qualities. Yet in the wake of the *Tribune* decision Ford's old optimism came only in spasms, which made it seem more like eccentricity than a coherent philosophy. For those who knew him well the public image was increasingly at odds with the private reality.

On the edge of old age, Henry had never really taken the time to think about his emotional life. Its debits and credits could be seen in his relationship with Clara. There was a comforting familiarity in their bond. Henry would come home from work every afternoon and whistle with a special trill which she would echo from wherever she was as she came to meet him. As a friend said, they were like partners or mates, that mutual longing of their first years together having gradually been replaced by a more staid affection. Henry had bought expensive gifts for her over the years—a cabochon emerald and diamond necklace insured for $322,000, a $135,000 string of pearls,

---

* He briefly considered making a run for the office, but Clara put her foot down. Storming into Ernest Liebold's office one day, seething over what she felt was the shame attaching itself to the Ford name, she declared, "I hate the idea of the Ford name being dragged down into the gutters of political filth.... If Mr. Ford wants to go to Washington, he can go, but I'll go to England."

a Russian sable coat valued at $75,000, and other jewels and furs worth nearly $1 million. Yet despite their great wealth, Clara remained a nouveau riche. She collected first folios of Shakespeare and original manuscripts of Dickens' novels, but when a visitor picked books off the shelves of her library he found that most of the pages were uncut. Her homey predictability had always been her virtue for Henry, but as he was subjected to pressures elsewhere in his life it became her liability as well.

They were both set in their ways. Henry typically got up before Clara, rode his bicycle down to the front gate of the estate and back, a distance of two miles. She hated exercise. One afternoon when she was having an arthritis attack, he took her out in a car on a deserted rural road. Stopping suddenly, he said, "I want you to get out and run. Run fast. It'll be the best thing for you." She became outraged, replying, "I won't do it!" and the matter ended there. They also had disagreements about the house and the grounds, which Clara insisted were under her command. Once, when she was gone on a trip, Henry had the library painted; she insisted on repainting it the former color when she returned. Another time he ordered the more than two dozen full-time gardeners to begin digging dandelions out of the Fairlane lawns, but Clara had a fit. "Look at them!" she cried. "Thirty men out there at six dollars a day picking dandelions! I can't spend that much money!"

Ford maid Rosa Buhler glimpsed an area of more serious conflict—what Clara referred to as her "female problems"—one Sunday afternoon when she came into the Fairlane library to deliver a telephone message. "There was Mr. Ford sitting on a chair and Mrs. Ford standing next to him. He said. 'Callie, sit on my lap.' He had to repeat it four or five times. And just as Mrs. Ford wanted to sit down Mr. Ford looked up at me and said, 'Oh, there's Buhler.' Poor Mrs. Ford jumped up. She didn't want to have anyone see her give her affection to Mr. Ford."

He squeezed the maids and the cooks, trying to cover his tracks lest Clara find out. (Once one of the women who worked in the house saw him stroking the hand of a maid named Agnes. Henry sent both women away for fear that his wife would find out, although Clara eventually heard the rumors and hired the Pinkerton Detective Agency to find Agnes and bring her back to Dearborn for an interrogation.) He had resigned himself to a diminished affective life when, at the age of sixty-one, he suddenly found himself in the middle of an illicit romance with an attractive young woman named Evangeline Cote which he was powerless to keep under wraps.

COTE WAS PERT AND ENERGETIC, part daughter to Ford and part lover. She got her ambition from her father, a French-Canadian immigrant, and her dark good looks from her mother's side of the family. (Matinee idol Tyrone Power was a first cousin.) She had come to work at the company in 1909 at the age of sixteen, starting as a clerk. She was working as Harold Wills' secretary when she came to Ford's attention: a petite young woman with a saucy tongue and bedroom eyes. Ford made her a personal assistant. Soon he and his pretty young aide were involved in an affair.

Unlike Clara, whose life centered around home and garden, Evangeline was a liberated woman who liked fast horses (she was the women's harness-racing champion of Michigan) and airplanes (she was also the first woman in the state to be granted a pilot's license). Even the nicknames Ford gave to the two women in his life were diametrically opposed: Clara's was the homey "Callie," while Evangeline's was the tomboyish "Billy." Clara's provinciality was apparent in her choice of charities—the Girl's Protective League, a group promoting morals in young women. Evangeline Cote was the type she would have liked to reform. At one stage of the affair Evangeline carried a pistol in her purse, telling friends that she was ready to kill anyone who tried to harm Ford.

Like most men, Henry underestimated the extent of his wife's knowledge of his secret life. Once he was talking to a young engineer about Harold Wills' fall from grace at the company. "Was it too many women?" the young man inquired. Ford may have had his own situation in mind when he answered, "Women? Why, women won't do you any harm. You can screw any woman on earth excepting for one thing—never let your wife find out." Clara pretended not to see what was happening, although she drew the line when Evangeline tried to select fabrics for her husband's suits. "I pass on what Mr. Ford wears," Clara declared, "and no one else will select clothes for him." If she winked at the romance with Evangeline it was because she regarded Henry's passionate side as a cross best borne by someone else. She knew that their marriage was otherwise secure.

Having Clara and Evangeline at the same time presented a problem which Ford finally solved by getting his chauffeur, Ray Dahlinger, to marry Evangeline, rewarding him with a job as head of Ford Farms. This marriage of convenience kept Evangeline near him and also provided a facade of respectability. In 1923 when she had a son, John, Ford's christening gift was the bed he himself had used as a baby. It was widely rumored in Dearborn that the child was Henry's. Interestingly, Ford had used the name "John Dahlinger" for years as an incognito, telling people whom he and Ray Dahlinger met during their travels that he was Dahlinger's uncle John. Young Dahlinger grew up thinking that Ford must be his father because he had been named after this "other self."

Ford couldn't give the Dahlingers stock in his wholly owned company. Instead he gave them possessions—a three-hundred-acre farm; a summer place near his own in upper Michigan; a tract of land next to Fairlane for a permanent "family" home. The Dahlinger estate, which took nine years to build, included an elaborate paddock, a lake with a skating house, a green-house, and a four-car garage complete with mechanic's rack for repair service.

More to the point, leading from a small room downstairs to Evangeline's bedroom there was a secret staircase of which her husband was apparently ignorant, although Henry was not.

Sometimes he would come to the house early in the day, gliding soundlessly up the Rouge in Clara's electric boat. Because of his well-known abstemiousness, the Dahlingers arranged for a watchman to press a buzzer at the gate when Ford appeared, sounding an alarm at the house which meant that cigarettes had to be extinguished and liquor hidden. Ford would walk up to the front door and say, "Hello there, Ray. Is Billy home?" Then she would come out and the two of them would go for a walk in the woods. When he was away on business, they would carry on lengthy conversations by radiogram, chattering away while a company operator typed out the conversation.

As John Dahlinger grew up there was gossip about how much he looked like Edsel. When Henry commissioned company artist Irving Bacon to do a series of paintings of his own early life, he suggested that John pose for scenes showing him as a boy. He gave the boy a little car like those he had had specially made for Edsel's boys—mini-Fords that went fifteen miles an hour. The situation did not allow Ford to show John paternal affection, but he did have an avuncular concern for the boy, habitually greeting him, "How's my little friend today?" He would take John on walks in the woods, stopping to sit down on fallen logs so that they could play duets on the Jew's harps he had brought along for the occasion. Young Dahlinger always remembered the strangeness of Ford's behavior the time his "father" Ray had tried to fix his model train several times and given up and then Ford repaired it in an instant. John had looked up and said, "Gee, Mr. Ford, you're a genius!" and Ford had laughed until the tears rolled down his cheeks.

FORD'S AFFAIR WITH EVANGELINE MAY have coincided with his late-life crisis, but it did not solve it. The relationship did not liberate him or enlarge his emotions; more than anything else, it was a symptom of the changes coming over him, changes which he could scarcely understand, let alone control.

There had always been talk about Ford's "mean streak." Most often it was manifested in a flash of temper or a rough practical joke. (He liked to come up behind an employee chewing tobacco in defiance of company rules and clap him so hard on the back that the man swallowed his cud; then, as the man began to go green, he would laugh hysterically.) However, the discordant elements in his personality had formerly been held in check by the strong personality of Couzens and by the minority stockholders. Now that these constraints no longer existed, the mean streak became more calculating and cruel; an imperiousness and grandiosity no one had seen before began to enter Ford's behavior. People wondered if perhaps Couzens had been right in his parting analysis of his old friend. Perhaps Henry Ford was two people: one generous and optimistic, the other paranoid and intolerant; one a caring and successful industrialist and the other an ignorant and powerful dreamer. If so, by the early 1920s the second persona was clearly starting to win out.

One thing that was clear was that Ford was obsessed with maintaining the control he had gained over his company. He insisted on taking credit for any advance that happened at Ford. He ordered its public-relations officers to mention only his name in its releases. As a result of the cult of personality he established, the company became a place of Byzantine power arrangements where two men especially rose to the top because of their zeal to serve Ford— Charles Sorensen and Ernest G. Liebold.

Sorensen had emerged as the preeminent Ford executive because of his bedrock loyalty to the enterprise and to Ford himself. (One coworker said, "Suppose Mr. Ford should suddenly say, 'People are crazy to go around the earth when the shortest way is digging through it.' Charlie would go back to the Rouge and start digging.") Operating out of the Rouge, which he had built and controlled, Sorensen had also developed a distinctive personal style, becoming a man of withering tirades and towering rages in which he would crash stools over the desks of foremen or jump into a car and drive it onto the factory floor, causing workers to scatter like a flock of chickens. Once he was walking through Highland Park and, noting that the windows were dirty, grabbed a handful of bolts from a bin, said, "I'll show you how to clean them!" and fired them through the windows, shattering the glass. His reputation was such that when he walked through the factory word of his coming would be broadcast ahead of him in a sustained whisper, "Here comes Sorensen!" He was the quintessential "driver," a word with meanings ambiguously straddling the operator of a car and an operator of men.

While Sorensen thrived on being the center of attention, even if it was negative, Ernest Liebold preferred the shadows. A short, squat man who talked in a low monotone and became angry if he was asked to repeat himself, Liebold brought the same Prussian sense of order to the office as he did to his home, where his eight children marched to the dinner table on his command and sat only when he gave the word. His iron hand was shown in an exchange with a clerk to whom he remarked, "You always get here exactly at eight o'clock." When the man said that he did so because he wanted to be on time, Liebold replied reproachfully, "Yes, but too close to on time," and told him to be there at ten minutes before eight. He was the sort of man who would stop when a subordinate wished him merry Christmas during the holiday season, and then, after considering the statement for a moment, would murmur, "Well, all right," as he walked on.

Discovered by Couzens when he was a teller in a Dearborn bank, Liebold was hired the day the company moved to its Highland Park plant. Six years later, on the afternoon Couzens quit, Ford asked Liebold for a photograph so that he could give it to the press to show them the company's new office manager. But while he had moved efficiently into this role, Liebold sensed a larger opening. Ford, bored and unnerved by administrative matters, had resorted to using a written code to deal with supplicants. If he noted for his secretary, "Please *see* this man," it meant he was enthusiastic; if the message said, "Please *sea* this man," it meant to throw him out. With Liebold's rise, such subterfuges were no longer necessary. Liebold barred access to Ford, taking over office procedure and also a large dimension of Ford's personal affairs, signing checks and answering correspondence in addition to controlling access. Those wanting to see the industrialist began to get neatly typed notes over Liebold's signature: "Mr. Ford is out of town."

Liebold's harsh candor sometimes rubbed Ford the wrong way. The two men would go for long periods not speaking to each other except for an acrimonious exchange of greetings. But Ford was aware of Liebold's value, noting to someone who had complained about his unpleasant nature, "You don't hire a watchdog to like people." A project like the Henry Ford Hospital proved that he had not only a watchdog but the ultimate detail man in Liebold.

Ford had initially pledged $100,000 in land and $10,000 in cash to a citizens' group in 1917 for what was then called the Detroit General Hospital. He distrusted organized medicine and was satisfied with his chiropractor Dr. Coulter, who pleased him by using automotive terms for treatment, saying that he needed to have his carburetor adjusted, his chassis aligned, etc. But he regarded the hospital project as a challenge. When the fund-raising drive became bogged down and all the other benefactors had withdrawn, Ford came to Liebold and said, "Well, it looks as if I'll have to take over the hospital. But if I do, I don't want any strings attached to it." Liebold took the project on, making a medical and financial success out of the only big charitable gesture in Ford's career.

The rise of Sorensen and Liebold coincided with a purge of other men who had made major contributions to the company but who, Ford thought, had perhaps known him too long and too well to be amenable to the new era of his absolute control. Ford indignantly denied that he fired anyone, although he noted archly that "every now and then we did drag a dead skunk across somebody's trail." Sociological Department head Samuel Marquis, who had appealed to Ford's better side in better times and who had been the conscience of the company, watched this process with dismay and wrote later of Sorensen and Liebold:

> To them the morale of the organization meant nothing. They also flouted loyalty on the part of employees as being of no value. They stoutly held that men worked for two reasons—their wage, and the fear of losing their jobs. The humane treatment of employees, according to these men, would lead to the weakening of the authority of the "boss," and to the breaking down of the discipline in the shop.... They were always thinking of themselves as little gods who were to be feared.

Among the first to go was Norval Hawkins, the ex-convict who was Ford's great reclamation project. The Ford Motor Company's first sales manager, he had begun 1903 with nothing and by 1919 had created a network of eleven thousand dealers selling nearly a million automobiles a year. Under Couzens he had learned a dogged loyalty to the company but also the courage to speak out in matters of concern. It was this last quality, which Henry interpreted as insubordination, that led to his dismissal.

Next to leave was Harold Wills. He had been with Ford the longest, helping create the 1903 car. He was still one of the greatest engineers in the auto industry, but Ford had the Model T and was no longer interested in engineering advances. Sorenson felt that one of the problems between them was Wills' inability to defer to Ford's growing ego. There was also the matter of Wills' hard drinking and high living, qualities which irritated Ford's puritanism. There was not just one woman, like Ford's own Evangeline, but dozens, most of them courted with ever larger rings and necklaces. Wills was not formally fired; the dead skunk across his trail involved an empty desk with no work on it. After he quit, Wills reminded Ford of a commitment he had made at the outset of their partnership, to give him 30 percent of Ford's own dividends because Wills had been unable to buy stock in the company at the time of its incorporation. The 30 percent commitment was never observed, although Ford did pay Wills some $3 million over the years. Now, as a sort of severance pay, Wills got another $1.5 million, Liebold writing him a check the day he left.*

After Wills it was the turn of Frank Klingensmith, vice-president and treasurer, who had become chief financial officer after Couzens' departure. He was independent, which Ford disliked. He had also helped train Edsel, and Ford was intensely jealous of anyone who had a private relationship with his son. Even worse for Klingensmith, Ford associated him with the postwar economic crisis that had rocked the entire auto industry. It was a time of sluggish demand on the part of consumers and cash shortages for manufacturers, which most of them solved by bringing banks into a closer partnership with their businesses. In the middle of these hard times, Klingensmith had suggested that the Ford Motor Company borrow some money from New York bankers, an anathema to Ford, who never forgave this trespass against the taboo of his populist economics. He also suspected that Klingensmith wanted to grow into Couzens' role, and he feared the rise of an alternative locus of power. After Klingensmith was gone, one of his colleagues tried diplomatically to find out what had happened. "I fired him because he forgot his mother," was Ford's enigmatic reply. When the employee said that he didn't understand, Ford applied the punch line: "He started out this life as a bookkeeper. Therefore bookkeeping was his mother profession. When he forgot to be a good bookkeeper I fired him."

Next to go was the Sociology Department's Samuel Marquis, who had become a one-man court of last resort against the increasingly autocratic

---

* Wills used this money to build one of the most elegant vehicles of the era, the Wills–St. Clair, a "Swiss watch" of a car which had the misfortune of coming out with a $3,000 price tag in the Depression year of 1921. Later Wills was hired by Walter Chrysler and worked for him for years, winning engineering awards until his death in 1940.

personality of the company. His leaving was occasioned by what he saw as the death of humane concern about the men on the line and the accession to power of "drivers" like Sorensen. Using the metaphor of the machine, Marquis' parting shot hit the mark: "If only Mr. Ford was properly assembled! He has in him the makings of a great man but the parts are laying about him in disorder." With Marquis gone, the Sociology Department lost whatever interest it had ever had in improving the workers' lot and became little more than an exercise in snooping and bureaucratic interference.

The most significant casualty of all, however, was William Knudsen, regarded as one of the most impressive of the young Ford executives because of his work in setting up fourteen branch factories. Jovial and easygoing toward others although tough on himself, Bill Knudsen seemed to embody the other side of the Danish coin from Sorensen. An inability to master office politics and to blandish Ford sufficiently got him into trouble. Ford began to ridicule him because of dental problems which, combined with a propensity to take a drink, gave him bad breath and led some to refer to him as "the goat." The crisis in their relationship came in 1921, when Edsel asked Knudsen to go to Europe to take over the company's increasingly prestigious operations there. Sorensen immediately went to Henry to get him to overturn the decision and bring down the only other man not bearing the Ford name whose power might rival his own. On the eve of his departure Knudsen was notified that he wouldn't be going.

One employee remembered the day Knudsen told him he thought he would be fired, saying, "I have a good friend over there [in the office]. He heard that when Mr. Ford gets back from lunch I'm going to be fired. I've never gotten fired off a job in my life. I'm just going to wait over there by his office, and when Mr. Ford comes in I'm going right up to him and resign." Ford was both cryptic and cavalier about the matter: "I let him go not because he wasn't good," he said, "but because he was too good for me." But the loss of Knudsen would haunt him later on after his former employee was hired by General Motors and quickly built Chevrolet into Ford's chief rival.

Some insiders saw the Ford Motor Company as a benign monarchy which, for reasons they couldn't fathom, was gradually turning into a despotism. Others more interested in global affairs found an eerie resemblance between developments in the company and in the totalitarian states beginning to spring up throughout the world in the 1920s. The comparison made was not unreasonable: first came the elimination of constitutional checks and balances at Ford, in the putsch by which Henry got rid of all minority stockholders; next there were purges of those who had helped make the company; and finally a dictator emerged, supported by a few tough lieutenants and a cult of personality. Interestingly, the *New York Times* called Ford "an industrial fascist—the Mussolini of Detroit." The company even had a prevailing ideology in the form of Henry Ford's anti-Semitism.

Later on it would be suggested by Ford apologists that anti-Semitism was a virus Ford brought back from Europe as part of his disillusion with the Peace Ship. In fact it predated that doomed voyage. Rosika Schwimmer recalled that during a luncheon when her antiwar collaboration with Ford was beginning, he had suddenly slapped a breast pocket containing one of his notebooks and blurted out, "I know who started the war—the German Jewish bankers. I have the evidence here. Facts. The German Jewish bankers caused the war. I can't give out the facts now, because I haven't got them all yet. But I'll have them soon."

Schwimmer thought the comment was "cheap and vulgar," although she didn't say so at the time for fear of alienating Ford. (Ultimately he came to believe that his mission to Europe had failed in large part because this "Jewess" led him astray.) But while the war hadn't caused his anti-Semitism, it did reinforce it. When he returned from Europe he told Liebold, whose Prussian background and character made him the perfect detail man for this new obsession, that he was "going to go after the Jews who had started the war." Soon after the Peace Ship fiasco, in fact, Liebold had hired a con artist named Stanley W. Finch to study the malign operations of "big money" in the United States. Formerly an aide to U.S. Attorney General George W. Wickersham during the investigations of white slavery which led to passage of the Mann Act, Finch told Liebold that he had learned that Jews were largely responsible for the abduction of women used in burlesque and prostitution.

In his work for Liebold, Finch developed a "cross system" showing the relationship between powerful individuals and institutions. A forerunner of the diagrams of interlocking directorates by which a later era would ventilate its paranoia regarding power arrangements in American society, the "green book" Finch assembled showed the links between directors of certain corporations, banks and investment houses—all of them Jews. Employed by Ford from 1916 to 1921, Finch was ultimately fired by Liebold only because he had submitted excessive expense accounts. (He claimed, for instance, that an expensive fur coat was necessary to maintain the proper image with the vulgar Jews he was investigating.)

There was a cultural factor in Ford's anti-Semitism: the notion that the Jew, with his presumed cosmopolitanism and money lending, was the villain in the populists' soap opera of American capitalism. His own personal prejudices extended to Catholics as well. Hearing that the Ford Motor Company's hiring department was controlled by Catholics favoring their coreligionists, Henry once had his brother William pose as a Mason in an employment interview and then fired those who refused to hire him. He would explain Jews and Catholics who were his friends as exceptions to the general rule of racial and religious inferiority. Ford might say of a Jew he liked, "Oh, he's mixed, he's not *all* Jewish." Or of a Catholic, "Well, you know, he's not a *good* Catholic." The difference between him and other respectable men who were also prejudiced was that he insisted on systematizing his bigotry, transforming it from a personal quirk to an architectonic truth he could demonstrate.

His proofs appeared in the *Dearborn Independent*, which he bought in 1919 when he became concerned about the quality of the press he was receiving. E. G. Pipp, a respected Detroit newsman hired as first editor of the *Independent*, didn't quibble with most of Ford's quaint notions—his belief, for instance, that the concept of the assembly line could be applied to a newspaper by having one editor writing facts, then passing the copy on to another who would add humor, and then to another who would add opinion, etc. But when Ford started to make the paper into an organ for anti-Semitism, Pipp resigned, becoming a dedicated Ford watcher and critic. He was replaced by the more compliant William J. Cameron, who began to deliver the anti-Semitic message under Liebold's direction.

The *Independent* was sold on the street, but Ford agencies across the country were the key to wide circulation. A dealer on the West Coast later recalled, "We had continual directives that they wanted the subscriptions to the DI increased and that everything possible should be done to give it the best possible coverage in the territory." Eventually most dealers capitulated and factored a subscription fee into the purchase price of a car to satisfy their quota. Since over a million Model Ts a year were being sold in 1919–21, this meant that the *Independent* went from a fortnightly filled with gossip about a sleepy suburb of Detroit to a mass-circulation weekly whose news was almost exclusively the Jews.

For ninety-one consecutive weeks it flogged "the Jewish question," excoriating the "International Jew" for grasping every lever of power and leaving nothing sacred, not even the Christian religion. Ford played an active role. He once wrote an editorial offering a reward of $1,000 to anyone able to give him an example of a Jewish farmer, part of his belief that Jews avoided "honest" manual labor in favor of "criminal" activities in the banking industry. But most of the material in the paper was far more serious and damaging in its implications than this piece of whimsy.

Liebold hired a New York detective agency to follow up on the work of Stanley Finch and break new ground in anti-Semitism for the paper. Messages to Detroit came in code. Liebold himself traveled to New York incognito— his code designation was "121X"—to receive the agency's findings. The biggest coup of this cloak-and-dagger effort was obtaining a copy of "The Protocols of the Elders of Zion," an alleged report about the secret meetings of Jewish leaders devoted to world domination. The document came from a woman calling herself Madame Shiskmereff, who had come to Liebold's office to discuss "the Jewish question." Concocting a phony genealogy for "The Protocols" (the pamphlet was actually written in 1905 by a Czarist agent trying to channel the revolutionary ferment in Russia into an anti-Semitic byway), she gave Liebold a copy and offered him the original, which she claimed was in a Shanghai bank, for $25,000. Thrifty even in his bigotry, Liebold said that the copy would do nicely for his purposes.

Claiming that the Jews had connived in everything from the discovery of the New World (Queen Isabella was a "Jewish front") to the destruction of Europe as a result of World War I, "The Protocols" was a sort of encyclopedia of ethnic virulence. Its assertions were repeatedly repackaged and inserted into the *Independent*. But the Ford-Liebold inquiry into Jewish iniquity did not stop with publicizing this forgery. The two of them broke new ground of their own, becoming convinced, for instance, that the Jews, working through the 1860s equivalent of the international-Jewish-bankers conspiracy, had been centrally involved in the assassination of Abraham Lincoln. Researchers they supported claimed to have discovered that a body embalmed in California in the late 1800s was actually that of John Wilkes Booth, who (according to this conspiracy theory) had been spirited off to the West Coast and given a new identity by the Jewish bankers who hired him to kill the President. Ford wanted to buy the mummy, bring it to Detroit and have it studied as part of a concerted attempt to connect the Jews with Lincoln's death, but even Liebold drew the line at this.

Edsel and others in the company were disturbed by the way the Ford name was being systematically linked to anti-Semitism. But Henry believe that he was purveying "science," not prejudice, and that the "truths" appearing in the *Independent* could not hurt individuals. In fact, he was convinced that the "good" Jews appreciated his efforts. Employing his best Jewish accent, he liked to tell about a time he went to a pawnshop in Washington: "The elderly pawnbroker kept looking at me. He said, 'Hey, you're Henry Ford, aren't you?' I said, 'Yes.' He said, 'Well, I been reading that *Dearborn Independent* of yours. It's all right. It tells the truth about us.' " Ford was genuinely hurt when Rabbi Leo Franklin, his friend and former neighbor in Detroit, sent back a Model T he had given him. Ford called him on the phone and asked, "What's wrong, Dr. Franklin? Has anything come between us?"

Ford's obtuseness was nowhere more apparent than in the section of his autobiographical sketch *My Life and Work* where he discussed "our work on the Jewish question." Helped by the pen of his ghost writer Samuel Crowther, he claimed that he was involved in this issue because:

> there had been observed in this country certain streams of influence which were causing a marked deterioration in our literature, amusements, and social conduct; business was departing from its old time substantial soundness; a general letting down of standards was felt everywhere. It wasn't the robust coarseness of the white man, the rude indelicacy, say, of Shakespeare's characters, but a nasty Orientalism which has insidiously affected every channel of expression...

Longtime Ford defenders in the press were disgusted. Former Presidents Taft and Wilson and other national leaders pleaded with him to stop. But he forged ahead. The Jews were a fixation that penetrated into the operations of the Ford Motor Company itself. A new employee was dumbfounded his first day on the job when he was told by an old-timer, "Don't ever let Mr. Ford see you using brass. It's a Jew metal." Foreman William Klamm later said, "There was a policy not to have Jewish boys working in the shop. Of course it wasn't outspoken, but you knew it when you were told to 'fire that Jewish fellow over there.' "

Ford formed the Dearborn Publishing Company to reprint a series of anti-Semitic pamphlets which were later called, when collected into a single volume, *The International Jew*. While the book had a modest circulation in the United States, it did better elsewhere in the world and fell on especially receptive ears in Germany, where it was a best-seller and where a *New York Times* reporter, during a visit in 1922, found it on the desk of the as yet largely unknown Adolf Hitler, along with a large photograph of Ford.

The anti-Semitism subsided only when Ford was threatened with another potentially embarrassing legal action. The focus of the *Independent* had shifted from the Jews' world plots to their alleged activities in the United States in areas ranging from baseball to bootlegging. In "Jewish Exploitation of Farmers' Organizations," the paper focused on one Aaron Sapiro, a lawyer who had organized cooperatives to help farmers escape the agricultural depression of the 1920s. Even Liebold had worried about the harshness of the attack. After going over proofs of one issue of the *Independent* he went to Ford and said, "You know, Cameron is going a little bit wild on this fellow Sapiro." Ford shrugged, saying, "That's just what I want. Don't you interfere with Cameron. If he can get me into a lawsuit with Sapiro, that's just what I want. I'd like to see that fellow start suit against me."

He soon got his wish, as Sapiro filed suit in Detroit. But then, a few days before he was to make an appearance in court, Ford claimed that his car had been run off the road near Fairlane. While he was recuperating from alleged injuries, his agents got a mistrial by spreading the story that a person with a "Jewish cast of countenance" had tried to corrupt one of the jurors. Once a date for a new trial was fixed, however, Ford, fearing a repetition of the *Tribune* ordeal, decided to end his long war against the Jews by having his lawyers work out a settlement in which he apologized to Sapiro individually and to the Jewish people as a whole in the *Independent*:

> I confess that I am deeply mortified that this journal, which is intended to be constructive and not destructive, has been made the medium...for giving currency to the so-called Protocols of the Wise Men of Zion which have been demonstrated, as I learn, to be gross forgeries, and for contending that the Jews have been engaged in a conspiracy to control the capital and the institutions of the world, besides laying at their door many offenses against decency, public order, and good morals. Had I appreciated the general nature, to say nothing of the details of these utterances, I would have forbidden their circulation without a moment's notice.

After the recantation, the "Journal of the Neglected Truth," as the *Dearborn Independent* had called itself, sank out of sight, leaving behind only an oil slick of bigotry.

Now that the anti-Semitic campaign had ended, a friend screwed up his courage to ask Ford why he had begun it in the first place. "The Jews have gone along during the ages making themselves disliked, right?" he answered. "They ignored their own splendid teachers and statesmen. Even they could not get their people to change some of their obnoxious habits."

"Well?" the friend prompted him.

"Well, I thought that by taking a club to them, I might be able to do it."

SIX

FORD'S IMMENSE CURIOSITY ABOUT the way the world worked had been stunted by the overnight adulation his company had brought him. He was a man who had once felt that he could produce an original philosophy, but had settled for the destructive, secondhand "knowledge" of "The Protocols." Among other things, the anti-Semitic campaign suggested the extent to which he was troubled by the modern world which he, perhaps more than any other individual, had helped create. The older he got and the more wounds he accumulated in the various combats he had undertaken, the more he came to accept his father's old dichotomy between the sinful metropolis and the pure countryside, finally proclaiming that "the *real* United States lies outside the cities."

From the early twenties onward, Ford spent a good deal of time and money trying to turn back the clock whose mainspring he had unknowingly put in place when he installed the first assembly line at Highland Park. Edison had given him the idea of creating an archipelago of village factories, rural plants that would allow men to work for the Ford Motor Company when they were not farming, thus keeping them from having to migrate to the vice-ridden cities. Ford established some plants with great fanfare, but lost interest when they were incapable of doing anything more than light manufacture and could employ only about two thousand workers, a fraction of those now on his payroll at the Rouge.

Although he never stopped promoting rural values, he realized that the attempt to keep people on the farm was a doomed idea, something like trying to close the barn door after the horseless carriage was out. So his obsession with the past became a haunting sentimentality, a lost Eden into which he retreated in his own personal life, peeking out dyspeptically at the modern world and then pulling down the shades. The old family homestead which he had been so desperate to escape as a teenager became the key to this vision of a prelapsarian state, having a power of evocation for him similar to what "Rosebud" had for Citizen Kane. Ford would occasionally find a half-dozen schoolboys and take them out to his birth-place, calling the caretaker in advance to make sure that there was a peck of apples on hand and that the hayrack was piled high enough so that they could all jump onto it from the top of the barn as he had done when he was a boy. One Ford employee happened to be at Fairlane when Henry burst in through the back door one afternoon, saying excitedly, "Well, I think I've done today what my mother wanted me to. I went over to the old residence and...I did things I used to do for my mother. I took her paisley shawl and laid it very carefully in the dresser drawer where she used to keep it." He decided to move the "old residence" closer to Fairlane and to restore it completely, cloning the interior from fragments of wallpaper and bits of rug; he had a complete set of his mother's china reproduced from the shards of an old plate he located during the excavation.

Company artist Irving Bacon once accompanied Ford to the homestead and found that it was like entering a time machine where the past was completely re-created and preserved: "He took me to the cool cellar where we ate apples, drank cider, and helped ourselves to hickory nuts.... We climbed the narrow stairs to his bedroom. It was small, just large enough to hold the patchwork quilt-covered bed that he slept in when he was a boy.... On the bench were tools used for repairing watches and clocks." Ford ordered Bacon to paint a scene of him as a boy sitting at his bench fixing watches.

The preoccupation with the house of his youth led to a larger project. For some time Ford had been collecting implements from the past—guns, clocks, shoes and the like—storing them in a little corridor off his Highland Park office which his clerks called "the chamber of horrors." During the *Tribune* trial, when he and Liebold were discussing the furor caused by his fateful statement about history: "History is bunk," Ford said, "I'm going to start up a museum and give people a *true* picture of the development of our country. That's the only history that is worth preserving. We're going to build a museum that's going to show industrial history, and it won't be bunk."

His collecting was as eccentric as were the theories behind it. He once spent $45,000 on what he regarded as an unusual highboy. It was said that he had one of every kind of shoe ever produced in America. Obsessed with showing the evolution of things, he discovered that a certain kind of engine had been made in New York and insisted that his agents find one of each of the twenty-four sizes it had come in, for his collection.

He decided to house all his treasures in a model village which would preserve the old ways in the face of the encroachments of modernity. As a philanthropic gesture he had already done a restoration of the old Wayside Inn immortalized in the Longfellow poem. This led to the idea first of building a replica of a typical New England village clustered around a common, and then of constructing a more generic village, which he decided to call Greenfield Village in honor of the place where Clara had been born. He bought two hundred of Dearborn's best farming acres and had architects begin to design a square into which he planned to transplant the house where he had been born, along with the homes of Walt Whitman, George Washington Carver, Stephen Foster and others he admired. William McGuffey's house would be there. So would the Scotch Settlement School that Henry had attended as a youth. He had Edison's laboratory dismantled brick by brick and rebuilt as the cornerstone of this village. ("Dear me," Mrs. Edison remarked as the workmen appeared, "I do wish Mr. Ford would keep out of our back-yard.") He wanted this project to outlast the flimsy modern structures he saw going up all around him, and demanded a wood for the floor of his museum that would last a thousand years, not quarreling with the $325,000 price tag for a rare variety of teak.

At the same time he was building Greenfield Village, Ford's increasingly militant antiquarianism led him to promote a rebirth of old-time dances that he remembered from his youth. He hired a dance master named Benjamin Lovett and invited people to come first to his home and then, as the crowds grew larger, to the Ford Motor Company ballroom to learn how to begin with a two-step and strike up a "gallop." Caught up in enthusiasm for a "clean" entertainment different from the decadent "sex dancing" that Edsel's genera-tion enjoyed ("A gentleman should be able to guide his partner through a dance without embracing her as if he were her lover," said the manual *Good Morning* which Ford had printed in defense of the old styles), he ordered foot-prints indicating the step of a particular dance painted on the floor of the Engineering Building so that he could force employees to practice with him. (A mortified Sorensen learned the *varsovienne* with Ford himself—a bear of a man being pirouetted about by his master.) The dances became formal weekly events, ordeals which Ford executives dreaded but dared not miss. Knowing that the teetotaling Ford would serve only fruit juice, they brought hip flasks which they nipped at all evening to help them through the ordeal.

FORTIFIED BY SEVERAL COCKTAILS, Edsel, too, would come to these events and stand silently on the periphery of the dancing, a crown prince present at a royal ceremony he didn't comprehend. Episodes such as his father's affair with Evangeline Cote, the anti-Semitic campaign and even the increasing retreat into the past each brought up in its own way the issue of his birthright. Born to the Ford Motor Company, he had always regarded it as a calling which ruled out any commoner's ambition or normal way of life. The company was like a sibling in one way, like a family totem in another. If it had made Edsel the man he was, it had also drained him of manhood because its powers could not be seized, only given. And the gift was always conditional, liable to be withdrawn. He was president of Ford, yet that office had been conferred on him not because he had earned it, but because it was a convenience for his father. He seemed stuck in the role of the good son. Real power, as one of Edsel's friends put it, was like a mirage of water the thirsty man sees just over the next sand dune.

His first insight into the price that might be exacted from him had come in 1917 in the much-discussed issue of his draft status. Happily married, with a young son and with other children planned, Edsel had thought to volunteer for the Army, knowing that all able-bodied men who did not would be branded slackers. But Henry had forbidden it, claiming that he was vital to the business. This gesture had brought a chorus of derision from people like Theodore Roosevelt, who, during the 1918 Senate election, had written an endorsement for his father's opponent, Truman Newberry, noting that his sons, at least, had enlisted: "The failure of Mr. Ford's son to go into the Army at this time, and the approval of the father of the son's refusal, represent exactly what might be expected from moral disintegration..."

Edsel had been badly shaken by the experience. When his second son was born, in 1919, he at first named him Edsel Jr., and then, as if overcome by self-doubt that he didn't want to pass on, even symbolically in a name, changed the birth certificate while the infant was still in the hospital, renaming him Benson. But if he doubted himself, he never doubted his father, accepting the Henry Ford myth as unquestioningly as any man on the street. Ernest Liebold always recalled the time when he and Edsel were talking about some complex problem and Henry walked into the office, listened to them a moment, then immediately came up with a solution and went on his way. As he left, Edsel looked up and said, "Isn't that marvelous? Isn't it a mystery? I don't understand how he does it."

As critics began to resurrect the old "Crazy Henry" persona of a prior era, this time with darker implications, Edsel refused to dissociate himself from his father. "I have not worked out a separate business philosophy for myself," he said. "It has not been necessary, for on all material points I agree absolutely with my father's philosophy. I do not merely accept his beliefs; I feel as strongly about them as he does." Yet such shows of loyalty did not close the growing gap between the two men. One day a Ford employee witnessed a scene of pathos as Edsel tried to establish a camaraderie with his father by telling him a joke about an old Jew ready to die who asked his wife to line up the children: " 'Children, I want to make a confession. Your mom and me never married.' There was deep silence until the oldest, a boy of fifteen, piped up to his brothers and sisters, 'Well, you bastards, aren't you going to say something?' " While his father laughed, Edsel reddened in shame at the price he had paid for this momentary closeness.

In certain respects he was an impressive young man, contemporary and stylish, the sort of person who photographed well in flannels standing in front of Art Deco buildings. Of medium height, with his father's long-legged body but without his robustness, Edsel had dark wavy hair and an appealing face dominated by bright and observant eyes which allowed him, one secretary said later, "to size things up without saying anything." Yet what he sized up, particularly regarding his father's behavior, seemed to perplex him, and throughout the 1920s his liquid brown eyes, in unguarded moments, conveyed a bemused quality, as if he considered his position at Ford an imposture. In addition, he had never outgrown the physical frailness of his youth, and suffered bouts of nausea which his few opponents in the company tried to magnify into a metaphor by saying he had "no stomach" for the hard going of the auto industry. In 1920 he had an appendectomy, but that didn't seem to improve his condition dramatically.

Yet Edsel tried to build a life apart from his father. He was interested by the people of wealth and power Henry found "phony." He met Franklin Roosevelt while vacationing in Warm Springs, Georgia, and became friends with the young man who had attacked the Peace Ship fiasco while serving as Secretary of the Navy. One afternoon Edsel and Eleanor and a friend from Grosse Pointe, Harry

Pierson, were about to leave for a picnic with Roosevelt, who had recently been afflicted with polio. On an impulse Edsel sat down and wrote out a $25,000 check for a swimming pool in Warm Springs to benefit Roosevelt and others who suffered from this disease. Too embarrassed to give Roosevelt the check himself, Edsel asked Pierson to do it. When FDR saw the amount, he struck his forehead with the palm of his hand and said, "Well, I'm just flabbergasted!"

Edsel had adopted a tight self-restraint as a survival tactic. He was proper and decorous, yet capable occasionally of an off-color drollery. (Once he was driving by a bridle path where a pair of brightly dressed and heavily made-up women were riding and quipped after glancing at them, "Nice horse.") Probably because of the contrast with his increasingly conservative father, he got a reputation as being something of a bon vivant and was said to have personally introduced the rumba to Detroit one evening at the Pontchartrain Hotel. But while he was "handsome enough to charm the dogs off a meat wagon," in the words of one woman, he was bonded to Eleanor and wrote to his mother after a stay in Florida, "Before leaving for home I want to [say] how sweet you were to write what you did in your letter about Eleanor. I think she is perfection."

Together they built a family into which Edsel burrowed as a way of escaping momentarily from his father's world. The children grew up in two units. One was comprised of Henry II and Benson, both of whom had inherited Eleanor's heavy-jawed fleshiness. The other unit contained Josephine ("Dodie"), born in 1923, and Bill, who followed two years later, both with Edsel's own lithe body and dark good looks.

There was never any doubt about who was the leader of this younger Ford generation. Henry II had been the chubby princeling of the Ford clan from the moment of his birth. Vacationing at the summer home she and Edsel had bought in the elite Maine seacoast community of Seal Harbor when Henry II was a baby, Eleanor had sent back postcards like this one to "Dear Sonnie," meant to be read aloud to him: "Just a week from today we expect to leave here and arrive home on your birthday.... I know you must be having a beautiful time at Dearborn so take good care of your grandmother. A big hug and kiss from Muddies."

As he grew up he adopted an imperious tone with his brothers and sisters, the tone of someone in charge of his generation but not particularly concerned about its well-being. This was clear in a note he sent to his sister Dodie in 1926 when he had been taken to Europe while she was left behind: "Are you having a good time in Dearborn? How's the weather? I am shure [*sic*] you would like to be here and see the funny little boys and girls. We will be home in a week or so. Mother and Daddy are very sorry they didn't write you. Love Hank."

Growing up into the power of the Ford name, Henry II took for granted the remarkable things that were happening to the family. Thus, at the age of eleven he wrote to his namesake from Seal Harbor, Maine: "Dear Grandaddy— How are you and Callie? Daddy said you went up with Lindbergh and then with him and Lindbergh.... The paper said you were the first passenger in the *Spirit of St. Louis*. Yesterday we went to the horseshow. Ben rode Laddie Boy but did not get anything. I rode and got first prize..." At about the same time he wrote his grandmother a note about a present he had gotten from the President's wife: "Dear Callie—I received the puzzle yesterday from Mrs. Hoover and the books from you.... Will write Mrs. Hoover a note of thanks today. Please excuse all the mistakes in this poorly written letter. Love Henry."

His brother Benson was different. When he was born, the doctors had put too much silver nitrate into his eyes, leaving him almost blind in his left one. Someone looking at him could not tell he had a physical problem, yet it marked him invisibly as a Ford apart, giving him some of the reticence of a disabled person. Growing up he never questioned his role as Henry II's side-kick and foil, as best supporting actor. There was no rivalry between them, because there was no contest. As one friend of the family said, Benson was the child who "looked most like the mother and acted most like the father." He was shy, diffident, somewhat disoriented. Yet there was a sweetness in him that Henry II didn't have. Tom Loughlin, a groundskeeper and sometime baby-sitter, once went with the family on a Caribbean vacation where gambling was legal. He thought that one of the slot machines was ready to pay off, and gave nine-year-old Benson three silver dollars to play. Benson hit a jackpot on the last one, and they split $118. When they got back to the hotel, the coins weighing down Benson's knee pants, Henry II begged his brother for half his share, and Benson gave it to him. Told at the breakfast table what had happened, Edsel smiled quizzically at Benson and said, "That's good, but I don't think I would have divided with Henry."

"EDSEL HAD EVERYTHING GOING FOR him," a friend once said. "He had everything a man could want—a good family, a good personality, a good life. There was just one problem—his father." Volatile, eccentric, self-absorbed, the Henry Ford of his adulthood seemed so different from the steady and affectionate figure he had known as a child that Edsel had trouble understanding him. Evangeline Cote had said that Ford liked to create the conditions by which he could possess people entirely. This was truer with Edsel than with anyone else.

Rather than battling his father directly, Edsel tried to find avenues in the company where he could prove himself. Henry was unpredictable in his hours, appearing suddenly in the Rouge among the assembly lines, tinkering with the machines and talking with the workers. Edsel saw this as the prerogative of genius. He tried to act the role of president, arriving precisely at nine o'clock, already having read his mail on the ride in to the office. He would lunch with his father—a command performance—and never leave the office until after five. His secretary later said, "He had the most orderly desk I've ever seen.... Never did I see him lean back in a chair and read a newspaper for entertainment."

It was owing to Edsel's influence that Ford bought the Lincoln Company in 1922 from Henry Leland.* Since his childhood Edsel had been fascinated by fine automobiles and wanted to add the Lincoln to Ford's line for this reason. "Father made the most popular car in the world," he said at the time of the Lincoln purchase. "And I would like to make the best car in the world." He wrote long detailed letters to Henry Braunn, head of the firm manufacturing the Lincoln body, specifying precisely the kind and color of paint to be used on the car, the grade of leather he wanted on the seats, and the placement of the trim on the body. Yet his father regarded the car as Edsel's toy and refused to put money into volume production; thus the Lincoln limped along as an elegant loser in the Ford stable of cars.

Edsel also looked at other areas where he might make a mark. He was interested in speedboats and had Ford engineers design and construct models such as the *Miss Dearborn*, a thirty-five-footer with an engine developing 1,000 horsepower which he entered in an international sweepstakes race on the Detroit River. His own career in racing ended when the boat he was driving burst into flames on Lake St. Clair and he narrowly escaped injury. But he still felt that he could use racing boats the way his father had used race cars—as a public-relations device to popularize a low-priced boat for the common man. He built prototypes powered by an engine similar to the one in the Fordson tractor. But he found that the boat did not plane the water adequately, and thus the idea of a marine Model T by which Edsel could establish his own identity as an industrialist went by the wayside.

He tried the same thing with airplanes. Even as a teenager he had been interested in flight. Shortly after the Wright Brothers made news at Kitty Hawk, Edsel had joined Charles Van Auken, another young man in the company, in designing a plane with a frame of metal tubing, wings of silk, a landing gear of bicycle wheels and a Model T engine. The plane had flown a

---

* Leland was the famed engineer who had been brought in by backers of Ford's earliest venture, the Detroit Auto Company, to increase the quality of its products. After the piqued Ford left that company, Leland had taken control and eventually turned it into Cadillac. After William Durant bought Cadillac to become the flagship of his General Motors combine, Leland and his son formed the Lincoln company.

few feet and then crashed into a tree. Edsel's involvement in aviation out-lasted this accident. Committed to the modern world his father was rejecting, he remained convinced that flight had tremendous commercial possibilities, a position to which he ultimately brought Henry as well. He built hangars and a tower where the dirigible *Shenandoah* could be tethered when it was in Detroit.

With his father, Edsel laid out an airport which was soon the center of local aviation activity, especially after Charles A. Lindbergh had come to give Henry and Edsel a ride in *The Spirit of St. Louis.* (Edsel telegraphed to Eleanor, who was vacationing at Seal Harbor: "Had 10 minute flight with Col. Lindbergh in the Spirit of St. Louis today. Hope you won't think too harshly of me but I just couldn't resist it, especially after Father had gone up with him.") Edsel tried to do his part for airplane navigation by asking all Ford dealers to paint the name of their town in large letters on the roofs of their buildings. By the mid-1920s he had made aircraft an important sideline at the company. The Ford trimotor was on the drawing board, an all-metal craft which was soon purchased by several commercial airlines, proving to be one of the most durable planes ever built. Edsel worked with Ford engineers on the design of a cheap low-winged monoplane, fuel efficient and not particu-larly fast, which would become the Model T of the air. It was his idea to build two thousand of these little planes and begin selling them at Ford agencies around the country. But his father, upset by the death of a Ford test pilot, stopped in at the engineering room one day and looked at the model of his son's "flivver plane." After Edsel had explained the plan to him, Henry shrugged dismissively, saying, "That's no good. No, don't do that," and walked out the door, dooming Edsel's attempt to enter aviation history the way he had doomed his attempt with automobiles.

Edsel saw his dilemma. "I have responsibility but no power," he said sadly to a friend. Still, as his father's attention wandered into obsessive byways, Edsel was left to provide whatever coherence the company had. At times he would try to exercise some of the prerogatives of a company presi-dent, but then something would happen which would call the whole enterprise into question. For instance, Edsel saw the demoralizing effects of Charles Sorensen's brutality and the dangers of his growing power, which often put the two of them at odds. (Ray Dahlinger told another Ford employee, "Sorensen's job here is to train Edsel for the big job when he can take it over. Edsel just isn't tough enough.") Finally one day Edsel had enough of Sorensen's arrogance and told him he was fired, but Sorensen merely went behind Edsel's back to his father, complaining of the mistreatment, and was promptly rehired. As one family intimate said, "This resulted in the suspen-sion of amiable relations between Edsel and his father, and for a good many months they never even spoke to each other."

Henry was caught in a paradox of his own making. He wanted Edsel to succeed in the company, but he didn't want to surrender control to him. Observers felt that there was something calculated in the humiliation of his son which resulted from this ambivalence. In one especially painful incident, Edsel decided that the company's growing clerical and executive staff made it necessary to build a new administrative building. Shortly after an excavation had been made for the foundation, Henry happened to notice it and asked, "What's going on here?" Told what it was, he said, "We don't need any more administrative space. If we're overcrowded, get rid of some people." He had the hole fenced in, and after it had served for a few weeks as a reminder of who was in charge he had it filled in.

Finally Edsel decided to make a serious bid for power with the support of his brother-in-law Ernest Kanzler. A graduate of Harvard law school, Kanzler was a broad-shouldered six-footer with a high forehead and eyes whose penetrating power was magnified by strong glasses. He and Edsel had gotten to know each other during their mutual courtship of the Clay sisters. Because Eleanor was so close to Josephine (they called each other every day on the telephone, even if they had been together the previous evening; Eleanor had named her daughter after her) it was natural that Kanzler should become Edsel's best friend after he married Josephine.

At the time of the Dodge brothers' suit, Kanzler was clerking for the law firm handling their case. Henry had talked about his defense freely when Kanzler visited Edsel at Fairlane. Kanzler warned him not to. Ford laughed and said, "You ought to be on my side. Why do you want to be a lawyer, anyway? They're parasites. Come to work for me. I'll give you a job." Eventually Kanzler decided to take him up on his offer and started at Henry Ford and Son, the tractor company, at $5,000 a year in 1919.

He insisted on beginning at the bottom as a mechanic, talking and acting like the other laborers except at lunchtime, when he went outside to eat on the lawn like everyone else, then opened an elegant lunchbox and mumbled to himself, "Well, let's see what the Jap butler has fixed me today." A burly man peering out of thick glasses, he was somewhat incongruous in overalls, but the men were impressed with his intelligence and intensity. "He was a very broadminded individual," one of them said later. "He could assimilate information...[and] surround you with the highest amount of data, history, or what have you and plow through it all and come up with the right answers. He had a terrific analytical mind."

Soon after Kanzler arrived it was obvious to everyone that there was only one person in the company his equal in drive and energy, Charles Sorensen, and that conflict between the two men was inevitable. Kanzler made it plain that he was Edsel's partisan in his losing Oedipal battle with his father, and one Sunday when he called on Sorensen at his home he criticized Ford for "keeping Edsel down." In an elaborate show of support for his patron, Sorensen immediately jumped up and showed Kanzler the door. When Sorensen told Ford about the incident Ford said, "You have not seen the last of him yet. He will be on Edsel's lap now."

Edsel did transfer his brother-in-law from the tractor company to Highland Park. Once again Kanzler insisted on learning from the ground up—going out into the plant at three o'clock every afternoon and putting on overalls so that he could watch the men build axles and motors, starters and generators. He had the office next to Edsel's and he saw his job as helping Edsel consolidate control over the company. Kanzler became Edsel's eyes and ears and, more often than not, his heart as well. Henry Ford was increasingly suspicious of him—not only because of his frank comments to Sorensen and the impact he was having on the organization, but also because of his connections with the hated Grosse Pointe "crowd," and the fact that he had convinced Edsel to join him in buying a summer place at Seal Harbor, where they both vacationed with the Rockefellers and other figures of the Eastern establishment Henry loathed. ("Kanzler and Edsel ought to be bankers," he told an associate in a comment revealing how deep his disillusionment was.) Ford considered it a betrayal when Edsel "defied" him, as Sorensen said, by forcing Kanzler's appointment as vice-president and member of the board of directors late in 1923.

As Kanzler worked with Edsel to make the company respond to the changing marketplace, Henry was behind the scenes, encouraging Sorensen's obstructionism and making the company into a caldron of infighting and intrigue. One climactic episode occurred when engineer Theodore Gehle, sent to England by Kanzler to survey the deteriorating situation there, concluded that the company's position had become vulnerable primarily because of a newly mandated "horsepower tax" that made the Model T impractical. In the spring of 1925 he wrote to Kanzler with his recommendations regarding the need for a modified vehicle and received a cable reading, "Sail at once." Arriving home, Gehle was met at the train by one of Sorensen's flunkies, who told him that Sorensen wanted to see him immediately. He protested that he was reporting to Kanzler, but nonetheless he allowed himself to be taken to the Rouge, where Sorensen gave him the "third degree" in an unsuccessful attempt to find out what he was thinking. Getting free, Gehle went to Kanzler and handed him his written report. After going into Edsel's office and talking to him for a few minutes, Kanzler beckoned for Gehle to follow him into the president's office. Edsel said to him, "We would like you to come to the Round Table for lunch tomorrow and bring this data with you. I'll ask you some questions and I want you to answer them just as you have in my office." As Gehle was leaving, Kanzler came up to him and said, "Of course, I may ask you to do things sometime that are disagreeable or unpleasant. In fact, we may ask you to do something you can be fired for. But we still want you to do it."

The next day the three of them went to Highland Park, Edsel driving and making nervous conversation. While they were eating in the executive lunchroom that Ford insisted on calling the Round Table, the conversation was amiable. Afterward Edsel cleared his throat and said, "Father, Ted's been over in England long enough to collect some information…. I would like to ask him some questions about it and have him answer." After the catechism was over, Ford, who had listened with rising irritation, began his own interrogation of Gehle, who knew that he had committed the ultimate heresy in suggesting that the Model T be modified in any way. In answering his question of what kind of car was needed in England, Gehle said candidly that it had to be smaller, lighter, less powerful and more fuel efficient. Ford leaped up and began to yell at him, "You're trying to tell me how to design an automobile for the English market!" After he had stomped out of the room, everyone else filed out. Kanzler took Gehle aside and whispered, "You've probably been hurt by this. My suggestion would be that you get back to England as soon as you can. Get out of Henry's sight."

Despite episodes like this, Kanzler worked hard to introduce rationality into the company's managerial structure, an element largely missing since Couzens had quit. Before Kanzler's emergence as Edsel's right-hand man, Ford production strategy, in the words of one foreman, "was simply a matter of build all the cars you can." Kanzler initiated inventory and production schedules specifying what kind of cars would be built, how many, when, etc. One executive said, "He was production manager in every sense of the word; he would take the forecasts of the Sales Department and then in a meeting including Edsel would decide how many cars to build and what to project for the following months. He would have schedules. He established the first Production Control Department the Ford Motor Company ever had."

Thinking that the president's office offered him protection, Kanzler understood too late that he was in danger of being outflanked by Sorensen. His rival had ceded control of Highland Park to Edsel and Kanzler, making the Rouge his own redoubt. He knew that someday the company's center of gravity would eventually shift to this industrial metropolis and until then all he had to do was burrow into its emerging structure, become identified with it and indispensable to its operation. By 1925 this was exactly what had happened. At this point Sorensen joined the battle with Kanzler in earnest, both of them recognizing that their personal confrontation was an allegory for the larger contest between Edsel and his father over the soul of the Ford Motor Company itself.

Even though he was better educated and more genteel than Sorensen, Kanzler was no less tough. At the time when the bulk of the company's work force was being shifted from Highland Park to the Rouge, Kanzler told one of his assistant superintendents to take a transfer to keep an eye on things at the new plant: "Now you go down to the Rouge plant. We want to get that son of a bitch Sorensen out of there. You understand what I mean?"

For a brief moment it seemed that Kanzler would win; that he would be able to unseat Sorensen and thus gain real power for Edsel's presidency. But there was one factor that resisted all his energy and resolution, and that was the Model T itself. Jokes about it that had once been affectionate now had a sharp edge. ("What does the Model T use for shock absorbers?" went one of them. "The passengers.") Although the car's appeal had begun to decline after a decade on the market, Ford still regarded it as the fulcrum of his personal myth and therefore unchallengeable. Late in 1922, at a national gathering of Ford salesmen, he had sat for two hours listening to pleas for an update of the Ford line. Yawning to express his indifference, he then rose to deliver his final word: "Well, gentlemen, so far as I can see, the only trouble with the Ford car is that we can't make them fast enough."

Two years later, however, the Model T's declining appeal had become critical. General Motors was steadily cutting into Ford's market, largely because of Bill Knudsen's assumption of control at Chevrolet, where sales had increased from 280,000 to 470,000 in 1924-25 and then to 730,000 in 1926, mostly at the expense of Ford. The statistics were alarming. In 1923 the Ford Motor Company had produced 57 percent of all the cars sold in the United States; by 1925 its share of the market was at 45 percent and falling. Ford's original goal had been to turn out a Model T every minute. In 1925 he was turning out one every ten seconds, but people were buying other cars.

Alfred P. Sloan, who had been brought into the presidency of GM by the Du Ponts and other large shareholders when William Durant became overextended in trading the company's stock, had seen something Henry Ford stubbornly ignored—that a new stage in the auto industrial age had been reached and consumers were ready to make a transition from a simple, practical car to an attractive, comfortable and higher-performance vehicle. While the Ford Motor Company stuck stubbornly by its utilitarian car and the slogan that showed how passé it had become, "It Gets You There and It Brings You Back," Sloan was taking decisions regarding the shape and color of GM's cars away from the engineers and giving them to stylists.

He had been steered in this revolutionary path by his associate Lawrence Fisher, youngest of the four brothers whose body business had been acquired by GM in 1926. In a Cadillac dealership in Los Angeles Fisher had discovered a man named Harley Earl making a small fortune off wealthy customers who came in to have their cars customized with unusual paint schemes, modified lines and occasionally whole new bodies. Fisher brought Earl to Detroit, where he did a quick make-over on the bodies of the 1927 Cadillac. Sloan was delighted. He saw Earl as the perfect figure to help in his strategy of raising styling to equal status with mechanics. Sloan appointed him to head an "Art and Color" section. Earl's work gave impetus to frequent model changes. Even more important, it acknowledged that the automobile had traveled from the workaday world into a cultural dreamscape and that the successful manufacturer of the future would be the one who would tap the hunger of the growing middle class for status.

Edsel, too, was sensitive to these new trends. With Kanzler he had designed an extensive remodel of the Model T in 1924, but when they showed it to his father, Henry snarled, "Rub it out!" In 1926, as the company entered harder times, Kanzler took it upon himself to write a six-page memorandum to Ford on the issue of the Model T. His language was diplomatic, even deferential. ("I can write certain things I find difficult to say to you. It is one of the handicaps of the power of your personality which you perhaps least of all realize, but most people when with you hesitate to say what they think.") Yet the memo did not avoid the hard truths, pointing out that production and sales were falling along with dealer morale:

> We have not gone ahead in the last few years, have barely held our own, whereas the competition has made great strides. You have always said either go forwards or backwards, you can't stand still.... The best evidence that conditions are not right is the fact that with more of the bigger men in the organization there is a growing uneasiness because things are not right—they feel our position is weakening and our grip is slipping.... The buoyant spirit of confident expansion is lacking. And we know we have been defeated and licked in England. And we are being caught up with in the U.S. With every additional car our competitors sell they get stronger and we get weaker.

After reading the memorandum, Ford first simply remarked, "That young man is getting too big for his britches." Then he began a concerted assault on Kanzler, snubbing him at the Round Table during lunch, brusquely interrupting his conversation and sometimes ridiculing him to his face. As part of this campaign, Ford's man Ray Dahlinger began casually remarking to other executives, "By the way, you know Kanzler is a Jew, don't you?" When this remark got back to Kanzler, who was not Jewish, he said calmly, "A lot of brilliant men are Jews." When Edsel tried to reinforce his brother-in-law's message about the Model T, his father became so annoyed that they barely spoke to each other.

The astute Liebold saw the truth of the situation—that it was a power struggle. "The trouble was that Mr. Kanzler...got a lot of those fellows working along with him.... They were *his* men. Mr. Ford finally figured he couldn't stand for two organizations in the company. These people were coalescing around Edsel. Mr. Ford thought they weren't the right influence." The end came when Edsel sailed to Europe with his family on a trip to collect antique furnishings for the estate he was building at Gaukler Pointe. Ford was visiting an old family friend and, after chatting for a while, stood up with a broad smile on his face and slipped on his overcoat, his reedy voice crackling with pleasure as he said, "Well, by this time I think Edsel is several miles out to ocean, so I think tomorrow we can get rid of Kanzler." He fired him and let Edsel know about it by telegram.

Upon returning home, Eleanor, who had seen the stakes of this struggle and appreciated the protection Kanzler had tried to offer Edsel, came to her father-in-law in tears to beg for her brother-in-law's reinstatement. But Henry wouldn't budge. Edsel, who had brought home several engraved Dunhill lighters from England for his key executives, as if to acknowledge their status as an elite within the company, put the gifts into one of the drawers of his desk and never took them out again. The battle for the soul of the company was over. As one person close to the situation said, "It was like a family tragedy. The full unraveling would take years. But at this point Edsel had the tragic recognition—that there was no way out of his dilemma except by death, his father's or his own."

SEVEN

I N A STUDY OF THE WORLD'S richest men published in the *New York Times* in 1926, Stuart Chase estimated the Ford fortune at $1.2 billion, which put Henry and Edsel at the top of his list. All the other great families of America got their wealth from a variety of sources; Ford's came from the Model T. But he didn't love the car for that reason, or even because it had changed the face of America. He loved it because it was the tool of his destiny, the concrete embodiment of the most daring and creative part of his life. Because of the astounding velocity of the auto age, the Model T had become involved with a past which Ford increasingly believed had to be defended at all costs. This reflex was reinforced when pressure to change came from people like Kanzler whom he despised. Years later, when the Model T was only a memory, Henry still couldn't understand why it was no longer being driven. "The only thing wrong with that car," he said to an associate, "was that people stopped buying it."

As the death of the once and future Ford became more likely, Henry tried to escape the fateful decision. Sometimes he would sneak away from the heavy security at Fairlane by hopping into a truck that had just made a delivery and hiding on the floor until the driver had passed through the front gate. Then he would get out and walk off into the woods, where he would be found by panicked security men a few hours later leaning on a fence talking to some old Dearborn farmer. He also spent days on end at Greenfield Village, where, to help preserve it as a hiding place from the company, he had refused to allow telephones to be installed.

Feeling that his father was fiddling while the company burned, Edsel commissioned designers to work on a new car. When he tried to show Henry the results of their work, the tension between them rose. At one point Henry told Sorensen to ask Edsel to clear out and go to California for a leave of absence, an order Sorensen diplomatically ignored.

Henry had always had what seemed a sixth sense of how to handle his competition. In 1914, Detroit companies began making small, two-person vehicles called "cycle cars." Noting the growing popularity of two models called the Comet and the Mercury (names which would later be appropriated by the Ford Motor Company), Henry decided that something must be done. So he built a smaller version of the Model T—streamlined and stripped down—and had it parked in front of the Pontchartrain Hotel. As Ernest Liebold later noted in telling this story, "Everybody saw it and assumed that Ford was going to build a cycle car.... That ended the cycle car era in Detroit."

But such stratagems were possible only when Ford was the undisputed leader of the auto world. Those days were long gone. In one last desperate attempt to stop the erosion of the Model T's position in the marketplace, Henry decreed a price cut in 1926. But this technique, which had worked so well during past sales crises, didn't work at all this time. GM sales continued to soar, particularly in the Chevrolet division. It was not just a matter of revenue; the Ford Motor Company was clearly losing its position as industry leader. GM had invested huge amounts of money in research facilities that had paid off with inventions such as the self-starter and hydraulic brakes which made Ford products seem especially antique. The Ford Motor Company had nothing—no engineering laboratory, no proving grounds. What passed for "road testing" involved Ray Dahlinger taking a new model for a drive and then returning with a laconic verdict, "No damned good" or "Goddamned good."

While other manufacturers were introducing four-wheel brakes, water-pump cooling and other innovations, Henry had made it dangerous even to mention such changes. So, while everyone saw the need to modernize the company's line, few dared mention it. The importance of hydraulic brakes, for instance, was a cause that united all the executives, even the feuding Edsel and Sorensen. After an emergency meeting it was finally decided that Edsel should try one last time to speak to his father on this touchy subject. He waited until after lunch, then approached Henry with an armload of substantiating data. "Father, I believe the time has arrived for us to give serious consideration to a hydraulic brake system—" he began. But before he could finish, Ford got up from his chair glowering, said, "Edsel, you shut up!" and then walked out of the room.

When dealers begged for styling and engineering changes, Henry's response was to order Sorensen to charter a large number of new dealerships, which meant that often there were now several shaky competitors in an area where before there had been one successful dealer. "Hell, he won't have a dealer left if this keeps up," Edsel said disconsolately. "I can't even face people. The whole thing is so silly and unfair."

One of the things the dealers wanted was a car with a six-cylinder engine. But Henry had hated the six since his earliest days in the company when Malcomson had forced him to build one for the "luxury trade." He came up with another solution—a revolutionary engine called the X-8, with four cylinders facing downward and four up. He had worked on this for years, although Kanzler had challenged the soundness of the design in a series of memos written before he was fired. The engineers pointed out the problem with the X-8—that its spark plugs were down at the bottom of the engine, which made them subject to mud and wetness—but Ford pushed the experimental engine nonetheless, largely because it was short and could fit under the hood of the Model T. But when it was finally road-tested, the X-8 became so badly fouled by dirt and moisture that he had to admit it wouldn't work.

All this time Edsel kept up the pressure for a new model. Finally, on May 24, 1927, Henry capitulated and announced that the Ford Motor Company would discontinue the Model T and build a new car. Even Sorensen admired the tenacity with which Edsel had argued his case: "He finally forced his father to give up the Model T. That was his victory." But it was a bittersweet triumph for Edsel, because it meant that Highland Park, the plant associated with his attempt to assert control over the company, would finally be closed and the people there, many of them his close aides, would be treated like a conquered army—some fired outright, others offered menial jobs at the Rouge under Sorensen.

Something was going out of the company. However advanced it had seemed when it first opened its doors, Highland Park had been in human scale. The camaraderie that had existed there evaporated in the impersonal vastness of the Rouge. Walter Reuther, a Ford tool- and die-maker at the time of the transition, said later, "Highland Park was civilized, but the Rouge was a jungle." Another oldtimer said, "At the Rouge you didn't know when somebody was going to come along and clip you and knock you down." When the workers who were brought there encountered some new process and said innocently that they were accustomed to doing things differently at Highland Park, some supervisor was sure to snarl, "Well, *this* isn't Highland Park!"

William Klann, a leading foreman for years at Highland Park, later said, "A lot of jobs were being moved to the Rouge plant and they didn't want the supervisors to come. They wanted to put in their own gang there. Sorensen was going around saying, 'We want to fire every Model T son of a bitch.' " Eventually it came to be Klann's turn. After following orders and firing over two hundred Highland Park men—many of them among the first Ford employees, whose connection with the company went back to its opening in 1903—Klann himself was fired, Sorensen prevailing upon a Michigan state trooper to break the news while Klann was upstate on a brief vacation.

Edsel and his aide Walter Fishleigh visited Klann at his home to find out what exactly had happened. When told how the firing had occurred, Fishleigh said he himself might as well quit right then because he was scheduled for vacation the following month.

"Don't be silly," Edsel said, trying to laugh it off. For the rest of the afternoon the two of them tried to figure out a way for Klann to return, eventually offering him a job in the Airplane Department.

"No," Klann said, "they'd just do it again."

On May 26, 1927, the fifteen-millionth Model T came off the assembly line, Edsel at the wheel and his father in the passenger seat. They made the ceremonial fourteen-mile trip to the Dearborn Engineering Laboratory, where the first Model T ever produced was waiting alongside the original car of 1896. Henry took the wheel of each vehicle and drove it around the plaza. A triumphant chapter in automotive history had drawn to a close. It was clear to everyone that future chapters would be written in a malicious and unstable hand.

WHEN WOULD THE NEXT FORD appear? What would it look like? Could the Ford Motor Company compete, or was it finished? These questions were asked not only by the business community but also by the average citizen. The end of the Model T and the shutdown of the Ford operations which followed while its successor was being readied were the great industrial soap opera of the day.

It marked a temporary revival for Henry Ford himself. In the early 1920s he had become alienated from the creative aspect of his company—hiding out at Greenfield Village, jiggling the strings of power from afar. But now he threw himself with some of his old gusto into the engineering challenge of designing a new car. For a time it seemed as though the challenge of the new car would wipe away all the ambivalence that had clouded his attitude toward Edsel and the entire Ford enterprise. Even though he was sixty-four years old, Henry pushed himself relentlessly. There was no longer a Harold Wills able to translate his ideas almost intuitively into blueprints, but there were good engineers—notably Lawrence S. Sheldrick, a young designer who had begun as a draftsman at the Hudson Motor Company and come to work for Lincoln after Ford bought it, distinguishing himself during the experiments on the doomed X-8 engine. While Henry and Sheldrick handled the engine for the new car, Edsel was involved in styling—interior and instrumentation as well as the body. Seeing his work, Henry grudgingly admitted that Edsel had real automotive know-how. "We've got a pretty good man in my son," he said to an aide, although the compliment was never passed on to Edsel himself. "He knows style—how a car ought to look. And he has mechanical horse sense too."

A prototype was ready by August 1927. But retooling for mass production was still to come. Changeovers of such magnitude as this one were unknown in American industry. Nearly six thousand new parts had to be made, involving an around-the-clock effort to build the new tools to make them. Early in October it was done. On October 21, the first example of the new model came off the assembly line. Henry called it the Model A, the name of the first car he had ever put up for sale, as if even in moving forward he couldn't resist a recapitulating look backward at his own history.

By December there was a burst of advertising—full-page ads three days running in all the nation's major dailies to put a final edge on the public's already keen appetite. (A mild recession had been attributed, in large part, to the fact that people were not buying cars in anticipation of the appearance of the new Ford.) On the day the Model A appeared, there were mob scenes at dealerships across the country; in some cases the press of people was so powerful that showroom windows were broken. Some fifty thousand cash deposits were received the first day in New York alone; an estimated ten million people saw the new car in the first thirty-six hours it was on display. In a year of American celebrities, the Model A was second only to Charles Lindbergh himself.

FORD ASSUMED THAT THIS CRASH program would give him another car that he would be able to keep in production for as long as the Model T. But times had changed. Chevrolet came out late in 1928 with a new six-cylinder model that strongly challenged the Model A for first place in sales, even though it was more expensive. Nor would it be a two-company race for long, Walter P. Chrysler having served notice that he intended to become a major factor in the auto industry. Chrysler had gone from the presidency of Buick to Willys and Maxwell before forming the Chrysler Corporation in 1925. He was putting out the De Soto and the Chrysler while the Model A was struggling to be born, and then in 1927 he picked up the Dodge Company, which had sunk badly after the deaths of the Dodge brothers, but which offered him the manufacturing facilities he would need to stage an assault on the inexpensive market. His entry was called the Plymouth, and it rose to third place behind the Model A and the Chevrolet with a rush which suggested that it would soon be challenging the leaders.*

There might be disturbing moments, but by October 21, 1929, Henry believed that the worst of his troubles were behind him. During the year, the Ford Motor Company had sold 1,851,000 cars—34 percent of the industry total and well ahead of Chevrolet's 20 percent. The company appeared to have stabilized itself, and on this day he was finally realizing the other great dream of his life by inaugurating the Edison Institute and opening the Henry Ford Museum and Greenfield Village. It was a national moment, with President Hoover presiding over ceremonies meant to celebrate the advent of man-made power and to commemorate the fiftieth anniversary of Edison's invention of the light bulb by a dimming of the lights across the country. A small contretemps developed when the eighty-two-year-old inventor sat down outside the banquet hall and refused to budge, finally breaking into tears and saying that he simply couldn't face the crowd, let alone the microphones that would carry his words across the country. His wife was summoned and pleaded with him, and finally he went into the banquet hall on the arm of his best friend, Henry Ford.

Things had never seemed better, but three days later, on the day that would become known as Black Tuesday, the stock market crashed, and Henry Ford's world, like everyone else's, changed forever.

---

* Rivaled only by Ford as a giant of the auto world, Chrysler paid homage to the master by bringing to Dearborn the third Plymouth off the assembly line. He took Henry and Edsel for a ride and then gave the car to them.

CARS, WHICH HAD RANKED twenty-first among industrial indicators in 1909, ranked first twenty years later. Automobiles had become the archetypal American business, and the manufacturers had participated in the glib optimism about an unlimited future which had helped bring about the Crash. Over the next few years, however, there would be an elemental sorting out in the industry. About one third of all automakers would go out of business, taking with them a whole ecosystem of suppliers and wholesalers. The Ford Motor Company seemed among the fittest and most likely to survive in this Darwinian world. As usual in times of adversity, Henry moved to lower prices. Even more audaciously, he also raised wages to seven dollars a day.* Nonetheless, by 1931 GM had 31 percent of the market, and Ford only 28 percent. Although it would cost some $50 million for design and retooling, Ford set out once again to update and upgrade his line with the V-8, his last great innovation. The car went on display in May 1932 in fourteen body types (a concession to Edsel) with gracefully curved lines and a 64-horsepower engine that was the wonder of the industry.

As with the Model A, Ford had thrown himself personally into the project. But he was five years older, and during the development of the V-8 his behavior became increasingly erratic. He threatened his engineers and designers because he believed they were giving trade secrets to Walter Chrysler. Yet when GM chief Alfred Sloan came for a visit, Ford took him to the engineering laboratory to look at a model of the V-8 engine. "You could never tell what he was going to do," one man who worked on the V-8 project said of Henry. "Some days he'd come into the office with a sort of dark, smoldering look about him—like he'd just been hit by lightning or something. When he had this look you knew there'd be hell to pay." He began to show up at work with leather patches on the elbows of his jackets, a quirk that puzzled executives until he told one of them confidentially that he wanted to help create a feeling of sacrifice and hard times among workers who were already beleaguered by the Great Depression.

The dumb-show was hardly necessary. The Depression had hit Detroit, fourth-largest city in the United States, with a tremendous impact. In 1929 the auto industry had made 5,294,000 vehicles valued at $3.7 billion; by 1933 only 1,848,000, valued at $1.1 billion, were produced. By this time, one third of all wage earners had been totally or partly unemployed for four years in succession. There were over 200,000 dependents on the city's relief rolls;

---

* The increase in wages was once again purchased by a speedup of the assembly line. One Ford foreman told the workers, "Go like hell, boys. If you're gonna get that raise, you gotta increase production." One worker calculated that to get the seven-dollar day, a 17 percent raise, his personal production quota rose 47 percent. In any case, the seven-dollars-a-day wage had to be rescinded within a year because of hard times.

another 150,000 people had fled the city. The suicide rate had risen precipitously. On January 3, 1932, newly elected Mayor Frank Murphy shocked the city by revealing that there were some four thousand children standing in breadlines every day. Not only had Henry been forced to take back his raise, but his workers' wages had even fallen below the previous standard of five dollars a day.

Ignoring these auguries of social breakdown, Ford claimed that hard times were a necessary purgative after the excesses of the Jazz Age. He stated publicly that the Depression was "a wholesome thing in general" and, more extremely, that it could represent "the best times we have ever had" if the people would simply recognize it as such. When his workers said they were suffering, his response in effect was to let them eat vegetables. He commanded each of them to plant a garden plot of his own or to sign up for one within the four-thousand-acre Ford Farms. Because of the compulsion, they became known as "shotgun gardens."

He had always been against philanthropy, feeling that it weakened the spirit of self-reliance he believed was the highest good. ("Professional charity," he wrote, "degrades the recipients and drugs their self-respect. Akin to it is sentimental idealism.") None of the ravages of the Depression could shake him out of this conviction. He promoted such views by sponsoring *The Ford Hour* on national radio—fifty-four minutes of Strauss waltzes and other light classics, followed by six minutes of philosophy delivered by William Cameron, former editor of the *Dearborn Independent*. The Ford-Cameron homilies were proposed as wisdom for hard times: "Unless we help ourselves, there is little hope of helping others"; "A society comprised entirely or in part of dependents has little on which to depend"; "If you would lift another, you must have a foothold yourself."

Although Franklin D. Roosevelt assiduously courted him, Ford hated the new President. Asked what Roosevelt had talked about at one private meeting at the White House, Ford snapped, "Well, he took up the first five minutes telling me about his ancestors. I don't know why, unless he wanted to prove he had no Jewish blood." The only good thing Ford had to say about the New Deal had to do with the appointment of Henry Morgenthau Jr. as Secretary of the Treasury, a move he supported because he felt it made sense to have the nation's money under the control of a Jew. Ford became the last holdout in the auto industry against the National Recovery Act, rejecting several embassies from Washington designed to bring him into the fold, including one from Pierre S. Du Pont, who said to him at a New York party, "Mr. Ford, I want you to go along with the NRA. That Blue Eagle is my baby." Ford, who had felt that the Du Ponts were out to get him since they had become prominently involved in the operation of General Motors, replied testily, "That's all the more reason I don't want to have anything to do with it," and walked out of the gathering. When the Supreme Court declared the NRA unconstitutional, Cameron crowed on *The Ford Hour* about the discomfort of the "busy young men who have been making picture puzzles of the American way of living."

Until the Depression, Ford had always remained a hero to the "little man" whose causes he had championed and whose viewpoint he had expressed. But his behavior in the thirties changed that. The Emersonian epigrams about self-sufficiency which had before seemed so profound now rang hollow in the face of widespread misery. Ford's panacea, decentralization of industry and a back-to-the-farm movement, seemed ridiculously inappropriate. As he fought against the NRA and other measures meant to rally the country, his following evaporated. It was as if the cuticle of common sense that had protected him over the years from his own worst tendencies had worn away, leaving him increasingly vulnerable to obsessions which brought back the "Crazy Henry" tag of his youth, now with more serious implications. A transition had been made: the man who had gained fame as the Great American Idealist was now the Great American Crank obsessed with his personal tics and hobbyhorses.

He continued to call himself a "practical scientist," but his "experiments" were increasingly peculiar. Edsel's daughter Dodie always looked into the sink of Henry's bedroom when she visited Fairlane, fascinated by the way her grandfather left old razor blades to rust in the water in which he then washed his hair, because he believed rusty water was a hair restorative. His maid Rosa Buhler, who had noticed that socks were disappearing from his drawer, once found him in the kitchen boiling several pairs. When she asked why, he picked up a sock one half its normal size with some tongs and replied, I've always wanted to find out why it makes wool shrink."

This eccentricity also manifested itself in spiritual matters. Henry had long since stopped any involvement in organized religion. While Clara was becoming attracted to the humanistic Oxford movement, he became increasingly interested in reincarnation, a concept he stamped with his own distinctive thought. Once, when driving along with one of his employees, he pointed at some chickens which had scattered at the approach of the car, noting that they had been "hit in the ass in a previous life" and had thus learned a lesson they were using in this one. He told a cousin, "You know, when a person dies I think their spirit goes into a newborn baby. I think that's why some people are so much further advanced in knowledge than others and are gifted. A man when he dies, if he is a genius, his spirit will go into a newborn baby and that person will be an expert like Einstein or Edison." He added that he himself had been a genius in a prior life.

He had always had peculiar ideas. One of his first workers spoke later about the lack of ventilation in the Ford shop: "It wasn't because of meanness that he allowed this type of working conditions. Mr. Ford always thought that for anyone who had heart trouble or tuberculosis the best thing in the world was to come in contact with monoxide gas. He said it was a cure for them." As he grew older, Henry was increasingly attracted to quackery of all kinds. Thinking that physicians at the Henry Ford Hospital were acting too "grand," he threatened to make his own doctor, a chiropractor, chief of staff there. He hired a man to help him work on his collection of antique clocks and watches, and while they were rebuilding a rare Eli Terry clock with worn bone bushings he tried to think up something to use as a substitute material. First he brought in horse joints, but they were too spongy. He tried deer antlers and other substances. Finally he got the idea of trying to find a Negro's skull, which he claimed had hard bone three quarters of an inch thick.

But chief among his obsessions was a concern with food which took on the status of a fetish. Ford's interest in health had begun years earlier, when he banned tobacco from his plant and waged war against alcohol because Edison had told him these substances destroyed the brain cells. But his old friend, the only person in front of whom Ford ever felt embarrassed by his prejudices and eccentric ideas, was dead now, and there was no longer anyone to check his bizarre thoughts. "If people would learn to eat the things they should," Ford now announced, "there would be no need for hospitals. Jails and prisons would have less to do." Proclaiming, "Quadrupeds are out," he rejected red meat. He refused to eat chickens, because they ate bugs. He claimed that eating sugar was suicide because its sharp crystals would cut one's stomach to shreds, a phobia that continued even after a scientist made him look through a microscope at sugar crystals being dissolved by water. When Ford added George Washington Carver's log cabin to Greenfield Village, he got the black scientist to come to Dearborn for the ceremonies and found that he, too, was interested in diet. People who overheard the conversation between the two men were astonished. Ford said that cows were on the verge of obsolescence because science would soon be making synthetic milk, and Carver vigorously assented. Then Ford said that if people would only breathe deeply they would rid themselves of most ailments, and again Carver agreed. As noon approached, Carver told Ford that every day he ate a lunch of weed sandwiches. Overjoyed, Ford went out with his guest, spent a few minutes picking weeds and made sandwiches which he sat under a tree munching like a ruminant.

But most of his attention was focused on the soybean, which he believed was a miracle substance. He spent over $1 million in research on soybeans in 1932-33 alone, planting three hundred varieties on eight thousand acres of the Ford Farms. There were some practical applications: soybean oil was used in enamels to paint Ford cars and in fluid for their shock absorbers; the meal was used in window trim and horn buttons. Company researchers made fiber from soybean protein and spun it into textile filaments which they used in upholstery and which Ford had made into a suit of soybean wool. But the dietary dimension was more important to Ford than the industrial one, and he began treating soybeans as a universal food. He hired scientists to produce a variety of soybean products—soybean bread and butter, soybean "meat," soybean ice cream. At Chicago's Century of Progress exposition he had cooks serve an all-soybean dinner: tomato juice with soybean extract; celery stuffed with soybean cheese; a main course of soybean croquettes; and a dessert of apple pie with soybean crust, washed down with soybean coffee. He tried to force some of his soybean recipes on executives at the Ford lunch table, and they nibbled at them in the spirit of resignation with which they had attended his old-fashioned dances. Only the sulphurous Sorensen defied Ford's "rabbit food," ostentatiously insisting on eating a huge rare steak every lunch. The rest of them tried the health foods but clearly didn't like them, which irritated Ford so much that one day he picked a piece of white bread off the lunch table, rolled it into a ball in his palm and then threw it at a window; when it shattered the glass, he exclaimed triumphantly, "*That's* what you're putting into your stomachs!"

He hired his boyhood friend Edsel Ruddiman, who had earned a doctorate in science since the two of them had gone their separate ways, to supervise his soybean research, outfitting him with an elaborate laboratory complete with white rats and glass beakers. Ruddiman's main task was to make a single "biscuit" of soybean extract containing all the nutrients necessary for daily life. One Ford employee recalled, "It was one of the most vile-tasting things you ever put in your mouth. Henry kept plates of them which he offered everybody. And after one taste they immediately slipped them into their pocket." The dispirited Ruddiman, bothered by the turn his career had taken, but hard pressed to turn his back on the largesse with which Ford supported his research, extracted a fluid he called soybean milk which, in the words of one person who tried it, made Milk of Magnesia taste good by comparison.

That this was not simply harmless faddism but part of the progressive deformation of Ford's character was clear in an incident involving designer Lawrence Sheldrick. Never one of Ford's favorites, because of his stubborn independence, his loyalty to Edsel and his ongoing battles with Sorensen, Sheldrick was perplexed when Ford came to his office one day at noon, half an hour earlier than the normal lunchtime, and said, "Come on, let's you and I go in and eat ahead of the rest of the group." Inside the lunchroom Ford insisted on sitting next to Sheldrick instead of across the table. "We're going to have some fun," he said, looking around in a conspiratorial way. "No one else is here today. We're going to eat what we damned please. We're going to go on a food drunk today." They had roast pork, potatoes, apple pie—Ford stuffing himself with items he usually condemned as toxic and insisting that Sheldrick do the same. When they were so full that they could hardly move, Ford asked Sheldrick to come with him to Ray Dahlinger's office. "Ray, where's that new laxative stuff that those pharmaceutical houses sent you?" he asked when they got there. Trying to suppress a smile, Dahlinger pointed at the bottle. Ford said, "Well, give Shel a bottle of it and give me one." As Sheldrick was handed some of the laxative, Ford gave a disguised order: "Let's take the stuff and see if it works." Sheldrick realized that Ford had wanted to try the new product but wanted someone to share the risk with him.

WHEN HE TURNED SEVENTY-ONE, Henry showed up to meet the press wearing two different shoes. Asked about it by reporters, he looked down and, obviously making up an answer on the spot, said that he always wore one old shoe on his birthday to remind himself that he had once been poor and might be again. He still had his loose-limbed walk and springy gait; the netted wrinkles around his eyes collaborated with his mouth when he smiled. He was still automatic news, charming even the reporters who came to "get" him. Even his rare refusals to do journalists' bidding were endearing. A photographer once asked him to pose between two boys with a hand on the head of each, and he refused. When asked why, he reminded the photographer about the picture of John Dillinger with an arm around the sheriff whose jail he later broke out of. "You can see for yourself the spot I'd be in if these two boys turned out badly," he said.

But if he was the same old Ford to the outer world, the employees close to him saw him as a different man. The practical jokes of a prior era had fermented into episodes of intentional cruelty; the belief in individuality and independence had become a sclerotic insistence on having his own way. It was Edsel who absorbed most of the punishment. It was clear to everyone that Ford loved his son deeply, but it was the same sort of love as when Edsel was the little boy to whom he had been unusually close. Henry could not relinquish the role of father, and as Edsel tried to find ground he could occupy Henry tried to push him back into dependence, capriciously overturning the decisions Edsel made as president and humiliating him in front of others. When Edsel learned that yet another of his orders had been countermanded, his jaw would tighten and his features cloud. "Well, I thought Father understood about this," he would say. "Apparently somebody talked to him about it...." Finally he would shrug and repeat the only explanation he had for such behavior: "Well, after all, my father built this business. It is his business."

Edsel's rebellions were small. He had an occasional cocktail when his father was not present. One day Clara appeared as he was about to take some friends out on Lake St. Clair in one of his boats and delivered a lecture to all of them on the evils of tobacco; Edsel agreed mildly with everything she said and then, once the boat had pulled away from the jetty, pulled out a package of Camels and passed it around. But circumstances always made his dependence humiliatingly clear. Just before the Depression, for instance, Edsel had become financially involved in the Guardian Detroit Union Group Inc., a holding company of banks. By 1931 they were in enough trouble that a $15 million emergency loan was required from the Continental and other banks, a loan made possible by security pledged by Edsel. By January 1, 1932, the Guardian Group owed him $8.5 million in advances and endorsements, but its fiscal position continued to erode to the point where by the end of the year the Guardian trust had assets of only $6 million against liabilities of $20 million.

The situation was growing desperate in the Detroit banks. On February 1, 1933, Commerce Secretary Roy D. Chapin was in Detroit to try to convince

Ford to help; Ford not only refused but said that he would not allow Edsel to place $7.5 million of company money in the Guardian, as Edsel had promised to do to ease the crisis. Chapin warned that this could mean the failure of the bank and the beginning of a chain reaction. Ford replied, "Let them fail! Let everybody fail! I made my fortune when I had nothing to start with, by myself and my own ideas. Let other people do the same thing. If I lose everything in the collapse of our financial situation I will start at the beginning and build it up again." Three days after the Chapin meeting, the Guardian Group declared a bank holiday.

At about this time, Edsel's friend Admiral Richard E. Byrd, whom he had supported on pioneering exploration of the Antarctic in 1929, asked for the loan of a Ford trimotor plane for another expedition. Edsel wrote an alarmed letter of refusal: "The present situation in Michigan has forced us to make every possible curtailment.... One does not know what is going to happen from day to day. Conditions may get better or may get worse and I feel that under the circumstances none of us should make any further obligations."

Edsel laid off all but four of the twenty-five employees who kept his estate running. As things went from bad to worse for the Guardian and other banks, he was very much "in the dumps," in Liebold's phrase. One morning he came into the office with tears running down his cheeks and said, "Well, I'm cleaned out." When Liebold told him he must be exaggerating, Edsel replied, "All that has to happen is for the Continental Bank to call on me for that five million and I'm cleaned out." Liebold asked him if he had talked to his father about it, and Edsel said he hadn't. Liebold went to Ford, who listened to the tale and then said, "Well, you'd better fix it up." After bailing Edsel out, he happened to pass him in the corridor and remarked casually, "Well, son, I see they took you to the cleaners." Nothing more had to be said: once again Edsel had been reminded which side his bread was buttered on and who held the butter knife.

Edsel never complained or lost his tight self-control, but others caught an occasional glimpse of the pathos that enveloped his life. Once he drove with Lawrence Sheldrick to upper Michigan to road-test a modified Model A. They stopped to eat in a hotel where it was required to register for lunch. Edsel's eyes lit up; he grabbed Sheldrick's arm and said, "You register under my name today and I'll use yours. Let's have some fun." For the rest of the afternoon Sheldrick, who everyone thought was the Ford heir, was the center of attention; Edsel just sat to one side and grinned. But this prince-and-pauper act was not possible in his workaday life. Edsel had two choices: to fight his father or declare a separate peace. He chose the latter, pursuing his private life as if living well was the only revenge.

One of his favorite places was his farm in upper Michigan, Haven Hill. It was built of logs hauled down from Ford properties at Iron Mountain; pine needles were bagged and brought down to be spread around the house to supply a mountain aroma. Edsel raised horses there and trucked them east each summer to the other vacation house he had bought in Seal Harbor,

Maine, near the retreat of his friend John D. Rockefeller Jr. A sense of life at Seal Harbor was conveyed in Edsel's twelve-year-old son Bill's letter to Clara in 1936:

> Dad and I have got another dog. He's a black and white cocker spaniel and his name's Happy. How is the weather? The weather here is pretty good now, but the first couple of days it was pretty foggy. We have seen 8 movies since we have been here.... We have tennis lessons in the afternoon and we go swimming in the morning. We ride horseback. The tennis tournament is on the 10th and the swimming race on the 9th. I am invited out so I have to go.

Edsel also bought a place at Hobe Sound, Florida. He wrote to his mother about it: "We have bought a piece of property here and are quite excited about it. It runs through from river to ocean and enables us to have our own dock and tennis beach on the ocean." He kept his 125-foot yacht the *Onika* in Florida, where its elegant Chippendale living room, Hepplewhite dining room and French Provincial staterooms made it something of a legend.

But the place that occupied the center of Edsel's life was his Gaukler Pointe estate. In 1925 Edsel bought the choice fifty-five acres from his father, who had once thought of building there before deciding that he couldn't stand the aristocratic pretenses of the Grosse Pointe "crowd." Edsel kept adding to this tract until he had almost a mile of frontage on Lake St. Clair, landscaped with full-grown trees brought from the Ford Farms by teams of horses leaving Dearborn at midnight and making the trip to Grosse Pointe by lantern to avoid daytime traffic. He had a lagoon dredged on his lake frontage so that his friends could moor their boats alongside the *Onika*.

Deciding that he and Eleanor would be most comfortable in an English home, Edsel sent architect Albert Kahn to the Cotswold district of England to study the stone houses that were part of that region's vernacular architecture. Kahn came back with pencil drawings of an elegant thirty-room home which managed to maintain the lack of pretense of a Cotswold "cottage." It took three years to build. Roughened stone was used on the exterior; the split-stone roof, made of slabs shipped from England, was put on by English masons who were also imported for the task. Every detail was correct: Edsel went to substantial expense and worry to make sure that "authentic" English moss grew on the stone. After the house was completed he built a separate powerhouse like the one his father had at Fairlane, to make sure that he would never be shut down by a municipal emergency. Unlike the bucolic wildness his father tried to preserve at Fairlane, however, the grounds at Gaukler Pointe were perfectly manicured, as if this would help provide at least an illusion of order in Edsel's life.

Similar care was expended on the interior of Gaukler Pointe. Edsel and Eleanor had returned from their 1926 trip to England with hundreds of thousands of dollars of furnishings. They found Jacobean chairs and Tudor tables, each piece with a brochure detailing its pedigree. They acquired whole rooms of wainscoting and paneling from old English estates which they had cut to fit their own downstairs living areas. (The only concession made to the modern world was in the boys' rooms, furnished in the latest Art Deco.) The net effect was one of casual opulence. Visitors were surprised to find that a mammoth chest containing logs to burn in the huge fireplace of the Gaukler Pointe ballroom was actually a rare fifteenth-century artifact.

For a time Edsel's children were the connection linking the separate worlds of Gaukler Pointe and Fairlane. While young they were chauffeured back and forth in units, Henry II and Benson one weekend, Dodie and Bill the next. (Dodie later recalled, "Bill and I were always sent to Fairlane by ourselves. I don't ever remember going with Henry and Ben.") "Callie," as they called Clara, built up an exquisite doll collection for Dodie, and had a chicken house built with four separate sections so that each of them could gather his own eggs. She also superintended the construction of the "Santa Claus house," a log cabin deep in the woods of Fairlane where a sleigh would take her grandchildren every Christmas Eve to see the mounds of presents that had been left for them.

Henry was instructive rather than loving. ("He was hard to talk to," Dodie recalled. "He always seemed to be thinking about something else.") He took them to the maple sugar shack he built at Fairlane and showed them how to tap the trees and boil down the syrup; he taught them each to drive. When he knew they were coming for a visit, he would get out easels and drawing paper and make them do writing and drawing exercises with an "educational" value, even though plump Henry II informed him saucily, "We would much rather saddle the ponies and take a ride." He built a tree house for the grandchildren, and after they had gone back home to Gaukler Pointe he would sometimes sit there alone writing in his notebook.

Henry sometimes added young John Dahlinger to the play group. People who knew him liked the boy because of his inquisitiveness and personability. For some, the fact that Dahlinger was mechanically adept only confirmed suspicions they harbored about his true parentage. But putting the boy together with his blood grandchildren was the wrong thing for Henry to do. Edsel's sons had either picked up some of the whispering about their grandfather and Evangeline or were resentful of the implication that John was improperly put into their class. Although he got on well enough with Bill, who was closest to his age, Henry II and Benson were hard on him, doing such things as "accidentally" smashing into trees when "borrowing" the scale-model roadster Ford had made for him, crumpling its bumpers and denting its fenders. For his part, young Dahlinger regarded Edsel's two older sons as "a couple of fatties."

Sometimes Henry became impatient with his grandchildren, particularly Henry II. (Once the boy accompanied him on one of the ships that delivered iron ore to the Rouge and discovered a box of candy whose contents he kept stuffing into his mouth, causing his grandfather finally to throw the box overboard in annoyance.) Yet for the most part Henry felt that the boys ought to be allowed to "run wild" because they were "held in" at home. He took Henry II and Benson to the plant with him on Saturdays, and they obliged him by getting into Model Ts and careening wildly through the Rouge, shuffling the workers' time cards, and manning the cash register in the cafeteria where they gave back more money than they took in. Dreading their coming, employees called them "the Katzenjammer Kids."

Henry taught all of his grandsons how to shoot a pistol and drive a car. Bill later recalled a time when his grandfather was speeding down a Dearborn street and was pulled over by a policeman, who called Fairlane to tell what had happened. By the time they got home Clara was waiting. Giving Henry a withering look, she said, "Bill, go upstairs. I want to talk to your grandfather." Bill left the room knowing that there would be "hell to pay."

But as they got older Edsel's children all felt an ill-defined sense of estrangement from their grandparents, and the trips to Fairlane became onerous obligations instead of good times. There was no talk at Gaukler Pointe about the way their grandfather treated their father ("It was the dirty little secret of the Ford family," said one of Henry II's childhood friends). It was not necessary that it be explicit; the subject was almost in the air they breathed. They may not have realized that Edsel's indulgence of them was a reaction against his own relationship with his father, but they saw him as someone to be protected and rallied around. As they grew up they tried calling him "Father" and "Dad," but they found it difficult to keep from reverting to "Daddy," however old they were. Denied and papered over, the problems between Henry and Edsel subtly infected the children's lives, too. Knowing that something was terribly wrong but confronted by a denial of the particulars, they grew up suspicious of strong emotion and given to concealment themselves. As one family friend said, "For most young people superficiality is the enemy. With the Ford kids you got a sense that they'd decided it was a survival mechanism."

Edsel could not talk about his relationship with his father, but he tried to be a good father himself. He had a special feeling for the two youngest. He built a playhouse at Gaukler Pointe for the very pretty Dodie—a remarkable structure in complete scale, with a functioning miniature kitchen and other realistic features. He sent her a sad cable on a birthday he had to miss: "I hope you will have a very wonderful birthday today. I can't realize that you are growing up and are a big girl 7 years old. I'm very sorry I'm not going to be there with you today. A great deal of love, Daddy." He shared a love for animals and the outdoors with Bill. Edsel knew that the boy looked most like him of all the children, and he sympathized with Bill for the harassment he had to put up with from his two older brothers.

But Edsel knew that the drama of the next generation would center around Henry II. Referred to as "Chief" by his playmates because of his compulsion to lead, Henry II also called the shots in the family. When the Prince of Wales, the future Edward VIII, came to Dearborn, a formal dinner was staged at Gaukler Pointe. Eleanor's mother, too flustered to meet him in the flesh, decided to watch from behind a screen. Dodie became ill from the excitement. When the royal guest finally arrived, the plump eldest child, Henry II, shook hands with him and gravely informed the Prince that his sister had just vomited and his grandmother was hiding behind a curtain.

Dodie had breathing room in the family because she was the only girl, and Bill because he was the youngest. Benson had none at all. Henry II was everywhere, monopolizing everything and taking more than his share. One incident that showed how power worked in the third Ford generation occurred in 1933 when J. Edgar Hoover was scheduled to come to Gaukler Pointe, a visit which conjured up visions of G-men and derring-do among the children. Henry suddenly contracted diphtheria and was quarantined to a cottage on the estate. Frantic with disappointment, he went through Benson's closet breathing on his clothing in hopes that he, too, would get diphtheria and be unable to see the FBI chief. "Young Henry was like a hyena," said one Ford employee. "He ate all he could and peed on the rest. Ben wasn't like that. He was a good and trusting boy."

Edsel selected the Hotchkiss School in Lakeville, Connecticut, as the place for the two older boys to enter the larger world after finishing the eighth grade at his own alma mater, Detroit University School. Hotchkiss was an upper-class prep school with traditional connections to Yale, yet isolated enough that for years it had not competed athletically against other schools, but only intramurally—fielding teams with names like "Olympians" and "Pythians." Its strong Christian traditions had left a mark on distinguished alumni such as Henry Luce, in large part because of the domineering presence of headmaster George Van Santvoord, "the Duke," a man of overbearing intelligence and equally profound obtuseness. (Knowing that student John Hersey had spent time as a boy in the Orient, Van Santvoord once asked him if some local children he had heard saying "Eeny, meeny, miney, mo" were counting in Chinese.)

Edsel smoothed the way for his sons by giving Hotchkiss a Ford ambulance for medical emergencies. Henry II didn't need much help. He moved right in, joining the staff of the Hotchkiss *Record* (his was the most noted line on the masthead of the magazine: "H. Ford, Business Mgr.") and writing letters home which showed his lazy progress:

> Dear Pop,
>   Just a reminder on the official paper of The Record that you promised to give me an advertisement for The Record of May 29. That as I think I told you is the upper mid-dance issue and we're going to make it a 12 page issue…. How's everybody at home? Things here are still going strong. I begin waiting on a table tonight. They take only two boys who wish to and when I asked I didn't know I'd be doing as much work as I am at the present point…. I think I'd better stop now as I have a little Record work before going out to my daily Dramat [sic] workout.
>   Love, Henry

He didn't bother to mention that his brother Benson had the measles, a fact that Edsel noted with irritation in his reply. Benson was having a difficult time at Hotchkiss, failing in almost direct proportion to Henry II's success.

The crusty Van Santvoord wrote to Edsel with an evaluation of his phlegmatic and somewhat disoriented second son: "The masters' comment is that though the boy is attentive and eager to learn, he is very immature in his powers of expression and needs to develop considerably before he will be able to do first-rate work."

Unlike Henry II, Benson did not affect a superiority to his schoolmates. In fact, he came home from his first semester at Hotchkiss noting happily that while most of the others already had Victrolas, he had to wait until Christmas to get his. He did not even try to be average in his schoolwork, failing so many courses by the end of his junior year that he was informed he probably would not be able to graduate with his class. Told of this, Edsel wrote to school officials in alarm: "In discussing Benson's problems with him and in having in mind his great disappointment in not being able to finish next year, the suggestion arose as to whether it would not be possible for Benson, with some summer work in English, to make up that upper middle course which he failed...[and to get] sufficient credits to enter Yale."

The strategy did not work and neither did Benson, and the following term he was moved from upper to lower class. Shortly before Thanksgiving he was showing signs of a mild breakdown—extreme nervousness and hysterical vomiting. On November 4, 1937, Frank Slodin, physician in chief at the Henry Ford Hospital, wrote to the Hotchkiss physician:

> His parents brought Benson Ford directly to us here on November 1 from New York City. If they haven't reported it to you, they found him very nervous and on their own gave him phenobarbitol.... He gave us the impression of being very high tuned nervously and yet of being in very low gear physically....

Reporting that after physical tests showed nothing wrong they had tested Benson's intellectual powers and found that he had an IQ of 124, Dr. Soldin continued:

> The emotional reaction to some of his experiences at school was quite enough to account for the recent attack of vomiting. In fact we were grateful that it took this form rather than a more distressing nervous break.... I do hope—and this is in the form of a prescription for him—that he will be restored to his own classmates and to associations with them. The demotion to a lower class has been a severe type of punishment and we feel that it is the etiological factor in this illness....

Henry II went on to Yale as planned. That Edsel was trying to groom him for a role at the company was clear from a letter he wrote to the dean of freshmen there, outlining a course of study such as he himself had never had an opportunity to take:

> I would like him to take a middle of the road course for his freshman year and possibly after that [a course in engineering].... My feeling is that for Henry's future career both types of education are important. I also feel that insofar as the mechanical and technical side of his work is concerned he can take that up in a practical way after college by some courses we have in our factory.

Benson did not get into Yale. Edsel managed somehow to get him into Princeton, but was soon receiving anxious letters from the dean of freshmen: "I am deeply concerned about Benson's standing thus far.... The midyear report shows that he failed his beginning course in Spanish and has also failed in English.... Not only are we disturbed but his undergraduate friends feel that he is taking a rather casual attitude toward his work." Benson was always making new beginnings, and toward the end of the year he optimistically wrote to Clara: "The work is going much better now than it was at the beginning of the year. If I can keep it up I won't have to go to summer school this year, so I'm working very hard because that doesn't look like a very pleasing way to spend the summer." The next letter home, to his grandfather, apologizing for forgetting his birthday, showed the outcome of this resolution: "Father told me when I saw him in New York that you weren't feeling too well. Hope by now everything is fine. I've been having a wonderful time in summer school. The work is hard but the weather has been so nice, I haven't had time to notice the work at all." Edsel seemed to understand his second son and wrote to a correspondent who asked about him: "He is shy about asking advice and would rather go blindly alone than to approach the proper parties for counsel." Half blind in one eye and not in control of his needs or desires, Benson was Edsel's amiable problem child. "Blindly" was the metaphor for Benson's life.

EDSEL NEVER REALLY QUESTIONED the destiny that bound his children to the Ford Motor Company. The company was like a family religion: it gave meaning to their lives. Whatever doubts he himself had, he never stopped believing. As his life at the company became more difficult, he tried to enlarge its secular dimension by becoming active in Detroit's cultural scene.

His father remained something of a primitive where culture was concerned, regarding fine art as a European affectation that was against the American grain. Thinking to make a collector of him, the famous British art dealer Lord Joseph Duveen had once presented to him a three-volume set of photographs of canvases of the old masters bound in fine calf. Duveen then came to Fairlane to follow up by trying to sell him some art, Ford gave him one of his foxy smiles, held up an album and said that he had no need of paintings, because he had the books. It was as part of a covert rebellion against his father that Edsel established himself as a major figure in the emerging world of modern art.

His mentor was William Valentiner, a German-born art historian who had come to the United States and gotten a job in New York at the Metropolitan Museum in the early 1900s, meeting Morgan, Frick, Rockefeller and other wealthy patrons. Later, after becoming close to Abby Rockefeller, a founder of the Museum of Modern Art, Valentiner was invited to Detroit by the Arts Commission, eventually becoming director of the Detroit Institute of the Arts.

Valentiner first met Edsel at a party where he gave him a letter of recommendation from the Rockefellers. He got to know him better after spending time studying an early Persian bowl in Edsel's collection about which he had been commissioned to write an article. After the acquaintance had been consolidated, Valentiner wrote home to a German friend: "I must say that Edsel Ford represents the type of lively young American who tries to go beyond the practical talents which come naturally to him and to appreciate the intellectual potentialities of life."

Edsel made his first significant gift to the Detroit Institute of the Arts in 1925—a rare Isfahan carpet of the sixteenth century—to celebrate his own appointment as a trustee of the Arts Commission. During the next few years, Valentiner's ambition to make the DIA nationally prominent intersected with Edsel's desire to have an identity outside the company, and the two men entered a creative collaboration. Edsel provided Valentiner with money he could use on European art-buying trips; Valentiner gave art seminars at Edsel's house, discussion groups replete with photographs of the great masters and other visual aids. "It was touching and a little pathetic," said one of the art historian's friends, "to see these uneducated midwesterners sitting in this incredibly sumptuous house trying to learn some culture." At the end of their education, when Edsel and Eleanor set out for Europe on an art-buying expedition of their own—the first of a series of trips on which they would buy works for the walls of Gaukler Pointe by Holbein, Renoir, Cézanne, Degas, Matisse, van Gogh and others—they did resemble Henry James' American ingénues traveling through the Old World with more money than culture.

Edsel became president of the Detroit Institute of the Arts in 1930 after a long line of gifts that included canvases by Titian, Andrea del Castagno, Verocchio and Caravaggio and sculpture by Donatello. During his tenure, Valentiner got the DIA to commission frescoes by Diego Rivera for the museum walls. Getting Rivera was a tremendous coup for Detroit. (Valentiner later said, "I felt I had to act quickly before New York and its enthusiasts for modern art—whom Rivera had not yet met—captivated him.") Edsel was wholly behind the project despite Rivera's controversial political views—a contrast to his friend Nelson A. Rockefeller, who eventually bowed to public pressure and removed frescoes by the Mexican artist from the walls of Rockefeller Center in New York. Edsel arranged for Rivera to come to the Ford plant to make sketches for his celebration of the automobile and its technology. Valentiner was struck by the impression that the Ford heir had made on the Marxist painter: "Diego confessed to me that Edsel had none of the characteristics of an exploiting capitalist and that he had the simplicity and directness of a workman in his own factories and was like one of the best of them."

Late in the project Valentiner talked to Rivera and discovered that he would be willing to do more frescoes on extra panels for an additional $5,000. Knowing that Edsel had been hard hit by the Depression, Valentiner dreaded having to ask him for the money, but felt that it was so important that he had to. Invited to a party at Gaukler Pointe, he found himself talking "intensely," if somewhat elliptically, about Rivera. Finally Eleanor called out gaily to Edsel, "William is very nervous. Can't you take him into a corner and find out what he wants to tell you?" After a brief chat Edsel agreed to put up the extra money, saying, "We must keep artists in good humor if we want them to do good work." Rivera eventually inserted Edsel into his stylized mural of the auto world, a quizzical face at the bottom of things.

Edsel's involvement in cultural matters singled him out in the nouveau-riche atmosphere of Detroit's auto world. (One automotive executive later said, "He was far above the rest of us in this monkey-wrench, perforated-shoe society of ours. Rivera could have been an outfielder for the Washington Senators for all we knew.") Nelson Rockefeller asked Edsel to be on the board of the Museum of Modern Art. He agreed and donated $5,000 a year to the museum, although he was rarely able to attend meetings.

All this activity cost Edsel increased turmoil with his parents, who regarded modern art as decadent. At one point the Edison Institute decided to show an exhibit of recent paintings by Michigan artists. When Clara came on opening day, the curator tried to steer her away from the modern canvases, but she finally saw one of them and exploded, "I don't like it! It just doesn't belong here." The curator tried to change the subject, but Clara continued to rail about Edsel and Eleanor, saying that they knew nothing about real art. She ended her tirade with the ultimate insult: "They get their idea of art and liking certain things from the Rockefellers."

But Edsel's interest in art was different from that of Nelson Rockefeller. Rockefeller viewed the emerging world of modern art as a place to exercise power and control and shape the artistic taste of the nation. For Edsel, involvement with art was part of a lonely odyssey toward self-discovery. Adept at drawing since he was a boy, especially sketches of cars, Edsel began painting canvases as well as collecting them, Valentiner having arranged for him to have lessons with a celebrated Detroit artist, John Carroll.

Lonely for company, Edsel sometimes invited Ford Motor Company artist Irving Bacon to Gaukler Pointe to paint with him. Under one of van Gogh's self-portraits and beside the man his father had commissioned to do realistic scenes from his childhood using young John Dahlinger as a model, Edsel tried to find himself in pigments. Sometimes he would set down his palette, go outside and stand on the vast lawns of Gaukler Pointe, staring with his wounded eyes into the middle distance of Lake St. Clair. There was an undefined loss amidst his plenty; a sense of bemused imposture as if he knew he was not the man everyone thought him to be. As one of his friends later said, "Even more than most men, Edsel's middle age had a tragic air. He was a character right out of Fitzgerald."

EIGHT

O N April 11, 1938, Edsel and Eleanor gave Henry and Clara a party to mark their fiftieth wedding anniversary. It was an extravagant show of affection. Temporary buildings were erected on the grounds of Gauk-ler Pointe to house a huge range and a mobile kitchen; dozens of uniformed serving people were hired for the night. Famed New York designer Walter Doran Teague supervised the decoration of a dance pavilion; a full orchestra played an evening of the traditional music the elder Fords loved, beginning with a waltz they started on the dance floor alone, with Edsel and Eleanor and then the rest of the guests eventually joining in. The only contretemps that occurred came when the large fans installed in the art gallery to take off the excessive heat caused the candles in the chandeliers to bend double and drip wax onto the guests' dinner clothes. Those hit were maneuvered inconspicu-ously into the kitchen, where maids worked feverishly to take the wax off by using hot irons over paper.

Standing in front of large reproductions of shots taken when they were married, Henry and Clara were photographed again. Except for his gray hair and a network of wrinkles around his eyes, Henry looked the same. Clara, wearing maroon—Henry's favorite color—was plumper, but the drawstring lines around her mouth suggested that the solidity and durability implicit in her character as a younger woman were now real achievements. The two were photographed with Edsel and Eleanor, as if to underscore the continuity between the generations. "It was a good evening," Edsel said wistfully to one of the last guests to leave. "Too bad there has to be a tomorrow."

In the workaday world of the Ford Motor Company there were no con-tinuities, only divisions. It could be seen in the personal geography of the two Fords at the helm. Edsel worked out of the Administration Building, trying to make the company run according to predictable routines. His father had a formal office next door, but never used it, going instead each day to his infor-mal office in the engineering laboratory—his way of saying that the only decisions that mattered were made not by executive drones such as his son, but by those coming out of the pioneering spirit of innovation he alone embodied. He had always opposed paying attention to the structure of the company, having dismissed that subject in *My Life and Work*: "No organization, no specific duties attaching to any position, no line of succession or authority, very few titles and no conferences." Edsel's position was summarized by Liebold: "Edsel felt that people ought to be given certain responsibilities in certain positions and that their authority should be designated and fixed. Mr. Ford didn't go along with that line of thinking. He often said that if he wanted a job done right he would always pick the man who didn't know anything about it."

This disagreement went deeper than management philosophy. It was finally about the nature of power itself, and how it would be wielded in the company. Edsel saw corporate structure as potentially protective—a formal arrangement of power that would shield him and his executives from his father's caprice. For Henry, on the other hand, corporate structure threatened the fluidity which was the key to his continuing influence.

The philosophical struggle between the Fords was thrown into relief by the emergence of General Motors as a prototype of the modern corporation. Alfred Sloan had pioneered a decentralized form of management in which the automotive divisions were set up as integral units, each with its own executive structure, but all working together in a coordinated effort. There was a new emphasis on expertise in fields other than auto manufacture—in the emerging field of finance, in the collection and interpretation of data essential to long-range planning.

In a vision of the corporation as potentially revolutionary for the industry as Ford's vision of the automobile had once been, Sloan said: "Any plan that involved too great a concentration of power upon a limited number of executives would limit initiative…and would reduce efficiency and development. Further it would mean an autocracy, which is just as dangerous in a great industrial organization as in a government…." The company was a machine whose moving parts were human and whose lubricant was merit: "Think of the corporation as a pyramid of opportunities from top to bottom with thousands of chances for advancement. Only capacity limited any worker's chance to grow, to develop his ability to make a greater contribution to the whole and improve his position as well." The fact that the exceptional figure would necessarily rise to the top in such a system was proven by William Knudsen, who had suffered in the autocracy of Ford but risen in the meritocracy of GM as his work at Chevrolet became the wonder of the auto industry.

Edsel saw Sloan's famous flow chart showing where everybody stood in the General Motors organization and felt that if he could create a similar one at Ford it would be a sort of Magna Carta for him and his loyalists. Hearing what Edsel intended, Henry became more set against formal structure than ever. Lawrence Sheldrick, who in this titleless institution came as close to being a chief engineer as anyone at Ford since Harold Wills' departure, once answered a subordinate's confusion about responsibility by looking around nervously and then pulling out of his desk a piece of paper on which he had listed names and duties. "Here," he said with an air of secrecy. "Don't let anybody ever see this, because we're not supposed to have an organizational chart."

Looking for other ways to counter his father's autocracy, Edsel suggested (even though it would mean a dilution of his own birthright) that perhaps there should be a stock offering that would make the Ford Motor Company publicly owned. Henry became livid. "I'll take every factory down brick by brick before I let any of those Jew speculators get stock in the company," he said. The subject didn't come up again.

The battle lines had been drawn in such a way that there could be no compromise but only total victory for one or the other of them. Henry's possessive love of his son, ever more unrequited as Edsel burrowed into his own private life, had hardened into an obsession with his son's limitations. The thin membrane of civility between them was often pierced by Henry's irrational jealousy of Edsel's friends at Grosse Pointe, a locale he increasingly regarded as a sort of Sodom and Gomorrah. The most casual reference to Edsel's life there was liable to touch off a violent response. Henry said that people like Kanzler were "piddling in Edsel's ear," and called them "ear piddlers." When he once asked where Edsel was and was told that he was watching one of his social friends in a boat race, Henry, who hardly knew the man, exploded, "Oh! That goddamned rotten puke!"

He said he wanted his son to succeed, but whenever Edsel gave evidence of doing so Henry immediately undercut him, often humiliating him in front of Ford executives in a demonstration clearly, if unconsciously, meant to show who was boss. He once said to Liebold, "The next time you see Edsel, tell him that you don't approve of the people he goes around with." Liebold replied, "That's going a bit far. I think Edsel would consider it an affront for me to make a suggestion of that kind." Ford insisted, "Well, you tell him. That's what I want him to know."

He constantly interrogated people who knew about Edsel's private life. Spotted whispering to one of the Gaukler Pointe servants in his office at the engineering lab, Ford admitted that the man was a paid informant keeping him abreast of his son's activities at home. To escape this constant surveillance, Edsel, although president of one of the largest corporations in the world, found himself trying to evade his father like a teenager. Sympathetic employees helped him in his petty deceptions. On one occasion, for instance, Edsel wanted to go to a formal party in the early afternoon. He got his tuxedo out of the trunk of his roadster, changed in the office and left. His aide Ed Harper knew that Henry would soon be calling to check on his son's whereabouts, as he did every day, and told a plant foreman to tell the old man that Edsel was at the foundry. When the foreman hesitated, Harper said, "Well, it's about time you learned to tell a white lie to help Edsel out." The man did tell Ford the white lie and, when he was found out, almost lost his job as a result.

Henry always justified his harassment of Edsel by saying that his son was not "strong" enough. (Those sensitive to the nuances of the situation and to the newly fashionable psychology of Sigmund Freud thought Ford was projecting his own weaknesses onto Edsel.) First it was Sorensen who was adopted as a surrogate son and made to engage in a symbolic sibling rivalry to "toughen up" Edsel. But Sorensen was interested primarily in controlling the Rouge, and after he had secured a power base there he backed away from the conflict. It didn't matter. Ford had found another person who relished the role Sorensen rejected, someone who could be the strong son Edsel couldn't be and also the strong man he himself was not. It was Harry Bennett, a figure who would drive the tragedy between father and son to a conclusion.

ENTERING THE FORD SAGA RELATIVELY late, Bennett changed it from the spectacle of an increasingly bitter and fitful old man unwilling to relinquish power into a Byzantine court drama filled with treachery and intrigue, dire struggles for power and real physical danger.

On the surface Harry Bennett didn't seem the one to play a major role in a major American corporation. A semi-orphan (his father had been killed when hit on the head with a chair during a barroom brawl when Bennett was young), he was raised by a working-class mother who aspired to culture. She insisted that her ancestors had come over on the *Mayflower* and forced her only son to sing tenor in the choir of the local Episcopal church when he was growing up. But Bennett was not interested in the false gentility, nor was he a choirboy; he ran away from home at the age of sixteen to join the Navy.

As a young man he was short, about five foot six, and even though he worked on his physique his stature dominated his life, causing him to be always on the lookout for opportunities to prove himself. ("I'd always wished that I were a big man and all my life took on jobs that were meant for a man bigger than I," he said after he had become notorious.) While in the Navy at the outset of World War I, he became a deep-sea diver and took on other hazardous jobs, and also boxed for the fleet as a lightweight, calling himself "Sailor Reese."

Bennett was twenty-four years old, about the same age as Edsel, in 1917 when he first came to work for the Ford Motor Company—square-jawed and pug-nosed, with thinning reddish hair, gelid blue eyes and a wary intelligence. One day in 1918 Knudsen, who was at that time in charge of the Eagle boat project, told a couple of Ford employees that he wished he had someone tough enough to keep an eye on watchmen he suspected of stealing building materials. One of them replied, "We have just the man for you—an ex-champion of the U.S. Navy named Harry Bennett." Knudsen told them to send him around, but when they brought Bennett to see him the next morning he took one look at the diminutive figure and said scornfully, "I thought you were going to bring me a big prizefighter."

Soon afterward Henry Ford was accompanying Knudsen through the plant when they saw a large crowd of shouting workers. When he asked what was happening someone pointed at a large man in the middle of the crowd and said, "We just brought this big brute in for beating a boy." Disturbed by the injustice, Ford asked, "Isn't there anybody around here big enough to beat that fellow up?" Bennett, overhearing him, jumped up as if by reflex and went at the man, hitting him with several solid blows in the face and finally knocking him down. From that moment on, knowing that he had made an impression, Bennett did something flamboyant every time Ford was in the plant. Once during the building of the Eagle boats he grasped a rope dangling down from an upper deck and climbed up hand over hand from the floor, knowing that every eye would be on him by the time he reached the top of his hazardous climb. Henry finally rewarded him by making him head watchman at the Rouge.

Bennett had immediately seen where the power was in the company in the mid-twenties, as Sorensen battled Edsel and Kanzler to a standoff and consolidated his position as czar of the Rouge once that great plant came onto line. He became Sorensen's man, taking on special duties, especially when danger was involved. Behind his back he was referred to as Sorensen's "puppy," although at times it seemed that "mad dog" would have been more appropriate. As one employee later described the relationship, "If Charlie Sorensen pointed his finger in a direction, Bennett would go into action without thinking.... If Charlie told him to fire this group or that particular man he wouldn't question Charlie in the least. I remember on one occasion Sorensen sent Bennett after someone he saw standing around apparently idle. He said, 'Go and get rid of that fellow.' Harry came running back boasting, 'I just fired fourteen men going down that aisle.' Very pleased, Sorensen said, 'Good boy, Harry, good boy.' "

The watchmen hired by Bennett eventually formed the nucleus of the Service Department, an organization which not only performed security functions but also roamed through the Rouge trying to control pilferage and maintain order among the men. Noting Bennett's willingness to do whatever was asked of him, however dangerous, Ford made him his fixer. Bennett was effective during the crisis caused by Ford's anti-Semitism, managing to get a mistrial in the Sapiro libel suit by making it appear that Jewish sympathizers had succeeded in corrupting a woman juror. Sometimes there were flamboyant acts of derring-do, as when Bennett jumped into a car and pursued some thieves who had held up a Ford office, driving close to their car while an aide crouched on the running board and fired shotgun blasts at them. He became the company's resident tough guy—a pugnacious little man talking out of the corner of his mouth who seemed to have stepped right out of the gangster movies of the era. Henry was attracted to his dark charisma. When some individual was making trouble in the plant, Ford would sidle up to Bennett and whisper, "Harry, let's you and him have a fight."

During the time that the Rouge was closed down to retool for the Model A, the relationship between the two men became more intense. Ford began to phone Bennett the first thing in the morning and would often have his chauffeur pick him up so that they could drive to work together. He liked the look of the man—the colored silk shirts, the Western belt buckle, and the snap-brim felt hat. He liked the Damon Runyonesque quality—the fact that Bennett had real experience in a masculine world. He was intrigued by Bennett's tics—how he wore nothing but bow ties because, as he said, "A four in hand gives tough customers a handle for steadying a man just before the punch." Henry was also intrigued by what he referred to as Bennett's "depth"—the fact that he was a talented artist and musician, playing saxophone in his own dance band. For a while Ford tried to get involved in Bennett's private life, getting Clara to help him try to patch things up between Bennett and his first wife when they separated. Henry and Clara then blessed Bennett's second marriage, to a Dearborn schoolteacher; but when that relationship too disintegrated and Bennett took up with an attractive nurse, Clara snubbed her at one of the old-fashioned dances, and that ended their social friendship.

When Henry played the autocrat at his luncheon table, arriving precisely at 12:59 to shake hands with everyone present and sitting down to the "rabbit food" he tried to coerce everyone else into eating, too, Bennett was never present. He ate with his own cronies in his own lunchroom, playing Ford to them. On most days, Henry quickly finished eating, left the executive lunchroom and went down to Bennett's office, waiting for him to finish so that the two of them could talk about what Ford called "cops and robbers." Bennett took the lead by telling tales about members of the Detroit underworld he knew. Some people thought that Henry's credulousness made Bennett exaggerate his mob associations; in fact, however, he was close to Chester "Chet" La Mare, known as the "Al Capone of Detroit," whose branch of the syndicate was said to be banking $3500 a day from bootleg liquor. Bennett awarded La Mare the concession to supply vegetables to the Ford kitchens not long before the mobster turned up dead in front of his home in a gangland killing. Joe Tosco, who sometimes came to visit Bennett in his office with a .45 tucked into his waistband, was also shot in a mob killing. Once Bennett took convicted murderer "Black Leo" Celuria with him to one of Henry's lunches where he knew the Governor of Michigan would also be present. He gave a job to Kid McCoy, a onetime boxer who had done time for murdering one of his ten wives. Henry would sit in Bennett's office talking compulsively to each of the men in his rogue's gallery, saying things like "How did you get into that?" and then, before the man could reply, blurting out, "I'll bet a woman got you into it."

Seeing this as a sort of crush on Henry's part, Edsel and the other executives were initially grateful to Bennett for distracting the old man's attention from the company. They assumed that the uneducated Bennett, a man with no apparent interest in the intricacies of the auto industry, had no ambitions and would be content with his sinecure as the company's most colorful figure. By the time Bennett's authority had begun to grow, it was too late to stop him. He had become a central player in the Ford drama, equally adept as a troubleshooter and as a troublemaker.

Ironically, it was the Fords' need for personal security and protection that gave Bennett a route to power inside the company. The kidnapping and murder of the Lindbergh baby in 1932 sent a shiver through every American family of wealth and prominence. The Rockefellers doubled the number of watchmen at their Pocantico Hills, New York, estate and put bars on the windows of their children's bedrooms. The Fords turned their well-being over to Bennett and his Service Department. Always before, the threats that were mailed or phoned to Ford headquarters had been dismissed as the work of harmless cranks. But by the early thirties, as the folder of menacing letters in what became known as the "nut file" grew larger and larger, the threats were taken seriously. "I can replace factories but not grandchildren," Ford said, and he gave Bennett authority to deal with all security matters.

One plot was hatched by a man who said he would kill all of Edsel's children if he was not paid a ransom. Bennett had a Ford employee pose as Edsel, go to the church named as the drop-off spot for the ransom and get out of Edsel's Lincoln with a dummy strongbox, which he left on a pew. When the extortionist went into the church to pick up the money, Bennett and his men nabbed him, calling the police only after they had roughed him up.

There were several similar episodes, always ending with Bennett exacting crude justice on people who threatened the family, and always leaving an ambivalent memory behind. Edsel's son Bill, for instance, never forgot the time a hoodlum threatened his brother Henry II. "Bennett said he'd handle it. Later on, the guy was found floating face down in the river."

While Edsel had no choice but to accept Bennett as chief protector of his family, he disliked having to rely on him, and so did his children. Bill was often driven to school in a car with a siren on it, and he would slide down in the front seat when he saw his schoolmates. A childhood friend of Benson's remembered how he drove around Grosse Pointe in the midget racer his grandfather had given him, shrieking with laughter when he managed to give his bodyguards the slip. A Ford employee whose job it was to escort Henry II and Benson back to Hotchkiss from weekends in Detroit was at first alarmed when Henry II looked out the rear window of their cab as they left Grand Central Station in New York and said, "Here come those rats now!" Then he realized that young Ford was talking not about criminals but about Bennett's men, who trailed him and his brother everywhere.

If the need for security provided Bennett with a foothold in the company's power structure, it was the growing labor unrest which put him into the top echelons of Ford. By the middle of the Depression, the company's reputation for being enlightened had been assaulted so often by Ford's insensitive statements that it had finally collapsed. In an industry where employment and wages were low, along with worker morale, the Rouge became an inviting symbol for labor organizers and political radicals. Henry left no doubt where he stood: "Unions are organized by Jewish financiers, not labor. A union is a neat thing for a Jew to have on hand when he comes around to get his clutches on industry." Harry Bennett was the weapon he decided to use on workers' organizations to keep them out of his company.

In March 1932, Communist organizers set up a "March on Hunger" through Detroit and Dearborn to the Rouge, attracting several thousand participants.* Dearborn police tried to disperse them with tear gas as they headed for the Ford Motor Company employment office, but the stiff spring wind blew the gas back into their faces. The police were unable to hold the line, and, despite the fact that fire trucks doused the demonstrators with water which froze on contact, the crowd broke through. As the demonstrators began to heave. bricks at the building, Bennett went out to try to talk to them. A young woman yelled, "We want Bennett, and he's in that building."

He replied, "No, you're wrong, I'm Bennett." Instantly he was showered with slag and bricks. Hit in the head, he instinctively pulled an organizer for the Young Communist League down on top of him as Dearborn police opened fire on the unarmed demonstrators; four of them, including the man shielding Bennett, were killed. Henry was at lunch with Edsel and Sorensen when word of the fracas came. The three quickly drove to the Rouge and saw the chaos. Bennett, just regaining consciousness, was still bleeding profusely from the head. Onlookers were impressed by the depth of Ford's worry. ("It was like it was Edsel lying there," one of them said. "Henry was white as a sheet; there were tears in his eyes.") He accompanied Bennett to the hospital and called him daily to find out how he was doing while also sending a new Lincoln to his home as a reward for gallantry under fire. Bennett, once he was released by the doctors, applied a bright splash of Mercurochrome on his bandages to keep attention focused on his head wound, and exploited all of Ford's fears about another, more serious worker assault. He stockpiled tear gas and constructed machine-gun emplacements at Gaukler Pointe and Fairlane. The budget for the Service Department was increased, and, as Bennett began to hire ex-pugs and hoods accountable only to him—a private army—his influence grew at an alarming pace.

BENNETT'S RISE WAS HARD ON everyone. Even Liebold suffered. He had been

---

* It was ironic, given the fact that the Comintern had given orders for the march, that the riot was witnessed by forty engineers from the Soviet Union whom Henry had agreed to train in auto production. Henry had been vaguely sympathetic to the USSR from 1928, when the first Soviet delegation arrived at the Rouge to arrange for the import of Ford autos. Later that year, Sorensen visited Russia and was given an elegant private railcar with his own chef and steward. He met Politburo members Anastas Mikoyan and Vyacheslav Molotov and discussed Ford operations with them. Henry's romance with the Soviet government continued for several years. By 1936, Ford transactions with the USSR amounted to some $40 million.

Ford's other self for years, but now he saw his power begin to wane because of the growing influence of "the little man." Finally he went over the edge, suffering a nervous breakdown in 1933, when he disappeared from work one afternoon, driving a company car until he was exhausted and then registering in a small hotel in northern Michigan under a pseudonym. He woke up the next morning disoriented and bathed in sweat. He bought a newspaper when he saw banner headlines, obviously inspired by Bennett, that he was feared kidnapped. Knowing that state troopers were looking for him, Liebold burrowed down under the covers of his hotel bed and slept for twenty-four hours. Finally the authorities located him and brought him back to Dearborn. After several days under sedation, Liebold came back to work. But he was never the same, knowing that he had been supplanted by Bennett.

Edsel couldn't escape as easily. Not only did he have to bear his father's erratic and often sadistic behavior, but he also had to cope with an upstart whose power was metastasizing throughout the company. Yet, in the middle of this deteriorating situation, Edsel nonetheless managed to come into his own as president of Ford. Through years of patient politicking, as well as by the acquisition of real expertise, he had come to the point where he could now have at least a limited impact on Ford products. Among his accomplishments was opening a new engineering laboratory at the Rouge under Sheldrick's direction, away from the pathological prying of his father. ("Henry couldn't pop in so often over there...." Sheldrick later said. "We were able to get things done, get things built up to finished form before he could upset them.") Edsel also finally got the company a test track.

Just as it had been Edsel's idea to buy Lincoln to give the company an elegant car to match GM's Cadillac, so in the mid-thirties, as Ford's competitive position continued to slip, he tried to get a part of the growing middle-priced market through the Zephyr. The Zephyr began as the Briggs Manufacturing Company "dream car," which Edsel saw in prototype at the 1933 automobile show. He was excited by it, having wanted for some time a car in price and quality between the Ford and the Lincoln. He bought the rights from Briggs and then brought in Eugene T. Gregorie, a former boat designer, to carry out his vision of a sleek auto for the middle-class buyer. Seen by one colleague as a "smart, cocky young fellow" whose attitude "kept him in continual hot water, especially with Henry Ford," Gregorie made his reputation as one of the major stylists in Detroit with the Zephyr and began a collaboration with Edsel that would last for years.

The Zephyr did not have large sales, because Henry denied Edsel access to the economies of the Ford line, forcing him to build and market the car within the more expensive Lincoln division. But it did force the issue of middle-priced cars to compete with GM, whose strength increasingly came from Buick, Oldsmobile and Pontiac. After the appearance of the Zephyr, Ford sales manager John Davis was able to badger Henry and Sorensen into building the competitor within the Ford division. The result was the appearance of the Mercury in 1937.

But Edsel's chief accomplishment was winning a role for styling in the company and taking control of this aspect of the business. He poured tremendous energy even into small things such as the selection of the proper hood ornament. One Ford draftsman recalled, "The changing of models was left up to Edsel. He would come in and tell us each year what the model was going to be. He came in practically every day. Edsel liked to criticize the first model made in clay.... He [might not] like the shape of the grille, the back end, and so on. He criticized the interior quite a lot and the instrumental work.... He was very particular about the riding qualities of the car. He knew what he wanted and insisted that he get it."

Defying his father, Edsel was finally able to create a design section outside the engineering group in 1935. Eugene Gregorie, who had begun to play a role for Edsel similar to the one Harold Wills had played for his father at the beginning of the company, was given an office in an old airframe building which had been used recently as a studio for auto interiors. Under his direction, the design section soon began to produce important innovations such as integrating the headlights and taillights into the front and back fenders in place of "can" appendage, a feature first appearing on the 1937 Ford. Edsel came into the design section every day after lunching at the Round Table, and Gregorie would show him what was happening. Noting that Henry never visited, one of the designers said later, "Well, we all wore smocks and considered ourselves *artistes*. The old man thought we were queer."

The major achievement of the collaboration between Edsel and Gregorie was the Continental. In a sense it was the end product of all the thinking about fine cars that Edsel had done since his youth, the end of a quest to capture the Grail of the auto industry—an American car that could hold its own against the great European touring cars. Coming back from trips on the Continent, he would talk to Gregorie about the cars he had seen there. He had Gregorie build prototypes of several sports cars on a Ford chassis—cars with sweeping front fenders, high narrow grilles, thin bumpers and piped-leather interiors. But his hopes that such cars would be included in the Ford line were repeatedly dashed by his father and Sorensen.

Then Gregorie got an idea. Ed Martin, who worked under him in the design section, said later, "One day when [Gregorie] and I came back from lunch he asked me to get out the tenth-scale sketches of the Lincoln-Zephyr convertible coupe. As I sat beside him he took out a piece of vellum, put it over the sketch, and began drawing.... After several minutes of silence during which he kept drawing, he told me that because it was impossible to build a sports car on a Ford chassis, he would suggest to Edsel that we build a special sports car on a Zephyr chassis." Edsel fell in love with the design. He allowed Gregorie to bypass the model stage and in effect hand-make a prototype that came out of the Lincoln plant on a blustery day in March 1939. The car, which Edsel had decided to call the Continental, was so beautiful that he drove it directly to Florida by himself to show it off. At first he intended to build only three Continentals, one for himself and one each for Henry II and

Benson. But by the time he had returned from his vacation, he found that over two hundred orders had been placed by people who had seen him on the road. He put the car into production and sold more than five thousand Continentals over the next two years.

Edsel was doing his best to bring the company into a competitive position, but his efforts added up at best to a holding action. Ford's position continued to deteriorate. In 1936 the company sank to a low point, winning only 22 percent of the U.S. market, which put it behind GM's 43 percent and, even worse, Chrysler's 25 percent. But external competitors bothered Edsel less than the chaos coming from within as a result of labor unrest.

Early workers' organizations had approved of Ford. But by the early thirties, when the company's high-wage policy collapsed and Henry became increasingly suspicious of his workingmen, the Ford Motor Company became labor's *bête noire*. Because of its collaborative style, the American Federation of Labor (AFL) unions had never been able to make an effective assault on Ford or the rest of the auto industry. But passage of Senator Robert F. Wagner's National Labor Relations Act in 1935, guaranteeing the right to collective bargaining, gave workers new hope. The plant locals originally chartered by the AFL were taken over by aggressive young organizers and rechartered as the United Auto Workers affiliated with the Congress of Industrial Organization (CIO).

It was clear that the UAW's effort to organize the auto industry would be different from that of its predecessors. The model for the UAW battle plan was the successful CIO assault on the steel industry. But it was also clear to all concerned that the auto men would not capitulate as easily as U.S. Steel had, and that Henry Ford would be by far the most difficult and dangerous target of all.

Edsel believed that the company and the industry should seek an accommodation with the UAW before the plants were convulsed in violence. But his father regarded these notions as just more evidence of his weakness. Henry's reaction to the labor movement was to make the Rouge into an industrial concentration camp overseen by Bennett's army of Service Department men. They followed workers into washrooms to make sure they didn't talk about union matters; they demanded that someone walking from one place to another tell them where he was going and why. While workers were at their benches their lunch pails and overcoats were ransacked for union literature. A meeting of any two workers was considered prima-facie evidence of a conspiracy. "Sniffers'" even stood at air registers to make sure workers did not break the rule against smoking in the washroom. Outside the plant, Service men skulked around the taverns and markets frequented by Ford workers, listening for damaging gossip.

There was no sitting, squatting, singing, talking or whistling on the job. Smiling was frowned upon. Workers learned to communicate without moving their lips, in what became known as the "Ford whisper." Their frozen features were called "Fordization of the face." The workers fought back by taping messages onto the parts moving along the assembly line, a technique that allowed them not only to communicate but also to uncover the informers in their ranks when the information on the messages was revealed to men of the Service Department. Not even Bennett's men could stop workers from picking up the notices of a union meeting which fluttered down from the sky after the UAW hired an airplane to circle the Rouge on March 23, 1936.

But such acts of defiance were rare. For the most part the men were disoriented by the intimidating situation Bennett had created. They understood, moreover, that it was part of a general philosophical change that made the company, once one of the auto industry's best places to work in, now one of the worst. Ford made his feelings clear: by even listening to union organizers the men had forfeited any claim to his old paternal concern. He turned his back on them entirely and urged Bennett on. Anyone even suspected of being a UAW sympathizer was not only summarily fired but usually beaten up as well. Even if not suspected of union sympathies, men with long seniority and earning high wages were fired and then, after being allowed to sit home and experience unemployment for a few days, rehired at starting pay. Absolute loyalty was demanded, not only to the company's antiunion ideology but also to the product. One supervisor said, "If we found a fellow who drove a Buick, say, we'd ask 'Is this your car?' 'Yes,' the employee would say. 'Well, you're through working here...' we'd say. 'You've been late three times this month and we're firing you.' The real reason was that he was driving a Buick." Bennett sent around a questionnaire to workers naive enough to admit that members of their families did not drive Fords. One man who wrote that his wife had bought a Chevrolet because she preferred the riding qualities of the back springs found that severance proceedings were immediately begun against him.

And finally the assembly line was speeded up once again, a fact which, when added to the paranoid atmosphere of the plant, began to break men physically and emotionally—causing a syndrome involving exhaustion and despair which eventually became known in Detroit medical circles as "Forditis." The regimented horror that Charlie Chaplin had shown beneath the slapstick of *Modern Times* was part of the workers' daily life, as they struggled to keep the items they were trying to assemble from whizzing by and ran back to the line cramming food into their mouths after fifteen-minute breaks during which they had to wash and go to the toilet as well as eat.

But the UAW continued its assault on Detroit. On December 28, 1936, a sit-down strike at GM's Fisher Body plant created a movement which swept through the company. Chrysler and Ford were not affected by the shutdown, but it was clear that their time would soon come. During a meeting at the Michigan Governor's office, Walter Chrysler said to CIO chief John L. Lewis, "This isn't fair. You shut us down one at a time." Lewis replied, "I agree with you. It isn't fair. And I'll tell you how we'll fix it. Tomorrow I'll close you down." In March, a few weeks after GM had settled, Chrysler was struck, and almost immediately it capitulated. That left the Ford Motor Company—the toughest for last.

Scornful of his competitors' weakness, Ford vowed to fight the UAW to the bitter end. Edsel was concerned about the adverse publicity, as he had been during his father's anti-Semitic campaign, and knew that the intensive radio campaign the UAW had begun against the company was having an effect. He saw unionization as inevitable and wanted to get recognition over with so that the company could focus on the other problems confronting it. When the Supreme Court upheld the constitutionality of the Wagner Act, the Roosevelt Administration expected that Ford would engage in collective bargaining. Edsel urged him to do so, and when he refused the two of them argued so bitterly that Sorensen, who watched the confrontation with dismay, had to leave the room.

One afternoon Ford called Edsel and Sorensen to his office and delivered what was clearly a summary statement on the whole issue: "I've picked someone to talk with the unions. I want a strong, aggressive man who can take care of himself in an argument, and I've got him. He has my full confidence. I want to make sure that you, Edsel, and you, Charlie, will support him. He's waiting in Charlie's office at the Rouge now, so let's go down there and see him." Acceding to the obvious pleasure Henry took in drawing out the suspense, they went with him to the giant plant, only to find Harry Bennett waiting in his office and bubbling over with excitement at his new assignment. Edsel was heartsick, but there was nothing he could do, his father having already told him that if he didn't have the stomach for a fight he should plan a long vacation that would take him far from Detroit.

Over the next few months Edsel tried to let the union know indirectly that he was not unsympathetic to the cause of the working-man. But his gestures were like semaphore signals sent from afar by a stranded man. Bennett was adding more employees to the Service Department payroll and tightening security at the Rouge to the breaking point. It was hard for Edsel to argue against success: by May 1937, the tactics of intimidation seemed to be working, because there was not sufficient backing at the company for the UAW to try the sort of all-out assault that had worked at GM and Chrysler.

When Walter Reuther, a former worker on the Ford assembly line who had gone on to a position as UAW organizer, obtained a permit to distribute literature outside the Rouge on May 26, Bennett immediately took countermeasures out of all proportion to the threat, posting brawny former fighters and wrestlers, as well as known hoodlums, at every gate of the plant. Reuther, Richard Frankenstein and a few other unionists drove to Gate 4. As they got ready to distribute leaflets, one of Bennett's men came up and shouted, "This is Ford property, get the hell out of here." The labor leaders started to leave, but as they did other Service men came up to block their exit. Suddenly Bennett's men rushed them. Slugged in the kidneys, Reuther went down and was kicked in the face, hit and kicked again, and then shoved down several stone steps. One Service man got behind the burly Frankenstein and pulled his coat down over his shoulders, immobilizing his arms so that he couldn't fight back. He was slugged repeatedly; when he finally went down, several of Bennett's men stomped him.

Others in the party were also beaten. A minister there as an observer had his back broken; a young woman unionist began to vomit blood after being kicked in the stomach. It would have been a complete victory for Bennett except for the fact that the cameras of newsmen had been clicking all during the violent confrontation, capturing pictures of the beatings as well as the aftermath, when the bloodied Reuther and Frankenstein tried to hold and comfort each other—images which gained immediate standing as metaphors for the whole union struggle in America.

NINE

ENRY FORD TURNED SEVENTY-FIVE in the middle of these troubles and, for the first time in his life, began to show his age. He had always prided himself on his youthfulness, often having his chauffeur stop when he saw a knot of boys alongside the road so that he could challenge them to a footrace and astound them with his speed. But not long after his birthday he suffered a mild stroke. It was hushed up and called a bad case of the flu. He himself treated it lightly, telling the chief of staff of the Henry Ford Hospital that he was being adequately treated by his chiropractor Dr. Coulter, and, when the doctor threatened to hospitalize him, countering by threatening to put Coulter on the staff.

The aftereffects were slight—more caprice, more eccentricity. There was also less ability to live in a world of constantly changing automobile styles, government relationships, union troubles—that vexing world of the present, containing the seed of a future which was so dramatically foreshadowed by the 1939 New York World's Fair.* Henry spent more time traveling. For twenty-five years he and Clara had taken their vacations with the Edisons, spending time in Florida after both men were too old for their camping trips. But that era had ended with Edison's death in 1931—an event so climactic for Ford that he had begged the inventor's son Charles to sit at Edison's deathbed and capture his last breath in a vial, which he kept as a talisman at Fairlane ever after. Now Henry spent several weeks a year at the four-thousand-acre plantation at Richmond Hill, Georgia, they had bought in 1934 at the suggestion of John Burroughs. Clara helped teach the local girls to cook; he gathered some of the boys living around the house and told nostalgic stories about his early days in the automobile industry.

On one of his visits, Henry went to Bascomb Mahaffey, caretaker of the plantation, and said he wanted to find a Model T so that he could remove

---

* Edsel moved temporarily to New York to be in charge of the Ford exhibit, which became one of the centerpieces of the fair. Occupying seven acres near the symbolic Trylon, it was centered around the "Road of Tomorrow," an elevated highway on which visitors could drive Fords, Mercurys and Zephyrs.

and study its transmission. Mahaffey scoured the county and finally found one, buying it for $25. As he drove the overheated Lizzie back to the Richmond Hill garage, Ford was waiting. He looked at the old car lovingly and whispered in awe, "Just think of that!" He got Mahaffey to take him for a drive, raving about the Model T as they went: "Now, this is responsible for everything. This is the car that did the work. I do hope that everyone appreciates what it has meant to the world. It meant a *good bit.*" Ford insisted that the car be taken apart. When Mahaffey had the parts spread out on the garage floor, Henry decided that he now wanted a Model A to take apart for a comparison. They went to the local wrecker, but there were no Model A's there. Surveying the cars lined up at the front gate of the wrecker's yard—Chevrolets, Plymouths and Dodges, all with staved-in radiators and crumpled fenders, he said proudly, "The world wouldn't believe that. Twenty-five hundred automobiles and not a Model A to be found among them. There's no other company that would give you a picture of that kind."

But these sudden accessions of sentiment did not mean that Ford had mellowed. He was still determined to control his company as long as he was alive, and his tool for doing so was Harry Bennett, who had become his man of all seasons: confidant and fixer; judge, jury and executioner; general in command of the Service Department, which the *New York Times* called "the largest private quasimilitary organization in existence." Ford liked him because he was a "real man." (Bennett bought pornographic movies with such titles as *The Casting Director, A Stiff Game,* etc., which he showed to some of his underworld contacts as well as to Ford himself.) But what impressed him most about Bennett was the way the cocky little man got things done. One day the two were driving to the Rouge when Henry noticed a Ford-operated service station. "Why are we in the gas business, Harry?" he asked querulously. Later that afternoon when they were driving home, Bennett made a point of going by the former service station, which had been razed by the bulldozer .he had called in, and replaced by a little park with a sod lawn, plants and trees. "That's nice, Harry," Ford said, smiling, as he studied his henchman's industry out the window.

Henry treated him like a son. When Bennett was on a trip, Ford called him twice a day. He became jealous at signs of the slightest civility between Bennett and Edsel. If the two of them did happen to talk without rancor, Henry would sidle up to Bennett not long afterward and say, "Now, Harry, you think you're getting along with Edsel, but he's no friend of yours." He was once riding in the backseat of his car with a newspaperman who asked him who was the greatest man he had known. Without hesitating, Henry nodded in the direction of the driver, Harry Bennett.

Henry gave his surrogate son a relatively small salary, but compensated him with several homes—a hundred-acre island on the Huron River and a summer place in Gross Ile where a succession of three yachts (the last one, a seventy-five-foot cruiser, eventually conscripted by the U.S. Navy) were moored. Bennett's chief residence was an estate he called his "castle" near

Ypsilanti, in the backyard of which he kept lions and tigers given to him by famed animal trainer Clyde Beatty. There was an underground tunnel connecting the house to his car for quick getaways. In the front door there were bullet holes which he preserved as conversation pieces, bragging that they had been left there after a mobster's assassination attempt.

Bennett had seen Ford use a combination of small wages and large gifts to make Ray and Evangeline Dahlinger dependent on him. He knew that the same thing was possible in his own case, that Ford's largesse was a devious generosity intended to create a debt. But he had his own agenda. He had become a sort of blue-collar Macbeth whose intention was to immobilize Edsel and perhaps someday replace him in fact as he had in Henry Ford's fancy. All he had achieved was a sort of serendipity, after all. No one had expected him to come this far. Why shouldn't he go all the way?

Bennett's machinations had taken their toll on Edsel. What young John Dahlinger called his "martyr's smile" had hardened to the point where, in repose, it looked like a knife wound. Always a bit frail, Edsel had become sickly by the end of the thirties, his face having taken on a pallor that even the sunshine of his Florida vacations couldn't hide. He got colds easily and had trouble getting rid of them. He had increasingly serious stomach problems. Bennett made fun of him for throwing up, implying that it was a little boy's response to tension. But there was more to it than that, a problem manifesting itself in repeated bouts of what Edsel called gastritis. The doctors told him he had ulcers and put him on a strict diet, while also watching him closely. "Dr. McClure and I were discussing the status of your health yesterday," Dr. Mateer of the Henry Ford Hospital wrote to him in 1940, "and we felt it would be a good idea at this time to obtain a progress X-ray examination, since it is now 19 months since you have had an examination of this type made.... The above X-ray, along with a routine blood and urine check, would apparently be all that would be indicated.... There would be no indication for any tube swallowing this time."

The combination of Bennett's increasing power over Henry and Edsel's increasing incapacity made the company founder. In 1937, it made a profit of $7 million on $848 million in sales, less than one percent, while Chrysler was making $51 million on $770 million in sales and GM $196 million on $1.6 billion. Because of his problems with Bennett, Edsel was powerless to reverse the downward slide. His rival never challenged him directly, but always went behind his back to Henry for a reaffirmation of his right to meddle. Unable to take it any longer, Edsel blurted out to a friend, "The hurtful thing is that Father takes Harry's word for everything and he won't believe me. Who is this guy anyhow? Where did he come from?"

But the provocations continued. One of the most serious involved John Davis, sales manager and one of the few remaining men of talent and integrity in the company. In a sales meeting, Davis got into an argument with Harry Mack, a Bennett crony who headed the Dearborn branch. After the two men came to blows, Edsel fired Mack. The following day Bennett went to Henry and not only got his friend reinstated but got Davis exiled to California with a demotion as West Coast sales manager. Edsel called Davis into his office in despair. "I want to support you," he said, "but I just can't fight any longer with Father. If I continue to support you in this manner I don't think I can hold out much longer."

All their married life Eleanor had tried to deny what was happening between Edsel and his father, drawing a silk curtain around their life together at Gaukler Pointe and pretending that whatever happened at the Ford head-quarters had no implications outside Dearborn. Even as Edsel's problems with his father became more serious and began to affect his health, she could not confront Henry directly, although a plaintive undertone could be heard in the bread-and-butter letters she sent him. "I do wish we were going to be with you for your birthday," she wrote from Seal Harbor when Henry turned seventy-five. "It is nice that Edsel will be there though, and we all send you very much love and the happiest of birthday greetings…. I wish I could ade-quately express how much Mrs. Ford and you have always meant to me [and] I guess you know how fond the children are of you both."

Eleanor meant to cauterize the family wounds, but her denial of the conflict between her husband and his father was disorienting for the children. "Mother would start to refer to it occasionally," Bill later said. "But then she'd sort of catch herself and change course, as if to say, 'Well, this isn't what I ought to be saying.' "

Clara was more direct. She had long been a spectator of the warfare between her son and her husband, watching with horror as it expanded, yet unable to affect it because, however sorry she felt for Edsel, she nonetheless believed that Henry was right in his condemnation of their son's Grosse Pointe lifestyle. But she always maintained cordial relations with Edsel, and even during periods of alienation from his father he always dropped by Fairlane to visit her when Henry was away. But now, distressed by Edsel's physical decline, Clara became so concerned that she made an appointment to see Sorensen at the Rouge and then broke down in tears, crying, "Who is this man Bennett who has so much control over my husband and is ruining my son's health?"

Sorensen, too, had seen the threat Bennett posed, and had made com-mon cause with Edsel in a last ditch attempt to keep the company afloat. But it was too late. The labor situation had given Bennett the whip hand and he didn't intend to relinquish it. He played the union struggle for all it was worth with Ford, using it to consolidate and then expand his power.

Finally, after three years of skirmishing with Bennett, the UAW readied itself for an all-out assault on the last great target in Detroit. By late 1940 the union was openly signing up men at the Rouge. Bennett's Service men would come by and tear off their UAW buttons, but the workers would put on more. The conflict came to a head on April 1, 1941, when Bennett fired eight work-ers for union activities and fifteen hundred others sat down in solidarity. Seeing the historic aperture they had been awaiting so long, Reuther and the rest of the union hierarchy rushed out to the plant. By the time they arrived there the whole of the Rouge was out—fifty thousand men, who quickly blocked the entrances and set up forests of pickets.

Hearing that his father and Bennett were massing the Service Department forces for a pitched battle, Edsel flew home from a vacation in Florida, where he had been trying desperately to recover his strength. Thin and pale, he argued the case for accommodation with a desperation that company executives had never seen before. To Bennett's disgust, Henry finally agreed to an NLRB election, largely because he had deluded himself into believing that his workers were still loyal to him. But only 1,958 workers, 2.5 percent of the force, voted for the "no union" option on the ballot. It was "crushing news," Sorensen felt after talking to the old man, "perhaps the greatest disappointment in his business career." His mind still fixed on the glory days of the five-dollar-a-day wage, Henry had forgotten all that had happened in the intervening years during Bennett's reign of terror at the Rouge.

When a formal agreement was readied for signing, Ford met with Sorensen and Edsel. "I'm not going to sign this contract!" he said in an irrational frenzy that Bennett had helped whip up the night before. "As far as I'm concerned the key is in the door. I'm going to throw it away. I don't want any more of this business. Close the plant if necessary. Let the union take over if it wishes." The next day, Edsel and Sorensen went to work with a heavy sense of foreboding, fearing that after all there would be the violence which they thought had been averted. Then they heard the news: Henry had signed a closed-shop contract and agreed to a checkoff by which union dues would be automatically deducted from workers' pay—and had also agreed to match the highest wages paid by the other automakers in each employment category.

Shaking his head in amazement, Edsel shot a quizzical look at Sorensen. "What in the world happened?"

Sorensen shrugged, "I was about to ask you the same thing."

A few weeks later, in a rambling conversation with Sorensen, Ford broke his silence about his sudden change of heart, saying that Clara had put her foot down when she heard of his threats to close the plant. "Mrs. Ford was horrified. She said she could not understand my doing anything like that. If that were done there would be riots and bloodshed, and she had seen enough of that.... She became frantic about it. She insisted that I sign what she called a peace agreement. If I did not, she was through. What could I do?.... I felt her vision and judgment were better than mine. I'm glad I did see it her way. Don't ever discredit the power of a woman."

KNOWING THAT HE HAD BEEN displaced in their sibling rivalry by Bennett, who flaunted the affections of his father at the same time that he continued to alienate them, Edsel had seriously considered quitting during the darkest hours of the union conflict. It may not have been the first time such a thought had crossed his mind, but it was the first time he had allowed himself to utter the words. When he told friends, they thought of it in terms of an abdication rather than an employment decision; a matter of state involving visions of a pretender to the throne in exile across the sea. Such thoughts projected Edsel into a dilemma with existential overtones: the Ford Motor Company had been the destiny he had embraced as a boy; if he was not heir to the company, who and what was he?

Fortunately, circumstances had kept him from having to pursue his threat to quit. The union contract was signed, and a tentative peace had been achieved. Moreover, in 1940 his father had suffered another stroke. Unlike the previous episode two years earlier which affected him minimally, this stroke caused an immediate and profound somatic change. Almost overnight, Ford became stooped and gaunt; his gray hair went white and his skin acquired the texture of vellum; one worker who saw him in the Rouge said of his eyes, "They looked like someone dimmed the power behind them." His mental processes, always acute however wrongheaded he may have been, also began to deteriorate. Evangeline Dahlinger's son John saw it. A cheeky teenager who went around Dearborn calling himself "Henry Ford's illegitimate son" (a claim given credence by the fact that he looked more like Edsel than Edsel's own boys), young Dahlinger was walking with his tutor, Harley Copp, one day when Ford came up to show them a dime whose embossed date was almost worn away. "What year is this?" Henry asked. When Dahlinger and Copp replied that they couldn't tell, he croaked, "It's 1896, the year of my car," and walked away in triumph. Dahlinger had a compassionate look in his eyes and said to Copp, "He may ask you that about the dime again sometime. If he does, act like you don't know the answer."

Those who heard rumors of Edsel's deep disillusionment now took one look at the old man and begged him to hold on. The company to which Edsel had given his life might soon be his, and when it was he could fire Bennett and his army of supporters and restore decency to Ford while he was also bringing it into the modern era.

There was another reason why Edsel had to hang on, of course: to protect the Ford heritage for his children. The company had come to resemble the morally infected realm of Shakespearean history cycles—a place where unnatural rulers refused to pass on the crown to their sons and where usurpers threatened to step in and cut off the line of legitimate succession; a place where fathers had to worry about the right of their sons to come into what was theirs. Edsel knew that if he abdicated, his boys would be cut off.

Executives who considered themselves part of Edsel's "team" would drop into his elegant office and sit under the Gilbert Stuart portraits of John Quincy Adams and General Henry Dearborn and try to convince him to confront the problem of his sons' inheritance directly: to tell them about the deteriorating situation and teach Henry II and Benson particularly the arts of statecraft and *realpolitik* which they would need to secure their place in the hazardous world of the company if something should happen to him. But to do this would have required Edsel to question the deep loyalty he still had for his father—the loyalty that had always defined him—and to admit that Henry Ford had degenerated into a dangerously foolish old man. Instead, Edsel tried to normalize his children's lives, to allow them to grow up outside the harsh and dangerous automobile world which had constrained his own youth.

Friends of the family noticed that the photographs of Edsel and his father were always posed in a car or alongside one, as if the automobile was the only medium of exchange between them. Photographs of Edsel and his children, on the other hand, were almost never near a car, but in family activities such as swimming, boating or playing tennis, or romping with the dogs and horses Edsel loved. But while a division between the world of work and the world of family might be the norm for most people, for Edsel it was difficult. The large questions involving their fate in the Ford Motor Company made his family fit both parts of Tolstoy's maxim: they were happy like all happy families and unhappy in their own distinctive way.

He was close to his daughter, Dodie. ("I could wrap him around my finger," she later recalled. "My mother was the no-sayer.") She was never considered for a role in the company, her mother having told her, "Nice girls don't work." So Dodie had instead concentrated on her social skills. She was an outstanding tennis player and popular with the smart set of Grosse Pointe, whose members considered her frivolous but fun. Eddie Stroh, a friend of Benson's who took Dodie out, always remembered the occasion when she wrote witty and obscene sayings on the windshield of his car with her lipstick while they were driving down Lakeshore Drive. Edsel loved Dodie especially, he said, because she reminded him so much of Eleanor as a young woman.

He felt that he hadn't been as close as he should have been to Henry II and Benson, and tried to make it up with Bill, his lastborn, who he believed had the best disposition of the boys and in many ways was the most promising of them all. Although small in stature, Bill was bright and an excellent athlete. Eleanor and Edsel called him their "pride and joy," a term that was half humorous but caused real envy in the other children. Edsel was particularly struck by a certain toughness in the boy's character. When he was ten years old, Bill asked the tennis pro who came to Gaukler Pointe to give lessons to his brothers to teach him how to play, too. Thinking to dismiss him, the pro gave him a wooden hoop and said that if he could roll it down to the gatehouse with a forehand motion and back again with a backhand by the following summer, he'd give him lessons. To his surprise, Bill did it.

By the time he was a teenager, he had become a good enough player to be invited to try out for the Junior Davis Cup team. By the time he reached Hotchkiss he was so good that many felt he could have had a national ranking if he had devoted himself entirely to the game. He was also a daring skier, perhaps too daring in his assault on difficult hills. (Advised of one of Bill's accidents, in which a slalom pole punctured his groin, Edsel wrote anxiously to the Hotchkiss doctor: "It was a strange mishap and couldn't have been in a worse place. I hope the cuts will not be of a serious nature and will not involve other parts closely associated with the scrotum.")

Edsel didn't flinch at the letters he received from Van Santvoord about his youngest son's failing grades. But when the crusty headmaster wrote about Bill having joined two friends in destroying the possessions of a schoolmate, and called it "an attack of petty spitefulness and enmity," Edsel jumped to his son's defense: "I do not feel that William has any of those unfortunate traits in his makeup and he has had plenty of opportunity to develop them with two older brothers and an older sister picking on him from time to time."

Bill was too young for there to be much talk about a career for him in the Ford Motor Company. But this was not the case with Henry II and Benson. The fact that their coming of age coincided with their father's growing impotence in the company made Edsel feel like the pivot in an imperiled dynasty.

Henry II in particular was on the edge of a manhood which carried with it the expectation of a place of influence in the family business. His mother, who considered herself more "worldly" than Edsel, believed that her eldest son needed to be "finished." When Henry visited Italy in 1936 before entering Yale, she had called Frances Cinelli, a good friend from Detroit who had married an Italian and was living in Florence, and said, "Frances, Henry is in Venice with two young friends. I don't think he knows which end is up. Would you send your son up there to show them the ropes?"

On his trip home aboard the *Normandie,* Henry met a young woman named Anne McDonnell who was returning home to enter the Academy of the Sacred Heart at Noroton, Connecticut. An athletic blonde, Anne had a witty effervescence that Henry II admitted made him feel a little ponderous. As the ship plowed toward New York, they spent time swimming and playing deck tennis during the day and danced all night in the grand ballroom.

Henry II was taken by Anne's zesty competence and also by the stories she told about her family, the celebrated "golden clan" of New York comprising the McDonnells (she was one of fourteen children) and their Murray cousins. Her parents were careful as to whom they let their daughters see (they had rejected young John F. Kennedy as a possible suitor for Anne's sister Charlotte because of his father's questionable reputation), but they decided early on that Henry II was a "regular fellow." Charlotte McDonnell was puzzled by Henry's attraction for her sister and eventually said to Anne, "What do you see in him? He's not that good-looking." Anne's answer was indisputable: "What do I see in him? What do I hear is more like it. Listen to the name. *Henry Ford.*"

Henry II was attracted to the boisterousness and vivacity of this large and closely bonded Irish Catholic family which was so unlike his own, where there were large, Midwestern spaces between family members. The McDonnell-Murrays were a family of accomplishment (the patriarch, Thomas E. Murray, was second only to Edison in patents filed and inventions produced), and when he was with them Henry II felt that being a Ford didn't count so heavily. As one friend said, "He liked Anne's looks and everything, but her chief attraction was that she could draw him out and make him seem less boring to himself and everyone else."

The romance simmered as Henry II returned to college. At Yale he was the manager of the crew, a member of Zeta Psi fraternity and of the Book and Snake Club, whose members called him "T" after his grandfather's most famous model. He began in engineering and switched to sociology, noting with characteristic insouciance, "I was flunking engineering, so I switched. Then I flunked sociology too." His academic life at Yale involved failure notices and tutors. (When Edsel finally received a note from a Yale dean during Henry's senior year saying his son was doing well, he replied ironically, "It is almost time for him to do so, having but a few months left.") Henry was far more interested in Boston deb parties than in school, once taking a suite at the Ritz for a postparty party which lasted until 5 A.M., when the manager called to threaten Henry's group with removal and Henry said to the friend who answered the phone, "Tell him to go fuck himself."

One afternoon Anne came home with a new dress she had bought for that night's date with Henry. Her mother began to scold her until she said, "I just know tonight is the night. I'm sure he's going to propose." He did.

By the time of his twenty-first birthday party in 1938—a sort of coming-out party at which Edsel paid $2,250 for bandleader Tommy Dorsey and Frank Sinatra, and another $1,250 for tap dancer Paul Draper—Henry II was secretly engaged, but did not make any public announcement because he wanted to have one last fling. Shortly after the party he wrote his grandparents a letter about his plans which glossed over the potentially explosive religious issue in a typically cavalier way:

> Dear Callie and Grandad,
>
> You will no doubt be surprised to hear from me at this time of year, but it so happens I have a very good reason for writing.... I am planning to announce my engagement to Anne McDonnell. You may have heard something about her from Mother and Daddy and I assume that you will learn a great deal more from me when I see you. She happens to be a Catholic, which I don't think was too pleasing to Mother and Daddy in the beginning, but now that they have seen her and the family I think they are completely reconciled to the fact that I shall no doubt become one. Hope that both of you will have a chance to meet her soon as I know you will like her. You did meet her at my 21st birthday but that was amongst many others....
>
> Much love,
> Henry

In fact his grandfather was extremely angered by the prospect of a Ford converting to Catholicism, and he believed that Henry II had fallen under the evil influence of Bishop Fulton J. Sheen, whom the McDonnells had gotten to give him religious instruction. When gossip columnist Walter Winchell wrote that Ford might follow his grandson to Catholicism, he was so angered that he looked for ways to sue and, when persuaded that this was impossible, had Harry Bennett arrange for him to become a very public Thirty-third Degree Mason.

The marriage took place at the McDonnells' summer home at Southampton, Long Island. It had taken two weeks to ready the place for the reception, including construction of a huge oblong dance floor across the front of the house on dunes overlooking the ocean, glassed in to provide protection from wind and sand. There were over a thousand guests. Edsel and Eleanor arrived aboard the yacht *Onika,* Henry and Clara aboard their private railcar, the Fairlane. Kathleen Kennedy, sister of the rejected suitor Jack, was one of Anne's maids of honor. The bride-to-be impressed everybody with her piquant sense of humor. When someone asked Sheen which robes he was wearing for the wedding, she wisecracked "pink taffeta" before he could answer.

On the morning of the wedding day, Henry II was baptized by Sheen in the family chapel. Old Henry (a term people had begun to use to distinguish him from his grandson) was on his best behavior and made a good enough impression to precipitate a postwedding letter to Edsel from James McDonnell, father of the bride: "Again I want to thank you for all the kind interest you and Eleanor and in fact all your good Detroit people took in Anne and Henry's wedding. Everybody was delighted with the great simplicity of your good father and mother. They are still talking about them."

Leaving their wedding gifts in the custody of several armed guards, along with a scrapbook of newspaper articles agreeing that their union was the "marriage of the century," the couple left for a honeymoon in Hawaii, as Eleanor and Edsel had some twenty-five years earlier. On the way back they docked at San Francisco and returned to Detroit via Canadian Pacific, stopping off at Banff and Lake Louise and then journeying over the Canadian Rockies. After returning home, they finally opened their presents. But the best one was not wrapped. It came from Edsel: a Georgian home in Grosse Pointe and 25,000 shares of Ford Motor Company stock. It was, Edsel wrote to his firstborn, "in recognition of the fact that you are finishing your college career this month and after being married will join the Ford Motor Company as your future business..."

Henry did finish his college career that month, but it was without graduating, having turned in a paper entitled "Folkways and Thomas Hardy" which the professor said he would have known was cribbed even if Henry hadn't neglected to remove from it the sale slip of the tutorial service where he purchased it. He did go to work for the company and was joined by Benson, who had simply quit Princeton after two borderline years there. "I signed up for courses I thought would be the easiest," Benson later said. "But I miscalculated. They were tough. Still, I wasn't worried. I figured I could always get a job at Ford."

Nothing in Benson's life seemed to have the fanfare that accompanied Henry II's milestones. When he married Edith McNaughton, a young Grosse

Pointe woman whose father had been a vice-president of Cadillac and whom he had known since they were in kindergarten together at Liggett School, it was far from his elder brother's royal wedding. As one friend said later, "Benson had seen Henry get married. He tried to do everything Henry did. He and Edie knew each other and he didn't really have anything else to do, so why not get married?" The most memorable incident of the wedding occurred when Edsel went to the basement with Benson's good friend Travers Smith to bring up several bottles of champagne for the reception and found that it had gone flat because the butler had stored it incorrectly. Edsel dispatched Smith on a hurried mission to buy fine champagne at liquor stores all over town. Benson "laughed like hell" when Smith told him about the contretemps after the reception, but then, typically, worried about the butler: "I hope the poor guy won't get fired because of this."

By late 1940 both Benson and Henry II were working full time at Ford. Since their childhood, it had been assumed as a matter of course, by Edsel and, he thought, his father as well, that the company ultimately belonged to the boys; that it was theirs to contemplate as young adults and to grow into as mature men. Henry had, in fact, taken the lead in making them see the company as their inheritance. No one had reckoned on the changes that had come over the old man, changes which called these long-held family assumptions into question. But by the end of their first week at the Engineering Department, where Edsel had asked Sheldrick to get them started, it was clear that actually working for Ford would be a different and more trying experience than the boys had anticipated. Their grandfather came by with Bennett one afternoon to see how they were doing and was shocked and angry to find that Sheldrick had put them under a black foreman named Leonard Williams. Bennett asked Sheldrick to step out of the room and then began to threaten and swear at him about "niggers." Sheldrick immediately reported the incident to Edsel, who was disgusted. "Don't pay a bit of attention to him," he said. "That's good for the boys. Keep them right there."

Not even Bennett could destroy the pleasure Edsel felt at having his sons in the company, and his hope that the continuity which had been so badly damaged in his own case might yet survive. Co-workers would catch him looking out his office window with pride and pleasure at Henry II and Benson as they worked on the line with tools in their hands and smudges of grease on their faces.

After they had worked in the Engineering Department for a few weeks, Sheldrick moved Henry II and Benson to the new Jeep development project—which Ford had taken on for the Army in 1939—so that they could participate in the final process of assembly and testing. As a sort of tribute to Edsel, Sheldrick and other executives arranged for him to be present for the Jeep's first test drive. It took place on a piece of Ford land covered by weeds four or five feet high and overgrown with scruffy bushes. When Edsel arrived, Sheldrick had a prearranged signal set up with the two boys, who were waiting in the Jeep well back in the woods. "They came tearing out of the underbrush," Sheldrick later recalled. "The Jeep just came out of nowhere up to their father. He got the biggest bang out of that. The fact that his boys were driving the first Jeep on its first test drive pleased him greatly. That was the one time I saw Edsel when he was enjoying himself thoroughly. He was awfully proud of the boys."

This pride was not shared by his father. His hearty grandsons seemed to remind Henry of his increasing fragility; their desire to be a part of the company seemed to indicate to him that mortality would inevitably rob him of his control over the thing he prized most in the world. Instead of counseling acceptance and resignation, however, these perceptions only provoked angry denial. Far from the indulgent "Granddaddy" of old, he became snide and remote, treating Henry II and Benson with brusque indifference.

Early in 1941, after the boys had been working at the company for a few weeks, old Henry, egged on by Bennett, suddenly and gratuitously ordered Sorensen to remove his grandsons from the premises; they could be kept on the payroll, or they could be transferred to some branch plant, but they had to be gotten out of his sight. This order roused Sorensen, who liked the boys and who, as Bennett's menacing accumulation of power continued, had tightened his mutual-defense pact with Edsel. He told Ford, "Edsel has given me your message about Henry and Benson. I am opposed to any such action and if you have any ideas that I'll carry it out, forget it. I refuse. Furthermore, if you do this to yourself, I am through. That's all I've got to say."

Ford dropped the matter. But a disturbing impression was left behind of a situation in which blood ties and kinship no longer counted. As one Ford executive said, "It was like watching a hog trying to eat its own farrow."

TEN

T HE INTERNAL DRAMA OF THE Ford family was soon caught up in the larger drama of war, a cataclysm which would tumble the people and crises of the company toward an angle of repose.

So much had changed in the twenty years since the last global conflict. The Ford Motor Company had emerged from World War I doing 60 percent of the nation's auto business; it entered World War II doing less than 20 percent. Henry Ford had been an important player in the prior war, but in the one beginning to unfold he would be at best a bit actor. His comment as Germany was getting ready to invade Poland sounded like one of Samuel Goldwyn's non sequiturs: "They don't dare have a war and they know it."

He was deeply anti-British, perhaps because of a traumatic occasion years earlier when he had met Winston Churchill in England and told him that most of his country's problems could be solved if farming was revolutionized, a notion which Churchill had ridiculed with patrician scorn. Ford was sympathetic to Germany, considering the nation clean, thrifty and technologically adept, qualities which had led him to accept, on his seventy-fifth birthday, the Supreme Order of the German Eagle from Hitler's emissaries. The highest honor any non-German could receive, this decoration had ostensibly been awarded because of Ford's contribution to mass production, although the symbolism, coming at a time when the Reich was beginning its campaign against the Jews, called up other associations.

Ford believed with Charles Lindbergh, whom he joined in the America First movement, that the United States should remain aloof from the deteriorating European situation. He found himself involved with figures such as the right-wing fanatic Gerald L. K. Smith, who, after Bennett had gotten him an interview with Ford, went back to his hotel room and began hopping around and vomiting bits of the lunch he had just eaten and saying, "Now I've got it in my power! Now I can rule the world!" Ford glided through the "phony war" with everyone else, taking it as an omen that there would be no real conflict. Even after the Nazi Blitzkrieg rolled over Europe, he was disturbed by the preparations for war in the United States, especially after his onetime employee William Knudsen was plucked out of his position as president of General Motors to mobilize private enterprise as Commissioner of Industrial Production.

Edsel, on the other hand, was enthusiastic about the idea of the company becoming part of democracy's arsenal. After conferring with Knudsen in Washington, he agreed to build nine thousand Rolls-Royce engines, with the possibility of designing a pursuit plane as well. His father at first reluctantly agreed to build the engines, but then suddenly changed his mind and decided that he didn't want to be on the side of a belligerent. Edsel was forced to call Knudsen and tell him, "Bill, Father just won't do it."

"Aren't you president?" Knudsen demanded.

"Yes, I am," Edsel said sadly, "but you know how Father is."

When Knudsen arrived in Detroit to make a personal appeal, Henry greeted him and then said, "You're all right, William, but you're in with a bad crowd back there in Washington." He added, "I won't make any of those Rolls-Royce engines for England."

"But, Mr. Ford," Knudsen argued, "we have your word that you would make them. I told the President of your decision, and he was very happy about it."

The mention of FDR, whom Ford loathed, was not tactically wise on Knudsen's part. The old man snapped, "We won't build the engines at all. Withdraw the whole order. Take it to someone else."

One of the results of this decision was that the United Auto Workers and other Ford enemies immediately charged him with being a Nazi sympathizer. When, in August 1940, the government asked Ford to build Pratt and Whitney engines, Edsel, who had been seriously scarred by the Rolls episode, managed to convince his father to do it only by emphasizing that the work was for the United States, not a foreign power. The company was also continuing work on the Jeep and taking on other projects that would implicate it in the arming of America despite Ford's antiwar sentiments. Notwithstanding Henry's autocratic rule the company had become integral to the American economy and subject to its crises.

At the end of the year General James H. Doolittle led a group that came to Dearborn to ask the company to build two hundred B-24 Liberator bombers. Ford, who believed that the war in Europe would be over before it really got started, was scornful. "These planes will never be used for fighting," he said. "Before you can build them the war will be over." Nonetheless, Edsel, Sorensen, Henry II and Benson went out to San Diego to look at the plant of Consolidated Aircraft, which had initially been scheduled to build the Liberator and wanted subassemblies from Ford. When they toured the plant, Sorensen immediately saw the magnitude of the problem: Consolidated was in effect custom-making planes, turning out one a day when the Army Air Corps (soon to become the Army Air Forces) needed thousands a year. He sat down that night and sketched out on paper a process by which the bombers could be mass-produced by breaking them down into assembly units. By dawn Sorensen had designed the floor plan of a plant that could handle the intricate operations. He showed his work to Edsel at breakfast, and Edsel realized that it was something absolutely new—use of a process perfected for cars adapted to something thousands of times larger and more complex. The two laid the plans before the startled Army officials and told them that Ford would make the whole plane or nothing; that they would require $200 million for a new plant and in return would guarantee 540 planes a month instead of Consolidated's 520 a year. Contacted in Dearborn, Henry gave his approval— not because he wanted to build weapons but because the grandiosity of Sorensen's plan piqued his interest.

A location was selected for the mammoth plant—a piece of Ford land near Ypsilanti where a stream called Willow Run meandered through a pastoral countryside. Ford architect Albert Kahn designed a plant which he called "the longest room ever built." But as the project came closer to reality the elder Ford became irrationally obstructive. After Edsel and Sorensen set the stakes at the building site, he came out and moved them. They reset the stakes; he again dug them out, complaining petulantly, "We're going to grow soybeans there. Build it someplace else." There followed a minuet of absurdity in which they would set the stakes one day and he would move them the next.

Finally Sorensen said, "We've got to do something about this. We've committed ourselves to production on the planes, and unless we get busy sometime we're never going to get to it."

Edsel replied, "All right. Let's go out tomorrow and settle it."

They put down the stakes one last time and brought in the steam shovels. Ford was furious and wouldn't speak to either of them for weeks.

By the time Roosevelt made his "arsenal of democracy" speech, the Ford Motor Company was already deeply involved in such projects as the M4 tank, antiaircraft gunnery, and amphibious vehicles which grew out of the Jeep project. Yet the project that really mattered was the production of the Liberator at Willow Run. During the early stages of operation it seemed at times unlikely that the company would ever meet Sorensen's ambitious production objectives. The Army brass decided to hold a meeting at the plant (which some critics were beginning to ridicule as "Willit Run?") and call Sorensen on the carpet. Everybody was there at 10 A.M. talking about how things must change and how the government ought to take the operation over. Then Sorensen walked in several minutes late, in what one observer euphemistically called "rough spirits." Before his Army critics could begin, he attacked: "The first thing I want to tell you fellows is there's not a goddamned man in this room, especially some young whippersnapper just out of college, who's going to come in here and tell us how to run the Ford Motor Company. *We're* going to run the Ford Motor Company...." Finishing the harangue, he abruptly walked out, leaving people in the room with their mouths open.

At the beginning of 1942, Edsel wrote to Under-Secretary of War Robert A. Lovett: "The Bomber Project at Willow Run is well ahead of construction schedule and we have something like 2000 production hands and tool makers working there now...." Lovett replied by return mail, saying that the progress, while welcome, was not fast enough. The correspondence continued with Edsel complaining of the difficulty the company was having in securing and keeping competent workers. Finally he wrote to Washington with statistics showing that in a single month the company had lost almost 1500 workers at Willow Run to the draft, and proposed a "manpower stabilization plan" by which workers would be inducted into the reserve while working. But Lovett wrote back: "It has been determined that the system of induction-deferment on inactive duty and subsequent induction into the armed forces presents complications which makes it unworkable at the present time."

The question of whether or not the plant would achieve its large purpose was still open when FDR arrived for a visit on September 18, 1942, alighting down from his private railcar on a ramp designed for his wheelchair and then being lifted into the large Lincoln waiting below. There he joined Edsel and the dyspeptic Henry, scrunched down in the backseat, annoyed because he had to sit with his old enemy instead of riding with Bennett in the open "security car" that led the motorcade around and into the giant plant.

The presidential visit marked a turnaround for the bomber project. Within a year Willow Run was beginning to meet its promise, turning out 190 bombers in June, 231 by August and 365 by December, and thereafter outdistancing even the epic projections Sorensen had made in what seemed a rash moment several years earlier.

DESPITE THE EVENTUAL SUCCESS at Willow Run, however, the Ford Motor Company remained a crippled giant, wasting from a malignancy of leadership. Although he was increasingly disoriented, Henry insisted on being involved in every aspect of the company, as he hadn't even a few years earlier when he was still in full possession of his powers. At times his confusion had a comic dimension. At the outset of the war, for example, the company was experimenting with synthetic rubber, a project close to Ford's heart. His obsession with the Du Ponts made him anxious to know whether or not they, too, were doing research, so he got Bennett to send a detective to Delaware to spy on them. This person had a heart attack while on the job. Bennett sent another man, and when he, too, died during his investigation Ford came to Bennett in panic. "Harry, don't send any more men down there!" he cried. "By God, they're killing them!"

Yet for people close to the situation such episodes were macabre rather than amusing. And Ford's obvious decline raised in an increasingly urgent way the problem of succession which had bedeviled the company for a generation. The only difference was that now much of the speculation centered as much on Bennett as on Edsel. Bennett had dedicated better than a decade to isolating and outflanking Edsel. He had become the Rasputin of the company, with a relationship to the old man that gave him ultimate authority over its operations. At first sensitive about criticism, he had come to relish his role as the dark presence of Ford. Once when a writer showed him an advance copy of an article about him, Bennett scanned it and then threw it down scornfully, saying, "No one will recognize me." Taken aback, the writer asked, "But why?" Bennett smiled caustically. "Because you don't say I'm a son of a bitch."

While Sorensen had always been feared and respected, Bennett was just feared. When not exercising his role as Henry's henchman and head of the company's secret police, however, Bennett was regarded as something of a buffoon. On one occasion planners failed to include him in a modest ceremony marking the maiden flight of a large glider the company had developed under contract to the Air Force. The glider was positioned; the tow plane was hooked on and took off, gaining altitude and then releasing the glider, which flew beautifully. About ten minutes into the flight, as everyone watched the plane inscribe lazy circles in the sky, an automobile came tearing up to the field and screeched to a stop, the front door practically flying off its hinges as one of Bennett's flunkies got out. "Nobody invited Mr. Bennett!" he shouted in agitation. "Nobody invited Mr. Bennett!" Ford, Edsel and Sorensen all merely looked at the man quizzically. Receiving no answer, he got back in the car and tore off again, leaving a bemused ripple of laughter behind him.

But the fact that Bennett was difficult to take seriously as an executive did not alter the fact that he had audaciously seized the reins of power inside the company. His unique status was suggested by the placement of his office—in the basement below the official company offices, as if to underscore the fact that he existed at a more profound level than Edsel and the other executives. Someone could enter only after Bennett had pressed a button under his desk buzzing the door open. The outer office had a control board about six feet square covered with signal lights, switch keys and buttons connecting him electronically to all the stations of the Service Department and making his office the command center that transmitted and received messages to and from all the company cars, including Ford's own, which were equipped with short wave. For executives like Lawrence Sheldrick, this board symbolized Bennett's stranglehold on the company. "You couldn't get a message to anybody without him seeing it," Sheldrick recalled later. "One could not hire, fire or transfer a man. I could not send a man on a trip. I could not make a long distance telephone call. I could not send a telegram if he did not wish me to do so. He had control of hiring and firing. He had control of transportation and communication. He had to approve all travel vouchers…. Regardless of where you were he knew about it. If you were in Europe he would know who you had dinner with on such and such an occasion. He had a spy system that was that thorough."

Bennett had trumped Sorensen in power, although his onetime sponsor in the company hadn't fully realized it until FDR's tour of Willow Run, which Bennett orchestrated and controlled. After that, Sorensen began calling around trying to keep tabs on Bennett. But it was too late. A few days after the presidential visit, Sorensen heard that William Knudsen was leaving Washington for a visit to the company. He asked another executive named Logan Miller to tell him when Knudsen arrived. The following day, Miller went to Bennett's office on an errand and saw Ford there. Miller told them of Sorensen's request. Ford responded, "Logan, don't pay any attention to Sorensen. Tell him to go to hell." It was clear that the old man was speaking for Bennett's amusement and approval.

Not long after this incident, Sorensen was at Willow Run for an inspection and found that someone had ordered soft-drink machines installed. Concerned that the empty bottles might be used as weapons if labor relations, still a volatile issue despite Ford's settlement with the UAW, ever deteriorated, he asked who had made the decision. Told that it was Bennett, he said, "I wonder what the hell business he's got giving those kinds of orders?" and told his aide Roscoe Smith to get rid of the machines. The next day Bennett came to the Rouge and baited Sorensen into an argument, at one point ripping off his coat and snarling, "For two cents I'd punch your face for you." Sorensen looked at him in disgust and said to Smith, "Come on, Roscoe, let's get out of here." As they walked out Bennett hit Smith in the jaw and knocked him down.

Bennett's effrontery now extended even to relations with Edsel. Always before he had been polite, although observers had seen a heavy load of contempt in his elaborately deferential manner. Now Bennett didn't bother to conceal his feelings about the man he scornfully referred to as "the weakling." In October 1942, during the last and most serious confrontation between the two men, Bennett began playing once again on the theme from which he continued to draw most of his power, threats to Edsel's family, saying that he planned to encircle the residences of Henry II and Benson, as well as Gaukler Pointe, with men from his Service Department to protect them from possible violence. Edsel, shaking with anger, shouted at him, "Stop this talk! Leave the boys alone! I don't want protection for myself or my sons!" He went on to say that he no longer believed in the kidnap stories and felt that Bennett had fabricated most of them for his father's benefit. Enraged, Bennett ripped off his coat and was ready to fight the sickly Edsel until Sorensen managed to hustle him out of the room.

The chaos spread outward from these closet dramas to infect the whole of the company. The ultimate consequence of Edsel's inability to create a managerial system like GM's, with a system of checks and balances, was a figure like Bennett who was able to operate in the shadows acquiring and exercising enormous power. As a result of Bennett's machinations, the company continued to lose its most promising executives to competitors. The Ford Motor Company was seen as a sort of madhouse; people like chief engineer Lawrence Sheldrick and sales manager John Davis who had kept the business going the past several years never knew where they stood.

Most executives stayed on only because of Edsel. Someday, they prayed,

Henry would die and Edsel would finally take over and cleanse the company of Bennett's brutality and larceny. The only problem was that Edsel's physical condition was degenerating more rapidly than his father's. For some time he had suffered from ulcers, and he spent hours each day lying on the couch in the executive washroom eating crackers and drinking milk. In November 1942 he had a stomach operation and then began a recuperation that didn't seem to work.

As his health failed, people who had never thought of Edsel as anything more than the Ford Motor Company's perpetual Prince of Wales began to appreciate his accomplishment. He had established himself as a presence at Ford, presenting a reassuring face to a world concerned by rumors it heard of the perturbations within the company. In the Continental he had made one of the most elegant cars in the history of the American automobile industry, a car already talked of as a classic. Perhaps most significantly, he had worked with Sorensen to make the Willow Run plant a reality and to fill the skies of Europe with Liberator bombers.

Edsel's illness dramatized a time of transition for his family. Dodie had married Walter Buhl Ford, Yale graduate and scion of a socially prominent Grosse Pointe family, early in 1943. Edsel had joked that his daughter's branch of the family would be known as the Ford-Fords. Not long after the marriage, Wally, as Dodie's affable new husband was called, had joined the Coast Guard.

Both Henry II and Benson could have claimed deferment from the armed services on the basis of the company's contribution to the war effort, but both had enlisted. Edsel was proud of them for being able to live as "regular guys" and happy that they would not have to endure what he had suffered for staying home during the previous war.

In his application to the Navy requesting appointment as an ensign, Henry II noted that he and Anne had their first child, Charlotte; listed four years at Yale and a fair command of French; and wrote "Only pleasure" at the question asking his seagoing experience. By the time he was stationed at the Great Lakes Naval Station, Anne was expecting again. He tried to be an ordinary officer, but it was difficult, especially when his commanding admiral asked for permission to come to Dearborn to have lunch with his grandfather. Henry II was trying to shuffle off the persona of the rather self-indulgent young man who had coasted through the earlier part of his life. His letters from Great Lakes revealed someone with a nascent sense of irony about himself and a keen interest in the goings on at the Ford Motor Company. "This man's navy is *plenty* tough," he wrote. "I have the duty three times this week which means I have to be there 24 hours.... This afternoon they gave us drill for over an hour and I was in charge of one of the two battalions. Of course I don't know how to lead this sort of thing, so I made plenty of mistakes and the thing turned out to be one terrible mess."

A few days later he was complaining of the monotony of naval life: "I've had two days with nothing to do and it certainly gets boring after a while. I wish I were back at Dearborn where there is something to do every second, so that you can't keep up even if you try...."

Benson was in the Army, although typically his route had been more difficult than his older brother's. Originally rejected as a volunteer because of his almost total blindness in one eye, he had been forced to obtain special permission from the War Department to enlist, going into the Army as a private and passing through his physical under the name "B. Ford." He went to officer candidate school and eventually rose to the rank of captain, although something of a scandal occurred when Harry Bennett, apparently acting on his own, got Benson posted to nearby Selfridge Field, under the command of Colonel William T. Coleman. A cushy desk job which Benson didn't particularly want was arranged anyway. ("Benson is in the public relations office," Coleman wrote to Bennett, "and is working up a historical record of the progress on the field, plus helping out with other details.") Later on, when Coleman was court-martialed for a number of offenses, including bringing Benson to Selfridge, Bennett testified that he had made attempts through General Henry H. "Hap" Arnold and others to get Henry Ford's grandson into officer candidate school.

Old Henry didn't seem to care much about his grandsons' armed service experiences. But he did have a long talk with young John Dahlinger as he got ready to enlist. The boy had given Ford one gift over the years of their relationship, a pocketknife with a cherrywood handle. As he was going into the Army Ford told him he wanted him to take it back for good luck. Dahlinger carried the knife all through the war and then gave it back to Ford when he returned home.

Edsel, too, was somewhat remote from what was happening to Henry II and Benson. Unable to rally after his ulcer surgery, he was weak and dispirited. Eleanor now begged him with a new sense of urgency to quit the company, but he carried on. He was still committed to managing the difficulties of his life with dignity, including the relationship with his parents. In March, after his daughter-in-law had given birth to a second daughter, named (like her) Anne, Edsel wrote to his mother and father to tell them that he had attended the baptism, performed by Bishop Sheen in Chicago: "I was godfather to baby Anne and Mrs. McDonnell was godmother. The baby is a beauty and didn't make a murmur during the ceremony, but Charlotte made up for both. She didn't stop talking and walking all the time. It was all fun."

Edsel continued to write to his parents, as if letters were the last hope of maintaining civilized discourse. Not long after the baptism of "little" Anne, he and Eleanor took the train to Florida for a vacation aboard the *Onika* at Hobe Sound. Edsel wrote back to Fairlane:

> We arrived Tuesday afternoon with the train only two hours late. Most of them have been five to seven hours late, so we were lucky. Everything is the same here—Lots of people at the club—lots of men coming from Washington for a rest. When we arrived Bob Lovett, Secretary of War for Air, was on one side of us, and on the other side of Ernie [Kanzler] was Di Gates, Secretary of Navy. We also

have two ex–Mrs. Roosevelts, one of Jimmy's former wives and one of Elliot's....
After three days I feel much better and am hoping I can put on about five pounds.

Still trying to justify the "liberal" positions he had taken at the company, Edsel enclosed with this letter a portion of a telegram to one of his aides from an Army official at Willow Run regarding an appearance he had made before a group of UAW committeemen:

> Some of the union officials told me [the Army officer had written] how pleased they were that Mr. Ford spoke to some of the committeemen.... He made a real hit by doing this. I just hope he will continue to [involve himself] in labor relations because more than anyone else in the Ford Motor Company he can help with the situation, as the union group has a lot of confidence in him. Of course they will try to reach him personally a lot and that should not be permitted, but the realization that he is interested in promoting better relations is having a swell effect....

Edsel struck a somewhat more personal tone in letters to his mother, talking about his health (a subject he avoided in more formal letters addressed jointly to her and Henry, lest his father once again perceive him as "weak"):

> Henry [II] had been here a week and Bill and Mademoiselle arrived yesterday. They all looked like Snow White when they arrived, but a few days in the sun will take care of that.... I'm feeling much better than I did the first two weeks. My gastritis is practically cured up but Dr. Mateer thinks it wise to stay a little longer for a build up....

This was, however, a sort of whistling in the dark. Everyone could see that Edsel was gaunt and unsteady, a very sick man. Those close to him understood that it was unlikely he would ever recover his health; they had finally to confront the situation they had denied so long. Realizing that the task of protecting the family's interests in the struggle against Bennett might soon fall to him, Henry II tried to be politic. He moved to reassure his grandfather by keeping up an air of false cordiality. After the first of the year he wrote Henry and Clara an almost obsequious letter of thanks for the handkerchiefs they had sent him for Christmas: "Both Anne and the baby are getting along well, in fact even better than last time. We have decided to call the baby Anne.... The girls are all named for the McDonnells and if we have any boys, we'll name them for the Fords." But Benson, as second born, didn't feel the need to be diplomatic and went into an uncharacteristic rage after hearing about Edsel's terminal illness: "Grandfather is responsible for Father's sickness, and I'm through with him!"

In mid-April Edsel had to return to Dearborn from Florida to deal with another crisis caused by Bennett. This time it involved one of the company's outstanding employees, A. W. Wibel, who had been hired as a machinist in 1912 and worked his way up to vice-president in charge of purchasing and director. In Edsel's absence, Wibel had been fired for refusing to fill a contract Bennett had awarded to one of his cronies. Immediately upon returning,

Edsel had a lacerating exchange with his father over Wibel and, as usual, lost. After the confrontation, old Henry phoned Sorensen and told him that Edsel must change his attitude toward Bennett, the company and life itself. Sorensen jotted down the five main points Ford made over the phone:

> a. Discord over handling labor relations [to end].
> b. Wibel and his attitude toward Bennett, says Wibel is through.
> c. Bennett in full accord with Henry Ford. Henry Ford will support Bennett against every obstacle.
> d. [Dealing with labor is] Bennett's job, no one else.
> e. Change relations with Bennett.

At this point Edsel finally decided that there was no point in going on. He was "fed up," in Liebold's phrase, and decided to quit the company. It was a momentous step—getting ready to turn his back on the inheritance which had hung over his life like a giant charge of static electricity for forty years.

But the moment of liberation came too late. Soon after the fight over Wibel, Edsel was hospitalized. The official explanation was that he was suffering from undulant fever. He had indeed contracted this disease from drinking the unpasteurized milk his father had insisted would cure his condition. But the truth was that Edsel also had cancer of the stomach. Doctors at the Henry Ford Hospital decided that an operation ought to be performed, but they were too wary of Henry to take responsibility for doing it themselves, and so a surgeon had to be brought in from the outside. Edsel was opened up and then closed, the surgeon reporting that he was beyond medical remedy. Eleanor came to the hospital to get her husband and took him home to the stone house they had built together as a redoubt to protect them from the wounding things of life.

The doctors' diagnosis had thrown old Henry into a fury. He commanded Bennett to drive him to Gaukler Pointe, where he went into the house and smashed all of the liquor bottles, screaming that Edsel's drinking had caused his condition. But it soon became clear to him that his son was dying and there was nothing he could do about it. Unable to bring himself to visit Edsel, Henry spent hours each day tramping the woods around Fairlane, a desperate guilt suddenly piercing his confusion. Clara stayed at home in patient grief, waiting for the news that was now a certainty.

Edsel tried to hold on so that he could see his youngest child, Bill, his "pride and joy," one last time. Bill's Hotchkiss graduation had been pushed up to March because so many of the students were enlisting. At Edsel's insistence, news of his ailment had been withheld from the boy. ("I didn't even know how bad it was until about three days before the graduation when I got a letter from him saying how sorry he was he wouldn't be there," Bill later recalled. "I was disappointed. I was not only getting a diploma but a trophy for being the school tennis champion and I wanted him there.") Bill got a sense that things were wrong when his sister Dodie, pregnant and living at home—her husband, Wally, was stationed in Florida—came to Florida as a proxy for their parents. After the ceremony, they hurried home. He saw his father and showed him the trophy. It was hard for Edsel to talk, but he grasped Bill's hand, mutely communicating his pride and love. The next morning he went into a coma. Doctors told Bill that they had expected his father to die two weeks earlier and that he had not only held on but disciplined himself to be coherent so that the two of them could have a last conversation.

For two days Edsel Ford lay in state, his plain coffin flanked by two clusters of roses and a large circle of gardenias sent by Local 600 of the UAW. There was a touching moment at the funeral when rank-and-file workers in overalls appeared by the hundreds to view the man they knew had tried to treat them with humanity. The immediate family was there. Ernest Kanzler broke down and had to be helped from the room. Old Henry Ford sat listlessly, his lips moving in a conversation with himself. He had tried to get Bennett to come, but Bennett had refused, saying that he was guilty of many sins but hypocrisy was not among them.

The pathos was similar to that following the passing of someone who had died before reaching his prime. Yet Edsel was forty-nine years old; he just seemed young because he had never come into his own. If his death was tragic it was because he had never really challenged the role he was given as Ford heir. He had been born to the cough of one of his father's engines. As a baby he had been taken for a ride in his father's first car. As a teenager he had worked with his father in the Ford plant. As a young adult he had been made president of the company so that his father could pursue his scheme for total control. As a man he had kept a steadying hand on the company while his father lurched from one scheme to another.

Henry had made his way by defying *his* father. Not so Edsel. If his different fate also involved character, it was clear that what distinguished his life from his father's was the existence of the Ford Motor Company. The company: the destiny he could never quite grasp. This was the beckoning green light that this poignant Gatsbyesque figure had stared at all his days.

EDSEL'S DEATH WAS DEVASTATING to his family. The night after his burial, Eleanor slipped into Lake St. Clair and began to swim out toward the middle, but was rescued and brought back to shore. She wrote to her mother-in-law: "Somehow I have a rather difficult time sleeping at night, so I'm writing you a line to thank you for the most wonderful husband and father God ever made...." Later on, after she and Bill had gone to Hot Springs, she again wrote to Clara: "I do miss him so terribly that at times it seems impossible to go on, and yet I feel so very close to him that this gives me comfort. I brought down so many pictures with me."

For Eleanor, Edsel was a lost love. For his children, he would be a lost cause haunting their efforts to grapple with the company and ultimately bedeviling their attempts to live in moral balance with it. For Henry, his son's memory was pure guilt. At first he sought solace in his belief in reincarnation, telling Bennett, "Well, Harry, you know my belief—Edsel isn't dead." But this wasn't sufficient to hold back the pain, and his defenses collapsed. "I never believed anything like this could happen to me," he said helplessly. He became obsessed with the death, bringing it up over and over again, stopping himself by saying, "Now we aren't going to talk about it anymore," and then starting to talk about it all over again. Running into one of his old employees who had known Edsel since he was a boy, Henry said, "I just can't get over it. I've got a lump right here in my throat. Clara sits down and cries and gets over it, feels a little better. I just cannot do it. I have a lump here and there's nothing I can do about it."

The distance that had separated him and Clara during the death watch widened afterward, as Henry spent days alone at Fairlane, hovering on the edges of the silence which he knew contained an accusation that implicated him in what had happened. As if to show that he knew the good times were over, he disbanded the old-time orchestra and sent dance master Benjamin Lovett away. There would be no more dancing; the music of their lives had stopped.

It was weeks before Clara could release him from his despair. It happened one day in July when she appeared with a pair of baskets and casually asked him if he wanted to help her pick flowers. They spent the day together chatting as they always had done. But the loss would always remain. The only thing Henry Ford had loved as well as his son was his company, and now that was all he had.

PART II

HANK THE DEUCE

He's not your typical great man. His greatness...if you could call it that...sort of sneaks up on you.

—Whitney Young

ELEVEN

FTER ATTENDING HIS FATHER'S funeral, Henry Ford II caught the train for Chicago to resume his job at the Great Lakes Naval Station. He had slimmed down during his time in the Navy, but he still looked large in his dress uniform, although the impression he conveyed was one of fleshiness rather than solid bulk. That unfinished quality his mother had noticed in him when she asked a friend to "show him the ropes" during a college trip to Europe was still a part of Henry II now that Edsel was dead and all eyes were trained on him. Punning on his current job in the Navy, one company employee who saw him at the funeral said that he looked "totally at sea."

Shortly after the train pulled out of the station, Harry Pierson, the old friend and schoolmate of Edsel's who had introduced him to Franklin D. Roosevelt during their joint vacation in Warm Springs in the 1920s, recognized Henry II. Although the train was crowded with military personnel, Pierson had miraculously managed to obtain a private compartment, and he invited the young man to join him for a moment. As Henry sat down, Pierson began to tell him how saddened he was by his old friend's death. Before he could finish, Henry immediately stood up in agitation and burst into tears. "He was a saint, just a saint," he said. "He didn't *have* to die. *They* killed him!" While Henry struggled to compose himself, Pierson realized that he had never seen such a passion from this young man. In fact he felt that he had never really *seen* him before. Henry's high-pitched voice seemed almost effeminate, and his large, slope-shouldered body conveyed a sense of softness rather than strength, but the penetrating blue eyes bored relentlessly into the subject of his father's death. Henry talked about Edsel not just as a father who had died, but as someone martyred to a large moral principle. It was only after he had left to go back to his seat that Pierson realized that his old friend's son actually intended to attempt the impossible—to pick up his father's fallen standard and try to reclaim the company that bore his name and reassert his family's honor as well.

For Henry, as for his brothers and sister, Edsel's death was the stone cast into the pool of family life—the event that would continue to make waves for years to come. Not only did it leave a moral vacuum for the next generation to deal with, but it also conveyed daunting messages about the dangers of power and the need to seize and hold the company against anything that might be interpreted as a challenge.

It was a pivotal time in his life, Henry II acknowledged later on, a time of heavy anger and confusion but also, paradoxically, of faint stirrings of hope and ambition. The day after his father's death, "Uncle Ernie" Kanzler had taken him down to Edsel's private safe in the basement of the Administration Building. The two of them had pawed through the deeds and records as if looking for the keys to the kingdom. Title to his patrimony did not exist on any piece of paper, however, but only in the chaos of the Ford Motor Company; it was a legacy that would have to be fought for rather than inherited. Was he powerful and capable enough to pick up his father's burden? And if he were to engage in a struggle for the soul of the company to which his father had devoted and, it seemed in retrospect, sacrificed his life, would it enlarge and define him or merely dwarf and drain him of significance?

These were pressing questions. But they also seemed academic given the reality at Ford. The status quo with which his father had wrestled for twenty years at the company still existed; if anything, his grandfather was even more tightly under Harry Bennett's grip than before. Shortly after Edsel died, the old man had begun to hint that he wanted Bennett to be the next president of Ford. Eleanor, who now controlled her dead husband's sizable block of stock, "had a fit," in the words of one family friend. To appease her, old Henry said that he would take over the office himself and called a meeting of the board of directors two days later to formalize the move. At this meeting he made Bennett and some of his cronies directors, diluting the power of Eleanor, Benson and especially Henry II, who had objected to the propriety of selecting a new president so soon after his father's death but was overruled. When the meeting ended, there was none of the usual congratulations and good wishes.

Old Henry moved quickly to reassert himself in the company. The day after the board meeting he came into the plant, announcing, "I'm going to fire everybody around here who worried Edsel." In fact he did just the opposite, harassing the men who had *supported* his son over the years. Fred Black, Edsel's close aide who had helped him set up the company's immensely successful exhibit at the 1939 World's Fair, was fired. So was Edsel's secretary and right-hand man, John Crawford. Then it was the turn of E. T. Gregorie, the brilliant stylist who had designed the Zephyr and the Continental.

It was a purge of ideas as well as men. One of the innovations Edsel had been working on with an eye to what he knew would be the changed conditions of the postwar world was a small economy car; old Henry killed it outright. An even more revolutionary project, under the direction of chief engineer Lawrence Sheldrick, was the creation of a car with front-wheel drive and independent suspension. When the old man found out about Edsel's experiment he ordered the Engineering Department to destroy it. (Mildly disobedient, they broke down the prototype, crated it up and hid it in the basement.) After weeding out these attempts to grasp new technology, Ford approached Joe Galamb, his favorite draftsman, and said, "Joe, we've got to go back to Model T days. We've got to build only one car. There won't be any Mercury, no Lincoln, no other car."

To the outer world Ford looked like his old self, decisive and in charge. But those close to the situation looked behind the facade and saw a sad and disoriented old man. "I never know where I'm going in the morning," he confided to one friend. "I just get up and go out in the car and just drive around someplace. I come to the right place and I get out and go in and see some people about something I had to see them about....I wouldn't know where I was going next but I would just drive along until I got the idea that I should go to some other office or drop in and see somebody else."

Soon his daily routine excluded the company almost entirely. Most of the time he was home at Fairlane, tinkering in his machine shop in the powerhouse by day and by night listening to *Amos 'n Andy*, *Henry Aldrich*, and other favorite radio programs. In the afternoon he would sit with his eyes closed while Clara read to him—novels like *The Yearling* or biographies of royalty. Sometimes he would go into the library and put a record onto the Victrola and dance by himself. He rarely read the war news on the front pages of the papers, but he always read the comics, especially *Little Orphan Annie*. When the plot got too suspenseful for him he had his secretary contact Harold T. Grey, the author of the strip, and find out what was going to happen.

The real presence behind the broken figurehead was, of course, Bennett. Balding and a little paunchy now, "the little man" tried to cultivate a more dignified air once he was elected to the company's board of directors, but it was beyond him. He still consorted with unsavory characters, still wore the brightly colored silk shirts and flashy bow ties; when he talked business the effect was of a Damon Runyon character self-consciously using polysyllabic words.

In the first days after Edsel's death Bennett had worried that Sorensen, the only figure in the organization who really knew about production, would try to take over the presidency, and he had sent emissaries to Willow Run to find out what his onetime mentor's intentions were. But Sorensen was so overwhelmed by the bomber project that he couldn't focus on the problems of succession at Ford. Having always relied on the power of his character to get his way, he ignored details of political organization inside the company. He didn't know, for instance, that his personal secretary, Russell Gnau, was having lunch with Bennett every day in his private dining room and, in effect, functioning as a double agent.

With Sorensen stuck at Willow Run, Bennett had the company to himself. Whenever an important issue came up he would disappear for a couple of hours and then return, saying, "I've been to see Mr. Ford and he wants it done this way." Bennett had so persuaded the old man of his indispensability that Ford remarked to an employee, "The Jews and Communists have been working on poor Harry until he's almost out of his mind...[but he] will keep fighting the ones who are trying to take over our plant." With this sort of endorsement from the founder, it was little wonder that Bennett didn't regard Henry II as much of a threat. When one of his cronies remarked that it might make good political sense to bring the Ford heir into the company, Bennett smiled condescendingly and said, "Sure, we could use him. I'll take him right under my wing." He believed that he had crippled any challenge to his power in advance by getting Ford Motor Company lawyer I. A. Capizzi to work with him in drafting a codicil to old Henry's will establishing a trust that would control the Ford Motor Company for ten years after his death. Sorensen, Lindbergh and Edsel Ruddiman were among the trustees; Bennett was secretary of the trust. The reason for this move, he told Capizzi, was that the old man was worried that if something should happen to him Ernest Kanzler and other devious individuals would exert undue influence on his grandsons.

Yet the Ford grandsons did not seem much of a threat. Bill was just eighteen years old. Bennett knew from the way Benson had allowed himself to be manipulated during his time in the Army that he was a pushover. And Henry II, for all his baby fat, seemed to him a lightweight, a spoiled young man who had failed in school and rushed into an early marriage and fatherhood; someone who didn't seem to care much about his family and had not been particularly impressive while working in the company during the brief time between leaving Yale and joining the Navy.

But while he may not have been articulate about it, in fact Henry II had taken his role as oldest of the Ford grandchildren seriously from the onset of his father's illness, and had become intensely interested in his heritage, although uncertain about how to claim it. Before enlisting in the Navy he had broken the taboo that had existed from his boyhood by going to his father and saying, in reference to the strange alliance between Bennett and his grandfather, that the company was in a mess and would have to be cleaned up. Edsel, a stricken look crossing his face, had agreed with his son's perception of the problem, but not with his solution. It would be impossible to deal with Bennett, he said; it simply couldn't be done. Henry II had nonetheless continued to gnaw at the edges of the company, trying to understand its complexities, trying to figure out how he could fit in when his time came.

While undergoing training in the spring of 1941 at the Great Lakes Naval Station, Henry II had carried on a correspondence with Sorensen's secretary Russell Gnau, showing sharp curiosity about the company as he tried to keep abreast of developments from afar by requesting material for his records and by speculating on developments:

> I rather imagine that things are moving quite fast around the plant these days what with more than a double increase in the R-2800 [Pratt and Whitney] motors and also the bomber job. If we also get into making turbines I don't see where there's going to be much automobile production the next year. I really miss getting out there and into all these things, and especially so as I was just beginning to understand how things worked.

The letters also contained complimentary references to Bennett showing that Henry was politically savvy enough to understand that Gnau was covertly working for his father's antagonist and would pass on the disarming compliments.

When Edsel had seen his eldest son's growing interest in the company, he had reacted ambivalently. One part of him wanted to shield Henry II and his other children from any contact with the Ford Motor Company, which had assumed the status of a toxic substance in his own life; but another part wanted his son to succeed in taking over. Not long before his death Edsel had talked at length to Ernest Kanzler, still his closest confidant, who was in Washington serving on the War Production Board. Edsel, too, created a sort of codicil to his will, by saying that when he died he wanted Kanzler to make sure Henry II got out of the Navy so that he could return to Dearborn to fight for his birthright.

After Edsel died, Kanzler arranged a meeting with Secretary of the Navy Frank Knox at which it was decided that Henry II would be allowed to muster out of the service and given a chance to tame the Ford Motor Company. The only problem was that Bennett had prompted old Henry to tell Washington that the company didn't need or want this favor, which Kanzler, by then a connoisseur of Bennett's skullduggery, later called "the dirtiest piece of work I've ever seen in my life." In the weeks following Edsel's death, the Roosevelt Administration became extremely concerned about the deteriorating situation at Ford. For a while there was thought of placing the company under the stewardship of Studebaker or even of nationalizing it. But Kanzler kept pulling strings, and then in late July Secretary Knox, after consulting once more with the President, finally hustled Henry II out of the Navy so that he could go back to Dearborn and try to slay the dragon.*

THE TASK SEEMED FAR BEYOND his grasp. "Henry seemed so young," one company executive said later on. "He seemed so shallow." At this point in his life he was very easy to underestimate. Most employees assumed that Bennett would chew him up. They took him as he presented himself, not realizing that even at twenty-six he was a man of masks—complex and cunning, energetic and ambitious. He was far more like the grandfather he hated than the father he adored. He was on a mission of vengeance and vindication, aware of the magnitude of what lay ahead of him: saving the company from extinction and saving Edsel's memory, and also, as a subtext to these challenges, proving himself as well.

Knowing that despite his name he would be in the position of an unin-

---

* Henry had the one-paragraph letter he received from Navy Secretary Knox framed and displayed it in the several homes he would live in over the next forty years: "You are hereby released from the Navy to get you back to work at the Ford Motor Company."

vited guest in the company, Henry II tried to neutralize his grandfather by writing an earnest and respectful letter as he was finishing mustering out of the Navy:

> ...I am very pleased that things have finally been decided and that I am now on the way back to the plant. I have always been extremely interested in working there and even more so than ever now. I hope that somehow and in some way I can be of some value to you and possibly relieve you of some few things and maybe in some small way do a few things daddy used to do."

Eleanor also tried to drum up enthusiasm for his return in a letter to Henry and Clara: "My, it will be wonderful to have him here. It seems almost too good to be true. I know he will grow up to make us all proud of him. Edsel had such confidence in his ability."

But the old man ignored his grandson when he showed up. When Henry II tried to move into Edsel's old offices at the engineering laboratory, his grandfather had them locked. Henry then took over Edsel's office in the Administration Building, knowing that this was a place his grandfather avoided like the plague. The image of Edsel was always before him. Almost four decades later he would recall his bitter feelings at this time during a conversation with a friend: "It was my grandfather who killed my father. I know there was cancer. But it was also because of what my grandfather had put him through."

For weeks Henry II did nothing but study his father's files, reading them, as one observer felt, "like a cryptographer looking for a clue." He thought back to all the times he had tried to talk to Edsel about "the Bennett thing," unable to fathom why his father had refused to answer his questions about the man whom he had now inherited as an arch enemy. Trying to make himself useful, he traveled to dealerships around the country to reassure them that Ford would still be in business after the war. But when he went out into the plants back in Dearborn and saw the bizarre combination of feudal laws and naked power that ruled them, he began to wonder. There was no real management, only Bennett's tyrannical caprice. There were thousands of unneeded workers in manufacturing, a woeful lack of engineers. There was no scheduling of materials, no cost control, no mechanism for establishing or checking plans. Financial statements were kept from all but a handful of executives because, as one of Bennett's lieutenants noted darkly, "You never know what someone will do with one of these."

Bennett, with feigned affability, condescendingly offered to help young Henry find his way through the company maze. The Ford heir allowed himself to be patronized. Bennett even tried to establish a social relationship, taking Henry up in his plane for a flying lesson. Benson was unremittingly hostile to Bennett, refusing to have anything to do with him. But as Henry II pointed out when Benson accused him of hypocrisy, consistency was a luxury he could afford because he was in the Army rather than in the Ford Motor Company. (Others pointed out that the emphasis in the sociology department when Henry had studied at Yale was in man's adaptation to his environment.) He went along with Bennett, hating him but affecting a hearty camaraderie nonetheless.

In mid-September Henry went to see chief engineer Lawrence Sheldrick, a man Edsel had admired and trusted, and asked him about his father's thoughts on a postwar car. After Sheldrick showed him some of the designs and layouts he had salvaged from old Henry's purge and kept hidden ever since, Henry II asked him if he thought it might be a good idea for him to establish contacts in Washington with people in the War Department for whom the company was making tanks. Sheldrick agreed that a trip to Washington and the Aberdeen proving grounds, where the tanks were being tested, might be in order and said that he would meet him there after taking care of some private matters on a trip east he had already planned. But the day before he was scheduled to leave, Sheldrick was summoned to Sorensen's office.

"What's the big idea of you filling the young man's head with all of these crazy modern ideas of yours on postwar cars?" Sorensen snapped. "Another thing, what's the big idea of you trying to make a warmonger of him and taking him to Aberdeen? You know how his grandfather feels about this."

Sheldrick could tell that Sorensen had been put up to the attack after a "workover" by Ford and Bennett, but he still felt that he had to stand his ground. By the end of the conversation he had resigned, and the company had lost a man generally regarded as one of the best engineers in the auto business.

Yet the tide was moving against Sorensen, too. Because of his inattentiveness to the realities of power at Ford, he had been outflanked by Bennett, who had gotten old Henry to appoint him as Sorensen's assistant for administrative affairs and his crony Ray Rausch as Sorensen's assistant for production. By the time Sorensen realized what had happened, it was too late. One afternoon he was trying to get something decided at Willow Run and asked old Henry a question which he wouldn't answer. In disgust Sorensen said, "Well, I guess I'll go down to Florida, where I can get some rest." It was clearly the offer of a resignation, meant to elicit a vote of confidence. But instead of asking Sorensen to reconsider, old Henry simply shrugged. The day before Sorensen left for Florida, he went to Ford to say goodbye. Ford shook his hand and said, "Well, I guess there's something in life besides work," thus dismissing the man who had been with him for thirty-five years and who, more than anyone else, had made the company what it was.

A few weeks later the other remaining relic of Ford's golden age, Ernest Liebold, had his turn when corporate counsel I. A. Capizzi showed up in his office, demanded the power of attorney Liebold had kept for Henry Ford for a quarter of a century, and, once it was handed over, fired him, too.

With all the other characters off the stage, it came down to a duel between Bennett and Henry II, with old Henry looking on.

HENRY II HAD HIS NAME. But Bennett had control of his grandfather and of the company. Possible allies of young Henry's who hadn't already been purged began to leave voluntarily. Sales manager Henry Doss was one, saying to Henry after finishing cleaning out his desk, "I don't like to leave you and I wouldn't leave you if something could be done about the Bennett situation." Henry reluctantly agreed: "I don't blame you a darn bit, but there's nothing I can do about it now. Someday I will."

But for now it was like fighting with shadows. When an important decision came up, Bennett would follow a familiar gambit by getting into his car and disappearing for a while before returning with the verdict: "I've been to see your grandfather and he wants...." After one of these episodes, Henry II checked with his grandmother and found that Bennett hadn't spoken to the old man for weeks. But when he tried to talk to his grandfather about the situation, old Henry cut him off, saying angrily, "I won't hear a word against Harry!" At times the old man and Bennett ganged up on Henry II, as when he returned from a speech in the East on the issue of government control over the auto industry and was brought to a meeting where Bennett lectured him about taking positions that didn't agree with his grandfather's, old Henry adding scornfully, "Aw, I don't care. Don't tell him anything. I don't want him to agree with me on anything." All pretense of cooperation vanished. Henry II accepted no more plane rides from Bennett, who he knew was referring to him contemptuously behind his back as "the fat young man wandering around with a notebook in his hand."

In his time of need Henry managed to find three men who would become his trusted allies. One was Mead Bricker, beefy production aide to Sorensen, who had taken over Willow Run and, unlike most of the other remaining executives in the company, refused to kiss Bennett's ring. A man of great energy and integrity, Bricker had mastered the art of production under Sorensen's tutelage, but had no grandiose personal ambition. He wanted only to see operations run efficiently, which was why he threw his lot in with Henry II.

Another ally was John Davis, the legendary sales manager whose run-in with Bennett a few years earlier had forced him into exile in California. While on the West Coast he had done good work, not only increasing Ford's market share, but also managing, after months of patient negotiation and cajolery, to convince Jewish executives in Hollywood's motion picture industry that old Henry's anti-Semitism was a thing of the past, with the result that Ford started getting free advertising once again as its cars began showing up as props in the films first of Paramount and then of the other major studios.

Davis was reluctant to come back to Dearborn, but Henry II tried to allay his fears about being betrayed again: "Put it on this basis. If I stay, you stay. If you go, I go. The Company and I need you. We shall share the same fate." Davis was impressed by the task the young man had taken upon himself: " I think he realized he just had to assume leadership. His brother Benson didn't seem to want to and Bill was far too young. Henry knew it was up to

him." So Davis joined up, ready to do battle with Bennett once again. As someone who had watched the development of power arrangements in the company
over the years, he was struck by the contrast between young Ford and his
father: "Edsel was far more the artist of the two, and had an excellent knowledge of business; but he had no aggressiveness, no push. He was sweet. He was
always receptive, courteous, pleasant. Henry II is ambitious, aggressive, fear-
less. He has a drive that Edsel lacked." There was a bottom line: "We would
have done anything for Edsel, but he never asked us. Henry asked."

The most significant member of Henry's new triumvirate was former
Detroit FBI chief John S. Bugas. Frequently commended by J. Edgar Hoover
during his successful career with the Bureau, Bugas had been involved in several important cases, most recently one involving "Countess" Dineen, a
glamorous German spy who had been trained in Hamburg at the beginning of
the war and sent to Detroit to try to pry secrets out of industrialists. But the
FBI had penetrated her cover and Bugas had "turned" her so that she became
a double agent. He set her up in a fashionable Detroit apartment filled with
two-way mirrors and microphones, and then filmed and recorded her encoun-
ters with other Hitler agents.

Tall and lanky, Bugas had been a standout basketball player at the University of Wyoming. His eyes were weak, but he had an inquiring face with a
sharp nose and chin which gave him a sense of being pointed toward information. He did not volunteer information about himself easily, but those
who were well acquainted with him knew the story of his Czech immigrant
parents who had gotten into debt in the twenties and had to mortgage the family ranch in Wyoming; and how Bugas himself had worked for years to help
retire the debt and then stood with his father in the chaparral weeping as
they burned the redeemed note. Bugas' wife, Maggie, felt that his leading characteristic was his "cowboy morality." She liked to tell the story of the time
when they were on a train and her husband saw a man verbally abusing a
woman. Grabbing him by the scruff of the neck, Bugas took him out between
the swaying cars to chastise him and, when the man swung at him, knocked
him down.

Bugas had actually been on the case at Ford since the beginning of the
war. In July 1940 he had interviewed old Henry because J. Edgar Hoover
believed that someone in the War Department was leaking classified information to Charles Lindbergh and wanted to find out who it was. ("When Charles
comes out here we only talk about the Jews," the old man told Bugas.) He also
talked on and off to Bennett, once telling Hoover that Ford's enforcer was "a
very valuable friend of this office and without question one of the best sources
of information along practically any line in the area." Bennett had gotten the
idea that Bugas was his friend, just as so many other law enforcement officers
were; but the FBI man was actually a sort of time bomb Edsel had left ticking in
Bennett's vicinity. Edsel had come to know Bugas when he called him in late
1941 regarding a theft ring which was taking millions of dollars of material
out of Ford properties every year. Some of Bennett's cronies had been impli-

cated. Before his death Edsel had mentioned to Bugas how vulnerable he felt his family was to Bennett's machinations. Afterward Eleanor had told Bugas about the precarious position Henry II was in. The seed of his future loyalty to the Ford heir had germinated before he was hired as director of "industrial relations." Bennett had offered him the job, thinking to create a sense of obligation by making it seem it had been his idea all along. Bugas had been hoping to go to work at Ford, but was worried that it would seem that he had used his FBI position as leverage to get the offer. After Bennett approached him he wrote an anxious letter to J. Edgar Hoover: "The offer came as a complete surprise and without any solicitation whatsoever at any time from myself with the thought in mind of feathering my own nest...."

Beginning by working as Bennett's aide in industrial relations, Bugas, together with his family, spent a good deal of time with Bennett at "the Castle." Bugas even rode his palomino as unofficial grand marshal of the rodeo Bennett staged every summer. There seemed to be enough of a closeness between the two men that Henry II was confused, saying later of Bugas, "At first I didn't know how to play him." But Bugas began to understand Bennett's true character when he took his wife out to dinner one evening and, instead of returning home to Dearborn, stayed with her in a Detroit hotel. The next morning he was summoned to Bennett's office and chastised for his "immorality." Bennett told him, "I have an eyewitness report right here that you checked into the Book Cadillac Hotel with a redheaded woman last night." After he had tracked down the spy and gotten him fired, Bugas found himself "as isolated as a tuberculosis germ." He began to understand the situation Henry II faced and to understand also the meaning of the dark hints coming first from Edsel and then from Eleanor Ford before he came to work for the company. He pledged his allegiance firmly to Henry II for what he knew was the inevitable struggle ahead.

As his triumvirate of supporters were forming late in the spring of 1944, Henry II finally found out about the existence of the codicil to his grandfather's will. He understood that it was Bennett's ultimate weapon and believed that it scuttled any hope he had of taking over at Ford. He was plunged into despair. "This thing killed my father," he said in reference to the Bennett situation, "but I'll be damned if I'm going to let it kill me. I'm going to get out before it does." He told Bricker, Davis and Bugas that he was thinking of quitting, selling his stock and going to Ford dealers around the country to tell them that the situation in Dearborn was hopeless and they should sever their connections with the company. Bugas counseled restraint. After calming Henry II he went to see Bennett. Bennett initially refused to discuss the codicil, telling him to come back the next morning. When Bugas did, Bennett stared at him a moment and then, with a wolfish smile, pulled out the typewritten document and a carbon, crumpled the papers, dropped them on the floor and then lit them with a match. When the ashes had cooled he scooped them into an envelope and said, "Take this to Henry."

It was not clear why Bennett had incinerated his one chance for taking over the company. Perhaps he thought that one of the melodramatic gestures he found so appealing would bring Henry close to him. Perhaps he felt that the codicil was not valid. (I. A. Capizzi later said that old Henry had carried the document around with him for months, scrawling biblical verses and bizarre sayings all over it, thus making the codicil almost a prima-facie case for his mental incompetence.) But whatever Bennett's reason for his gratuitous act, it was clear that the odds had suddenly shifted. Bugas realized that the battle had been joined when he came to work the next day and found that his desk, previously in an office next to Bennett's, had been moved into Bennett's washroom and was separated from the toilet and wash basin only by a flimsy partition.

As World War II dragged toward an end, old Henry wrote in a spidery hand in one of the notebooks he had kept for years: "Should find out who crated [*sic*] Hitler and the war mongers." But in the spring of 1945 the first uncut footage of the Nazi death camps began to reach the United States. At a showing in the Rouge auditorium the old man watched in horror as the atrocities flashed across the screen. Swamped by guilt and paranoia, he bolted from his seat, later claiming that government agents were out to get him. From this point on, he insisted that his chauffeur be armed.

The old man was largely oblivious to the struggle for succession between Henry II and Bennett, which was about to reach its climax. Once Bugas had brought evidence of the destroyed codicil, young Henry gained enough confidence finally to move against his rival. Using his apparent ineffectuality to disarm Bennett, he had gotten himself named executive vice-president of the company several weeks earlier. Now, as the great bomber project at Willow Run was completed, he turned his attention to cars. He began to talk about the design of the postwar Ford and overturned his grandfather's decision to scrap the Mercury and the Lincoln in an attempt to reenter the lost paradise of one chassis and engine. The middle- and large-sized cars restored, he pondered the next move against Bennett. Once again Bugas provided the direction: "First get your grandfather to sign a piece of paper saying that nobody can get fired around here without your permission."

But his grandfather sensed the plot brewing against Bennett and refused to give Henry II the authority he needed. It seemed as though the rebellion would stall, but then, at this crucial moment, the women of the family, silent during Edsel's long humiliation, threw their weight onto Henry's side. Clara made it clear to her husband that denying Henry II power in the company would snap already damaged family ties once and for all. Then Eleanor set aside the deference which had always characterized her relationship with her father-in-law and issued an ultimatum: if her son was not put in charge of the company immediately, she would sell all the stock she had inherited from Edsel, some 41 percent of the company.

This last threat got the old man's attention. After days of pressure he reluctantly called his grandson to Fairlane to offer him the presidency of the company. Instead of immediately accepting the offer, however, the cagey Henry II gave him a hard look and upped the ante: "I'll take it only if I have a completely free hand to make any change I want to make."

The old man bristled, but after a stern look from Clara he grudgingly came to terms. Henry II returned immediately to the office and had Frank Campsall, his grandfather's secretary, draft a letter of resignation for the old man to sign. He also called a board meeting for the following day. He knew that Campsall, who was Bennett's man, would immediately inform his rival. And, indeed, there was soon a telephone call. "Henry, I've got wonderful news." Bennett's voice was unctuous. "I've talked your grandfather into making you president of the company!"

The board convened on September 21, 1945—a day to remember for the Ford family, although Benson boycotted the meeting, having sworn never to be present in the same room with Bennett. Henry II was there with his mother and grandfather, who was so frail that he had to be helped to his seat. As the old man's letter of resignation was read aloud, Bennett got up in agitation, looked at Henry II, snarled "Congratulations!" and then rushed out of the room. Later that day, young Henry ran into Bennett in the hall. "You're taking over a billion-dollar organization you haven't contributed a thing to," his father's old enemy snarled. Henry, suddenly fearful that he might not be able to make an outright firing stick, told Bennett that he was reassigning him to other duties.

It was left to Bugas to administer the *coup de grâce*. Sticking a .38 into his belt, he went to Bennett's office. As he walked in, Bennett looked up, shouted "You son of a bitch!" and pulled a .45 automatic out of his desk. Bugas pulled his own gun out and said calmly, "Don't make the mistake of pulling the trigger, because I'll kill you. I won't miss. I'll put one right through your heart, Harry." In agitation Bennett changed his tone altogether and offered to take Bugas for a ride in his airplane. Bugas declined, then turned around and walked to the door, wondering, he later admitted, if he would be shot in the back.

For the next few hours smoke drifted out of Bennett's office as he burned his private papers. By the end of the day he was gone.

It was as if a curse had been lifted. Everyone was jubilant, but none more so than sales manager John Davis, who had felt Bennett's lash most sharply. "Now can I fire somebody?" he asked Henry II after Bennett had left.

"Who?"

"Harry Mack." Davis named the Bennett crony he and Edsel had fired years earlier only to have Bennett overturn their action and use it in a power move against them.

"Sure," Henry said, "Go ahead."

Getting Mack on the phone, Davis said, "You're fired—and this time you can't get back, because your boyfriend Bennett is gone too."

A few days later Bugas went to Bennett's home to recover furnishings, building materials and other Ford property that had been taken there over the years. Bennett tried to punch him, but Bugas simply reached out a long arm and held him by the chest as he windmilled his fists impotently. After Bugas' men had loaded up what they came for, he let the broken Bennett go.

A few weeks after leaving the company, Bennett got word from a reporter friend that old Henry was trying desperately to get in touch with him but couldn't because he wasn't being allowed access to the phone. Finally one day Ford managed to get through. "Harry," he said in a quavering voice, "I want you to go to the plant and shut it down...." But before he could finish his thought, he broke down in tears and became incoherent. He called several times later on, but Bennett refused to come to the phone. The old man missed him, but in one of his lucid moments he said with an air of bemusement, "Well, I guess Harry is back where he started from."

TWELVE

THROUGHOUT THE SUMMER OF 1946, a time when many Americans were putting their names on waiting lists for automobiles, Henry Ford II came out of the red brick Georgian home at 300 Provencal Road every morning, stepped briskly down the walk, grabbed the open door of a Ford from his chauffeur and slammed it, his head cocked critically to hear the sound, then opened and slammed the door again before finally getting in. It was a different Ford every day, and during the ritual ride to work Henry II ignored the new foliage of the majestic Dutch elms of Grosse Pointe, concentrating instead on the inside of the car. To people in other vehicles pulling up alongside him at stop signs, he looked like a child having a tantrum—bouncing on the seats, rolling the windows up and down, pushing and pulling at the ashtrays, the cigarette lighter and other gadgets. But it was always the doors that bothered him most. When he got to the plant he would sometimes walk down the production line angrily opening and slamming the doors on the skeletal vehicles, telling the workers, "Don't you know that Chevrolet salesmen take prospects out to a Ford salesroom and slam a car door? When it sounds like tin, they just say, 'See—tin!' and take them back and sell them a Chevrolet."

It was nearly eight months since John Bugas had walked into Bennett's office and ended his long usurpation of the Ford birthright. In retrospect, Henry II had decided that it was a mistake for him not to have done "the dirty work" himself, and when Bugas offered to take the next step in cleaning out the Bennett loyalists embedded deeply in the company, he said, "That's not the way. I'll have to do it myself or I'll be known as a guy who couldn't face up to his responsibilities."

Working from a list of Bennett supporters Bugas had prepared, he walked down the corridor of the Administration Building, going from office to office and firing men as he went. To dramatize the meaning of what he was doing he went to the Rouge, where one of Bennett's most abusive cronies had maintained a secret entertainment lounge, and with an ax broke down the partition concealing the room. Henry's wrath didn't stop at the gates of the Rouge, but reached into the divisional and branch offices. When it was over, more than one thousand men had been fired. It was a clear sweep except for four well-known Bennett stooges who were spared because they had become informants in identifying the hundreds of key men Bennett had hired over the years.

Far from acting like the pampered princeling Bennett had joked about, Henry II had established a demanding routine for himself, arriving at work at eight-thirty and staying until after six—often seven days a week. He was in charge and in the public eye, displaying an earnest desire to learn ("I am green and reaching for answers," he had told a *Fortune* writer soon after taking over) as well as a nice sense of locker-room badinage, as when he finished fielding reporters' queries one evening at Detroit's Off the Record Club and then said, "Now I want to ask *you* a question. Where's the men's room?" If it wasn't quite charisma, it did add up, in the words of one observer, to an "unpolished charm." The press began referring to him as "Young Henry," as if he were the prince from across the water who had returned to assert a rightful claim to a family throne. With John Davis he had made a tour of Ford dealerships across the country, telling them of changes he intended to make, delivering inspirational messages about how the company would be number one again, and most of all letting them see and touch a human Ford. He drove the pace car at the Indianapolis 500, the first time a Ford had been there since Edsel drove in 1932. At a more practical level he and Bugas had negotiated a precedent-setting contract with the UAW in which the company paid top dollar and in return the union acknowledged that the wildcat strikes and work stoppages that had plagued Ford for several years would have to stop. Through Bugas' Industrial Relations Department, Henry II launched a training program to bring college graduates to Ford.* And finally, on October 26, 1945, a day designated as "V-8 Day," Henry II brought out the first postwar American car. It was only a 1942 model prettied up with a little extra trim and a few engine modifications, but it symbolized the return to business as usual that the company, its customers and indeed all of America had been waiting for.

As the energetic young man asserted his family's right to control Ford and asserted himself, too, displaying more strength and leadership than anyone had assumed he possessed, old Henry faded into the background, confirming suspicions that what had seemed his robust presence in the period after Edsel's death had actually been Bennett's ventriloquism. He seldom came to the Rouge. On the rare instances when he showed up there, workers who had known him were taken aback: he was a parody of what he had been, hollow-cheeked and drawn, his gray eyes staring into confusion, and his long fingers moving in constant spidery motion on his pants legs. At home he was totally dependent on Clara, never leaving her or letting her leave him, following her around Fairlane with a palsied hand on her arm as if he were a

---

* It had been agreed to bring in only fifty recruits in this first class of 1945, but a young engineer from Allentown, Pennsylvania, named Lee Iacocca insisted on being included and became the fifty-first.

blind man who needed her to steer him from place to place. He got up in the morning and almost immediately went into the sunroom that looked out onto the Rouge River, and began to catnap on a couch, standing up quickly when Clara came into the room because he knew she wanted him to appear alert. All his life he had been a heavy sleeper, so heavy, in fact, that his snoring had amused the household help in the rooms below. But now he had trouble even dozing at night. He was so restless that Clara finally switched to twin beds, a move he hated. To get some relief from Henry's dependence, she occasionally asked Ray Dahlinger to take them for a drive through Greenfield Village. Sunk deep in the backseat, Henry would look longingly out at the craftsmen he had installed there and wave in slow motion as the car passed by.

Henry II never visited Fairlane, and he spoke about his grandfather only on ceremonial occasions. The memory of his father was constantly with him—a cautionary ghost counseling wariness and advising him to surround himself with a modernized corporate structure as quickly as possible. Yet while Henry may have told himself and others that he was taking over the company to preserve it from Bennett and to make it efficient once again, there were other motives, too. Despite his apparent lack of pretense and personal ambition, Henry II wanted to become a *Ford* and somehow to inhabit his grandfather's mythic stature in the automotive world, which was waiting once again to become Ford country.

In fact, Henry II had begun thinking about his image shortly after going to work for the company, when Bennett still seemed firmly in control. He commissioned pollster Elmo Roper to do a study on Ford worker attitudes, and Roper suggested that he contact Earl Newsom, pioneering public-relations expert who had worked for the Rockefellers and other powerful families conscious of the way they were perceived by the public. When Henry approached him, Newsom put him off after discussing the company with other auto executives, one of whom told him that "nobody could resurrect that pile of junk, least of all that socialite." Instead of an outright refusal, however, Newsom had put what at that time seemed an impossible condition on his acceptance, saying that he would consider it only if Henry II managed to gain control of the company. After firing Bennett, Henry immediately called the Newsom agency. "The first thing I did was fire Harry Bennett," he said. "The second is to call you. Do I go there or do you want to come here?" Newsom went to Detroit.

After a brief examination of Ford, Newsom told Henry that whatever campaign he began would have to be personalized: "The company is you, it is not an organization." The magic in the Ford name and the richly complex history surrounding it made the Ford account a public-relations man's dream. One of the associates who helped Newsom design his campaign saw the possibilities for drama: "You could play Henry II off against the grandfather, for instance. In Ford's labor relations everyone remembered the Battle of the Overpass, so if Henry showed signs of a different attitude toward the work force, that would show progressive management."

Labor was indeed the first focus of Newsom's efforts. In January 1946, while talks with the UAW were in progress, he wrote a speech polished through a dozen drafts for Henry to deliver to some four thousand members of the Detroit Society of Automotive Engineers, calling for "industrial statesmanship" on the part of owners and unions. "The public is 'boss,' not management or labor," Henry II said. The industrial problems of the postwar era could be solved "by giving the same hardheaded attention to human factors that we have given so successfully in the past to mechanical factors," and contracts ought to be negotiated "with the same efficiency and good temper that marks the negotiation of a commercial contract between two companies." As Newsom had predicted, the contrast between Henry II's conciliatory tone and the violent rhetoric that had characterized his grandfather's pronouncements on the subject of labor immediately won him national attention. The speech put Henry II on the cover of *Time*. The U.S. Jaycees named him the outstanding Young Man of the Year, he was hailed as a model of the businessman of the new era and several universities offered him honorary degrees.

Henry's stature grew when he took on Chester Bowles of the Office of Price Administration. He made several trips to Washington to argue against the prices the OPA had set for 1946 cars (although they were, on average, no higher than prices for 1942) and against production controls which allowed Ford to produce only 35,000 cars despite the fact that it had 300,000 orders. He went back and forth with Bowles, who accused him of trying to undermine the OPA, which he called "the American people's bulwark against economic disaster." Henry responded that the Washington bureaucracy was keeping the auto industry from accelerating the postwar recovery. After the smoke had cleared, Henry was being referred to as a future leader of the entire automotive industry.

It was a heady experience for a young man who hadn't yet reached his thirtieth birthday. But he understood that all the public-relations savvy in the world couldn't change the fact that the Ford Motor Company, which hadn't turned a profit in fifteen years, was now losing money at the rate of some $1 million a day. The 1946 car was merely a stopgap measure, a way of showing that the company was still in business. The signs reading "Beat Chevrolet" that Henry had ordered posted all over the Rouge were really empty bravado unless something concrete was done. "Clearly," he said to Newsom out of the blue one day, "I just don't know enough...to run this damn place." Desperate for expertise, he took one of the biggest gambles in contemporary business history by hiring a group of ten young former Air Force officers who became known as the "Whiz Kids."

Their leader was Charles B. "Tex" Thornton, a charismatic and ambitious young colonel who was the youngest man ever to win this rank in the Army Air Forces. One ancestor had designed the Capitol building for George Washington, and another was a signer of the Declaration of Independence, but Thornton was closest in temperament to his father, a legendary figure in the

Texas oil business who had made a living shooting wells and blowing out fires. Graduating from Texas State Technical Institute in the middle of the Depression, Thornton had a keen knowledge of the new principles of accounting and statistics. But he wanted to be more than just another bookkeeper. Figuring that Washington was the place to be during hard times, he booked a compartment on a train headed there after getting letters of introduction from his Congressman.

Thornton was working as a statistical clerk at the U.S. Housing Authority when Under-Secretary of War Robert Lovett discovered him. After listening to him talk about the way in which statistics might be used in wartime planning, Lovett immediately conscripted him for his office, and he worked in the War Department for the duration.

Noticing that although the Army Air Forces brass talked about arcane points of strategy, they never really knew at any given moment how many planes they had, where they were or in what state of readiness, Thornton formed the Statistical Control Group and arranged for the Harvard Business School to help train young officers in management. In effect treating the AAF as if it were a corporation, Thornton's group of bright young men worked like gifted junior executives in centralizing the materials for decision-making and in manipulating the "inventory" of bombers and fighters. In so doing, they revolutionized air warfare.

General "Hap" Arnold never appeared before a congressional committee in Washington before being briefed by Thornton or having him at his side. Going from one triumph to another, Thornton soon became known, not without a certain envy on the part of older officers who used the nickname, as "Young Napoleon." He used his arts of persuasion in small matters as well as large. For instance, when one of his most promising young officers, Francis C. "Jack" Reith, became morose because his romance had gone sour, Thornton called Reith's girlfriend in Oklahoma from his office in the War Department. "Now please don't hang up on me," he pleaded. "The truth is that my office is grinding to a halt because Jack Reith can't reach you. He's just come apart at the seams. Do you realize you're jeopardizing my whole operation and impeding the war effort? For God's sake at least let him come down and see you. It can't hurt." The girlfriend started to protest, but Thornton ignored her. "I'll get him aboard an airplane tonight. There's some official business in Oklahoma he can take care of for me."

As the war wound down, Thornton, now thirty-two, got the idea of keeping together a group of his best young officers for a postwar venture involving a company that had fallen on hard times and needed a quick infusion of order and progress. "If you went in with one or two people you could get lost or chewed up...," he said later, explaining his decision to assemble a team. "To convert a really large company quickly you need a group." Along with Reith, those he picked to accompany him on this venture included Charles Bosworth, Arjay R. Miller, Ben D. Mills, George Moore, James O. Wright, Wilbur Andreson and J. Edward Lundy. The last member was a reluctant

Robert S. McNamara, who had been an assistant professor of accounting at Harvard before the war and had intended to pick up his career there afterward, until he and his wife contracted polio in 1945. His case proved to be mild, but his wife's was more serious, involving a lengthy hospital stay and mounting medical bills. Thornton didn't hesitate to twist McNamara's arm when he said he wasn't sure he was interested: "You'd better get interested. Didn't you tell me you were broke? You owe it to your wife."

The group's first preference was becoming involved with a service rather than a product—something similar to the A. C. Neilsen Service, which at that time rated radio programming. Thornton offered the group's services to the Alleghany Company, an ailing conglomerate. Its president, Robert R. Young, was interested enough to make them an offer, but not all the group found the prospect of working for the virtually anonymous Alleghany exciting, and Young, for his part, wanted to hire only two or three of them. Thornton wanted to keep the unit together, not out of sentimentality but because he intended to *take over* a company, not merely get some executive jobs. One of his group, Arjay Miller, saw a *Life* article about the Ford Motor Company's precarious situation and convinced Thornton to approach Henry II by way of a "dramatic" telegram.

> I REPRESENT A GROUP OF ASSOCIATES WHO HAVE SERVED UNDER ME AT THE OFFICE OF STATISTICAL CONTROL, ARMY AIR FORCE. WE WOULD LIKE TO DISCUSS WITH YOU PERSONALLY A MATTER OF MANAGEMENT IMPORTANCE AND REQUEST EARLY MEETING. THE HONORABLE ROBERT A. LOVETT CAN GIVE YOU MY BACKGROUND IN DIRECTING THE ACTIVITIES OF THREE THOUSAND SPECIALISTS IN ADVANCED MANAGEMENT TECHNIQUES DURING WW II.

The day after he sent the telegram, Thornton received a call inviting him to come to Dearborn.

Before the group arrived, Kanzler arranged for Henry to speak with Lovett about them. The Under-Secretary enthusiastically endorsed Thornton and his men. When they arrived at the Ford Rotunda in late November, Henry was prepared to like them and did. They were all about his age and shared his philosophy about the role a modernized business community could play in postwar America. Admittedly they knew nothing about cars, but they had known nothing about airplanes either, and had nonetheless revolutionized the Army Air Forces' concept of strategic bombing. Henry believed that they were just what he needed.

Studying the Ford heir hard during their meeting, Robert McNamara got the feeling that while Henry had a circle of intimates, he didn't really feel that any of them could take him the final step in rebuilding the company. It was clear to everyone in Thornton's group that John Bugas, chief of these intimates, felt threatened by them. At one point in the meeting he said, "Well, Henry, if you hire the group I—" Ford interrupted him, "Now, John, what do you mean *if* I hire them? I *told* you I wanted to hire them. Now let's get on with it." Bugas was still opposed. After the meeting he took the AAF group to dinner at the Detroit Athletic Club and interrogated them over cocktails to make sure they were not opportunists. The questioning was so sharp that afterward the group decided that Jim Wright, the only lawyer among them, should research the question of whether or not they should demand a written contract. Wright's opinion was that such a document wouldn't accomplish much; if they couldn't trust Henry Ford II, they were in an absurd situation.

The group was scheduled to report for work on February 1, 1946. Thornton arrived a few days early and bought a home in a township near Bloomfield Hills. The rest of them arrived with their wives on January 31, taking up quarters in the Dearborn Inn. When they reported for work the next day, Bugas' Industrial Relations Department forced them to take a two-day battery of psychological, achievement and intelligence tests. McNamara felt it was just another attempt on Bugas' part to see whether they were dangerous, although he was amused by questions obviously intended to catch possible homosexuals, such as "What would you rather be, a florist or a coal miner?" All of them "passed," achieving some of the highest scores ever recorded on these tests, yet this episode inspired a certain paranoia which affected the wives back at the Dearborn Inn as much as the men. "We would open the doors between our rooms and talk in hushed tones," Ben Mills' wife, Helen, later said, "because we didn't know who might be listening in the next room. The men would come home every other evening and say, 'Don't unpack your bags yet.' "

As the weeks passed, their lives became normalized. One couple after another, they were offered homes in the Spring Wells Park complex (which became known as the "Ford Foundation" because of their presence), the first vacancy going to Jack Reith, whose wife, Maxine, the reluctant girlfriend Thornton had helped win over, was pregnant. The men were getting into things at the company. After a long orientation process, they began going around to various departments asking questions and scribbling notes on their pads. What they found out was shocking. Thornton soon discovered that old Henry had millions of dollars in non-interest-bearing accounts in banks all over Michigan. Arjay Miller went to the Accounting Department to get figures that would allow him to begin making forecasts and projections, and found that old-fashioned bookkeepers kept piles of bills up to four feet high and estimated accounts payable by measuring the stack with a yardstick. It was an administrative dark ages: Ford workers were still being paid in cash because old Henry had once tried paying by check and found, by studying the endorsements, that many of them had been cashed in saloons and places of ill repute. One of the group asked someone in the controller's office what he projected some figures to be in six months' time and the man replied, "What would you like them to be?"

Soon they had collected more data than any group ever had about the company. Someone called them the "Quiz Kids," after the child prodigies on the radio. Someone else made it "Whiz Kids," a name that stuck.

Talking about things like polling, statistical analysis and market research, the Whiz Kids were something new in the industry—executives whose claim to leadership would be based on financial know-how and sophistication rather than a feel for the product itself. McNamara was their representative man—someone who would have been just as happy, one observer noted, selling widgets or ladies' undergarments. He was calculating, if not cold, and cared only for the bottom line, a trait he shared with other men coming into the industry—"bean counters," in the auto-world jargon to come.

In time Thornton's group would provide the Ford Motor Company with two presidents and six vice-presidents. But in the spring of 1946 they were green. Henry II recognized this, and he understood, too, the ambitiousness of Thornton's team. This quality, in fact, rang an alarm bell in Henry, making him aware once again of the precariousness of his own situation, which was, after all, based on no real knowledge or expertise, but only on his name and ownership position. In what would become a characteristic gesture for one susceptible, because of his father's experience, to a view of the company as an area of Byzantine intrigue and struggles for power, Henry moved to hedge his bets. He talked to his indispensable Uncle Ernie Kanzler about bringing in someone who could both help the company take a great leap forward, as the Whiz Kids could not, and also balance their obvious ambition. Kanzler, who happened to be on the board of Bendix Aviation, told Henry that Bendix President Ernest R. Breech, star of the GM system and protégé of the great Alfred Sloan himself, was just the man he needed.

FROM THE OUTSET, ONE OF the things that fascinated Henry II about Ernie Breech was his self-madeness, the fact that he seemed almost to be an illustration of one of old Henry's homilies about self-reliance. Small but muscular as a result of having worked, as a boy, for his father, who was the blacksmith in a sleepy village in the Ozarks, Breech had been an avid reader of *Struggling Upward* and other Horatio Alger books. He made spending money in high school trapping rabbits and selling their skins, and supported himself at Drury College ironing other students' clothes and selling Victrolas door to door out of the back of a borrowed Model T.

Breech got a job as a bookkeeper in Chicago after graduating, and earned a CPA degree by attending night school. He became controller for several companies and was finally hired by GM, joining a group of accountants who pioneered the comprehensive financial-control systems Sloan used to revolutionize the auto industry. After establishing himself as Sloan's chief problem-solver by turning around failing GM properties and overseeing complex mergers, Breech was made president of Bendix on the assumption that he was a likely future president of GM. But during the war the Sloan faction of which he was a part had been stalemated by the Knudsen faction, and by the time he was contacted by Henry II, Breech—a dapper little man with a pencil mustache who at the age of fifty was one of the acknowledged giants of American business—was stalled in his present job.

Meeting with Breech, Henry worked hard to sell him on the company, outlining the plans for reviving Ford which he had discussed with Kanzler and with Thornton's impressive group. He told Breech that he had come to him because he was "the logical man"—someone who had been schooled in the General Motors system and who understood the procedures that had made GM the best managed company in the business. When he said that he wanted to hire him, Breech asked, "In what capacity?" Henry answered, "As top man." Although he was flattered, Breech told Henry he really didn't want the job. "Well, I'm not going to take no for an answer," Henry said, asking Breech at least to come to Dearborn to look things over and give him some advice.

When he looked the company over, Breech was astonished at its condition and at its balance sheet—"about as good as a small tool shop would have," he remarked later. The visit was daunting, yet intriguing. He left Dearborn feeling that if he "ducked" this challenge, he would regret it the rest of his life. He was also affected by Henry himself, who, despite the fact that he was nearly thirty years old with children of his own, seemed somehow fatherless and adrift. The day after looking over the company, Breech called his wife, Thelma, who was visiting relations in Missouri. "I couldn't sleep last night," he told her. "Our son is just one year younger than Henry. I lay there awake and said to myself, 'I wonder, if [he] got in trouble, do I have a friend to help him out?' It came over me that I should help the kid out." With Thelma's encouragement, Breech called Henry and agreed to come aboard.

Breech's seniority over him in age and the fact that he was a star of the mighty GM made Henry anxious in a way he hadn't been when he hired Thornton's group. He later admitted that the moment of sudden panic he experienced after negotiating the contract with Breech was probably caused by the memory of having seen the company snatched away from his father by strong outsiders. Had he just signed away his birthright by bringing in a strong figure like Breech? He set up another meeting and asked Kanzler to be there. When Breech, too, expressed new fears and second thoughts about the arrangement, Kanzler had to calm both men down. The relationship was finally cemented: Breech would not be named president but executive vice-president, second in command as far as the world was concerned, but with the authority to make corporate decisions. The relieved Kanzler was driving home down Woodward Avenue when he glanced up into the rearview mirror and noticed Henry weaving through traffic behind him in a frantic attempt to catch up. After Henry had pulled alongside him and tried to communicate by way of agitated hand gestures, Kanzler finally stopped.

Henry came up breathlessly to the window. "My lawyer says I'm abdicating by making Ernie vice-president!"

Kanzler repeated what he had said before: "You can't give him the power. You must make it understood that you are to retain the power."

In one final meeting Breech reassured Henry that there would be "no misunderstandings" on that score and, for his part, received assurances that he would be "set up financially for life" in case the company went bankrupt. The deal was finally made, and Breech agreed to come aboard on July 1.

This awkward *pas de deux* between the two men survived two early tests. The first one involved personalities. John Davis and John Bugas were miffed at having been displaced. But the real problem was Thornton. One of his Whiz Kids, Ben Mills, later said, "Tex had in mind that he wanted to be president of the Ford Motor Company. When Breech was brought in, there was immediate conflict, not so much between him and Tex personally, but between him and Tex's ambition." Thornton tried to recoup his losses by an end run. He drafted a letter for Henry II proposing that his Planning and Control Group should essentially oversee all the vital operation of the company and possess a veto power to secure its authority. Henry showed the letter to Breech, who read it and handed it back with a shrug, saying, "If you sign it there'll be no need for me." The letter was returned to Thornton unsigned.

The next challenge was from Earl Newsom and involved the larger-than-life imagery he had been creating for Henry. While Breech was attending his final stockholders' meeting at Bendix, Newsom called to inform him of a major press conference planned for the day he formally took over in Dearborn. The conference would center around Henry II, Newsom said, adding that if the press happened to ask Breech a question he should respond, "Well, I don't know," or "I can't answer that question," and defer to Henry. Breech blew up, telling Newsom that his cursory examination of company books and operations had shown that it was imperative to *avoid* a news conference. "Furthermore," he added, "I *know* the Detroit press and I believe I have their respect, and I am not going to sit there and be a Charlie McCarthy for your benefit or anybody else's." He thought that ended the issue, but a week after he came to work for Ford a Newsom aide came into his office with an agenda for a press conference. Breech hurried him unceremoniously into Henry II's adjoining office and said, "If you wish to risk yourself with the press at a time when things are in such bad condition at the Ford Motor Company, you may do so without me . . ." Suddenly it was Henry who was being tested. He looked Newsom's aide in the eye and said quietly, "There will be no news conference."

THE SCHAEFFER ROAD ADMINISTRATION Building, set in swampland with its back to the Rouge, was a modest three floors arranged in a U shape. About as imposing a structure as a high school or a city hall in a moderate-sized Midwestern town, Ernie Breech thought. Henry had the office originally meant for his grandfather, which old Henry had never really used. Breech modernized Edsel's old office, which was next door to Henry's, and moved in there.

Breech had thought that he knew what he was getting into. But one

morning about a month after taking over he stopped his company Lincoln outside the Administration Building and sat at the steering wheel momentarily
unable to move as he considered the magnitude of the task ahead. The Engineering Department was archaic and chaotic. The dealer organization was in
shambles. All of the executive talent at Ford had been purged by Bennett after
Edsel's death. Breech had learned, moreover, that old Henry had not bothered to file the disclosures legally required of defense contractors at war's end,
with the result that the company had been slapped with a $50 million tax sur-
charge for excess profits at Willow Run. Vast sums of money were being lost to
employees who, sensing the end, were carrying off tools, parts and anything
else they could lay their hands on—a problem symbolized by the crane that
had to be rented to retrieve a piece of equipment one Willow Run executive
had stolen and then reassembled piece by piece in his basement. Breech had
always been up to any challenge, but this one seemed impossible to handle.
"For the first time in my life I was over-whelmed," he said later on. "I was
not afraid exactly, but very disturbed. Our problems seemed almost insuper-
able."

But while he sat there in his Lincoln, sunk in depression, he thought of
an old Ozarks saying from his boyhood about how one goes about breaking
an unmanageable bundle of sticks: by doing it one at a time. Bugas was
already trying to get the theft problem under control by stationing security
guards at the gates and searching the men as they left work every day. Ford
lawyers were negotiating with Washington over the $50 million tax surcharge.
So the real issue was corporate structure and identity.

Breech had gotten to know Peter F. Drucker when the sociologist was
doing research for *Concept of the Corporation*, a study of General Motors
and the way it had implemented the new accounting techniques, theories of
decentralization, etc., which had been pioneered at the Harvard Business
School in the 1930s. Breech now bought dozens of copies of the book and
distributed them to key employees throughout the Ford organization. Even
Henry II, who hated to read, took *Concept of the Corporation* home and sul-
lenly plowed through it. But Breech knew that Ford could not be refashioned
by literature alone, and so he began a program of "hijacking" top executives
from GM. Within months Ford had hired over 150 executives off its bonus list,
leading GM President Charlie Wilson to complain to Breech in a meeting. The
problem was not that he was stealing his top older executives soon to retire,
Wilson said, but that he was taking the younger men from the second and
third managerial levels whom GM regarded as its top men of tomorrow.

Among the men brought to Ford were future heads of the engineering,
manufacturing and legal divisions—Harold T. Youngren, Delmar S. Harder
and William T. Gossett. These men would make significant individual contributions. (Harder, for instance, coined the term "automation" and helped
streamline the concept.) Even more important, they brought more recruits
with them, tempting them with the image of a young, robust president, a
growing sense of corporate mission and the drama inherent in Ford's dire

straits. In weaning a young attorney for his staff away from the prestigious New York law firm of Milbank, Tweed, for instance, William Gossett articulated the challenge this way: "Look, we're rebuilding an empire here. Something like this will never happen again in American business." The attractions were practical as well as existential. Gerald J. Lynch, a finance man who came from GM's Fisher Body Division, recalled, "When I was leaving I made the rounds of the fourteenth floor of the GM building. People said that I had a big future and they couldn't understand why anyone in his right mind would join that bankrupt outfit on the Rouge. I answered that I was gambling on Breech's ability to turn it around. I also pointed out that they were seven deep at every position at GM and zero deep at Ford."

Of all the people Breech hired, the key figure was not a young man at all but fifty-two-year-old Lewis D. Crusoe, a legendary GM executive in semi-retirement. A man of starchy morals and restless intelligence (at thirteen he had written an essay arguing the necessity of giving women the vote), Crusoe had worked as a "cruiser" as a young man, scouting Michigan's forests with a canoe and an ax and marking trees for lumber companies. Getting his college degree at night school, he went to work for the Fisher Body Division of GM and rose in the hierarchy until he had become controller. Hair silvering at the temples and severely parted just off center, eyes magnified by thick rimless glasses, Crusoe may have had the appearance of an accountant, but he had the bold imagination of the old-fashioned auto man—someone with a feel for the product and for the romance of bringing it to market. As one of the young men who worked for him at Ford said later, "He inspired great loyalty because unlike so many other executives he wasn't just pushing himself forward. When you worked for him, you were *making cars.*"

In 1945 Crusoe had retired early to his ranch in Cheboygan, but soon afterward Breech had asked him to help at Bendix, a job Crusoe self-effacingly called "making the pancakes and the syrup come out even." When Breech asked him to come to Ford with him, Crusoe shrugged and replied, "I can try it. I can't get hurt." But he went with the understanding that it would be an all-out enterprise. He said to a young man he recruited from GM to come with him, "If you want to swim away from the shore, okay. I don't know where I'm going." Crusoe came as Breech's executive assistant and was quickly made head of Finance, the most pressing of Ford's corporate trouble spots. Like Breech and everyone else who had looked over Ford's problems, Crusoe was shocked, especially by the fact that there was no breakdown of costs to indicate which aspects of the business were doing well and which badly. "Everything ran together like stained glass," he said later.

THE COMPANY HAD GOTTEN AWAY with one warmed-over prewar model. Breech knew it couldn't afford another one. At the same time that he was assem-bling a new management group, he worried about this problem. He came to the Engineering Department with Henry II to see what was being worked on as the next Ford.

"What's this car going to compete with?" he inquired after looking at drawings and models.

"Chevy and Plymouth," was the stylists' answer.

"What's it going to cost?" he asked.

Nobody could answer that question.

Breech looked at Henry and then shook his head. "We've got to find out what this car's going to cost. Unless we do we'll end up either losing our ass or abandoning the low-priced field to General Motors and Chrysler."

Breech asked Crusoe to hire a group of experienced estimators from GM. After they had examined the proposed new Ford, Crusoe concluded that even under manufacturing methods identical to GM's, which was not possible given Ford's obsolete plant, there was a built-in loss of $400 to Ford on every car. Getting this information, Breech said that the model he had seen would do for the new Mercury but not for the new Ford. Aware that it normally took three years to conceive, design, tool and produce a wholly new model, he decided that Ford had to go for broke. "I have a vision," he told the Policy Committee. "We start from scratch. We spend no time phonying up the old Ford, because this organization will be judged by the next car it produces and it had better be a new car. So we'll have a crash program as if in wartime!" The target date he set was just fourteen months away, June 1948, which would give Ford a jump on its competitors, whose new models would not be introduced until the fall. It was a gamble of money as well as time—$72 million in retooling costs for a new chassis, body and engine.

The 1949 model would be only the fourth major incarnation of the Ford, following the Model T, the Model A and the V-8. It would contain a number of the innovations Edsel had wanted in earlier Fords, such as an independent front suspension and a reengineered transmission with overdrive. Edsel would have liked the design as well—a grille built around the futuristic bullet shape, and the abandonment of front fenders in favor of "pontoon" sides. But would old Henry like it? Early in 1947 he and Clara came in to see the first full-size painted clay model produced by the designers. The model was so realistic that Clara tried to grab the door handle and open the car, then stepped back and said sheepishly, "It looked so real." Henry stood there awhile looking confused and then blurted out, "What engine are you going to put in this car?" When an engineer said that they planned one eight-cylinder model and one six-cylinder, observers who knew of the founder's hatred of six-cylinder cars flinched. But he merely mumbled something to himself and shuffled out the door. In the Engineering Building he ran into George Holmes, grandson of the midwife who had delivered him. "George, who are these men?" he asked, pointing at the dozens of young employees. Holmes replied, "They're engineers and draftsmen." Then old Henry asked, "Who are these women?"

Holmes said, "They're the secretaries to the engineers and draftsmen." Henry shook his head and went away mumbling a non sequitur, "If only my father could see me now."

He had been a legend in his own time and now he was a relic of that legend. His days were running down like the clocks he had continued to work on until his eyesight began to fail. In February and March 1947, he and Clara vacationed in Richmond Hill, Georgia. On the way down in their private railcar he forgot where he was and kept asking if it was time to "go upstairs" until Clara came along with a steady hand and forced him to sit. By the time they returned to Dearborn in early April, his condition seemed to have improved. On the morning of April 7 he seemed particularly well, almost like his old self, although the day was gray and rainy, as it had been all week. After getting up, he got a report from John McIntyre, head man of his private powerhouse, who said that the motors were underwater and that it would probably be best to go to the Dearborn Inn for the night. Henry laughed and replied, "My gracious, we have fireplaces. In Scotland and Ireland they cook *everything* in the fireplace." After a late breakfast, he asked Ray Dahlinger to drive him around town to look at the effects of the flooding. First they went down the road alongside the airport he had built many years earlier and from there to the Rouge itself, where they watched the rising waters lapping over the river's banks. Before going home Henry asked Dahlinger to swing by the Ford family cemetery on Greenfield Road, not giving a reason but saying he felt he ought to see it.

By the time he got home, the high water had receded somewhat. He walked down to the powerhouse, where workers were trying to fix the motors and restore electricity to the house. "Boy, you fellows been having a devil of a time here," he said. "I got a couple of radio programs I'd like to listen to tonight." After the workers said they'd try their best, Ford said, "Okay, well, I think I'll go back up to the house and see what they got to eat." The power went on long enough for him to listen to his favorite radio shows, then it abruptly went off again, leaving the big house in darkness. Henry and Clara went to bed by candlelight shortly after nine o'clock. A few minutes later he came out and asked for some milk. "I sleep so well when I have a glass of milk," he said. Then he went back to bed.

The Fords' maid, Rosa Buhler, was awakened about midnight by a frightened Clara. "I'm afraid that Mr. Ford seems very ill," she gasped. Buhler got the chauffeur to go for the doctor and then rushed up to the bedroom. Ford was sunken in the bed, breathing harshly, with Clara sitting next to him caressing his forehead. The maid realized at once that he was dying. She put another pillow under his head, and he tried to sit up, then put his head on Clara's shoulder like a tired child.

Clara kept saying, "Henry, *please* speak to me."

After a while they laid him back down. The harsh breathing slowed and Buhler said, "I think Mr. Ford is leaving us."

Refusing to understand, Clara said, "I'd better get dressed before the doctor comes," and went into another room to put on her clothes.

When Henry tried to fold his hands as if in prayer, Buhler called Clara back and they held each other as he died, the figure who had done more than any other to make power a fact of man's daily existence departing his life in darkness as he had entered it eighty-four years earlier.

As with the passing of any mythic figure, Henry Ford's death made the world slow down a moment and take notice. There were eulogies by President Harry Truman, Winston Churchill, Joseph Stalin and other world leaders. Over a hundred thousand people passed through the Henry Ford Museum, where the body lay in state. Ford had both made history and lived the history he made in a way that few other individuals ever had; he had changed the human map by discovering and colonizing the terra incognita of the machine. When he left the farm as a young man, one in five Americans lived in the city. When he died, the proportion was exactly reversed, largely because his Tin Lizzie had extended human range. At the time of his passing, Ford had made about as many cars as there were people in the United States when he was born. Largely because of him, one in seven American workers now had a job making automobiles or in a related industry. He had provided the engine that had powered his country into the American Century. He had begun his life with an open heart and an inquiring mind; eventually his mind had closed and his heart had hardened. He had been creative and destructive almost in equal parts, embodying the best and the worst of which an individual is capable.

These and other sentiments were echoed in the days before the first Henry Ford was buried. Yet when his grandson and namesake came out of the funeral services at St. Paul's Cathedral in Detroit with Clara on his arm, the speculation was less about what the first Henry Ford had been than what the second Henry Ford would become. "Ford is dead!" one voice in the crowd cried out. "Long live Ford!"

THIRTEEN

ENRY FORD WAS THE FIRST and last great giant of the auto industry. Even as his company was sinking in the thirties, he had continued to stand above it like a colossus. During his life he made the automobile an American innovation and conquered the world with it. And although it may not have seemed so at the time, his death was a recessional for that time of industrial conquest in the nation's life. In the years ahead this American hold on the identity of the automobile which he more than anyone else had established would weaken and finally slip. Even though it had been fraught with eccentricity and destructiveness, his time would come more and more to seem a golden age by comparison with what came after.

His death also marked the end of an era for the Ford family. It was ironic: old Henry had never been an emotional center for the rest of them. He was too peculiar a person for that, too much the Midwesterner requiring large emotional spaces; too deeply involved in his own strange drama to have time to create a dynastic imperative for his family. Yet he had defined their lives, if only in a negative way, dominating the family experience by his forceful grappling with his destiny and most of all by his treatment of Edsel. While he was alive, the rest of the family saw themselves in terms of their relationship to him. After his death, the intensity and drama he had provided for them by his negative presence evaporated. They were somehow ordinary, except for his name and company, and the unhealing scar of the memory he left behind.

They had all felt an ambivalence toward the old man. He was like some god of Oriental mythology—simultaneously creator and destroyer, the one who had made them significant but who also threatened that distinctive status. He dominated them not only in his acts but in the company he had built. This was the central fact of their lives, the purple to which they were born. The Fords might not be an aristocracy of demeanor and attitude in the way of other American families of great wealth and power. They were too green and isolated, too close to their rural Midwestern origins ever to have been gathered up into that notion of a special mission that distinguished other great American families. Yet they were far more like a royal house than all the rest in that they had a real kingdom—the Ford Motor Company—whose power and glory controlled their aspirations and achievements. This realm might be imperiled by a mad king like old Henry. It might have the tragic drama of a doomed prince like Edsel who would have proved the most noble if ever put on the throne. It might have dangerous usurpers like Harry Bennett. Yet the realm itself was eternal. And those Ford males who had survived its cataclysms—Edsel's three sons—saw it not just as a world of ceremonial roles, but as one of real power as well; a place where one could distinguish himself as a person and a Ford, which is what they set out to do in the postwar era.

GIVEN THE ROLE CLARA AND ELEANOR had played in getting old Henry to step back from the company, there was considerable speculation after his death that the men in the company would be controlled by a matriarchy, or at least a regency of women. This was a misreading of internal realities from the outside. Clara had never wanted influence at Ford; the only power she ever had was that of restraint and homey common sense. Early on, Clara had chosen her husband over her extended family, and after Henry's death her life was diminished. For a while she was something of a queen mother. But Henry II was too bitter about what had happened to his father to allow this image to be anything more than public relations. The only member of the next Ford generation really close to Clara was her granddaughter Dodie, who often brought her own children to Fairlane to spend the day baking apple pies and gossiping. ("We talked about everything under the sun, except my father," Dodie said later.)

So Clara lived on alone at Fairlane, as much an artifact as the giant collection of memorabilia clogging the fifty-six rooms. As the years passed she shut one room after another, finally spending most of her time in the wicker-filled sun porch or outside in the rose garden, sitting by herself and crying silently because of her loneliness. Eleanor never visited; and the grandchildren hated the place, even if they didn't say so, because it had been the lair of the man they believed had contributed to their father's death. Sometimes the company's Public Relations Department would try to schedule an event there, but one of Henry II's assistants would say, "God, no. You know he hates that place. He'd be just as happy if it collapsed in an earthquake."

In 1950 Clara became sick and went into the hospital for minor surgery. She came back home but was never really well after that, never able to get back into the garden which had been her refuge during the difficult years of her husband's domination by Harry Bennett and her own solace after his death. Her maid, Rosa Buhler, watched Clara sit in the breakfast room staring out with wrenching melancholy at the white peacocks she and Henry had allowed the free run of the place. Buhler brought food to her; Clara pushed it around on her plate and said sadly, "You know I can't eat." A few days later, on September 20, 1950, she was dead.

Henry II had wanted to get rid of Ray Dahlinger since his grandfather's death, but had kept him on the payroll out of deference to his grandmother. A few days after she died, Dahlinger's office was emptied and locked, and Ray and Evangeline were left on their own to spend the rest of their days as people who had been brought inside the eccentric circle Henry Ford drew around his life.

Not long after Clara's death, a search team headed by Deputy U.S. Archivist Robert Bahmer entered Fairlane and walked through the musty rooms like archaeologists who had stumbled onto the petrified remains of a remarkable life. The greatest collector in American history had amassed tons of material in addition to that which filled the Henry Ford Museum and Greenfield Village. There were antique hand tools, rare books, stacks of antique firearms. But most significant of all were the scores of boxes filled with papers which were packed so tightly into a dozen basement rooms that the doors hardly opened. On that first day of exploration Bahmer plunged his hand at random into one of those boxes and drew out a letter from the *Chicago Tribune*'s Robert McCormick asking old Henry's forgiveness for libeling him in their celebrated trial. The next thing he picked out was a telegram from Calvin Coolidge thanking Henry for supporting his election.

The dig into the Ford papers would last for years, finally allowing archivists and scholars to establish the documentary record of a remarkable American life. But if historians were ecstatic over the find, the Ford heirs were less enthusiastic about this part of their inheritance. For them, Fairlane was something of a white elephant. A few days after his grandmother's death, Henry made his first visit to the estate in months, saying to two of Fairlane's workmen, "You know, a lot of my grandfather's stuff is turning up missing. I'm going to put a chain on this [entry], and only you guys are going to have a key. Don't let anybody in there." Appraisers from the government arrived. Orders were given that nothing was to be touched for three months. Then the servants were told to lay everything out so that the four Ford heirs could come with their families to mark what they wanted and take it away.

If Clara was not a major influence on the next generation, neither was Eleanor. Her sons loved and respected her, but because she had never really dealt with the tragedy at the core of Edsel's life, instead seeing her role as filing away the sharp edges and making things as palatable as possible, she lacked the credibility to deal with the dynastic question. Her life after Edsel took on an aura of genteel loss. For a time she was escorted to social events by Hunter McDonnell, a bachelor uncle of Henry's wife, Anne. Someone raised the possibility of remarriage, but she said, "Oh no, I could never do that. Edsel is always at my side." She retreated deep into Gaukler Pointe. She continued to be close to her sister Josephine, wife of Ernest Kanzler, and to her daughter Dodie. The two women had formed an especially tight relationship in the months after Edsel's death, when Dodie was living at Gaukler Pointe with her infant son, Buhl, while her husband was serving in the Coast Guard. After the war ended, the "Ford-Fords," as Edsel had jokingly referred to Dodie and her husband, settled in Grosse Pointe so that Wally could set up a consulting business in interior design and she could be close to her mother. Eleanor called her every day, spending hours talking about trivialities.

Asked about her plans for her sons, Eleanor smiled naively and said, "The boys are on their own. They're good friends and things will work out." For a while it seemed that she was right. Benson had been elected to the board of directors the same time as Henry, June 1, 1943. He and his new wife, Edie, had had a rocky start; she had felt that the role of Ford consort was claustral and had briefly left him, coming back largely because Eleanor intervened to patch up the marriage. Now things were better between them. In 1943, not long after Benson became a member of the company's board of directors, Edie had written proudly to Henry and Clara: "A week from today we will be home. Ben will be a magnificent new second lieutenant.... Wait until you see him in his new uniform. He is handsomer than ever." Benson had been a little surprised when Henry II was named president. He didn't know in advance and wasn't consulted. Yet it was not in his temperament to worry about it. "Sweet" was the word people used for him as an adult, as they had when he was a boy. There was a sense of bemused melancholy about him, accented by his long face. It was not apparent to someone who didn't know him that he had an eye problem. Yet his bearing was slightly off compass, a way of compensating for his disability that made him seem slightly out of kilter.

Upon leaving the Army in 1945, he had come to work at Ford without definite duties but assuming that his brother would make a place for him. He did an apprenticeship in various aspects of the business over the next couple of years. He was punctual, impressing people with his three-piece suits and then causing them amusement when they realized he still wore his square-toed army-issue shoes. Some things were hard for him. Angriest of all the Ford grandchildren at old Henry during Edsel's final illness, he nonetheless couldn't stand to see the old man's decline. At one point he called his close friend Eddie Stroh: "I got to get out of here. Everyone is waiting for my grandfather to die. It gives me the creeps." He and Stroh drove to Chicago in one of Edsel's Continentals, registered at the Ambassador and spent the weekend making the rounds of night-spots.

On the executive "fast track," Benson worked for a while as part of Tex Thornton's planning office and, in 1947, was put on the Policy Committee. The other members were struck by the fact that never once did he say anything at the meetings; he just sat there, happily dominated, as he had been since he was a boy, by Henry II. Early in 1948, Henry announced Benson's election to a vice-presidency and his appointment as chief executive of Lincoln-Mercury. This appeared to be a key move, for his appointment came at a time when there was a big push to make the vexed division work by establishing a separate Lincoln-Mercury dealer organization, along with three new plants. ("This appointment comes when the division is on the threshold of its greatest expansion program," Henry announced. "There are very definite plans for the future of Lincoln-Mercury. We intend to go after the business in the medium- and high-priced fields more aggressively.") Yet it was really a sort of mirage. Lincoln-Mercury was not really an independent division, its policy and finance still being controlled by central staff. His wife, Edie, said, "Finally Ben is getting a chance to get out from under Henry's thumb." Yet he was still passive, as he had been when he and Henry were young. His close friend Carlton Higbie remembered traveling with him to Los Angeles on business shortly after Benson had gotten his title at Lincoln-Mercury. They stopped at the dealership there, and Benson happened to note during the conversation with the general manager that the building looked a bit run down. When they came back for another meeting the next day, they found that the building was being painted, inside and out. Horrified at having been taken seriously, Benson muttered to himself, "I'm going to have to learn to keep my goddamned mouth shut."

Next it was Bill's turn. He had never had the same relationship with Henry as Benson because of the difference in their ages. As the youngest child he missed some of the drama in his father's life and death. He had never seen the tension between Edsel and old Henry, for instance, and therefore never hated his grandfather as his older brothers had. In the months immediately after his father's death, the responsibility for Eleanor had fallen to him, and he had escorted her through the first days of her long mourning, first in Florida and then back in Grosse Pointe. ("Bill had to cope with my mother when Father died," Dodie said later, "because he was the only one around. Ben was in the Army and Henry was taking over the company. I was married and had a baby. The whole load got dumped on Bill.")

After Eleanor had begun to recover, Bill, just nineteen, had enlisted in naval cadet training. He had hoped to see action immediately in the Pacific, but was stationed in New York. While there he was visited more often than he wanted by his mother. On one of her trips, she discovered that her old friend Isabel Firestone was in town and arranged for her and her daughter Martha, a Vassar student, to come to lunch at Voisin. Petite and blond, barely five feet tall and wearing a size two shoe, Martha was perky and attractive, and she had a brittle humor that led Bill to feel she wore her college nickname "Stoney" well. After the lunch Mrs. Firestone remarked about Bill, "He's so good-looking!" Martha told her that she was allergic to the idea of dynastic marriages and so not to try to matchmake, but later on, when Bill was stationed in California, the two corresponded secretly.

Although he had grown up somewhat pampered as his mother and father's "pride and joy," Bill was the only Ford of his generation who had enjoyed competitive athletics. ("I always liked sports because they involved a democracy of talent," he said later on.) Flight training was extremely rigorous, involving swimming, running, boxing and mastering an obstacle course. On graduating from preflight school each cadet had a number put on his back and took part in a competition designed by former heavyweight champion Gene Tunney. Of all the hundreds of cadets entered, Bill finished first. It was a moment he never forgot. "Without anyone knowing my name or who I was or whether I had a dime," he recalled later, "I did it on my own."

As the war ended he left the Navy and enrolled at Yale, where he captained the soccer and tennis teams. He and Martha Firestone continued to date, keeping their relationship secret from their respective mothers as long as possible. Both twenty-two years old, they finally decided to get married. The ceremony took place in Akron on June 17, 1947. Just outside the entrance of the hotel where their reception was held sat a Model T from 1908—the year old Henry had first met Harvey Firestone, his future good friend and, with Edison and John Burroughs, camping companion. Among the wedding presents was an architect's drawing of a house from Eleanor with this note: "Perhaps it won't look like this but it will be your home—Momma."

People who looked only at Bill's small size and gracious manner missed the toughness that had made him such a good athlete. But if they crossed him, they soon learned their mistake. When he was twenty-one, for instance, Bill went to Pierre Heftler, the Fords' family attorney, for information about his financial status. "Well," Heftler said, "of course you've got your father's estate and your grandfather's and we'll keep them in trust for you till you're thirty-five." Bill said calmly, "I want it now." The attorney was taken aback and Bill repeated, "I want it right now. I'm legally entitled to the money at the age of twenty-one." He got it.

If anything, Bill was so sure of himself that there was a touch of arrogance in his character. Tennis great Bill Talbert, who had played with Bill, saw this flaw in his tennis game. "He was an excellent player, but he had a problem. He would go for too big a shot before he was ready for it."

He had studied engineering at Yale. He wasn't particularly interested in the subject, but he kept at it because he believed it would be relevant to working at Ford later on. As a child, he had never been as close to the company as his older brothers were, but he had always known that he, too, was ultimately headed there. "That's all there was since I can remember," he said later. "It never occurred to me that I wouldn't work there. I had loved cars ever since I was a boy. That's the only line of work I had thought about from the day I was born. I thought about it in boarding school. I knew I would end up in the company. There was never an alternative."

In June 1948 he was made a director of Ford. While finishing at Yale he had worked summers on the assembly line at the Rouge and loved it. After graduating he went to work full time, Henry making the announcement: "In order to become acquainted with the Company my brother will spend considerable time in each of the staff and operating divisions before becoming assigned permanently."

For a while he worked under sales manager John Davis. When labor negotiations with the UAW began in June 1949, Bill sat in on the company team headed by John Bugas. The negotiations turned out to be a test of his mettle. Reuther and his men constantly heckled him about his grandfather. His face flushed with anger, Bill wanted to strike back at them, but members of Bugas' team counseled restraint. "No, you can't win this," one of them told Bill. "You'll have to sit there and take it." He did take it in an impressive show of strength that won the respect of Reuther, although Bill continued to think of the labor leader as an unprincipled demogogue.

The closest Eleanor or anyone else ever came to specifying the form of the next generation was in something she said to Bill. "She told me that Henry, being the oldest, would probably be boss. But she said that Benson and I would sit beside him, his right and left hands, his young brothers on whom he would be able to depend." But this sort of constitutional arrangement didn't hold much appeal for Henry, who had already sensed the power in his name. While his brothers were learning how to be Fords, he was already playing the role to the hilt.

Henry was automatically a major figure in Detroit. In 1948 he went to Europe. For his wife, Anne, it was an opportunity to go on a clothes-buying spree and to hobnob with royalty. For Henry it was a chance to step into the great affairs shaping the Cold War world. At a stopover in Scandinavia he said he had thought about opening a plant in Finland but decided against it because he didn't want "to get involved with the Russians." Yet it was Ford Motor Company politics that proved most important on this trip. He and Breech tried to buy 51 percent of Volkswagen, but were turned down. Afterward they went to England to visit the great Ford plant at Dagenham and contemplate the Fords' European holdings, which were now in partial ruins as a result not only of Nazi takeovers during the war but also of a seriously obsolete organization and management. Old Henry had made English Ford a proconsul for his empire, giving it a large ownership in the other European companies. Henry II now decided that the company would reacquire this interest from English Ford and that European headquarters from Stockholm to Lisbon would be controlled from the United States. Later that spring the new Ford International Division had a meeting in Dearborn attended by representatives from all over the world—a multilingual gathering of the greatest industrial empire since the heyday of Standard Oil.

Back home Henry and Anne adopted a royal lifestyle of their own. The birth of their son, Edsel II, in 1948 was regarded as the appearance of an heir apparent to the throne of Ford. When the King of the Belgians visited Detroit, Henry and Anne went to meet his plane at the Detroit airport, afterward entertaining him lavishly. Anne found such power in the Ford name that one society matron remarked cuttingly, "She started out being one of fourteen kids and she wound up being Queen of the U.S.A." Some people who remembered the first dinner she had given in Grosse Pointe years earlier, when she insisted on saying grace as the meal was served, were amused by her newly acquired regal airs.

In his social life, Henry was trying to fulfill his father's idea of what a Ford should be, just as he was trying, through his rehabilitation of the company, to fulfill Edsel's notion of what a corporation should be. But Henry was a different type of person from his father. His repressed side, fun-loving and irresponsible, kept popping out even as he was taking on one obligation after another—an episode of vulgarity, a night of too much drinking. His sense of duty to his father's memory was real. But what if he did not really fit the genteel image through which Edsel had tried to discharge what he regarded as the duties of a Ford? It was a question others asked, but one which Henry, so much closer in temperament to his grandfather than to his father, never considered.

Henry was forced to act older than his years. But sometimes it seemed that this behavior was only skin deep. At heart there was something vulnerable about him, an unresolved immaturity that endeared him to older men like Breech. On a golfing and business trip to Florida, the company men went to dinner one night while Henry was at a meeting. Walking out of the restaurant, they saw him spot them and come running in their direction. He jumped on Bugas' shoulders for a piggyback ride, shrieking, "This company is fun!"

THERE WAS GOOD REASON FOR exuberance. The 1949 Ford, a car whose futuristic lines embodied a kind of optimism about the postwar tomorrow, was a tremendous success. When it was introduced on June 8, 1948, at the Waldorf-Astoria in New York, nearly fifty thousand people crammed into the gold-and-white ballroom to inspect it. Breech's gamble had paid off, as the car came off the assembly lines three months sooner than its competitors. Sales figures reflected the head start. In 1949 the company sold 807,000 Fords—the most since the Model A was introduced twenty years earlier—along with 187,000 Mercurys and 38,000 Lincolns, sending it over the one million mark. It was still in third place, some five thousand cars behind Chrysler, but profits were rising—$94 million in 1948 and $177 million in 1949.

This triumph ensured the company's survival, which had been so much in doubt when Henry took over. It also allowed Ernie Breech to consolidate his control. For the first time in company history, it seemed, there was no internecine strife among the top men at Ford, and a new generation of executives could do their work without fear of purges or coups. A transition generation was already making way for them. After running the Rouge for years with the efficiency of a true Sorensen disciple, Mead Bricker was ready to retire. John Davis, who had been a mentor to Henry II in the dark days of the Bennett battle, suffered a heart attack and, while maintaining his position as vice-president, began to play an emeritus role. John Bugas, the remaining figure of that original triumvirate on which Henry had relied, had trouble adjusting to the Breech regime. He knew that Breech thought he was out of his depth because he was not an auto man. He arranged to accompany Breech on a European trip, telling an aide, "Well, I'm going to have him five days on the boat, and if I don't get him to change his mind about me, it's all over." During the voyage he used his considerable personal charm to good advantage on Breech, and by the time they returned the two were social friends.

Tex Thornton presented a somewhat more difficult problem. He had been reporting directly to Henry when Breech came on board and brought

Lewis Crusoe with him. One of the first items of business for the two General Motors veterans was how to bring the ambitious Thornton and his Whiz Kids into line. Breech announced that the group was to be broken up and assigned to various duties and departments under Crusoe's jurisdiction. Most of the Whiz Kids bowed to the inevitable, regarding the GM people as older and wiser figures from whom they could learn; Thornton saw them as competition. As he maneuvered for leverage, an odd relationship developed between him and Crusoe. Thornton, who had managed somehow to get one of the scarce company cars, would pick up fellow Whiz Kid Jim Wright and then Crusoe every morning. They would talk all the way to the office, Crusoe telling Thornton about the "realities" of the auto business and Thornton telling him that "organization and positive management" worked whatever the industry they were applied to. The symbolism of this ongoing conversation, Wright felt, was that Crusoe wanted Thornton to know he had a lot to learn, while Tex wanted the older man to know that he already knew a lot.

Meanwhile, Thornton warred with Breech through memos, proposing strategies which Breech pointed out were flawed. Thornton, still popular with Henry, often went outside the official line of communication to talk to him.

It seemed to many that Henry, anxious to maintain his own primacy in the corporation, unconsciously encouraged the situation, which blurred the lines of authority and set his executives in conflict. Sometimes he would summon Thornton over the intercom and ask him to come to his office, where they would gossip about what the other Whiz Kids were doing and where Thornton would give him an uncensored view of his thoughts about Breech and the company's future. Although Thornton attended these debriefing sessions eagerly because they kept his ambitions alive, he would have preferred it if Henry had found a more discreet way for them to meet, since the intimacy of the Ford Administration Building made secrecy impossible. Every time he was summoned to Henry's office, Thornton had to pass under the gaze of Breech, who purposefully left his door ajar so that he would know when these conferences took place.

Feeling that Crusoe was more vulnerable than Breech, Thornton concentrated his fire on him. "Crusoe should have been smarter than that," he would say about some decision. Or "Crusoe should have seen that this was the wrong way." Finally Crusoe had enough of it. His face constricted with anger, he walked into Breech's office and said, "I've been here awhile and I think I've made a contribution. If you want me to stay, get rid of that son of a bitch."

Seeing the handwriting on the wall even before this confrontation, Thornton had already begun looking for an escape hatch. He had heard about an eccentric genius named Howard Hughes and arranged a meeting in which he told Hughes that he believed there was a big future for advanced electronics in the postwar period, in both the civilian and the military areas. Hughes agreed and told him that perhaps the two of them could do business. Nonetheless, Thornton was unprepared when the final blow came at Ford. He appeared at a Whiz Kid party one Friday night with a long face, finally explaining, "Ernie Breech called me into his office today. He said, 'Tex, you've been running around here getting into everyone's hair and acting like you're the executive vice-president of this company. You're not. I am. So you're going to leave.' "

After Thornton finished there was shocked silence. Then Jack Reith said he'd quit in a show of support. Most of the others agreed—all but McNamara, who stood up and said with the emotionless clarity for which he was already well known, "We ought not to do anything in haste. Let's wait and see what develops." Thornton agreed. By the time he cleaned out his office and came to say goodbye to his old AAF friends, he was his usual irrepressible self. He told them that he was going to do something big with his life, that it would probably involve building a company from scratch, and when he succeeded any of them who needed a job could always come to him. *

THESE PERSONNEL MATTERS SEEMED important but were dwarfed by larger issues. The 1949 Ford model was a success in styling and sales, but Breech knew it was because of the pent-up demand on the part of consumers who hadn't been able to buy cars since before the war. Moreover, the car was not good in terms of quality. Breech was fond of repeating what a friend had told him: "This car is a piece of junk. The body doesn't even fit. Water and dust always get in." He himself had listed well over a thousand different defects. The problem was that no one person could be held accountable for the problems plaguing the car.

At this point, Breech decided to press on with the next step in the decentralization plan—a step that Lewis Crusoe had proposed when he was first hired but that until now had been impracticable: to create a separate Ford Division whose head would be responsible for the development and sales of all Ford cars. The division would have its own engineering and finance people, its own sales staff. This bold move brought the Ford Motor Company a step closer to the GM model, which had succeeded largely because of its division structure—a galaxy of what were in effect independent minicompanies within the larger company. It was a conceptual as well as organizational jump, allowing Breech and Henry, in the moments of confidence about the future that were becoming more frequent, to speculate about a time when the Ford would not be the only viable product of the company, but one of many truly competitive cars.

The creation of the Ford Division and the improved balance sheet allowed the executives who had come in with Breech and Crusoe to congratulate themselves for having taken a chance. It also allowed them to dream of

---

* Later on, after he had started Litton Industries, Thornton did put out feelers to several Ford executives, including many of the Whiz Kids.

a day when the slogan "Beat Chevrolet," which Henry had made his battle cry, would be replaced by "Beat GM." They all dreamed of a bigger and healthier company with more and better-paying executive jobs at the top. For the time being, however, it was clear that whoever ran the Ford Division, which was for all practical purposes the company, would be a force unto himself. There was only one real candidate—Crusoe himself.

After Thornton's departure Crusoe had taken over responsibility for organizational planning, while, as head of Finance, he oversaw the introduction of the new systems of financial control and the development of a central corporate staff that had brought Ford into the modern era of accounting and management. Henry acknowledged that Crusoe was the driving force at Ford. After agreeing to his appointment as head of the Ford Division, Henry walked up to him and shook his hand, commenting, "Well, Lewis, you'll be running practically the whole Ford Motor Company."

Breech remained a sort of overlord for Ford. He was interested in everything. When his wife, Thelma, found that her mink coat stuck onto the upholstery of the Ford, Breech devised a "mink test" which all seat covers of the future had to pass. While attending church in Dearborn one Sunday, he noticed several company cars in the lot. Bothered that they were being used on a weekend, he went out with a clipboard during the sermon and took down license numbers, and he dealt with the offenders the next day.

But Crusoe became the ramrod of corporate operations. Upon being named head of the new Ford Division, he immediately set up his headquarters in the old Parts Depot and began to assemble his team. Three months later at a meeting of the Product Planning Committee, Breech, realizing that he had created a job close to his own in power, tried to backtrack and reclaim some of the power he had given away. Crusoe picked up the gauntlet immediately, serving notice of his intention to protect the integrity of his new domain. He would welcome advice, he told Breech and Henry at this meeting, but he intended to "guard the independent thinking of the division as though it was an entirely separate company." Breech acquiesced. Using a metaphor from football, a sport at which he had excelled as a young man despite his diminutive size, he said he would be the coach, but Crusoe would be the quarterback calling his own plays and having the responsibility for getting across the goal line.

Henry had followed his grandfather's tradition of hosting a daily "round table" lunch at the Rotunda. Crusoe was conspicuously absent from these meetings, eating with his own men at the Parts Depot—a gesture that seemed to say that the real work of the company took place away from the executive suites. Capable of a laconic humor that belied his severe appearance, Crusoe once took a look at an exhaust pipe a designer was proposing for a tail of a Lincoln and said to him, "Gee, looks like a guppy's anus, doesn't it?" But he was also capable of harshness to people he felt didn't cut it. Upset with stylist George Walker for what he felt were poor design elements in the 1949 Ford, he once asked him to line up the models he had made for the next year's Ford.

Looking the candidates over, he said, "George, which model do you like?" Walker looked hesitantly at the three models and said, "Well, Mr. Crusoe, I like Model B." Crusoe looked scornfully at his choice and then said, "You know what, George? Model B looks like it has been in an accident."

Crusoe took under his wing younger men he considered promising. He created a special élan among members of his staff by staging get-togethers at his Bloomfield Hills house and his Cheboygan, Michigan, ranch. His sayings had the status of holy writ, and his young men were always quoting the statements of "Lewie." ("This is a nickel-and-dime business," was his rationale for cost-cutting on every item that went into a car. "A dime on a million units is $100,000. We'll practically cut your throat around here for a quarter.")

Chief among Crusoe's young men was former Whiz Kid Jack Reith. Almost too handsome, with wavy hair parted in the middle, a flashing smile, and a combination of shyness and aggression which made women notice him, Reith radiated a sort of kinetic charm. His flamboyant gestures had an element of will. Like other Depression babies—his father, a Midwestern land developer, had lost everything after the Crash—he had made caution and conservatism the cornerstone of his world-view. Yet people thought of him as reckless. They didn't realize that he took risks not so much for the thrill as because they promised a shortcut to the security that would keep him from ever suffering the want he had grown up with. As his wife, Maxine, later said, "Jack was driven to make sure the same thing didn't happen to me and the kids that had happened to him and his family."

Reith had always prided himself on a sure entrepreneurial touch. While at college, he had rented a house and then rented out rooms to other students. After graduating in 1936 he was interviewed for a position with General Electric. When they didn't contact him, he sent them a wire saying he had been offered another job and if they wanted him they'd have to act fast— a ploy that worked. Even after he was employed he continued to make money on the side, buying cars on the East Coast and hiring people to drive them to California, where they could be resold at a profit.

Reith had been Thornton's unofficial second in command in the AAF until supplanted by Robert McNamara. The same thing happened in the Whiz Kids' first day at Ford, when Thornton put Reith in charge of the reorganization plan he began drafting for Ford but soon replaced him with Jim Wright in a move that seemed to indicate a lack of confidence. But Crusoe saw Reith as a young man of promise and made him his chief of staff for the new Ford Division. It was a show of confidence that gave Reith more daring and more commitment. He responded by putting in seventeen hours a day, seven days a week. One of the men who worked under him recalled later a particularly stressful period when they were working their fourth Sunday in a row. Reith's team walked into the office and saw him at a desk with a big easel covered with a sheet. He said, "Well, boys, we're going to start with a little Sunday service. I want you all to bow your heads but keep looking up here." They did and he ripped the sheet off to reveal a painting of a cathedral. "OK," he continued, "we get one minute of silence and then I want you to get your asses to work." This was vintage Reith. He liked to appear flinty and tough, fearful that anyone would see even a hint of weakness. But whenever there was a firing that had to be done he delegated the job to his aide Chase Morsey. "You do it, Chase," he would say, "I can't stand the sight of blood."

Using Reith and others like him, Crusoe made the Ford Division into his own private realm. He rode herd on design and styling. He set up an executive training program whose first recruits included future Ford presidents Philip Caldwell and Donald Petersen. Breech watched all this with ambivalence. He understood that the Ford Division would probably succeed, and no one appreciated Lewis Crusoe's formidable talents more than he. But he also saw how independent Crusoe was becoming. It was a tendency that concerned him not only because of the headstrong tendencies Crusoe had shown in his pre-Ford past, but also because of the recent change he saw in Henry. Breech knew that he could no longer count on automatic backing from Henry in the conflicts that inevitably came up at company meetings. He had watched Henry tilt toward Crusoe on the question of authority for the Ford Division. As Henry's confidence in Crusoe grew, Breech could not be sure how far the tilt would go. The authority Crusoe had taken for the Ford Division was authority taken from Breech. He tried to contain the loss by having the Finance Department of the central office oversee Crusoe's activities. His chief agent in this effort was the new company controller, Robert McNamara, *his* favorite Whiz Kid.

McNamara was called "the nay-sayer" by other men. Even his appearance—hair slicked down and precisely parted as if by calipers, granny glasses like impenetrable disks, the bulldog jaw—suggested pugnacious negation. McNamara was a bottom-liner whose job, as Breech saw it, was to use figures to rein in the imagination of product men like Crusoe and his team of zesty young designers and engineers.

The struggle was almost metaphorical. On one side there were the "bean counters" like McNamara, with no feel for the product. On the other side were the product men like Crusoe, men with "gasoline in their veins" whom the bean counters derided as "hot dogs." Gene Bordinat, who would become one of Ford's great stylists, said later, "To be a good product man you have to be ruled in part by your emotions. We assume that all cars *work*. But people *buy* cars, the product man understands, because they see in them *something that turns them on!*"

Because of these secret alliances and unacknowledged struggles for power that entered the Breech-Crusoe relationship, the company became a genteel battleground. No sooner had the Ford Division opened shop than Crusoe discovered that the "bean counters" in Finance had decided, for reasons of economy, to scrap the V-8 and produce only six-cylinder models as Chevrolet did, in order to save a few dollars. Jack Reith's aide Chase Morsey launched a passionate protest, saying that ever since he was a boy he had owned a V-8, that it was a beautiful engine, and that as far as the public was concerned, he

believed, the V-8 *was* Ford. It was the sort of personal testimony most executives would have dismissed. But Crusoe took Morsey seriously and
commissioned a survey of all Ford dealers which revealed that over 90 percent of them wanted a V-8 if the added cost was only $100 or less. Armed with
the results of the survey, Crusoe went to Breech and got the decision of the
bean counters reversed.

But if the battle for the V-8 was a normal skirmishing within the corporate planning system, the conflict behind it between the company's two most
powerful executives—a struggle Henry had helped instigate by his inclination
to create subtle conflicts that would preserve his own power—had significant
consequences. Quality had been the paramount public complaint about the
'49 Ford, and it was to remedy this situation that Crusoe approached Finance
with a request for funds to modernize the plants in which the cars were produced. While McNamara and his aides stalled on the request, Crusoe did his
best to keep Ford competitive, a job made harder when Chevrolet came out
with the rakish new 1950 Bel Aire—the first "hardtop convertible." The tooling costs for the 1949 Ford had been so large that McNamara and Finance
would allow Crusoe only minimal funds to respond with a "facelift" on the
1949 over the next two years, until the production of the all-new model
planned for 1952. "We are going to have to live in sin with this shell until we
get the '52 out," Crusoe told his executives. To offset Chevy's styling coup,
Ford designers quickly developed the "Crestliner," coming in three colors and
with a loop on the side reminiscent of the classic Bugattis and Duesenbergs.
Crusoe walked into the studio, saw what they had come up with and said,
"That's it! I don't want one thing changed!"

His efforts worked. The facelifted 1950 model sold 1,519,000 cars, pushing Ford ahead of Chrysler and closer to Chevrolet. In the spring of 1951, the
all-new 1952 was introduced. A little boxier, with a discreet scoop around the
rear wheels to suggest fenders and Ford's first one-piece windshield, the
model had a feeling of newness, particularly because GM and Chrysler did not
introduce new models that year. The production controls instituted because
of the Korean War held down total sales, yet Ford captured 17.6 percent of the
market, closing in on Chevrolet's 20.5 percent. GM was now taking them seriously. Its sales manager came into the display room at the Rotunda to see the
sleek 1952, stared at it as if weighing its substance and said with gruff admiration, "How much does that son of a bitch weigh?"

Crusoe's personal velocity was now carrying the entire company with
him. Liberated from his career of accounting and recognizing that he had the
chance of a lifetime, the chance to go all the way, Crusoe pushed Ford ahead.
With Reith at his side, he began an audacious assault on the market, chasing
the great consumer explosion of the 1950s. The 1949 Ford had two lines and
seven models. By 1953 there were four car lines and fourteen models. The
era the industry had entered was an auto man's heaven replete with chrome,
gadgets and a huge menu of extras. Part functional necessity and part fantasy
object, the automobile had become a sort of siren beckoning men like Crusoe.

Marshaling his forces like a general in battle, he began what he called the Competitive Analysis Department, part of which involved clandestine spying against GM. "Their job was getting pictures," Chase Morsey later recalled. "We knew GM was testing out in Arizona. Our guys would climb fences out there at their proving grounds with telephoto cameras strapped to their necks."

One of the things Ford spies saw was something brand-new and radically different from anything else on the market—a prototype of what became the Corvette sports car. Like a chess player, Crusoe immediately reacted with a gambit of his own—not simply a competing sports car, but a more comfortable automobile with a sporty image, what he called a "boulevard car." McNamara and the finance people in the central office said that the new car couldn't make money and tried to kill it by holding back funds for tooling. Crusoe beat them back by the sheer force of his conviction. It wouldn't be necessary for his boulevard car to pay its way by volume sales, he pointed out. It could help Ford by functioning as an "apple in the window"—the stunning machine that would build traffic in the dealers' showrooms. When it appeared, the Thunderbird, as he named his creation, outsold the Corvette three to one.

Crusoe's great achievement as head of the Ford Division was to make Ford, hitherto a car of the masses, respectable for the middle class. He created a range of Fords so that those in the upper price range began to compete with GM's middle-priced car, while those in the lower price range competed with Chevrolet. Because of Crusoe the "Beat GM" hung up a few years earlier began now to seem less like empty bravado.

THE BENEfiCIARY OF ALL THIS creativity was, of course, Henry. The days when he was pitied as the outmatched inheritor of a declining kingdom were long gone. He was now regarded as the leader of one of the most powerful industrial organizations in the nation, the man who had resurrected the Ford Motor Company. And the effort was given historical resonance by the fiftieth-anniversary celebration of 1953. The event was a cultural event marked by a special edition of *The Ed Sullivan Show* and by hour-long specials on both NBC and CBS television. A commemorative medallion was struck showing the joined profiles of old Henry, Edsel and Henry II. A Norman Rockwell painting showing the three men in profile—versions of a single Ford face in old age, middle age and youth—was commissioned.

To the degree that it was useful public relations, Henry willingly allowed himself to be gathered up into this glorified Ford tradition. To the degree that it involved a *real* past, however, he was monumentally ambivalent. The fiftieth-anniversary celebration was partly based on materials in the Ford archives which had been developed out of the tons of material dis-

covered at Fairlane when Clara died. Old Henry's papers were thoroughly catalogued, and so were Edsel's. When Henry II went through Fairlane, at that
time temporary headquarters of the archives, on one of his rare visits in 1952,
he noted the series of boxes containing the papers. He stopped for a moment
and flipped through the collections. He wasn't interested in his grandfather's
files, considering them "dead history," but the "Edsel B. Ford Papers" were
something else again, history that continued to cut to the bone. Henry opened
one of the boxes, which happened to contain some of his father's personal correspondence. Muttering, "Oh, no, Mother wouldn't like this," he directed that
all of his father's papers be forwarded to his attorneys, who ultimately ordered
that 90 percent of them be destroyed. Ford archivists pleaded for a stay of exe-
cution for the material, pointing out that it was tantamount to erasing Edsel
Ford's contribution to the company, as well as his biography. But Henry could
not be moved. Ernest Kanzler later commented, "I think Henry felt that there
had been enough questions asked, enough poking around." Yet Henry II was
not just concerned about propriety; he wanted to obliterate that dimension
of the family life involving his father's humiliation, a story which had become
the Ford's dirty little secret. His grandfather had said that history was bunk;
Henry II made it bunk by systematically destroying it.

The net result of the fiftieth-anniversary celebration was to allow Henry
II to inhabit the Ford legend, thus increasing his stature as a national business
leader. In return for his support in the 1952 election, President Eisenhower
appointed him an alternate delegate to the United Nations.

"I went to the UN to learn about the world," Henry would later say of his
motives for taking the post. "I was just a kid. I didn't know anything about
the world. I had worked like hell for Eisenhower. Otherwise he never paid any
attention to me. But he did ask me to go to the UN."

Henry made his maiden speech on free trade and soon afterward clashed
with members of the Soviet delegation. Later he described his relations with
the Russians: "When I met them in the hall in the morning, they'd smile at me.
I suppose somebody told them to do it." Asked whether he smiled back,
Henry said he did. Did someone tell him to do it? "Yes." Who? "My mother."

There was no doubt that his celebrity had achieved critical mass in the
outer world. But how much power did he have in the company, the only place
where it counted for a Ford? There it was not so clear. The advantage of the
GM system that he had worked so hard to implant in the company was that
it could eliminate arbitrary decision-making; the disadvantage for Henry was
that it threatened to make him just another executive, a figurehead secondary
in importance to Ernie Breech. One day in 1953 corporate counsel William
Gossett overheard Henry dressing down P.R. man Earl Newsom for giving
Breech so much credit for the company's turnaround: "What do you think *I*
was doing all that time?" He hired Charles Moore, until then on Newsom's
payroll, as his own personal public-relations director, signaling his intention
to begin taking credit for the company's achievements himself. He also

opened a personal office in Washington, an indication that he intended to wheel and deal in the larger political world.

In fact, Breech was no longer the supremely important figure inside Ford that he had been. With Crusoe's success, the erosion of his authority had become more and more obvious. As one Ford executive said later on, "All the Fords, even Dodie, were always talking about what a great job Crusoe was doing." Whenever Breech proposed something, Henry would immediately ask, "What does Lewie think about this?" Those close enough to make a judgment knew that in matters concerning operations and product, Ernie Breech was no longer the top executive, after Henry, in the company. Lewis Crusoe was. Yet the official hierarchy remained unchanged. Crusoe did not challenge Breech directly. He did not want Breech's job. He wanted to make Ford cars and to make Ford's battle plan against GM.

With each new sales record that Crusoe broke, Breech watched Henry's inbred caution recede a little further. He knew that as long as Crusoe succeeded, his power would grow. Product made money. Finance, which was the seat of Breech's power, could only count and spend it. Crusoe's success caused a shift in the company as well as in the marketplace. From now on, the corporate leadership at Ford would belong to those who had proved themselves in the end-product divisions where the money was made. It was a prospect of concern to Breech not only because of his own situation, but also because of the cloud it cast over the future of McNamara, his chief aide in the struggle against Crusoe.

McNamara was brilliant, puritanical, and arrogantly self-confident; a little like one of George Eliot's smug parsons, somebody remarked, a man mesmerized by his own virtue. He stunned listeners with his critical acumen. He prepared for Executive Committee meetings as if cramming for Ph.D. orals, poring over minutes of previous meetings to see who had said what and arming himself with arguments for the coming debate. Gerry Lynch, his chief aide for two years, once had an unusually intimate discussion with McNamara, who asked for Lynch's evaluation of his future chances with the company.

"You want me to be frank?" Lynch asked.

"Yes," McNamara answered.

"Well, you could go all the way to the top except for two things. First, you don't have sensitivity to people as people. Second, you're never wrong."

McNamara paused a moment before replying: "With respect to people, I agree that I don't have the rapport that some of the backslappers do. I can't help it. With respect to never being wrong, I just analyze every situation with all the tools at my command. When the decision is made, that's it."

But McNamara was somewhat more devious than he gave himself credit for. For instance, he once made a decision regarding the number of bolts in an engine against the judgment of engineer Harley Copp. Stung less by the decision itself than by the cavalier fashion in which McNamara had spurned his expertise, Copp wrote down the details of the argument in an *aide-*

mémoire. Subsequently, McNamara's decision cost Ford in money and reputation. Hearing that Henry was on the warpath, Copp mentioned to another executive that McNamara was responsible for the mistake. "How do you know?" the man asked. "Because I wrote it down in a memo to myself," Copp answered after describing the incident. The next day the executive came to Copp and said, "I told Bob what you said and he asked me to tell you that he wants all copies of your memo."

When he had been made controller, the title seemed perfect for McNamara. He wanted to control everyone and everything; he wanted to control the company itself. Yet there were certain obstacles in his path to higher offices. Stubbornly insisting on living in the university town of Ann Arbor instead of in the auto executive enclave at Bloomfield Hills, he maintained an emotional as well as spatial distance from the company that was interpreted as haughtiness. A more serious drawback was his aloofness from product. Walking through a styling studio in the mid-1950s, McNamara was asked by designer George Walker which of the models on display he liked. McNamara pointed at one and said quite seriously, "That one, but it doesn't move me like the stained-glass windows at Notre Dame." After he had left, Walker shook his head incredulously and said to one of his colleagues: "Shit, man! These guys who buy these cars never heard of Notre Dame. They just want something that looks like it's laying down rubber and going ninety while it's standing still."

Jack Reith was very much McNamara's opposite, both personally and professionally, and their clash had been almost preordained once Reith had seen McNamara displace him as Tex Thornton's chief aide. An almost obsessive risk-taker working largely from intuition, Reith was outgoing and social. While McNamara was sitting quietly at home listening to chamber music, Reith was likely to be banging on the set of drums he kept in his family room, or practicing with the jazz combo he sometimes played with. McNamara was a confirmed monogamist; Reith, it was rumored, had a "zipper problem."

But the most significant difference between the two men had to do with automobiles, which Reith, unlike McNamara and the other Whiz Kids, loved as much as any Detroit product man. He had shown his ability as head of the Ford Division's spectacularly successful product programs. And more than anyone else, he had shared Crusoe's triumphs. Crusoe, who was not profligate with his emotions, had adopted Reith almost as a son. When Reith was hospitalized with polio for two months in 1952, Crusoe had called Maxine every day. In return, Reith had named his son born in 1953 after his mentor— Charles Crusoe Reith. McNamara called the homage "shameless brown-nosing," but the gesture endeared Reith to Crusoe even more. On more than one occasion Crusoe had said, "If I could have only one man in this company it would be Jack Reith."

Continuing his shadowboxing match with Crusoe by pitting McNamara against Reith, Breech worried that Reith was becoming too visible. McNamara was an acknowledged genius in finance, but unless he had experience in operations the top leadership of the corporation might be out of his reach. Already humiliated by Crusoe in the present, Breech looked to the future for a victory. He began to think of how to place his protégé in an end-product division. Benson's Lincoln-Mercury Division did not offer the required opportunity, not so much because it was Benson's as because it was overwhelmed by the Ford Division and had no prospect of similar power in the corporation. Breech began to think of trying to place McNamara as assistant general manager in the Ford Division, thus making him next in line after Crusoe.

In order to make this move, however, Breech had to arrange for Jack Reith to be somewhere else. And so he began talking up the serious management problems faced by Ford's troubled French subsidiary and the need to get it into shape so that it could be sold before what he regarded as a likely future Communist takeover in France. He took Henry and corporate counsel William Gossett to Paris for an on-site inspection, and while they were there, worried about the situation, he decided to strike. Putting through a transatlantic call to Crusoe in Dearborn, he explained that the well-being of the French subsidiary had become an urgent matter. Then, seeming to change the subject, he asked Crusoe who the best young man in the company was. "Jack Reith," Crusoe answered without hesitation. Then Breech sprang the trap: "Do you think he can handle the French situation?" Ben Mills, who was present at the Dearborn end of the conversation, saw Crusoe go white and then snap out a tight-lipped answer, "Yes, he can handle it." After hanging up, Crusoe called Reith, who happened to be on vacation, and told him that he had to be in Paris in three days. Soon after Reith left, Breech had McNamara installed as assistant general manager for the Ford Division.

FOURTEEN

WITH FORD GAINING ON CHEVROLET, what had seemed in the earliest days of Henry's reign an impossible dream now became an intriguing possibility—finally to go head to head with the company's great rival. But this meant entering the middle- and upper-range car market, which had grown during the postwar years so that it now accounted for some 30 percent of total car sales. ("We're just growing customers for General Motors," Crusoe had said despondently after seeing surveys which showed that Ford owners "graduated" to Pontiacs and Buicks.) Edsel had seen the beginnings of this trend as early as the mid-thirties when he tried to make the company competitive in the middle-range market by introducing the Zephyr and the Mercury, but old Henry had wanted only one car, the Ford, and had sabotaged his son's efforts. As a result, by 1951 Mercury had only 4.5 percent of the market and wasn't making much headway against GM's middle-priced powerhouses. The company lacked the product and the dealer organization—the so-called "stalls in the marketplace"—to compete with its giant opponent's formidable five-car lineup. It also lacked an overall strategy, which was why Henry, early in 1952, created a committee headed by respected emeritus John Davis to study alternatives that Henry acknowledged at the outset might include "the introduction of another car name, a new dealer organization, and an additional car division."

It was the pivotal moment in the postwar history of the Ford Motor Company. Four months later the Davis Committee issued recommendations. They were very cautious despite the almost apocalyptic promptings in Henry's mandate. While GM might seem infallible, the committee pointed out, in fact it, too, had attempted to introduce new lines, such as the Marquette, the La Salle and the Viking, which had failed. Instead of a new car, therefore, the Davis Committee recommended beefing up the Mercury line. In addition to the Mercury, which was taken off the Ford shell, there could be a larger and more luxurious one taken off the Lincoln shell. This one, the Davis Committee suggested, might be called the Mercury Monterey. The smaller Mercury could compete with Buick at the lower end of the middle-priced range, while the Mercury Monterey could compete with Oldsmobile at the upper end.

On the surface the Davis Committee recommendations seemed like a windfall for Benson, in that his Lincoln-Mercury Division would be the focus of the expansion and the place where the Mercury Monterey would be built. Playing a more significant role in the company was exactly what he had always hoped for—an escape from the nagging feeling that he was in a leadership position merely because of his last name. Yet he had never asserted himself and had trouble with strong personalities. When Breech sent him aggressively worded memos, Benson's aides begged him to respond in kind, but he would demur: "Really, how important is this? Is it worth having a rhubarb with Ernie over?" They told him that it was symbolic: he had to establish himself as a leader and a Ford in the mold of his elder brother. But Benson just shrugged and said, "Henry's good at that sort of thing. I'm not."

Benson had retreated from the Ford family, forming his own circle of friends, a circle which kept getting tighter as old loyalists like Carlton Higbie dropped out for fear that the late nights and the drinking would damage their career at Ford. As he was thrown more and more onto his own resources, Benson's uncertainty about himself became almost pathological. It manifested itself in small things. Every year he went to the Mexican road races in Juárez, always making reservations under the name "Ben Jones" because he didn't want to admit who he was, and then, after he got there, always having to spend a half hour or so convincing the skeptical hotel manager that he was really Ben Ford. It was this same emotion that a Lincoln salesman saw when he ran into Benson sitting alone in a New York nightclub after a dealer meeting. The man came over and held out his hand, saying, "You're Benson Ford, aren't you?" Alarmed, Benson looked around furtively and then whispered, "Yes, but for God's sake don't tell anyone!"

His wife, Edie, felt he was "too sensitive for his own good" and that he had been wounded in his youth by having to play second fiddle in Henry's one-man band. Yet despite his position as the Fords' weak link, Benson seemed to be doing well at the time the Davis Committee recommendations were being discussed. His Lincolns had run far better than expected in the Mexican road races, almost beating the formidable Cadillacs. His Mercury, advertised on *The Ed Sullivan Show*, was poised to be pushed as the company's next glamour product. People close to him felt that Benson was finally coming into his own. His brother Bill, keenest observer of people in the Ford family, said later, "Ben really worked hard at it. He loved the road races, getting out there with the mechanics and getting his hands dirty. He was great with the Lincoln-Mercury dealers. He got to know them by their first names, and had them working their tails off for him. It was the time of his life."

Yet Benson's modest achievements had gone virtually unnoticed in the tidal wave of Crusoe's success. For Crusoe, Mercury's failure to keep up with the sales of Ford was more proof that Benson's division was an anomaly in a company that was supposed to be run like GM. Crusoe tried to convince Henry that the time had come to put a sharp executive in charge of L-M. And so a rising young manager named Richard E. Krafve was assigned to help Benson work out some of the Davis Committee recommendations on the new

Mercury Monterey and to deal with the question of perhaps eventually splitting it off as a model unto itself.

Dick Krafve's brilliance was such that people assumed he was a Whiz Kid, although he had come into the company after them. With him running things for Benson, Mercury took a significant step forward.

IF BENSON FELT HE HAD THE potential for new importance in the company because of the Davis Committee recommendations, so, too, did Bill, who felt that he had been "treading water" at Ford so far. While concentrating on the need to compete with GM in the middle-priced range, the committee had also included a proposal close to Bill's heart: reviving Edsel's Continental. The idea was not to compete in another "stall" in the marketplace—the car the committee envisioned would cost far more than the Cadillac—but to produce a low-volume luxury automobile that would enhance the company's reputation for quality.

The idea of reviving the Continental had surfaced from time to time since Edsel's original went out of production at the beginning of the war. As far back as 1946, $1 million had been spent on a design and a clay model. But as one of the stylists left over from the heyday of the collaboration between Edsel and E. T. Gregorie said, the result looked less like the Continental than Buck Rogers' skyrocket. Breech had kept the issue alive in casual car talk around the executive dining room. "You know," he would say to Bill, who he knew had inherited his father's love of design, "we keep getting letters about the old Continental. That was a great car. Are we ever going to bring it back?" Bill would say, "Yes, I definitely think we ought to do it." He didn't think anything would come of the talk, even though Breech kept coming back to the subject: "Well, if we ever decided to do such a project, would you be interested?" and Bill always jumped at the idea: "You bet I would!" Now, after getting the Davis Committee's report, Breech came to Bill one last time and told him that a Continental Division would be formed. "Okay, the project's been approved. You've got the ball. Now run with it."

The first person Bill hired was a young engineer named Harley Copp, whose life was oddly enmeshed in Ford history. Meeting him when he was a young man and finding out that he was distantly related to William Holmes McGuffey, author of his beloved reader, old Henry had given Copp a job as a guide at Greenfield Village and later made him tutor to John Dahlinger. Now Copp's involvement with the family and its cars was to take a step forward. He and Bill set up shop in the old Henry Ford Trade School, a place where Bill's grandfather had trained a generation of Dearborn boys in manual arts. The building was near the old experimental soybean gardens, and so it was immediately dubbed by other Ford employees "the country club."

The term was intended to be derisive, but it contained real envy of the independence and élan that distinguished the Continental's team the moment it was assembled. There was an elegant car to be made; there was also a sense of family mission on Bill's part that affected all the men he hired. "Bill Ford came to this task with stars in his eyes," said John Reinhardt, the Continental's head stylist. "His earliest memories were of sitting at a desk beside his father doing watercolors of fine cars. Now he was going to design his father's car! He was just overcome by the enormity of it. It was almost like being asked to design a headstone for Edsel. All the time we were designing the Continental he kept talking about the trips the two of them had taken to Europe when he was a boy and how they had always spent time looking at the great European cars."

A large and friendly man with a taste for $200 suits and sharp automobiles, Reinhardt faced unique design problems. First, the Mark II, as the car was being called, had to be recognizable as a lineal descendant of Edsel's Continental, whose classic status had recently been authenticated by a retrospective exhibit mounted by the Museum of Modern Art. But it also had to be contemporary and capable of refinement so as not to be caught in a "frozen design" like that of the Rolls-Royce. Bill himself was something of a problem, too. Although he had no formal design training, he had an instinctive feel for cars, just like Edsel. This led him to meddle. Sometimes he would come into the design studio and take a sculpting knife, for instance, and score new lines on the evolving clay model of the Continental, leaving a note on the "windshield" apologizing for having done so but also asking Reinhardt whether he didn't think his suggested revision was an improvement.

The short deadline for a final design made the Continental a crash program. Often Reinhardt would work until dinnertime, then take his stylists out for a quick meal and return to work some more until midnight. Before a crucial presentation to the Executive Committee he would stay at the office all night, going into Bill's office to catch a few hours of sleep before getting up to put on a clean shirt and go to the meeting.

On December 18, 1952, Breech and John Davis came to the trade school with Henry II and Benson to look at the preliminary design. Breech expected something flashy; Henry wanted something sporty with a strong Italianate flavor; Benson didn't care. After the curtains on the design stage had parted to show Reinhardt's "classic" design, none of the executives was particularly enthusiastic. Henry was especially negative, grumbling, "I wouldn't give you a dime for that." Stunned by the reaction, Bill went back to his office and wrote a letter to the Executive Committee lecturing them on the car:

> Delicacy in treatment of design detail in contrast to massive detail is a predominant feature of European cars. No example of this theme exists in contemporary American car design. With the style of the Cadillacs, Lincoln, Packards, and Chryslers trending toward the spectacular "Car of Tomorrow" theme, we believe the [Mark II], embodying the modern formal [design] described herein, will stand out in tomorrow's market, just as the Continental Mark I did in yesterday's market. Such a car will appeal to its owner not only as a work of art but as a symbol of affluence.

The Executive Committee ordered a "shoot off" between Reinhardt's design and several others. Largely as a result of Bill's persuasiveness, Reinhardt's design was chosen. But as he had tried to do with Crusoe and the Ford Division, Breech suddenly tried to pull back from the autonomy granted to the Continental Division, saying that now that the design was completed the division should perhaps be "folded back into the mainstream." He also attacked the idea of building a special plant to turn out the Continental. Bill felt that this was crucial to the integrity of the car, and he won over other Executive Committee members in behind-the-scenes lobbying.

By the time the Continental was in production, Bill had established himself as a power in the company, albeit a somewhat eccentric one. His personal style involved an iconoclasm unusual in executive ranks and far different from his brother Henry's impeccably conservative style. He was nocturnal, arriving at work at noon and staying until nine or ten. He frequently missed appointments. Even the august John Davis had to cool his heels for two hours when he arrived on time for a ten o'clock meeting.

Bill's mordant wit and sarcasm also stood out in the behavioral conformity of the auto industry. In the same way that he casually referred to Henry II as "lard ass" just at the time when his elder brother was reaching for an imperial persona, so he didn't bother to deal diplomatically with other executives he felt had wronged him. Suspecting, for instance, that design elements of his Continental had been "stolen" for the Thunderbird, which preceded it to market by a few months, he called the T-bird's "father," Lewis Crusoe, and offered to buy him some tracing paper. He felt that his Continental had a chance to become a classic just as Edsel's already was, and he defended every detail tenaciously. When Crusoe, anxious to give a common identity to all Ford Motor Company products, decreed that the Continental hood should have a plastic ornament similar to other Ford vehicles', Bill refused, defending the Mark II's special hood ornament although it cost $150, the price of an entire Ford grille. "If you see the hood ornament of a Mercedes," he pointed out, "you never have to ask what kind of car it is. The same is true of the flying lady of the Rolls. That's what kind of identification I want for the Continental."

When the prototype was almost ready, Harley Copp brought in John Dahlinger (with whom he had maintained a relationship since the days when he was his tutor) for a look. After he left, Bill growled, "What was that creep doing here?" He didn't want anyone to see the car until it was ready, especially not the man who went around Dearborn introducing himself as "Henry Ford's illegitimate son."

The first Mark II was finally ready to be driven the week before Christmas 1954. Bill invited Henry and Benson to the Ford proving grounds, where they all took it around at speeds of better than a hundred miles an hour. Afterward Bill had the prototype trucked to Gaukler Pointe so that he could take his mother for a drive. Eleanor giggled like a girl, proud of Bill and his homage to Edsel's memory, and also happy that her youngest seemed to have won his spurs in the company. "She was especially pleased that I could get so excited about something like a hood ornament," Bill said later. "She said that it reminded her of my father."

THE DAVIS COMMITTEE SEEMED TO have elevated Benson and Bill to positions of importance similar to what Eleanor had envisioned when she said that they should sit at Henry's right and left hands. A cautious step had been taken toward a deeper penetration into GM's virtual monopoly of the middle-priced market by beefing up the Mercury. A luxury car had been created for the company. All this happened at a critical juncture in Ford history—a time when the corporation was finally going public.

Negotiating the rapids of a public stock offering had been particularly difficult in Ford's case because of decisions that went back to 1936, when old Henry and Edsel had tried to figure out an ownership structure which would help avoid the massive taxes that would become due when either of them died. Working with attorneys, they created two classes of stock—a large block of nonvoting Class A stock and a much smaller block of Class B stock which had voting privileges and thus controlled the company. They also created the Ford Foundation and then willed their Class A stock to it while willing their Class B stock to the family. (If they had not done this, according to one estimate, their heirs would have had to pay $321 million in estate taxes.)

An unintended byproduct of this decision was that the foundation, until the mid-1940s a small-time family charity giving yearly gifts to cover the operating costs of Greenfield Village, the Henry Ford Hospital, etc., suddenly became huge and powerful once it had acquired the Class A stock of Edsel and old Henry.* Henry II established a study group on "policy and program" to figure out ways to spend this mammoth windfall in behalf of "human welfare." Headed by former New Dealer Rowland Gaither, the group recommended five areas of focus: the establishment of peace; the strengthening of democracy; support for education; and research into individual behavior and human relations. Paul G. Hoffman, former administrator of the Marshall Plan, was named foundation president and began to initiate innovative programs such as the Fund for the Republic, an organization to defend civil liberties, headed by former University of Chicago President Robert Hutchins.

Challenging the Rockefeller Foundation as the most influential charity in the country by the mid-1950s, the Ford Foundation played a large role in

---

* In forming the foundation in January 1936, Edsel said: "The Ford Foundation will take care of the various charitable, education, and research activities that I don't care to personally. It will be on a small scale and I have no intention of making it larger."

the decision of the family to take the company public. Its administrators were not content to receive income from the foundation's 88 percent ownership of the company in the form of annual dividends. They felt they should have full control of their assets, including the ability to sell Ford stock on the open market. But the foundation's interests were not wholly congruent with those of the Ford family. Resistance to going public was headed by Bill. "For me it was a matter of 'If it ain't broke, don't fix it,' " he said later. "But Henry was living it up and always strapped for cash. He always needed more money than the dividends gave him. He was for going public because it would allow him to raise money by selling his stock in the open market."

Eleanor lined up with Bill. Dodie, who also always seemed to need more money, lined up with Henry. Benson was somewhere in the middle in the family discussions, which often became quite heated. Wall Street wizard Sidney J. Weinberg was brought in to broker between family members and between the family and the foundation. He eventually worked out a deal whereby the family would retain 25 percent ownership—enough, he said, to ensure control. Henry was elated. Benson was resigned, saying, "Well, all right, dammit, if I'm going to have to sell it, somebody's going to pay for it pretty good." Bill was still doubtful. At the eleventh hour he said to Henry, "I don't think twenty-five percent is enough." Henry was annoyed: "Aw, hell, Bill, the deal's done." Bill was not moved: "Listen, forty percent is better control. I don't think twenty-five percent will keep us in the position of calling the shots." Henry responded, "Look, I've already told Sidney what the percentages are. If you want to change it, you take him on."

Bill went to the redoubtable Weinberg and talked to him about the ratio of common stock to Class B stock, which would determine the Fords' percentages. Weinberg told him, "If you don't accept a ratio of five to one, the thing will never fly." Insistent that the ratio should be higher, thus increasing the importance of the family's Class B holdings, Bill answered, "It's going to be fifteen to one and I frankly don't care if it flies or not. That's the way it's going to be." After a few days, Weinberg tried to haggle one last time: "You might want to come down to twelve to one." Bill responded, "Sidney, I'm not talking compromise here. I'm not bargaining. I've laid it out for you. If the other people involved don't like it, my heart's not broken. I'd just as soon walk away with no deal." Finally Weinberg gave in.

It was the biggest stock issue ever. People stood in lines outside brokerage houses in 1956 to be able to buy Ford stock, thus owning a piece of the company which still had an almost magical quality for the average American. As for the Fords, it made them all very much richer and, as Bill had feared, changed the nature of their company forever.

MONEY WAS POURING IN FROM THE public issue. For the first time in twenty-five years, Ford was neck and neck with Chevrolet. In the unbounded confidence that had taken over, it was little wonder that the Davis Committee study suddenly seemed far too conservative. As one Ford executive later said, "We believed we could catch up with GM tomorrow if we had a good enough plan. We were just waiting for someone to come along and say that we needed to do something ten times more ambitious than anything we had yet considered." This was exactly what happened late in 1954 when Jack Reith returned from France.

His nearly two-year stay there had been designed by Breech as a sort of exile or at least a move sideways so that McNamara could consolidate his position as heir apparent after Crusoe and Breech himself retired. But Reith had turned the no-win French job into an unmitigated triumph. The subsidiary had been clearly on the verge of bankruptcy when he arrived in Paris. Resented by the French Ford executives, whose honesty he doubted, Reith and his family found themselves isolated and alone. "I never really visualized my life in these terms," his wife once said to him. "I can't even talk about it," Reith answered. "I'm in a nest of thieves and robbers. We're walking the razor's edge." When he did take time to reflect on his life, his thoughts always went to Dearborn: "I have a picture of them back there walking around the halls saying, 'Wonder whatever happened to Jack Reith.' "

But Reith took charge of the situation in Paris. He brought out new French models good enough to make the subsidiary attractive to possible buyers. He began negotiating with other manufacturers and soon had made a difficult sale of French Ford to Simca. While he was out of sight, Crusoe made sure Reith was not out of mind. He kept talking up his protégé and describing his French exploits. And when he talked, other Ford executives listened because Crusoe was at the height of his power. "Lewie was sort of running wild," corporate counsel William Gossett later recalled. "He was doing what he wanted without discussing it with Breech or any committees. Breech called him in two or three times and gave him hell about getting too far out in front of everyone else and free-wheeling, but Crusoe just went to Henry, and Henry went to Breech and said it was okay."

At the June 1954 Greenbrier Management Conference, first of a series of get-togethers in which top Ford executives from all over the country were flown to the White Sulphur Springs, West Virginia, retreat for brainstorming sessions, Crusoe loudly sang Reith's praises. He said publicly that Reith was the best man Ford had and ought to be given any job he wanted.

His job in Paris concluded, Reith was recalled to Dearborn a few months later. He was triumphant but not certain what his next step should be, especially given the fact that his rival McNamara was obviously slated to get the plum job as head of the Ford Division once Crusoe moved up to the newly created super-executive job of vice-president for cars and trucks early in 1955. But within days of getting back, Reith realized that the Davis Committee's much-discussed plan to create new products in the middle-priced range represented an opportunity for him. His thinking became clear in a meeting with a young executive named Paul F. Lorenz, who was working under Dick Krafve at Lincoln-Mercury on the "E-Car," as the Mercury Monterey envisioned by the Davis Committee was now known. "Reith asked me about our plan, and when I told him he said, 'You're not thinking big enough.' The next thing I knew he was making his own study."

Reith had seen the obvious: his chances of getting to be head of a division depended on there being more divisions. So he came up with the daring strategy of bypassing Lincoln-Mercury altogether and creating a new division for the E-Car, giving it its own shell and its own staff and dealers. It was a drastic departure from the Davis Committee's cautious attitude toward building a brand-new car. Reith had also determined what he wanted for himself: a Mercury Division split off from Lincoln. As an executive who worked closely with him said later, "Jack chose Mercury because he knew that heroes aren't made of guys who handle cheap cars. Heroes are made of guys who handle cars in the middle- or high-priced range. Jack was fascinated by Red [Harlow H.] Curtice of GM, who became a hero by taking Buick from 250,000 cars a year to over 800,000, and went from there to become head of GM. Jack set his sights on Mercury and let everyone know that his game plan—for the company and for himself—was to beat the hell out of Pontiac and Buick."

Reith proposed two models of the E-Car, one below the Mercury in price and one above it. There would be separate Mercury, Lincoln and Continental divisions in addition to one for the new car. This way the company, in one great leap forward, could fill all the stalls in the marketplace and finally go head to head with GM. He ridiculed Dick Krafve for plans which had called for a mere $100 million to be expended in launching a new vehicle within Lincoln-Mercury according to the Davis Committee strategy. He boasted that his own plan would cost $250 million.

On February 7, 1955, Reith appeared before the Product Planning Committee with an audacious proposal that was part of his overall strategy. He wanted to scrap the Mercury planned for the following year. He showed a clay model of the car Benson Ford's stylists had designed and then unveiled another model representing his own idea of what the Mercury *ought* to look like—an upgraded version allowing the company to move into contention with GM immediately. There were risks, of course. Up until now Mercury had been, in effect, a prettied-up Ford using a Ford shell. The car Reith was proposing had a noninterchangeable body, which meant wholly new production facilities and plans. Hearing of this proposal, one engineer said to Reith, "Man, you're really smoking opium on this one. The risks so far outweigh the potential benefits that it isn't even funny." Reith's performance before the Product Planning Committee was so persuasive that they bought the package, deciding to discard Benson's car and go with the new model, almost immediately referred to as "Reith's Mercury." He justified his vision in terms he knew would appeal to Henry: it brought Ford one step further to market parity with GM.

Next on the agenda was the Big Plan, as Reith's supporters and detractors alike were calling it. It was the most ambitious proposal ever put before

Ford or perhaps any other automotive company, but getting it approved at an Executive Committee meeting on April 7, 1955, a scant two months after conceiving it, was scarcely more difficult for Reith than displacing Benson's Mercury had been. Years later, after it had gone terribly awry, people in the company would speculate about why the Big Plan had encountered so little opposition. They overlooked the obvious explanation: that Crusoe and Reith had bypassed the formal committees meant to pass such an idea up through the hierarchy—the elaborate GM system Henry had labored for a decade to install at Ford. The two most charismatic of Ford's executives presold the Big Plan in informal one-on-one sessions with the key players, especially the player whose vote counted for more than all the others combined—Henry himself. Henry was hooked on the vision. If the Reith-Crusoe plan succeeded, it would make him a Ford in the epic mold. He would have picked up the ball his grandfather dropped when he let GM sneak ahead of him in 1924; he would have fulfilled his father's unrequited dream of becoming number one again. "This is what we've been waiting for," he said in one discussion of the Big Plan. "This is our mission."

Crusoe, now at the peak of his power, had become a man possessed. To express doubts about the feasibility of the Big Plan in informal conversation, as Whiz Kid Jim Wright attempted to do, was enough to send Crusoe into a rage, an indication that far more was at stake than a judgment about market opportunities in the middle-priced range of automobiles. Other executives mindful of their future saw that they must play their cards close to the vest. And so the only serious opposition to Reith and Crusoe was voiced by Benson's staff men, Dick Krafve and Emmet Judge. When Judge told Reith that the idea was too big, too sudden, based less on market realities than on wishful thinking, Reith became flushed with anger. "We're going to do it," he said. "And we're going to get the market-research specialist to *make* it work."

The logical point of resistance should have been the central staff, Finance and their overseers, Breech and Henry. But Henry was already on board, and Breech was a prisoner of the situation Henry had created. To have gone to the mat against Crusoe and lost would have meant the end of Breech's career at Ford, a career which had just recently been sweetened by a newly created title Henry had offered: chairman of the board. As he would say to a friend later, "It was a time when I didn't have any choice but to bite my tongue and swallow my doubts."

McNamara, who had stood in for Breech on other issues, was convinced that his rival Reith's plan would not work. In his usual workmanlike way, he ticked off its defects in private talks with Jim Wright and his other Whiz Kid allies: "You can't break into a market dominated by well-established brands unless you provide something those brands don't. We're not going to have great price or mechanical advantage, and I have my doubts about styling." But McNamara had been promoted to head of the Ford Division and was no longer on the central staff with an actual duty to make his feelings public. And fellow

Whiz Kid Ed Lundy, his successor as controller, did not have the force of personality or the inclination to go all out against a project Henry backed.

And Henry did back it. William Gossett later said, "He was so excited by the company's successes that he knew no boundaries. He wanted to beat GM and he wanted to do it in a hurry. He was ready to shoot the works."

At the April 15 meeting for final approval of the Big Plan, the tireless Reith administered the *coup de grâce* to opposition to his plan by citing statistics: Ford had 43 percent of low-priced automobiles, but only 13 percent of middle- and higher-priced ones. Of Ford buyers "trading up," one in three bought GM cars. As the vote came, Breech was the only one to voice any doubts. "This could be a great tragedy for this company if it is not a success," he cautioned. "It is a mistake to gamble everything instead of testing the market gradually as the Davis Plan proposed to do." He alone raised his hand against the Reith-Crusoe plan when the question was called, although afterward he said he would retreat and go along because everyone else seemed "so heady" about the prospects for success. It was the first time since the days of old Henry Ford that the company's governing council had ceased to be the forum of reasoned argument, functioning instead, as it had so often in the past, as the instrument of the crystallized will.

Three days after the meeting, Crusoe announced the establishment of separate Mercury, Lincoln and Continental divisions, as well as a Special Products Division which would build the new E-Car. The person most immediately affected by this shuffling was Benson. In February, he had run afoul of Crusoe when he failed to show up for a Lincoln-Mercury meeting. Crusoe had asked Benson's aide Krafve where he was. "He's out on the lake in his boat," Krafve said. "If it's important I can get ahold of him." His face reddening, Crusoe had snapped, "Get ahold of him!" After Krafve had called Benson on the boat, Crusoe came on the line: "What the hell are you doing out on the goddamned lake? Don't you know there's a meeting here? You're supposed to be running this operation. You're either going to run it or you're going to get the hell out!"

Despite this dressing down, the first time anyone could remember a non-Ford talking to a member of the family like this in public, Benson felt he would get the Mercury Division after it had been split off from Lincoln. As one of his aides said, "He thought he was the natural person because he'd done so well with Mercury in the past two years." Everyone else realized that the decision had already been made and that Benson was out, replaced by Reith. When Henry made the formal announcement, he also announced that Benson had been "promoted" to work with Crusoe in the newly created position of group vice-president in charge of the Mercury and E-Car Divisions. But Crusoe simply ignored him, bypassing his line of authority and making it clear, if it had not been before, that Benson didn't count. As Bill Ford said later, "It was a fancy-title nonjob they gave Ben. He had absolutely nothing to do. He hated it. There was never any discussion about it. It just happened." One of

Benson's closest friends said, "This was the worst thing that ever happened to him. He realized that his career at Ford was basically over. He never saw what hit him. He was devastated."

It was not just that he was kicked upstairs into a position lacking authority. It went deeper than that. Others had seen the problem, but Crusoe was the first to act on it: Benson himself lacked all authority. He could not bring authority to the new position any more than he could invest the Ford name with authority. The only power he ever had was what people gave him, and the stakes had been raised so high in the company that power was no longer being given away, not even to a Ford. It was not so much that Henry had abandoned him, as Benson came to believe, as that Henry could no longer protect him as he had done in the past.

BENSON WAS DEPOSED. REITH had Mercury. These were Henry's acts, but Crusoe's decisions. In his next move, Crusoe made Dick Krafve head of the Special Products Division, which barely existed on paper but was charged with designing, developing and producing an all-new car and bringing it to market in two years. Krafve's appointment was the first sign of the peculiar atmosphere that soon grew up around the E-Car, for no one had opposed building a wholly new car more than Krafve himself. This opposition was not forgotten by Crusoe. "I could fire you," he said to Krafve when making the appointment, "but I'm going to make you head of the E-Car Division instead." Crusoe asked Emmet Judge, who had worked with Krafve and Benson, to become chief aide to Reith at Mercury. When Judge insisted instead on going with Krafve into the terra incognita of the Special Products Division, Crusoe said ominously, "Okay, but remember, if I'm forced to choose between making the Mercury succeed or the E-Car, I'm going to sacrifice the E-Car."

Seeing that the project was the riskiest the company had yet attempted, other executives also moved to isolate themselves from Krafve. McNamara, sending his aide Chalmers Goyert to the companywide committee overseeing the E-Car's development, told him that when he was asked how the Ford Division voted he was always to say, whatever the issue, "The Ford Division passes." He kept checking with Goyert to make sure that no commitment had been made in his name. "Bob didn't want to be part of the E-Car," Goyert later said. "He built a wall between it and him. He felt it might not succeed. He knew that the Ford Division's own Fairlane model was going to be a chief competitor of the E-Car when it came out."

The E-Car was surrounded by high secrecy as Krafve's stylists worked for a unique design. Locks to the design studio were changed immediately when a key was reported lost. Security men stood guard around the clock outside the styling studio's doors. A man periodically swept with a telescope the high terrain around the studio, checking for spies. By late summer 1955 the design was established, including some of the features that would make the new car distinctive: a grille which detractors claimed was shaped like a horse collar; horizontal wings in the rear of the car that were at odds with the vertical tailfins then dominating the market; a unique transmission arrangement in which gears were shifted by a cluster of push buttons at the center of the steering wheel. On August 15 the curtain rose for a showing of the clay model of the new car, and the Product Planning Committee burst into a standing ovation.

Some questions remained unanswered. How to sell the new car, for example? "The smart car for the younger executive or professional family on the way up," was the suggestion of the advertising agency. Far more important was what to call it. Market-research firms conducted interviews and free-association sessions. There was even a detailed correspondence between Ford executives and poet Marianne Moore, whose suggestions for a name included "Utopian Turtletop" and "Andante con Motor." Finally a thick folder was delivered to Krafve containing six thousand potential names, alphabetized and cross-referenced. Several weeks of study brought the list down to four finalists—Corsair, Citation, Pacer and Ranger. Early in 1956 Breech dismissed them all at a board meeting: "Let's take another look at some of the others."

One of the names that was not on the list of six thousand but had been mentioned prominently during the months of the E-Car's development was "Edsel." Benson's response was, "Over my dead body." He knew that his father had disliked the name enough to change his mind about naming him Edsel Junior. Bill was against it, too, arguing that the Henry J (Kaiser) and other cars named for individuals had a poor record of success. Eleanor hated the idea. When public-relations man Charlie Moore came to Gaukler Pointe to talk to her about it, she slammed the door in his face. Nonetheless, Breech now brought the name up once again to the board of directors, saying that it would be a nice homage to the man who had played such a crucial role in the company's history. He put in a call to Henry, who was vacationing in Nassau, and, after hearing all the arguments, Henry agreed with Breech. As one of his aides said, "Henry was so pumped up over the Reith-Crusoe plan, so much into the certainty and *grandiosity* of it, that he really did believe this car, a guaranteed success, would be a way of honoring his father. A great car for a great man."

The E-Car was now officially the Edsel. It was as if the jaws of fate clamped shut on the new automobile the moment this decision was made.

FIFTEEN

IT WAS ALMOST LIKE SOME Greek myth. As soon as the men of the Ford Motor Company staked their all on the Reith-Crusoe plan, the gods of the auto world decided to punish them for their hubris. 1955, the year the plan began to be put into effect, marked the apex of the Detroit boom. By 1956, when the plan was tested in the market, the times had soured, and an impending recession was cutting through the previous year's optimism. Almost immediately the plan was in trouble and the angry gods began to demand sacrifices.

The first victim was Bill Ford's Continental. A portent of what was in store had occurred during the groundbreaking for the plant Bill had fought so hard to get. Henry, who almost missed the beginning of the ceremony, walked by his brother and said out of the corner of his mouth, "Sorry to be late for your funeral." The remark was forgotten as the Mark II went into production in June 1955. The formal introduction came in October when five hundred press and television representatives came to a preview at the Ford Rotunda, where the Continental was showcased under a miniature replica of the Eiffel Tower serving as a canopy of elegance. Seven hundred orders were received the first day the car went on sale; by November, *Business Week* noted, "Ford's new Continental is selling like hotcakes."

But despite the initial optimism there were underlying problems. In the middle of the project, Breech, feeling more pressured than ever by Crusoe and generally wary of breaking new ground, had sent Whiz Kid Ben Mills of the Finance Department with orders to "get control" of the Continental project. Mills told Bill's chief engineer Harley Copp, "You know, Harley, we're going to be selling stock in the company in the near future and Mr. Breech doesn't want a car line losing money." Even though price had been an acknowledged obstacle in the path of the Continental from the outset, Mills and others from the central staff pushed the break-even point farther off by raising the price from $8,500 to $10,000, some 35 percent higher than Cadillac, at the same time they were cutting back on many of the "goodies" that made the car so special.

Even as the first Continental was coming off the production line, decisions were being made that would kill the car in its crib. The plan Bill had developed called for the 1955 model, which came only in a two-door version, to be followed immediately by a four-door version. "Historically four-door sedans have always dominated the high-priced market," he had stressed in his initial presentation. "The four-door has more formality; it furnishes much greater convenience of rear-seat entry; it can be chauffeur driven; it can be converted to a limousine." But now Breech decreed that they would not build the Town Sedan, as the four-door was called. As Bill said later, "This was a mortal blow to the whole project."

The Continental was never intended to be a volume product, or even a money-making one. And it couldn't really support the division structure. But its own contradictions were far less of a problem than the Reith-Crusoe plan of which it had become such an unwilling part. The embattled Breech had increasingly come to believe that because of Reith-Crusoe the company was overextended and over-committed; he began to worry about short-term profitability of the Continental, never before a criterion in discussions about the car. "I'm not going to go to my first public stockholders' meeting with a division that's planned to lose money," Breech grumbled. The more authority he saw slipping through his fingers, the more tightly Breech grasped what remained. The first stockholders' meeting was scheduled for May. This loomed as a D-Day for Bill as well as for Breech.

The initial assumption on which the Continental was based—that it was important for the company to have a luxury automobile that would allow Ford to trade on the remembered elegance of Edsel's Mark I—was forgotten. Forgotten, too, was the promise Breech and others had made at the outset of the project: even if the Continental lost money it would nonetheless be regarded as a worthwhile "marketing expense," just like advertising.

"They're moving the goalposts on us after the game has begun," Bill said despondently to aides after another depressing meeting with Breech. He knew he also faced opposition from Crusoe, who, feeling the heat of expectation about the plan, was looking for something to get tough with. If Crusoe hadn't hesitated to tell Krafve that he would sacrifice the E-Car, how much easier would it be to sacrifice the Continental? Bill later said that he began to feel queasy the minute Crusoe began telling him stories about Harold Wills' famous Wills–St. Claire and other well-engineered luxury cars that had failed.

Bill tried to talk to Henry during a family meeting at Gaukler Pointe. When his elder brother avoided the topic, Bill exploded: "If you'd just quit listening to goddamn Crusoe for a minute and listen to me for a change, it might help." But Henry didn't offer to help him. Bill felt that his brother wasn't particularly interested in having him succeed in the company. But he knew that Henry hadn't torpedoed him, either, no more than he had Benson. Henry was like the watchmaker god of the company: he had wound up the Reith-Crusoe plan as well as the tension between Breech and Crusoe, and he was now sitting back and letting the gears turn toward an outcome.

What had begun as a personal gesture—a homage to the martyred father through an elegant automobile Edsel would have loved—ended as one, too: a testament to Bill's impotence in the Ford Motor Company. His personal life fell to pieces in tandem with the disintegration of his corporate life. In early December 1955 he snapped a tendon playing paddle tennis. A wheelchair was brought into his office at the Continental Division, but, with his leg in a hip cast, he couldn't get into it. He felt helpless as well as immobile as sales of his car began to fail after a strong start. He blamed the failure on another promise on which Breech had reneged—that sales of the Continental would be handled only by select Lincoln-Mercury dealers, thus preserving the "prestige" of the car. But the excluded dealers complained and Breech allowed all of them to get at least one Continental. When it didn't sell immediately, they tended to discount its price, thus affecting the ability of the dealers with the proper clientele to sell their stock.

Everything seemed to conspire against Bill. In the spring of 1956 he snapped his Achilles tendon a second time when the physical therapist working to help him recover from the first injury asked him to stretch to test his recovery. He was in constant pain; even worse for a good athlete, there was a prospect of a lifetime of diminished activity. Deeply depressed over the twin assaults on his car and his body, Bill went to see golfer Ben Hogan, who had just recovered from a serious auto accident in which both of his legs had been shattered. "Do you see any point in my having another operation," Bill asked, "or would you just leave well enough alone?" Hogan advised him to go ahead with another operation.

There was no mercy killing for the Mark II. It was condemned to a lingering death. The car was still being built and sold, but it existed in a strange limbo. The four-door had been canceled; the elegant Mark III that Reinhardt's team had envisioned as the next model of the Continental never got off the drawing boards. One day Bill asked Harley Copp what he should do.

"If it were me," Copp answered, "I'd throw in the sponge. I'd say to Crusoe, 'Okay, Lewie, you want to kill this thing. We can't get our plans approved, we can't get our money. Why don't you get on with it? Kill it and get it over with.' "

Bill said dejectedly, "Do you really think I should do that?"

Copp shrugged. "What other choice do you have?"

A climactic Executive Committee meeting took place shortly after this conversation. Crusoe said that doing anything more with the Continental would be "throwing good money after bad." Still pursuing his "stalls in the marketplace" theory, he added that a large Lincoln with some of the Continental's panache might make a dent in Cadillac's market, and proposed that Continental be "folded into" the Lincoln Division, which would produce a Lincoln Continental Mark III. Everyone around the U-shaped table supported Crusoe, McNamara holding back until they all had their say and then developing his usual devastating summary of the consensus. Then there was a hand vote on Crusoe's motion. Bill, sitting with his leg spread across a couple of chairs to support his heavy hip cast, was the only one who voted against the motion. "I hope you heard my no and recorded that," he said loudly to the secretary. Then he struggled up onto his crutches. Crusoe moved to assist him but was repelled by the anger in Bill's glance. Feeling betrayed by Henry, Bill shot one last hard look at his brother and then dragged himself out of the room.

It was ironic. Just as Ford stock was being sold to the public, and the company was being reorganized along the lines of GM so that it was no longer a family business in the same sense that it had been for over a half century, the family drama involving the isolation of Benson and Bill reached its denouement. Both of them now watched happenings at Ford from the sidelines, a drink in their hands as they slid toward alcoholism. Bill, the family's high achiever, began a long night of the soul in which he would test his lower limits. In 1957, Benson, just thirty-nine, suffered a heart attack which doctors said was caused by a congenital defect, but which people close to the family believed was caused by Benson's perception that whatever honorific posts Henry might throw his way in the future, his career at Ford was over.

One afternoon not long after the Continental had been killed, Bill and Benson were visiting Eleanor at Gaukler Pointe. In the course of the conversation, she asked why they weren't being of more help to Henry. Bill looked at Benson and smiled bitterly. "Because he doesn't want us to, if you really want to know the truth," he said.

Henry had set out to save the company for the family and to purge it of personality. He had instead purged it of family and filled it with himself. Inside the framework of the corporate rationality he had imported from GM, he had reproduced his grandfather's compartmentalized, personalized authority structure and had unleashed the force of the individual will. Chief among the multiplying ironies was the fact that he had done this not as a naked power grab—even Bill, by now a connoisseur of his brother's faults, did not believe this—but out of his instinct for survival. The fear that the Fords would be replaced in the company, even stronger than his fear that a single Ford would begin a cult of personality, had created the fault line that threatened to undermine his stewardship.

Henry's instinct for survival manifested itself as craftiness combined with a kind of weakness. He had endowed Crusoe with the power to do virtually whatever he wished. By withdrawing his grace from Breech and bestowing it on his lieutenant, he had made antagonists of the two men most vital to Ford's success. While Henry had lost confidence in Breech, however, he had left him officially in charge because this increased his own maneuverability. And, as Crusoe's official superior, Breech could be useful if Henry wanted to keep Crusoe in check. But this same ambiguous authority gave Breech an opportunity to put checks on Crusoe that crucially hindered his efforts to make the Big Plan work. As one Ford executive said, "Henry was walking this tightrope he couldn't even see. The way things were arranged was a prescription for disaster. Bill and Benson just happened to be the first victims."

THE DEATH OF THE CONTINENTAL WAS the first blow to the great enthusiasm that had washed over the company at the time of its passionate embrace of the Reith-Crusoe plan. Suddenly everyone was playing it safe. Breech continually said that he was "withholding judgment," a phrase implying that a day of judgment might soon be at hand. McNamara, as head of the Ford Division, was now not just standing apart from the plan, but using his position to undermine it. One of his first moves was to introduce a "luxury" Ford—an extended Fairlane that, with a 120-inch wheelbase, would be larger than the largest Mercury. Next he rushed to produce the four-seater Thunderbird, which Crusoe had initiated before leaving the Ford Division. Most Ford executives thought it odd that McNamara, apostle of efficiency, should become committed to two large and gaudy cars, but gradually part of his reasoning became clear: the Fairlane and the four-seater Thunderbird provided devastating in-house competition for Reith's Mercury and Krafve's Edsel. It was more in character when McNamara decided to kill the classic "little" Thunderbird even though it had sold well enough in three years and had captured the imagination of auto buffs everywhere. McNamara told product planner Tom Case, "I don't want anything to prevent us from making a profit on the four-passenger bird, so we're not going to continue the Little Bird. We're going to stop it." Case saw this as a tragic mistake and on his own tried to find out if it was possible to get better prices from some of the subcontractors on the car. McNamara found out about this and chewed him out: "The car is dead! I don't want to hear about it again."

The Edsel was scheduled for the fall of 1957, but the Reith-Crusoe plan called for Mercury to pick up a few points of the middle-priced-market share before the new car was introduced. This was to be done by adding new styling features and being more daring and aggressive in marketing, a responsibility Reith took upon himself. In fact, however, his 1956 models lost ground instead of gaining. GM beat Reith to the punch with promotion and advertising, and their middle-priced cars pounded the Mercury. Reith's 1957 model fared even worse.

Suddenly Crusoe saw that he was in trouble. A conservative man all his business life, he realized that, in the supercharged atmosphere that had characterized Ford in the "Beat GM" period when he came to power, he had uncharacteristically acted out of motives that had little to do with business. He had acted from the heart because of his fondness for Jack Reith. He had moved too fast, made too many enemies, left himself too vulnerable. The extent of his jeopardy was clear in a memo bearing the scent of the *auto da fé,* which was circulated on October 25, 1956, over the signature of Whiz Kid Ben Mills who had been given the new Lincoln Division, but obviously with the blessing of Breech and McNamara:

> In the last few months, the top management of the Ford Motor Company has faced the realization that the launching of its 1957 models has been unsuccessful and

extremely costly. Naturally, members of management have asked very pointed but more than fair questions as to what happened. Why did we miss schedules so badly? Why was management not informed by people who certainly must have known that the programs were unsound?

As sales and earnings dropped along with the price of Ford stock (the latter a new and volatile element in decision-making), Breech began to move against Crusoe. Long unable to challenge the man who had begun as his subordinate and become his equal while he was flying high, Breech now felt free to call him on the carpet. He began to accuse Crusoe of exceeding his authority. He began to question him about small details. Even the most insignificant issues took on a heavy portent. When changes in the 1957 Lincoln's side moldings, for instance, came before the Product Planning Committee, which normally would have disposed of the matter in ten minutes, Breech made it into an ordeal that lasted for over two hours. He forced Crusoe to bring in the drawings and unroll them on the floor, and then he got down on his hands and knees to ask questions about them. "What's this, Lewie?" he pointed. "How about this? Why is this here?" As he went through his answers, Crusoe began to get red in the face. Others in the room were hoping that Henry would ask to move on to the next agenda item and force the two men to solve their problem on their own time. But he let the argument go on. When it was finally over, Crusoe left the room looking shaken and muttering, "I don't have to take this shit."

Now Crusoe was not only fighting to make the plan he and Reith had designed succeed, but fighting for survival as well. "That son of a bitch Ernie Breech is trying to get rid of me," he said to one of his executives, "but I'm not going to let him." Apparently forgetting how he had treated Benson in the past, Crusoe went to him with tape recordings of conferences he had had with Breech and others. Benson realized that something was "preying" on Crusoe, but refused to become involved. Crusoe tried by sheer force of will to dig himself out of his dilemma, working longer and longer hours. He insisted on making all decisions himself, taking everything into his own hands and trying desperately to maintain his reputation as Ford's miracle worker. His executives noticed that his hands had begun to shake, and that an angry rash was crawling up his chest to his neck. His secretary, Mary Crecy, noticed that although his face was engorged with redness Crusoe still conveyed a sense of pallor. In late October, he suffered a massive heart attack.

WITH CRUSOE BARELY CLINGING TO life in the hospital, the first one to hear the whisper of the ax was Jack Reith. Even though his Mercury had not succeeded as he had predicted, he had assumed that Crusoe would be there to help him out of the jam. But with Crusoe out of the picture, Reith was exposed. The assumption on which his plan had been based, that the Edsel and the Mercury would not be over-whelmed with competition from the Ford Division, no longer held true. It was now dog eat dog, and McNamara, whom Henry named as Crusoe's successor, was now top dog in the company.

Starting in early 1957, after disappointing introductions of the new Mercurys, McNamara began to hammer on Reith, obviously acting with Breech's authorization, and emphasizing problems in quality and poor sales—issues which clearly symbolized the larger question of Reith's judgment. As one observer said later, "McNamara seemed to be talking about cars; he was really talking about character." Breech weighed in on February 5, 1957, with a letter listing twelve quality defects on the Mercury—such things as the transmission microswitch shorting out in wet weather, water leaking into the deck at the taillight assembly, etc. After three weeks of investigation, Reith answered in a memo stating that these problems "were prevalent on early production cars and have since been corrected." He circulated among members of the Executive Committee a review of the 1957 Mercury that had appeared in *Consumer Reports*, underlining the salient passage:

> On and off and particularly during the last few years, Mercury has had a hard time concealing the fact that it was essentially a Ford with not much more than a difference in nameplate and styling.... But 1957 changes all that. The Mercury Montclair, which [we] have just finished testing, is very thoroughly non-Ford, having its own chassis, body and suspension, all of which are new for 1957. Unlike previous Mercurys (or Fords) it is an outstanding car in its road behavior.

Breech kept up the attack, accusing Reith of deceiving him with regard to sales. Reith tried to fight back, sending a letter to the Executive Committee on June 4 showing that while the market for the middle-priced cars had shrunk from 31 percent of the auto industry in 1955 to 24 percent in the second half of 1957, Mercury's share of this market had risen steadily from 17 percent to 21 percent. But all this was to no avail. McNamara moved in on Reith, demanding veto power over everything he did, circumventing and second-guessing him.

It was the final act in the rivalry that had existed between the two men since they competed to see who would be second Whiz Kid behind Tex Thornton. From the outset, their struggle had always been about personality as well as policy, McNamara always having trouble with Reith because of his grandiose ambition and his flamboyant personal style, including what McNamara regarded as Reith's sexual self-indulgence. It was a no-holds-barred struggle, with McNamara's ally Ben Mills spreading rumors that in the battery of tests Bugas had administered to the Whiz Kids in 1946 Reith had scored below 100 on the IQ test. William Gossett later said, "McNamara wanted to make Reith say 'yessir' and 'nosir.' Reith wasn't about to do that. He refused to be diminished." Reith appealed to Henry, who backed McNamara.

When Reith was offered a face-saving job as head of Ford of Canada, John Bugas went to Maxine Reith and told her to try to convince him to take the job: "It's just a wrist-slapping. Get him to take it. He'll be able to come back." But Reith regarded it as too great a fall for someone who had flown so high. After spending a few weeks in a small office away from the executive suites—a sort of limbo for those who had no future at Ford—he decided to leave. On August 30, 1957, the memo announcing his resignation also noted that the Mercury Division had been merged back into a single unit with Lincoln.

THE FINAL ACT IN THE DRAMA that had begun with Reith's Big Plan centered on the Edsel, which came out at about the same time he was let go. There could hardly have been a worse time to introduce an expensive new product. The recession had set in. GM had beefed up Pontiac, Buick and Oldsmobile in anticipation of the challenge; McNamara's big Fairlane had become successful and posed serious competition within the corporation.

In an attempt to boost profits, the company had decreed a $200 across-the-board increase on all of its 1958 models. McNamara insisted that it must begin with the Edsel, although it was coming out three months earlier than the others and was technically a 1957 model. Edsel Division chief Dick Krafve complained, but McNamara held fast, rubbing it in during a confrontation with Edsel sales chief J. C. Doyle at the executive lunch table: "You can't possibly think that car will be successful, can you? How can you expect to sell it against our Ford, which is a better car and sells for less?"

As the launch date approached, McNamara's aide Paul Lorenz reported that the Edsel Division had signed up only 550 out of a projected 1,000 dealerships. "With just two months to go before the introduction date, I'm very much concerned that we won't reach that goal."

McNamara gave him a significant look. "My concern is a bigger one," he said. "I'm afraid they might actually come close to getting a thousand dealers by that time."

On August 27, a week before the car went on sale, the first photos were released to the public, showing the three Ford brothers sitting in false amity in an Edsel convertible. The next night, at a dance staged as part of the press introduction, Fairfax Cone, head of the ad agency handling the Edsel account, asked McNamara what he thought of the new car.

"I've got plans for phasing it out," McNamara said without further explanation.

The public saw none of this struggling for position inside the company. It did see the most expensive new-product launch in history. There was wild, almost febrile enthusiasm on "Edsel Day." One Ford public-relations executive went so far as to find a fireworks company in Japan willing to make, for nine dollars apiece, five thousand rockets that would release nine-foot scale models of the car, which would inflate and then descend by parachute after a midair explosion. Krafve was constantly on the road that summer with other Edsel executives, speaking to community groups, bankers and investment companies they hoped would loan money to prospective Edsel dealers. As a final flourish on press day, they let seventy-one automotive writers drive Edsels back to the headquarters of their newspapers.

Edsel Day was September 4, 1957. There were four lines: the Corsair and the Citation had 345-horsepower engines, largest of any American car; the Ranger and the Pacer were six inches shorter and narrower and had engines with 305 horsepower. Some critics were taken with the push-button gear cluster at the center of the steering wheel, the standard-equipment tachometer and other features. But discussion about the car was dominated from the outset by its looks. The grille was compared to a man sucking a lemon, to a toilet seat, to a horse collar. Most of all it was compared to the female sexual organ. (One auto writer said that it ought to be called the Ethel instead of the Edsel; and a joke went around the Ford Design Center that if a Cadillac with its protruding taillights backed into an Edsel, the resulting hybrid offspring could be called an Edsellac.) There was also what one critic called "a sinister personality change" occurring somewhere between the grille and the back of the car, where rear fenders swooped outward and angled taillights gave the appearance of a "slant eyed grin."

From the outset there were doubts about its workmanship. Then a devastating review appeared in *Consumer Reports*:

> The amount of shake present in the Corsair body on rough roads went well beyond any acceptable limit.... The Corsair's handling qualities—sluggish, over-slow steering, sway and lean on turns, and a general detached-from-the-road feel are, to put it mildly, without distinction.... The "luxury loaded" Edsel—as one magazine described it, will certainly please anyone who confuses gadgetry with true luxury.

Sales began encouragingly. On October 13, 1957, Ford paid CBS to preempt *The Ed Sullivan Show* with "The Edsel Show" featuring Bing Crosby and Frank Sinatra. But by November, sales were off. At first there was panic, then despair. By December Henry had to go on closed-circuit television to ask worried dealers to hold fast. The same day he was telling his captive audience that the Edsel was "here to stay," however, McNamara was writing the first of a series of memos calling for the termination of the Edsel at the earliest possible opportunity. Over the next few weeks he handed out analyses of the figures which showed that they would never come close to the 200,000 cars projected as the break-even figure for the first year. He had also removed Krafve, a capable and independent executive whom McNamara had always hated, as head of the Edsel Division, consolidating it with Mercury and Lincoln to make the M-E-L Division.

Only two years had elapsed since the most massive restructuring and product investment in Ford's history, and now all that was undone. The five divisions of the Reith-Crusoe plan were two again. The fall of Crusoe and his man was accompanied by the rise of McNamara and the other Whiz Kids (Arjay Miller was head of Finance, Ed Lundy was controller, James Wright was head of the Ford Division, Ben Mills would become head of M-E-L).

The next year's Edsel was an improvement. Even *Consumer Reports* relented, calling it a "respectable and even likeable automobile." Sales improved marginally. But by July 1, 1959, almost two years after the Edsel had been introduced, only 84,000 had been sold. On November 19, the car was discontinued. Gene Bordinat, who watched the whole drama unfold, later said, "They could have made it if they'd hung a little tougher. There was room for that car. The mid-priced market came back. Those stalls in the marketplace Lew Crusoe used to talk about are hard to come by. In time the Edsel would have gotten one. Some of us told Breech he could save the Edsel by making it more a Ford and less of a Mercury and he said, 'I don't disagree with you. But I've made up my mind.' "

The company had suffered a net loss of some $350 million on the Edsel. Ford stock had dropped $20 a share. But the trauma went deeper. What had begun as a tribute to the unknown soldier of the Ford family had wound up maiming his memory. As Bill Ford said disconsolately, "You're always sensitive when your father's name becomes a synonym for failure."

The Reith-Crusoe plan became a cautionary tale that was branded deep into the identity of the company. Part of the moral was subliminal, having to do with the fate of the men who had sponsored this Big Plan:

Lewis Crusoe recovered from his heart attack but never returned to the company he perhaps more than any other individual had helped revive. He stayed incommunicado, not even bothering to claim credit for a delayed triumph when the 1957 Fords, last of those he had designed in his old role as head of the Ford Division, beat Chevrolet—the first time this had happened in more than thirty years.

Jack Reith got a job as head of Avco. But he too never recovered from the feverish days at Ford. He had periods of bleak depression that he was unable to shake. He complained about the fact that he was an auto man working in a nonauto job. On the July Fourth weekend, 1960, he was cleaning his gun and shot himself in the head. Ben Mills' wife, Helen, said, "For insurance purposes they had to say it was an accident. And of course Jack was Catholic. But everyone knew." Not long before he pulled the trigger Reith said to a boyhood friend, "When the Edsel went down I took the rap." But it wasn't so much the death of an automobile that disturbed him as the death of the dream he and Crusoe had shared. There would never be another chance to create that epic vision.

SIXTEEN

A SEA CHANGE HAD WASHED OVER the company. When the 1950s began, Ford had not only been revived but was about to launch an audacious assault on GM for leadership of the auto world. At the end of the decade, after the failure of the Reith-Crusoe plan, Henry was resigned to the fact that the company would never really challenge its great rival again.

A similar passage had occurred in the Ford family. At the beginning of the fifties Eleanor's dream of a company in which each of her three sons would play a major role seemed to be coming true. By the end of the decade, however, the dream was dead. Benson had been removed from any real power and given a demeaning job as head of the Dealer Policy Board. Although barely forty years old, he already had a bad heart and was drinking heavily and, in the words of a friend, "just rotting away."

After the death of the Continental, there had been some talk of offering Bill the job of head of Ford International. But Henry had put an end to that, saying, "He wouldn't make the necessary sacrifices—travel, meeting people, building up the individual companies." So Bill was made head of the Design Center, a job comparable in influence to Benson's on the Dealer Policy Board. Realizing that he would always be "blocked" at the company, Bill simply with-drew. Like Benson, he had become an alcoholic, but his involvement with the bottle, unlike his brother's, was almost a conscious process. "I remember the exact moment when it happened," he said later. "The Continental had been killed, and I saw that it was really over for me in the company. I was sitting at home with my leg still in this huge cast one afternoon when a friend called. He asked what I was doing. I said, 'Sitting here feeling sorry for myself. In fact, hold on a minute, I think I'm going to get up and get myself a drink.' That was the beginning."

Henry alone was left. He was the only Ford.

He had planned a new headquarters for the company—a building imposing enough to fit a destiny that had outgrown the offices he inherited. As the twelve-story structure went up, he was transfixed by it and sometimes asked his executives to come over and take a look and then write memos with their impressions. Ready for occupancy in the spring of 1957, the new headquarters was immediately dubbed the "Glass House" because of its modernist structure, although the nickname also suggested a pun on the saying about people who live in such buildings.

The advent of the Glass House marked a change in the company's identity. In the heady postwar period, executives had barged into one another's offices in the old Schaeffer Avenue Administration Building without much regard to etiquette, or held impromptu hallway conferences upon running into one another on the way to the water coolers. But all this camaraderie now disappeared. The headquarters of a company which was no longer struggling for an identity but had achieved one, the Glass House was antagonistic to this kind of intimacy. It was cold and formal, a place that made distinctions rather than blurred them. Onetime corporate counsel Alan Gornick says, "Suddenly there were 'grades' of people. If a fellow on my staff was just a starting attorney he couldn't have an office that exceeded so many square feet. If he was in the next echelon he could have an office with a window, then, at the next level, an office with a plant. Really—a plant!"

The twelfth floor was "executive heaven." The visitor emerged from an elevator into a huge carpeted room with security guards at the central desk. To the full-length portraits of old Henry and Edsel that had always been the centerpieces of Ford headquarters there had been added another painting—of Henry II.

Henry now saw the Whiz Kids, the ones he had hired before Breech arrived on the scene, as *his* team, the men he would use during the golden age of his reign. They had worked only for Ford; dealing with them would be different from dealing with the GM men, who would always be father figures. Henry had even picked out the man he believed should lead the company: Robert McNamara.

Shortly after Crusoe's heart attack, Henry had begun to hold secret meetings with McNamara to discuss structure, organization, planning—processes in which the Whiz Kids had been interested since their arrival. Even though these conversations were secret, the fact that Breech—his sometime patron— was bypassed made the keenly political McNamara nervous. To cover himself, he confided in a Ford executive who was also an Ann Arbor neighbor that after each meeting with Ford he wrote and filed an *aide-mémoire* so that Henry could not later distort what had been said. One of these memos (they were all stamped "Confidential"), dated March 13, 1957, suggests how wide-ranging the talks were. McNamara said that Henry had asked him to think about a reorganization of the company with regard to end-product divisions, manufacturing plants and engineering staffs. "Mr. Ford recognized that the present organizational structure leads to unresolved controversies.... [He] does not expect an immediate answer to his questions from me, nor does he wish the matter discussed with others."

Always listening and responding, always subtly dominating these and other discussions, McNamara was like a new toy Henry wanted to show off. Another executive remembered walking with McNamara down the twelfth-floor corridor of the Glass House one day when Henry approached, stopped him and told him about an idea he had had. McNamara listened and then began with one of his typical responses, "Well, Mr. Ford, the following advantages would flow naturally from such a policy:..." As he was enumerating them in descending order of importance, Henry was beaming with pride at the abilities of the man who had become his new back-channel executive.

If Henry was elated by McNamara, however, Breech was alarmed. He had thought that once Crusoe was out of the way his undisputed leadership of the company would once again be certain. His onetime protégé reassured him that he had the greatest respect for him. But it was clear that something profound had changed. Henry told Breech that he realized he was "using" McNamara more, but urged Breech to interpret it as part of a gradual executive transition that would take years to complete. Yet Breech saw that he was losing out to McNamara in the here and now. Despite all the reassurances, Breech suspected that Henry blamed him for the Edsel, perhaps because he had *named* the disaster.

A watershed moment occurred at the Greenbrier Management Conference of 1958, when Henry gave an opening speech whose tone was belligerent and whose implication was that people were disregarding *his* leadership. Onlookers—Breech among them—became more puzzled as the speech went on, until Henry finally said in a voice filled with passion, "I am the captain of the ship and I intend to remain captain as long as my name is on the bow." In the dead silence that followed, one executive noticed that Breech had turned white.

Over the next few months many found themselves wishing that Henry would simply put Breech out of his misery and fire him. Instead he toyed with him, countermanding his orders and upstaging him during meetings. There was more than a little pettiness. For years, for instance, Breech had as one of his perks a block of tickets to the Detroit Lions football games. Bugas' aide Bob Dunham had often called to ask for them if Breech had decided not to go. Now he did this one Friday afternoon and Breech said sadly, "Bob, a lot of things are changing around here, and one of the signs is that I don't get football tickets anymore."

Henry was at center stage now—unpredictable at meetings, always saying things like "My name is on the building" to justify his peremptory decisions. He was a volatile presence, the growing pressures in his private life showing at the office. At one Product Planning Committee meeting he suddenly turned around from his front-row seat and looked at the others, his reading glasses slipping ominously down his long nose. "I have stopped recommending our cars to my friends," he said with a violent undertone in his voice. "Do you want to know why? Because every time they buy one I spend all my time on the phone trying to get the goddamned thing fixed."

Even McNamara was not immune from the lash of Henry's tongue. As a result of his displeasure with Ford quality, Henry appointed onetime GM production man John Dykstra as a "quality czar" reporting directly to him. At one point in a meeting at which Dykstra proposed adding an average of $25 to each car in "quality costs," McNamara took the floor after sharpening his intellectual pencil for several minutes. "Mr. Ford," McNamara began as Dykstra nervously fished for a cigarette, "I'd like to propose that we have a system whereby every penny that's added to this car is put down on a list with the reason for it and the person who proposed it." Ford glared at him and said, "Well, Bob, that's really the controller's job, isn't it? It's a controller's function to keep track of these things. You should know that better than anybody."

THERE WERE CHANGES IN HENRY'S personal life, too. Enriched by the public stock offering, he had bought a mansion on fifty acres in Southampton, Long Island, in 1955—a place that one neighbor referred to as "a miniature Versailles with warmth." The following year he bought the mansion on Lakeshore Drive in Grosse Pointe that had been built for his father's old friend Roy Chapin, one-time head of the Hudson Motor Company and Secretary of the Treasury, whose son Roy Junior had inherited his position as head of American Motors. In 1927 Chapin had commissioned John Russell Pope, architect of the Jefferson Memorial, to design a home for him. The result was a pillared two-story house incorrectly called Georgian by some—it was really "monumental Colonial"—which was arguably the most beautiful home in Detroit.

The old house on Provencal Road that Edsel had given Henry and Anne as a wedding present had been awkwardly designed and not suitable for entertaining, but the Chapin place was perfect for the head of what was now the fourth largest company in the United States. Visitors walked into a fifty-foot-wide foyer filled with so many canvases by Corot, Degas, Renoir and other nineteenth-century French painters that they could imagine they were in a small Parisian art museum. It had an almost intentional magnificence. Anne had furnished it with one of the finest furniture collections in the country, a collection that included pieces once owned by Marie Antoinette and Catherine the Great.

A sign of the Fords' social arrival was the coming-out of their eldest daughter, Charlotte, in 1959. She flew in from Florence, where she had been attending school, and people noticed that she was still pretty but perplexed, always tense around Henry—as if she held him responsible for some deficit in her life. Some of her strongest recollections were of those childhood Christmases at Fairlane when she and other great-grandchildren of old Henry and Clara were taken by sleigh to the log cabin deep in the woods. A man dressed as Santa Claus would invite them in and show them mounds of presents, saying, "It's all for you. Help yourselves." Everything was there; it was symbolic of their possibilities and limitations.

As children Charlotte and her sister Anne had often set up a stage in the living room and put on a talent show for their father—singing, dancing, and telling riddles. Later she would say that the conclusion she drew from this experience was that it took a performance to get her father's attention.

"We didn't see much of my father," she complained. "He was always away or coming in from work after we had gone to bed. We had a Christmas tree and presents and birthday presents and all that. But looking back on it, I think I'd have been happy to have fewer presents and more parents."

Charlotte and "little" Anne had been protective of their little brother, Edsel, whom the other children teased because of a weight problem which eventually became so severe that he had to go around supported on crutches for fear he would damage his hips. Once the girls left for convent school, Edsel was on his own. He relied for affection on his governess, "Zelly," the pet name he made out of "Mademoiselle." She was a strict disciplinarian, but very warm. As he became so fat that he sat on the sidelines while the other children played, Zelly tried to do something to help him. A child whose food problem was so bad that he kept a bottle of chocolate malt in his personal safe, Edsel was difficult for her to help.

Edsel II had been given the obligation of dancing the first dance with Charlotte at her deb party. But when it came time, he refused, saying petulantly, "It's a free country." Henry took his place and athletically whirled his daughter around the replica of an eighteenth-century court ballroom that he had paid French designer Jacques Frank $150,000 to create. The evening was an unqualified success, with luminaries like Gary Cooper and Lord Charles Spencer Churchill having been flown in from all over the world, and with Nat King Cole singing songs directed especially at Charlotte. By the time the evening had concluded, her coming-out was already being called "the Party of the Year."

It was another in a series of triumphs for "big" Anne, her mother, who had achieved a status in the Ford family similar to Henry's in the company. She had been able to trump Bill's wife, Martha, simply by her seniority. She had intimidated Benson's wife, Edie, more intentionally. The two women had been close when Anne first arrived in Detroit, Edie showing her the ropes from a native's point of view. But as young women married to Ford men they had been equals for only a brief time. As Henry rose in the company and Benson failed, Anne had pushed Edie to one side. In time she had even cowed her mother-in-law. Eleanor had always bought her clothes at Hudson's until Anne began wearing Christian Dior dresses and made the discussion of clothing labels, once thought vulgar in Grosse Pointe, chic.

By the late fifties, Anne had become a social arbiter of Grosse Pointe as well as head of the family. When she sent her daughters, Charlotte and "little" Anne, to dancing school in red leather Mary Janes, the other children, until then content to wear traditional black or perhaps white shoes, immediately changed so that, in the words of one observer, "it looked as though the feet of Grosse Pointe's little girls had measles; you've never seen so many red leather dancing pumps in your life."

Anne had always been a dutiful if somewhat remote mother, exacting religious devotion from her children. (Charlotte later remembered with some bitterness going to Mass every day: "It was a good twelve years of Mass. It was like prison.") She was less good as a company wife, however. She was ill at ease with shop talk, never having bothered to master the rudiments of the automobile culture. She was haughty toward the other executives' wives, especially Thelma Breech, who had a warm, earthy sense of humor and occasionally told stories dealing with such things as the outdoor privies she and Ernie had grown up with in the Ozarks.

Yet Anne made up for her inability to engage in small talk with the wives of Henry's subordinates by a social activism that connected the Ford name with the right causes. She was "launched" in 1956 when she got Henry to make their first big gift to the Detroit Institute of the Arts, a Holbein portrait of the English period which led Edsel's old art mentor William Valentiner, now an old and sick man, to write in his diary: "I am glad the Museum in Detroit is getting another masterpiece.... I am more pleased, however, that the friendship of Edsel Ford, which was so essential for the development of the Museum, resulted in an interest in art among the children." Like Edsel and Eleanor before them, she and Henry took informal "seminars" in art from Valentiner. They also got instruction in classical music. Henry tolerated art, which, as he said to one friend, "you could at least buy and sell," but not music. Anne was quite different. In the words of a catty female acquaintance, "She was an eager student because she knew the social rungs of Detroit were like a musical clef."

Asked to head the 1959 opera season, Anne said, "I talked it over with Henry and he says I can do it. He has given me ten thousand dollars for expenses and loaned me two men from the company public-relations staff." She was nervous at her first luncheon, saying, "I've taken six Libriums. I'm scared to death. I've never talked to more than a couple of people at a cocktail party." But three weeks later she was talking to eight hundred with perfection. Her success left Henry behind. A friend says, "It wasn't exactly his idea of fun to come home after a hard day at the office and then have to sit around talking with opera manager Rudolf Bing." He hated opera and quickly left their box after the first act on opening night and headed for the bar. Asked what his favorite part of the performance was, he quickly answered that it was the second act. Why? "Because I spent it getting drunk."

Edie called Anne "the Ice Queen." Indeed, for all her social success in the wider world, she had allowed a glacial quality to enter into her relations with her husband. As a Catholic friend said, "She had already had her children, so the welcome sign was not exactly hung out on the bedroom door every night." She was easily offended by Henry's high spirits. After an evening of carousing at Southampton, he came in with Charlotte's sixteen-year-old friend Charles Cudlipp, whom he had met in town. "Go up and get her out of bed and bring her down," he commanded. Cudlipp went up, wrapped Charlotte in a comforter and carried her down the stairs giggling. "All of a sudden Anne appears at the top of the stairs," he recalls. "She started putting things in order right away. She lashed out at me, reminding me that I was a guest. Henry stood up sort of disgusted and said, 'I asked him to do it. We were just trying to have a little fun around here.' "

Henry felt that he was owed something. He had struggled to fulfill obligations that were imposed on him without regard to whether he was suited for them by talent, intelligence or character. Now he had entered a new phase of his life in which he became aware of obligations of a different order, obligations to himself. These would be more difficult to fulfill.

He began to drink heavily—not, like Bill and Benson, as an escape, but as a way of bringing on the high spirits that would intensify his life. But it was difficult for him to regulate his quest for "a little fun." Sometimes he lapsed into the outrageous behavior of one who had slipped his moorings. A social friend remembers, "We were at a restaurant and when the waitress came over to take our order, Henry just ran his hand right up her dress. She wasn't especially attractive. She was just *there* and he decided to do it. Anne was sitting right there in her beautiful pearls pretending not to notice." Another well-remembered incident took place at one of his wife's impeccable dinner parties. Midway through the evening, one of the female guests felt Henry's stockinged foot stroking her under the table. Annoyed, she pulled the sock off and passed it to the guest next to her. The sock was passed from person to person until it reached Anne. As the men got up to retire to the study for brandy and cigars, she said with disgust, "Henry! I've got your sock!" Bad drinking and bad language became part of his distinctive signature; Anne started to leave parties without him.

Feeling stifled at home, Henry turned toward Europe, whose *dolce vita* atmosphere fascinated him. As Charles Cudlipp recalls, "He couldn't really show all his money around the company. A little bit at Southampton, maybe, but not in Detroit. He could show his money in Europe, where everyone else who had it did. He discovered Europe as if it were *terra incognita*. When he discovered it he couldn't get over it."

Italy was the place. Henry was treated deferentially in Detroit, but he was treated like royalty in Italy. One Italian aristocrat who watched the rake's progress of this young American industrialist was present at a party where actress Virna Lisi was at a table with Henry, Reggi di Piaggio and Gianni Agnelli. "Here I am with the three kings of Ford, Vespa and Fiat," the actress said. "I have all these cars at my disposal. What should I get next, maybe a Learjet?"

His perception of his friend and opposite number at Fiat, Gianni Agnelli, had the largest impact on Henry. While Agnelli's wife was sitting happily at home with the kids, Gianni was on his yacht with a bevy of women. As one observer later said, "Henry was entering his forties. Time was moving. He saw Agnelli screwing these girls on the boat and in his private apartment. Then he saw him going back to his wife and children as if nothing had happened. He saw the emptiness of his own life back in Grosse Pointe, where Anne would say 'No!' whenever he tried to goose a secretary in the elevator."

Henry started visiting high-class bordellos in Paris during business trips there. One of his favorites was on Rue Paul Valéry. People in Grosse Pointe would ask what he had planned for his European visits and he would reply, "I'm going to visit Paul Valéry," a comment that left them perplexed because they were sure he didn't know French poetry from French perfume. He became a little like Fitzgerald's Dick Diver, losing his way in Europe not just because of Old World depravity but also because of his own susceptibility.

It was a midlife crisis which, as one friend pointed out, had less to do with life than with sex—"Sex with a capital S." When someone complimented Henry on what a wonderful "lady" Anne was, he said ruefully, "Yeah, but did you ever try to get into the sack with a *lady*?" In addition to sex there was guilt. "I think he felt guilty for all the water he'd allowed to go under the bridge," a Ford executive later analyzed him. "He felt guilty for destroying his brothers, and for making a laughingstock of his father's name by letting the Edsel disaster happen. But he also felt that he was the one who'd stepped in and devoted his whole life to the company when it was going to hell in a handbasket. Now life was slipping through his fingers. He felt he was *owed*. This is what gave him that weird quality. He was like a time bomb—you could almost hear the ticking."

HENRY WAS UP TO 250 POUNDS. He was drinking prodigiously. He was dangerous when crossed. His executives knew to stay out of his way when he was "in a mood." At the Greenbrier Management Conference of 1959 Henry discovered that Whiz Kid Arjay Miller had quashed the purchase of a property he thought a potentially valuable asset. Getting drunk after one of the afternoon sessions, he suddenly asked, "Where's Arjay?" Those present knew where Miller was, but they knew, too, what would happen if he was found: Henry would attack him in front of everyone and then fire him. Various people went off pretending to look for Miller but returned to say that they couldn't find him. The next morning Henry had forgotten about the night before.

But the worst thing was the way Henry treated Breech. Even though Breech had long since been shunted aside, Henry had tried to keep up appearances. When he gave Crusoe the green light to push the senior man aside, he had compensated Breech with the chairman-of-the-board title and by appearing on an episode of the television show *This Is Your Life* devoted to Breech and making flattering comments about his work at Ford. (Bill Ford, still smarting over the Continental, had gotten up from the studio audience midway through the show, said, "This is awful. How can Henry say that shit?" and stalked out.) But now he began to grow impatient and seemed angry at Breech for not resigning. As Breech hung on, the situation grated on Henry. He began to contradict Breech openly in committees, shocking the other executives present. He ignored the older man. But he would not—or could not—ask him to leave.

Everyone thought he should have saved Breech's face by telling him he'd done a great job over the years but had to step aside now. But he didn't do that. Finally Breech realized he would have to take the initiative. He came to Henry early in 1960 and said, "Henry, now you've come of age. You want to take over and I want to step aside." Henry replied, "Yes, Ernie, I've graduated." He called Breech's wife, who he knew had been trying for months to get Ernie to step down. "I've got what I think you will call good news, Thelma," he told her. She asked, "Did he do it?" Henry answered, "Yes, he did. You know we're all sorry."

WITH BREECH OUT OF THE WAY, there was only one choice to replace him—Robert McNamara.

By training and cast of mind he was representative of the other young executives moving to positions of power. Yet personally he was something of an anomaly. Other executives in the auto industry were anxious about the symbols of power. Not McNamara. He made his own airline and hotel reservations, traveled commercial instead of reserving a company plane. One day he showed up for work with a bandaged hand. One of his executives heard him on the phone with his wife: "No, I'm all right, darling. There's nothing to it. Don't worry." Then after hanging up he explained, "This morning I was getting into the car and slammed the door on my hand. Of all things, I fainted. My wife was very much against my coming to work." Designer Gene Bordinat remembers McNamara once showing up on a Monday morning with a program from Ann Arbor's First Presbyterian Church on which he had scrawled the dimensions of a new Fairlane the previous day: "It was conceived in the presence of God, who McNamara worried might have been upset with him if he had wasted that Sunday morning in religious meditation."

Even during Breech's last days, McNamara's vision had come to dominate the company. It was the antithesis of what Reith and Crusoe saw. Theirs had been a vision of the early 1950s, a time when the primacy of the American Century was as yet unquestioned. McNamara's was a vision of limits shaped by the recession of 1957 and the USSR's successes with Sputnik and intercontinental ballistic missiles. He also differed from his GM predecessors in his idea of the executive role—which he saw as an almost judicial function rather than inspirational leadership. People noted that every time a product didn't do as well as anticipated, McNamara insisted on doing a "white paper" to fix the blame. "Bob had a deep desire to say who was right and who was wrong," another executive said later on. "It was part of that moral prissiness people saw in him."

It also led to the disturbing tendency to want to *appear* right even if he had been wrong. A few years earlier, upon taking over the Ford Division, McNamara asked engineer Harley Copp to fire one of his staff, a man named Bennett, because of a small error in his work. Copp protested that Bennett had otherwise been a valuable member of his team. "Okay," McNamara said, "then I want him on special assignment reporting to you, and I want his salary reduced for ninety days." Copp told him he was making a mistake and McNamara replied, sneering, "What's the matter, Harley, are you getting chicken?" The day before the demotion, one of the GM division heads called Breech to tell him that he would jump at the opportunity to hire someone with Bennett's talents. Hearing of this, McNamara called Copp in a panic: "This Bennett thing is out of control. Don't say anything in your office or over your phone you wouldn't say directly in front of Mr. Breech!"

McNamara had little feel for cars, and his stewardship of the company reflected the same philosophy that led him to state as Secretary of Defense, "There is no strategy; there is only crisis management." There were younger people in the company who were real car men. One of them was actually a McNamara protégé, a man named Lee Iacocca who was swiftly moving up the executive ladder. Iacocca, people said, was one of those old-fashioned auto men with gasoline in his blood. For such men the great challenge was to figure out what people *wanted* to buy; for McNamara it was trying to design what he felt they *ought* to buy. Once he took a Thunderbird home as part of the program whereby executives tried to familiarize themselves with the company's products. Usually these cars were filled up with gasoline by the company garage. For some reason his wasn't; McNamara had to stop at a service station. The next day, according to one of his aides, "he came back horrified at how much gas this car used and how much it cost to fill it up. He came to us saying that we had to do something about fuel economy. It was a great idea, but, Jesus, everybody knew that you didn't expect fuel economy in a T-bird kind of car."

Everybody else saw the failure of the Edsel as a complex matter. For McNamara, however, it was a simple thing. Reith and Crusoe had gone after a well-established market instead of trying to locate a new, untapped one. As he saw it, this was why Dr. Ferdinand Porsche's Volkswagen Beetle had become such a success in the fifties. McNamara was not inclined to make the same mistake as Breech, who had snidely dismissed Volkswagen: "What they sell in a year is not one day's production here." The German manufacturer was exporting nearly one million vehicles to the United States by 1958. Furthermore, McNamara *liked* the car. He had once asked Jim Wright and other executives to drive a Beetle and had come to work the next day filled with anticipation, only to become crestfallen when they told him they didn't share his enthusiasm for the Bug.

Now that he was in the driver's seat at Ford, he decided to do his own small economy car. On March 19, 1958, he had Wright circulate a memo: "As you know, for over a year Bob McNamara and I believed that the Ford Motor Company should manufacture a 'small car' in the U.S. At various times considerable opposition has been expressed by various segments of the Company to such a proposition.... [But] today the Product Planning Committee formally approved a small car program."

Engineer Harley Copp recommended a six-cylinder car. McNamara insisted on a four-cylinder. Del Harder of the board of directors came to Copp one day and asked why the car they were working on was a four-cylinder model. Copp responded, "Because Bob insists on a four-cylinder because it is $13.50 cheaper." Harder said he would take care of it. McNamara immediately caved in under the political pressure from the old operations man, and it became a six-cylinder. Another symptomatic episode came when Tom Case, chief stylist, stuck his neck out by saying that the car was too short and narrow. McNamara was furious and told him, "I'm going to prove to you this is a six-passenger car." He grabbed six workers and forced them into the mock-up of the car, where they sat hunched together with their knees practically to their chins while McNamara shot Case a look of irritation. Later on, when the car was presented to the other executives, McNamara could see that Henry was not too taken with his model. He got up and said, "Mr. Ford, the reason you don't like this car is that it is too short and narrow. That's why we're recommending that it be lengthened and widened by three inches."

There was not much enthusiasm in the auto community for the Falcon, as the car was called. The press immediately recognized it as a "modern version of the Tin Lizzie" which had been born out of the ashes of the Edsel. (In fact, McNamara closed down the Edsel's plants while the car was still technically in production, to make them available for the Falcon.) One auto writer said of McNamara, "He wears granny glasses and puts out a granny car." But it had great appeal to buyers whose pocketbooks were pinched at the end of the Eisenhower era. The Falcon sold over 400,000 units its first year on the market, and on June 3, 1960, McNamara, who had been functioning as a chief executive since Breech's departure, was appointed president.

It was a triumph for Henry, too: McNamara was *his* man in a way Breech had never been. But scarcely five weeks after announcing the appointment Henry heard that R. Sargent Shriver, chief headhunter for newly elected President John F. Kennedy, had talked to McNamara. At first the news was not too bad: McNamara had been offered the job of Secretary of the Treasury and had turned Kennedy down. But then Henry discovered that Kennedy had offered to make him head of Defense and that McNamara would probably accept. Henry had influential figures at Ford try to dissuade him, but McNamara put each of them off with the same little speech in which he said that he had come from a relatively poor family and he had already made more money than all the McNamaras before him. Then he said that America was a fantastic country because it allowed a poor boy to go as far and as quickly as he had and that he felt he owed it to America to go to Washington.

When he left, it was a tremendous blow to Henry, who had assumed that McNamara would be working with him for years to come. Charles Cudlipp, his daughter Charlotte's friend, was at the Ford home the day McNamara's resignation was announced, and happened to pass by Henry's study when the door was open. As Cudlipp passed by, Henry asked him to come in. Just then his wife, Anne, walked by and asked, "Are you doing any better?" Henry shrugged. "Well, not really. Chuck and I are going to sit here for a while and have a chat and then we'll join you." He closed the door and Cudlipp noticed that he had been crying. "This may be one of the worst days of my life," Henry said, pouring himself a drink. "I can't believe it happened. You've heard the news about Bob, haven't you? Well, I spent years training him. He's the first president outside the family. After all those years of training he's leaving. I can't believe it. Now what do I do?"

SEVENTEEN

THAT QUESTION—NOW WHAT DO I DO?—was the keynote of what became the first chapter in the second part of Henry's life, the part in which he would be confronted with a more difficult problem even than getting the company onto solid footing: how to locate himself, how to try to square the circle of responsibility and desire, to balance the claims of the corporation and the claims of the self. He was entering a new complexity. He would no longer be seen as the young man who, in an episode reminiscent of Western shootouts, had come back to clean out the town filled with bad guys and restore the family honor. He had outgrown that. The problems involved with rescuing the company were solved; now there was a new set of problems centered on the issue of whether or not he could rescue himself. It was an altogether more dangerous enterprise as far as his public imagery was concerned. Mastering a company, especially a company like Ford with historical resonance and international importance, was visible and attractive, a heroic enterprise. Trying to master a life and a self, the task that lay ahead, was not so visible, especially in one so closemouthed about his emotions, and therefore not so attractive.

Now what do I do? It was also the unarticulated theme of Ford's fourth Greenbrier Management Conference, held the third week of November 1960. There was no climactic moment equal to the one at the previous meeting when Henry had stunned Ernie Breech and everyone else by saying that he was the captain of the Ford ship. Yet there was an air of uncertainty and suspense that gave the conference its own drama. Breech was gone now. McNamara's crisp and insightful keynote address laid out a market strategy for the coming decade, but the speech was a tease because everyone knew that McNamara was going to become JFK's Secretary of Defense.

The uncertainty had to do not just with the question of who would occupy the top positions at Ford, but with Henry himself. Ironically it was McNamara, temperamentally impatient with matters of the heart, who stumbled onto the truth, although he didn't realize its full importance. As Ford's president he had been placed in a room adjoining Henry's suite at the Greenbrier. As he later told a colleague, he was astounded when his sleep was interrupted night after night by the sound of Henry's voice, talking with a

238

tenderness and a passion that were apparent even through the wall; talking as if he was trying to penetrate the static of a transcontinental telephone cable and a foreign culture as well. Without really wanting to, McNamara found himself eavesdropping, trying to guess who was on the other end of the line. It was clearly a woman, and, because Henry kept repeating the word *bambina,* McNamara surmised she was an Italian.

She was Cristina Vettore Austin. Henry had been introduced to her in Paris the previous March by Ernie Kanzler's new wife, Rosemarie. Kanzler had met and married the beautiful Swiss-born Rosemarie Ravelli, a onetime manicurist, in 1955, not long after his first wife, Josephine, Eleanor Ford's sister, had been found floating face down in their swimming pool at Hobe Sound, dead (and, according to Grosse Pointe gossip, dead drunk), and naked except for white gloves. Bald and a little stooped now, no longer the imposing figure he had been in the 1920s when he and Edsel tried to seize control of the company, Kanzler said of the thrice-married Rosemarie—who was almost twenty years younger than he but far more experienced in the ways of the world—"She has recharged my batteries."

Coming to Detroit after the marriage, Rosemarie had felt snubbed, especially by Anne Ford, now a social arbiter among the Right People, who was also exacting a kind of proxy revenge in behalf of her mother-in-law against someone she regarded as a gold digger who had dishonored the memory of Josephine Kanzler. But in Europe Rosemarie's adroit use of Kanzler's money had given the two of them a first-class ticket with the jet set. When Rosemarie decided to throw a party at Maxim's in Paris, she invited Henry and, as revenge against Anne for blocking her in Grosse Pointe, Cristina Austin as well. Henry had seen the young Italian woman the previous night. Even though Anne and his daughters were with him, when he arrived at Maxim's he took his name card, which had been put next to that of Princess Grace of Monaco, and moved it so that he would be sitting next to Cristina.

With her exaggerated Italian features—a long aquiline nose and a wide sensual mouth—Cristina was pretty in an off-balance sort of way that made her striking as well. She had tawny hair and Seurat eyes—amber with a pointillism of green and blue specks—set deeply above high cheekbones. It was a beauty that people immediately assumed came from an aristocratic background. In fact Cristina was quite self-made. Her father had died from meningitis when she was two hours old, and her mother had raised her and her sisters by playing the piano and singing in a bistro. Cristina had married a wealthy Canadian and later, after divorcing him, had returned to Europe to become a longtime companion of Count Marco Fabio Crespi. It was a relationship which had recently reached dead end when Crespi's aristocratic family asked him to stop seeing her.

Henry didn't know anything about Cristina's background that first night at Maxim's. But he wouldn't have cared if she had been a Gypsy fortuneteller. After dinner was over he asked her to dance. Midway through the song he tilted his head back, looked down at her and said, "I'm going to marry you."

The words seemed to escape him almost accidentally. Thinking he was joking, she laughed and tried to change the subject. Henry smiled nervously and kept on saying, "No. Really. I'm going to marry you." He continued to dance with her for the next hour, pressing his body against hers with a suggestiveness she found embarrassing, until his daughter Charlotte came by and pinched him on the arm.

"Sit down with your family," Cristina said. "Your wife is looking."

Henry shrugged. "I don't care. I'm going to marry you."

The next day, when Anne and the girls were off to Dior's on a shopping expedition, Henry called her. Cristina said she was going to church. He asked if he could come. When she cautioned him she was a Catholic, he said laughing, "I'm married to one. I have to go to confession every week." They went to Notre Dame. While she took communion, he knelt and prayed. The next day he had to leave for London, but he called when he got there and every day thereafter.

Two weeks later, after Anne and the children had returned home, Henry, carrying an extravagant bouquet of orchids, met Cristina in Geneva. He tried to buy jewelry for her, but she refused. They rented a car and wound their way back to Paris through the château country of southern France. Henry was so concentrated on her during their intimate dinners at the small inns where they stayed that he almost shuddered with intensity. People around them smiled and repeated the phrase "*un coup de foudre.*" Henry asked what it meant. "A strike of lightning," Cristina said in her broken English. "They are saying that you act like one hit by a strike of lightning."

John Bugas met them for dinner in Paris. Head of Ford International now, Bugas was the only executive in the company with the kind of relationship that would allow him to talk to Henry on a personal level. After Cristina had left to go back to the hotel, Henry began to tell Bugas about her—how in love with life she was, so intense and sensual, so different from Anne, who was uptight and in control. He said that he wanted to be out of control emotionally for once in his life, and that he had outgrown Anne, just as he had outgrown Breech. In a way it was all Anne's fault: if she hadn't gotten to feel that she was "better" than Detroit and hadn't wanted to take the family international, he never would have met Cristina.

Bugas remained unmoved. "You're emotionally involved with that girl," he said. "I've known you all these years, and I've never seen you emotional like this. But you'd better cut it out, because you're married, with three children. Keep her as a mistress if you have to, but don't divorce Anne."

Later on, when Henry told Cristina what Bugas had said, excluding the final piece of advice, he cautioned her not to take it too seriously. "John's marriage is in trouble, too, but he won't do anything about it. He has this saying, 'Better the one you know than the one you don't know.'"

Even though he was opposed to the relationship and felt that it would lead his friend to grief, Bugas reluctantly allowed himself to be conscripted into the affair as Henry's confidant and beard. Back in Dearborn a few weeks after the Paris meeting, he told chief stylist Eugene Bordinat to pack his bags for a quick trip to Europe. They flew to Cologne, checked into a hotel and the next morning met Henry and talked briefly with the head of Ford of Germany. That night they had a quick drink with Henry, and the following morning they left for home. "What the hell's going on here?" Bordinat asked as they sat on the plane. "This was the most unnecessary trip I've ever taken." Bugas smiled cynically and said, "Come on, Gene, you're a big boy. Henry's going down to meet Cristina in Paris again. We're just a device so he can 'legitimately' be in Europe."

By the time of the Greenbrier meeting when McNamara heard Henry wooing his *bambina* over the phone, the affair was well advanced and had taken on an intercontinental flavor, with trysts one week in Paris and the next in New York. It was clear to Cristina that Henry was trying to break the chrysalis that had constrained him all the years of his earnest labor at the company, so that he could emerge a different, freer person. It was also clear that he was worried about where the affair would lead, and guilty about Anne. And despite the attraction the libertinism of Europe's *dolce vita* held for him, he was at heart still a provincial American who had difficulty with "arrangements" and double standards. When he and Cristina registered at hotels as husband and wife he would blush nervously—less because he feared scandal, Cristina felt, than because he was simply uncomfortable with the deceit. Once they were forced to wait in the foyer of an exclusive New York restaurant while the maître d' flitted around them nervously before finally whispering to Henry that his daughter Charlotte was dining inside; Cristina was struck by the look of guilt that washed over Henry's face, something she knew she never would have seen in a European man.

Henry tried to take stock, to look at himself from the outside for the first time in his life. He saw what everyone else saw: a man in his early forties who looked older; whose face was jowly and bottom-heavy, bloated and red from drinking; whose weight was over 250, although it gave him no sense of real gravity. ("I feel like I'm floating up above reality," he once told Cristina when discussing his weight problem, "like one of those balloons in the Macy's parade.") Instead of enjoying the relationship with Cristina and the sensation of being in love again, he became more and more agitated. Even those who didn't know about Cristina felt that he was driving himself too hard. On May 10, 1961, he was at the Company Styling Division, having been dragged there by the energetic Lee Iacocca, whom he had just appointed head of the Ford Division, to view what Iacocca believed was Ford's answer to the Chevrolet Corvair. After being shown a clay model of the car that would eventually become the Mustang, he was taken out into the parking lot, where Iacocca had reinforced his point by lining up Chevy's line on one side and Ford's line facing it, leaving a hole on the Ford side opposite the Corvair. Henry looked dyspeptically at the dramatic tableau and then turned away. "Don't give me this shit, Lee," he said. "Just don't talk to me about it." He got into his limousine and went directly to the hospital, where he was admitted for what the doctors diagnosed as mononucleosis but referred to among themselves as a nervous breakdown.

He was bedridden for nearly a month, getting back on his feet in time for his daughter Anne's coming-out on June 19. More free spirited than Charlotte, with none of the first child's existential baggage, "little" Anne had always been Henry's favorite. Once again he spent an immense sum, $250,000, for what the papers, alluding to their own earlier hyperbole on Charlotte's coming-out, called "the Second Party of the Century." This time designer Jacques Frank did a replica of an eighteenth-century English garden with elaborate bowers and huge tents made to look like summerhouses. It began to storm about an hour before the affair began, and cars were backed up for miles along Lakeshore Drive. Because Anne was crazy about roses and butterflies, there were thousands of roses in vases all over the ballroom and a huge cloth balloon suspended overhead which, at the dramatic moment, opened to drop fifty thousand butterflies, many of them dead. Henry, drunk before the party began, fox-trotted the first dance with his daughter to "My Heart Belongs to Daddy." He got drunker and wound up conducting the band in his favorite song, "When the Saints Go Marching In." When singer Ella Fitzgerald finished her program he asked her to sing some more. "Thank you, Mr. Ford," she replied with firm politeness, "but it's time for me to go." He yelled at her, "But I *paid* you!"

People left the party talking about his behavior. But it was a sort of catharsis. On the eve of the debut, his wife had picked up a phone and heard him talking to his lover and saying that he would marry her. It did not occur to Anne that he seemed much like his grandfather at this point in his life: two wives, two lives. Unlike old Henry, however, it was difficult for him to maintain the deceit, let alone institutionalize it. It was also difficult for him to confront the situation directly, just as he had been unable to stop the Reith-Crusoe plan or to fire Breech. Angry as she was at the revelation of Henry's infidelity, Anne might have agreed with one of her female friends: "Henry is willful like his grandfather, but he suffers and wants to please like his father. This combination makes him interesting."

The night after the coming-out, Henry and Anne told their daughters that they had decided to separate. It was the first emotional scene the family had ever had. "It was crushing," Charlotte said later, "especially since none of· us was prepared. I remember thinking, What do I have to live for now?"

Yet, having taken this step, Henry pulled back, appalled at the pain he was causing and the emotional fissures that were opening up around him. He wavered, wooing Anne and Cristina at the same time—trying to undo the damage that every act seemed to do. As one friend later said, "Henry was not quite the brute everyone thought at the time. He was very human. He found himself in a situation where all he could do was hurt people. He didn't know how to stop. He didn't see he was hurting himself more than anyone else. He might have been like a bull in a china closet, but he was the one getting gored."

HENRY SET CRISTINA UP IN A Park Avenue apartment in New York. But he was conflicted about what step to take next, a man who was caught in an attraction-repulsion syndrome and was about to repeat every cliché of the midlife crisis, especially where it applied to the Wife and the Other Woman. Cristina later recalled, "Henry always come to me and say, 'I want a divorce.' But then he did not get one. A Jekyll and Hyde who doesn't know who he is or what he was doing." Waiting for him to make up his mind, she worked for Eileen Ford's modeling agency, where her feet and her face, which she considered her chief assets, were photographed for magazine layouts. "If I am a kept woman," she told a friend, "I am not kept very well." She said that Henry didn't spend extravagantly on her, perhaps to keep his guilt about infidelity under control. She bought secondhand Dior dresses for $100 apiece from Rosemarie Kanzler, who scissored the labels out before handing them over, a gesture Cristina regarded as the cruelest cut of all.

By the fall of 1961, as "blind" items were beginning to appear in gossip columns about a famous U.S. industrialist and his Continental sweetheart, Henry panicked. He told Cristina that the relationship was over. She must go back to Italy. He gave her $10,000 to close out her expenses and pay her way back to Italy. Having done this, he tried to repair the damage with Anne. "He wooed her like a lovesick kid," says one Grosse Pointer. "There were presents, flowers, a rush of attention. But she was mad as hell. They didn't call her the Ice Queen for nothing. It was pretty clear that she might forget, but she would never forgive." Ernie Kanzler's son Robert spent that Christmas with the Fords and never forgot the chill—literal and figurative—in the air: "Anne left the house cold, about sixty degrees. When the guests asked, she said it was good for the paintings. After dinner we went to the basement to watch a movie. There was a lot of rustling around to keep warm. Because of this, someone knocked over an ashtray. Anne switched on the lights and said, 'Okay! That's it! Everybody out of here!' Henry tried to calm her down: 'Oh, Anne, come on, don't be foolish.' But she kept it up. We left."

Stuck in his in-between state, unable to commit himself to either woman, Henry became almost pathetic. Helen Bogle, an old friend of the Ford family, ran into him at the Otsego Ski Club late that fall and noted his aura of sadness. "Anne was in New York on one of her charities. He was trying not to see Cristina. He seemed terribly alone. He got frightfully drunk one night and kept saying, 'I just wanted to come up here skiing.'"

But the pressures to force a decision were building. In November 1961 his old friend Nelson Rockefeller announced that he was getting a divorce from his wife of thirty years, an event Henry later said had a profound impact on him because it was the first time someone in his circle, someone with strong family tradition and a public identity, had done such a thing. Also,

Cristina hadn't left for Italy at all, but had become involved with another man in New York.

The affair had begun when she went into the drugstore of the hotel where she was living, to buy some lipstick. She asked for Revlon, that being the only brand name she knew. The clerk said they didn't carry it, but a man who had been watching her from the corner of the shop said he would see that she got what she needed. The next day a huge pack of Revlon products arrived at the hotel. The man turned out to be Revlon's owner, playboy Charles Revson himself, as smitten by Cristina as Henry had been at Maxim's. But before he could arrange an introduction, Cristina moved out of the hotel into the apartment Henry had set up for her. Revson had a composite drawing made of her from memory and circulated it at the best New York restaurants, offering a $1,000 reward to anyone who could tell him who the woman was. Finally a waiter recognized her and tipped Revson off. For two weeks he sent her three hundred roses a day without a card. Finally he called her and introduced himself. Cristina stammered out an excuse: she couldn't go out with him because she was in love with a man from Pittsburgh. But Revson kept bombarding her with attention, and finally, as she was giving up hope on Henry, she relented. She and Revson began spending an occasional weekend together at his country place. He said that he wanted her to marry him; she said that he, like Henry, was toying with her affections. As a token of his good intentions, Revson offered to put $1 million in escrow which would be hers if he didn't marry her.

When Henry found out about all this, his resolution not to see Cristina again melted. He telephoned her in desperation. "Do you really like him?" he asked.

Cristina replied, "He's a tough guy, but with women he's rather sweet."

Henry pleaded, "Don't see him again, *bambina*, please. Ever. Because I'm going to marry you."

Cristina hesitated, then answered wearily, "Okay. I don't care if you marry me or not. See me when you are in New York."

She broke off the liaison with Revson and returned to the status quo ante with Henry, functioning as his sometime consort while he tried to exorcise the uncertainty that few people saw, certainly not those who said that he was willful like his namesake. When he and Cristina were together, the subject of Revson would sometimes come up and she, unable to resist the dig, would refer to him as "Le Beau Charles." Finally Henry was unable to put up with it any longer and exploded, "Make that Le Beau Kike!"

One evening they rented a car in Manhattan and drove to Westchester for dinner. They were returning late at night when a policeman pulled them over for possessing a stolen vehicle. Initially confused, Henry finally realized that the parking attendant at the restaurant had brought him the wrong car when they were leaving. He couldn't keep the incident out of the paper, nor the fact that his rented car was a Chevrolet, although he managed to keep the reporter from mentioning that Cristina had been with him. He was not so lucky a few weeks later when he was in New York dining with Cristina and the maître d' showed his wife Anne in. Everyone froze for a moment, then Anne, ever the proper lady, paused at their table, and said genteelly, "Well, this was bound to happen sometime," and took her leave.

AT ONE OF THOSE TIMES WHEN he was trying to tell Cristina why it was so difficult for him to make a decision about her, Henry blurted out, "I've got the company. I've got to think about the company first. There's you and Anne, but I'm really married to the company. That's the one relationship in my life that will always be there." Indeed, that was his special burden. He might be a man in love, but he was also captain of the ship. Whatever happened below deck, he had to remain at the helm and try to steer a steady course. But as the emotional turbulence increased, he found that it was not easy to maintain the compartmentalization as he wished.

Some people had thought that Henry overreacted at McNamara's leaving. They said that the partnership would never have worked; that McNamara, staid and conservative, never would have been able to put up with Henry's lordliness and profligacy. Yet McNamara was very politic, much more so than his young protégé Lee Iacocca, who would eventually enrage Henry by his uncontrollable ego. It is equally possible that McNamara would have been the perfect counterbalance for Henry, the stabilizing force he needed during this difficult period in his life, and that the two of them, yin and yang, would have made the perfect team.

In any case, it was clear that McNamara's departure was a portentous moment. His resignation took a strong figure, one that Henry could have relied on for a long time, out of the picture. It ended the rise of the Whiz Kids to the highest echelons of the company, and it set the stage for the emergence of the first generation of young executives hired after the war. But most of all it meant more difficulty for Henry at a turbulent stage of his life. He seemed to be gloating when he chatted with reporter Bob Considine about the subject. "McNamara gave up a bundle of stock options," he said, pulling a little leather book out of his breast pocket. "He gave up thirty thousand shares of $33 options and, let's see, another thirty thousand shares at $23.71. He'd be worth three and a half million if he hadn't left."

McNamara's leaving threw his plans for Ford into doubt and gave the impression that the company was mired in confusion. By early 1963, *Business Week* was writing, "In today's auto sales race, the Ford Motor Company must feel like the man in a bad dream who races like mad only to find himself farther behind than ever. Ford is enjoying good car sales...yet its share of the market—the ultimate measure of competition performance—has dropped to a five-year low."

Between 1959 and 1963, GM's market share had gone from 41 percent to

57 percent, most of it at the expense of Chrysler. But in 1962 half of GM's gain had come out of Ford's hide, with Chevrolet alone outselling all the Ford products. Henry had a right to be doubly angry with McNamara because economy, an important element in the success of the 1960 Falcon, had vanished as a consumer issue. In the brief prosperity of the Kennedy years, buyers were once again asking for styling, luxury, accessories, but Ford was stuck with McNamara's legacy of austerity and utilitarianism. It had to sell the stripped-down compacts and family sedans that auto writers snidely referred to as "Plain Macs" while GM was making money with sporty models like the Corvair Monza.

Having always wanted to build an organization like GM's, Henry, in what he would later acknowledge was a kind of low-key desperation after McNamara's departure, called General Motors Chairman Fred Donner and set up an appointment. "I went down to New York and spent a whole day with him," he later recalled, "and he helped me a hell of a lot. I just wanted to learn, and the best one to learn from is your competition. I said, 'Fred, there's a lot of stuff I don't know, and there's a lot I can learn if you give me a little of your time.'"

But advice, even from the head of GM, was not enough. Henry saw that he needed a strong right hand, someone he could rely on to stabilize the leadership situation at Ford. Flailing about, he turned to Ernie Breech and implied that he would welcome him back at the company. But Breech said that he was happily retired, although shortly after their conversation he accepted a post as the chief executive officer of TWA. Henry then selected as president John Dykstra, whom Crusoe had brought into the company with the first wave of GM executives and who had functioned as "quality czar" since the Edsel disaster. Former Whiz Kids Arjay Miller and Ed Lundy were brighter; John Bugas felt that he deserved the top spot. But Henry liked Dykstra and felt that he had handled himself well during the debate over quality. It turned out to be a case of bad judgment on Henry's part, as he discovered that Dykstra might be a good manufacturing man but lacked leadership qualities. As William Gossett said, "Dykstra couldn't talk. He couldn't read a speech. Henry realized the mistake immediately. He couldn't wait to get rid of him."

To compensate for his bad choice, Henry found himself drawn into the nuts-and-bolts management of Ford. Trying to expand the company, he masterminded the purchase of the Philco Corporation for $83 million, a move that was intended to get Ford into advanced electronics and defense work, but soon proved a failure. At the same time, however, he spent over $350 million buying the publicly held shares of Ford's European companies, thus virtually reassembling the international empire begun by his grandfather, a maneuver that would later be seen as a stroke of genius.

When Dykstra reached mandatory retirement, in April 1963, Henry tried to recruit Semon E. "Bunkie" Knudsen, son of the old Ford and GM executive, who had followed his father's footsteps by making a spectacular success at Pontiac. Feeling that he was in line to become head of GM, Knudsen turned

Henry down. Desperate to solve the leadership problem, Henry created what he called the Executive Office, a "troika" comprised of himself as chairman, Arjay Miller as president, and Charles "Pat" Patterson, another manufacturing man, as vice-president. John Bugas spoke for most in the company when he dismissed the Executive Office by saying, "This is a camel with three humps for sure."

What Henry didn't seem to realize was that Ford faced a crisis of identity as well as a crisis of personnel. The whole product team of the late 1950s which had briefly put the company at the top of the industry—Crusoe, Reith, Krafve and others—had been mowed down by McNamara's relentless scythe. As Harley Copp put it, "Lewie Crusoe planted the seed corn and McNamara ate it up. With Crusoe we competed head 'n' head with GM. After Crusoe we just marked time." The consequences were obvious. The Ford Motor Company no longer had autonomous divisions competing in the marketplace. Ford was its one division and its one automobile line, as it had been in the days of old Henry. "The real problem," according to Copp, "was that there was no idea man at the top, no charismatic figure."

The one bright light in the executive ranks was a young man named Lee Iacocca. He had come of age in the organization in 1959, which was not a good year for the industry. At the last minute, Iacocca, just thirty-six years old, had slapped a four-seater Thunderbird roofline and engine onto the chassis of a Ford Galaxie and had an ad made showing the two cars in white standing next to each other under a "Just Married" sign. The strategy had worked, and Iacocca was summoned to Henry's office. He later recalled, "Mr. Ford called me over at ten-thirty A.M.—you never forget these things—on November 3, 1960. He said, 'We like what you are doing, but we have something else for you.' Then he said, 'How would you like to be a vice-president and general manager of the Ford Division?' "

Ford-watchers felt that Henry had found his next back-channel executive, someone who would play a role similar to the one Crusoe and McNamara had played. Yet Iacocca was different from both of the other two. He was more driven, more self-assured and, most crucially for future events, more distant from Henry himself. While Henry had been growing up in Grosse Pointe, separated from others in his family by large WASP distances and taboo subjects, Iacocca had been a boy in Allentown, Pennsylvania, so close to his immigrant mother and father and his sister that the family felt like "one person with four parts." If the Fords embodied one part of the American myth, the one having to do with self-reliance and rugged individuality, the Iacoccas represented the other, having to do with upward striving and the attempt to crawl out of the melting pot into the mainstream.

Lee's father, Nicola, arrived in America in 1902, returning to Italy in 1921, when he was thirty-one, to meet and marry a young woman of seventeen. While the first Henry Ford was using his Sociological Department to try to raise his immigrant workers by their bootstraps, the first Iacocca was doing it himself—parlaying a hot-dog stand into respectability and even modest wealth. He was also a tough guy, once screaming at a crossing guard who cited him for almost running over a child in a crosswalk, "You whore! Why don't you go home and work in your kitchen?" He communicated both these values, entrepreneurship and bull-headedness, to his son. Under Lee's picture in his high-school yearbook was this statement: "When you aim at anything you are sure to hit it."

Lee's first vision of Ford was dreamlike: the sleek black Continental driven by the recruiter whom Henry sent out to interview college students in 1946 when he was trying to find young men to help him rebuild Ford. "One glimpse of it," Iacocca later said of Edsel's classic car, "and one whiff of the leather interior were enough to make me want to work at Ford for the rest of my life."

Although trained as an engineer, Iacocca had realized during his training that he would have a better chance of succeeding if he could apply the human touch than if he was stuck at a drafting table. He talked himself out of the Engineering Department and into Sales. He did well in fleet sales, but during the recession of the early 1950s he was demoted although he was doing a good job. This so depressed him that he briefly considered quitting and getting into the nascent fast-food business. But he stuck it out at Ford and by 1953 had worked himself back up to where he had been. He was promoted to a position in which he taught other salesmen, and he wrote a handbook entitled "Hiring and Training Truck Salesmen."

Iacocca was on the executive fast track in 1956 after coming up with the sales idea that buyers should be able to get a Ford for $56 a month. His "56 for 56" campaign caught the eye of McNamara, then vice-president of the Ford Division, who brought him back to Dearborn from Washington, D.C., where he had been working as district sales manager. Once back at Ford's headquarters, Iacocca enrolled in a Dale Carnegie course to improve his speaking and self-presentation for what he firmly believed would be the crucial years ahead.

McNamara and Iacocca were odd allies. Both were deeply political, but while this trait was the root of their alliance, they recognized that otherwise they were quite different. It was not just a matter of character—the cold and calculating Whiz Kid versus the bold and brash immigrant's kid. It involved automobiles as well. As Ford designer John Najjar later said, "With McNamara, despite his intelligence, you had to explain certain things over and over. For instance, why there had to be a vertical post on the rear door of the four-door hardtop convertible. He'd keep asking, 'But why does that thing have to be there?' Not so with Iacocca. He *knew* cars."

In the field during the Reith-Crusoe plan, Iacocca returned to Dearborn when heads were rolling but was associated with neither the victims nor the headsmen. He had a style all his own. As a young sales chief he had planted microphones around his salesmen to see if they were aggressive enough in closing their deals. Another time he was speaking at a sales conference and snarled at his sales force, "You either get into the black in this business or you get out." He might rub people the wrong way, but even his enemies admitted that he did *know* cars. After becoming head of the Ford Division he recognized immediately that the austere McNamara had badly miscalculated the mood of Americans, mistaking a transient economic trend for a basic characteristic. One of his first moves was to jazz up McNamara's Falcons with accessories, fancy trims and styling extras like hardtops, which most observers believed was the only reason the car continued to sell past the first year. He showed himself to be master of the "quick fix"—a cosmetic makeover that didn't involve costly basic mechanical changes. The word given to this technique was "packaging"—manipulating the surfaces that were so crucial in an age of media.

Taking control of the Ford Division, Iacocca moved quickly to kill the Cardinal, McNamara's attempt to make an American Volkswagen, which Iacocca regarded as a designing disaster despite the new V-4 engine, front-wheel drive and great mileage. "The Cardinal is a loser," Iacocca told Henry. "To bring out another lemon so soon after the Edsel will bring this company to its knees. We simply can't afford a new model that won't appeal to younger buyers." Iacocca talked Henry into resuming the Ford racing program, which had been disbanded in 1956, as another way of gaining the attention of the youth market. His frequently repeated watchwords, "Youth, power, performance," struck the same chords that John Kennedy was composing into an anthem for his administration.

With his hawkish face, his raspy voice and the large Ignacio Hoya cigars he used as a prop in the manner of George Burns, Iacocca had a rough charisma. Added to his undisputed auto sense, it made him a compelling individual in a company that seemed to have lost its way. Ford Division Product Planner Donald Frey later said, "Lee was the first guy at the top of the company since Crusoe to go up there and say, 'Look, here's what the public wants, here's how to build it, here's how to sell it.' Henry was surrounded by people who had every ability except for that." People might not agree about Iacocca as a person, but there was a consensus that he was close to the heart of what the company purpose was or ought to be, certainly more than the men of Finance, the "bean counters" who had played an important and (their critics claimed) largely negative role in the postwar auto era. He was the only executive who was a strong motivator. As one of his colleagues said later, "When Lee had to make an appearance one of his guys would get together fifty pages of facts and analyses, and then he would throw it away and make a great speech. Whatever level you were in the company, he made you want to go out and sell a Ford to the first ten people you ran into on the street."

When he first became head of the Ford Division, Iacocca began to lunch frequently at the Detroit Athletic Club. People sometimes joked about the way auto executives there furtively took snapshots out of their pockets, showed them to colleagues and then hid them away suddenly if someone approached. It looked as though they were passing around porn; actually they were photos of competitors' cars. At one of these sessions Iacocca found out that

Chevrolet had taken its much-criticized Corvair, outfitted it with bucket seats, wheel covers, a standard-equipment tachometer and other sporty extras, and was going to market it as the "Monza." (His aide Hal Sperlich recalled, "I remember sitting there and thinking, 'Son of a bitch, the bastards have turned defeat into victory.' ") Iacocca felt that GM was once again beating Ford to the punch and decided to act on the mandate Henry had given him to get some life back into the Ford Division. He described the car he wanted to do as "a poor man's Thunderbird for the working girl."

The new project began in the spring of 1961. It was, in fact, an early prototype of the new car, called the Allegro at this point, that Iacocca had shown Henry the day he came down with mononucleosis. Iacocca liked early, two-seater versions of the car, but told designers that he couldn't sell a two-seater car in volume. Word went out through the company that Iacocca wanted something "bold and brassy," and that the Design Department had struck out. One day product planner Don Frey was stopped in the hall by Joe Oros, head of truck design. Although trucks were the Siberia of styling, Oros and his men had been coming in after work and on weekends, excited by the prospect of getting involved in the sweepstakes for the new car. "I've got your sporty car," he told Frey as he showed him the drawings. Frey was amazed: "There it was—exactly what we wanted."

Ironically, Frey was able to save on tooling costs by using the basic engine, transmission, axles and drive lines of the dowdy Falcon. He changed the floor plan, but even used the instrument cluster. He built a prototype, knowing that it was a tough time for new products in the company, a time when the Edsel was still being used as a cautionary tale. He showed Iacocca the finished product, telling him it was a winner.

"How do you know?" Iacocca asked.

"Because the people who run the experimental garage—the testtrack people who've seen everything—go ape over this car," Frey answered. "When we bring it onto the track this car collects crowds."

Iacocca ordered Frey to bring in a dozen of the best auto writers in the country. When they reacted with unanimous enthusiasm, he agreed that they had a winner. He hired the J. Walter Thompson agency to help name the car. Their first choice was "Torino." But then a call came from Charlie Moore, Henry's personal publicity agent inside the company, telling Iacocca he would have to find another name because anything Italianate might remind people of the gossip they might have heard about Henry and Cristina. Henry himself had strongly suggested "Thunderbird II." But the Thompson agency recommended "Mustang"—their concept came from the great World War II fighter plane, not the horse—and that stuck.

In politicking for the Mustang inside the company, Iacocca disdainfully ignored one third of the ruling troika, "Pat" Patterson. He dummied up market research regarding the new youth market to convince Scroogish Arjay Miller that the expenditures were necessary. Then he concentrated on the top man. As the car went through development, sales projections had been steadily raised. Iacocca came to Henry with visions of huge sales. He told him of a study the Ford Division had conducted in which a group of fifty-two Detroit couples were invited to the styling showroom and their reactions to the new car were taped. The white-collar group was impressed by the styling, the blue collars by the status and prestige the Mustang promised. When asked to guess about its price, both groups overestimated it by an average of $1,000. Henry, who had still not gotten over the Edsel catastrophe, was impatient. "Enough of that shit, Lee," he growled. "We got our ass lost on the last one. Who needs another?" He finally allowed himself to be dragged to the styling studio and glanced at the car dyspeptically. "You guys got to sell this thing," he said finally. "I'm going to approve the goddamned thing to get rid of you. But once I approve it you got to sell it, and it's your ass if you don't."

Iacocca put together a "Mustang team" to iron out production problems that had helped kill the Edsel. But it was in launching the Mustang that Iacocca showed his genius. About four months before the car's debut, he got Ford public-relations man Bob Hefty to invite *Newsweek*'s Detroit Bureau chief, James Jones, to lunch. Jones was shown the first pictures of the Mustang, which Hefty called the most significant car of the generation, and was offered an exclusive story in return for a major space commitment. Jones checked with his editors, who invited Iacocca to the magazine's New York headquarters and, after their meeting, decided to schedule the Mustang for a cover story. Meanwhile, Hefty was secretly contacting *Time*'s Detroit Bureau chief, Leon Jaroff, and inviting him to meet Iacocca at Ford Division headquarters. Jaroff was shown the Mustang and given a similar promise of exclusivity in return for space in his magazine. [*]

Both cover stories featured Iacocca as much as the Mustang. *Time* called him "the hottest young man in Detroit" and even gave its readers a lesson on how to pronouce his name: "*rhymes with try-a-coke-ah.*"

After his publicity coup, Iacocca had emerged a megafigure in the company and in the auto industry. His image as a rising star would be solidified when the Mustang (whose "father" he would thereafter be called) sold over 418,000 units in its first year on the market, adding over one half billion dollars to company sales. Iacocca made it clear that he thought this was the start of something big: "I see this as the start of a new golden age for Ford that will make the peaks of the past look like anthills."

HENRY WAS TAKEN ABACK BY IACOCCA'S self-promotion and his appropriation of the company's public-relations machinery for personal advancement, pub-

---

[*] Jones later claimed he was "double-crossed," although he acknowledged that Hefty probably would have been fired if he hadn't done what he did.

licity that virtually ignored Henry himself. Not only did *Time* and *Newsweek* feature Iacocca on their covers, but the articles within hardly mentioned the captain of the Ford ship. Yet Iacocca had been willing to devote the endless hours for the interviews and the posing, time which Henry was unwilling to give because of his increasing absorption with his private life. And so, even though Iacocca may have staged a minor coup within the company, ultimately Henry had to be grateful. The Mustang gave Ford the appearance of being reoriented and on track. It also gave Henry some breathing space for the decisions he knew he would have to make in his private life.

In the year since he had weaned Cristina away from Charles Revson, he had continued to live with his ambiguity. On the surface he appeared even-handed in juggling relations between his wife and lover. For Christmas he had given Anne a $65,000 necklace of pearls the size of marbles. But it was like a pre-alimony payment, because at a deeper level of his emotional life he was preparing for a breakout. Soon after the new year he spent $700,000 on a 109-foot yacht he christened the *Santa Maria*. When asked why he had picked that name, he shrugged. Some close to him felt that the symbolism was clear: he intended to set sail for new worlds of the emotions.

In his case this meant a voyage to the Old World. He and his family arrived on the Côte d'Azur in August 1963, anchoring off Cap Ferrat. What struck Europeans about the *Santa Maria* was the discipline of the boat: watching the crew stand at attention, a Greek jet-setter compared them to members of a German U-boat. What struck them about the Fords was that Henry and Anne seemed utterly at sea with each other. In fact, after the vacation was over and the *Santa Maria* had returned to the United States, Anne packed her bags and moved to New York, taking a suite at the Carlyle Hotel. It was impossible to keep up the charade any longer, she told members of her family, the McDonnells; she had been humiliated long enough. However well prepared Anne may have felt as a result of her knowledge of Henry's affair, however, she was still traumatized, as a believing Catholic, when it came time to begin the divorce. When she had her first meeting with William Hadley, senior partner in the blue-ribbon New York law firm of Milbank, Tweed, she broke down in tears. Hadley looked at her and said, "Well, Mrs. Ford, I see that you're not in any condition to discuss the matter today, so we'll have to make another appointment."

She had gathered herself together well enough to go to Hotchkiss with Henry in the Ford plane to bring Edsel II home for Christmas, telling him what his older sisters already knew—that the marriage was over. Edsel went with Anne to Sun Valley for a skiing holiday the day after Christmas. He returned, but she stayed in Idaho for the brief residency that led to a formal divorce on February 12, 1964. By this time she was reconciled to the breakup, telling a friend, "I should have done this earlier. It was wrong to hold him."

Once Anne had left, the press, which had so far not published much about Henry's private life, suddenly "discovered" Cristina. ("A Ford for an Austin," read one headline.) Henry was relieved that the deception was over.

But he still felt that he had to live up to the institution he had worked so desperately to possess, and so he continued to try to keep the relationship with Cristina private. She occupied herself in New York in the spring of 1964 by making the rounds and doing a little modeling. (Photographer Richard Avedon shot her in profile without makeup or jewelry for a spread in *Harper's Bazaar* entitled "An Eclectic Beauty.") Henry saw her in New York as often as possible and on a couple of discreet skiing weekends. She made a few clandestine trips to Dearborn, staying at John Bugas' house, where she sat with her hair in curlers watching television and chatting distantly with Bugas' wife and daughters while waiting for Henry to call. She did not know that he had asked Bugas to do a background investigation on her, or that, even though he had not found anything incriminating, Bugas still advised Henry, "Don't marry her."

"It was a strange time in Henry's life," a friend later said. "It was hard for him to cut through the ambiguity; it was like walking in water." Partly it was Cristina. His daughters were scarcely speaking to him because of her; they referred to her cuttingly as "the Dago." Benson's wife, Edie, taking out on Cristina her aggressions over what had happened to her husband, called her "the Pizza Queen." Even Eleanor Ford was upset. She had never been emotionally close to Anne, but she had appreciated the social functions she had performed, especially because Anne had taken the pressure off her to be the Ford representative at art and charity functions. Now Eleanor was distraught over the divorce, holding several uncharacteristically harsh discussions with Henry about the chaos he was creating inside the family.

Yet Henry's malaise went deeper than lack of approval for his love life. It was also the case that when he looked around in the family he saw he was the only one succeeding and his success was precarious. His sister Dodie had become retiring and private. She once said, "What else is there for a girl who wasn't competitive to do but try to escape all that Ford stuff?" The irony, of course, was that because of whom she married, Walter Buhl Ford, she didn't really escape the name. But the marriage was good. By profession an interior designer, her gentle and unassertive husband had made space for Dodie which insulated her from family pressures. He fulfilled her civic responsibilities, allowing Dodie to concentrate on her small circle of friends. She had trouble with alcoholism—it was something like an inherited genetic disorder for her Ford generation —but not to the same degree as Benson and Bill. Dodie was friends with everyone in the family, trying to keep them together as a group. She was one of the few Fords who didn't blame Henry for what had happened to his brothers.

The person he had been closest to as a boy, Benson, was now a virtual stranger, someone Henry felt he had to shout to across a vast emotional chasm. Since suffering his heart attack in 1957, Benson was often in pain, gulping nitroglycerine pills with about the same frequency that he did glasses of Canadian Club whisky. He was still heading the Dealer Policy Board—a body that heard and adjudicated Ford dealers' complaints and problems. For a non-Ford it might have been a worthy job; for Benson it was clearly a make-work position which reinforced the message he had already received that as far as the company was concerned he was only a ceremonial Ford. Yet he doggedly tried to fulfill the job. When scheduled to speak at a dealer convention, he would become so nervous that he vomited, not being able to relax until after the ordeal was over and he had downed three or four shots of Canadian Club. The most fragile and intensely personal of all the Fords, Benson seemed not to regard these qualities as virtues. Another executive who watched him at Dealer Policy Association meetings says, "They loved him. He was the one Ford who would sit and talk to them. Ben didn't realize how appealing he was."

The aides who worked for Benson all became irredentists, trying to get him to become more aggressive and reconquer territory he had lost during the Crusoe era. But Benson wouldn't try. Becoming more and more insecure, he talked them out of their ambition for him: "I don't want to make waves. That's my problem. You've got to get in there like Henry does and beat the hell out of them. You've got to do what Henry did with Bennett—face the sons of bitches and beat them. I can't do that."

His problems were magnified by what had happened at home. Edie had long since realized the exact nature of the problem. In her brother-in-law Bill's formulation: there could be only one Ford in the company at a time. While Benson plodded doggedly ahead, not naming the absurdity of his situation, Edie could not deceive herself so easily. At first she had tried to get him to fight back. Their friends remember her pleading with him, "Please, Ben, don't let them push you around." But Benson knew that exerting himself would inevitably put him in conflict with Henry. He would shrug her off, saying, "I'll do it my way." After a while her attempts to support him fermented into bitterness. "Aw, tell those guys to go screw themselves," she would say when he mentioned some problem at work. "Why ruin your health? They'll never let you have any real power."

Edie took the lead in drinking. Sleeping until noon before getting up to have cocktails with her friends, she would be drunk by the time Benson got home from work. He would pour three fingers of Canadian Club into a glass and, tossing it down, say, "Well, I see you have a head start. I'll have to catch up with you." They became a pair of people talking past rather than to each other. Edie drank at home with women friends; Benson went out on the town and drank himself into stupefaction. Occasionally Ford officials would be called to rescue him from one of Detroit's raunchy downtown bars.

The effects on the children, Benson Junior and Lynn, were noticeable. They were essentially raised by maids and governesses who made their meals, bought their clothes, put them to bed and kissed them good night. One family friend said of Lynn; "She had this pixie cut when she was a little girl. It was cute. But when she became a teenager and didn't change the style and looked ridiculous, it was obvious that nobody was looking after her in the family."

The toll on Benson Junior was even more apparent. As a boy, he had been a great favorite of his father's, who referred to him affectionately as "BF" and "the young man." But as things went badly at the company, the nature of their relationship changed, Benson shrinking from his son as if fearful he would see his failure mirrored in the boy's eyes. He occasionally delivered what Benson Junior came to think of as The Lecture: "Someday you're going to grow up and be a very important person with the Ford Motor Company. And the way you act now will affect your future." If it was delivered by Edie instead of Benson, The Lecture would conclude with this admonition: "And don't argue with Dad, he's had a heart attack." What was the point? Benson Junior wondered. What could he do at this stage of his life about being a Ford, anyway? He was struck less by the benefits of being part of a great family than by the liabilities. He would always remember the way servants laid out his clothes in the morning and cleaned up after him at night—efficient, invisible. Sometimes he would get up out of bed after everyone was asleep, go downstairs and make a mess in the kitchen. But every morning when he got up things would be clean again, his attempt to leave a thumbprint on things eradicated.

When they were small, Lynn and Benson Junior had been raised close to Bill Ford's children and Edsel II. But as their parents' lives drifted into defeatism and drunkenness, they were the first to be sent away to boarding school. It affected young Benson particularly. As his father withdrew from the company and began splitting his time between Detroit and Florida, Ben Junior was often taken out of school for long periods. He fell behind at the Grosse Pointe School and had to repeat a grade. Sent at the age of thirteen to the Fessenden School in West Newton, Massachusetts, Benson Junior tried to communicate his state of mind to his parents symbolically by dropping tears onto the pages of the melancholy letters he wrote back to Dearborn, hoping that this indication of his distress would make them realize how miserable he was and bring him home. When nothing happened, he ran away from school. He was returned and held back another grade. When he flunked out, he was enrolled in another prep school, Suffield Academy.

People close to Benson knew that he would have liked to do something about his son and daughter, but he was too involved in his own tragedy to see theirs. As his close friend Eddie Stroh said, "Benson could take the punches. But as time went on even he had to admit that he was losing the battle at the company. Ford had meant everything to him, but he began finally to pull away. He just gave up." He had become a dedicated sailor over the years, buying a forty-two-foot yacht in the early fifties, trading it in on a fifty-footer, and then, in 1959, buying an eighty-five-footer he christened, after Edsel's boat, the *Onika II*. With no hope at the company, he retreated to the yacht, sailing the Great Lakes and, as often as possible, making the trip to Palm Beach. Stroh says, "The boat was the one place Ben felt he was in command. He'd get aboard and say, 'What the hell am I fighting all this for? I've got everything I want right here.' But he knew that wasn't right. Everything he wanted was at the company and he couldn't have it. That's what ate at him."

Bill had taken the opposite route from Benson's, choosing to withdraw from the company rather than try to prove himself within it. After the Continental was terminated, his life seemed to switch to slow motion. He had bought a piece of property on Lakeshore Drive in 1959 but took until 1964 to finish a house. (Some people ascribed the delay to his ambivalence at living in the same neighborhood as Henry.) He also boycotted the Glass House, regarding it as Henry's monument to himself. He maintained the office at the Design Center, whose nominal chief executive he had become after his Continental was canceled. He came in every afternoon, still keeping his own hours. But people assumed that he was never there and made a joke of his absence: "Where can you always park at the Design Center? In Bill Ford's space."

The death of the Continental—Bill continued to think of it as a murder—took on status as a metaphor for him. When younger he had always thought of the Ford Motor Company as his destiny. Now he saw that it was a malign fate he couldn't affect. He did not bother, as Benson did, to restrict his heavy drinking to after working hours. Almost consciously, he embarked on what amounted to a bruising ten-year lost weekend. His eyes took on an alcoholic glaze; the sharply handsome face became bloated, and his slender athlete's body looked as though it had been injected with some heavy whitening agent. Drinking most of the day, Bill made only a few concessions to appearances, such as pouring Baccardi into a partly filled Pepsi bottle which he carried with him when people were present, as if it were soda pop. "Bill may have thought he was punishing Henry," a friend observed, "but he was really punishing himself."

"What I needed most of all," Bill said later, "was something to do." Partial salvation came from an unexpected source—the Detroit Lions football team. Bill had been a stockholder since 1956, when the ubiquitous "Uncle Ernie" Kanzler got him involved. Then in 1961, when two other candidates got embroiled in an ugly proxy fight, Bill was asked to become the Lions' president. When the team went up for sale in 1964, he issued an ultimatum reminiscent of his grandfather's decision to buy out the original Ford Motor Company investors: either he would be allowed to buy out the other Lions stockholders or he would resign. It cost him $4.5 million, but after the deal was consummated he said, "I always wanted something that was all mine and mine to do. This was it."

The team was like a passing piece of driftwood he had grabbed at while going down a final time. He told his wife, Martha, "I couldn't do a car again. But this is something that can be my business, and I can run it the way I want to. I won't even have stockholders to tell me what to do." But it didn't solve his problem. A fellow board member recalled, "He drank hot gin—no ice. Oh, Jesus. He'd get himself really swacked. But he wasn't a fun drunk. He'd look at me and say, 'You son of a bitch, you drank a bottle of whisky and you don't look like you had a drink.' I'd say, 'Well, it agrees with me and it doesn't agree with you.' Henry had fun when he drank. He'd go out and raise hell. Bill would just get stewed. He was black, no fun at all. He'd go in his room and lock the goddamned door."

All during this time the company got calls from the Detroit police regarding Bill's drunkenness. Ford executive Bob Dunham fielded many of them, including an expression of deep concern on the part of the police leadership when Bill applied for a permit to carry a concealed weapon. Dunham always reported these incidents to Henry, who said he would handle them. More than once Henry called other Ford executives and asked them to take Bill's car keys away from him. Sometimes when this happened Bill incoherently repeated the phrase that had become the cornerstone of his worldview: "The trouble is that there is only room for one Ford at a time."

AT THE EXACT MOMENT HENRY WAS trying to become authentic, trying to locate himself within the Ford persona, everyone was making him a symbol—an almost totemic figure responsible for whatever happened to them. This was true within his family. It was also true with his friends. They all seemed to want something, to expect some royal touch that would improve their lives. "I got into a situation where all I could do was hurt people," he said later. "I didn't want to, but because of the company I couldn't help it."

His old friend John Bugas was a case in point. John Davis and Mead Bricker having retired, Bugas was the last of the triumvirate who had stood beside Henry during the dark days of the Bennett struggle. Bugas had been wounded by being passed over for the Ford presidency in favor of Dykstra and then being excluded from the troika. Some people in the company thought that Bugas' ambitions were unrealistic. He was, after all, only a former FBI agent who had been made a millionaire by Henry as a result of the stock options he had been given over the years; a man with no background in the auto business who had nonetheless been made head of Ford International, that part of the company closest to Henry's heart. Yet as Bugas saw it, he was as good as any of the men recently elevated above him. He had been loyal to the company. (When Harry Bennett had been about to publish a book of reminiscences about his years with the company in 1955, Bugas called the office of J. Edgar Hoover to say that he had contacted Bennett's ghostwriter and thought he could make a copy of the manuscript for a couple of hours if the FBI would loan him some photographic equipment.) And loyal to Henry personally. Despite his own doubts about Cristina, for instance, he had become a facilitator of the relationship.

At a dinner shortly after the troika had been formed, Henry came up to Bugas and said that he had heard he was upset. When Bugas said he was, Henry told him, "I've been meaning to talk to you about it. Not here. Not tonight. But I do want to get together with you…and I want to tell you about the considerations I had in mind." He never did have this conversation, which made Bugas all the more nervous as the months passed, especially when he looked around and saw the velocity in the careers of a younger generation of executives led by Iacocca. What Bugas didn't know was that Henry had discussed the matter of his possible appointment to the presidency with Sidney Weinberg, the Wall Street banker who had brokered Ford's public issue, and that Weinberg had said adamantly that Bugas didn't have the right background.

Bugas remained loyal. He prided himself on this quality, not just in his relations with Henry but in his life. At about the same time that his relationship with Henry was sinking into crisis, he was playing golf with young John De Lorean, a GM executive who had made a name for himself by bringing to market the Pontiac GTO, which was based on the "street machines" he had seen teenagers racing in Detroit. As they teed off at the Bloomfield Hills Country Club, the talk turned to the civil-rights struggle erupting in the South. Bugas said that he had recently spoken to "the Director," as he called his old friend J. Edgar Hoover. "The Director was telling me that he refused to shake Dr. King's hand and that Martin Luther King is stealing money from the SCLC. Not only that, but he's a sexual pervert." In the course of the conversation Bugas told De Lorean that Hoover had asked him to contact the Ford Foundation and try to get them to terminate King's funding, which he had done. De Lorean attacked Hoover's civil-rights policies, and Bugas was so angry that he ended the golf game.

But now Bugas felt that his loyalty to Henry and his attempt to look out for him, particularly where Cristina was involved, would hurt him. "It was the biggest mistake in my life," he said when telling a friend how he had acted as a cover for Henry in Europe, kept Cristina in his house and also investigated her background. The subject of Cristina immediately surfaced when he and Henry met in England for the British auto show in October 1964. During dinner at Les Ambassadeurs the talk quickly shifted away from the company. "She's gone through great agony the past three years," Henry said about Cristina. "Don't be surprised if I get married soon."

Bugas knew that Henry was inviting a reaction. He tried to be careful, but the puritan in him won out over the pragmatist. "You shouldn't ask for advice, because you don't want it," he said. "You never take advice unless it happens to coincide with what you've already decided you want to do.... But since you've asked, I might as well tell you that you'd better fish or cut bait. You can't go on traveling around the world with a woman, unless she's your wife, without hurting the Ford Motor Company.... This situation of yours and the great stresses and strains that have resulted have been bad for you as a person."

Looking deeply into his brandy snifter, Henry replied, "I know. I've been absolutely torn apart. I want my family on the one side and Cristina on the other. It has been a living hell for the last few years."

Perhaps because he was still angry at what he regarded as the betrayal of his ambitions, Bugas gave the knife a turn: "It's obvious. You haven't applied yourself. You've neglected your job.... Hell, Henry, you haven't put in over half your time on your job during the last two or three years." Henry flinched, but Bugas kept on: "Because we've been friends a long while, I do have a concern about you as an individual. My concern here is for the Ford Motor Company. You'd better get this personal situation of yours cleared up, because nobody, even with the Ford name behind them, can run this company without working at it."

Because of the intensity in their relationship, it was especially difficult for Henry to take the next step with Bugas. But Arjay Miller and the Whiz Kid group in Finance had never taken to the outsider from Wyoming. And now, feeling the incipient challenge of Iacocca, Miller and his supporters moved to extend their control over Ford International. Miller and Ed Lundy made the case against Bugas' performance there, employing an argument Henry could not help but heed: the company was increasingly dependent on International as a profit center and must have top men in the top jobs there. Miller demanded that the staff of International be "folded into" Finance, which was controlled by Lundy. Bugas saw that this would take away his power base and refused to go along with the change. In a February 15 meeting Henry criticized Bugas' choice of executives. Two days later, he summoned his old friend to his office. He was visibly shaken, a gray pallor on his face. "It must come as a surprise to you," he began, "but maybe it's been my fault. But I'd like to have you step out of Ford International. I want to put somebody else in to run it. You've made a great contribution. I want you to stay on as a VP and member of the board of directors."

Bugas replied cautiously, "I know you. I've seen you operate around here and I've never seen you be happy with cripples. That's what I'd be around this place."

Henry reassured him that there would be real work and real responsibility. Bugas said he'd like to take a while to make his decision. Henry said that there was no hurry because he'd be leaving for Switzerland at the end of the week. The question of Bugas' future could wait until he got back.

Bugas thought his old friend had been cavalier on a matter of importance to him. He didn't know how difficult a moment it had been for Henry. His daughter Anne happened to be in Detroit for a visit, and on the eve of his departure for Europe he had stayed up until 4 A.M. talking with her about Bugas. He was in tears as he concluded the conversation: "It's not easy to fire your best friends."

What he didn't say—to his daughter or to Bugas—was why he was going to Switzerland. He had finally decided to marry Cristina, in hopes that his life would become easier and better. The next day he called his Washington public-relations man James Newmyer and told him that he planned to get married, but that because his divorce from Anne had been so difficult he wanted to make this move in privacy. Newmyer arranged it, obtaining a suite in the Shoreham Hotel and a justice of the peace to perform the ceremony. He and Hildegard Czerner, a friend of Cristina's who ran a chic Washington boutique, stood up as witnesses. After it was over Henry smiled enigmatically and said, "It's a long way from the Wedding of the Century to this, isn't it?"

EIGHTEEN

I F A MAN GETS THE FACE HE deserves by the age of fifty, Henry had apparently earned one that was heavy and mapped with lines, one whose pouchy eyes looked ironically down over the half-glasses riding low on his nose, and whose mouth tipped up at the corners in what seemed a gesture of faint disapproval, as if he had just smelled an unpleasant odor. When he was a young man first stepping into power at the company his face had been unfinished—chubby with baby fat, his forehead frowning as if in perpetual consternation, his bottom lip puffed in an adolescent pout. Now he had not only found his look—the large head, slim hips and deep gut of a Midwestern man of power—but he had also finally found his identity as well. He was "Hank the Deuce." The nickname given to him by the Detroit auto community conjured up perfectly the confidence of the man of the world, as well as the comradely masculinity of the heir who had at last come to terms with his power and, most of all, with his name and was ready, like his grandfather before him, to make a bid for power and glory.

Never before had he been so much himself. The monogram "HFII" appeared on the pocket of his dress shirts, the door of his Lincoln limousine and the toes of his house slippers. It was about the time he was settling into the persona of Hank the Deuce that he went to Australia for a tour of the Ford subsidiary there. Leaving a meeting, he had to run a gantlet of aggressive newsmen. One of them yelled, "How does it feel to be Henry Ford the Second?" Without breaking stride, Henry said over his shoulder, "I don't know. I've never been anyone else."

If he seemed finally to have found a center of gravity, it was largely because his own personal impossible dream, marriage to Cristina, had finally come true. She was his Everywoman—the earthy peasant who would tend to his needs at home, the effervescent beauty who would adorn his social life, and the sophisticated European who would understand his requirements for personal adventure. Her worldliness had been seen as a defect by John Bugas, who warned Henry that she had "been around." But it was exactly this quality which had always attracted him—the promise she embodied of personal freedom within the sympathetic structure of marriage. The two of them had discussions, exhilarating in their frankness, in which she candidly described her past and he admitted the attractiveness of the sort of relationship he had first witnessed on Johnny Agnelli's yacht. He told her that above all he did not want another "American" marriage such as the one he'd had with "Garcia," the code name the two used for his ex-wife, Anne.

When both of them were excommunicated during their honeymoon at St. Moritz, Cristina was bothered but Henry was pleased, regarding the action of the Church as a further loosening of the chains that had bound him for so long. During their stay at St. Moritz he tested the elasticity of what he hoped would be a "European" marriage. At the end of an evening of drinking Cristina found him dancing closely with a woman she didn't know. She said, "Henry, let's go." He grinned at her and nuzzled deeper into his dancing partner's neck. "Don't be like Garcia," he said.

He could cut loose on the Continent, but back home he was a king and was forced to behave like one. He had already introduced Cristina to his Grosse Pointe friends at discreet dinner parties. Returning from his honeymoon, he began to show her off at larger social functions. She was an immediate hit; people who were prepared to be critical found themselves charmed by her simplicity and openness and by her amusing struggles with the English language, which were always accompanied by hand-waving and anguished facial gestures. Obsessed with physical fitness, she began to ride a bicycle around Grosse Pointe, stopping at the homes of her new friends and tinkling the bell on the handlebars to let them know she was there. They would come to the door and find her in an old sweater, without makeup, her hair in appealing disarray. She tried to do something about Henry, too, luring him to a physical exam at the Henry Ford Hospital by saying she had an appointment and was afraid to go alone. Soon she had him riding a bicycle, cutting down on food and liquor, and accompanying her on regular trips to La Costa. He restricted himself to a bottle of red wine with dinner, although he backslid on his promise to quit smoking, asking photographers not to snap pictures of him with a cigarette because he'd "catch hell" from his new wife.

Cristina was a business asset in a way Anne had never been. She became involved, for instance, in an effort at a joint promotion between Ford and Puritan Fashions, which was doing the interior of the new Thunderbird. At a reception given to kick off the campaign, she arrived in a dress designed by Puritan and immediately attracted a huge crowd of reporters. One of them noted that she had recently returned to her suite at the Regency Hotel to find that a $40,000 necklace Henry had given her had been stolen. "Yes," she said, laughing nonchalantly, "this is my problem. I like having jewels but I don't like wearing them."

But it was in her efforts with his children that Cristina most impressed him. Charlotte was the leader of the next generation, the one Cristina knew she had to win over. She was less attractive than her sister Anne, perhaps, but more ambitious. While Anne occupied herself studying French and piano, Charlotte had worked in Lyndon Johnson's presidential campaign, at the Society for the Prevention of Juvenile Delinquency and at other jobs, which people close to the family felt were an attempt to prove that she could be her father's heir, although Henry himself never seemed to get the picture. ("If Charlotte had been a man," he once said, unconsciously turning the knife, "she would be running the Ford Motor Company.")

Hearing some of the details of the courtship of Cristina which followed her mother and father's divorce, Charlotte had told the more forgiving Anne that if she ever even spoke to Cristina it would be the end of their sisterly relationship. The resulting freeze between New York and Dearborn had kept Henry from telling his daughters about his wedding plans. But he did phone them after the brief ceremony in Washington so that they wouldn't find out from the press, and, still anxious to knit the splintered parts of his life, he told them rather pathetically that he had reserved a suite for them at the Palace Hotel in St. Moritz in case they wanted to visit him during his honeymoon. After a struggle in which Anne argued strenuously against Charlotte's continuing vindictiveness, they decided to go—not to celebrate the marriage, they insisted, but to demonstrate forgiveness.

Once there, the *dolce vita* atmosphere that had so intrigued their father caught them up, too. Charlotte was especially affected. She had long since wriggled out of the constraints of her strict religious upbringing. ("I used to go to Mass every day," she told a friend. "Now I know better.") But she had never before practiced the art of letting go as she now did with Greek shipping magnate Stavros Niarchos. She had met him a few years earlier. It was when her father had first discovered Europe, and her then boyfriend, George Livanos, brother of the third Mrs. Niarchos, introduced them at St. Tropez. Charlotte had visited Niarchos' *Black Creole*, the largest private yacht in the world and a virtual floating museum of van Goghs, Renoirs and Gaugins. At that time Charlotte had left the yacht in a huff when Niarchos laughingly said she was "cheap" for refusing to buy a new dress so that she could stay for one of his dinner parties. But now, shortly after arriving for a visit with her father, she accepted an invitation to visit Niarchos at his residence in St. Moritz, largest in the city.

It was the opportunity Cristina had been looking for. She paid almost as much attention to Charlotte as Niarchos did, appealing to her at the subtle level of feminine cooperation by saying to her conspiratorially, "Did you notice how Stavros was looking at you?" after the dinner had ended. Charlotte had indeed noticed, although she was not sure anyone else had. She was anxious to talk to someone about what it meant that this fabulously rich man, older than her father, had paid such attention to her. At first hesitantly and then with greater interest, she began to talk about it with her new stepmother. It was the moment when Cristina knew that she had gotten a foot inside the door of Charlotte's emotional life.

The day after the party Henry was surprised and pleased when his daughter and Niarchos joined him and Cristina on the ski slopes. The sudden romance may have perplexed others. ("I guess she hasn't kissed him yet," one wag said after looking at the knobby Niarchos face. "He's still a frog.") But Cristina understood: she, too, had been courted by an older man of great power and wealth. In this sense she was different from Charlotte's own mother, who heard about the fling with rising alarm. By the time the honeymoon was over, Charlotte and Cristina were on their way to becoming intimate friends, Charlotte saying of her vital and diverting stepmother, "She's the funniest person alive."

Now that Charlotte had been won over, the more pliable Anne was easy. Cristina then made a similar effort with young Edsel when they all returned to Grosse Pointe. He was still an overweight and socially awkward young man who had flunked out of Hotchkiss. But Cristina courted him, carefully drawing him out. She changed the décor of his room from French style to a jazzy contemporary look with black-and-white walls and a zebra rug. Edsel II, who, in the words of a friend, "lived in his car" during visits to see his father before the marriage to Cristina, loved the room and loved her. She made friends with his friends—becoming a confidante and confessor who drank Cokes with them in the summer and cocoa in the winter. For the first time since the separation of his parents, Edsel began to look forward to summer and holiday visits to Grosse Pointe.

The spirit of reconciliation Cristina embodied gave Henry the feeling that his fragmented life was coming back together. He understood at some level that a second marriage in midlife was a graft that could never really take, yet Cristina had changed things for him. Simple and open personally, she had made his social life rich and complex. As one observer of Detroit society said, "With Cristina you were just bathed in sunshine. She had all this royalty coming to Grosse Pointe—the Princess Luciana Pignatelli, Princess Irene Galitzine and others. There was Evelyn de Rothschild, Imelda Marcos, Van Cliburn. Everyone was just dazzled."

She was also an asset in Washington. Henry's personal political interests had been dormant since his stint at the UN during the Eisenhower administration, but he had covered the corporation's bases beginning in 1953, when he first realized that the company needed a presence in Washington. Six months after the Korean War he called in his aide Gerry Lynch and told him, "We've been screwed by the Truman Administration. They told us that if we'd hold the line they'd take care of us. We froze our prices but they let the suppliers in under the umbrella and so our costs went up 10 percent. We've been double-crossed." He asked Lynch to go to Washington and represent him and the company. By the end of the decade, however, he understood that he needed more than an office. Dealing with the rising tide of criticism of the auto industry required a complex lobbying effort. So he started a Ford Motor Company Government Affairs Organization to augment Lynch's Washington operation. This office worked against what Henry regarded as harmful legislation; it also gave contributions to candidates, loaned them company planes and performed other courtesies.

Although Henry had halfheartedly backed Richard Nixon in 1960, he allowed the Kennedy Administration to use him as a source of free cars. Former Congressman Patrick J. Hillings, who had become an employee of the

Government Affairs Organization, later recalled, "When JFK's bunch went to California we'd supply them with vehicles. It was a never-ending party. We found out who everybody was sleeping with by where the cars were left. Pierre Salinger, for instance, always ordered a T-bird. We always picked it up in front of a certain girl's house in San Francisco after the presidential party had left town." Yet this service didn't win the company or Henry himself any respect at the White House. Punning on Henry's girth, Kennedy always called Grosse Pointe "Fat Point" and made it clear that he regarded the Fords as bumpkins. (One amusing moment had occurred with Bill Ford at a White House dinner. The President had said he liked Lincolns but felt that the back-seat was too small. Bill had innocently said, "For what?" and the look JFK gave him brought the house down.)

With Lyndon Johnson, however, things changed. He and Henry hit it off well. Both were coarse and earthy, both with a sense of being outsiders even as they acquired places at the center of things. Henry's endorsement of LBJ in 1964 had come on the spur of the moment while he was standing at a urinal in an airport talking to a reporter. Asked whom he was voting for, he replied, "Lyndon," and then walked out. It was a casual comment, but it wound up on the front page of Detroit newspapers and Henry wound up playing a significant role in the Johnson campaign. After the election his friendship with the new President was solidified. Johnson asked him to visit at his Texas ranch; when Henry arrived he brought with him a Model T exactly like the one in which LBJ had learned to drive as a boy. There was talk of Henry possibly getting an ambassadorship. The notoriety of his divorce and remarriage weighed against the offer of such a post, but did not keep him and Cristina from being ornaments at the Johnson White House.

At a White House party for Princess Margaret of England in 1965 Cristina showed up in a low-cut strapless white gown, so low, in fact, that one breast slipped out while she was dancing. She nonchalantly stuffed it back into her dress and kept on dancing while everyone gaped at her. After dancing with LBJ that evening, she remarked, "I am the only one to give the President of the United States a hard-on dancing, yes?" The evening belonged to Cristina. "Washington will be talking about the White House dinner dance for Princess Margaret for weeks to come," the *Detroit Free Press* wrote the next day. "And not just because of the honored guests, either. It was Mrs. Henry Ford II who was the sensation of the evening. The Italian born blond, so full of fire and animation that she intrigued every man who danced with her, made such an impression that she was toasted in absentia at a dinner party the very next night." The *New York Times* was struck by her very real star appeal: "She symbolizes, as does movie actress Julie Christie, the return of uncontrived sexiness to fashion. With their leadership, bosoms and unlacquered hair may be back in style. So may dancing cheek to cheek."

FOR YEARS HENRY HAD BEEN HAUNTED by the thought that he would have to choose between self and company. But now, because of Cristina, he began to believe that he could have both; that in fact these two realms were not antagonistic but complementary. The feeling of imminent liberation and personal transcendence were part of the 1960s. So, too, were the second thoughts, the sense that the giant enterprise of the self could have unintended and possibly destructive consequences. If Henry did not yet see these consequences in his own life, he did see them in the lives of his daughters.

In the summer of 1965, six months after his marriage, Charlotte and Anne had joined him and Cristina on the *Shemera,* an elegant yacht he had chartered, for a summer cruise along the Côte d'Azur. When they moored in Villefranche, Niarchos' *Black Creole* was only a couple of waves away. The passion that had begun that past winter blazed anew.

Every Thursday Niarchos flew from his office to the *Creole* so that the boats could sail together. At first Henry was taken aback: the twice-divorced Niarchos, who, at fifty-five, was eight years older than he, had been married to his present wife for eighteen years and had four children by her. Niarchos' affair with Henry's twenty-five-year-old daughter seemed almost a parody of his own relationship with Cristina. When Charlotte said, upon returning home to America, that she was "madly in love," Henry hoped this emotion would pass, a hope that persisted even after she flew to London a few weeks later to be with Niarchos. Henry was the last to notice that Charlotte was becoming thick-waisted; that while others were drinking liquor at cocktail parties, she had started asking for milk. Finally his other daughter, Anne, called to tell him that there was a crisis. When Henry arrived in New York two hours later, she told him that Charlotte was pregnant. "Well, I guess we'd better talk to Stavros," he said.

Niarchos couldn't come to the United States because the government was seeking $25 million in taxes he had evaded. So the next day Henry and his two daughters flew to London to meet him there. After a long negotiation in which Niarchos calmed Henry's fears that he might be interested only in getting a large block of Ford stock through his relationship with Charlotte, Henry agreed to try to help him in his tax problems and the Greek agreed to seek a divorce from his wife. Henry's efforts brought him the admiration of his daughters ("It was Daddy who handled everything," Anne said. "He was there when we needed him.") The girls flew back to New York, where they and their mother had been booked for a fashion spread in the *Herald Tribune.* Anne and "little" Anne sat on a Louis XV chaise, with Charlotte standing behind to hide her expanding midsection.

The McDonnells were stunned, as were the other Fords, particularly Eleanor. She had become a sort of grande dame in the years of her widowhood, the last of the elegant ladies of a bygone auto era to drive through Grosse Pointe in a limousine with a glass partition separating her from her chauffeur. She was a center of the family, her Gaukler Pointe home having strong symbolism. Too self-effacing ever to try to play the role of matriarch, Eleanor nonetheless now called a family conference to find out how her first grand-child—the upright convent girl—had gotten into trouble with a man older than her father, an international playboy in trouble with the Catholic church and with the American government. Eleanor saw the truth that Henry's own quest for liberation had blinded him to: that the appearances she and Clara and all the other Ford women had labored to maintain for so many years in the face of the derelictions of the men—old Henry's secret affair with Evangeline Cote and his destruction of Edsel, the alcoholism of Benson and Bill, and Henry's divorce and remarriage—had now ended in defeat. It was one thing for the men to act this way, but quite another for women, who had historically preserved the double standard in the Ford family.

As if Charlotte's dereliction was not enough, Anne, too, had disturbed them by announcing her intention to marry an unacceptable mate, a thirty-one-year-old Florentine named Gianni (Johnny) Uzielli. The pressure was off Henry in this relationship: "little" Anne had met her fiancé through playboy Ted Bassett, with whom her mother had taken up to revenge herself against Henry.

Most of the Fords liked the Harvard-educated Uzielli, who had been born a Jew in Italy but raised as a Catholic in America. The problem was that he had been briefly married to model Marie Deschodt, later wife of French film director Louis Malle, and if there was no annulment or papal dispensation Anne would become the second person in the family to be excommunicated that year. Eleanor joined her former daughter-in-law in begging the couple to wait for the Vatican bureaucracy to act in their behalf. But they refused, saying they would be married on December 27, 1965. "Big" Anne told a friend with some bitterness that, thinking about it in retrospect, she wished she had never allowed the girls to be taken to the Continent and become attracted to shiftless European men: "We'd have been much better off taking them down to Wall Street and putting sandwich boards on their backs reading, 'I'm the daughter of Henry Ford. I'm worth this many million dollars. This is my telephone number, et cetera.' At least the young men on Wall Street are working. At least they *do* something."

Anne McDonnell was eventually reconciled to what had happened, but Eleanor Ford was not. Henry was jolted by the depth of his mother's despair during family discussions—an emotion he hadn't seen in her since his father's death. Since she could not approve of the marriage, Eleanor finally said, she would not be present at the wedding. Henry understood that this was a judgment of him as much as of his daughter.

While arrangements for Anne's wedding were going forward, Eugenie Niarchos arrived in Juárez, Mexico, to complete her divorce from her husband. When the decree was issued on December 14, Charlotte apologized to her sister, whose maid of honor she was to have been, and boarded a Ford company plane headed for Juárez, where she met Stavros. He gave her a $600,000 diamond ring she immediately dubbed "the skating rink" because of its size, and then married her in front of a justice of the peace. They left for a honeymoon in St. Moritz, where they had to stay in a hotel because Eugenie and the children were staying in the Niarchos chalet. Charlotte couldn't ski because of her pregnancy, so Stavros spent his days on the slopes with his ex-wife.

Alone, Charlotte placed calls back home to America for news about her sister. She heard that 445 guests at the top of the Social Register had filed into Delmonico's for a prenuptial party. Henry stood sweating in the reception line with Anne McDonnell, danced with her as well as Cristina, and proposed toasts to the absent Charlotte and Stavros as well as to his daughter Anne and Uzielli. The wedding took place the next day at Anne McDonnell's Fifth Avenue apartment, an amplified civil ceremony instead of a religious one because of the Church sanctions. The only jarring note occurred when the newlyweds went out to the car that would take them on their honeymoon and a photographer yelled at Anne, "Hey, Charlotte, give us a smile." When Anne and Gianni were on their way to Acapulco, Henry was oblivious to the shell-shocked friends and relatives left behind. He smiled at a reporter and said, "Well, it all worked out."

It all worked out. If Henry's successes always seemed to contain some hidden problem, it was also true that his problems contained unexpected elements of success. Even the things that seemed to call for a severe judgment—his divorce and remarriage, Charlotte's and Anne's choices of husbands—only added to his celebrity. Rather than stigmatizing him, the moral chaos he had passed through (and led his daughters into) only put his family at the center of what was being called the "in" crowd. Thus a *New York Times* fashion reporter wrote at the end of 1965: "This was the year of the Fords."

IN WASHINGTON, HOWEVER, IT WAS the year of Ralph Nader, and this marked a big change from business as usual for Henry and the entire auto industry. Always before there had been a presumed identity of interest between government and the automakers, a presumption that had reached its apogee in the fifties with Charles E. Wilson's notorious observation that what was good for GM was good for the nation. But that assumption was now under challenge, largely because of the efforts of a somber young lawyer who could not even drive a car.

Until Ralph Nader arrived on the Washington scene, automotive safety was the sort of subject that was periodically recycled and ignored in Sunday supplements. He made it important by writing articles that appeared in *The New Republic* and *The Nation*, and later by his book on GM's Corvair, *Unsafe at Any Speed*. Nader was hired as a consultant to Senator Abraham A. Ribicoff of Connecticut, whose subcommittee had opened hearings on auto safety in the spring of 1965. The controversy boiled down to a contest between two star witnesses—the sincere, public-minded young attorney and James P. Roche,

bumbling and arrogant head of General Motors. Even after their confrontation the issue might have remained isolated if GM hadn't been caught hiring a
detective in an attempt to discredit Nader. The outcry that followed set the
stage for national legislation.

Although Ford and the other automakers knew they were invisible
defendants along with GM, Henry could take solace in the fact that Ford cars
hadn't been tainted. It was also true that as far back as 1956 the company
had pioneered an attempt to make safety features, including seat belts, a selling point of its automotive line, finally abandoning the innovation only
because of poor consumer response. It was because it was relatively
unscathed on the safety issue that Ford was asked by the other automakers to
take the lead during the crisis. Henry called on John Bugas, in his new executive role as "special assistant," to represent Ford with the other companies to
hammer out a common front and then to present the industry position to the
Senate.

Fear of antitrust action had always prevented such a summit as the one
Bugas now convened. As they got together to plan their response to impending legislation, auto company representatives also talked about upcoming
negotiations with the UAW, which had adroitly exploited its postwar momen-
tum by dividing and conquering the various companies through selective
strikes. But this took a backseat to the safety issue—actually a crisis, Bugas
believed, because it threatened to "put the government into the auto-manu-
facturing business." When he showed around Dearborn the hard-line
statement he had drafted with the other industry representatives, the initial
response was enthusiastic. When he showed it to Ford's Washington office,
however, the people there who knew the mood of Congress were dismayed.
As James Newmyer later said, "What Bugas proposed to say was something
to the effect that they had been making safe cars all along. They had gotten the
message that Congress expected them to make cars better than they had in
the past, great as their cars had always been. And since they had gotten the
message, federal legislation was unnecessary."

Newmyer and Rod Markely, head of Ford's Washington organization,
knew that this statement wouldn't be well received by Congress. The movement whose banner Nader was carrying had gone too far to be satisfied by
such palliatives. Markely's recommendation was that rather than oppose legislation, industry representatives should regard it as inevitable and devote
their energies to trying to shape it into a more acceptable form. But Bugas
stood fast, lobbying others in the Ford hierarchy until they backed his position. Henry was out of the country during this intense round of politicking,
and he asked Newmyer and Markely to present their position when he
returned.

Taking place in the spring of 1966, this meeting involved some forty
top Ford executives. Bugas began by summarizing the position he intended
to defend in upcoming hearings. Then Henry, who with Arjay Miller was the
only one in the room not yet to have taken a position, asked the men from

the Washington office what they thought. "Mr. Ford," Newmyer replied, "I think that the Senate committee will just laugh when they hear this statement from the auto industry." Henry asked Theodore O. Yntema, an old Ford hand who had been called out of retirement for this meeting, what he thought. The onetime economics professor, who had joined the company in the Breech era, reminded the audience about Ford's failed attempt to sell safety in the fifties. He said it was possible that Nader and Naderism would go away; if so, the industry could go back to the old ways. However, if they were really determined to make cars safer, as Bugas said in his statement, they should welcome rather than fight government involvement, because the government would take the safety issue out of the realm of competition and establish standards to which all companies would be subjected equally.

Yntema's common sense fell on deaf ears. The other executives were still lined up with Bugas. Every time there was a "kidney break," they would walk by Newmyer and Markely and make snide remarks such as "Well, how are the doves doing?," borrowing the term from the early debate on the Vietnam War. It was obvious to Newmyer that Henry agreed with his position. But he was also concerned about the fact that his friend Bugas had put himself on the line for the company. When the meeting was over, Henry called Newmyer and Markely into his office. "I think you're right," he said after telling them about the role Bugas had played during the Bennett firing. "I'm really sorry it's gone as far as it has without my knowing about it, but now it has gone too far. I can't pull the rug out from under John."

At the Senate hearing four days later, Bugas did read the statement. The second person to question him was Senator Maurine B. Neuberger of Oregon, who made Newmyer's prophecy that he would be laughed at come true: "Mr. Bugas, all I can say is, ha, ha."

After this fiasco, Henry saw that a Pandora's box had been opened and that the pollution caused by auto emissions would be the next issue to pop out. He took upon his shoulders responsibility for defending the industry. He put stockholders on notice in the 1966 annual report: "In the past our success has depended primarily on our response to the test of the marketplace. In the future, we shall be severely tested by the need to respond at the same time to the requirements of the market and the requirements imposed by the federal government's safety and air pollution regulations." Then he went on the offensive, charging that attacks by Nader and the Naderites were "irresponsible and uninformed." He argued that they had exaggerated the potential for improving safety by legislating design while ignoring gains that could be made by highway improvement, driver training and better enforcement of traffic laws. In contrast to the sanctimony of the statement Bugas had read, however, he said, "With the benefit of hindsight, I wish that we in the industry had done more, sooner. We did not act soon enough and vigorously enough to help combat the rising toll of highway accidents."

Nonetheless Henry said that the new standards of the National Traffic Safety Agency were "unreasonable and arbitrary." Nader replied that Henry was "the most obstinate man in the industry when it comes to safety." Henry said that the Ford Motor Company had met its responsibilities for safety before Nader even published his views: "We can build a tank," he said. "If you want to ride around in a tank, you won't get hurt. You won't be able to afford one, though. And neither will I."

FAR FROM BEING SIMPLY A RESPONSE to circumstance, the leadership that Henry now asserted was the result of a long preparation. He had been ready to assume the role of spokesman for American industry since telling Ernie Breech that he was captain of the ship, but his family and personal problems had distracted his attention. Now, with those problems resolved, he stepped forth as the most effective and powerful industrialist in the country, a man of his time.

He saw that the Vietnam War was causing deep divisions in American society similar to those he had already seen in the anticorporate attack of Nader. But the war was a deeper problem, with leftist critics calling for a new scrutiny of American business and its covert role in making foreign and domestic policy. Henry answered by calling for a "better understanding between the profit motive and the public welfare." This was not simply the defensive reflex of most industrialists. In a sense, the uncharted territory the nation was now entering was familiar to him. If he was at odds with the growing tendency of the late sixties to hold business responsible for every evil, real and imagined, he was also at one with the hunger for change and liberation which was also part of the temper of the time.

One incident showing what sort of person he had become occurred in 1966 when Time-Life's Andrew Heiskell invited Henry to be part of a group of national business figures touring Eastern Europe and the USSR. Heiskell later reported on the trip to Bill Curran, a friend of Henry's: "Henry was, as usual, in his Jekyll and Hyde mode. The first part of the trip he was crocked all the time, raucous, talking constantly about pussy, et cetera. Then when we got down to business he changed. He was sober, dependable, insightful. He outweighed every other heavyweight—and there were plenty of them—on the trip."

The National Urban League's Whitney Young had joined the group in Paris. Over cocktails one evening the black civil-rights leader told Henry that they were linked by history. Henry asked how. Young said that as a result of old Henry's liberal employment policies his father had been hired at Highland Park for the five-dollar wage; influenced by the Ford philosophy of thrift and self-betterment, his father had saved enough while working at the company to go to college at night and eventually became a teacher. Henry enjoyed this story, and over the next few days, he and Young became constant companions.

Everyone on the Time-Life trip was struck by an incident that occurred as the group passed through the Iron Curtain at a checkpoint in Hungary. A guard boarded the chartered bus, scowling at each capitalist boss as he took his passport and looked at the photograph on it. When he came to Young he beamed to see one of the oppressed sitting among the powerful. Next he came to Henry Ford, a name to conjure with even behind the Iron Curtain. The guard's face fell as he concluded that Young was a valet for Ford. Finally the group was allowed to get off the bus. Before Young could get his bags Henry reached up and grabbed them off the overhead rack along with his own. "Instead of seeing me leave the bus with a ball and chain," Young later recounted the incident, "this Communist guard saw Henry Ford carrying my suitcase. Man, you should have seen that fellow's face fall then."

As head of the National Urban League, Young was under fire from radical blacks as an "Uncle Tom" who spent too much time cozying up to members of the white ruling class. But he pursued Henry because he believed him to be one industrialist who was educable; a figure whose involvement would help support the Urban League position of progress through racial cooperation and real achievements. "We're at a perilous stage in our history," he told Henry as they continued to talk during their trip. "We can't leave the solution to our problems up to the kooks.... We can't let a crazy bunch of irresponsible people take over. You've got to come in with us. You've got to take the lead." When Henry showed an interest, Young continued grandiosely, "Listen. I'm going to make you the white Moses. You're going to be known in history as the businessman who turned the critical period of black and white relations around."

That Christmas, Young received a note from Henry: "You are a great guy and run a wonderful organization." Included in the envelope was a check for $100,000 made out to the Urban League. In their continuing relationship, Young continued to press him about the need of the auto industry to hire more blacks. Henry talked to Arjay Miller, who was hesitant about any such program. Shrugging off his president's doubts, Henry invited Young to Dearborn to talk to top Ford executives. "I didn't talk long," the black leader later said. "I just said that there were two reasons why I was there. One was my respect and affection for Henry Ford personally, and the second was that I owed my father's debt to the Ford Motor Company for opening up its gates to him as a professional man." Young asked Ford executives to give blacks a chance and not to expect them all to be like Ralph Bunche. His speech won over Miller and other doubters. Ford began a hiring program for blacks which became an industry standard. Young later estimated that fifty thousand jobs for blacks resulted from this one visit.

The following summer the Detroit ghetto erupted in the most violent and costly race riot in American history. Henry got his Urban and Community Affairs Department to come up with a comprehensive program entitled "How Industry Can Help Detroit." He became active in the New Detroit Committee. While radicals were claiming that hard-core unemployment was a result of "institutional racism," he moved to begin a program which made hiring the hard-core unemployed a corporate goal, the first such program in the country. "Equal employment opportunity requires more than the elimination of deliberate racial discrimination," he said. "Opportunity is not equal when people who would make good employees are not hired because they lack the self-confidence to apply, or because the formal hiring criteria screen out potential good employees as well as potentially poor ones." As a result of his commitment, the company ultimately hired over fourteen thousand of the hard-core unemployed in Detroit. In 1969 Henry admitted that 40 percent of those hired had failed, but he emphasized that this meant 60 percent had succeeded. "If they weren't working," he said proudly, "they'd be scrounging for a buck here or there, or on relief. Maybe both. Relief carries with it no dignity, no pride. These men can hold their heads up." It could have been his grandfather talking.

Surveying Henry's actions during this critical time in American history, a respected urbanologist said: "Given the system of values in this country and the system of values in his company, he's more willing to take risks than any other top industrialist in America." Early in 1968, LBJ acknowledged this work by appointing Henry to head the National Alliance of Businessmen, an organization mandated to mobilize the resources of the federal government and private industry to find jobs for the hard-core unemployed.

It was a highpoint for him. All through this period, rumors had continued to percolate about a job in the Johnson Administration as an ambassador or perhaps a Cabinet officer. But Henry knew that he had acquired too much baggage to be able to have the sort of political appointment he might have wanted. Realistic about his prospects, he knew, too, that he could never persuade his ambitious wife to be similarly realistic. "Henry likes to sit under the fig tree and let the figs fall into his mouth," Cristina said. "No ambition at all. I push him. We push him, the children and me. We say we want you to be U.S. President. Nothing. He says he has the Ford Motor Company and that is enough."

Henry's acceptance of limits, thrown into relief by Cristina's complaint, was a sign of new maturity. This is what I am, he seemed to say, and it is enough. But his wife was right about the company being a sufficient scope for his ambition. When Henry went abroad it was as a head of government, the government of Ford, whose absolute sovereign he was. He was born to it; he had earned it. Ford Country was his country, the only place he really wanted to rule. Thus it had been for as long as he could remember; thus it would ever be.

NINETEEN

ENRY WAS A PARADOX. IN MANY ways he was a throwback to his grandfather: a figure of tremendous power; an industry giant of the old mold who had outgrown the auto industry. Yet he was more his father's son than those who judged him on his surfaces could have known; and while the power he had accumulated was attractive to him, it was also vaguely disquieting. It was not that he felt he hadn't earned this power: he knew that his contribution in reviving Ford had been significant and real. It was not that he had been unable to use this power. His unease came rather from the fact that he was wary of power itself, particularly in the context of a family business, remembering how his grandfather had been affected by the power he had wielded, and how it had affected his father when it was wielded against him. Thus he continued to be interested in installing the GM managerial system, which he saw as an antidote to the cult of personality whose prerogatives he was otherwise happy to enjoy. The "Beat GM" signs that had adorned the Rouge during the Breech era had long since disappeared, but "Imitate GM" was a slogan that was still engraved on the walls of Henry's mind. As a counterweight to his own almost incalculable power, he continued to look for a strong leader in the executive office, a role that had not been filled since Robert McNamara's departure in 1960.

In the years since then things had gone from bad to worse. In 1965, shortly after his heart-to-heart talk with John Bugas, Henry had disbanded the troika involving him, Pat Patterson and Arjay Miller and had appointed Miller president. Adroit with figures, as all of Thornton's Whiz Kids had been, Miller was nonetheless product-blind and utterly without charisma, as one of Iacocca's men suggested in the jibe "Arjay would announce the end of the world in a monotone." If not as bright as McNamara, however, or as creative as Iacocca, Miller was still far above the average auto executive. Henry respected him, but knew that he was only a temporary solution.

Henry was not the only one who sensed a vacuum at the top. While he was mulling over the leadership problem in Dearborn, a former employee in Washington was floating a trial balloon. It was McNamara himself. The exemplar of the can-do mentality of the New Frontier, whose computer mind had charted a course for two Presidents into the lightless tunnel of Vietnam,

McNamara had begun to have doubts about the whole enterprise by 1966, and by late 1967 he was confiding to friends that the policy whose chief architect he had been was heading the Johnson Administration toward disaster. One of these friends was Robert F. Kennedy, agonizing about whether or not to begin his doomed quest for the Presidency. Kennedy appealed to McNamara to use his resignation from Johnson's Cabinet to make a public break with the war. It would help him run all out against Vietnam, Kennedy said, and yet protect him from the stigma of party betrayal. But McNamara refused. He wanted to leave without making waves and was looking for a civilian job to slip quietly into. Dearborn seemed to him exactly the right distance from Washington. Running into Ford chief counsel William Gossett at a White House function, McNamara let it be known that he was thinking of leaving the Defense Department and wouldn't mind being invited to come back to the company. Upon Gossett's return to Detroit he told Henry about the conversation. "That's very interesting," Henry said with uncharacteristic irony, "but I don't know that we could find a place *worthy* of him." When Gossett asked what he meant, Henry gave a politic response, saying that McNamara had been away from the auto business too long to be effective any longer. "I could make him president of the Ford Foundation," he added. "But then it wouldn't be the Ford Foundation any longer; it would be the McNamara Foundation."

Henry believed that Arjay Miller was still a valuable asset to the company, as was controller Ed Lundy. But he knew that the era of the Whiz Kids was over. He thought Ford needed a different kind of executive to boost the company out of its doldrums. After he had punctured McNamara's trial balloon, circumstances delivered exactly the man Henry had always wanted for the top job at Ford. It was Semon E. "Bunkie" Knudsen. The nickname had been given by his father, the legendary William S. Knudsen, who had such a close relationship with his son that he regarded him as his bunkmate. Bunkie's earliest memories were of the Ford Motor Company—climbing on the Eagle boats his father was helping build during World War I before he was fired by old Henry. His fondest memories, however, were of General Motors, where his father had gone after leaving Ford and where he had driven the Chevrolet to glory, becoming president of the mammoth corporation. Following in his father's footsteps, Bunkie had worked all his life for GM, quickly climbing the executive ladder that led to the top office.

In 1963, Henry, despairing of the troika arrangement and impressed with the way Knudsen had transformed stodgy Pontiac into the hottest car in the industry, had offered him the top job at Ford. Feeling that he had an inside track for the top job at GM, Bunkie had turned him down at that time. But in 1967 his lifelong ambition had been dashed when his competitor, Ed Cole, was selected as GM president. Realizing that Knudsen was ripe to be picked off, Henry contacted him about a meeting early in 1968. Knudsen asked if he should come to Grosse Pointe, but Henry said, "No, my wife has some people here and they're all talking Italian." He said he would come to see

Knudsen at his home in Bloomfield Hills. He arrived early one Saturday morning, driving an Oldsmobile so that he would not be recognized in this GM enclave. The offer he made was $600,000 a year. Knudsen, already a multimillionaire because of investments his father had made in Bloomfield Hills land, immediately accepted. Henry was elated: he had not only solved his executive problem but also gotten an experienced GM man who could finish the job of making Ford the mirror image of its competitor.

The unpleasant side of the deal was having to fire Arjay Miller. Henry summoned him back from a tour of Ford holdings in South America for an urgent meeting in his office on Sunday morning. Then he told him he was through, although he tried to soften the blow by telling Miller he would make him a vice-chairman of the board and head of the Finance Committee. It was a poignant moment: the end of the rise of the Whiz Kids, Henry's own postwar team and a group he associated with that extraordinary period when he had remade the company against all odds. But while he found this Sunday session with Miller difficult, Henry was so buoyed by his coup in getting Knudsen that at their joint press conference the next morning he uncharacteristically personalized the occasion and tried to make it seem an instance of historical necessity: "About fifty-six years ago, a man named Knudsen became associated with a man named Ford in a young automobile company. Their relationship became one of the legends of this industry. The senior Knudsen eventually parted company with my grandfather and joined General Motors, where he became president. Today the flow of history is reversed."

THE NATIONAL PRESS GAVE HENRY rave notices. "A managerial masterstroke," *Time* called it. "The nation's most audacious executive raid in years." The business community saw it through Henry's eyes—as the solution of the problems that the lack of a strong executive had created at Ford over the years. Thus *Fortune* wrote: "In one deft stroke Chairman Ford reshaped the management of his company...remedying a managerial weakness." As a subtext to the effort to strengthen the company's management, Henry also thought that he was winning a measure of maneuverability in his private life. Knudsen, at least, believed that one of the reasons he was hired was that Henry believed he had the experience to run the company if Johnson should finally appoint Henry himself to the one post he really wanted—ambassador to England.

But within a month of Knudsen's appointment LBJ announced that he would not run for reelection. And while there might have been enthusiasm in the press about Knudsen, there were pockets of sullen resentment in the company. There was murmuring in the congregation at central staff and at Finance, places in the organization where Arjay Miller had functioned as leader and teacher over the years. The anger was focused less on the firing than on the way it had occurred. The flame of discontent were fanned by McNamara, who, his own subtle bid to replace Miller freshly rejected, now hypocritically got on the phone from Washington to let his old colleagues know that he regarded Henry's move as "cruel and unconscionable."

From another sector of the company came an even more serious complaint: that Henry had gone over the head of the entire Ford hierarchy in selecting an *outsider;* and that in his rush to pay homage to GM he had violated the central principle of his leadership—that merit would be rewarded and ability would rise. From this perspective, the executive most hurt was the irrepressibly ambitious Lee Iacocca.

After the success of the Mustang, Iacocca had become "Henry's boy," taking over where Crusoe and McNamara had left off before him—bypassing the chain of command to report directly to Henry, circumventing the colorless Miller, whom he dismissed as "just another bean counter." When Miller refused to pick up the gauntlet, Iacocca stopped criticizing him and was content to sing his own praises. "*I* am the product man in this company," he once said when the issue of executive succession arose. "I am the one who moves the iron." Aggressive and domineering in large matters and small (he so terrorized his wife about smoking that she posted a friend outside the airplane lavatory when traveling with him so that she could sneak a cigarette), Iacocca had become a force unto himself at Ford. Some of his enemies felt that he worked overtime creating illusions about himself.

One such illusion involved the Lincoln-Mercury Division, which Henry had asked Iacocca to take over and "rub some of that Mustang ointment on it." Yet Paul Lorenz, head of Lincoln-Mercury at the time, recalled later that the bloodiest confrontation he had in his years at Ford was with Iacocca over Lorenz's plan for a new model, to be called the Cougar: "At that point Lee was still just head of the Ford Division, and the meeting we had set a new high-water mark for having general managers go after each other. We had our fight in the Product Planning Committee. We had developed a hell of a sleek model in the Cougar. Iacocca argued that all we were doing was taking sales away from the Mustang." Yet later on, when the Cougar was introduced, Iacocca, now group vice-president, staged an extravaganza of De Mille proportions for the car. The unveiling took place at St. Thomas in the Virgin Islands. A World War II landing craft pulled up to a beach lit by brilliant torches; the audience of press and industry people who had been flown down for the occasion watched breathlessly as the ramp lowered and a white Cougar drove onto the sand, stopping to allow singer Vic Damone to get out and begin to sing as everyone watched, transfixed. The Cougar became the first Mercury to establish itself as a big seller, and Iacocca, who had opposed the car at the beginning, made himself its "father" by an act of forced paternity different from the way he had sired the Mustang before it.

The most serious doubts about Iacocca didn't have to do with his corporate machinations, however, but with his treatment of people. He had used a ruthless style to solidify his position in the company. He exhibited an almost Sicilian loyalty to *his* men, but had no qualms about abusing those who were not part of his team. He humiliated subordinates in front of others, and routinely used threats and profanity as management tools. One executive remembers a vice-president coming out of Iacocca's office looking as though "someone had just told him he had cancer." Iacocca followed him out with the swollen look of someone who has just won a fistfight. "That fucking prick!" he growled, as he chewed his cigar angrily. "You know what I just told him? That he was a fucking prick!"

When Leo-Arthur Kelmenson, president of the Kenyon & Eckhardt Advertising agency made his first visit to the Glass House in 1967 to take on the Ford account, he was told by an Iacocca man to disregard Arjay Miller altogether: "Lee makes the decisions around here, and Henry approves them." By Iacocca's own calculations he was "the odds-on favorite to become the next president of the Ford Motor Company." He had acquired dozens of disciples in the vast corporate terrain he had covered in marketing, production and public relations. One of them, Jacques Passino, head of the Ford racing program that Iacocca had helped revive, spoke for the rest when he said of the hiring of Knudsen, "To bring in someone over Lee is beyond comprehension. It's unbelievable."

Henry had anticipated such a reaction and sent his private plane to bring Iacocca to his office the day the announcement about Knudsen was made. He told him that the primary reason for the decision was that Bunkie would be bringing his vast knowledge of the GM system to Ford. A few years of leadership by such a high-level executive, Henry said, would make a big difference for the company. He pointed out that Knudsen was twelve years older than Iacocca and that Lee should therefore not interpret bringing him in as a block to his career. "Look," he concluded, "you're still my boy. But you're young. There are things you have to learn."

It would have mollified most people. But not Iacocca. He fretted that Knudsen would bring in John De Lorean, the only other rising young executive in the industry with anything like his own reputation. The perceived injustice was like a canker. As his close associate Don Frey later said, "The day Bunkie was hired, Lee declared war."

THERE WERE SOME SET BATTLE SCENES. One of them came when Knudsen proposed to import a small European Ford for the domestic market and Iacocca immediately countered with a plan to build a comparable car more cheaply in Dearborn. Knudsen maintained that the Europeans had the technology and experience to do it better; Iacocca, with his usual flair for the selling slogan, insisted that he could bring his car in "under two thousand pounds and under two thousand dollars." Because of the powerful self-confidence of his presentation, no one pointed out to Iacocca that he was reversing the normal procedure for auto design, putting a price on a car that hadn't yet been designed, although some engineers grumbled that having to work within these rhetorical figures could compromise the safety of the car.

Nonetheless, Knudsen's small European car was put on hold and Iacocca's small American car, to be called the Pinto, was given the go-ahead.

But for the most part Iacocca waged a guerrilla campaign which he summarized under the rubric of "making life miserable for the son of a bitch." It was the sort of effort he was best at. Ford chief counsel William Gossett says, "Lee did a lot of swimming under water. You never quite knew where he was going to come up." Drawing on the loyalty of the group of executives he had surrounded himself with, he developed the idea of a "red team" (the term came from Army Air Forces war games) that would function as the real power in the company. As Paul Lorenz later said, "The red team was naturally his team. It was not so much that they were against Bunkie's team, because Bunkie really didn't have one. It was the red team against everyone else in the organization."

Knudsen made Iacocca's task easy by underestimating his ambition. ("He was so much younger than I," he said sadly later on. "I thought he'd be able to wait.") It was clear that he lacked a power base inside Ford, but, even so, Bunkie brought in only three trusted aides instead of a group that could have protected him against Iacocca and his "red team." Because he thought he had Henry's imperial seal, Knudsen became careless, disregarding the dangers posed by Iacocca's animosity, and ignoring the chain of command in the orders he issued to second-level management. He was insensitive to Ford pride, provoking a general outrage by ordering designers to place what amounted to a Pontiac grille on the revered Thunderbird. One executive compared it to what was happening in Vietnam: "Every time Bunkie screwed up like this—accidentally stepping on somebody's toes or doing something dumb—he made recruits for Lee in just the same way we were making recruits for the Vietcong. The people who had been offended by Bunkie would immediately go to Lee and he would feed their outrage." Finally there was the charisma factor. While Iacocca was an excellent speaker and an inspirational leader, Knudsen, a product of the GM system with its deemphasis on self-promotion, was a step backward even from the colorless Arjay Miller; he was the sort of person who went to press interviews with three-by-five index cards which he thumbed through laboriously before answering a question.

It was impossible for other high-level executives to maintain neutral ground between the two men. Don Frey, who had succeeded Iacocca as head of the Ford Division, tried and failed. Something of a protégé of Iacocca's, he nonetheless formed a casual friendship with the isolated Knudsen because of similarities in their training as engineers. Often Knudsen invited Frey to the Styling Department, where he would point out changes he wanted made on designs Iacocca had already approved. "It was like being the meat in the sandwich," says Frey, who had to deliver the bad news to Iacocca. "In Lee's mind he was at war with Bunkie. That made me guilty of fraternizing with the enemy. I'd tell Lee that Bunkie wanted some changes, and Lee would tell me to tell Bunkie to 'shove it up his ass.' " When Iacocca "promoted" him to the meaningless position of head of the Product Planning Committee, Frey, who had spearheaded the development of the Mustang and other cars, decided to quit although he was second only to Iacocca among the company's bright young stars. In a farewell conversation with Henry he told him about Iacocca's campaign against Knudsen and said, "Man, you got problems here." Henry shrugged and gave a weak laugh.

At about this time, Iacocca was playing his trump card. Within weeks of Knudsen's arrival, he had gotten Herbert J. Siegel, a classmate from Lehigh and now chairman of CrisCraft, to offer him a job. When the time was right he began to use it as part of what one Ford employee called a "Chicken Little strategy"—telling his colleagues that the sky was falling and they had better think about finding other jobs for themselves. As Gene Bordinat says, "Lee began to hold counsel with anxious executives, telling them that Bunkie was going to take the company down the goddamned tubes and warning them that if they didn't want to go down, too, they ought to do something. He would let them know that he was listening to the corporate head-hunters himself and would use the CrisCraft offer as an example."

The company became polarized at its upper reaches. Finally, as one old Ford hand later said, "it got to be voting time." At the moment it became clear that the new Maverick, another car which bore the Iacocca stamp, was going to be an enormous success, a group of Ford's top executives presented Henry with a dossier containing a list of Knudsen's mistakes, along with an ultimatum: "Either he goes or we go."

Faced with the prospect of a mass defection, Henry had no choice. On September 3, 1969, the day after Labor Day, he came into Knudsen's office and said, "Bunk, I'm sorry to tell you this, but you'll be leaving."

Knudsen was stunned. "Well, why?"

Henry shrugged, trying to conceal his discomfort. "Well, it just didn't work out the way I hoped it would."

Knudsen pressed him. "Henry, that's no reason. That's only a statement."

Henry mumbled something about the organization not pulling together, and although Knudsen continued to probe for the reason for his firing, he could get nothing more.

Once the news was out, one of Iacocca's men quipped, "Henry Ford once said that history is bunk. But today Bunkie is history."

Knudsen's bewilderment and disbelief, widely reported in the press, made Henry seem cruel and arbitrary. On the day that the firing was officially announced, over a hundred journalists crowded into the Ford auditorium. Henry, sitting on a dais with Iacocca beside him, said, "I had no personal conflict with Knudsen." Iacocca said he hadn't, either: "We had our differences of opinion from time to time, but nothing earthshaking, nothing important." Henry, who would take the rap for the chaos at Ford, was telling the truth; Iacocca, who would emerge from the affair appearing blameless, was not.

It was an odd twist which showed how limited Henry really was, despite the imperial image; how constrained even in his own company. The press, which had been enthusiastic about the hiring of Knudsen, saw the firing as bizarre. The affable man of power "Hank the Deuce" was recast as a captious and whimsical Henry the Eighth. (A friend who had ordered a plaque reading "Hank the Deuce" kept it on his desk, as an ironic comment on what had happened, when it came back from the engraver misspelled "Duce.")

The thing Henry had tried most to avoid in his business life was being compared to his grandfather. It was almost a phobia, as Cristina noticed when, after discovering that in the dozens of photos on the walls of his home there was not one of old Henry, she innocently tacked up a shot of the two of them when Henry II was a boy. When he saw it he burst out angrily, "Take that away and burn it!" But now the *New York Times* accused him of having as much power as his grandfather and of exercising it as capriciously. When he was hiring Knudsen, Henry had said that it was a case of history being reversed, but the lesson that the *Times* and other newspapers drew from the episode after the smoke had cleared was that history was repeating itself, and that the only difference between Henry and his grandfather was the Roman numeral after his name. When Cristina suggested to Henry that he had perhaps done the wrong thing, she hit a raw nerve. "You think *I'm* bad?" Henry raged. "You think I'm bad? Compared to my grandfather I'm good, I'm a kind man. Hell, when my grandfather fired people, he just put their severance pay in an envelope in their desks, put their desks in the hall, and locked the door of their offices!"

HENRY'S LIFE HAD BECOME AN ILLUSTRATION of Oscar Wilde's maxim that there are two types of tragedy—one resulting from not getting what one wants, and the other resulting from getting it. The year 1970 marked the twenty-fifth anniversary of his rehabilitation of the company, one of the most remarkable achievements in postwar American industry. He was a man of power and national influence—diminished somewhat, perhaps, since Johnson had decided not to stand for reelection, but substantial nonetheless, enough certainly to mark him as far and away the leading business figure in the United States, perhaps the only one who would write an article on the first Earth Day praising government regulation.* He had come far enough that he could even make fun of himself during a 1969 speech at the Yale Political Union. Unfolding the typescript, he looked out at the crowd he knew had probably heard of his expulsion for plagiarism as an undergraduate and said, "I didn't write this one either."

---

* "Without it, the company that spends nothing for pollution control gets rewarded by lower costs and higher profits than its more conscientious competitors. It is futile to rely entirely on corporate good citizenship if the system encourages the poorest corporate citizen."

Still, even though Henry seemed, in the words of one friend, to be "at the top of his game," something was wrong. The Knudsen affair was part of the problem. But it went deeper than that.

The most obvious symptom was the change in his marriage. Cristina had not turned out to be what she had seemed. She had changed, as Anne had changed before her, once she got the title of Mrs. Ford. John Bugas' daughter Patty had seen it: "Before they got married, her hair was wild, she wore no jewels, she was *natural.* Then things seemed to change. Her hair was always done up beautifully and she looked like an ad for precious stones." Another observer, Helen Bogle, says, "I think what happened is simply that she sort of got stuck up. Good old-fashioned term, 'stuck up,' but it describes what happened."

If Henry had missed the obvious about her it was not so much that he was fooled by Cristina's stratagems—the staged peasant simplicity; her calculated indifference to being wooed by an earnest American—as that these things spoke to his own powerful desire to escape the complexity in his own life. But after a while the escape itself became tiresome. As one observer of the Fords said, "When he was married to Anne, Henry would get upset about how she kept everything so perfect, herself included. After he married Cristina they could come in from the pool and actually *make a mess*, he with a wet bathing suit on and she with dripping hair. At first he found this charming and beguiling. But then I think it became boring."

One of the things agitating Cristina was that she was forced to spend so much time alone. Henry left home by eight o'clock every morning and didn't get back until seven at night. She was left to her own devices all day, speaking imperfect English, never really able to integrate herself into Grosse Pointe society. She did not take up Anne's cultural pursuits. The only exception was when she began the Committee to Rescue Italian Art, an effort to raise emergency funds for the flood-stricken cities of Florence and Venice. The rest of the time she spent on herself, telling a reporter, "Women have to work hard to keep looking well…. I have a massage at ten-thirty every day, so I have to wake up at least by ten. Then I take an hour of gymnastics: pushups, stretching, ballet. I used to do it a lot more. My God, I had a figure like Brigitte Bardot. But in the last six months—goodbye, no more."

Once the bloom was off the relationship, her attempt to keep Henry healthy and trim through exercise and moderation in food and drink began to seem like nagging rather than concern. And she had become so concentrated on herself that she was no longer a good corporate wife. (Once Henry took her with him to visit an important dealer, but Cristina ordered the flowers which the man's wife had placed in her room out, claiming that they "ate the oxygen," and at mealtimes she refused to eat anything but honey for the duration of their stay.) And while she may still have been an ornament in society, she was far from a success at home. Because of her background and lack of language, she couldn't run the house. Ernest Kanzler's son Robert said, "The whole thing was a kind of disaster from the start. Cooks and butlers, people to get the groceries and run after this and that—she couldn't handle any of it. Henry wound up doing a lot of it himself." As things mounted, he became more and more irritable with her. One day they were out for a drive and pulled up alongside another car. Cristina said, "Oh, what a beautiful Mustang." Henry pounded the steering wheel in exasperation, shouting, "It's a Chevrolet! I've told you ten times that's a Chevrolet!"

She tried to pressure Henry into spending time with her in Europe. They did go to Windsor Castle for lunch with Queen Elizabeth II and Lord Mountbatten, whom Cristina charmed and wound up calling "Dickie." They also spent time with the King of Sweden and other people with titles. What she failed to take into account, however, was the function Europe had always had for Henry. It was not somewhere to act like royalty; he could and in fact *had* to do that at home. Europe was a place where he could be somewhat anonymous and, more important, free. He thought that this was part of a prenuptial understanding between them, and a safety valve for their relationship that would keep it from becoming just another constricting middle-class marriage. Cristina later recalled one of their conversations on this subject: "He said, 'I want to go alone to England to see the girls.' I say, 'What am I going to do by myself?' He said, 'We discussed all this before we got married. I married a European because I wanted to be a little free. Not completely free—a little free.' " He was not asking for an "open" marriage so much as a relationship which incorporated the emotional equivalent of an occasional paid vacation. When Cristina kept pressing him he finally shot her a hard look and said, "I already left a wife because she was always questioning me. If you do like Anne—always looking over my shoulder, always asking what I'm doing—I will leave you too."

Since he would not go to Europe under her terms, Cristina brought a little bit of Europe to Grosse Pointe. She made the Lakeshore Drive house a stopover for the jet set. Ford family friend Helen Bogle says, "The Agnellis were there, people from the theater, people from the arts. There were some Henry liked. But most were hangers-on, people with no visible means of support. It was pretty awful for Henry. I think he felt used."

Sophia Loren had once told Cristina, "Remember, your husband married you because you are Italian." Now Henry could not forget her nationality. The house was always filled with people speaking Italian, people he didn't understand who didn't understand him. Because the Beautiful People, as Cristina called them, could not spend as much time in Michigan as she wished, she began to seek them out in their habitats, punishing Henry for not traveling with her by traveling by herself. In mid-February 1970, a day before Henry left for London for a lengthy business trip, she took off for a two-week visit to Mexico City, to be there for festivities which were part of the visit of Philip, Prince of Wales. From there she went to a White House dinner, escorted by Henry A. Kissinger, who kept looking at her neckline nervously and muttering, "I've got to get home to my computer," while she told reporters who asked why she was there with the national security adviser, "My husband is in London making more money so I can buy more couture."

A month later, when Henry led a delegation of Ford executives to the USSR to meet with Premier Aleksei Kosygin and explore the possibility of building a truck factory there, Cristina insisted on going along and convinced Charlotte to accompany her. The party took advantage of the private plane and limousines the Russians had put at their disposal, and of the beautiful house in Leningrad with five servants. Journalists covering the trip played it up as another of Cristina's public-relations triumphs, writing about how when she and Charlotte went into the Moscow subway Russian women stared enviously at their long blond hair and their shapely legs revealed by miniskirts, finally coming up and asking to touch the fabric of their clothing. What went unreported was the tension in the marriage, which was obvious when the Fords were out of the limelight. As one company executive later said, "While they were cloistered there in the compound, Cristina would have a few drinks and then start screaming at Henry. He'd scream back, of course, because he wouldn't take that crap from anybody. She would keep ranting, usually in Italian. This made Henry even madder. He'd yell back, 'I can't understand you! Talk English! Talk English!' "

What had happened was largely his fault. But nonetheless a poignant sense of deficit entered Henry's life. He had staked everything on the relationship with Cristina, and once it began to crumble he had nothing. Even Bunkie Knudsen, not noted as a particularly observant individual, had been struck by Henry's loneliness. Before Bunkie was fired, he and Henry would often have week's-end conferences on Friday afternoons in the chairman's office, and almost invariably Henry would wander off from whatever topic they were discussing to ask Bunkie what he had scheduled with his family for the upcoming weekend. After Knudsen had told him, Henry would say that Cristina was off again on her travels with the jet set, or that they had just spent another evening with her Italian friends in which he had felt left out. "He was always trying to put together some sort of family vacation such as the ones he had enjoyed as a boy," Knudsen recalled, "but it never seemed to happen." Henry never really mentioned his private life directly, but he did say to Knudsen with a sadness in his voice, "Some things don't work out the way they should have."

Things hadn't worked out as they should have. Because he—like the rest of the Ford family—had never mastered the art of self-inventory, because the unexamined life was, in some sense, the condition for his forward movement in the world, people misunderstood Henry. They assumed that he was trivial, a good-time Charlie of the automotive world, another Midwestern vulgarian. They didn't realize the extent to which his personality had been formed by the obsessive concealment and denial of his family, although the fact that all the Fords seemed to need alcohol to feel free should have been a tip-off to the truth. People looked at Henry and saw only a man of power. They didn't see the yearnings that made him far more interesting than his control of the Ford Motor Company did.

He had not only tried to assert his own sense of self against the Ford juggernaut that had crushed his father, but had tried also in his emotionally tongue-tied way to clear a space for individual lives within his family. The results were disappointing—for him and the rest of them. Both his daughters had become parents—Charlotte having given birth to a baby girl, Elena, five months after her marriage, and Anne to a son, Alessandro, the following November. Charlotte in particular continued to generate publicity of such a bizarre and demeaning nature that Henry wondered if it was a carom shot aimed at him. Shortly before the baby was due, Niarchos had arrived in New York for the first time in a decade, the Johnson Administration having agreed to settle his $25 million debt for $1.5 million. ("It helps to have friends in high places," columnist Drew Pearson noted snidely in a barb aimed at Henry.) Niarchos had left after the christening, and when Charlotte took the baby to Cap d'Antibes to meet him in his villa there she found that he had already left on an African safari. Eventually he sent a friend to tell her he wanted a separation. She agreed, but, just as she was about to leave for Juárez, Niarchos showed up in New York and took her to his home in Nassau for a "honeymoon." The morning after their return, Charlotte did leave for Mexico, where she got the divorce. Niarchos continued a desultory courtship over the next few months, but she finally dropped him for good when he gave her an expensive diamond pin and then had the bill forwarded to her, an episode that led her to conclude, "Greeks don't like to see you dead. They like to watch you dying." She went on to date Frank Sinatra, Cary Grant, skier Jean-Claude Killy and others, while working for Henry's friend Whitney Young in the Urban League and giving fund-raisers for figures like United Farmworkers Union leader Cesar Chavez. "Charlotte likes names," Henry told one reporter. She retorted to another, "I only like people who have accomplished something."

Nor did the extended family offer much solace to Henry. His mother made it clear that she was deeply disappointed in him. His sister Dodie, while remaining close to him, had not made much of a success of her own life, metamorphosing from a slender beauty into a large woman with an alcohol problem who seemed at times a professional eccentric. She was in a unique position as far as her generation was concerned—a Ford with no ambitions to be part of the company. Her relationship with the company was largely ceremonial, and, aside from the dividends it brought, she regarded it all as something of a mystery. In the days when Ford officials still gave new models to family members to try out, she had been given a Mustang with strict orders not to let the new car, which had not yet been "launched," be seen by photographers. Her son Buhl had to go to the dentist and asked to take the Mustang. While it was parked in front of the dentist's office, a photographer saw it and snapped pictures that were all over the papers the next day. Dodie called her mother in a panic to ask, "What will I do?" Eleanor told her to call

Iacocca and apologize. Dodie said she'd prefer to call Henry. "No," her mother said sternly, "your brother didn't have anything to do with the Mustang. You must call Iacocca."

Dodie's son Alfred ("Alfie") had joined Krishna Consciousness, going to India, where he was photographed among rose petals, chanting mantras. Her daughter Eleanor ("Nonie") was so uncertain about the family that she sometimes denied she was a Ford. When a young man named Henry Hay dated her, there was an exclusive club at Hobe Sound that sent pink sweaters to acceptable guests and black sweaters to unacceptable ones. Hay and Nonie were walking on the beach when they passed a woman with a raspy voice who had obviously been drinking. He said, "I'll bet she got a black sweater." Nonie said coolly, "That's my mother."

But it was with his brothers that Henry most sensed the distance that had come to separate all the Fords. Benson had deteriorated further. "He spends a lot of money, drinks a lot of booze, and is miserable," Henry told a friend, speaking in such an agonized way that it could only be assumed that he held himself partly responsible. Benson had trumped Henry by spending over $500,000 for his daughter Lynn's debutante party, literally turning the grounds of his Lakeshore mansion into a three-ring circus, filled with life-sized velour animals. Bandleader Les Brown performed for the adults, and British rockers Bonnie and Delaney for the young people. But despite the lavish display, the party was a disaster, partly because it was the wrong cultural time for a deb party and also because of Benson's bad karma. A family acquaintance who was there said, "The adults stood around and got drunk; the kids went outside and smoked pot and got high. It was just a disaster."

Edie stood in the receiving line next to Benson. One of her old friends said, "She had been so witty and entertaining, so good at one-liners. Now she was a wreck. Being a Ford wife had done her in. She had that alcoholic flesh—so bloated that it looks like you could poke your finger into it and it would leave a hole. This gaudy emerald necklace was sinking into her chest. Her arms and legs were thin as sticks, while her stomach was bloated. She just smelled awful, poor darling. Booze was just oozing from her pores." She and Benson had set up minibars in almost every room of their immense house. During the day they would go from one room to another and drink, sometimes going outside to get into their golf cart and drive to the pool house to drink some more. Asked by a friend what he was doing with his life, Benson had given him a look that was meant to be jaunty and ironic but was merely sad. "Waiting for the end," he said.

If Benson embodied a fate that he had avoided, Bill showed Henry a life that might have been. He had made a remarkable recovery from his alcoholism and, in his own words, "gotten into the clearing." His personal crisis had come in November 1965 when his eldest daughter, Muffy, came home from boarding school for the Thanksgiving holiday and became so worried by his condition that she tried to withdraw from school to take care of him. Bill remembered the incident later on: "I'd always thought, Oh, what the hell, it's my privilege to wreck myself if I want to, especially if I'm not hurting other people in the process. My wife never mentioned the alcoholism to me. But then there was this confrontation with my daughter and I thought, God, if it's getting to the kids I've got to do something about it."

He went to the Donwood Clinic in Toronto, suffered through a terrible case of the DTs, and kicked the bottle cold turkey through an act of sheer will. The costs of his long debauch were obvious: his face was gaunt after he lost forty pounds of bloat, and the silky good looks of his youth were gone forever; he had heart trouble, for which he had to pop nitroglycerine pills that he kept in a little gold box in his pocket. But after coming back home to Grosse Pointe from Donwood he never drank again. He joined Alcoholics Anonymous and held meetings at his own house, his son Billy sometimes answering the door in his pajamas and showing other recovered alcoholics into the Ford parlor.

How could he do it when Benson couldn't? They had both been desperately disappointed in their careers at Ford, both outflanked and outshone by Henry. But Benson had always been, in the words of one person close to the family, "second fiddle in Henry's one-man band," while Billy had been so much younger than Henry that he didn't compare himself with him. Benson had kept on plugging after being emasculated at the company; Bill was cynical, not paying full attention to his job at the Design Center, and even giving back his executive bonus one year because he felt he hadn't earned it.

The final difference between the brothers was that Bill had a support system that Benson did not. The Detroit Lions football team was something that he owned and controlled, something that was uniquely his own and gave him a sense of independence from the company. During the 1967 Detroit riots he worried that that season's tickets would be looted and asked the company to send over a couple of vans to help him move out the tickets and other important items. When a Ford executive refused, claiming that no company driver would take the risk, Bill got a trusted black janitor and former Lions defensive great "Night Train" Lane to help him do it.

The team was his pride and joy. Henry would sometimes come to a game. Bored, he would suggest that his brother stage a rock show at half time. Bill would simply laugh at him, saying, "You've got the company. You can do that hokey stuff there. The Lions are my show." The team was not an unforgiving obsession as the company had been for Henry. It was an intense interest which Bill could also stand back from when he needed to. It was important to him that the franchise was successful, for a brief time becoming a contender in the late sixties, and a large money-maker as well: as football became the quintessential American sport during the Nixon era, the team became worth ten times the $6 million that Bill had paid for it earlier.

But Bill's primary support had been his family. His wife, Martha, never badgered him about his alcohol problem, trusting that he would eventually do something about it himself. Coming from a dynastic family herself and having watched the Firestones struggle with their name, she had never hungered for

the social power that attracted her sisters-in-law Anne and Edie. At the outset of their marriage, she and Bill had made a pact not to allow their
relationship to be affected by the expectations that were part of their respective names and family backgrounds. When Bill entered what she called his
"bad time," Martha arranged the family like insulation around him, giving the
children a snack late in the day so that they could all eat dinner together when
he returned home late in the evening. She insisted on this ritual even if Bill
was drunk and unable to contribute much; it was a way of keeping him
grounded, preventing him from spinning off into the alcoholic's deep space.
"Martha is a strong woman," one of her friends said, "but isn't poisonous
about it like some strong women. She was always at school lunches and functions. Her children stood out from the rest by their poise, grace and charm,
and by the way they presented themselves."

Bill's eldest child, Muffy, who had triggered his rehabilitation by offering to quit school and take care of him, was a high achiever academically
and athletically, setting a standard of excellence for the other children in the
family. Her sister Sheila was state junior tennis champion. A little awed by the
success of his two sisters, William Junior ("Billy") was somewhat at sea. As
Bill recovered from his alcoholism, he took Billy on as his project. Remembering the role sports had played in his own life, he encouraged Billy to play
Little League baseball with all the public school kids and to play hockey
with boys from a local blue-collar neighborhood.

Billy grew up to be scrappy and aggressive. His first-grade teacher, Jean
Harris, later to gain notoriety for killing her lover Dr. Herman Tarnower, wrote
on his report card: "Whether Billy is under, beside or over the desk, he seems
to know what's going on." When, during his teens, it seemed that the boy
might not live up to his sisters' achievements, Bill took him for a drive in his
Continental. ("The only way we could talk was to get into the car, lock the
doors, and go fifty miles an hour.") He asked Billy to name someone who
stood for something or who had made an impressive achievement, someone
he would like to pattern his life on. "His answer took me aback: hockey star
Gordie Howe. But then I talked to him about how a man like Howe had obviously chosen goals that required dedication and hard work, and how he
would have to do the same thing."

Bill no longer envied Henry. If anything, he saw the poignancy of
Henry's life, a life in which controlling the company had exacted a price of
loneliness. Bill did not condescend with pity—Henry was too powerful for
that—but he did feel sorry for him because he had never had a chance to experience his children's growing up, missing the little dramas of athletic and
social achievement. Bill could not communicate these feelings to Henry. The
issue of his Continental was still between them. Also, Bill had fallen outside
Henry's social orbit, having no interest in or sympathy for the jet-setters
Cristina had brought into his life. "I've got no use for that group. I don't particularly enjoy the foreigners he's apt to get associated with. We lead our own
separate lives."

The difference between the three Ford brothers was summarized by their positions in the 1968 elections. While Benson was contributing without enthusiasm or personal involvement to the Nixon campaign, Henry went with the power, an LBJ man down the line. But Bill had nagging doubts about Vietnam which crystallized early in 1968 during the annual National Football League owners' meeting, held in Hawaii. He took the family with him for a vacation and got into a discussion with his daughter Muffy, who was already working for Eugene McCarthy. She explained the Minnesota Senator's position on Vietnam in detail, thinking she would have to convince her father. But Bill told her immediately, "Well, anybody who's against this war can't be bad. Maybe I'll go to work for him, too, when we get back home."

They arrived back in Detroit the day Lyndon Johnson announced that he had decided not to run again. A speech which caused Henry a metaphysical lurch was welcome news to Bill. He called McCarthy headquarters in Detroit to say that he'd like to volunteer. Before, his name had always opened doors. Now it didn't help.

"Who are you?" the voice on the other end of the line asked after Bill said he wanted to volunteer.

"William Ford."

"Are you William Ford the Democrat from the Fifteenth?"

"No, I have no party connection."

"Do you know the Senator?"

"No, I don't."

"Well, what do you want to do?"

"Anything I can."

Nobody asked him to do anything. In frustration he finally called McCarthy's Washington headquarters. He got the runaround there, too, someone finally telling him to call Detroit. He tried once again. This time he told in detail who he was. "Oh, *sure*," the man at the other end answered in disbelief. Bill earnestly insisted that he was *the* William Ford. The man he was talking to happened to be a Lions fan and subjected him to a snap quiz on the team. When Bill passed with flying colors it finally dawned on the McCarthy forces exactly who it was who had been trying so hard to volunteer.

Bill worked for the rest of the ill-fated campaign, giving some speeches to businessmen and hosting dinners and fund-raisers. "I had a wonderful time," he recalled later. "It was one thing for Henry to pal around with Johnson. His politics were business politics. But I was doing this thing *voluntarily*. That's what made it fun. My mother particularly thought I was off my rocker."

For Eleanor Ford, Bill's recovery from alcohol had been a sort of Lazarus experience. She was closest to Dodie, speaking with her by phone every day if she didn't see her, but Bill had remained her "pride and joy," the one on whom she had most depended in the long years of her widowhood. As he and his family thrived she began to take heart and believe that perhaps the Fords had a future after all. She had given a large reception at Gaukler Pointe for each of her granddaughters on the eve of their debutante seasons. On December 21, 1969, she invited six hundred people to honor Benson's shy daughter Lynn and Bill's dazzling daughter Sheila, an honor student at Yale. It was a grand affair which she said reminded her of the parties they had staged before she and Edsel were married. But Eleanor knew that those days were over. She had no choice but to blame her firstborn, whom she still called in moments of affection by the pet name she had given him when he was born, "Sonnie." Henry had saved the family; yet at times it seemed that he had cursed it, too. "He is more like his grandfather than any of us would like to admit," Eleanor once said to a friend in perplexity.

TWENTY

ANOTHER MAN MIGHT HAVE BEEN shaken by such criticism—by the fact that he had been given the responsibility of being the family's leader and then was censured for being its black sheep. But whatever other faults he might have, Henry had none of the self-pity that had dragged down his brothers Benson and Bill. His stewardship of the Ford Motor Company might have begun as a necessity; but if so, he had long since embraced it as a choice. One of the deficits in his past that he felt most acutely was the fact that Edsel had suppressed the painful side of his life to such a degree that he left no lore or wisdom Henry could use for charting his own course. So he took to heart the advice Bunkie Knudsen said *his* father had given him at the outset of his career in the industry: "In this business, the competition will bite you if you keep running; if you stand still it will swallow you." Henry kept running, in his private and his public life.

Years earlier he had told Ernest Breech that he was the captain of the ship. Indeed, as he moved from one adventure to another—corporate as well as personal—he came to resemble a crafty Ulysses, seizing the main chance in his quest for survival, but also ready to strap himself to the mast of the ship when necessary and face the discordant music his journey caused. He had never been an intellectual. Mistrustful of pretense, he still stopped executives whom he suspected of affectation by asking them to define a polysyllabic word they had just used. But during his personal voyage he had acquired a kind of wisdom that people often didn't credit him with. It had less to do with the world at large than with himself. Beneath the inarticulate, roisterous persona he had adopted, there was someone able to deal with the truths about himself without flinching—a quality that gave him real strength in his midlife passage.

On the occasion of his twenty-fifth anniversary as head of Ford, a reporter asked him how he liked his job. "I like it," Henry replied. "I think there's a lot to be done and a lot of things to be accomplished. And I just like it. I'm probably standing in the way of a lot of people. But until I get thrown out, I don't particularly want to leave..." He went on to some quite remarkable musings about the industry which no other auto executive could have gotten away with: "The fact is that we didn't foresee what the hell the demands were going to be on us for safety and emissions, and the fact that we've created a credibility gap for ourselves [is a major failure]. Maybe we don't listen to our customers. Maybe we're not awake enough to really listen to what the hell our problems are."

His critics might bark—within the family and without—but the balance sheet by which he measured his performance, the Ford Motor Company balance sheet, was healthy. The company he now headed was more than three times larger than the one he had inherited. In 1970 it was reporting record sales of $15 billion despite a recession and lowered domestic sales. This showing, moreover, was the result of a good performance by Ford International, which for the sixth consecutive year led all U.S. automakers in car and truck sales abroad. The foreign operations, strengthened by his 1967 decision to consolidate worldwide operations, had always been the part of the business for which Henry was most responsible.

If there was a problem with the company, in fact, it was not Henry himself, but the leadership vacuum below him. After Knudsen's departure, he had appointed another troika—one of those sideways crablike moves he made in times of crisis. The three chief executives were Robert Hampson, in charge of Diversified Products (including Philco-Ford); Robert Stevenson, head of International; and Lee Iacocca, chief of North American Operations. As with previous troikas, this one didn't work. ("It was a dumb, dumb, dumb darn thing," Henry later said.)

People assumed that it was an ad-hoc arrangement to block Iacocca, which in fact it was. By creating such chaos in the organization that Henry had to fire Knudsen, Iacocca had, in Henry's view, shown contempt for his judgment and thwarted his plans for Ford. By installing another troika, Henry attempted to keep from capitulating entirely to Iacocca's ambition. Yet the fact that he chose a "system solution" rather than confronting the authority problem directly showed his ambivalence about asserting his full power, his tendency to put off what close observers realized even then would be a day of reckoning between the two of them.

In the meantime, the troika required Henry constantly to adjudicate disputes among the three men. It was also clear that there was an asymmetry in the triangle, with Iacocca's leg carrying more weight than the two others. His fame as an auto man had spread. His Maverick had first-year sales close to those of the Falcon and the Mustang. Comparably successful was the Pinto, the two-thousand-pound, $2,000 car Iacocca had used so adroitly in his war against Knudsen. Also the Lincoln Continental Mark III, which he had developed, as he put it, "on the cheap," using a Thunderbird base along with a design reminiscent of the older Continentals. Iacocca's car had none of the elegance of the ancestors designed by Edsel and Bill Ford; in fact, some people said that it looked like a Mafia staff car. But the Mark III outsold Cadillac's El Dorado and had such a huge profit margin that Iacocca could legitimately crow, "We make as much selling one Mark as from ten Falcons." He could also claim that Lincoln had made its first profit since old Henry bought out Henry Leland in 1921.

Iacocca had lowered his own sideburns to exactly the same place below the earlobes as Henry's. He had also adopted a baronial style he thought to be Fordesque, bringing wines from France with him to restaurants and brow-beating his guests into agreeing that they had never tasted anything like it. He invited Henry and Cristina to his home for dinner and glowed when Henry spent the evening graciously telling his parents, who were there, too, how important their son was to the Ford Motor Company. He blandished Henry in his press interviews. Asked about the company's "maverick" image by a reporter from the *New York Times*, Iacocca replied, "Yes, they say that over the years we have done more innovative things, product and quality wise, than other companies have. That's probably true. A lot of that is a tribute to the man Henry Ford."

Clearly his time in the company had come. But Henry seemed to be ambivalent. It was not easy to put his finger on the problem. "There was just something about Lee that rubbed him the wrong way," another Ford executive said later. But it was there nonetheless. Iacocca finally had to nudge Henry, about a year into the unwieldy reign of the troika, by suggesting that he might have to look for another job if he wasn't soon promoted to the top spot. Henry recognized that he couldn't afford to lose him, and so, on the day of the annual Ford press conference in 1970, he called Iacocca to his office to say that he was giving him what he had long since claimed as his right—the pres-idency of Ford. The two men sat there, Iacocca taking luxurious drags on his cigar, Henry puffing nervously on a cigarette. As the smoke obscured the space between them, they fell into an extended silence, as if acknowledging an estrangement from each other even at the moment when their destinies were firmly joined.

For Iacocca it was a dream finally come true. His wife, Mary, had revealed to reporters that at home he kept a piece of paper on which he graphed his business future—target dates for promotions, salaries, perks. The Knudsen appointment had set the schedule back, but now he had reached his destination. It was satisfaction in itself; it was also a stepping stone to the ultimate prize: actually *running* the company after Henry stepped down; becoming the first non-Ford to inhabit the Ford majesty. Gaining the presi-dency was also an illustration of the Italian maxim he liked to quote, "Revenge is a dish best served cold." When Knudsen had gotten the top job over him, there had been talk about how the aristocracy of the auto world would always triumph over a social climber like himself. But now he had broken through that barrier. Shortly after the announcement of his appoint-ment was made, he lunched at the Grosse Pointe Yacht Club with Leo-Arthur Kelmenson, head of the Ford advertising firm of Kenyon and Eckhardt. They were midway through their meal when Iacocca suddenly looked up, sur-veyed the room and then said with boundless satisfaction, "Shit, Leo, do you realize that ten years ago neither one of us could have gotten into this god-damned place?"

ONCE IACOCCA NOTICED A PHOTOGRAPH of Henry taken by Yousuf Karsh and asked for an autographed copy. Henry's assistant said he would get him one, but never did. Later Iacocca was in Henry's office and reminded him with a broad hint, "This is a great photo." Henry replied, "Actually this one is for you. I just haven't gotten around to signing it yet." He never did sign the photo or give it to Iacocca. It was almost like some primitive tribesman's taboo: if Iacocca got hold of his image, Henry feared he himself would disappear.

Yet the aggressive and talented young man offered advantages, too. Chief among them was the fact that with him tending the store Henry was free to branch out. To some degree the directions he took were determined by a man named Max Fisher. The saturnine and sad-faced Detroit financier had become Henry's closest friend by the late 1960s. Eleven years older than Henry, he had one foot inside the establishment while nonetheless being something of an outsider because of his Jewishness. It was the same ambiguous standing Henry had earned by tarnishing the Ford name with his eccentric behavior.

If he saw the two of them as being on the edge of the establishment, Henry also found Fisher's Algeresque rise interesting. Growing up in a Christian fundamentalist town (he was called "Goosegrease" in the Boy Scouts and "Rabbi" as a star center on the high-school football team), Fisher had gone to work out of college for his father's tiny oil company, later starting his own firm along with two partners. The Aurora Gasoline Company, as they called it, had grown large enough over the years so that in 1959, when it was bought by Marathon Oil Company, Fisher's take was over $100 million.

Fisher had become friends with John Bugas in the early 1950s, joining with him and Ernest Breech in successful oil-leasing ventures. But although Bugas was president of the Bloomfield Hills Country Club, he was unable to overcome its anti-Semitism and get Fisher admitted as a member, so Fisher founded the Franklin Hills Country Club for Jews. He went on to be such an effective fundraiser for Jewish and Israeli causes that Benson Ford, when he was Detroit chairman of the United Way, defied the unwritten anti-Semitism keeping Jews out of high positions in that cause by asking Fisher to join its board.

Fisher had been in Henry's social circle for some time. But they became especially close after 1962 when both were active in George Romney's campaign for the governorship of Michigan. From then on the relationship had involved politics and power, although Fisher was unable to overcome Henry's dislike for Richard Nixon (he himself gave $400,000 to the campaigns of 1968 and 1972 and became an influential figure in the Nixon Administration).

As Henry became more lonely and isolated because of Cristina's jet-setting, he turned to Max and his wife, Marjorie, for support. Fisher was the first person he called after the Knudsen firing, for instance, saying, "Are you sitting down? Because I just fired Bunkie." He had trust in Fisher—and trust

had always been the hardest thing for him to give. Fisher saw this vulnera-
bility and was able to talk to him about it. In the aftermath of the Knudsen
affair, when the press was attacking him mercilessly, Henry said, "It doesn't
bother me, since I can't do anything about it anyway, Max." Fisher, who knew
how much Henry had been hurt, simply said, "You're full of shit."

In 1972 they took a trip to Israel. The highpoint came when their heli-
copter was forced down in the desert. Fisher took a walk. When someone
asked where he was, Henry quipped, "Max is looking for oil." Later on, when
they talked with Israeli leaders, Fisher was impressed by how well Henry
had prepared for the trip, how genuine his interest was in meeting Prime Minister Golda Meir and other leaders and in talking about their politics and
personalities. After these meetings Fisher would ask him what he thought,
and Henry would give a self-deprecating smile and say, "It was over my head.
I didn't understand half of what they were saying." Fisher would give him the
same old response: "You're full of shit." He was impressed by his friend's
toughness as well as his acumen—the way Henry had insisted on setting up
a Ford assembly plant in Israel in defiance of the boycott by the Arab League.

Fisher and Henry got involved in entrepreneurial schemes, some of
them with a mutual friend, Detroit real-estate developer Al Taubman. One was
the Fairlane development, consisting of twin towers serving as Ford office
buildings (and immediately dubbed the "Washer and Dryer" by architectural
critics of the project), the Fairlane Town Center—a hotel and a shopping center linked by monorail—an apartment and condominium complex, and
several smaller office buildings. Henry was criticized because of the environ-
mental implications. Unnoticed were the Oedipal implications of the
project—the fact that it was built on 2600 acres that had once been part of
his grandfather's great estate and the farms adjacent to it. Henry was as ruthless about the land as he had been about Fairlane itself. *

Another project, closer to Henry's heart and more a matter of self-
definition, was the Renaissance Center. This was the outgrowth of his
long-standing involvement in urban affairs and in Max Fisher's Detroit
Renaissance, an organization consisting of the chief executive officers of large
Detroit corporations committed to projects that would revitalize the city. The

---

* After Clara's death the estate had been maintained for a time by the Ford Motor Company. Then Breech had become upset at the cost, $500,000 a year. There was some
vandalism: Clara's old electric boat the Callie B. was stripped and finally scuttled, the
statue of old Henry's friend John Burroughs was thrown into the river, and the Santa Claus
house was burned. Because the Ford brothers refused to support it, Fairlane, along with
two hundred surrounding acres, was finally given to the University of Michigan in
December 1956 for a Dearborn campus. On the occasion of the transfer of the deed, a
moment of high rhetoric about the importance of the estate as a landmark, Henry told
one of the university officials who had asked him what his hopes for Fairlane were, "I
don't care if you tear the place down."

Renaissance Center was by far the most ambitious project—a downtown development costing $500 million which Henry saw as "a catalyst for the total redevelopment of Detroit's central downtown district." J. L. Hudson Jr. and other prime movers favored a complex spreading throughout the city center, but Henry appeared one day with his own design involving waterfront towers, which was adopted. He raised $24 million of the required $35 million equity financing in four weeks, putting pressure on major businesses to relocate to the "Ren Cen" as tenants. (An executive of U.S. Steel groused, "The logo of the Renaissance Center should be a twisted arm.") He personally committed Ford to $12 million, twice the investment made by GM, the second-largest partner. As ground was broken it was noted that this structure stood a few hundred feet from the site of the Malcomson Coal Company business where the papers beginning the Ford Motor Company were signed in 1903. The parallelism in the careers of the two Fords was very much in the mind of Detroit Mayor Roman Gibbs when the plan was unveiled. "Henry Ford," he said, "is synonymous with Detroit. I think Henry Ford II will become synonymous with the rebirth of Detroit."

Henry had often been assumed to have power he didn't really experience. But as this development took shape, Henry could see his power. The towers going up gave it tangible form. If it were not for him, they wouldn't exist. All of his life he had hidden inside the identity of the Ford heir, a fact of life that imposed its own caution. Now he threw that caution to the winds. He not only twisted arms for the Renaissance Center, which was altruistic in the sense that it was "for Detroit," but also for the Henry Ford Hospital, which was for the family.

The hospital didn't have the negative charge of most of old Henry's ideas. It was his one unqualifiedly good idea. Unlike the Mayo Clinic, the only other hospital resembling it, the Henry Ford Hospital had always delivered quality service to a community population rather than special care to the elite. However, the deterioration of the inner city and the trauma of the Detroit riots had taken their toll. By the early seventies the hospital was underfinanced, inadequate in facilities, and dangerous in location.

Benson had gotten responsibility for the hospital in the loose and informal division of noncorporate responsibilities among the brothers. (Bill had gotten Greenfield Village and Henry the Ford Foundation.) But by the time the hospital reached its crisis, Benson was no longer able to cope even with his own problems: Edie was diagnosed as having throat cancer, his heart condition was getting worse, and his alcoholism had become so bad that Henry had finally asked him to stay away from the office.

Because Benson was unable to provide leadership, the hospital languished. Cristina had gone there a couple of times for minor treatment, and doctors who had given up on Benson as the hospital's savior entreated her to help. She asked her brother-in-law why he hadn't gone to the Ford Foundation for money. Benson said that he had gone to them three times and had been turned down. "What else can I do?" he said, shrugging impotently.

"You'll have to fight," Cristina answered. "If you do you'll get the money."

Benson gave one of his crucified smiles. "Oh, well, it's not so easy. They just turned me down. I'm a weak man."

At that point, Cristina went to Henry and told him that the hospital needed $100 million and he must get it from the Ford Foundation.

Henry had faithfully attended meetings over the years as the foundation was growing into one of the most powerful institutions in American life. Yet he had recognized that he could not stay on top of it and the company at the same time, and had resigned as chairman of its board in 1956, saying that this power should be held by someone able to spend full time on foundation affairs.

First it had been Rowland Gaither, and then Henry Heald. By the time New Frontier refugee McGeorge Bundy took over in 1966, the foundation had resumed the course of liberal activism that had gotten it into trouble with Senator Joseph R. McCarthy and other right-wingers in the 1950s. In 1967, for instance, it made a grant to CORE to register voters in Cleveland's inner city, which helped the campaign of black mayoral candidate Carl Stokes. This brought an outcry even from liberal Representative Wright Patman and other congressional watchdogs of the giant foundations. Undeterred, Bundy made what some observers regarded as "sweetheart" grants to some members of Robert Kennedy's staff following the Senator's assassination. He then got the foundation involved in New York City's bitter school fight, putting its resources behind black radicals attempting to wrest control of local school districts from the central school board. Yet when Henry approached Bundy for the hospital he was told that "giving to hospitals is not part of our program."

In an attempt to rehabilitate her crumbling marriage from without— repair from within apparently being impossible—Cristina became involved in the struggle. "How can you do this?" she assaulted Bundy. "Do you forget that the old man left three billion dollars to the foundation? He gave it to you instead of to his own children!" Getting no satisfaction, she went to foundation board member Robert McNamara, whom she had gotten to know during the frequent trips she and Henry made to the Johnson White House. She told him that it was a disgrace that the foundation had just spent $45 million on its new headquarters when it would not give anything to the Henry Ford Hospital. McNamara responded, "Cristina, I'll try to talk to Bundy. But you know how stubborn he is."

As Cristina was agitating the rest of the family and threatening Bundy to show up at the next meeting with Eleanor and all the other Fords, Henry, in the words of one trustee, "was really pounding the table," willingly using his influence even though he knew he would be criticized for institutional nepotism. Finally Bundy gave in, agreeing to give the hospital $100 million. Yet he made it clear that this was a "terminal" grant, the last money the foundation would give, and that it was given only because Henry and Cristina had thrown their weight around.

When the battle was won, Eleanor called her eldest son to congratulate him. He generously demurred, "No, Mother, don't congratulate me. Cristina did it." Eleanor said that she appreciated her daughter-in-law's efforts. Then she said she was worried about Henry's brother Benson, who had worked diligently, if ineffectually, with the hospital. "There ought to be something in this for Benson," she told Henry, who said he'd take care of it. The "something" turned out to be the Benson and Edith Ford Research Center, which required $25 million of the total Ford Foundation grant.

IN MAY 1973, *FORTUNE* PUBLISHED A celebration of "Henry Ford, Superstar." The article portrayed him as a sort of national resource—industrial statesman, political insider and community leader. He was a businessman who had become a celebrity in an age when business had lost its luster: "Ford even enjoys remarkable acceptance among the young, although he epitomizes the 'system'—the wealth and middle age they so often scorn." *Fortune*'s editors pointed out what he had accomplished at Ford—sales in the past year which had reached a record $20.2 billion, up 23 percent from 1971, with profits of $870 million, an all-time high.

May was a good month for him. In addition to the encomium from *Fortune,* he saw ground broken for the Renaissance Center, and on the first of May, Charlotte was married in her sister Anne's Park Avenue apartment to Anthony Forstmann, an investment banker and Yale man. Although Forstmann was the divorced father of three children, Henry regarded him as stable and trustworthy, someone who would heal the wounds his daughter had suffered in her relationship with Niarchos, an episode in her life for which he held himself obliquely responsible. There was an air of acceptance in the family generally, with all the grandparents—Eleanor Ford and the McDonnells—in attendance at the wedding. Henry gave an enthusiastic toast: "Hurray, hurray, the first of May, Charlotte and Tony are getting married today."

Not long afterward, there was a further healing when his son, Edsel II, finally graduated from Babson College after a five-and-a-half-year struggle. This allowed Edsel finally to begin an engagement with his Ford heritage after years of vacillation and uncertainty. His friend Billy Chapin, another heir to a Detroit auto tradition, who was at Babson with Edsel, said later, "There were a lot of business-oriented courses you could take that were applicable to the things that interested you. In my particular case it was cars and American Motors, and in his case it was cars and Ford. As he got going at Babson, Edsel also got going at Ford for the first time in his life, especially during the summer breaks. It might be working for [race car driver] Carroll Shelby, or working in the Marketing Department. Whatever it was, suddenly he was able to relate to his family as well as to the business."

Queried by reporters at his graduation, Edsel II said that he planned to join the company full time and was especially attracted to marketing. But he was realistic: "Unfortunately, it isn't like it was in the days when a Ford just walked into the company. I'll have to go out and prove myself, which I really want to do. I hope someday to run the company. But if I can't, I can't." Alluding to the bashes Henry had given for his daughter, the *New York Times* called the party he threw for Edsel "the graduation party of the century." Dress was black tie and sneakers. Henry's sneakers were navy blue.

IF IT HAD NOT BEEN FOR HENRY'S marriage, everything would have been working out well. But the relationship with Cristina had become a piece of unfinished business Henry could not deal with. As a consequence he began to engage in the bizarre behavior one friend referred to as "acting out." Some of it was simply sophomoric. At a fashionable Grosse Pointe restaurant Henry became bored with the repertory of the pianist and blew a shrill blast on a police whistle to show his displeasure. But some of his antics had more disturbing implications. Drunk at a Detroit Athletic Club affair, he careened from woman to woman with lewd comments. One observer saw him stop a Grosse Pointe social arbiter with an amiable grin on his face and say, "Hi, Maggie, want to see my cock?" As the woman blanched, he lurched away and stopped another matron he knew saying, "Hi, do you want to fuck?"

A friend present at this party shook his head and said of Henry, "Some people think he's a bastard. The fact is he's a lonely man. He's trapped. He doesn't want to hurt his mother again." Cristina had shrewdly exploited Henry's dilemma, telling Eleanor of progress she had made with him in cutting down his alcohol intake and his weight and otherwise reforming him. While she postured as the dutiful wife, however, she was no longer really a factor in Henry's inner life. Her occasional trips away from home—part of the mutually agreed-upon elasticity of the marriage—had become long sojourns. Visiting the British royal family on summer holiday, attending the wedding of Generalissimo Francisco Franco's granddaughter—there was always an event. To some degree it was Henry's own fault for requiring an "understanding" of her at the outset of their marriage. But some of her behavior seemed out of bounds; he had become especially upset and jealous over the fact that Cristina's trips increasingly seemed to involve the Philippines and her friend Imelda Marcos, wife of Philippine President Ferdinand Marcos.

Her relationship with Imelda had been forged when Cristina accompanied Henry to Manila in 1971 to hold discussions with Marcos about the possibility of building an automobile stamping plant there. Later that year Cristina was a guest in Imelda's tent at the Shah of Iran's $100 million gala celebration of the 2500th anniversary of the Persian Empire. Not long afterward, Cristina came back to the Philippines for the dedication of a new arts center in Manila. In return Imelda made visits to Dearborn. During one of them another guest went into Imelda's bedroom and saw her suitcase, which contained what she claimed was $1 million in cash for a shopping spree.

In 1972 Henry had hosted his fourth quadrennial presidential inaugural at Washington's F Street Club. At the previous one in 1968 he had gotten drunk and gone outside to talk to college students and eventually had grabbed Senator Edward M. Kennedy's arm and shouted, "Here's *my* choice for the next President!," a gesture which had annoyed Richard Nixon. Afterward he and Nixon had made a cold peace, and at the 1972 party the F Street Club was filled with administration personalities such as Secretary of State Kissinger and Attorney General John N. Mitchell's garrulous wife, Martha. But the big stir of the evening was created by the grand entrance of the Iron Butterfly of the Philippines, whose husband had declared himself president for life at his own inaugural three days earlier. By now Cristina's closest friend, Imelda had been the target of a knife attack by a would-be assassin a few weeks earlier. As she swept through the party attended by Secret Service agents and her own personal physician, her right hand was bandaged in splints, and her arm, with the newly healed scars of the attack bared melodramatically for everyone to see, rested in a long gold chain which served as a sling. For much of the evening she and Cristina whispered to each other intimately in a corner of the room.

As Cristina continued to get away with behavior she knew bothered Henry, she became bolder about what she considered his weakness. ("His problem is that he has the inferiority complex and the big ego," was her diagnosis, "and that is the worst combination.") In their increasingly brutal arguments, she made it clear that *she* was responsible for his success: "When we met, you were *el borracho*, the drunkard. Now you are Henry Superstar! Because of *me!*" Befuddled, Henry alternated between his "acting out" and supplication. One night Bonnie Swearingen, whose husband, John, was board chairman of Standard Oil of Indiana, was visiting as a house guest. She and Cristina continued talking after Henry had gone to bed. Shortly after midnight he came to the head of the stairs in a nightshirt and implored Cristina, "Bambi, come to bed. Come to bed, please." She replied, "No, you're drunk. Go to bed by yourself. Bonnie and I are talking." Not long after this, in Nassau at a small party, Henry was dancing with an eighteen-year-old model and said to her loudly enough for others to hear, "Let's fuck!" When Cristina tried to intervene, he lashed out at her: "You're just jealous, you old cunt."

Most of Henry's friends simply ascribed this vicious talk and erratic behavior to the "Crazy Ford" syndrome—that gene for bizarre self-indulgence he had presumably inherited from his grandfather. But Max and Marjorie Fisher, who had drawn particularly close to Henry at this time, saw what was happening. Henry was unhappy over Cristina's relationship with Imelda Marcos; she was taking advantage of the fact that he feared the scandal of another divorce, especially because of the impact it could have on his mother, to do what she wanted. Moreover, the Fishers knew that Henry had fallen in love again.

The woman was Kathy DuRoss, a thirty-three-year-old former model whom Henry had first seen at a party given by Cristina for the Italian ambassador. Kathy had left early that night with her escort before Henry could talk to her. Smitten by her earthy beauty, he had made several attempts to reach her afterward, but she had ignored him. A few months later the Fishers invited Henry and his house guest Evelyn de Rothschild to dinner. Henry told them to include Kathy as Rothschild's date. She happened to be in Toronto at the time, but Marjorie Fisher paid her air fare to Detroit to make the evening possible. She seated the young woman beside Henry and noted that the energy between them was "electric." Although Kathy later called him "delightful and polite, a jokester who made me laugh," she flew back to Toronto vowing not to get involved. But Henry was persistent, repeatedly calling her to ask whether he could come over. "He said he wanted to come over as a friend," Kathy recalled later. "Cristina was gone, sometimes a month at a time, and he was lonely and wanted someone to talk to."

It was easy to see why he was attracted to her. Unlike Cristina, who had spent her life imagining what she might become, Kathy had learned exactly what she was. She came from a working-class background. Her father, an auto worker at Chrysler, had settled in a blue-collar neighborhood bordering Grosse Pointe yet worlds away. Kathy had studied violin from the time she was eight, eventually making Detroit's all-city high-school orchestra. She was also a cheerleader at Cass Technical High along with classmate Lily Tomlin. Her flashing blue eyes, honey-colored hair and lithe leggy body made her popular with boys. At the age of fifteen she fell in love with an eighteen-year-old horn player named David DuRoss. When she became pregnant during her sophomore year, she quit school and married him, the two of them moving in with her parents. A year and a half after her first child was born she had another daughter. By this time Kathy was finishing high school at night and David was taking college extension courses and playing with a jazz band. On a freezing December night in 1959, David DuRoss was returning from practice when his car skidded into an abutment on the Edsel Ford Freeway, killing him and another band member who had been riding with him.

Kathy had tried to complete a music degree at the Detroit Institute of Technology, but it was too much for a nineteen-year-old with two small children, and so she had tried to make a living off her good looks by turning to modeling. Never making it to the New York fashion houses where models made six-figure incomes, she instead had posed for supermarket ads and car show promotions, supplementing this income by working as a secretary. She became popular with the city's most eligible men, dating various members of the Detroit Lions football team, business executives, and lawyers. She had many proposals of marriage over the years, but remained single. Women were catty about her; men were interested. What made her attractive was the fact that she was sensual without being vulgar; there was an innocence about her that far more innocent women didn't possess. She was also capable of a bedrock honesty about what she was and what she wanted. An attorney who almost married her summarized this quality: "Kathy fought and scratched through life and wasn't going to take second-class treatment for herself or her daughters. She would say, 'I'm tired of being poor. I want to live in a ninety-nine-room mansion with servants.' "

This was the sort of frank admission that Cristina, more the adventuress than Kathy, couldn't have made. Kathy was more like Henry himself, although they had started life from opposite sides of the track—a tough emotional survivalist who knew her mind, yet was still capable of captivating informality and warmth. As their relationship grew from its small beginnings, he was constantly surprised by her ability to equal his own hard candor. Once when something she did annoyed him he said, "You're just like my first wife." Without missing a beat she replied, "I could say you're like my first husband, but that would be a compliment."

What might have been a relatively brief encounter turned into something more serious largely because of Cristina's absences. As the Fishers had noted, Henry was emotionally needy and Kathy offered him a safe haven. Often he would go directly from an elite gathering to her apartment, bringing Dom Perignon and caviar, still hungry in a literal and a figurative sense, and ask her to cook him his favorite meal—a hamburger with a side dish of peas. Sometimes she would delight him by already being at the stove, clad only in a scanty apron, when he arrived.

AT THE SAME TIME THAT KATHY DuROSS was entering his life, his old friend John Bugas was returning to close the circle of their relationship. Their friendship had deteriorated over the years. There was too much indebtedness on Henry's part and too much unrequited ambition on Bugas' for them to feel comfortable with each other. Never an easy relationship of equals like the one with Max Fisher, the friendship with Bugas had always been charged with expectation that was bound to be disappointed. For this reason, Henry had begun to hold Bugas at arm's length, and finally they had become estranged. After the fiasco with the auto safety issue in 1968, Bugas had done little for the company, spending each day sitting in his office in an ostentatious sulk. Henry had gotten angry, once telling Cristina, "I could kill John. He just sits there at his desk reading the newspaper with the door ajar so I can see him as I go by." Others in the company had wanted him fired, but each time the matter came up Henry had repeated the pledge he had made many years earlier, "As long as I'm alive, John Bugas will have a job at the Ford Motor Company." But as the long silence between them deepened, Bugas finally took the initiative, quitting the month Bunkie Knudsen was hired. He moved into an office in the Standard Oil of Indiana Building and worked on oil leases, some of them involving a partnership with Max Fisher. He became more deeply involved in the management of his Wyoming ranch, Sunlight Basin, traveling there every May and October for the cattle drives.

For nearly four years Bugas and Henry didn't see or speak to each other. Then Maggie, Bugas' wife of thirty years, died. The relationship had been vexed by her alcoholism and indiscretion, yet he had stayed with her to the end even though their children had urged him to seek a divorce. He had carried on an affair with a married woman for some years, but had remained faithful to his wife in some more profound way, and for some time after she died he continued to grieve, a shy and lonely man turning deeper inward. Then, in late 1972, he and Henry began meeting in tentative lunches that reestablished their bonds, which had been bent but never broken. One day Henry called Bugas and said he wanted to ask a favor: he wanted to meet Bugas secretly at his Bloomfield Hills home and bring someone with him. He arrived at the house with Kathy DuRoss. He asked Bugas for his Nieman-Marcus catalogue and began to thumb through it while Kathy, who was just as puzzled as Bugas, looked on. Finally Henry came to a page featuring a $10,000 mink coat. He said that he wanted to buy it for Kathy and asked Bugas to order it for him.

Once again Henry was in a situation where he needed his old retainer's secret service. Their friendship revived, and their lives began to run along parallel courses. Not long after helping Henry meet Kathy, Fisher had introduced Bugas to another former model, Joan Murphy, divorced mother of three who had worked for the Eileen Ford agency as a slim blonde with a look of cool elegance. After her modeling days had ended, she ran a kitchenware store called Murphy's Landing in an Ann Arbor mall built by Henry's friend Al Taubman. In his matchmaking Fisher showed himself a shrewd judge of character. Henry's connection with Kathy was based on shared sensuality, Bugas' with Joan on a joint sense of propriety and restraint. While Henry had assaulted Kathy, almost the minute he saw her, with requests to see him, it had taken the stiff and formal Bugas a long time even to ask Joan Murphy to go out with him. He told her he was worried that she was so young—only five years older than his own daughter; he worried also that she was so attractive that he would lose her to a younger man.

By the summer of 1974 their relationship had developed to a point where Bugas asked Joan to come to his Wyoming ranch for the July Fourth weekend. It was going to be their first big weekend together, but by the way he talked to her it was clear to Joan that it would be something more than that. In the roundabout way she had come to realize was his basic mode, Bugas told her about what would happen: "There is going to be a friend who is going to join us. He is very well known and famous and it might upset you." Then Bugas finally came to the point: it was Henry Ford and he was going to be accompanied by a woman who was not his wife. He didn't say who she was and swore Joan to secrecy about the whole situation.

Bugas and Joan were alone on the twelve-thousand-acre ranch for a couple of days before it was time to make the three-hour drive to the airport. On the way there Joan learned that they were actually to meet two planes, Henry's and that of the secret lady with whom he dared not be seen. The consort's plane arrived first, and Joan stood with Bugas at the gate looking at the incoming passengers. She recognized an old friend from her modeling days. "Kathy DuRoss!" she called out. "What the hell are you doing here?"

Kathy looked at Joan and laughed. "What the hell are you doing here?"

Joan pointed at Bugas. "I'm with this very nice man."

Kathy's glance indicated that she already knew Bugas. "I'm with Henry Ford," she said.

Since Henry's plane was not due for another hour, they had lunch. When they arrived back at the airport parking lot, they heard Bugas being paged. Leaving the two of them in the car, he hustled inside. After a few minutes, he came hurrying back with an anxious look on his face. "That was Henry. He was calling from the plane. An old friend of his happens to be on the flight and will be getting off with him. Kathy has got to disappear." Joan asked where Kathy could go. Kathy, by now used to the routine, shrugged and said, "Down on the floor of the backseat of the car, where else?" Bugas parked the car far away from the airport and went in to meet Henry alone.

It developed into a weekend of relaxation for Bugas and Joan, who surprised and delighted him with her excellent horsemanship and appreciation for ranch life. Both of them were struck by the strong interaction between Henry and Kathy. He was nervous and impatient, sometimes criticizing her hair or something else with such a cutting edge to his voice that it brought her to the verge of tears. But she gave back as good as she got. And in any case there was something deep in the relationship—a real familiarity and domesticity. After they had boarded their separate planes and were heading back to Detroit, Bugas said, "Well, now Henry has two wives instead of one."

It was a dilemma. Henry wasn't happy at home, but he didn't want to admit that a second marriage had failed. He made furtive attempts to make the relationship with Cristina tolerable. They took a trip to Sardinia to visit their friends John and Bonnie Swearingen. It was almost idyllic. The four of them would have leisurely dinners and then stay up late chatting. Swearingen and Cristina both slept late every morning. Henry and Bonnie were up early, and after a cup of tea they would go out into a little cove, Henry rowing the boat and telling her about his days as manager of the Yale crew. Bonnie would get out to swim and he would row back beside her, not diving in himself until they were closer to shore because, as he admitted, he was afraid of deep water. Sitting on the dock while the sun dried them, they talked. Bonnie told him that because he had had the courage to get a divorce from Anne it had been easier for John to get one and then marry her. Henry laughed and said, "It's funny you should mention this. I said the same thing to Nelson Rockefeller." Bonnie noticed that Henry kept buying pretty necklaces at local shops. She kept expecting to see Cristina wearing one of them. Then she realized that they were not for Cristina.

The moments of reconciliation were perfunctory. Back in Detroit he and Kathy "played house" during Cristina's long absences from Henry's Lakeshore Drive mansion. Ironically, the comfortableness of their relationship made

Kathy increasingly anxious about continuing what she saw as an "underground" existence. Henry said he was going to leave Cristina, but there was always a good reason for delay—a stockholders' meeting, his mother's birthday, some other crisis. Finally Kathy said to him with the toughness he had come to expect from her, "Look, my life is going ahead. One way or the other. Either you do or you don't. But I'm going forward." It was clearly an ultimatum.

TWENTY-ONE

T HE PERSONAL DRAMA WHICH NOW monopolized Henry's life was played out against a backdrop involving the large historical forces that had overtaken the auto industry. On the Day of Atonement, 1973, Egyptian tanks crossed the Suez Canal and Syrian forces attacked the Golan Heights as the Yom Kippur War broke out. The fourth and largest of the Arab-Israeli wars was far from Detroit, but the auto world was one of its incidental casualties. It marked the rise of the OPEC cartel, the end of cheap gasoline, and the death of U.S. auto supremacy.

Passing over this epic cusp, automakers could not help but reflect on their recent history. In the 1960s they had produced a range of comparatively small cars to compete with Volkswagen and other cheap imports. These cars—especially the Falcon and the Corvair—were the original American compacts, and they succeeded in reducing the market share of the European competition. Then, during the economic boom of the mid-sixties, American cars once again became large, elaborate and expensive. By the depressed times at the beginning of the seventies, consumers once again had to look to imports from Europe to fill their needs. Behind the times again, domestic auto producers once more had to scramble to deal with the small-car threat from abroad. This time they were not successful. Ford and GM rushed out the Pinto and the Vega—overweight and underpowered vehicles unable to compete with such classics as the VW Rabbit and the Honda Civic, not to speak of the new models from Toyota and Datsun. Detroit auto executives believed that small cars simply were not an American thing; that small cars were sub-sized deviants whose days would inevitably end in a return to the *real* world of larger, more profitable, more *normal* autos.

But in 1973, as the Mideast explosion rewrote the rules of the game as it had been played since the days of old Henry Ford, Detroit was convulsed in a crisis of identity which was clear in advertisements from the foreign competition that moved to take advantage of the uncertainty. An ad for Fiat stressed the safety problems of American cars: "In the 30s and 40s in the U.S. the automobile began to change. Instead of remaining a practical and efficient means of transportation it became a symbol of wealth and power. The number of deaths and accidents increases each year...." Referring obliquely to the

1972 "alienation" strike at Lordstown, Ohio, against GM in which workers protested the monotony of the job rather than low wages, Saab featured an ad pointing out that "bored people build bad cars." Even American automakers were tempted by the trend toward self-denigration. A Ford "concepts manager" speculating about the future of auto travel in the early seventies produced a bleak scenario involving roads built on three levels of office buildings; commuters driving small "urban" cars which served as "security vaults" against city crime; cars which were loaded for vacation travel, three hundred at a time, onto jumbo jets and deposited at common tourist locations, to save gas.

The impact of all this on the Ford Motor Company and on Henry was immense and immediate. At a time when he was pushing his personal limits in ambitious projects like the Renaissance Center and in his deepening affair with Kathy DuRoss, his economic base had suddenly contracted and his industrial options had drastically diminished. As oil prices skyrocketed, Ford financial analysts warned that there would be a sharp decline in earnings in the fourth quarter, reversing the three-year trend of record-setting profits. The actual drop was 75 percent—from $240 million for the fourth quarter of 1972 to $57 million in 1973. This was followed by another 66 percent drop in earnings for the first quarter of 1974, a decline that continued for the rest of the year, culminating in an actual loss of $12 million for the fourth quarter of the year—the first such loss since the Edsel disaster sixteen years before. The avalanche of bad news created tremendous pressures inside the corporation, especially affecting Henry's increasingly tense relationship with Lee Iacocca.

In any other company it would have been just another struggle for power. But because Henry was one of the principals, it involved something deeper—the whole Ford heritage. The world at large had always compared him to his grandfather. A colossus astride the industry, he had certainly played a symbolic role for his era similar to the one the old man had played for his. Yet for Henry the grandfather represented a taboo: far from cultivating an identity with him, he had always despaired at the comparisons. And in certain crucial ways he had remained his father's son. In part it had to do with temperament—a certain phlegmatic quality even more visible in his brothers and sister. ("They all had Edsel's conflict-avoidance syndrome," a family friend said.) But another part of it was situational. The role he had taken as eldest son had forced Henry to suppress qualities he actually did share with his grandfather and to "play" his father. Yet Edsel's dilemma—unresolved at his death—was centered around the question of how to assert himself in a world his father had created. Henry inherited a modified version of that dilemma: how to re-create his grandfather's world, making it over again and better, but without appearing to be an incarnation of the old man, another "Crazy Henry."

Iacocca inserted himself into this Oedipal drama by saying that the company was no more than its product, and that he, more than anyone else, was the one who brought the products to market. According to this persuasive illogic, he *was* the company and had a legitimate right to be its head, certainly more than someone whose only claim to leadership was that he had inherited a name and some stock ownership. The only problem with Iacocca's vision was that Henry refused to allow his legitimate right to be the head of Ford to be questioned by someone he increasingly saw as another Harry Bennett—a potential usurper. In every sense, therefore, the relationship between the two men had to come to grief.

Henry had been suspicious for some time about what he saw as Iacocca's empire-building within the company. In 1972 Iacocca had placed his own aide Hal Sperlich in the Ford International Division as a vice-president, a move Paul Lorenz, then chairman of International, regarded as an attempt to "side-saddle" him. When Lorenz was rotated back to Dearborn as executive vice-president, Iacocca had tried to boost Sperlich into International in his place, but Henry insisted on putting his own man, Philip Caldwell, in as head of that part of the company which was closest to him.

In Iacocca's view, Henry had twice tried to block him—with Knudsen and then with the troika—only finally to have to give in. Making him president was only a confirmation of his view of reality at Ford: *he* was the product man; *he* made the money. By elevating him, according to Iacocca's logic, Henry had recognized his indispensability and proved his own impotence. Iacocca tried to be deferential in front of Henry, but elsewhere he had trouble concealing his contempt. Ford advertising executive Leo Kelmenson later said, "There wasn't any question that he didn't have respect for Henry. Behind his back."

Class difference was not important to Henry. Even his bitterest enemies never accused him of elitism. (On the contrary, the charge against him was that he was too vulgar, too common, insufficiently appreciative of his name and patrician responsibilities.) But class was important to Iacocca. He adopted a grand air himself—a sort of swaggering immigrant's parody of aristocratic taste and comportment. He scrutinized Henry's habits closely—both for behavior to emulate and for behavior to criticize, some hint of condescension that would justify his growing antipathy. (He was puzzled by Henry's preference for hamburgers over all other foods, until he triumphantly discovered that the hamburgers were made of ground New York steak.) Iacocca saw his own rise as confirmation of the efficacy of the Puritan ethic, but Henry's high position as the result of inheritance, not talent. "Henry Ford never had to work for anything in his life," he said later. "Maybe that's the bane of rich kids who inherit their money. They go through life tripping through the tulips wondering what they would have become without daddy." He was the first person since Bennett to adopt the view that Henry Ford II was nothing more than a spoiled rich kid, plump and self-indulgent and in no way deserving of the legacy that had fallen into his lap.

Feeling his oats inside the company because of his product successes and his unparalleled good press, Iacocca made the mistake of revealing his feelings for Henry. He made meetings into a showcase for his own expertise, ostentatiously demonstrating that he was in touch with the ins and outs of the automobile world, and aware of its lingo and intricacies in a way that Henry was not. Ford executive Chalmers Goyert recalled being in Henry's office after a meeting of the Product Planning Committee. "Henry would say to me, 'What the hell was Lee talking about? What was the point of all that? Who was he showing off for?' Lee worked closely with the product. He used the shorthand of the engineers and designers in his presentations. Although Henry approved every model we ever put out and knew the business inside out, he wasn't up on this shorthand and therefore couldn't follow Lee. I went to Iacocca a couple of times and told him, 'For Chrissakes, Lee, slow down. Mr. Ford isn't as familiar with this stuff as you are.' He'd sort of smile and promise to stop. But then he'd just do it again. It helped Lee's ego. You could see what he was thinking while he did it: 'Boss can't keep up with me, eh?' "

For the most part Henry kept his reactions to this sort of treatment below the surface. Sometimes his annoyance burst through, however. When Iacocca's right-hand man Hal Sperlich and Ford designer Gene Bordinat came up with the idea for a car called the Minimax, the young product planner trying to sell it to Henry cited supporting market research and then concluded, "Mr. Ford, we really have to do this. It's another Mustang." Henry scowled and said "Who needs another Mustang?" Everyone present knew what he meant: Do I need another merit badge for Iacocca, another product for which Iacocca could take sole credit?

If Iacocca had read Henry as someone who was weak and insecure, Henry had taken Iacocca's measure as someone tainted not only by overweening ambition but by hypocrisy as well. Knowing that Iacocca liked to present himself as a God-fearing family man, for instance, Henry seemed to go out of his way to talk about his sexual conquests when they were together. He bragged about having "made it" with the wives of certain auto executives, embellishing his tales to the extent of claiming that he had had one of them on the diving board of her husband's swimming pool. Looking directly at Iacocca, whose "goody-goody" image he mistrusted, he would say he didn't understand how, with all the "stuff" around, some of the executives remained faithful to their wives. He also chivvied Iacocca about going to church and believing in God.

At a more serious level, he also questioned Iacocca's cronies. One of them was Alejandro De Tomaso. Argentinian by birth, De Tomaso had been a race car driver in Italy when he married Elizabeth Haskell, granddaughter of one of the original GM partners. In 1963, his racing career going nowhere, De Tomaso turned to building sports cars, but had no success until 1967, when he was able to use his wife's money and connections to buy the famous Italian company Ghia, which had fallen on hard times and was producing only five cars a day.

Iacocca had originally become friends with De Tomaso because of his impressive social and political connections in Italy. Beginning in the mid-sixties Iacocca had pressed other Ford executives for the purchase of an Italian company. (Gene Bordinat, chief of styling at Ford, said, "Lee was real crazy for anything Italian. Knowing my French background, he used to razz me, 'You got to go to Italy to get any car worth a shit. You fucking Frenchmen, look at the kind of cars you turn out—Citroën.' ") For a while he had pushed for the purchase of Ferrari, but the complex negotiations eventually fell through. Then Knudsen came in and brought with him a GM stylist named Larry Shinoda, who designed a European-style sports car called the Mach 2. As part of his program of undermining Knudsen at every step, Iacocca encouraged De Tomaso to develop a competing design called the Pantera which he could use to shoot down Shinoda's design. When Knudsen was fired, Iacocca told Henry that Ford should buy a 30 percent interest in De Tomaso's company and distribute the Pantera in the United States. Henry allowed himself to be persuaded to go ahead when Iacocca and De Tomaso insisted that the Ghia plant was capable of volume production.

The relationship between De Tomaso and the Ford Motor Company began in April 1970, but orders went unmet for several months while production was being geared up in Italy. When the first shipments of Pantera arrived in Long Beach, California, Ford officials were shocked by the cars' condition. There were dents in the bodies, missing parts, engine problems, and suspensions so poor in quality that when Ford drivers began testing Panteras on their tracks six of them broke up.

While all this was happening, the brother and the brother-in-law of De Tomaso's wife, men with a controlling interest in Ghia, were killed in a small-plane crash in Indiana. After this, Iacocca once again went to work on Henry, persuading him that the only way to protect the company's investment was to buy out the dead men's interest. Henry finally agreed, and Ford had 80 percent of De Tomaso's company.

Originally De Tomaso reported directly to Iacocca. As the Pantera began to develop into a disaster, however, Iacocca "delegated" this responsibility to Bill Ford, whose executive assistant George Haviland later noted: "Iacocca is no dummy. He realized that he had a dog on his hands. He arranged it so that those in charge of the program would report to Bill Ford and thus leave him holding the bag. Looking at the reports coming in, it was clear to me that not many Panteras were being sold. Those that were being sold were mainly going to Ford as company cars, even though they were sports cars!" One Lincoln-Mercury employee who went to the lot in Baltimore where the Panteras were stored came back and told Haviland that they were rusting and that those that dealers did manage to sell cost hundreds of dollars to put into shape before they could be delivered to the customer.

It was another example of Iacocca's cunning—realizing, in this instance, that Bill was so disaffected from the company that he wouldn't pay attention to what was happening, and realizing also that any program involving a Ford would automatically mute criticism. And it was this cunning that Henry hated. He was annoyed, too, that De Tomaso proved to be such a roadblock in getting the defective automobiles repaired that the company finally had to buy him out. Nothing seemed to make the ill-fated deal come out right. In 1971, the number of Panteras sold was 130. The next year the figure was 1,552. In 1973 it was 2,033, and then in 1974, when the assembly lines finally stopped, 712. De Tomaso walked away with $3 million in Ford Motor Company stock for his 20 percent of Ghia, having, in Henry's estimation, been made a rich man at Henry's expense by Iacocca.

AS THE OIL CRISIS CONTINUED TO SPILL red ink onto the Ford Motor Company balance sheet and shorten tempers, the conflict between Iacocca and Henry, until now in a latent stage, began to break into the open. Henry became suspicious of Iacocca's increasingly imperial persona, and Iacocca decided that Henry was out to get him and began a guerrilla war to save himself.

Some of his strongest criticism of his boss involved the Renaissance Center. Originally Phase I of the project was calculated to cost $237.5 million. But inflation and other factors forced the price up to $337 million, an upward revision coming just as the auto industry and its suppliers, chief backers of the Ren Cen, were suffering through the worst automotive downturn since the 1930s. In January 1975 Henry went to Washington to raise the $100 million deficit. After getting $54 million from other sources, he increased Ford's equity by $46 million to make up the rest of the shortfall. He shifted the offices of 1,700 Ford employees to the building, thus increasing advance office rentals from a disastrous 35 percent to 60 percent of capacity. Iacocca sniped at Henry all during his work on the Ren Cen, accusing him of "building a monument to himself" while working behind the scenes to build a consensus against the project at Ford.

Henry responded with an attack of his own involving one of the perks Iacocca most enjoyed—the 727 jet purchased from Japan Air Lines as flagship for the Ford airline. Iacocca had urged its purchase in the first place even though, according to one calculation, the company's air force was already equivalent in size to the seventeenth largest airline in the country. Flying Ford was an exercise in luxury: executives coming into the freezing Detroit winter from tropical climates were taxied into the corporate hangar, where solicitous customs men came to them, and then they were whisked into a heated limo and driven home without having to change out of their summer clothes. Iacocca had redesigned the 727 with himself in mind. On top of the $1.5 million the plane originally cost, another $3.5 million was spent to bring it up to Iacocca's specifications— bedroom, bathroom, living room and galley, with half the luggage compartment converted to fuel tanks to make transoceanic flights possible.

Iacocca had used the 727 as his private plane. But as their relationship began to sour, Henry saw it as an indulgence which could not be supported. He would come home at night and log Iacocca's trips on a yellow legal pad.

Soon the entries added up to several pages. One night Cristina asked him why he was doing this. "Iacocca makes too many speeches," Henry grumbled. "He has a big mouth, talks too much. I don't like him using my plane." Soon Henry decided to get rid of the 727, selling it to the Shah of Iran for $5 million.

But beneath the competing pettiness there was a real issue between the two men—the company's capital investment program. Ever since the great gamble that led to the Edsel disaster in 1958, Henry's hallmark had been caution. This tendency was only accentuated by what he saw happening in the world beyond the company—oil crises, Watergate, America's disorderly retreat from Vietnam. To a man like Henry who had learned to navigate the rapids of corporate life, it was a necessity to be prudent, to wait out bad times. But Iacocca was urging the opposite course, insisting in 1974 on maintaining the capital-investment plans developed in previous years, before the world caved in on the car industry. Specifically he wanted to plunge ahead with the front-wheel-drive small-car program for the Topaz and the Tempo. When Henry opposed this program because of the poor economic climate, Iacocca began to go around the corporation delivering homilies about how management had almost failed to fund the Mustang a decade earlier. The implication was clear: Henry didn't have the knowledge of product or the guts to take the risks that made for leadership at a place like Ford.

Henry was not oblivious to the fact that the oil crisis had created a growing market for fuel-efficient cars. (In his "Letter to the Stockholders" in the 1973 annual report, he wrote: "We are convinced that the switch to smaller cars is not a passing phenomenon but a permanent feature of the North American car market.") Yet small cars were simply not as profitable as larger ones. With company earnings shrinking and the future clouded with global uncertainties, he was wary of committing scarce capital to a program which, even if successful, would not significantly increase earnings. But Iacocca felt that the company needed to cover the lower end of the market even if it didn't make high profits. Chalmers Goyert, Iacocca's executive assistant, recalled later on, "Lee saw it as a golden opportunity to steal market shares from GM. He resented the restrictions Henry was putting on his program." This ambition vis-à-vis GM seemed to Henry reminiscent of the Reith-Crusoe plan, which was exactly what worried him about it. It had been the ambition of his youth, the dream whose failure had injected a whole new set of responsibilities into his life. He had respected the experience of the Reith-Crusoe plan and determined that he would learn from it.

In Iacocca's mind it was another replay in the eternal struggle in Detroit between the gifted product man and the Lilliputians of finance who always tried to tie such figures down. With the imperiousness for which he was now becoming notorious, he reminded those who backed Henry's caution that the product men made the money which the others knew only how to count. When they repeated their concerns, he dismissed them as parasites. In effect he was accusing Henry of being the biggest parasite of all. By denying the nature of his contribution over the years Iacocca called into question the entire basis for Henry's governance of the company. As he said later on, after their apocalyptic blowup, "In terms of everything that really counted, I was far more important than Henry."

While Henry was in Washington trying to raise money for the Renaissance Center, Iacocca was in the Middle East on a *Time*-sponsored tour of Arab countries. Henry got back to Dearborn first and called a special meeting of top management to tell them that he believed the economy was headed for a depression, and that he wanted $2 billion cut from the capital-investment program.

Iacocca was shocked. Later he said, "Henry had waited until I was thousands of miles away in order to call a meeting where he usurped my power and responsibility...." In using the word "usurped," Iacocca revealed something of himself. As another Ford executive later asked, "How can the head of a company be a usurper? This is a sort of Freudian slip indicating what was on Lee's own mind."

He returned from the Mideast in time to be present when Henry asked for final approval on his bailout of the Renaissance Center as well as on his decision to cut the budget. There was no real fight, only the anguish in Iacocca's voice when he complained privately to Ford board member Franklin Murphy about what he regarded as Henry's abuse of power. Attempting to be sympathetic, Murphy tried to shift the focus from corporate issues to Henry himself: "He's under a lot of pressure. You have to be charitable. He's having a helluva time with his wife."

THIS WAS TRUE. LATE IN 1974, HE HAD seen his son Edsel get married—to Cynthia Neskow, a secretary in the Kenyon & Eckhardt advertising agency in Boston. By early 1975, John Bugas, free in a way Henry himself was not, had decided to marry Joan Murphy. Henry felt that he was surrounded by wedded bliss but denied it himself. But events were about to drive his situation to a climax.

Cristina was off on another visit to Imelda Marcos at the Malacañang Palace, part of a celebration for South African doctor Christiaan Barnard, who was opening a hospital for heart surgery in the Philippines. After the ceremonies, Cristina and Imelda flew on to Nepal for the coronation of twenty-eight-year-old King Birenda.

Henry went to San Francisco on business. Kathy, who had turned thirty-five the week before, followed him—as usual on a separate plane. After his work was completed, they rented a car and drove down California's romantic Highway 1, an idyllic trip which culminated in Santa Barbara. It was also the tenth anniversary of Henry's marriage to Cristina. When Henry had asked Cristina whether she wanted to celebrate, she answered, "I'm going to Katmandu." He had shrugged and said, "Well, fine. You just do what you want to."

In contrast to Cristina's jet-setting, he and Kathy stayed in a Howard Johnson's Motor Lodge. On their last night—Saturday, February 22—they had a leisurely dinner at a steak-and-potatoes restaurant a few miles from town and drank one and a half bottles of wine. It was a good evening. The fact that it was his anniversary made a strange association enter Kathy's mind: *I am his wife now.* By midnight they were tired and decided to go back to the motel. Confused by poorly lighted streets, Henry accidentally pulled onto a one-way street. His new Ford Escort was almost immediately flagged over by a policeman. He was given curbside sobriety tests, which he failed; then he was taken in handcuffs to a local hospital, where a blood test determined that he was legally intoxicated. He was booked and spent four hours in jail until Kathy could hire a lawyer to post the $375 bail. As soon as he was released he returned to the motel a nervous wreck.

"Go home," he told Kathy, who had been waiting there for him. "Don't open the door. Don't talk to reporters. But be prepared for an avalanche of publicity." Meanwhile he called Max Fisher to discuss damage control.

The arrest was global news. Cristina read the headlines in Katmandu, where she and Imelda were staying, and called her friend Bonnie Swearingen. After finding out the details, she stonewalled friends and reporters, claiming that Kathy was actually a family friend and that everything was fine. She made plans to come home immediately.

As Cristina was on her way back to Detroit, Henry was attending an Economics Club luncheon. It was two days after the incident, and he was still shaken by the furor it had caused. He was extremely nervous beforehand, but all the men applauded as he entered to take a seat at the head table. After lunch, when a journalist asked him about the Santa Barbara incident, he shrugged and commented, "Never complain, never explain."

Privately he was not so nonchalant. The incident had broken the membrane which had kept the parts of his life separate for the last several years. This separation had been his survival strategy. ("I thought I could compartmentalize my life," he said later on. "But I was wrong.") Now the already tense family situation would get out of hand. The first divorce and remarriage had been difficult enough for his mother to handle. But the news from Santa Barbara was doubly disquieting to Eleanor because of the onset of angina—a disorder running in the Clay family and in her own children—that had complicated her old age. But Eleanor Ford was not the only problem. Largely through Henry's own tireless efforts, his daughters were now close friends of Cristina's and sure to be resentful if he sued for divorce. There was also Cristina herself. Unlike Anne McDonnell, she could not be counted on to go gently back into the anonymity in which Henry had found her. He knew that she enjoyed her status as Mrs. Ford and that she would not shrink from making an ugly scene to maintain it if necessary. And, finally, he had to consider the fact that his conflict with Iacocca meant that an attempt to divorce Cristina would involve him in a two-front war.

So when his wife returned from Nepal his first tendency was to try to mollify her. He encouraged her to believe that Kathy was just a passing fancy, a momentary indiscretion. He swore he would never see or talk to her again and urged Cristina to join him in trying to rebuild the marriage.

Seeing the juggernaut Henry faced at the company and at home, Kathy relented in her ultimatum, giving him time to work things out. As he tried to recompose the surfaces of his life, she poured her energies into a plan she had come up with several months earlier, to open a Detroit nightspot. Entering a partnership with an attorney who was putting up the money, she began planning L'Esprit, as she decided to call it, working up to twenty hours a day transforming a dingy basement which had formerly housed a Greek restaurant into an elegant disco. Her friends gathered on Saturday nights to help paint and sweep up the week's sawdust. When the nightclub opened in late May, Henry didn't show up, but Edsel II came as stand-in for his father in a show of respect for Kathy, who had been acting as an intermediary between father and son for some time, trying to help Edsel in his efforts to be a good son and make his father an ally in his company ambitions. L'Esprit was an immediate smash hit—the trendiest club in Detroit.

But all of Henry's quick repairs couldn't keep his marriage from coming unraveled. There was a sort of Last Supper in the Lakeshore house, with a dozen people present, among them John and Bonnie Swearingen. After dinner the men made their ritual exit to the library to talk business while the women remained behind to talk about other things. Bonnie Swearingen, a blond former Miss Alabama with a brittle wit and an inquiring intelligence, was unable to keep from picking at the scab of the Ford's domestic discord, a subject which had been assiduously avoided during dinner-table chat. As the women came together, she suggested that they play Truth, a game in which the participants alternated as interrogators and interrogated, the only ground rule being that they agreed to tell the truth, whatever was asked of them. Bonnie began with Cristina, initiating a line of questions about her relationship with Imelda Marcos.

"Is it true that you like women?"

"Yes, I like women," Cristina answered after a moment's pause.

"Do women satisfy you?"

"Yes, they satisfy me."

"Do you prefer women to men?"

Eyes flashing, Cristina turned the tables: "First tell me about your *husband*. Does he satisfy *you*?"

Increasingly graphic in questions and answers, this game of Truth was still going on when the men rejoined the women—all of them except Henry, who had tired of the superficiality of the evening and gone upstairs to talk to Kathy on the telephone.

He had started seeing her again—at the Fishers' place, at Bugas' and even at his son Edsel's. He also visited Kathy in a town house she had bought in Grosse Pointe. The arrival of this girl from the other side of the tracks in the privileged sanctuary had raised eyebrows. Even before the headlines about the night in Santa Barbara, this house had made her a subject of small-town gossip. After news of the arrest had flashed through Grosse Pointe, she was an instant celebrity. Everyone watched her. They called her place the "Ten Thousand Dollar Screw House," on the erroneous rumor that Henry had loaned her that sum for a few days of ecstasy, and in ignorance of the fact that for years she had supported her two daughters and also the mother of her dead husband, David DuRoss. In addition to whispering about Kathy they watched for Henry. When a large figure in a red wig got out of a car and hurried up the steps of her home, nobody was fooled, no more than they were when an ambulance sometimes arrived in the evening to spirit this red-wigged man away. Watergate was still fresh in everyone's mind, and a local wit began referring to Henry as the "E. Howard Hunt of Grosse Pointe."

IT WAS AS IF HE HAD BEGUN PERFORMING in his own private theater of the absurd which enforced a floating unity on his private and corporate lives. At the same time that he went to war with Cristina, he and Iacocca were treating each other as open enemies. In the aftermath of Henry's unilateral decisions regarding investment strategy and the small-car program, Iacocca had to revise his notions of him as a weak man suffering from the moral hemophilia of inherited wealth. For his part, Henry realistically evaluated his adversary's strength in the corporation—an intensely loyal network of executives known as the Iacocca Mafia, reaching into the highest levels of the organization. Only International and the nonautomotive divisions had not been infiltrated. And in Finance, Iacocca had a sometime ally—Ed Lundy, last of the Whiz Kids and an increasingly powerful figure who, in reaction to the replacement of his close friend Arjay Miller, had joined with Iacocca in the effort to "get" Knudsen later on.

Under normal circumstances Iacocca's expanded "red team" could not have threatened Henry's control. But circumstances were not normal. On top of the other disasters of 1974 there had been whistle-blowing by Ford executive Harley Copp regarding the fact that Ford engineers, unbeknown to Henry, had developed two separate computer systems for testing new cars to see if they met EPA standards. As Copp pointed out to government investigators when Ford officials refused to do anything about it, the inaccurate system was for EPA records and the accurate one was for the company. The result of Copp's revelations was a $7 million fine for Ford and $60 million in retooling costs to honestly meet government reporting standards.

Further evidence that the time was out of joint for the industry had awaited Henry on his return from his Santa Barbara tryst with Kathy. Choosing a day when Iacocca was absent, he convened a special meeting of top management to discuss how to deal with news that had just leaked out: that Ford executives had paid Indonesian officials a $1 million bribe to get a $29.6 million satellite communications contract with the Indonesian government.

Not strictly illegal, such "commissions" in fact had been accepted as part of doing business in the Third World until the advent of the post-Watergate morality. But because of his struggle with Iacocca, Henry realized that he faced dangers inside the Ford organization as well as outside as a result of this leak, and he moved forthrightly to deal with it. Indeed, when Iacocca learned of the situation he called Paul Lorenz, the executive with responsibility for the Indonesian contract, into his office and began probing for details, pressing particularly for a smoking gun that would link Henry to the bribe. He would later claim that Lorenz told him Henry had winked at the bribe. Lorenz always denied that he had said any such thing and insisted that he would have sued Iacocca for libel if he hadn't been dissuaded by the Ford board of directors, who were anxious to put the Indonesian affair behind the company.

It was at about this time that Henry, realizing the depth of Iacocca's enmity, began amassing a file on him. Henry began by inquiring into the ties between the company and another Iacocca friend, William Fugazy, who handled Ford's lucrative travel arrangements and dealer tours. Fugazy was a family friend, his father having helped Iacocca's father get settled upon arriving in America. Iacocca had been able to persuade Henry to give Fugazy the Ford contract in 1965 after Fugazy arranged for Pope Paul to use a Lincoln instead of a Cadillac on his trip to the United States. But Bunkie Knudsen had discovered that Fugazy had overbilled Ford by some $300,000, and Henry believed that he was once again overcharging the company.

The investigation of Fugazy soon matured into a full-fledged probe of Iacocca. He learned about it when his loyal secretary told him, "I've just learned that every time you make a call on the company credit card, a record of it goes to Mr. Ford's office." A couple of weeks later she informed him of her suspicions that the papers on his desk were being examined between the time he left the office in the evening and when he arrived the next morning. The situation became so filled with paranoia that Iacocca and his loyalists went outside the Glass House to make phone calls to one another in which they traded their own intelligence. What they didn't know was that Henry's investigation was being coordinated by Henry's old friend John Bugas.

In August Henry launched a full-scale internal "audit" of Iacocca's doings, under the supervision of Theodore Souris, a former justice of the Michigan Supreme Court. Investigators conducted fifty-five interviews of Ford executives and suppliers at a cost of $1.5 million, focusing especially on dealer meetings and the link with Fugazy. "Aren't you afraid of Fugazy?" Henry asked Iacocca when he informed him that he was investigating his friend. "Aren't you scared of ending up in the East River with a pair of cement boots?" When Iacocca asked him what the problem was, Henry said of Fugazy, "I think he's mixed up with the Mafia." The situation had stirred up the primal soup of his youth, reminding him of a time when goons and criminals had gotten an upper hand in his family's company.

Iacocca was outraged, but he decided to turn the other cheek and bide his time. As far as he was concerned, his antagonist's days were numbered.

Henry's personal life was a disaster. Moreover, Iacocca knew that he himself had a solid base of support in the Ford family, all of whom were disturbed by Henry's behavior. After all, Henry's own mother had come to Iacocca to thank him for his work in the company, saying, "You have made my sons look good." And he talked frequently to Bill Ford, who had more Ford stock than any other member of the family and had encouraged him in the fantasy that he would someday come to him and say that Henry had "gone nuts" and that together they had to replace him.

WHILE HENRY WAS CONDUCTING HIS investigation of Iacocca, Cristina was investigating Henry, particularly his lengthy absences, suspecting that he had reestablished his liaison with Kathy DuRoss. Unlike Henry's detective work, hers met with instant success. As she saw what was happening, all the energy with which she had suppressed the truth—continuing to insist to her closest friends, for instance, that Kathy was just a brief encounter for Henry—now rebounded with a rage against her rival's invisible presence. Arguments in the Lakeshore Drive household escalated into screaming matches. The servants were scandalized. According to one account, Henry was said to have called a guard and asked him to bring in a large male dog and then commanded Cristina to allow the animal to mount her.

Henry said that Kathy offered him what Cristina no longer could—companionship, sensuality and domesticity. "She's a *whore!*" Cristina shouted. But Henry, who felt that he knew for the first time in his life what he really wanted, came back with a comment that rocked her: "Yeah, she's a whore. And a call girl. And a streetwalker. And whatever else you want to call her. She's fucked everybody in Detroit. Seven guys an hour. But you know what? She *fits me!*" Even though, as with other recent outbursts of Henry's, Cristina couldn't tell whether he was mocking her, it was clear that his words were not self-deprecating but part of a bedrock insight into who he was and what he wanted from life. They were also a declaration of personal independence from a superficial and failed marriage and from the social proprieties he had unquestioningly accepted along with the Ford name and power—values that in some way no longer fit him.

Domestic life at the Lakeshore Drive house came to resemble a road-show engagement of *Who's Afraid of Virginia Woolf.* Socialite Kitzie Eaton was invited for dinner one evening. Afterward there was a movie downstairs in the screening room, an area soon gaseous with the rhetorical violence that now characterized the Cristina-Henry relationship: "Anything she said he would disagree with. Toward the end of dinner he started making remarks about Mrs. Marcos, accusing Cristina of having a lesbian affair with her. He'd go upstairs, then come back down to the movie for a little while, and then leave again, saying, 'This is too boring.'" At times Henry seemed almost to put on an antic disposition. While shaving in the morning he would sometimes call out to Cristina in a singsong voice, "Remember, *bambina,* I am the King and the King can do no wrong."

In the past his derelictions had always been followed by contrition. "I am the King" marked a real departure—a sort of luxuriating in his acts which made Cristina desperate. Always before she had enforced a discretion, insisting to the world, however lacerating their private struggle, that everything was all right. Now she gave that up and began to drink heavily, and had no reluctance about dragging everything out into the open and playing on Henry's fear of public scandal. Bobby Kanzler remembers, "We were at a dinner party at a friend of Henry's one night. Cristina burst in alone, screaming and yelling, obviously quite drunk. 'Where's Henry? Is he with that *whore?*' "

As Henry weighed his choices, another complication arose that he hadn't counted on and couldn't control—his health. During the pressure of the past year he had begun to have chest pains. In a secret visit to a cardiologist at the Henry Ford Hospital, he had found that the angina which had affected his brother Benson twenty years earlier, then Bill and his mother, had now struck him. He was given Nitrostats to carry for attacks of pain and was told to avoid stress, which he nonetheless continued to get in toxic doses.

He had been told to follow a strict plan of diet and exercise. One day when he was taking what had become his constitutional—a two-mile walk from his house to his sister Dodie's place and then back again—he had gone a couple of blocks when he was suddenly stabbed by a pain so intense that he stopped dead in his tracks. Before he could get a Nitrostat pill out of his pocket the pain seemed to crush him. Feeling as though a giant hand were pushing him down, he slipped down to the curb. As the waves of pain washed over him he was still unable to get the pill out of his pocket. He tried to concentrate on one act: gripping his pants legs to keep the water in the gutter from getting them muddy. He finally got a Nitrostat into his mouth and, after waiting a long time, fought the pain back enough to be able to walk home. He felt a new resolve: he couldn't procrastinate any longer, because time was not on his side.

By the middle of the Christmas season Henry was ready for a decision. His mother was ill; in any case, large family celebrations had lapsed in recent years and none was planned now. Earlier he had let Cristina persuade him to spend the holidays with the Mountbattens in England. But the conflict with Iacocca over the capital-investment program was still simmering. A few days before they were supposed to leave he told Cristina, "I've got to make the biggest decision of my life. Do I make the small car or the big car?" Only half listening, she said, "Build the small car." He said he was going to the office, but she assumed that he was going to visit Kathy, whom she now referred to as "Miss Porno." As Henry went out the door, Cristina thought to herself, I'll bet Miss Porno will say, "Build the big car."

When Henry returned a few hours later he went upstairs to Cristina's dressing room, where the maid was packing her bags for the England trip. "I'm not taking you to England," he said. "I've made other plans and they don't include you."

"What are you talking about?" Cristina said, shocked at the baldness of his announcement.

"I'm fed up. I've had enough of you." Before she could answer he continued, "Besides, you can't handle one man and I've got a woman who can handle ten."

"You've gone mad," she shrieked. "People say you're crazy. They're right. You can't marry a whore!"

He got a strange smile on his face—at once foxy and self-deprecating. After staring at her a moment, he said calmly, "Remember, *bambina,* I am the King. The King can marry a whore. If the King marries a whore, every man on the street will bow down to her. The commoner can't do it. But the King can."

The next day he left for England. This time Kathy was on the same plane with him.

TWENTY-TWO

AFTER SPENDING CHRISTMAS WITH Kathy at the Mountbattens', Henry decided to work out of an office at Ford International in London for a few weeks while the domestic scene back in Grosse Pointe cooled off. He grew a beard; he was changing on the outside as well as within. When John and Joan Bugas visited him and Kathy at his London flat, they were struck by the rigors of his schedule. He was up very early each morning to catch a plane for Paris or some other European capital, where he would spend the day on company business. Returning to London in the evening, he would insist on staying up late into the night talking with Bugas. His old friend's help in the Iacocca investigation had brought them closer together than ever, repairing the damage done when Bugas was passed over for the company presidency a decade earlier. Often Kathy and Joan would fall silent and listen to the two men reminisce, their inhibitions loosened by several bottles of Bordeaux. They talked about the improbability of an impoverished Wyoming rancher's son winding up the close friend of the heir to the world's greatest industrial fortune; about the glory days when they undertook what seemed like an impossible struggle against Harry Bennett and won; about the even bigger triumph of rebuilding the company.

"Always it comes back to the company, doesn't it?" Bugas said during one of these sessions.

"Yes," Henry answered with a sly glance at Kathy. "The company has been my mother, wife and mistress."

Bugas shook his head in wonderment. "Why *did* you take on the terrible burden of running the company?"

Matter-of-factly, concealing as usual the depth of his feeling, Henry answered, "I did it for my father, to make it up to my father. My grandfather caused him so much anguish. I wanted to show the world that my father's seed was made of good-enough stuff. I *remember* my father." This last sentence was so obviously deeply felt, a rare acknowledgment by Henry of what had obviously been a dominating theme in his life, that everyone fell silent. It was an odd moment of homage to Edsel and to his eldest son's sense of fealty to him.

One day Henry had another episode of heart pain. After watching him double over, his skin becoming ashen, Bugas, who had recently had his own heart trouble, put in a call to his cardiologist in Ann Arbor. When he told him how many Nitrostats Henry was taking, the doctor said, "It doesn't sound too good. How long will it take him to get here?"

Bugas persuaded Henry to fly home immediately. He checked in at St. Joseph's Hospital in Ann Arbor for an examination; when Bugas' doctor saw the results of the tests, he refused to release him. He argued for a bypass operation, but Henry refused. The hospitalization provided disheartening news about his family as well as his cardiac condition. While he was there his brothers and sister did not visit him; neither did any of his children. No one in the family came or called. The doctors on the St. Joseph's staff were shocked.

What hurt most was that his mother boycotted his illness. But the separation from Cristina had been the final straw in the long disappointment he had become for her. Three days after Henry left to spend Christmas with Kathy in England, Eleanor had asked Ford officials to reserve a company plane for her and then flew Cristina to Sun Valley to spend the holidays with Charlotte and her family, paying for the trip herself. "I can't believe my son did that," Eleanor complained. "Before Christmas! He's crazy! He hasn't got any heart." In light of what had just happened to him, Henry found the last comment particularly ironic.

Yet while he was saddened by his outlaw status in the family, Henry was not shaken from his course. Emerging from the hospital after a three-week stay, he frequently visited Kathy at her town house in Grosse Pointe and occasionally invited her to spend the night with him in the penthouse atop the Glass House that had been built to accommodate directors attending board meetings. Someone noted that the view from the window there was magnificent. Henry agreed, saying pensively that it was a good vantage point from which to contemplate the future.

⟡

"MORTALITY IS THE GREAT CLARIFIER," Henry told Bugas in one of their lunches early that spring. His old friend noticed that he talked now more than he ever had before, reaching out for wisdom, for generalizations about his experience. Rather than depressing him, this particular perception about mortality had a tonic effect on Henry, halting the furious rush of his multiple lives and making him feel that it was time to set things straight and finish his work. In the early weeks of 1976 he rode his stationary bicycle, took long walks and spent quiet days and nights with Kathy in an attempt to strengthen his ailing heart for what he now realized was the summary task of his late middle age—resolving the dilemmas of his private life and putting the company into shape to pass on to other hands. He was still not anxious to talk about himself; he continued to be emotionally tongue-tied. But Bugas, Max Fisher, Kathy and others close to him noticed that a recurring phrase kept creeping into his conversation. It was part prescription for his body, part mantra to lead him in the right direction: "*I need to simplify my life.*"

When Henry officially returned to work on March 1, he had decided that it was time for him to leave the company. His decision put a new item at the top of his agenda. Who would replace him when he quit? The Dearborn grapevine sensed that the great drama of his career was heading toward its end, a catharsis that would affect all the players currently on the stage. The Detroit rumor mill assumed that Iacocca would benefit, but that the successor would come from the Ford family; it worked overtime grinding out gossip about which Ford would follow Henry and how this chosen Ford would work in partnership with Iacocca. But all the speculations were wide of the mark, because they ignored the decision Henry had made thirty years earlier to remake the Ford Motor Company in the image of General Motors. He had repeated his intention over the years, most recently in his "Henry Ford Superstar" interview with *Fortune* in 1973: "I've always been envious of GM because they have an organization that Mr. Sloan established.... We never really got a basic system.... I hope that by the time I retire we'll have one." The unsuccessful troikas he had installed periodically since McNamara's abrupt departure had actually been ineffectual attempts to emulate the executive pyramid at GM, where the chairman was chief executive officer, standing over the president and the chief operating officer and another figure who was the chief financial officer. This was the structure he wanted for Ford. But because he himself had become a Ford in the epic mold no one believed him when he said that this was his objective.

His first act when getting back on the job was to call in the high-powered management consultants McKinsey and Company to help him with the task of reorganization. This choice annoyed many executives at Ford simply because it involved outsiders, but no one could claim that calling in a consultant when a momentous executive change was being considered was not state-of-the-art management.

In April, Henry met the press for the first time since his hospitalization. He told them he was confident and optimistic, noting that his prediction for 1976 sales, $9.6 billion, had been unduly bearish and he was revising it upward to $10.2 billion. He also said that first-quarter profits were headed for $343 million, a dramatic recovery from the $11 million loss for the first quarter of 1975. But reporters didn't really want to talk about sales figures; they were more interested in the human story of the succession at the company, and especially about who would be the next Ford. Henry noted that while the family had 13 percent of the common stock and 40 percent of the voting stock, Ford "had to be run as a public company regardless of how much ownership we have." It was as if the decision to bring the company closer into line with the GM model had freed him, paradoxically, to depart from the suppression of the Ford self that had characterized his reign. In a woolgathering mood, he went on to say, "I think the public really wants, after I go, to see somebody called Ford somewhere right at the top of the company in some kind of position." Then he added, as if suddenly aware for the first time of the significance of this comment, "I have never said that before."

Although he had decided to complete the transformation of the company from a family business to a modern corporation, these remarks were taken as proof that he intended to continue the dynasty. The rest of the family fueled this speculation by their comments about the succession. Benson said, "It's just something to think about with the view to having someone from the family at the top of the company." He added sadly, "I'm afraid I'm not available, because of my health. That sort of leaves it up to Bill and I think he would be receptive."

Bill was indeed the logical candidate: a Ford of Henry's generation, although eight years younger—the perfect transition figure while the next Ford generation, notably Edsel II and his own son Billy, was learning the company ropes. Moreover, Bill's candidacy was backed by his mother, who had told her sons of her hopes for the company in a rare meeting at Gaukler Pointe in March, not long after Henry's release from the hospital. Sick herself, gasping for breath because of a worsening heart condition, she had concluded the parley with the typically laconic recommendation "It ought to be Bill." The son who had been the pride and joy of her youth ought to have his chance.

But Bill had been for too long on the outside of the company looking in. Although still resentful about his treatment during the era of his Continental, he had seen the importance of not being Henry. So had his wife, Martha. As she said later on, "We've had a nice oblivion. People ask if we're related to Whitey Ford or Gerald Ford. That's perfect. Henry hasn't been able to have this." Remaining remote from the company—heavily involved financially but only lightly in terms of responsibility—had been Bill's way of handling things. He was emotionally tied up with the Lions, having moved the team to Pontiac even though Henry had begged him to keep them in downtown Detroit. He prided himself on the fact that the franchise for which he had paid $6 million was now worth $75 million and making $5-$7 million a year. Stylist Gene Bordinat later said, "Bill did not enjoy being around the Glass House. He didn't want to participate in executive luncheons up in the penthouse and things like that. He'd come in occasionally, get a haircut at the barbershop, which happened to be a door away from his office, and then leave." A family friend playing golf with Bill shortly after he was made vice-chairman found him irritated at all the work that was involved, saying, "God, I can't believe it. Every time I walk into the office there's a stack of briefing books to go through. I do a couple and it gets pretty tiresome. Then all of a sudden I turn around and there's another dozen briefing books."

When the idea of his younger brother succeeding him came up, Henry told Bugas, "Bill's a professional dilettante." This assessment seemed confirmed by Bill's new venture into politics; he agreed to be the vice-presidential candidate in Eugene McCarthy's 1976 independent run for the presidency and then withdrew after six days. As far as the company was concerned he responded candidly when asked about succeeding Henry, "If it meant simply serving as chairman, chairing the company and stockholders' meetings, okay. But as far as actually running the company—no, I wouldn't want the job on an everyday basis."

Whom did this leave? Speculation centered on Edsel II. It was assumed by Iacocca and others that Henry's every decision was based on a desire to secure the top job for his son. In fact, however, Henry had been far less encouraging than his son had wished. "When I graduated from Babson," Edsel later remarked, "my father said, 'Don't ever feel you have to join the Ford Motor Company.' That wasn't said casually over a glass of wine. For years he said this." One of the reasons Edsel did go to work for the company was to solidify his relationship with Henry—so that they would have something to talk about other than "how much weight I should lose or why I didn't get better grades in college."

When he came to the company, Edsel had moved immediately into a fast-track management position. From 1974 to 1975 he had worked as a product planner in Dearborn. In 1975 he had moved to Ford Division marketing and sales in California. Then he was an assistant manager for the Lincoln-Mercury district sales office in Boston. In 1976 he was posted to Australia as assistant managing director, a job that Henry told him was good because it would allow him to oversee an entire operation, although Edsel worried about being so far away from the action in Dearborn. Asked about his son's prospects in the company, Henry was purposely ambiguous, saying that he'd like Edsel to succeed him someday, but emphasizing that he'd have to "earn it."

In the middle of all this speculation about the future of the Fords, Eleanor gave the discussions about mortality and succession a sudden reality. She had been admitted to the Henry Ford Hospital shortly after Henry's bout with angina, suffering from severe chest pains of her own. She was soon released, but the poor health she had suffered over the past few years prevented a recovery. As her daughter Dodie said later, "She was always putting those pills under her tongue. We couldn't even take walks anymore."

Since Clara's death Eleanor had been known as "the Mrs. Ford," the definite article differentiating her from her daughter and her daughters-in-law: a relic from a bygone era of auto elegance traveling around Grosse Pointe in her Lincoln limo with the glass partition. Now she couldn't go out any longer. She looked out her bedroom window at the vast lawns which shone like green glass. The great estate was a monument to her love for Edsel, a love that had never died in the years since his death. She had provided for Gaukler Pointe in her will, making sure that, unlike Fairlane, which had been gutted and forgotten, her home would live on.

When she died, on October 18, 1976, her son Henry, in whom she was bitterly disappointed, said it was one of the saddest days of his life.

HENRY NOW MOVED TO ACHIEVE closure on what he regarded as the most important piece of business left to him: simplifying his life. His first big step came in December, when he attended his first meeting of the Ford Foundation since his mother's death and surprised everyone by resigning.

Some assumed that his leaving had something to do with the struggle with McGeorge Bundy over the $100 million grant to the Henry Ford Hospital. That episode had indeed contributed to his feelings of alienation, but his concerns about the foundation's direction had begun long before. Over the years, he had come to see Bundy as a philanthropic analogue of Iacocca— someone devoted to self-aggrandizement and empire-building at the expense of the institution itself. He had contempt for Bundy's stewardship of the foundation, noting bitterly that during his reign its capital had been diminished by $1 billion, a third of its assets, because of risk-taking investment policies always trumpeted as "bold departures" from the "timid conservatism" of the past. He saw Bundy's attitude as an arrogant denial of the Ford family's contribution to the foundation and of the vitality of capitalism itself, which had provided money for the enterprise.

He arranged that at the December 16 trustees' meeting all his colleagues on the board would find a letter from him. In it he noted that while he took pride in the foundation generally, "it has also been a cause of frustration and sometimes plain irritation." Making it clear that he found it hypocritical to deny that its rich harvest had come from the fruits of American business, he added: "I'm not playing the role of the hardheaded tycoon who thinks all philanthropoids are socialists and that university professors are communists. I'm just saying that the system that makes the Foundation possible is very probably worth preserving." In the envelope with the letter he included a Xeroxed *New Yorker* cartoon showing a young foundation executive throwing dollar bills out the window while a horrified older colleague said, "Just a minute, young man, that's not quite the way we do things here at the Ford Foundation." Henry had appended a handwritten comment: "To my fellow trustees with warm and high regard. Maybe this fellow has a better idea."

Perhaps a resignation from the foundation was to be expected; after all, it had been clear for some time that he regarded service there as an obligation rather than a pleasure. But not so Henry's announcement two months later, on February 11, when he told the press that he would name a successor as head of the Ford Motor Company before the end of 1977 and that for the first time in its seventy-four-year history it would not be a member of the Ford family. The family and the company had been as one, their lifeblood flowing through a common vein; separating them from each other was like cutting apart Siamese twins joined at a sensitive spot of their anatomy. Aside from the shock value, this announcement pushed the succession question to center stage and the battle with Iacocca to its final round.

THERE HAD ALWAYS BEEN AN OEDIPAL element in the relationship. Phlegmatic and

aloof like his father, Henry had been fascinated with the sheer drive and innovative power of Iacocca, which was so like his grandfather's. He had taken
pleasure in the spectacle of it as long as he could. But when the point was
reached at which he began to feel, like his father, menaced by this power, he
decided to move against Iacocca rather than passively accept his force as
Edsel had accepted the forces arrayed against him.

Henry's investigation of Fugazy had been completed just before he left
Cristina. He had thought it might turn up a crime connection or proof that
Iacocca was taking kickbacks from firms with lucrative Ford contracts. It did-
n't. Confronted by an audit report, Fugazy did agree to return several hundred
thousand dollars in overcharges, but investigators had failed to confirm
Henry's deeper suspicions of Mafia connections. Yet that didn't deter him.
As Bugas said, "Before the heart attack, Henry would have retreated because
of the lack of evidence. But after the heart attack he had become a different
man. He knew what had to be done and went ahead and did it even though
he knew that without the smoking gun he'd be cast in an unpleasant light.
He reminded me of the end of *The Godfather* when the Don's plan went into
effect and they began to take care of business that had piled up over the
years."

One of his first acts upon returning to work after leaving the hospital
had been to appear before his board of directors to try to get Iacocca fired. He
told the group about his heart problems. He proposed one scenario that presumed his total incapacitation and another which assumed only a mild
incapacity. Neither of them included Iacocca. He didn't deliver a bill of particulars. He just said that he didn't like Iacocca and didn't want him working
at Ford. But this plea deeply alarmed the directors, who were already traumatized by Henry's health problems, by his public break with Cristina and
embrace of Kathy, by the bad press the company was receiving for the Pinto
and by the red ink spilled over the balance sheet in recent years.

Undeterred by the ambivalent response of his board, Henry made up his
mind to move ahead. He called Iacocca into his office and ordered him to can-
cel the contract with Fugazy. Iacocca protested, once again reminding Henry
of the good work his friend had done by getting the Pope to use a Lincoln
during his visit to America. Dismissing this episode as "ancient history,"
Henry concluded the meeting by growling, "Get rid of him."

His next move was against Bill Winn, an affable advertising man who
had built his own promotion company into a great success at Ford, largely
because he and Iacocca were old friends. (They had roomed together in the
late 1940s when Iacocca began at Ford.) As Iacocca rose in the organization,
he had thrown business Winn's way. Just as Fugazy had gotten contracts to
provide transportation for dealer organization meetings, so Winn's company
had gotten contracts to put on the spectacular shows for the dealers' annual
conventions. But Henry had become suspicious of the whole issue of dealer
conventions. (One target of the investigation of Iacocca had been a dealer
meeting in Las Vegas at which dealers allegedly had been provided company

funds for gambling and women.) And when he heard that Winn had sold his promotion agency to Kenyon & Eckhardt, the giant Madison Avenue agency that handled the Lincoln-Mercury account, Henry exploded. Getting on the phone with Kenyon president Leo-Arthur Kelmenson, he screamed at him about Winn, "Keep that son of a bitch peddler the fuck out of my company!"

Henry next set his sights on the man closest to Iacocca in the company—Hal Sperlich, chief product planner and veteran of the Mustang team. Knowing that Sperlich was his opponent's right-hand man, Henry had been watchful of him for several years, at least since he had blocked Iacocca's attempt to insert him into the presidency of Ford International. He also knew that Sperlich had a calculated disdain for him. (As designer John Reinhardt later said, "Sperlich was a smart-ass. He and Iacocca used to sit around and ridicule Henry behind his back.") After the other executives had swallowed Henry's decision to cut back the small-car program, Sperlich alone continued to complain about how wrong the decision had been. Henry was no longer in a mood to take his insubordination. After one meeting of the Product Planning Committee, always chaired by Iacocca with Henry on his right side and Sperlich on his left, he called Iacocca into his office and told him, "I hate that goddamn Sperlich, and I don't want him sitting beside you. He's always pissing in your ear. I don't want the two of you ganging up on me like that."

Iacocca gave Sperlich some tasks abroad to get him away from the heat. But Henry continued to bore in. Not long after their first confrontation over Sperlich, Henry said he wanted him fired.

"You got to be kidding," Iacocca protested. "He's the best we got."

Henry was unyielding. "Fire him now…. If you don't can him right now, you'll go out the door with him." He interrupted Iacocca's last-ditch attempt to argue for his friend. "Don't give me any bullshit. I don't like him. You're not entitled to ask why."

Iacocca hardly had time to assimilate this development when Henry moved again. At a press conference on April 18, 1977, he announced that there would be a major change in the managerial structure of Ford in accordance with the recommendations of the McKinsey consultants he had retained. He was creating an "Executive Office" which would consist of himself, Iacocca and Philip Caldwell.

In this new troika all eyes were focused on the third and largely unknown member. A onetime Navy man who had graduated from Harvard Business School and joined Ford in 1953, the long-faced and saturnine Caldwell, a protégé of Henry's in the same way Iacocca had once been, was a steady but unspectacular executive who had nonetheless established a reputation for reliability and predictable success in the various posts he held during his rise in the company. "If Phil Caldwell were Secretary of State, the United States would never go to war," Iacocca's red-team loyalists joked in the same way that they had said Arjay Miller would announce Armageddon in a monotone. Yet they could not deny Caldwell's accomplishments. Appointed to his first big post as general manager of North American truck operations in 1968, he had waged a meticulously organized campaign to overtake GM's lead in truck sales. This and other achievements had led Henry to elevate Caldwell to the presidency of Ford International in 1972. And his achievements there, continuing International's success as the company's primary profit-maker, led Henry to bring him into the new Executive Office. Caldwell would be vice-chairman, and in his own absence, Henry told the shocked press corps, ultimate authority would rest with the vice-chairman. It was another way of saying that Iacocca had been demoted to the number-three position in the company. Iacocca saw the move in terms of his personal melodrama: "It was a real crack in the face. Every time there was a dinner Henry hosted table one, Caldwell hosted table two, and I was shoved down to three. It was public humiliation, like the guy in the stockade in the center of town."

Given the strong personalities involved, it was hard for observers to see that this act was not only a personality conflict but also the culmination of a decision Henry had made twenty years earlier, when Lewis Crusoe's audacious gamble to beat his old employer GM at its own game had ended in the disaster of the Edsel. At that point, Henry had seen the lesson: the battle his grandfather lost to GM in the 1920s was probably lost forever. His executives would continue to pay lip service to the struggle, and some would pursue it as an existential errand, but GM's strength in the American marketplace was too great; plans to challenge his great competitor there would inevitably fail. The domestic market simply seemed intractable. As one Ford executive remarked, "Since 1960 the Ford Division has had three sales bonanzas. First came the Falcon, then the Fairlane, and finally the Mustang. When we started we had a twenty-three percent share of the market, and now, after all the hoopla, we got a twenty percent. So what the hell did we prove?"

But this realization hadn't meant settling back into second spot. Henry also understood that the European market was a new frontier where the Ford Motor Company could compete and win. In the late 1960s and early 1970s, while Iacocca was joking with Sperlich and other close aides about Henry's weakness and failure as an executive, his European gamble was paying off. Ford International, in effect, had saved the company.

In the weeks after Henry's announcement, Iacocca tried to dismiss Caldwell as an inept plodder, just as he had Miller and Knudsen before. But the business analysts saw something different. In 1977 the profits of Ford International, which Caldwell had headed for five years, amounted to 42 percent of the company's consolidated net income, while Iacocca's North American operations contributed 37.5 percent. Since 1972, when Caldwell was first posted to International, overseas profits were up 380 percent, more than double GM's 180 percent increase in foreign operations over the same period. But during that time GM had expanded its domestic net income by 50 percent, while Ford under Iacocca had failed to advance at all. This was not just a propaganda picture painted by Henry. In a communication to its clients the blue-ribbon brokerage house of Donaldson, Lufkin and Jenrette noted, "The contribution made by [Ford] overseas operations to overall profit growth and stockholders' equity during the last five years was large and dominant. It is equally apparent that Mr. Iacocca failed to match the corresponding performance of General Motors in his principal area of responsibility. North American automotive operations made no contribution at all to the Company's strong earnings expansion."

THE FIRING OF SPERLICH AND HIS OWN demotion marked a moment of truth for Iacocca. Until now he had felt that he could wait Henry out. After all, in Iacocca's view he was just an aging man with a leaky heart and an inexhaustible appetite for self-indulgence. But a passive strategy was no longer viable because of the iron that had suddenly entered Henry's spine and Iacocca saw that he had to act before Henry fired him. But even as he began to go on the offensive he was making a crucial error of self-aggrandizement by imagining that the McKinsey report and all the rest of Henry's maneuvering were simply some elitist plot to get rid of him. "When Henry began to realize his mortality he turned animal," Iacocca later said. "I imagine his first impulse was: 'I don't want that Italian interloper taking over. What's going to happen to the family business if I get a heart attack and die? Before I know it, he'll sneak in here one night, take my name off the building and turn the place into the Iacocca Motor Company.' " Many observers were surprised that Iacocca stayed. They didn't realize that he did so because he felt he could do the impossible—unseat Henry and take control of the company.

For several months he fought Caldwell just as he had Knudsen before. But this time it was different. Caldwell was no outsider, but rather a Ford man with a constituency of his own. In any case, Iacocca realized that even if he had been able to defeat Caldwell it would have begged the question. This was a confrontation between him and Henry, and if he was to prevail he would have to go right after the top man.

He began to curry favor with the outside directors, who, unlike the inside ones, were a center of power not directly under Henry's control. He also moved to solidify his strength with the dealers' organization, which had always been a base of personal power for him because of his success with products. (A resolution in the minutes of one of their meetings showed how successful he was in getting his views across: "Henry Ford II is not at this time offering the type of quality leadership that his dealers expect from him.")

But the pivotal figure in his plan was Bill Ford. They had always been compatible because Bill, too, considered himself a product man; a product man, moreover, who had also had his creativity damaged by Henry. He had supported Iacocca in the Knudsen firing and had let himself be used in the Pantera debacle. He was indispensable to any plot because of his huge ownership position, largest of all the brothers'.* If he could be brought into a loose confederation with the outside board members and the dealers, Iacocca believed, Bill's influence could be decisive.

The final piece in Iacocca's puzzle was Henry himself. Because of his erratic behavior in his personal life, he could perhaps be portrayed as another "Crazy Henry"—an embarrassing philanderer and drinker who created sleazy scandals with his wives and mistresses, someone who began paranoid investigations of his executives and made disreputable business decisions such as the Indonesia "bribe." Iacocca felt that he could use these perceptions of Henry in his struggle, and he launched an investigation of his own, starting with the bonus list, where he found that Paul Lorenz, who had been "retired early" after the Indonesia affair came to light, had been given $100,000 that same year as a bonus. He stored up this information for the time when push would come to shove, as he knew it would.

THREE DAYS AFTER THE PRESS CONFERENCE at which Henry announced the McKinsey changes in the company's hierarchy, there was a lavish dance downtown on the waterfront in the ballroom of the Detroit Plaza, the world's tallest hotel and one of the centerpieces of the Renaissance Center. The dance was part of the dedication of this symbol of Detroit's civic rebirth. The shimmering towers of the Renaissance Center were a monument to the city's determination to recover from the trauma of the 1967 riots. However, the 650 members of Detroit's social, business and political elite who gathered to hear comedian Bob Hope quip, "How do you like Henry Ford's rumpus room?" knew that it was also a monument to Henry himself. But Henry was not even there for the ceremonies. He was at the Martha Mary Chapel in his grandfather's Greenfield Village, standing in as father of the bride for Kathy DuRoss's daughter Deborah, who was getting married.

Solving the succession problem—Vice-Chairman Philip Caldwell was now the executive who would replace him in the event of his death—had simplified Henry's corporate life. Now he turned his attention to private matters. He was ready to divorce Cristina. It was done in his mind, just as the firing of Iacocca was. But in both cases he found himself involved in an emotional chess match whose endgame eluded him.

He waited for Cristina to act first. But she was waiting, too. Although for much of their married life together she had complained about the smallness

---

* As of 1978, Bill had 2,243,805 shares of Class B stock, the special family stock worth 4.7 votes per common share. Benson held 1,830,639, and Henry, who had sold some of his holdings over the years to support the grand lifestyle his two wives had demanded of him, had 1,258,226. Josephine owned the second-largest block, but because she was not an officer of the company she was not required to report her stock ownership.

and provinciality of Grosse Pointe, she now made public statements about how important the community and her home were to her, employing her remarkable theatricality to present herself as a seduced and abandoned woman whose predicament caused her now to wander wraithlike through the fifty-one-room mansion alone. At the same time that she was creating this image, however, she was also making frequent trips to New York and abroad to such ports of call as Manila, where in the summer of 1977 she celebrated Imelda Marcos' birthday, an event she had faithfully observed each of the five previous years.

The irony was that while Cristina cared little for the Lakeshore Drive house but nonetheless occupied it by squatter's rights, Henry, who loved the place, was barred from it. When he thought she might be about to take a junket away from Grosse Pointe, he would call one of his old neighbors and say, "Is Cristina going to be out of town this week? If she is, come over for dinner." He would exercise visitation privileges when she was away, letting himself and Kathy in with his key and then entertaining as if they were the married couple. They would sleep in the master bedroom, leaving telltale signs of their lovemaking on the sheets for Cristina to discover, a quid pro quo on Henry's part for what he believed to be going on during her extended stays in the Malacañang Palace.

Except for these rebellious gestures, Henry suffered in silence. Then, almost exactly a year after his mother's death, acting as if a prescribed term of mourning had elapsed and he was finally freed from the identity of son that had cramped him all his life, he made his move. While Cristina was off on a long trip to Rome, he hired moving vans to pull up to the Lakeshore Drive house and emptied it of its contents—$10 million worth—with the intention of putting it all up for auction. The legal battle was finally joined. Cristina returned home to file for an injunction to block the sale of the property.

The court hearing over this issue provided a glimpse of the two protagonists at a crucial passage in their lives.

"I would go in there and sit and look at all my beautiful things," Cristina told the judge. "The dining room was so feminine, so beautiful—a little corner of Versailles." She said that she was so shamed now by the emptiness of the place that she no longer invited friends to visit; that she was so distraught she took Librium.

During his four hours on the stand, Henry talked about his desire to simplify his life: "I'm getting older, not younger. I'm on the downgrade, not the upgrade. I thought it was foolish to have them [the furnishings and artifacts] sitting around. I want my holdings more liquid so my estate is in better shape."

After the court decided that he had the right to proceed with the sale, Henry filed for divorce.

THERE WAS A CERTAIN SYNCHRONISM between Cristina and Iacocca. Both had assumed that they *knew* Henry; that he was as weak as they had seen him in his weakest moments. They both thought that they could take advantage of the flaws they had perceived in his character. When he proved to be stronger than either had believed, both of them dug in and resolved to fight to the end, doing all the damage they could in a rearguard action even if their cause was lost.

Iacocca had waited all his working life for the moment when he would pull the sword from the stone at the Ford Motor Company. Now it was clear that this moment would probably not come. If he could not be the once and future king of this industrial realm, he would be its Mordred, precipitating a destructive crisis which would allow him to usurp Henry's leadership.

Fate seemed to have intervened on his side, laying a presumptive foundation for his challenge, when a California jury awarded an unprecedented $128 million in a claim against the company as a result of an accident in which Mrs. Lily Gray was killed and her thirteen-year-old passenger Richard Grimshaw was burned over 90 percent of his body when her Pinto, stalled on a Los Angeles freeway, was hit from behind by a car traveling at thirty-five miles an hour and burst into flames. Of the amount, $600,000 was to Mrs. Gray's survivors and $2.8 million was for Richard Grimshaw's condition; the remainder of the huge award was punitive damages, as the foreman of the jury said, "so that Ford wouldn't design cars that way again."

This was not the only action involving the Pinto. There had been a series of rear-end collisions resulting in fuel tank explosions, causing other fatalities and leading to other lawsuits. *Mother Jones*, a small left-wing magazine, made national headlines by charging that "secret documents" revealed that the design problems which made the Pinto especially susceptible to explosion and fire had been known to the team developing the car. During the Gray-Grimshaw trial a confidential company memo was introduced into evidence showing that Ford was fully aware of what might happen to the Pinto. The author of the document estimated that 180 people could die as a result of the Pinto's defects during the life span of the car, and another 180 be severely burned. These deaths and injuries, the analyst calculated, had potential "social costs" of $49.5 million compared to the $137 million it would cost to fix the Pinto immediately. Thus the modification would not be "cost effective."

During the public outcry against Ford over the Pinto, Henry had borne up with his usual stoicism. He was, however, aware of the irony: he was taking the blame while Iacocca actually bore the responsibility. In Henry's eyes, and those of many other executives, Iacocca was actually the midwife of the Mustang, rather than the father he claimed to be; but there could be no doubting his paternity of the Pinto. He had designed its "package" years earlier in his campaign against Bunkie Knudsen, claiming that he could build a subcompact "under two thousand pounds and under two thousand dollars" when Knudsen wanted to import a comparable car from Europe for about $2,400.

Onetime Ford engineer Harley Copp, who was "retired early" for providing expert testimony when the company tried to mislead the EPA on mileage figures, and who helped the plaintiffs in some of the Pinto suits, later said, "Iacocca assured Henry Ford that he'd do the car for two thousand pounds and two thousand dollars. But he didn't tell Henry that he was going to make an unsafe car. He was a smart operator. He figured that the Pinto was a way to put Knudsen in a box, to dramatically outshine him. Knudsen smelled something fishy. He knew the costs of the engine, the transmission, the axle, et cetera in the car Lee was proposing. He said, 'Something's wrong. It can't be done for that price.' Well, Lee did it. He actually brought the car in at 1995 pounds, $1,995. And the car was a success until the safety problems caught up with it. The thing is, they knew even before they produced the car that the fuel-system integrity wasn't up to standards. But because of the cost Iacocca had come up with in his end run around Knudsen, there was no money to be spent to protect the fuel system. The engineers all knew this."

The Pinto—Henry's Pinto, as it had become known when it failed, not Iacocca's—was very much in the background of a stockholders' suit filed on April 27, 1978, charging the Ford board of directors and especially Henry with acting as "agents of an illegal and fraudulent conspiracy" and of having countenanced a "gross waste" of corporate assets. Filed by Roy Cohn, onetime bad boy of Senator Joseph McCarthy's investigating committee, the suit sought $50 million in damages and recovery of $992,000 paid to Henry for the previous year's salary. The action, filed in behalf of the children of one of Cohn's law partners who had some Ford shares in trust, alleged that Henry had accepted $750,000 in kickbacks from a Chicago-based catering concern in return for exclusive concessions to provide food and beverage at the company's office and factories. It alleged further that he had awarded contracts to family members—a veiled reference to the interior-decoration business of Dodie's husband, Walter Buhl Ford—for furniture for personal residences which was billed to the company. The suit finally charged that the Ford Motor Company had wasted more than $1 million in company funds by paying maintenance charges and personal expenses in connection with Henry's six-room duplex apartment in New York's Carlyle Hotel.

Henry indignantly denied all these charges. It was ridiculous to assume that someone with his wealth would take a kickback, he said. While his brother-in-law's interior-decoration company had been on retainer to the company for years, it never did any personal work for Henry himself. And as far as the apartment was concerned, it had been primarily for business; when he used it for personal matters he had reimbursed the company. He aired his grievances at a May 1 press conference. "I have been criticized for a lot of things in my life and most of the time I just don't pay any attention to what was said about me," he said. But charges made in this suit "went beyond the pale." What he didn't say was that he knew that Cohn was a crony of Iacocca's good friend Fugazy and that Cristina had been in touch with Cohn about a divorce, and that he had therefore concluded that the suit was a joint production of his two nemeses.

On May 11, the annual stockholders' meeting was convened at the Ford Auditorium in downtown Detroit. Henry was in the chair, Iacocca beside him with other Ford officers and directors on the stage. Henry made an emotional opening statement: "The Ford Motor Company has been far more than a place of employment or a source of income for me. It's been my life. It absorbs virtually all of my time and attention in one way or another. It is a personal and family responsibility—a private and public trust that I have carried out as chief executive officer for nearly thirty-three years. To suggest that I would commit or condone any action harmful to the company's reputation or my own is preposterous.... The charges in this lawsuit are untrue. If left to stand unchallenged they would not only harm my reputation but could do incalculable damage to the company.... I deplore the need to dignify the blatant untruths by responding to them so publicly, but to do less would be to disregard my obligations to the company and its stockholders."

Cohn got the floor and began to attack Henry on a variety of issues from the Pinto to the Indonesian "bribe." When the aggressive tactics he had used twenty years earlier in bullying witnesses before the McCarthy Committee drew a chorus of boos and calls for him to be ejected, Cohn responded, "I realize I am in the Ford Kingdom and I am not a subject." He went ahead trying to interrogate Henry, who refused to answer. Finally John Bugas stood up in the audience and asked for the floor. He had just celebrated his seventieth birthday, but he still had the quiet power that had first attracted Henry some thirty-five years earlier, the same sincerity and forthrightness. What he said was moving for its autobiography as well as its history:

> I worked for the Ford Motor Company for nearly twenty-five years, beginning in January 1944. I am retired. I am on Ford pension. My appearance here today is totally unsolicited.... I and my family own and control approximately one hundred thousand shares of the Ford Motor Company. I state that to show that I have an interest in the affairs of this company. I read with interest and trepidation and disgust the lawsuit that Mr. Cohn has talked about so elaborately here today.... I came into this company shortly after Mr. Ford. Together, after the so-called "revolution at the Rouge," in which Mr. Ford...took control of the company, we spent the ensuing two or three years rooting out the type of corruption that Mr. Cohn's lawsuit is accusing him and the directors of today.... There is no one who knows better than I do the contribution on this one particular thing Mr. Ford has made to this company.... He had all kinds of money. He could have gone off on his yacht if he liked, but for some reason that I have never been able to completely understand, he dedicated himself to the Ford Motor Company...

At the same time that he was attacking Henry in front of the stockholders, Cohn was filing amendments that made his suit more serious and more clearly an Iacocca product. The new version flatly accused Henry of having personally authorized the $1 million Indonesia bribe and then attempting to cover it up by having "forged, altered and backdated" records involved in the bribe. In addition Cohn accused Henry of having tipped off "close personal and business associates" including Max Fisher about the Renaissance Center and Fairlane projects so that they could make large profits. Finally, the amended suit alleged that Henry had used company planes to transport Kathy from one place to another and had used the company's advertising firm to pay fees to a modeling business in which she was supposed to have an interest. The case was almost thrown out of court because it was not supported by enough voting stock, but then Iacocca's old crony De Tomaso put his holdings behind Cohn.

IT WAS AT THIS TIME THAT HENRY finally decided that Iacocca was "morally unfit" to be president of the Ford Motor Company and that he must be fired. His first step was a cautious one—enlarging the Executive Office by making his brother Bill "chairman of the Executive Committee," which meant that Iacocca was now reporting to Caldwell as number four instead of number three in the hierarchy. The change had the desired effect of demoting Iacocca another step, but it was also meant to find out whether Bill could play a role after Henry retired, and in this it was less conclusive. It was obvious that Bill would never forget about his Continental, nursing feelings which were still bruised after nearly thirty years. Not long after he got the new title, Bill was standing with his executive assistant George Haviland in front of a big window in his twelfth-floor office, looking down on the cornfield where the Continental had begun twenty-five years earlier. Haviland said, "You know what we're looking down on, don't you?" Bill replied with his usual cynicism, "Yeah, the thought crossed my mind." With both men thinking about the Mark II, Bill, who had boycotted the Glass House for twenty-five years, taking space there only because of the vice-chairman appointment, gestured at his elaborate office and said, "Quite a story, isn't it? Local boy makes good."

Many observers felt that in spite of his undoubted power, Henry's decision to remove Iacocca had come too late. The assault on the corporation and on him personally had drastically weakened his position. The company was experiencing its worst publicity since the Bennett era and was facing legal action on three fronts—the unresolved Indonesia matter, Cohn's stockholder's suit and the ongoing investigation of the Pinto and the Mercury Bobcat that had resulted in Ford's announcement on June 9 that it was recalling 1.5 million vehicles.

Amid all this bad news, Ford board members convened in Detroit on June 12 for a directors' meeting. As was his custom, Henry met with the outside directors on the Audit Committee chaired by Arjay Miller. Usually such meetings were a courtesy—a time for socializing as much as for business. This time Henry dropped a bombshell: he planned to fire Iacocca and wanted a recommendation from them to the full board that this should be done. Sensing resistance, he let the committee know that it would ultimately have to choose between him and Iacocca. But the group could not bring itself to back him. Associates who saw him after the meeting said that he was "white as a ghost." The next day he left on a business trip to Asia.

Iacocca seized on the fact of Henry's absence to push ahead with his audacious plan not just to survive at the company but to prevail. Once again he traveled east to lobby the outside directors, especially Boston banker George F. Bennett. But the key to his plan was still Bill. As his executive assistant Chalmers Goyert later said: "The Iacocca people wanted Bill to do something for Iacocca. Everybody wanted Bill to do something."

Bill went to several executives and asked them what to do when the big moment arrived. One of those he asked was Goyert, who told Bill, even though he worked for Iacocca, that if he went up against Henry it could cause untold damage to the company. It was another occasion when Bill's ambivalence toward the company came into sharp focus, an occasion which called up the fact that he had virtually boycotted the company after his disappointment with the Mark II but now was back a quarter century later considering backing Iacocca's challenge.

While Bill was checking his options, Iacocca was trying to enlarge his. At a meeting with the outside directors he lobbied to be reinstated to his former position. He loaded his guns for the July 12 board meeting. Two days before it was convened, unknown sources leaked material to the *New York Times* for an article on new developments in the Indonesia case. The big new piece of information was the $100,000 bonus Henry had authorized for Paul Lorenz. Lorenz himself said later, "Information in that article would have been known by no more than a handful of people and in one case no more than three." Henry, when he met with the Audit Committee again, accused Iacocca of having committed the leak, as well as having gone behind his back to outside directors. When he was once again opposed by some of the committee, who asked that he reinstate Iacocca, Henry became livid and said, "It's him or me. You have thirty minutes to make up your minds. If you don't give me your vote of confidence, I'll resign. You have thirty minutes to think about how *that* will look in tomorrow's *Wall Street Journal*." Then he left the room.

This was the moment when he reconquered his board, which backed him with a reluctant consensus. The next afternoon, with Bill sitting tearfully beside him—a way of indicating that there was no longer any need to consider splitting the Ford brothers apart—Henry summoned Iacocca to his office and told him that it was over. When Iacocca pressed him for the reason, Henry said, shrugging, "Well, sometimes you just don't like somebody."

At the end of a terse conversation Iacocca taunted him, "Your timing stinks. We've just made a billion eight for the second year in a row. That's three and a half billion in the past two years. But mark my words, Henry, you may never see a billion eight again. And do you know why? Because you don't know how the fuck we made it in the first place."

Henry didn't respond with the cutting remark he might have made: the company's success in the past two years was due far less to Iacocca than to Phil Caldwell, the man who would get the job as the first non-Ford to run the company for which Iacocca had campaigned so tirelessly.

TWENTY-THREE

FOR THE WORLD AT LARGE, the firing was an act of impotence on Henry's part. But those who knew him well understood that it was something quite different for him: a final ritual, marking both a passage toward old age and the final attainment of manhood. He didn't complain or explain, although Iacocca's wrath and that of the media he had cultivated over the years came down on Henry immediately. The most he said was a comment in an interview in *Fortune:* "When I got angina in January 1976, I suddenly discovered I wasn't going to live forever. I asked myself 'Where does the Ford Motor Company end up without me?' I came to the conclusion that Iacocca would not succeed me as chairman."

Iacocca saw it simply as a matter of family: Henry wanted to protect the throne for his son Edsel. He was correct that Henry's act had to do with family, but wrong to assume that it was anything so simple as ensuring an inheritance. It went back to the archetypal family drama: Henry didn't want the company to be the tool of a man who reminded him of his grandfather in his lust for power and of Harry Bennett in his deviousness.

There was speculation in the press about his brother Bill as a successor, and especially about Edsel II. There was even talk about Charlotte. But she remarked bitterly to reporters who asked her if she'd be getting involved in the company, "I have no desire to be on the board of the Ford Motor Company. I have never said that I wanted to be on the board. Anyway, I was born a girl and that takes care of that."

The one member of the family about whom there was no speculation was Benson. He had become the lost Ford. As his friend Eddie Stroh said, "Benson kind of was just there. You know, he was always fighting for visibility. Finally he just got tired of fighting." In 1973 Benson had called Stroh and told him that a common friend had terminal cancer and he himself had a worsening heart condition, so he had decided to stage a "last roundup." He had chartered a 240-foot yacht to cruise the Mediterranean for several weeks with all his close friends. He said to Stroh, "Let's go. I've chartered the first-class cabin of a Pan Am jet. We'll have a few drinks at my house, go to the airport, get on board and have a few drinks on the way over." By the time they arrived in England everyone was loaded. Benson had arranged for transportation to Paris and for a fleet of Lincoln limos to pick up his party there and drive them to the Côte d'Azur. They got aboard the rented yacht and stayed drunk for most of the rest of the trip as the boat meandered through the Mediterranean.

The cruising continued when he returned home. Henry had finally become so upset with his drinking that he asked him to stay away from the company and the make-work chores he had done there. Benson now spent most of his time with Edie aboard the *Onika II*. He was a sort of Ancient Mariner under a curse he didn't understand, condemned to endless sailing. From June to March they sailed a circuit from Detroit to Palm Beach and back. With the first refugees beginning to flow out of Vietnam, Benson said to his wife with unaccustomed bitterness, "You know, Edie, we were the original boat people." Their oldest friends saw them fade from view and considered them lost at sea. On July 27, 1978, he was cruising the Cheyboygan River when he suffered a fatal heart attack.

His death was as anticlimactic as his life, the news overwhelmed by the continuing aftershocks of the Iacocca firing, which continued to register heavily in the local media. Even at his own funeral Benson seemed relegated to the supporting cast. Henry arrived alone. Cristina, whom Edie had never liked and still referred to as "the Pizza Queen," was not invited. When Kathy arrived with Max Fisher it set the Ford-watchers to gossiping. However elliptical, it was her first introduction to the family.

Wasted by her long bout with cancer, Edie held the post-funeral reception at the Lakeshore Mansion. Attention immediately focused on her son Benson Junior. He looked like his father—there were the same large frame and pleasant oblong face, the same heavy jaw paradoxically conveying uncertainty rather than strength. When he arrived at the reception, he asked querulously, "What is this, a funeral or a social gathering?"

Speaking painfully through the squawk box an operation for her throat cancer had made necessary, his mother replied, "This is what your father would have liked, would have wanted."

Ben Junior seemed less worried about disrespect than about whether the same attitude of disdain that had followed his father would attach itself to him, too. It was a reasonable concern: while Benson had lived in suspended animation, young Ben had made his life, by the age of twenty-nine, into a bizarre, picaresque tale. The quality they had in common was failure.

As Ben Junior said in a summary he gave of his youth, his memories of growing up Ford involved none of the power of his heritage and very little of the glory.

> Until I was 14 I was always in a car with a goddamn guard or governess. My parents were usually traveling. I'd go to school in Palm Beach for three or four months in the winter. I had to repeat the third grade and flunked the seventh. So they shipped me off to Fessenden, a snatch-proof pre-prep school in West Newton, Mass. I was 14 and had never before been out of protective custody. Now I was in an environment where you had to fight to survive.

He finally managed to graduate from Suffield Academy, last in his class. Late that summer he drove out to California and enrolled at Whittier College, choosing the "party time" of a West Coast school instead of the rigors of an Ivy League college, which his father had pressed him to attend. California's ambiance of the late 1960s was a toxic substance for him, and in his own words he went "totally berserk" on alcohol and drugs. In his sane moments he tried clumsily to deal with family pressures. He talked to a classmate named Dave Gruennert about what he saw as the suppressed but intense rivalry among the Ford cousins—specifically himself, Henry's son Edsel II and Bill's boy Billy—for future dominance in the company, a contest in which he felt himself at an almost genetic disadvantage. "He felt like there was a real barrier," Gruennert later said. "His cousins, he thought, had the inside track and he had the attitude that his family just kind of was down on him—just didn't think he'd be successful."

In May 1971 young Ben was arrested for possession of drugs and driving under the influence. After bailing him out, his father called Bill Stroppe, his old friend from the Lincoln-Mercury racing days, who now lived in Southern California and had a successful racing equipment business, and asked him to help his son. Under Stroppe's influence, Ben got excited about racing and drove a Ford Bronco in the Baja 5000. But while Stroppe was friendly and concerned, he didn't fill Ben's need for a father figure. That role was soon played by a charismatic middle-aged man with a shaved head and a Zapata mustache, named Louis Fuentes.

Ultimately Benson would accuse Fuentes of having a "Svengali manner." Actually the appropriate analogy would have been Fagin. Parlaying a degree in social work and night-school therapy sessions into a counseling business called the Whittier Human Relations Center, Fuentes began to specialize in the lost children of the rich. (Most of his "patients," by his own account, were "unhappy kids with good intellects who came from wealthy homes.") He involved them in his social life and business ventures. Some, like Ben, went to live with him for a time in his Hacienda Heights home.

Fuentes was intrigued in almost equal measure by Ben Junior's Ford heritage and Bill Stroppe's lucrative business. He proposed to expand this business by forming a three-way partnership involving Stroppe, young Ben and himself. Ben's inheritance from his grandmother, worth close to $20 million, would finance the move. At first Benson and Edie resisted. But then in a December 20, 1972, meeting at the Glass House involving the two of them, Fuentes, Ben Junior and Ford family lawyer Pierre Heftler, they agreed to let their son have access to the money, although Heftler wrote a peeved letter to Ben Junior afterward: "The fact is that no part of this fortune is due to your own efforts; it is a family fortune which has come down to you through the efforts of others..."

Within a year, using the leverage of a smaller inheritance from Eleanor Ford, Fuentes and Ben had taken over the business that Stroppe had laboriously built up over twenty years. When Stroppe sued, Benson Senior, feeling bad about the havoc his son had caused his old friend, gave him $5,000 to help pay legal fees. But Stroppe was small fry compared to the leviathan Fuentes wanted to hook. He believed that he could attain influence at the Ford Motor Company itself by getting young Ben into his rightful place in the Glass House executive suite. This plan synchronized with Benson's own deferred dreams that his son should "play the role" of a Ford in the way that his elder brother Henry had played it but he hadn't. After Ben Junior agreed to embark on a five-year apprenticeship in the company, his father arranged for him to do a tour of Ford International's plants. Ben was on his way from Mexico to Argentina when Benson died.

Ben's overbearing attitude at his father's funeral came from his belief that because Benson had fewer children than his brothers and sister, he stood to inherit more of the Class B stock than his male cousins, whose stock inheritance would be diluted. But shortly after the burial Ben found out that his father had changed his will before his death, largely because of his mistrust of Fuentes. Half of the $100 million fortune would go to Edie and half would be held in trust for Ben and his sister, Lynn. Edie was to have absolute control of the trusts while she lived, and Henry and Bill would take over after her death.

Fuentes fed Ben's disappointment and anger by pointing out that this meant in effect that he'd never come into his inheritance. In November, a lawyer whom Fuentes had found for Ben filed a court action to have the will set aside. Ben's testimony opened the curtain that had been discreetly drawn over Benson's derelictions during his life. "My father was an alcoholic," he said. "During the last several years of his life, my father was known to drink as much as a fifth of liquor a day.... I talked with my mother privately and asked her how my father could have signed such an estate plan. She shrugged her shoulders, pointed her index finger toward her temple, and rotated it in the usual manner of indicating to me that she believed my father was not of sound mind." The testimony so incensed Edie that she virtually terminated her relationship with her son.

HENRY HAD REMAINED ALOOF FROM all this, even though in the minds of Ben and particularly Fuentes he was the shadowy nemesis of their tragedy. He had other problems—such as the fiery death of three teenage sisters from Indiana in a Pinto, leading to the most serious court case Ford had yet faced when a local district attorney accused the company of "reckless homicide," the first time a corporation had been charged with murder. Yet he kept a weather eye on his nephew, especially when he learned that Ben Junior and Fuentes had entered into a loose confederation with Roy Cohn and his stockholders' suit.

Also there was still fallout from the Iacocca firing. Iacocca stayed on at Ford until October 15, 1978, although Henry was so worried about the security threat he represented that he brought in auditors, investigators and retired

FBI men to prevent leaks and forced his lame-duck enemy to move from his executive suite in the Glass House to a remote office in the parts warehouse. But Iacocca had a phone there and continued to wheel and deal. He had concocted a grand design—some felt it was a megalomaniacal one as well—which he called Global Motors: a consortium of European, Japanese and U.S. companies which he believed would challenge GM. ("I envisaged myself as the new Alfred Sloan," he later said of this dream.) The foundation of this consortium was to be Chrysler, the offer of the top post there having been made to him, shortly after his firing, by J. Richardson Dilworth, the Rockefeller representative on the Chrysler board. Iacocca's initial idea was to use Chrysler as an "engineering base" in his global corporation. But when investment bankers told him his dream would never survive scrutiny by U.S. antitrust lawyers, he settled for taking the top job at Chrysler itself. As a final thrust at Henry before leaving Ford, he whetted young Ben's sense of having been wronged by telling him he found it "shocking" that Benson Senior had altered his will to shut him out.

Concerned that his former president would cooperate with a federal probe of the Indonesian affair, Henry encouraged Bugas, who had remained friendly with Iacocca over the years, to sound him out. Bugas invited Iacocca to dinner shortly after Thanksgiving. Bugas' daughter Pat was struck by the fact that Iacocca had the same stunned look on his face as her father had had a few years earlier when he was experiencing his troubles with Henry. Joan Bugas was struck by how bitter Lee's wife, Mary, was: "I've never seen anyone so furious, so enraged. She sort of assaulted me verbally. Referring to John's troubles at the company, she said, 'How can you be friends with anyone who did that to your husband?' Referring to Kathy she said, 'How can you be friends with that whore?' " Talking to Bugas, Iacocca called Henry a "bastard." Bugas, drawing on his own experience, tried to cool him off: "Maybe one day you'll thank that *bastard* for doing this to you." Iacocca's lip curled: "Never!" he said.

Two months after this meeting, at about the same time that Harry Bennett, whom he had come to resemble in Henry's mind, died at the age of seventy-nine in his Arizona home, Iacocca agreed to cooperate with federal investigators.

ON MAY 3, 1979, THE FORDS MET AT Bill's house to try to iron out their problems. Family meetings had become a rare occurrence over the years. Before Henry's divorces there had been an occasional get-together at Gaukler Pointe, but through the years these events had become infrequent. They all told one another that it was because they had families of their own. In truth, however, they stayed away from one another because the strains had become too great.

But now it was clear that the family was in a state of disarray and that the Fords' future in the company was unclear. Eleanor, the only stabilizing force in the family, was gone. Ben Junior was making dangerous and potentially damaging statements and now had hired Roy Cohn to represent him. When he arrived at this meeting he was wired for sound; the recording device was discovered because it touched off an alarm in Bill's doorway which Ben Junior had erroneously assumed was a metal detector able only to pick up weapons.

Henry and Bill took their nephew upstairs and made him take off the recording device. When he came back down again, the whole family turned on him, especially Charlotte. Once calm was restored, Henry announced that he was going to take the next step in his retreat from the company by relinquishing to Caldwell his job as chief executive officer.

It was as if everything was falling into place. Two days after the meeting, the *New York Times* reported that informed sources were saying that no top Ford executives would be prosecuted in connection with the Indonesian case. Ben Junior had gone home from the Ford family meeting with a tape recording made before his uncles took off his wire, and he played it for a delighted Iacocca, who encouraged him in his enmity; but on May 8 his suit against his father's will was thrown out of court.

Henry began the Ford stockholders' meeting by asking for a moment of silence for his brother Benson. Then he announced that he was retiring effective October 1. "Next year," he told the nearly three thousand people in the Ford Auditorium, "you'll find me in the audience." Benson Junior stood up to champion his lost cause and was told that the Audit Committee had turned down his request to be a board member. When someone in the audience asked why, Henry growled, "Not qualified," to general applause. When Roy Cohn took the floor to berate him for the second year in a row, Henry could have pointed out that Ford had just recorded a robust first quarter, with earnings rising 28 percent, while Chrysler had suffered sharp losses. But he held his tongue until Cohn said that the top Ford executives who had followed Iacocca were "leaving a loser and joining a winner," whereupon Henry snapped, "You put your money in Chrysler and go to their meetings, okay?"

Then it was Henry's turn to speak. "There are no crown princes in the Ford Motor Company and there is no privileged route to the top," he said in an oblique comment on Benson Junior and the rest of the family. "Until recently, I had not thought that there would be any worthwhile purpose in making that statement. The considerations involved in the appointment of top management seemed to me to be self-evident. But clearly this is not so—at least not to everybody—and since this is a time for frankness, I decided to make it clear beyond any doubt."

After the meeting things continued to come together. Cohn's stockholders' suit, thrown out of court in New York by a judge who believed that Michigan had jurisdiction, was turned down on appeal. Iacocca had motivated it from the outset; when he left the company the steam went out of the suit. Young Ben's charges had injected momentary life into it, but now that action, too, was over and Cohn's suit began to look like what it always was: harassment.

With things going so well, Henry decided to step down as chairman of the board, too, his resignation to be effective after the stockholders' meeting on March 13, 1980. He was thinking of himself and especially of Kathy. He knew that the difficulty of squaring the circle of his life—giving equal weight to company and self, obligation and desire—had contributed to the destruction of two marriages. He had now reached a point in his life where he could begin the last leg of his journey, and he had to do it without the encumbrance of the company. He had worn long enough the mantle handed down to him; what mattered now was, as he had said to Cristina in one of their last conversations, what fit him.

"After thirty-four years on the job I am ready to stand aside," he said. "The period I have been closely identified with is nearing its end...." It was a historic, even a melancholy moment. If his grandfather had been there from the creation of the automobile, Henry's career had paralleled the growing complexity of the auto industrial age. Detroit, once the pride of industrial America, had become a paradise lost. When Henry took over, the United States produced 80 percent of all the passenger cars in the world. When he left, it produced 28 percent. When he began, the industry had been trying to recover from the war. When he left, it was obsessed with an aspect of the postwar recovery it had never thought it would have to worry about and didn't understand how to handle: the invasion from Japan. Detroit seemed blind to the fact that the Japanese were doing what the first Henry Ford had done seventy years earlier—building smaller, more efficient cars in mass quantities; that they were willing, as Ford had been, to accept less money per unit to further the ends of mass production, putting the Americans in Alexander Malcomson's position of wanting higher-priced, bigger cars.

Once Henry made his announcement, all eyes turned to Bill. Finally it was his chance. The issue of his someday becoming chairman had come up the previous year in the family meeting to which Ben Junior had come wired. There had been a loose understanding that he would succeed Henry as chairman, but Henry continued to have doubts. He wanted Bill to be chairman *and* chief executive officer; Bill just wanted the chairman's job. Guilty as he sometimes felt for helping crush Bill's aspirations in the mid-1950s, Henry still worried about his dilettantism. Chalmers Goyert said, "Bill disappointed a lot of people. One of the most disappointed was Henry. If Bill had made an effort to prepare himself and had indicated a real interest in succeeding him, Henry would have been pleased. He wanted to keep the Fords at the top. But things had changed from the days when he took over. It was a public company now. You couldn't inherit the top position; you had to earn it. Henry resented Bill's withdrawal. His attitude was something like, 'Where have you been all these years?' He once talked to me about it. The way he put it was, 'If only I had been able to *qualify* Bill to be my successor.' "

Actually, despite the drama surrounding Bill in the public eye, Henry had already ruled him out. An hour before the March 13 stockholders' meeting was to take place, he came into Bill's office and told him he had decided that the chairman's job would go to Caldwell, who would be chairman and chief executive officer.

Shocked, Bill said, "Well, that's wonderful. Where does that leave me?"

Henry replied, "Well, I guess it leaves you vice-chairman."

Bill shrugged. "I guess it does. I wasn't aware that this is what we'd talked about."

Looking away, Henry said, "Well, no, but this is the way Caldwell wants it and that's the way it's got to be."

Bill watched his brother stand up and leave the room and thought, Holy Christ, what just hit me?

Bill hadn't realized that Henry really did intend to "professionalize" the organization and take the family element out. (Moving up to chairman, Caldwell would be replaced as president by Donald Petersen, head of Ford International, who had started in Lewis Crusoe's first group of apprentice product planners in the fifties.) He felt alienated from his brother. Yet the two men were much alike. Henry had found survival in the company while Bill had found it in his family, but each had acquired a stubborn integrity in his private life the other wasn't able to recognize.

Some weeks after this confrontation, Bill and Martha visited Henry at the estate he had acquired in Henley-on-Thames, England, to indulge his love of pheasant-hunting and things English. John and Joan Bugas were there, too. Easily bored as always, Henry wandered in and out of conversations. Bugas and Bill spent a lot of time talking intensely about the past. It was almost as if Bill was trying to understand the processes that he had been part of; processes that had taken his life, and all their lives, in directions he had never really been able to understand. After Henry made one of his periodic exits from the room Bill said to Bugas, "I think my brother hates me." Joan happened to be passing through the room and caught the remark. She looked at Bill and saw such a look of bewilderment and pain on his face that she had to stifle an urge to put her arms around him and offer comfort.

THERE WAS ONLY ONE THING LEFT for Henry to do. Divorce proceedings had been delayed because of Cristina's inability to settle on a lawyer. Finally a trial date was set for February 19, 1980, which happened also to be their fifteenth wedding anniversary. Henry arrived at the Wayne County Circuit Court with a secret weapon—his "Aunt" Rosemarie, widow of Ernie Kanzler. (Ernie had died in 1969.) Alluding to her role in introducing him to Cristina, he had only half jokingly told her, "You got me into this thing, now help me get out." Rosemarie hardly needed to be urged. Already she and Cristina had gone to war in the press. Cristina said she was a good wife, slimming Henry down from 250 pounds and getting him to exercise and eat health foods. Rosemarie had a different version: "She's a night bird. She never wanted to go to bed before three or four in the morning and she lived [in the Lakeshore Drive home] as a guest. She was off to New York every chance she had." When Cristina said she had no idea that Henry was seeing Kathy and was shocked by the news, Rosemarie responded, "She never loved him. How can she accuse him of adultery? And she loathes Grosse Pointe, but now she is squatting in the house. It is a sort of Italian vendetta." The media argument had become so heated, in fact, that Cristina had finally slapped Rosemarie with a $10 million libel suit.

Cristina arrived for the trial with her golden hair cascading onto her shoulders, dressed in an oatmeal-colored wool suit and suede boots. ("The suit is from Balestra," she told a reporter. "He's a well-known Italian designer.") Her lawyers had subpoenaed Ford executives and friends of Kathy's. With both sides so well armed, the press expected a sensational battle. One rumor had it that Cristina was going to try to get a court order allowing a doctor to examine the state of Henry's nostrils for possible signs of cocaine addiction. But after a routine morning session the case was adjourned for lunch, and the lawyers got together and settled, Henry agreeing to pay Cristina $15 million to be rid of her.

Now that the last roadblock was removed he began to talk of marriage to Kathy, who had become his Wallis Simpson, the woman he had given up a throne for. Both of them had wanted to get married for a long time; now that it was finally possible both of them found that they had tremendous doubts. His principal fear was that once she got the title of Mrs. Ford she would change as his other two wives had changed. She didn't bother to reassure him because she wondered whether marriage would change what had become a durable and comforting relationship without it.

In New York, while taking her home from dinner one evening, he nonchalantly asked, "Will you marry me?" She didn't think he was serious and didn't bother to answer. Almost two months later he said, "Will you answer my question?" She asked, "What question?" He said, "The question about marriage I asked you a couple of months ago." Kathy shook her head in disbelief. "That was a proposal?"

Without telling her, he had hired a lawyer to determine whether they could be married abroad. He had in mind the Mediterranean cruise they had planned for midsummer. His lawyers told him he could get married, but he decided against doing it in any of the cruise ship's ports of call for fear that reporters would catch wind of it. On the way back on the *Queen Elizabeth II* he asked the ship's captain to perform the ceremony, but he said he couldn't do it because Henry and Kathy weren't British subjects.

The last few years had been so filled with false starts and ambushes that Kathy wanted the best possible circumstances for their new life. She worked with her Ouija board and visited an astrologer to chart the best day, time and place for the wedding. ("Henry thought I was crazy," she says. "But I figured, Why not have as much going as possible?") The decision was for Tuesday, October 14, 1980, at 10:40 A.M. Henry chose Carson City, Nevada, as the place so that they could get married immediately and without publicity. They flew to Lake Tahoe in a private jet and drove down to Nevada the following morning. Only Kathy's daughters, Debi and Kim, were with them when Henry finally said his vows to the woman he loved.

TWO WEEKS AFTER THE MARRIAGE he and Kathy met the Bugases in Madrid, where they had planned to go on a partridge shoot. As always they stayed up late into the night, Joan and Kathy chatting and John and Henry drinking red wine over long moments of silence. Finally Henry began to talk about his children and how much they had hurt him. It was not so much Edsel II. He was in Australia and had an excuse for not attending the wedding. In any case, he had proved his fealty by naming his first child Henry III and even calling him "Sonnie," which had been Eleanor's nickname for Henry when he was a baby. It was his daughters' refusal that hurt. Anne had said she couldn't get a babysitter. Charlotte had said she had an engagement she couldn't break. She had made bitter comments about Kathy in Grosse Pointe, gossip which rivaled in venom anything Cristina had ever said. When Henry told Bugas how important his daughters were, his old friend replied, "Please don't let Charlotte and Anne keep you from your relationship with Kathy. They're not going to be there when you need them, but Kathy will be. Don't let them mess up your life with her."

The women retired early. When Henry staggered upstairs to his room, he found that he didn't have his key. He wakened Kathy by pounding on the door. She got up, let him in and started to go back to bed. Not yet really domesticated, he stood in the middle of the room, disoriented by the wine, and said, "Call a cab. I want to go home." Kathy replied, "We *are* home." He refused to believe her and kept insisting that she call a cab. Finally she stopped trying to reason with him. "Look," she said, "wherever we are together is home. Now come to bed."

EPILOGUE

HOME AND FAMILY: THESE WERE the hidden themes of this great industrial epic. They were what had been jeopardized when Crazy Henry Ford pounded a hole in his garage wall and drove his machine out into the world. The rural life he left behind in his mad ride to fame and riches had home and family as its ultimate good. The new urban world he helped create would be dominated by individuals and their discontents. Old Henry hitched his own individual star first to a machine and then to an industrial empire that replaced the family. For him and his heirs the Ford Motor Company became mother, brother, child—the source of fulfillment and meaning in life. It was a perfect creation, as Aldous Huxley had seen when he had people in *Brave New World* date natural cycles as the Year of Our Ford, cross themselves with the sign of the T, and comfort themselves by reminding themselves, "Ford's in his Flivver, all's right with the world."

It could even be said that this world had its martyr in Edsel, Henry's only begotten son, who died for mankind's industrial sins. Edsel had tried to reestablish home and family at Gaukler Pointe. But life there was always darkened by the shadow of the company. Not until Henry II performed the operation that removed the family from the company could the Fords really come home again.

In some sense the drama of the Ford story had been based on the family's exile. After Henry left the chairmanship and went home to Kathy, the drama went out of the Ford Motor Company. There might someday be another Ford at the top, but he would not be in the epic mold of Henry II or the old man whose name he had inherited and whose power he had resurrected. After he left the company, the story he had dominated for nearly four decades had that slow movement toward stasis that comprises the last chapter in a Victorian novel.

Least affected of the Fords was Dodie. Insulated from the ominous qualities of being a Ford because as a woman she was never considered for a role in the company, she had a strategy for survival that resembled Bill's retreat to privacy. She continued to drink heavily, but never allowed herself to become self-pitying or tragic as her brother Benson had been. Actually, she was something of a madcap—as Henry would have been without the responsibility of the company, some people said. There were food fights in which she would sometimes flip pats of butter onto the ceiling or, sitting next to a grandchild, ask him what was in his spaghetti and then when he looked down push his face into the plate. Wherever she went she took her dogs with her. Her son Buhl says, "Like maybe after a Thanksgiving dinner she might bring fifteen dogs into the room and they'd be jumping all over the furniture, crapping all over and barking. She loves dogs and keeps on buying them. When she decides she doesn't like a dog, she'll give it away."

Her daughters Eleanor ("Nonie") and Josephine ("Jolie") were private like her. Her sons were set back by the odd circumstance of her marriage to a man named Ford which nonetheless took them out of any consideration for the Ford succession. Buhl ("Buhlie"), the oldest, was unassuming and phlegmatic, plagued with a Ford ambition which was like a low-grade fever in its effects. He tried to strike an independent path in several business ventures, including beginning a film company in Detroit. But his businesses all failed and so did an early marriage, which yielded four children and a Ford-sized divorce settlement of $5 million. He finally took a low-level marketing position at the company, had problems with drugs which kept him from moving up, and decided, in his late forties, that it was a triumph for a Ford of his generation simply not to self-destruct.

Dodie's other son, Alfie, found his path in the 1960s garden of alternative lifestyles. He spent time in Krishna Consciousness in India. Then, with the daughter of Walter Reuther, he provided the funds to convert the old Fisher mansion at the edge of Grosse Pointe into an ashram. He took the name Ambarish Das, after the ancient Hindu king who gave up his kingdom to serve Krishna, god of love.

If Dodie's family had reached a compromise with the Ford fate, Benson's family continued to deteriorate after his death. Edie's throat cancer worsened so that she could only gasp. She maintained contact with the family through her brother-in-law Bill. When he came to visit she would write him notes which he would read and toss into the trashcan, until she became worried that the servants were reading them, whereupon he bought her a paper shredder. When Edie died, in August 1980 aboard the *Onika II*, she had not reconciled with Ben Junior. She left her money, house and belongings to her daughter, Lynn; to her son she left a used car.

Ben Junior continued to be one of the walking wounded. He was always upstaged, as when he had a stag party at the Little Club in Grosse Pointe before getting married and the forty guests all gathered around his successful cousin Edsel II, leaving him on the edge of things. In November 1982 he was driving home from a session at a local tavern and smashed his Lincoln Town Car into a concrete wall, suffering a variety of injuries including a shattered leg that required major surgery. While recuperating he saw that he would never be "an important person in the Ford Motor Company" as his father had wanted. He had dropped his challenge to his father's will and paid back all the money the family had spent fighting the suit. Now he severed his fortunes from those of Louis Fuentes, whom he denounced and ultimately sued for extortion. He did this by way of paying dues so that he could gain reentry into the family. Yet this was hard. As a friend said, "Ben kept thinking that he could do something that would get him back into the family. But he had burned his bridges. For Ben there really wasn't the possibility of a family anymore." He finally got a job in the company, but his burning desire to be taken seriously as a Ford seemed doomed to failure.

If Benson's life seemed cursed, Bill's seemed blessed. Two months after Henry told him he wouldn't be chairman of Ford he had a quadruple bypass operation. He saw a sort of karma in that, saying wryly, "Actually, things worked out for the best both for me and for the company." He continued to maintain his office at the Glass House—a place decorated with a brace of antique pistols given to him by his grandfather, a gold football inscribed by the Lions, and side-by-side photographs of his father's Continental Mark I and his own Mark II. But the center of his business life continued to be the hapless Lions, which he moved to Pontiac after cold-shouldering the pleas of Henry and his business friends not to desert Detroit in time of need. Games were a family ritual and recreation. Martha was at his side every time the Lions played and afterward when he compared notes on the game with the coaches. Family and business were harmoniously knit in a way that contrasted with Henry's bifurcated existence at the company. If the Lions were never a top team, they at least remained competitive.

So did Bill. He was a scratch golf player and a keen boatsman in his twenty-four-foot powerboat *The Sea Lion*, which he fearlessly plowed through freighter wakes on Lake St. Claire, scaring his passengers. He engaged in elaborate video-game competitions with his son Billy, playing on machines in his basement until four in the morning to get a better score and then calling Billy with the news.

Billy had gone to Princeton, successfully majoring in political science, although he felt alienated by left-wing professors who confused indoctrination with teaching. He had not given the company much thought in college. In fact, in his senior year, when all his friends were looking for jobs, he also scheduled interviews with a couple of banks. But then he saw the lure of the company: "I realized that everything I have comes from the Ford Motor Company. And so I thought I owed it to my heritage, so to speak, to give the company my best shot. I approached it with the notion of going one step at a time. If I liked it, okay, I'd stay. If I didn't like it, I'd leave." Billy went home after graduation and during a game of pool told his father what he had decided. Bill was silent a minute and then asked, "Are you sure that's what you want to do?" Billy said that it was. Bill shrugged. "Well," he said, "you don't have to do it on my account. Life's too short to be miserable. Do what you want. But do it well."

Billy took what he calls "shit jobs" just to prove himself. He was cynical about the Ford bureaucracy. He had studied his great-grandfather and felt that the need to "do something big" was in his blood. He sometimes thought of beginning a company of his own, perhaps a mail-order company for fly fishermen. But he stayed with Ford, progressing so quickly that by 1987 he had caught up with his older cousin Edsel II. He was finally given a position as head of truck marketing for Ford International, traditionally a proving ground for top executives.

Most observers felt that Billy was the "smartest Ford of his generation," the one who, if merit alone was the determining factor, would have the best shot at the top job someday in the future. ("He is the Ford to watch," the *Detroit Free Press* wrote.) While he wants the chance to compete for the presidency someday, he knows there is a different relationship between the family and the company today than there was for his father's generation. "If it happens for me it will have to be because of my own ability," he says. "I wouldn't have it any other way."

Bill was a spectator at the competition between Billy and Edsel II, which provided most of the company-related Ford gossip in Dearborn now that he himself had stood back from any ambition in the company and Henry had retired. He felt that the competition, which was referred to frequently in the local press, was a little ridiculous because even the top man at Ford could no longer have the kind of power Henry had inherited from their grandfather: "It's too big for one man anymore. One man can't rule the thing now. It has just become less of a personal thing."

Bill was still wary of Henry, and his resentments over the defeats of the past still showed: "I feel sorry for him. He doesn't have any friends. He just has people who kiss his ass." The distance between them, a distance caused by the company, was a permanent fact of their lives and they accepted it as such. Yet they were closer than either could acknowledge. They shared an insight into the family secret: that the primal Ford act which welded man and machine and displaced family was destructive. In their different ways— Bill saw that the family had to be purged of the company, and Henry that the company had to be purged of the family—they had tried to do something about it.

For his part, Henry had reached an angle of repose. There could never be a complete healing with his children. His daughters had trouble accepting Kathy. Edsel still felt that Henry might have done something more to fuel his rise to the top of the company. He often made unintentionally wounding comments about Henry, as when he told a Detroit magazine that the biggest obstacle in the way of his move to the top of Ford was the fact that he could never allow himself to be quit of his father. "Edsel says he will never be the kind of parent his father had been," the interviewer wrote.

Henry had found it difficult to disengage from the company. He had to watch what he called the "reputational degradation" of Ford because of the Pinto debacle. The recalls, the soaring interest rates and the high gasoline prices of the Carter years took their toll, triggering an import invasion and losses for the company that peaked at $1.5 billion in 1982—the largest loss any corporation had suffered up until that time, and the first time since it went public in 1956 that Ford paid no dividend. Yet the whole industry was hemorrhaging. GM was hurting. Chrysler was on the verge of bankruptcy, and there was talk of it merging with Ford, a continuation by other means of Iacocca's dream of joining with Bill to run Ford. Yet although he no longer had line authority, Henry was still by far the leading director of Ford and used his influence to make sure that when Iacocca made a proposal it was rejected so quickly that Iacocca was never even sure it had been made.

Continuing his strange obsession with Henry, Iacocca then tried to buy the house next door to him on Provencal Road, but Henry saw to it that the bid was rejected. However, in 1986 he couldn't keep Iacocca from buying his old home, which had been given to him as a wedding present by his father when he was married to Anne and which he had lived in until 1956.

At one point, Ford stock went down to 13. Chrysler survived with a bailout, and it seemed for a time that Iacocca would have a sort of triumph over Henry. But while the Ford Motor Company had made a mistake in delaying downsizing, it was nothing like the catastrophe Iacocca had prophesied. GM downsized with dispatch, and it, too, was badly beaten by the Japanese. The problem with all the companies in Detroit was that they never understood about the Japanese, and assumed that their cars sold only because they were less expensive and more fuel efficient when in reality their appeal came from the fact that they were well made.

Imports had established a permanent foothold, and Henry's vision of multinational production had proved right. Ford bought 25 percent of Mazda. With the coming of the Reagan Administration, interest rates began to fall; by 1983 the auto picture had turned around. Iacocca's exit line on leaving Ford—that the company would never again see a $1.5 billion profit—was proven wrong in 1983 when Ford's profits were $1.9 billion.

What now took place at Ford was more than a case of Iacocca being proven wrong; it was Henry's vindication. In the years that followed his resignation, his achievement was dramatized by events. It had always been conceded that he had saved the company in the 1940s. But even this accomplishment had been punctuated by a question mark in the dark days that followed his resignation. What was the verdict on the years after he had disposed of Ernie Breech, the years in which he had been in sole command of the Ford ship? The answer was provided by the balance sheet after he retired. The success of 1983 was followed by profits of $2.9 billion in 1984, $2.7 billion in 1985 and $3.3 billion in 1986. What was striking about this record was that it came at the same time that the profits of GM and Chrysler were in decline. In 1986 the great dream of beating GM had finally come true, the first time it happened since 1924.

Elements of this success were clearly Henry's legacy—the emphasis on product and quality; investment in individual talent; and emphasis on the European operations. Henry had always tried for a creative tension between the conservatives of finance and the product adventurers. This was why he had created competing pairs of executives like Breech and Crusoe, McNamara and Reith, Miller and Iacocca. The balance could never be complete, because he was there—a Ford with affections to be competed for, a force to try to conquer and overcome. But after he left, his last pair of executives did strike this balance: Caldwell and Don Petersen, a man who had begun his career in 1952 as a product planner in the first group of bright young men Lewis Crusoe had installed at the Ford Division. A healing figure after the bruising fight with Iacocca, Peterson was willing to submerge his personality into the company. Together he and Caldwell tried to guess about the future of the market after the last of Iacocca's Fords, the spare and boxy Fairlanes, came out in 1980 and 1981 and contributed to the company's big losses. Peterson concluded that it was necessary to do more than try to catch up with the high-performance European cars sweeping the market; it was necessary to jump ahead of them.

Just before Christmas 1985, the company introduced the Ford Taurus and the Mercury Sable. Sleekly aerodynamic, with high angled windshields, headlights that flowed around the corners of the front of the car into the body, and air intakes slitted into the bumper instead of a traditional grille, these cars represented something new in the industry—domestic models meant to duplicate the high performance and status of a car like the Audi 5000, which cost about $10,000 more. They also represented new thinking at Ford. Jack Telnack, head of design at Ford, who had plotted out on a computer the cars' new look, later recalled how Caldwell and Petersen had come through the studio asking, "Are you really proud of what you're doing? Is it the best you can do?" In the past, such exhortations had been largely rhetorical, and designers who went to the executive committee meetings with truly new concepts could expect blank stares and muttered cynicisms such as, "You've got to be kidding!" But Caldwell and Petersen had meant their challenge. They were willing to gamble.

Iacocca scoffed at the Taurus and the Sable as "flying potatoes" when he first saw them, but in their first year on the market, the cars sold more than 368,000 units, and soon Chrysler had joined the rest of the industry in trying to "go aerodynamic," too. But the new company slogan, "Have you driven a Ford *lately?*" was an allusion not only to a new look but to a new quality as well, a J. D. Powers survey having said that Ford now produced "the best American car." Because of the Taurus and Sable, the great dream was finally realized in 1986 when Ford beat GM for the first time since 1924.

Early in 1985, Peterson succeeded Caldwell in the first smooth transition of power there had ever been at Ford. If there was a final irony in the struggle between Henry and Iacocca, which continued to be waged in print long after it had ended in fact, it was that while Henry finally succeeded in making Ford a "regular" company unaffected by the character of any one individual, Iacocca had created a cult of personality at Chrysler, making the corporation an extension of himself.

TIMES WERE CHANGING. John Bugas died in 1982, the closing of a chapter in Henry's life. They ended as close friends. Not long before Bugas' death, Henry had visited him at the Wyoming ranch. At the end of an evening of wine and reminiscence, he had stood up and walked over to his old friend's chair, then bent over and kissed him on the forehead and said, "I love this man." Until the day he died, Bugas and Henry loved to sit and talk about the past in a conversation that would sooner or later meander back to the great days when they had conquered Harry Bennett. "Those were the days," Bugas would say. "We might have been killed."

Bill Ford was right: Henry did have only a few friends—mainly Max Fisher and Al Taubman, Jews and fellow pariahs. But they were good friends and sufficient unto his needs. Increasingly they saw him in Florida. Unable to get the $2 million he wanted for his Grosse Pointe home, Henry had demolished it and had one-family cluster homes built on the site. He bought a smaller home up the road, but decided to change his legal residence to Palm Beach. This caused grumblings about Henry's desertion among Grosse Pointers. Henry replied that he wouldn't even keep a place there if Kathy didn't like to make visits. "I don't care if I ever see that goddamned place again."

There was continued friction in his life. But he was, for the first time, a happy man. By turns he had played the role of Prince Hal and King Henry. Now he was a sort of Falstaff. He had tremendous interest in gossip—the big question of "who's sleeping with whom," as his daughter Charlotte put it. Arjay Miller, on the board of the *Washington Post* as well as on that of Ford, always had lunch with members of the paper's editorial board before meeting with Henry, so that he could bring him little tidbits.

Defying doctors' orders, Henry smoked ten cigars a day. His laugh was heartier, his voice deeper and more gravelly. He had given in to his paunch. His face was lined in a way that made him look like some old sailor who had weathered heavy seas; the captain of a ship whose sailing days were done. He was partly deaf but refused out of vanity to wear a hearing aid. One of his prize possessions was a pillow, given to him by a friend, with the needle-point inscription "Don't postpone pleasure." His family now was not with the other Fords but with Kathy, who was able to be his wife—baking cookies at Christmastime and playing a violin duet with the concertmaster of the Detroit Symphony for charity—without ever straining after the grandiose role of Mrs. Ford.

He was neither the put-upon hero his aides and allies made him out to be nor yet the villain portrayed by Iacocca and his other enemies, but a man more complex and therefore more compelling. There was something ultimately appealing in him because of the conflicts he had faced and the course he had steadfastly steered. Born to a sort of royalty, he had tried to deal with dilemmas common to every man—between self and family, past and present, the public and the private life; between responsibility and desire, duty and friendship, obligation and love. He was not an intellectual or even a particularly articulate man, but a man of pragmatic and instinctual bent who had dealt with these conflicts in action. He had put the Ford family into reverse and backed into the garage his grandfather had broken through nearly a century earlier. As captain of the company ship for all those years, he had braved all the elements. After his odyssey was over, his reward was finally to come home, purge his life of adversaries and enjoy his Penelope at last.

At the end of his journey, when he had finally released himself from all the obligations and duties that had encumbered but also enriched his career, he undertook one last task. Feeling time closing in, Henry began a systematic tour of Ford installations around the world that would take three years to complete—an opportunity to say farewell to the men and women he had known and worked with. At one of his stops, one company officer remarked, "Well, Henry, there'll be no more Fords like you."

Henry gave him a characteristic look over the half-glasses riding low on the bridge of his nose and said, "So what?"

AFTERWORD, 2001

HEN HENRY FORD II DIED in 1987, the epic, intergenerational story of creation and decay, enterprise and madness stretching back over a hundred years to the beginnings of his grandfather's inspired tinkering seemed to have come to an end. The two Henrys were bookends for a narrative unlike any of the other dynastic sagas produced by America's industrial revolution. The Fords and the company Crazy Henry built composed a unique chapter in our nation-building chronicle—in large part because this chapter was also about a family chasing its own myth.

We focused here on these two interlocking story lines—family and company—and on Ford's renaissance under the leadership of Henry II. At the time *The Fords* was first published, the latter theme represented a somewhat contrarian view. The prevailing opinion of Henry II was that of his great rival Lee Iacocca, preeminent auto salesman of the second half of the twentieth century, who was then at the pinnacle of his power as an American cultural icon. Iacoca's judgment—that Henry II was a capricious and meddling autocrat who caused his company's decline by making it his plaything—had attained the status of conventional wisdom. Yet the dramatic success of the Ford Motor Company during the past decade (compared with Iacocca's failures as head of Chrysler) vindicates Henry II and the story we told.

Iacocca was not alone in failing to anticipate the revival of the Ford Motor Company, of course. *The Reckoning,* David Halberstam's book on the auto industry which was published about the same time as *The Fords*, also missed this big picture. In fact, in what amounts to a meditation on American "declinism," Halberstam selected the Ford Motor Company as his example of why the creative capital of the American auto industry was spent, and Nissan, a company that has become virtually invisible in the last decade, to symbolize the inevitable victory of the automotive division of Japan Inc.

Like so many others, Halberstam mistook the blip for the screen. By the early 1980s, Ford had indeed declined from its glory days under the first Henry, when it was the largest industrial corporation in the world. It was also true that the company had been wounded in the 1970s, along with the other Detroit automakers, by a perfect storm of bad developments: foreign oil embargoes, new requirements for fuel efficiency and safety, and the advent of downsizing. And Japan had indeed filled the vacuum created by the contraction of the American auto industry. Yet Halberstam, writing inside this trend, missed the less obvious (but more profound) story of how the American auto industry, with Ford in the lead, was, at this time of maximum jeopardy, creating the conditions for a comeback of epic proportions. Halberstam was blinkered by his thesis—an outgrowth of seeing Ford as having suffered irreparably under the seigneury of Henry II—that the American carmakers' decline was caused by the rise of "bean counter" financial men whose only interest was pushing up stock prices. In fact, the eventual renaissance of Ford was inspired by great product men like Lewis Crusoe working together with marketing visionaries like Iacocca under the overall leadership of Henry II himself.

It is not surprising that figures like Iacocca and Halberstam—one for personal reasons and the other anxious to find a metaphor for American "overstretch"—focused their critique on Henry II. He was indeed an anachronism in an era when other American corporations had only a ceremonial relationship to their founders and their heirs. And it was assumed after his passing that there would be no other Fords in the Ford Motor Company's future. Yet in writing this book we were struck by the symbolism of the company acquired for family members—an existential mother's milk; an Everest of ambition to be conquered; a realm whose kingship was the only thing that could make a man truly a Ford. It was pursuit of this *Fordness* that had precipitated the dark and vengeful struggles characterizing the family's relationships with each other for so long, each assault producing an equal and opposite reaction over time. There was Old Henry helpless to keep from destroying his son, Edsel; Henry II returning from World War II to fight for the company not only because it was his birthright but because it would vindicate his father; William Clay Ford suffering a ruthless rejection at the hands of Henry II when he tried to achieve a handhold in the company; and eventually his son Bill outmaneuvering his cousin Edsel II to become the Ford in the company's future.

This drama in the fourth generation was an important motif of our book, but it was a drama just beginning to ripen as we finished our narrative. Before his passing, Henry II had tried to boost his son's chances to play a dominant role in the company. Meanwhile, his brother William's son Bill, smarting at the way his father had been excluded from a leadership position, was also making a bid for power. As both of them began to work their way through the ranks of the company during the late 1980s in an extraordinary executive training course, handicapping the chances of these two young men became something of a parlor game in Detroit, especially after they were both given seats on the board of directors in 1988.

At that time, CEO Donald Petersen denied the two young Fords important committee assignments and tried to marginalize them as dilettantes who happened to have inherited the Ford name and large blocs of voting stock. Bill and Edsel fought back, going public with their hard feelings, until Petersen

allowed them a more influential role and eventually threw in the towel by taking early retirement in 1990. Then the drama of the competition intensified.

We saw Bill as most likely to succeed, and we were right. In his progress
through the ranks, he had demonstrated a tenacity and political skillfulness
that his cousin couldn't match. (He also had his father, William Clay Ford, to
act as his *consigliere.*) Yet establishing himself as the leading member of his
generation was one thing; the larger question was whether, after the turbulent reign of Henry II, there would ever be room at the top in the company
for another Ford. Donald Petersen hadn't thought so. And the executive who
powered the company through the mid-1990s, Alex Trotman, actively "anti-
royalty" in the words of *Fortune* magazine, was even more anxious to cap
Bill Ford's rise. Yet Bill persevered, buoyed by the Fords' extraordinary power
in the company (4 percent of voting stock) and the fact that the family was
anxious to keep a hand in the operation of Ford and protect its estimated $5
billion in stock. Besides being adroit in his long apprenticeship at Ford, he
had become an effective politician within the family—along with Henry's
daughter Charlotte an organizing power in the fourth Ford generation, which
had twice-yearly family meetings and set up a proprietary website for keeping
in touch.

That Bill was making a serious bid for power was clear in 1995 when
he abandoned the executive climb that had taken him to every corner of the
company's business (in heading the heavy truck division he had gone to the
extent of becoming a licensed operator of an eighteen-wheeler), and, defying
Trotman, sought to become head of the powerful Finance Committee, which
controlled the company's $22 billion in reserves. Backed by William Clay and
his aunt Josephine, the two remaining members of the third generation, he
won this prestige job—the role Henry II had denied his father—and increased
his profile significantly. Trotman had clashed with Edsel II and effectively
blocked his ambitions. He tried also to block Bill's ascent, but others on the
board respected Bill and saw the value, both real and symbolic, of having a
family member in a highly visible position. In January 1999, Trotman's effort
to decide the succession after his retirement foundered when the Ford board
appointed Bill its new chairman (two months later Edsel II resigned from the
board) and Jacques Nasser as the new CEO. But transitions are never easy at
Ford. According to *Fortune,* Trotman said to Bill after the vote, "You have
your monarchy back, Prince William."

Trotman's contempt notwithstanding, it was a historic moment. Bill was
the first Ford to be chairman since his uncle Henry stepped down. The $154-
billion company he took over was the most profitable of the automakers, with
$5.9 billion in net income. It had 365,000 employees. Thanks to the purchase
of Volvo and Mazda, it was poised to overtake General Motors in global sales.
It had long since left the Japanese in the dust.

Still in his early forties, the Ford in his company's future, Bill, a straight-
laced family man and outdoorsman, was unlikely to continue a family
tradition of scandal, psychodrama, intrigue, cruelty and alcoholism. And as

he regularized the Ford family story, he took some of the drama out of it. Yet in some respect he was a throwback to the first Ford, the eccentric grandfather who died before he was born. Like old Henry, Bill had a global vision and also believed that "a great company goes beyond profits and makes the world a better place." In his case it involved passionate environmentalism. He instituted reforms to make areas of the Ford plants green. He personally believes that he will see the end of the internal combustion engine. He is a vegetarian and a Buddhist. His rise to prominence at Ford may have seemed unlikely, but as Jacques Nasser remarked when chosen to join Bill in joint control, "this is not just another company."

BIBLIOGRAPHIC NOTE

D ISCUSSING OUR NEXT PROJECT with us some years ago, our editor smiled, "Well, you've done the Rockefellers and Kennedys. What, or should I say who is left? The Fords. If you did a book on the Fords, you could say you'd completed a trilogy on the great American families. You might even get a boxed set in paperback."

Boxed sets and trilogies: consummations devoutly to be wished. In fact, we had already considered a book about the Fords and saw that it might offer an opportunity to explore further the subject matter of our other works—the effects of time, ambition, and success on the generational linkages of American families of great wealth and power. Like the Rockefellers and Kennedys (but unlike other families with money, influence, and longevity), the Fords had an internal drama that matched their external significance; they, too, had come to play a symbolic role in American life.

As we thought about it, we came to feel that there was a special relationship among these three families that had affected the cultural, political, and economic life of the country in an unparalleled way. The Rockefellers had given away a billion dollars in a canny philanthropy that had helped build the crucial foreign and domestic policy-making institutions of modern American society. The Kennedys had injected personality into our national life, personalizing the politics of this country in a way that altered it forever. And the Fords, meanwhile, had been intimately involved with America's industrial epic of nation building and with the economic transformation of its national life.

As we got into the project, of course, we began to see the particular dynamics that have driven the Fords and therefore to appreciate their uniqueness as individuals and a group. They were centered in the American heartland, apart from the arc of power joining New York and Boston with Washington and thus with national political ambition. If the story of the Rockefellers and, particularly, the Kennedys was about people who had given up citizenship in the place of their origins and become nomads living in the American imagination, the story of the Fords was about home, about the costs of staying put and also of straying too far, about the dangers of cosmopolitanism and deracination and also those of insularity and provincialism.

It was a difference we saw most dramatically in the homes where these people had lived. Visiting Pocantico Hills, the Rockefeller estate in Westchester County, was a sort of ceremonial experience, like going to Blenheim. Going to Hyannis, on the other hand, was like visiting a cultural Arlington: one couldn't help but hear the voices of dead Kennedys echoing on that storied lawn, voices that drowned out those of the living. Both places were launching pads as well as homes, places which the inhabitants used to stage their assaults on the American Dream.

Not so the residences of the Fords. Fairlane and Gaukler Pointe conveyed a sense of place and belonging. They were not mere beginning points, places to leave on a larger journey. They were also places that remained important, places to which the Fords retreated while struggling to control the only realm that counted, the realm of the Ford Motor Company. It was possible to imagine old Henry and Clara listening to the radio in the living room of Fairlane, to see him tinkering in his little workshop and her working on her beloved rose garden. Similarly, Gaukler Pointe, Edsel's formidably manicured estate which has become the first stop on the great homes tour of Grosse Pointe, has a permanence not simply as a local monument but also as the place where Edsel Ford tried to build a life of his own. One can easily imagine Henry II, Benson and Bill tearing around in their little scale-model Fords, and Dodie in the extraordinary playhouse her father built for her. One can almost see Edsel himself, happier here than anywhere else, gazing out onto Lake St. Clair with a perplexed and wounded look on his face.

The rootedness of the Fords' lives not only had to do with place, however, but also with occupation. The rich are different—from the rest of us and also from each other. The Rockefellers and Kennedys are philanthropists and politicians, semi-professional cultural figures. The Fords have had real jobs. They have been involved in *making* something, in producing something real and useful. That this product, the automobile, had become a part of the dreamscape of America as well as a utilitarian item may have given their productive lives another dimension, but they have never focused on that fact. For them, the business they're in is nothing more grandiose than "making cars."

As we became more deeply involved in our research, we discovered some of the same themes we'd found in our other books—eternal themes such as the conflict between parents and children, between the needs of the self and those of the family. Yet the existence of the Ford Motor Company gave these themes a weight and gravity. Whether or not Edsel Ford could assert his birthright against the destructive and irrational opposition of his father was a matter that had consequence for a company and an industry as well as for an individual. The ability of Henry II to assert himself against his grandfather in 1943 would affect the postwar economy of America as well as his own personal destiny and that of his brothers.

This project was a different sort of challenge, then, one in which we had to deal with an institution as well as a family. It was also different in the attitude we ourselves encountered. For the Rockefellers and Kennedys, writers were special people—people who are able to determine the reaction of the public and therefore people who must be dealt with. Long before we arrived on the scene, both of these families had developed an elaborate machinery for dealing with writers. Writers were part of their lives, part of their entourages; technicians intimately involved with their power and glory. Both families had, in effect, become literary artifacts—what writers had written about them, what they hoped writers would find attractive. They blandished writers and, almost in the same gesture, felt contempt for them.

The Fords, by comparison, are literary primitives. A writer might be useful in publicizing company products but was otherwise regarded as a nuisance with his own agenda. Certainly no Ford would cultivate a writer or take him into his confidence. This is not to say that writers were strangers to the family, of course. Old Henry had a brief and intense fling with the press, following the maxim of Thoreau, one of his favorite writers, that when a dog barks you should run at it. There was a tremendous amount of popular literature written about him in the 1920s and 1930s, a literature he cooperated with and indeed courted at the beginning of his mythomania, although later he scorned and tried to ignore it. Since old Henry's time, the popular literature has dried up, but there has been a continuing flow of academic books about aspects of the Ford Motor Company, many of them following Allan Nevins' authoritative three-volume work, *Ford: The Times, the Man, the Company*. But few of these writers, popular or scholarly, have understood the degree to which writing about the old man is like handling mercury. He was like a fox—back-tracking, sidestepping, and covering his trail. During his life, he gave writers only a whiff of what he really was. After his death, family members kept their counsel, fearful of rattling the skeletons he had left in the Ford closet as a result of his odd adultery with Evangeline Dahlinger, his destruction of Edsel, and his passage over the line that separates eccentricity from madness. "Behind every great fortune there is a great crime," Balzac once said. Old Henry, perverse as always, reversed things: the fortune came first and then the crimes.

After he died, of course, the Ford family retreated from publicity altogether except during those moments such as the renaissance of the company under Henry II when it was an absolute strategic necessity. Thus there has been almost nothing written about Edsel, the crucial figure in this story. Henry II has also remained a mysterious figure, willing to accept the blackguarding of Iacocca without reply, equally indifferent to friendly pieces in business magazines and critical ones in the popular press.

The challenge for us, therefore, was to penetrate the Fords' private lives but also to tell the story of the Ford Motor Company. We had to see what had traditionally been regarded as two separate stories as a synchronous and interlocking whole. Along the way we experienced the special pleasure of the biographer—stumbling onto that undiscovered country no other writer has yet set foot on, following the random paths that sometimes open onto underground caverns of meaning.

We had this sensation when we felt that we had finally gotten behind the masks of Henry I and seen that the genius who was the absolute monarch of the Ford empire was also the insecure man who felt that he had to keep reconquering the institution that was finally more important to him than his own flesh and blood. We had it, too, when we realized the central importance of Edsel in this story, the wounded son whose personal tragedy created the decline of the Ford Motor Company and also the conditions, in the vengeful veneration of his sons, for its regeneration.

Most of all we had a sense of discovery when we saw the real stature of Henry II, unlikely hero of the Ford epic, a man who cagily downplayed his shrewd intelligence and created unappetizing personas that were like the squid's ink in the way they covered his disappearance. The general view of Henry II, even before it was codified by Iacocca, was that he was a boorish oaf, the inheritor who might have saved the company in his youth but had long since become the consummate vulgarian and corporate figurehead. On the contrary, we discovered a shrewd and vigorous man who was, in the context of his times, equal to his grandfather, a colossus who had dominated American business from the time he left the Navy as a green twenty-four-year-old until his recent retirement.

Henry II also interested us because he seemed so roundly to disprove Fitzgerald's notion that there are no second acts in American lives. As a young man he discharged his obligations to his family and to his father's troubled ghost with fealty and honor. He might have coasted for the rest of his life, but he continued to wrestle with the company. Then, in his mid-passage, he turned his back on that staid and conventional persona as family man and corporate chief he had worked so hard to create. His drive to fulfill newly discovered appetites and, even more, to locate a real and authentic self within the ceremonial name and identity he had been given, seemed to us a story of great drama. Because of who he is, his answer to the question that bedevils most middle-aged men—"Is this all that there is?"—had some of the resonance of a character in fiction, a Saul Bellow character, perhaps, Henry the Rain King.

Henry himself, of course, would dispute the allusion. Other members of his family are un-literary; he is anti-literary, someone who neither trusts nor particularly likes books. (His attitude toward writers and their works, as well as his gruff humor, was revealed when he agreed reluctantly to write a preface for an adulatory 1969 biography by Booton Herndon and gave the author a piece of paper with these words written on it: "I'm not interested in this damn book. I'm only cooperating because I've been asked to. I don't care if anybody reads it or not.") It is hard to know the precise sources of this antagonism: perhaps because of the flattering picture writers had painted of his grandfather, ignoring the dark truths of which he, as a young man, was aware; perhaps because writers had stung him so badly when his private life was coming unraveled in the early 1960s.

Whatever the reasons, the consequences were clear. We had hoped, for instance, to tell the story of Edsel Ford, whom we believed to be the pivot of the entire Ford saga. We were shocked when Ford archivists told us that Edsel's papers had been catalogued and boxed in the early 1950s and were on the verge of being made available to researchers when Henry II found out about their existence and had them destroyed. He has done the same thing in advance with his own literary remains, telling Barbara Walters in a 1980 interview, "I've always thought...that I could separate my private life from my business life. And I found out a long time ago I couldn't do that, so now I want to make sure that nobody knows anything about me except from what's in the public domain."

In our interview with him, Henry II began by informing us, "I've spent thirty-four years doing a hell of a lot of things I don't like. Now I've got what's left to me—it's not long—and I don't see why I shouldn't do pretty much what I would like to do." What he would like to do, quite obviously, was not be interviewed by us or any other writer. When he did talk, it was less a conversation than a performance marked by strategic lapses of memory, feigned deafness, intentional *non sequiturs*, and other tactics of a man refusing to accept the subpoena of history and literature to testify about such things even as the struggle against Iacocca about which it was in his interest to speak. "There's a lot of stuff that you're never going to know about me," he told us. "And the reason you aren't going to know is not necessarily because I don't want to tell you. But it tears down other people, and that isn't fair. I can't 'come clean' or 'bare my soul,' or whatever the hell the expression is, out of fairness to the people I've worked with and who've relied on me. You have differences at all times with all kinds of people and that's a problem. I'm not going to tell you that so and so's a shit. I'm just not going to do it."

After being blandished by various Rockefellers and Kennedys, we were intrigued by his stoicism and almost appreciative of someone who saw writers as "sons-of-bitches." So we had a fencing match in the pale spring sun of Florida. We were asking; he wasn't telling. There were exchanges like this with his wife, Kathy, kibbutzing from the wings:

> HFII: Well, in answer to your question [about why he had created a troika after firing Bunkie Knudsen], I've tried to figure out a lot of things about myself, and there are a lot of things I can't figure out. I think people should figure themselves out. They ought to figure out what makes them do the things they do. When I do a very dumb thing, I ask myself what the hell I did that for. Sometimes I can figure it out; sometimes I don't know what I did it for.
>
> C&H: You are hard on yourself.
>
> HFII: That's okay. What's wrong with being hard on yourself? I think that's good for you. It's good for you to be hard on yourself. I'm not hard enough, otherwise I'd lose more weight.
>
> KATHY: [from the kitchen] How's the coffee in there?

HFII: The interview's terrible. [laughs] That's the way some interviews go, I guess. I don't know what you do about it. If I did what I wanted to do I sure as hell wouldn't be sitting here. I can tell you that.

KATHY: That's okay. You're making someone else happy.

HFII: You know that is probably never going to be found out.

KATHY: You've got to trust a few people in life, honey.

HFII: I'm very pragmatic. That's one thing I'll say about myself. But I don't think much. You want to know the truth. She says I never think. Now that's not quite true. I do think a little. But I don't think much.

C&H: Maybe you don't think much about what you do, but think about the consequences.

KATHY: [laughs] Especially after he's done them.

HFII: This book's going to be a disaster, I can tell you that.

KATHY: It can't be any worse than the ones that have been written already, darling.   Wait till I write my book.

HFII: Well, wait till I write a book about you. [laughs] I'll do it first because my life span is going to be shorter....

And so it went. We tried to pin him down; he created confusion to cover his escape. Yet in every interview one looks for revelations of character as well as actual information. These we got.

Henry Ford II will never write his book. He doesn't like books. One of his friends who saw our work in manuscript form said, "Henry ought to like this. Not because it is flattering—it is far from that—but because it tells the whole story of the family and the company and because it shows him whole and shows him true. But first off he'll probably never read it. Second, if he does happen to read it, he'll hate it. That's just the way he is. There are good books and bad books about the Fords, but from his point of view, the only great books are those that never get written."

WE DID MORE THAN TWO HUNDRED interviews in reconstructing the story of the Fords and the Ford Motor Company. We spent considerable time working in the company's Industrial Archives and in the public archives at the Edison Institute. This second place is a historian's paradise. One especially interesting part of the collection, even after thirty years of being picked over by researchers, is the so-called Fair Lane Papers which comprise the correspondence and rat-packings of Henry and Clara. The oral histories done by Allan Nevins when he was beginning his three-volume project are an even richer resource. In these oral histories, since called "Reminiscences," Nevins and his aides debriefed the old-timers who had witnessed the Ford saga from its outset. Nevins used only a fraction of the material he gathered. Underutilized since then, the "Reminiscences" provide an extraordinary account, tantamount to a composite eyewitness view, of the company and the people in it.

We want to thank Dave Crippen, archivist at the Edison Institute, and a man devoted to the notion of free inquiry on the Fords. Also Darlene Flaherty of the Ford Industrial Archives, Laura Berman of the Detroit *News* and Mary Joseph of the Ford Motor Company News Department. We are appreciative to Cynthia Read-Miller of the Henry Ford Museum, and Jim Muncey, R. W. Williams, and Dave Scott of the Ford Motor Company, who, along with Kathy Ford, all helped with the photos, and to Ben Horowitz, who helped assemble our research files. We want to acknowledge the good work of Georges Borchardt, our agent, and the patience of Jim Silberman, Wendy Nicholson, Lisa Baron and the others at Summit.

Finally, we each lost a parent during the writing of this book. As sons, our lives have been impoverished; as writers we were deprived of two incisive readers whose reactions we had come to count on over the years. We write in memory, therefore, of Doris Collier and Philip Horowitz, who, for quite different reasons, would have been intrigued by what we have tried to accomplish in this book. We think of them as being out there someplace, waiting for us, readying their points for a long discussion.

NOTES

PART I

p. 1 "It was raining...": Ford's account of the first car ride is reported by Samuel Marquis in *Henry Ford: An Interpretation* (Boston, 1923), p. 26.

p. 2 "Crazy Henry": Authors' interview with Ford Bryant. Mr. Bryant is a Dearborn historian who has extensively studied Ford family backgrounds.

p. 3 "the great speed...": Margaret Ford Ruddiman, "Memories of My Brother Henry Ford," *Michigan History*, September 1953, p. 267.

p. 3 William Ford's disappointment: Margaret Ford Ruddiman says, "Father may have resented a bit the success of Henry's machine, which proved that Henry had been right in telling us that horses were not necessary..." Ibid.

p. 6 Ford genealogical details: See Allan Nevins, *Ford: The Times, the Man, the Company* (New York, 1954), I, pp. 30ff. Also see Ford Archives, Accession 1, for memo by Charles Bateman, distant Ford relative who remained in Ireland, written for Ford genealogists.

p. 7 "A Turk, a Jew...": Nevins, I, p. 23.

p. 7 "There was Big Sam...": Reminiscences of Clyde Ford, Henry's cousin, born in 1889.

p. 8 "i like the Climate...": Nevins, I, p. 43.

p. 8 "brown hair and dark eyes": Margaret Ford Ruddiman, "Memories," loc. cit., p. 235.

p. 8 cargoes worth a billion dollars: See Carol Gelderman, *Henry Ford: The Wayward Capitalist* (New York, 1981), pp. 5ff.

p. 9 Phil Sheridan mustaches: See Sidney Olson, *Young Henry Ford* (Detroit, 1963), p. 8. Henry Ford later located the bandstand on which his fife-playing uncle and namesake played and placed it in the Henry Ford Museum.

p. 9 Mary's brothers at Fredericksburg: Reminiscences of Artemus Litogot, the son of the wounded and surviving brother.

p. 9 The first Ford to afford a buggy: Reminiscences of Clyde Ford.

p. 9 William on committee to Cleveland: Margaret Ford Ruddiman, "Memories," loc. cit, p. 245.

p. 9 "The first thing I remember...": Ford dictated some of his childhood remembrances later in his life. They can be found in Accession 1, Ford Archives.

p. 9 "Life will give you many unpleasant tasks...": Edgar Guest, "Henry Ford Talks About His Mother," *American Magazine*, July 1923.

p. 10   "of that rarest type...": Allan Benson, The New Henry Ford (New York, 1923), p. 19.

p. 10   "Do you remember...": Nevins, I, p. 43.

p. 10   "A boy in school...": Ford told this story to company artist Irving Bacon. Reminiscences of Irving Bacon.

p. 10   exploding teakettle: See Louise Clancy and Florence Davies, *The Believer: The Life Story of Mrs. Henry Ford* (New York, 1960), p. 16.

p. 11   fascination with watches: J. G. Hamilton, *Henry Ford* (New York, 1927), p. 71.

p. 11   "Every clock... shuddered": Margaret Ford Ruddiman, "Memories," loc. cit., p. 240.

p. 12   "You see that home?": Reminiscences of Edward Litogot.

p. 12   William Ford fondness for drink: Authors' interview with Ford Bryant.

p. 12   "Henry is not much of a farmer...": Reminiscences of George Holmes, grandson of the midwife who delivered Henry Ford.

p. 12   "The great miracle of America...": Margaret Ford Ruddiman, "Memories," loc. cit., p. 227.

p. 13   "My feeling...": Ibid., p. 255.

p. 13   "All right, if that's the way you feel...": Hamilton, p. 81.

p. 13   "I learned then...": Ford said this to his longtime aide William Cameron. Reminiscences of William Cameron.

p. 14   "Henry perhaps you will get helped...": Nevins, I, p. 89.

p. 15   "He's different...": Clancy and Davies, *The Believer*, p. 20.

p. 15   Henry was also impressed: Ibid.

p. 16   "Dear Clara...": HF to CBF, n.d., Accession 1, Ford Archives.

p. 16   "Hitch your wagon to a star...": Margaret Ford Ruddiman, "Memories," loc. cit., p. 261.

p. 18   "Have you got a piece of an engine...": Reminiscences of Lee Cusin.

p. 18   "Invariably my father would call...": Reminiscences of Clyde Ford.

p. 19   Birth of Edsel: Clancy and Davies, p. 37.

p. 20   "Henry is making something...": Cited in Nevins, I, p. 156.

p. 21   "Everyone thought Henry was crazier than heck...": Reminiscences of George Holmes.

p. 21   "I suppose there is a letter waiting for me...": CBF to HF, n.d., Accession 1, Ford Archives.

p. 22   "This young fellow...": Nevins, I, p. 167.

p. 22   "Young man...": Ibid.

p. 22   "Well, you won't be seeing much of me...": Olson, *Young Henry Ford*, p. 91.

p. 22   "Electricity, yes...": Nevins, I, p. 175.

p. 23   "The body is built...": *Detroit Journal*, Feb. 16, 1900.

p. 23   "There has always been...": *Detroit News Tribune*, Feb. 4, 1900.

p. 24   "I never really thought much of racing...": Henry Ford with Samuel Crowther, *My Life and Work* (New York, 1922), p. 50.

p. 24   "I was learning something...": Benson, *The New Henry Ford*, p. 69.

p. 24   "You'll never make a go of it....": Reminiscences of George Holmes.

p. 24   Ford's spiritual longings: Reminiscences of Oliver Barthel. As Barthel notes, Ford still remembered reading *A Short View of the Great Questions* some thirty years later. "When I was a young man," he said, "I was bewildered. I found myself asking the question What are we here for? I found no answers. Then one day a friend handed me a book. That little book gave me the answers I was seeking. It changed my whole life, changed my outlook upon life."

p. 25 Ford notebooks: Accession 1, Ford Archives.

p. 25 "My dear little son...": HF to EBF, 1/5/1900, Accession 1, Ford Archives.

p. 25 "Dear Papa...": EBF to HF, 1/18/03, Accession 1, Ford Archives.

p. 26 "We had a peach tree": Reminiscences of Faith Beebe.

p. 26 "Charley, Edsel is interested...": Ibid.

p. 26 Clara's diary entries: Accession 1, Ford Archives.

p. 26 "Dear Husband...": Ibid.

p. 27 "Edsel is growing...": Ibid.

p. 27 "Boy, I'll never do that again...": Booton Herndon, *Ford* (New York, 1969), p. 65.

p. 27 "Henry has been covering himself with glory...": Cited in Olson, p. 146.

p. 28 "Dear Santa Claus...": EBF to HF and CBF, n.d. Accession 1, Ford Archives.

p. 28 "He wanted another racing car built...": Reminiscences of Oliver Barthel.

p. 28 In 1900 thirty-eight new companies: Nevins, I, p. 234.

p. 29 "Well, this chariot may kill me...": Clancy and Davies, p. 60.

p. 29 Talk of calling it "The Daisy": See Harry Barnard, *Independent Man: The Life of Senator James Couzens* (New York, 1958), p. 39.

p. 30 "Mr. Ford, of this city...": The Anderson letter was first printed by James Martin Miller in *The Amazing Story of Henry Ford* (New York, 1922), p. 74.

p. 31 Ford and Wills keeping warm by boxing: Alfred P. Sloan, *Adventures of a White Collar Man* (New York, 1941), p. 72.

p. 31 Couzens' early life: See Barnard, pp. 15ff.

p. 31 "I won't stand for that!": Barnard, p. 38.

p. 31 "What do you think we ought to ask... ?": Barnard, p. 48.

p. 32 "The most reliable machine...": Cited by Keith Sward in *The Legend of Henry Ford* (New York, 1948), p. 20.

p. 32 "That's right...": Reminiscences of Louis Kinietz.

p. 33 "That ice was seamed...": Ford, *My Life and Work*, p. 57.

p. 34 Ford's hatred of the Model K: "Ford was definitely against the Model K. He carried it on because the stockholder wanted it. He didn't like the Model B either.... His idea was always just one car." (Reminiscences of Joe Galamb.)

p. 34 "A car should not have any more cylinders...": Joe McCarthy, "The Ford Family," *Holiday*, June 1957, p. 72.

p. 34 "The way to make automobiles...": Nevins, I, p. 276.

p. 34 "This is a great day...": Reminiscences of Fred Rockelman.

p. 35 *The Nation* diagnosed the situation: *The Nation*, Sept. 7, 1916.

p. 36 "Get a good lock...": Reminiscences of Joe Galamb.

p. 36 "Mr. Ford first sketched out...": Ibid.

p. 36 Ford altered sights on rifles: See Charles E. Sorensen, *My Forty Years with Ford* (New York, 1956), p. 25.

p. 36 "He was like a kid...": Reminiscences of Leo Brown.

p. 36 "God, he could get anything...": Reminiscences of George Brown.

p. 36 "I will build a motorcar...": Cited in Olson, p. 186.

p. 37 "some of the characteristics of a mule...": Garet Garrett, *The Wild Wheel* (New York, 1952), p. 59.

p. 37 rural people assaulted cars: See Reynold M. Wik, *Henry Ford and Grass Roots America* (Ann Arbor, 1972), pp. 14ff.

p. 37 "Ford Clinic": Wik, p. 38.

p. 37 Model T promotions: Wik, p. 35.

p. 37 "I have solved the automobile problem....": Robert Conot, *A Streak of Luck* (New York, 1979), p. 392.

p. 53 "like a planet that had adopted Edison...": Ibid.

p. 54 "Selden can take his patent...": Theodore McManus and Norman Beasley, *Men, Money, and Motors* (New York, 1929), p. 56.

p. 38 "We will protect you...": *Detroit News*, July 28, 1903.

p. 39 "No, my friend...": Nevins, I, p. 417.

p. 39 "I invented nothing new...": William Greenleaf, *Monopoly on Wheels: Henry Ford and the Selden Automobile Patent* (Detroit, 1961), p. 138.

p. 39 "Your Honor...": Gelderman, Henry Ford, p. 37.

p. 39 Charles Duryea testimony: See Olson, pp. 62-63.

p. 40 Details of transcontinental race: "1909 Transcontinental Race," Accession 717, Box 1, Ford Archives.

p. 40 Guggenheim speech: Nevins, I, p. 406. Edsel had gone to Seattle to see the finish of the race with a friend, meeting his father there. He wrote home to Clara about the aftermath of the race: "We are having a nice time and wish you were here. Burt [driver of the other Model T entry] arrived here last Wednesday and was cheered by 150,000 people. The streets were packed. Mr. Guggenheim is a fine fellow and the cup is great, but I'm afraid we won't get it. The Shawmut has protested Scott for changing axles. But he has protested the Shawmut for leaving Toledo and Chicago before the scheduled time. So there is a scrap on." (EBF to CBF, 6/26/09, Accession 1, Ford Archives.)

p. 41 "Tell him he can have it...": For an account of Durant's offer, see William C. Richards, *The Last Billionaire* (New York, 1948), p. 350.

p. 42 "A customer can have a car...": Nevins, I, p. 452.

p. 42 "After Mr. Ford had shown...": Reminiscences of George Brown.

p. 43 "I'll bet I can throw this...": Reminiscences of Georgia Bayer.

p. 43 "Well, Mr. Ford...": For an account of Ford's anger on this occasion, see Reminiscences of George Brown.

p. 44 "My first clear recollection": *Detroit News*, Aug. 4, 1921.

p. 44 "Have you seen Ed?...": Reminiscences of George Brown.

p. 44 "Yes, I have a fine son...": Clancy and Davies, *The Believer*, p. 121.

p. 44 Edsel notebooks: Accession 6, Ford Archives.

p. 45 "They forgot to teach...": This illustration of Ford's scorn for a college education appears in Sorensen, p. 63.

p. 46 Sorensen and the assembly line: Sorensen writes that the idea of the assembly line originated at the Piquette plant. "It was there that the idea occurred to me that assembly would be easier, simpler and faster if we moved the chassis along, beginning at one end of the plant with a frame and adding the axles and wheels; thus moving it past the stockroom to the chassis. (*My Forty Years with Ford*, p. 18.)

p. 46 "Time loves to be wasted...": Garrett, p. 101.

p. 46 Sales figures: see Nevins, I, p. 475.

p. 47 "Men now hardly past middle life...": *The Nation*, Sept. 7, 1916.

p. 48 "You fellows sit back...": Barnard, pp. 96ff.

p. 48 "Look at Henry Ford's boy": Richards, p. 15.

p. 48 "Each of us realizes...": Barnard, p. 90.

p. 48 "No, it's five or nothing.": Ibid. There has been some controversy over who should get credit for the $5 wage. Sorensen says it was Henry's idea, which he helped shape. He claims that Couzens agreed to the plan only for reasons of personal ambition and quotes him as saying, "I want to be Governor of Michigan, and this will help elect me." (*My Forty Years with Ford*, p. 136.) The truth seems to be otherwise. McManus and Beasley, in *Men, Money, and Motors*, a book based on interviews with pioneers of the auto industry, say that the prime mover was Couzens. In trying to substantiate their account of Couzens' central role, biographer Harry Barnard contacted onetime Ford Motor Company treasurer Frank Klingensmith, who said of the McManus/Beasley account: "[It] is an absolutely authenticated book.... While the incident of the wage raise is told in narrative form, the facts are there and I will stand by every word..." (*Independent Man*, p. 337.) Samuel Marquis also substantiates Couzens' role: "In 1914, Mr. Ford agreed with Mr. Couzens that in view of the earnings of the company, the men in their employ should be given an increase in pay. Mr. Couzens dared him to make the minimum pay five dollars a day, and Mr. Ford agreed." (*Henry Ford*, p. 21.)

p. 49 "He's crazy...": Garrett, *The Wild Wheel*, p. 75.

p. 49 The new system worked for the company: See Sward, *The Legend of Henry Ford*, p. 63.

p. 49 Employees wore identification badges off duty: Reminiscences of E. G. Biondi.

p. 49 "Give him a better job...": Reminiscences of Irving Bacon.

p. 50 "If some young fellow...": Reminiscences of H. C. Doss.

p. 50 "Rules of Living" pamphlet: citation

p. 50 "Let me lay my hands...": Marquis, p. 152.

p. 50 "When we got through...": Marquis, p. 114.

p. 51 Money was a way of keeping score: For an insight into Ford's theory of business, see Ford, *My Life and Work*.

p. 52 Ford's false whiskers: Reminiscences of Ernest Liebold.

p. 53 "Will, how's things going?": Ibid.

p. 53 Henry's relationships with his brothers: Authors' interview with Ford Bryant.

p. 53 "Take that danged thing...": Reminiscences of Artemus Litogot.

p. 53 "Keep away from your damned relatives...": Reminiscences of J. E. Thompson. (Thompson was the Fords' butler.)

p. 53 "I have a million in gold...": See Gelderman, p. 250.

p. 54 Lunch with Lochner and Schwimmer: See Louis Lochner, *Henry Ford* (New York, 1925), pp. 15ff.

p. 55 "Men sitting around a table...": Ibid., p. 18.

p. 55 "Why not a special ship... ?": Ibid.

p. 55 "You are looking very well...": The account of the meeting between Ford and Wilson comes from Lochner, pp. 23ff.

p. 55 "as little harm as good": *New York Times*, Nov. 25, 1915.

p. 56 "one of the cruellest jokes...": *New York Herald*, Nov. 26, 1915.

p. 56 "Out of the trenches...": Lochner, p. 41.

p. 56 "Do you want to know the cause of war?...": Sward, p. 86.

p. 57 "the tenderest of the tender...": Cited in Sward, p. 91.

p. 57 "J. Pierpont Morgan was dead...": Lochner, p. 63.

p. 57 "Guess I had better go home...": Ibid., p. 109.

p. 57   "I believe the sentiment...": *New York Times*, Jan. 1, 1916.

p. 58   "Until he saw a chance...": Cited by Jonathan Daniels, *The End of Innocence* (New York, 1959), p. 176.

p. 58   "I wanted to see peace....": William Stidger, *Henry Ford* (New York, 1923), p. 245.

p. 58   "If we had tried to break in...": Richards, *The Last Billionaire*, p. 48. Liebold claims that after the Peace Ship debacle Ford said to him, "Well, we got a million dollars worth of advertising." (Reminiscences of Ernest Liebold.)

p. 58   "Sir—I hereby forbid...": William Simonds, *Henry Ford: His Life, His Work, His Genius* (Indianapolis, 1943), p. 147.

p. 59   "I had put you down...": Barnard, p. 51.

p. 59   "I'll show you a good way...": Reminiscences of Harold Cordell.

p. 59   Couzens' loss of his son: After telling his family that the boy had died, Couzens insisted that they sit at the dinner table as usual, saying, "We must not give in to our feelings." Later he took Frank Klingensmith, Ford Company accountant, to see the body. "Wasn't he a fine big boy?" he kept repeating. But he refused to cry. (Barnard, p. 98.)

p. 59   "If you say the word...": Barnard, pp. 80ff.

p. 60   "You can't publish this.": Ibid., p. 5.

p. 60n "Man minus the machine": Cited in Wik, *Henry Ford and Grass Roots America*, p. 101. In its own way the Fordson tractor was as dramatic a success story as the Model T. Although he had despised farming as a boy, Ford became a prophet of the fields. He made the tractor a necessity rather than a curiosity, just as he had the automobile. But the Fordson was not quite the dependable machine that the Tin Lizzie was. It had a high frequency of repair. It was also dangerous because of a tendency to rear up and flip over backward if a sudden resistance created excessive torque in the transmission. *Pipp's Weekly*, a farm publication, in a story with the headline, "Fordsons Are the Huns of the Field!," claimed that the tractor had been responsible for 136 deaths by August 1922.

p. 61   "We arrived yesterday morning...": EBF to CBF, n.d., Accession 1, Ford Archives.

p. 62   The wedding took place: For accounts of the wedding see the *Detroit Evening News*, Oct. 31, Nov. 1 and Nov. 2, 1916.

p. 62   "Henry, I don't envy you...": Gelderman, p. 61.

p. 62   "The ride out here...": EBF to CBF, 11/8/16, Accession 1, Ford Archives.

p. 62   "I have been buying Detroit papers...": EBF to CBF, 11/17/16, Accession 1, Ford Archives.

p. 62   "Your conscience would not let you...": For a summary of the interrogation of Ford, see transcript of Dodge Trial, Ford Archives.

p. 63   "Practically gained every point...": HF to EBF, 12/23/16, Accession 1, Ford Archives.

p. 63   "Seeing as how we live...": EBF to CBF, 3/26/17, Accession 1, Ford Archives.

p. 64   "to devote my time to... other organizations...": Nevins, II, p. 106.

p. 65   "The Ford Motor Company has no mortgage...": Nevins, II, p. 107.

p. 65   "If Ford allows the rule...": *Chicago Tribune*, June 23, 1916.

p. 66   "Now don't forget this...": Cited by E. G. Pipp in *Henry Ford* (Detroit, 1926), p. 48.

p. 67n "I don't know anything about history…": Cited by Roger Burlingame in *Henry Ford* (New York, 1954), p. 3.

p. 67 Ford defined "chile con carne": Sward, p. 104.

p. 67 "A slight boyish figure…": Burlingame, p. 5.

p. 67 "Did you ever hear of Benedict Arnold?": Gelderman, p. 18.

p. 68 "They forced us to open the mind…": Ibid.

p. 68 "The fun of playing with matches…": *Detroit News*, May 18, 1920.

p. 70 "By the way…": Simonds, *Henry Ford*, p. 176.

p. 70 "How can a man over sixty years…": Couzens' statement was reported by the *New York Times*, Nov. 1, 1923.

p. 71 Collier's poll: see *Collier's*, Aug. 8, 1923.

p. 71n "I hate the idea…": Reminiscences of Ernest Liebold.

p. 71 solved a rear-axle problem: *Detroit Times*, July 16, 1915; *Baltimore Evening Sun*, Sept. 27, 1915.

p. 71 Henry had bought expensive gifts for her: See insurance policy, Accession 13, Ford Archives.

p. 72 "I want you to get out…": Reminiscences of J. E. Thompson.

p. 72 "Look at them!…": W. R. Brewer reminiscences, Ford Archives.

p. 72 "There was Mr. Ford…": Reminiscences of Rosa Buhler, Ford Archives.

p. 72 Evangeline Cote's background: See John Cote Dahlinger, *The Secret Life of Henry Ford* (New York, 1978).

p. 73 "Was it too many women?": Reminiscences of Harold Hicks.

p. 73 "*I* pass on what Mr. Ford wears…": Reminiscences of Ernest Liebold.

p. 74 "Hello there, Ray.…": Dahlinger, p. 41.

p. 74 "Gee, Mr. Ford, you're a genius!": Ibid., p. 46.

p. 75 "Suppose Mr. Ford should suddenly say…": Richards, *The Last Billionaire*, p. 223.

p. 75 "I'll show you how to clean them!" Reminiscences of Harold Cordell.

p. 75 "Here comes Sorensen!": Reminiscences of E. G. Biodi.

p. 75 "You always get here exactly at eight o'clock.": Reminiscences of J. L. McCloud.

p. 75 "Well, all right.": Ibid.

p. 76 "Please *see* this man.": Marquis, *Henry Ford*, p. 71.

p. 76 "You don't hire a watchdog": Reminiscences of William Cameron.

p. 76 Henry Ford Hospital: For details see Reminiscences of Ernest Liebold.

p. 76 "every now and then…": Sward, p. 186.

p. 76 "To them the morale…": Marquis, p. 141.

p. 77 Wills got another $1.5 million: Reminiscences of Ernest Liebold.

p. 77 "I fired him because he forgot his mother.": Reminiscences of Harold Hicks.

p. 78 "If only Mr. Ford was properly assembled!…": Marquis, p. 11.

p. 78 Knudsen's dental problems: Reminiscences of Ernest Liebold.

p. 78 Knudsen notified he would not go to Europe: Reminiscences of George Brown.

p. 78 "I have a good friend over there.…": Reminiscences of Charles Kruger.

p. 78 "an industrial fascist": *New York Times*, Jan. 18, 1921.

p. 79 "I know who started the war…": Cited in Gelderman, p. 219.

p. 79 "going to go after the Jews…": Reminiscences of Ernest Liebold.

p. 79 Stanley Finch's work for Ford: Ibid.

p. 79   "Oh, he's mixed...": Harry Bennett, *We Never Called Him Henry* (New York, 1951), p.43.

p. 80   "We had continual directives...": Reminiscences of Clarence Bullwinkel.

p. 80   Liebold hired a New York detective agency: According to John Lee, *Henry Ford and the Jews* (New York, 1980), pp. 22ff., one of Liebold's agents was C. C. Daniels, a lawyer and brother of Navy Secretary Josephus Daniels.

p. 80   Ford and "Protocols": For the fullest discussion, see Lee, pp. 27ff.

p. 81   Jews and assassination of Lincoln: Reminiscences of Ernest Liebold.

p. 81   "The elderly pawnbroker kept looking...": Reminiscences of Irving Bacon.

p. 81   "there had been observed...": Ford, *My Life and Work*, p. 250.

p. 82   "Don't ever let Mr. Ford...": Reminiscences of Harold Hicks.

p. 82   "There was a policy...": Reminiscences of William Klann.

p. 82   "You know, Cameron is going a little bit wild...": Reminiscences of Ernest Liebold.

p. 82   "I confess...": Cited in Gelderman, p. 234.

p. 83   "The Jews have gone along...": Richards, *The Last Billionaire*, p. 98.

p. 84   Ford jumped into hayrack: Reminiscences of Harold Hicks.

p. 85   "Well, I think I've done today...": Ibid.

p. 85   "He took me to the cool cellar...": Reminiscences of Irving Bacon.

p. 85   "I'm going to start up a musuem...": Reminiscences of Ernest Liebold.

p. 85   Ford's eccentric collecting: Reminiscences of Harold Cordell.

p. 86   "Dear me...": Cited by Robert Conot in *A Streak of Luck*, p. 443.

p. 87   "The failure of Mr. Ford's son...": *Detroit Saturday Night*, Oct. 26, 1918.

p. 87   changed the birth certificate: A copy of the original birth certificate naming Benson "Edsel B. Ford Jr." is in Accession 6, Ford Archives.

p. 87   "Isn't that marvelous?...": Reminiscences of Ernest Liebold.

p. 87   " 'Children, I want to make a confession....' ": Reminiscences of Irving Bacon.

p. 88   He met Franklin Roosevelt: Authors' interview with Harry Pierson, May 14, 1985.

p. 88   "Nice horse": Reminiscences of E. J. Farkas.

p. 88   "handsome enough to charm...": Authors' interview with Jane Schermerhorn, March 21, 1985.

p. 88   "Before leaving for home...": EBF to CBF, n.d., Accession 1, Ford Archives.

p. 88   "Dear Sonnie...": Eleanor Ford to HF2, n.d., Accession 1, Ford Archives.

p. 89   "Are you having a good time...": HF2 to Josephine Ford, n.d., Accession 1, Ford Archives.

p. 89   "Dear Grandaddy...": HF2 to HF, 8/23/27, Accession 1, Ford Archives.

p. 89   "Dear Callie...": HF2 to CBF, 8/13/30, Accession 1, Ford Archives.

p. 89   "Edsel had everything going for him....": The friend who said this was Ernest Kanzler. Authors' interview with Robert Kanzler, Jan. 24, 1986.

p. 90   "He had the most orderly desk...": Reminiscences of A. J. Lepine.

p. 90   "Father made the most popular car...": Gelderman, p. 255.

p. 90   He wrote... letters to Henry Braunn: The letters are in Accession 6, Ford Archives.

p. 90   he narrowly escaped injury: *Detroit News*, Sept. 1, 1929.

p. 90   Edsel planned marine Model T: Reminiscences of Harold Hicks.

p. 91   "Had 10 minute flight...": Telegram, EBF to EF, July 18, 1927, Accession 1, Ford Archives.

p. 91   "That's no good....": Reminiscences of Harold Hicks.

p. 91 "I have responsibility...": Authors' interview with Robert Kanzler.

p. 91 "Sorensen's job here...": Reminiscences of Harold Hicks.

p. 91 Edsel tries to fire Sorensen: Reminiscences of Walter Griffith.

p. 91 "This result in the suspension...": Reminiscences of Harold Cordell.

p. 92 "What's going on here?": Reminiscences of L. E. Briggs.

p. 92 "You ought to be on my side....": Nevins, II, p. 62.

p. 92 "Well, let's see what the Jap butler...": Reminiscences of William Mielke.

p. 92 "You have not seen the last of him...": Sorensen, *My Forty Years with Ford*, pp. 301ff. Also, Reminiscences of A. H. Weibel.

p. 92 Kanzler insisted on going out into the plant: Reminiscences of William Klann.

p. 93 "Kanzler and Edsel ought to be bankers.": Reminiscences of Ernest Liebold.

p. 93 Gehle story: Reminiscences of Theodore Gehle.

p. 94 "... a matter of build all the cars you can.": Reminiscences of William Klann.

p. 94 "He was production manager...": Reminiscences of Daniel Hutchins.

p. 94 "Now you go down to the Rouge...": Reminiscences of Ernest Liebold. The assistant superintendent was a man named Charlie Hartner.

p. 95 "Well, gentlemen...": *Detroit News*, Oct. 24, 1922.

p. 95 Chevrolet vs. Ford: For information on the contest between the two companies see Alfred P. Sloan, *My Years with General Motors* (New York, 1963).

p. 95 Fisher discovered Harley Earl: See Brock Yates, *The Decline and Fall of the American Automobile Industry* (New York, 1983), pp. 182ff.

p. 95 "I can write certain things...": Nevins, II, p. 404.

p. 96 "That young man is getting...": Ibid., p. 409.

p. 96 "... Kanzler is a Jew...": Reminiscences of E. J. Farkas.

p. 96 "The trouble was that Mr. Kanzler...": Reminiscences of Ernest Liebold.

p. 96 "Well, by this time...": Reminiscences of Georgia Bayer.

p. 96 Edsel brought back Dunhill lighters: Reminiscences of A. A. Backus.

p. 97 Stuart Chase study: Richards, p. 352.

p. 97 "The only thing wrong...": Reminiscences of Bascomb Mahaffey.

p. 97 Sorensen to ask Edsel to clear out: Sorensen, p. 219.

p. 98 "Everybody saw it...": Reminiscences of Ernest Liebold.

p. 98 "Father, I believe the time...": Reminiscences of Theodore Gehle.

p. 98 "Hell, he won't have a dealer...": Bennett, *We Never Called Him Henry*, p. 44.

p. 98 Story of the X-8 engine: Reminiscences of Lawrence Sheldrick.

p. 99 "Highland Park was civilized...": Reminiscences of William Klann.

p. 99 "At the Rouge...": Nevins, II, p. 294.

p. 99 "Well, this isn't Highland Park!": Reminiscences of William P. Baxter.

p. 99 "A lot of jobs...": Reminiscences of William Klann.

p. 100 "We've got a pretty good man...": Nevins, II, p. 447.

p. 101 Walter Chrysler career: See Walter P. Chrysler with Boyden Sparkes, *Life of an American Workman* (New York, 1950).

p. 101 Edison's breakdown: Reminiscences of Ernest Liebold.

p. 102 Effects of Depression on Detroit: See Nevins, II, pp. 571ff.

p. 102n "Go like hell, boys....": *New Republic*, March 3, 1932.

p. 102 Henry took Sloan for a visit: Bennett, *We Never Called Him Henry*, p. 90.

p. 102 "You could never tell...": Reminiscences of Harold Hicks.

p. 102 In 1929 the auto industry had made 5,294,000: Nevins, III, p. 4.

p. 103 "Professional charity...": Ford, *My Life and Work*, p. 207.

p. 103   "Unless we help ourselves...": cited by Richards, p. 265.

p. 103   "Well, he took up...": Richards, p. 382.

p. 103   Ford and the Morgenthau appointment: Dahlinger, *The Secret Life of Henry Ford*, p. 107.

p. 103   "Mr. Ford, I want you to go along...": Richards, p. 265.

p. 104   "I've always wanted to find out...": Reminiscences of Rosa Buhler.

p. 104   Clara and the Oxford movement: She eventually became disenchanted and stopped attending meetings because of what she regarded as an excessive emphasis on public confession of sins. "The first public confession can be stirring," she said, "but the tenth strikes one as the same old thing." (Clancy and Davies, p. 170.)

p. 104   "You know, when a person dies...": Reminiscences of Artemus Litogot.

p. 104   "It wasn't because of meanness...": Reminiscences of Frank Bennett.

p. 105   "If people would learn to eat...": Nevins, II, p. 489.

p. 105   "Quadrupeds are out": Dahlinger, p. 171.

p. 105   Ford and Carver eat weeds: Reminiscences of Irving Bacon.

p. 105   Ford and soybeans: Richards, pp. 297f.

p. 106   "*That's* what you're putting into your stomachs!": Reminiscences of B. R. Brower.

p. 106   "It was one of the most vile-tasting...": Reminiscences of Harold Cordell.

p. 106   Ford and Sheldrick lunch: Reminiscences of Lawrence Sheldrick.

p. 107   Ford wearing two different shoes: Richards, p. 145.

p. 107   "You can see for yourself...": Richards, p. 157.

p. 107   "Well, I thought Father...": Nevins, II, p. 273.

p. 107   Edsel pulls out a package of Camels: Reminiscences of Al Esper.

p. 107   Troubles of the Guardian Detroit Union: See Robert Conot, *An American Odyssey* (New York, 1975), pp. 385ff.

p. 108   "Let them fail!...": Barnard, p. 229.

p. 108   "The present situation in Michigan": EBF to Richard E. Byrd, 2/22/33, Accession 6, Ford Archives. The relationship between the two men had begun in the spring of 1924 when Byrd, then a naval lieutenant and an accomplished pilot, called on Edsel to tell him about a flight to the North Pole he had planned. Edsel eventually pledged $30,000 to help defray costs. This commitment helped Byrd get a similar pledge from John D. Rockefeller Jr. Before leaving, Byrd wrote to Edsel: "You are the father of the expedition..." Edsel gave Byrd $90,000 for his expedition to the South Pole in 1929. Byrd christened his plane (a Ford trimotor) the *Josephine Ford*, after Edsel's daughter Dodie, and named after Edsel one of the arctic mountain ranges he discovered.

p. 108   "Well, I'm cleaned out.": Reminiscences of Ernest Liebold.

p. 108   "Well, son...": Reminiscences of Irving Bacon.

p. 108   "You register under my name...": Reminiscences of Lawrence Sheldrick.

p. 108   Edsel and Haven Hill: See Reminiscences of A. A. Backus.

p. 109   "Dad and I...": William Ford to CBF, n.d., Accession 1, Ford Archives.

p. 109   "We have bought...": EBF to CBF, n.d., ibid.

p. 109   full-grown trees brought: Reminiscences of F. W. Lakowske.

p. 110   The grandchildren visited in units: Authors' interview with Josephine Ford, March 3, 1986.

p. 110   He built a treehouse: Reminiscences of Leland Avery.

p. 110 Suspicions of John Dahlinger parentage: Reminiscences of Irving Bacon.

p. 110 "a couple of fatties": Dahlinger, p. 36.

p. 110 Ford throws candy overboard: Reminiscences of Robert Temple.

p. 110 Henry felt grandchildren were "held in": Reminiscences of Lawrence Sheldrick.

p. 111 "Bill, go upstairs....": Authors' interview with William Ford, May 30, 1985.

p. 111 "It was the dirty little secret...": Authors' interview with confidential source, Feb. 16, 1985.

p. 111 "For most young people...": Ibid.

p. 111 "I hope you will have...": EBF to Josephine Ford, 7/7/30, Accession 6, Ford Archives.

p. 111 Prince of Wales at Gaukler Pointe: *Detroit Free Press*, Oct. 24, 1965.

p. 112 "Young Henry was like a hyena....": Authors' interview with confidential source, Oct. 23, 1985.

p. 112 "Dear Pop": HF2 to EBF, 4/30/35, Accession 6, Ford Archives.

p. 112 Edsel noted in his reply: EBF to HF2, 5/7/35, Accession 6, Ford Archives.

p. 113 "The masters' comment": George Van Santvoord to EBF, 10/21/37, Accession 6, Ford Archives.

p. 113 Benson had to wait until Christmas: Authors' interview with Travers Smith, Nov. 12, 1985.

p. 113 "In discussing Benson's problems...": EBF to Lawrence Keiply, 7/12/37, Accession 6, Ford Archives.

p. 113 "His parents brought Benson...": Dr. Frank Slodin to Dr. H. E. Wieler, 11/11/37, Accession 6, Ford Archives.

p. 113 "I would like him to take...": EBF to Edward Noyes, 4/10/36, Accession 6, Ford Archives.

p. 114 "I am deeply concerned...": Radcliffe Heermance to EBF, 2/17/39, Accession 6, Ford Archives.

p. 114 "The work is going...": Benson Ford to CBF, 4/19/39, Accession 1, Ford Archives.

p. 114 "Father told me...": Benson Ford to HF, 8/12/39, Accession 1, Ford Archives.

p. 114 "He is shy...": Cited in Nevins, III, p. 183.

p. 114 Ford and Duveen: Gelderman, p. 310.

p. 114 Edsel and William Valentiner: See Margaret Sterne, *The Passionate Eye: The Life of William Valentiner* (Detroit, 1978).

p. 115 "I must say...": Ibid., p. 154.

p. 115 Edsel's gifts to DIA: Clyde Burroughs (secretary of DIA) to Fred Black (Edsel's aide), May 13, 1938, Accession 6, Ford Archives.

p. 115 "I felt I had to act quickly...": Sterne, p. 192.

p. 115 "Diego confessed...": Sterne, p. 194. For more on Rivera's feelings about Edsel on his trip to Detroit, see Bertram Wolfe, *The Fabulous Life of Diego Rivera* (London, 1963).

p. 116 "William is very nervous....": Margaret Sterne, "The Museum Director and the Artist: Dr. William Valentiner and Diego Rivera in Detroit," Detroit in Perspective, Winter 1973, p. 107.

p. 116 "He was far above the rest of us...": Joe McCarthy, "The Ford Family," *Holiday*, June 1957, p. 121.

p. 116 Rockefeller asked Edsel to be on the board: EBF to Nelson Rockefeller, 4/9/36, and other correspondence in Accession 6, Ford Archives.

p. 116   "I don't like it...": Reminiscences of A. B. Ablewhite.

p. 116   Edsel invited Bacon to paint with him: Reminiscences of Irving Bacon.

p. 117   Edsel and Eleanor gave a party: Reminiscences of A. A. Backus.

p. 117   "No organization...": Ford, *My Life and Work*, p. 207.

p. 118   "Edsel felt...": Reminiscences of Ernest Liebold.

p. 118   "Any plan...": Sloan, p. 132.

p. 118   "Think of the corporation...": Ibid., p. 153.

p. 118   "Don't let anybody ever see this...": Nevins, III, p. 58.

p. 119   "I'll take every factory down...": Gelderman, p. 362.

p. 119   "The next time you see Edsel...": Reminiscences of Ernest Liebold.

p. 119   "Well, it's about time...": Reminiscences of William Klann.

p. 120   "I'd always wished...": Bennett, p. 14.

p. 121   "We just brought this big brute...": Reminiscences of Irving Bacon. Bennett's own rather flamboyant account of his first meeting with Ford is somewhat different. He says that he was still in the Navy and had just returned to New York after maneuvers in Vera Cruz. He was involved in a fight which Hearst newspaperman Arthur Brisbane witnessed. Finding out that Bennett was from Ann Arbor, Brisbane invited him to come with him to meet Ford, then visiting New York. Ford, says Bennett, was so impressed by him that he offered him a job. (Bennett, pp. 5ff.)

p. 121   "If Charlie Sorensen pointed his finger...": Reminiscences of Philip Haglund.

p. 121   Bennett jumped into a car: Bennett, p. 17.

p. 121   "Harry, let's you and him have a fight.": Ibid.

p. 122   La Mare banking $3,500 a day: See Sward, p. 30. Also Bennett, p. 69. Some people in Detroit dismissed Bennett as a crime "groupie." Yet his relationship with the city's mobsters was strong, and in the 1950s, when U.S. Senator Estes Kefauver's committee was holding hearings, Bennett was subpoenaed.

p. 123   "I can replace factories...": Nevins, II, p. 504.

p. 123   Bennett had a Ford employee pose as Edsel: The extortion plot is discussed in Reminiscences of A. A. Backus.

p. 123   "Bennett said he'd handle it....": Authors' interview with William Ford.

p. 123   "Here come those rats now!": Reminiscences of A. A. Backus.

p. 124n   Comintern had given orders: See Nevins, III, pp. 32ff. Sorensen's visit to Russia: Sorensen, pp. 192ff. In *My Life and Work*, Ford had been negative in his appraisal of the Soviets: "Russia is at work but it counts for nothing. It is not free work. In the U.S. a workman works eights hours a day—in Russia 12 to 14 hours. In America he lays off if he wants to—in Russia he goes to work whether he wants to or not." But a few years later he had begun his romance with the USSR. Hearing that Albert Kahn, architect of Highland Park and other Ford edifices, had been asked to design an auto plant on the Volga, Ford phoned him and said, "Glad to hear of your new business, Albert. We'll give you every help we can." In the course of the conversation he added, "You tell those fellows they can have our patterns, models, anything they want and we'll send some fellows to Russia to show them how to make cars." (Richards, p. 341.)

p. 124   "We want Bennett...": Nevins, III, p. 33.

p. 125   Liebold breakdown: See Reminiscences of Ernest Liebold, Ford Archives.

p. 125   "Henry couldn't pop in...": Reminiscences of Lawrence Sheldrick.

p. 126   "The changing of models...": Reminiscences of Joe Galamb.

p. 126 "We all wore smocks…": Authors' interview with Eugene Bordinat.

p. 126 Origins of the Continental: See "The Birth of the Continental," unpublished ms by Ed Martin written Sept. 3, 1951. (A copy was kindly provided to the authors by John Najjar.)

p. 127 1936 sales statistics: Nevins, III, p. 183.

p. 127 "Sniffers" stood at air registers: Authors' interview with John Najjar, May 24, 1984, and Jan. 18, 1985.

p. 127 "Fordization of the face": James Flink, *The Car Culture* (Cambridge, Mass., 1975), p. 86.

p. 128 UAW hired an airplane: Reminiscences of J. E. Bossardet.

p. 128 "If we found a fellow who drove a Buick…": Reminiscences of William Klann.

p. 128 "This isn't fair.…": Garrett, *The Wild Wheel*, p. 35.

p. 129 "I've picked someone…": Sorensen, p. 260.

p. 129 "This is Ford property…": For an account of the brawl, see Victor Reuther, *The Brothers Reuther* (Boston, 1976), p. 201.

p. 131 Henry and his chiropractor: See Gelderman, p. 338.

p. 131 The Fords at Richmond Hill: See Reminiscences of Bascomb Mahaffey.

p. 132 "Just think of that!": Ibid.

p. 132 "the largest quasi-military organization…": *New York Times*, June 26, 1937.

p. 132 Bennett's pornography: See memo dated 11/20/44, Harry Bennett FBI file.

p. 132 "That's nice, Harry.": Bob Considine, *The Fabulous Henry Ford II*, a series of articles reprinted by the Hearst Corp. (1964), p. 13.

p. 132 "Now, Harry…": Bennett, p. 25.

p. 133 Bullet holes in the front door: Authors' interview with Harry Pierson.

p. 133 "Dr. McClure and I…": Mateer to EBF, 11/5/40, Accession 6, Ford Archives.

p. 133 1937 sales statistics: See *Fortune*, October 1945.

p. 133 "The hurtful thing…": Nevins, III, p. 244.

p. 134 "I want to support you…": Herndon, Ford, p. 160. (Herndon interviewed Davis.)

p. 134 "I do wish we were going…": Eleanor Ford to HF, 7/26/30, Accession 1, Ford Archives.

p. 134 "Mother would start…": Authors' interview with William Ford.

p. 134 "Who is this man… ?": For Clara's reaction, see Sorensen, pp. 270ff.

p. 135 "perhaps the greatest disappointment…": For an account of signing of the UAW agreement, see Sorensen, pp. 268ff.

p. 136 "What year is this?": Authors' interviews with Harley Copp, Oct. 28, 29, Dec. 17, 1984; Jan. 22, Feb. 7, 1985.

p. 137 "Nice girls don't work.": Authors' interview with Josephine Ford.

p. 137 Dodie writes lipstick sayings: Authors' interview with Eddie Stroh, Jan. 23, 1986.

p. 137 the pro gave him a wooden hoop: Authors' interview with William Ford.

p. 137 he could have had a national ranking: Authors' interview with Frank Donovan, May 14, 1985.

p. 137 "It was a strange mishap…": EBF to Edward Hall, 4/25/40, Accession 6, Ford Archives.

p. 138 Edsel didn't flinch: George Van Santvoord to EBF, 2/11/41/ Accession 6, Ford Archives.

p. 138 "I do not feel…": EBF to Van Santvoord, 11/22/39, Accession 6, Ford Archives.

p. 138   celebrated New York "golden clan": For McDonnell-Murray backgrounds, see John Corry, *The Golden Clan* (Boston, 1977).

p. 138   "What do you see in him?...": Authors' interview with Charlotte McDonnell Harris, Sept. 23, 1985.

p. 139   "He liked Anne's looks...": Ibid.

p. 139   "I was flunking engineering...": Herndon, p. 60.

p. 139   "Tell him to go fuck himself.": Authors' interview with Carleton Higbie, July 1, 1984, and Aug. 12, 1985.

p. 139   "I just know...": Authors' interview with Charlotte McDonnell Harris.

p. 139   "Dear Callie and Grandad...": HF2 to CBF and HF, n.d., Accession 1, Ford Archives.

p. 140   "Again I want to thank you...": James McDonnell to EBF, 8/2/40, Accession 6, Ford Archives.

p. 140   returned via Canadian Pacific: EBF to James McDonnell, 8/8/40, Accession 6, Ford Archives.

p. 140   "in recognition...": Cited in Nevins, III, p. 184.

p. 140   Cribbed term paper: See Herndon, p. 43.

p. 141   Incident of champagne: Authors' interview with Travers Smith.

p. 141   Ford brothers work under black foreman: Reminiscences of Lawrence Sheldrick.

p. 141   "They came tearing out...": Ibid.

p. 142   "Edsel has given me your message...": Sorensen, p. 315.

p. 143   "The Ford Motor Company had emerged...": For statistics see *Fortune*, October 1945.

p. 143   "They don't dare have a war...": Nevins, III, p. 168.

p. 143   Ford sympathetic toward Germany: Bennett, p. 121.

p. 143   Ford and Gerald L. K. Smith: See Harry Bennett FBI file.

p. 144   "Bill, Father just won't do it.": Richards, p. 203.

p. 144   "I won't make any of those Rolls-Royce engines...": Sorensen, pp. 273ff.

p. 145   "We're going to grow soybeans...": Reminiscences of Charles Sorensen.

p. 145   "The first thing I want to tell...": Reminiscences of Al Esper.

p. 145   "The Bomber Project...": EBF to Robert Lovett, 1/14/42, Accession 6, Ford Archives.

p. 146   Lovett reply: Lovett to EBF, 1/22/42, Accession 6, Ford Archives.

p. 146   "manpower stabilization plan": EBF to Lovett, 11/30/42, Accession 6, Ford Archives.

p. 146   "It has been determined...": Lovett to EBF, 12/14/42, ibid. Manpower was one issue; womanpower was another. The hiring of large numbers of women at Willow Run caused problems. Ford Sociological Dept. worker A. B. Ablewhite later recalled: "The big problem was that you suddenly had a great group of women, the largest group of whom had never worked in a factory. Suddenly they were making considerable money.... There was of necessity a great deal of 'sharing the ride.' I think that the combination of men being exposed to women working very intimately and then vice versa caused [our] 'explosions.' As an illustration, a man would come and say his wife had insisted on going to work. He hadn't wanted her to work, but she wanted to.... He began to nose around and found out maybe she was getting too intimate with a foreman in the shop or a man riding back and forth to the shop. He'd come in raving, demanding that we fire the woman." (Reminiscences.)

p. 146 FDR visit to Willow Run: Reminiscences of Logan Miller.

p. 146 "Harry, don't send any more men...": Bennett, p. 150.

p. 147 "No one will recognize me.": Burlingame, *Henry Ford*, p. 82.

p. 147 "Nobody invited Mr. Bennett!": Reminiscences of Norman Benson.

p. 147 "You couldn't get a message...": Reminiscences of Lawrence Sheldrick.

p. 148 "Logan, don't pay any attention...": Reminiscences of Logan Miller.

p. 148 "I wonder what the hell business...": Reminiscences of Ernest Liebold.

p. 148 "Stop this talk!...": Sorensen, pp. 256ff.

p. 149 Edsel spent hours on the couch: Reminiscences of A. J. Lepine.

p. 149 his commanding admiral asked to come to Dearborn: HF2 to Russell Gnau, 4/30/41, Accession 6, Ford Archives.

p. 149 "This man's navy...": HF2 to Russell Gnau, 5/5/41, Accession 6, Ford Archives.

p. 149 "I've had two days...": HF2 to Russell Gnau, 5/11/41, Accession 6, Ford Archives.

p. 150 "Benson is in the public relations office...": William T. Coleman to Harry Bennett, 11/17/42, Accession 1, Ford Archives.

p. 150 Bennett testified at Coleman's trial: *Detroit Free Press*, Sept. 11, 1943.

p. 150 Dahlinger carried the knife: See Dahlinger, p. 6.

p. 150 "I was godfather...": EBF to HF and CBF, 3/8/43, Accession 1, Ford Archives.

p. 150 "We arrived Tuesday...": EBF to HF and CBF, 3/20/43, Accession 1, Ford Archives.

p. 151 "Some of the union officials...": This telegram is in Accession 6, Ford Archives.

p. 151 "Henry had been here...": EBF to CBF, n.d., Accession 1, Ford Archives.

p. 151 "Both Anne and the baby": EBF to HF and CBF, n.d., Accession 1, Ford Archives.

p. 151 "Grandfather is responsible . . !": Sorensen, p. 321.

p. 152 Sorensen jotted five points: Sorensen, p. 320.

p. 152 Edsel had decided to quit: Reminiscences of Ernest Liebold.

p. 152 Henry smashes liquor bottles: Gelderman, p. 210.

p. 152 "I didn't even know...": Authors' interview with William Clay Ford.

p. 153 Eleanor had to be rescued: Authors' interview with confidential source, March 22, 1985.

p. 153 "Somehow I have a rather difficult time...": Eleanor Ford to CBF, n.d., Accession 1, Ford Archives.

p. 153 "I do miss him so...": Ibid.

p. 154 "Well, Harry...": Bennett, p. 165.

p. 154 "I just can't get over it...": Reminiscences of Gus Munchow.

PART II

p. 156 "totally at sea": Authors' interview with confidential source, Sept. 13, 1985.

p. 156 "He was a saint... !": Authors' interview with Harry Pierson.

p. 157 Henry took on the role of president: Charles E. Sorensen, *My Forty Years with Ford* (New York, 1956), pp. 324ff.

p. 157 "I'm going to fire everybody...": Reminiscences of Ernest Liebold.

p. 157 Henry killed the economy car: Reminiscences of Joe Galamb.

p. 158   "Joe, we've got to go back...": Ibid.

p. 158   "I never know where I'm going...": Reminiscences of Howard Simpson.

p. 158   Henry's radio programs: Reminiscences of Rosa Buhler and J. E. Thompson.

p. 159   codicil to old Henry's will: See Bob Considine, *The Fabulous Henry Ford II*, a series of articles reprinted by the Hearst Corp. (1964), p. 13.

p. 159   Henry II goes to Edsel: Interview with Henry Ford II, Accession 975, Ford Archives.

p. 159   "I rather imagine...": HF2 to Russell Gnau, n.d., Ford Archives.

p. 160   Not long before his death: Authors' interview with Robert Kanzler.

p. 160   Kanzler arranged a meeting with Knox: Interview with Ernest Kanzler, Accession 975, Ford Archives.

p. 160n   Letter from Navy Secretary Knox: Authors' interview with Henry Ford II, Jan. 28, 1986.

p. 161   "I am very pleased...": HF2 to HF, 8/1/43, Accession 1, Ford Archives.

p. 161   "My, it will be wonderful": Eleanor Ford to CBF and HF, 8/1/43, Accession 1, Ford Archives.

p. 161   Henry II took over Edsel's offices: Reminiscences of Irving Bacon.

p. 161   "It was my grandfather...": Authors' interviews with Joan S. Bugas. (The friend was John Bugas.)

p. 161   "The Bennett Thing." Authors' interview with Henry Ford II.

p. 161   state of the company: See *Look*, June 30, 1945, p. 39.

p. 162   Henry II went along with Bennett: Reminiscences of Irving Bacon.

p. 162   "What's the big idea... ?": Reminiscences of Lawrence Sheldrick.

p. 162   "Well, I guess I'll go...": Reminiscences of Ernest Liebold.

p. 162   "I don't like to leave you...": Victor Lasky, *Never Complain, Never Explain* (New York, 1981), p. 64.

p. 163   "I won't hear a word... !": Ibid., p. 63.

p. 163   "Aw, I don't care....": Harry Bennett, *We Never Called Him Henry* (New York, 1951), p. 174.

p. 163   John Davis and the movie industry: Interview with John R. Davis, Accession 975, Ford Archives.

p. 163   "Put it on this basis....": Nevins, III, p. 265.

p. 163   "I think he realized": Herndon, p. 203.

p. 164   "Edsel was far more...": Interview with John Davis, Accession 975, Ford Archives.

p. 164   Bugas' career at FBI: Authors' interviews with Robert S. Dunham, April 23 and 27, June 2, Aug. 1, 1985. (Dunham was an FBI agent with Bugas in the Detroit office.)

p. 164   Bugas family backgrounds: Authors' interviews with Pat Bugas Harris, Bugas' daughter.

p. 164   "When Charles comes out...": Harry Bennett FBI file.

p. 164   "a very valuable friend...": Ibid.

p. 164   Some of Bennett's cronies implicated: Reminiscences of Ernest Liebold.

p. 165   "The offer came...": John Bugas to J. Edgar Hoover, 12/18/43, Harry Bennett FBI file.

p. 165   "At first I didn't know...": Considine, p. 17.

p. 165   "I have an eyewitness...": Booton Herndon, *Ford* (New York, 1969), p. 178.

p. 165   "This thing killed my father": Robert Couglan, "Co-Captains in Ford's Battle for Supremacy," *Life*, Feb. 28, 1955.

p. 166 Bugas' office moved to washroom: Considine, p. 18.

p. 166 Henry insists that his chauffeur be armed: Carol Gelderman, *Henry Ford: The Wayward Capitalist* (New York, 1981), p. 375.

p. 166 "First get your grandfather...": Considine, p. 20.

p. 167 "I'll take it only...": Ibid.

p. 167 "Henry, I've got wonderful news....": Ibid., p. 21.

p. 167 "You're taking over...": Herndon, p. 67.

p. 167 "You son of a bitch!": Authors' interview with John Carlyle, who was a newspaperman friend of Bugas. There are other accounts.

p. 167 "Now can I fire somebody?": Herndon, p. 186.

p. 167 Bennett and Bugas confrontation: Reminiscences of Irving Bacon.

p. 168 "Harry, I want you to go...": Bennett, p. 174.

p. 168 "Well, I guess Harry is back...": Herndon, p. 187.

p. 169 "Don't you know...": *Time*, Feb. 4, 1946.

p. 169 "That's not the way...": Couglan, "Co-Captains," loc. cit.

p. 170 four Bennett stooges: Authors' interviews with Robert S. Dunham. (Dunham, a former FBI agent in the Detroit office, had been hired in December 1945 by Bugas and had become his right-hand man in the Ford Motor Co. Industrial Relations Dept.)

p. 170 "I am green...": "The Ford Heritage," *Fortune*, June 1944.

p. 170 "Now I want to ask you...": Gilbert Burck, "Henry Ford II," *Life*, Oct. 1, 1945.

p. 170 he had made a tour of Ford dealerships: Authors' interview with Holmes Tuttle, June 11, 1985.

p. 170 a precedent-setting contract: Nevins, III, p. 302. There had been 773 strikes at Ford during the war years, and the efficiency of Ford workers had dropped 34% according to figures released by the company. (Authors' interview with Mel Lindquist, June 25, 1985. Lindquist was a former FBI man who had been hired by Bugas in 1945 to conduct labor negotiations for Ford.)

p. 170 he was dependent on Clara: Reminiscences of Rosa Buhler.

p. 171 He commissioned Elmo Roper: Authors' interviews with Jack Newsom, June 25 and 27, 1985. (Son of Earl Newsom, Jack Newsom was a member of the firm of Newsom and Associates during its association with Ford.)

p. 171 "nobody could resurrect...": Herndon, p. 188.

p. 171 "The first thing I did...": Ibid.

p. 171 "The company is you...": Interview with Ernest Kanzler, Accession 975, Ford Archives.

p. 171 "You could play...": Authors' interview with James Newmyer, Oct. 4, 1985.

p. 172 "The public is 'boss'...": Henry Ford II, "The Challenge of Human Engineering," *New York Times*, Jan. 10, 1946. For full text see *Vital Speeches* XII, Feb. 15, 1946.

p. 172 "the American people's bulwark...": Allan Nevins, *Ford: The Times, the Man, the Company* (New York, 1954), III, p. 300.

p. 172 "Clearly, I just don't know enough...": Herndon, p. 205.

p. 173 they revolutionized air warfare: Authors' interviews with Charles Bosworth, Nov. 28, 1984, and Jan. 18, 1985. ("Before Tex, the Air Force didn't know how many planes it had, let alone how many were combat ready—*worldwide*.") Also, authors' interviews with James O. Wright, Jan. 7 and 23, 1985. ("Tex was the moving force behind Statistical Control as much as any one person can be.

There were glimmers of this type of organization in the Air Force prior to his taking it over, but he seized upon it and brought it into being.")

p. 173 "Hap" Arnold never appeared: Interview with Ben Mills, Accession 975, Ford Archives.

p. 173 "Now please don't hang up...": Beirne Lay Jr., *Someone Has to Make It Happen* (Englewood Cliffs, N.J., 1969), p. 64. Also authors' interview with Maxine Reith Andraea, Jan. 11, 1985.

p. 173 "If you went in with one or two...": David Halberstam, *The Best and the Brightest* (New York, 1972), p. 229.

p. 174 "You'd better get interested....": Herndon, p. 203.

p. 174 "I REPRESENT A GROUP...": Lay, p. 79.

p. 174 "Well, Henry...": Authors' interview with Robert S. McNamara, Sept. 17, 1985.

p. 175 Wright should research the question: Interview with James O. Wright, Accession 975, Ford Archives.

p. 175 "What would you rather be... ?": Authors' interview with Robert S. McNamara.

p. 175 "We would open the doors...": Authors' interview with Helen Mills, Dec. 13, 1984.

p. 175 workers were still paid in cash: Reminiscences of J. E. Bossardet.

p. 175 "Whiz Kids": Interview with Ernest Breech, Accession 975, Ford Archives.

p. 176 just the man he needed: It was William T. Gossett, later Ford general counsel, who made the suggestion originally. "I was going down to New York with Kanzler. We were in the diner and I said to him, 'You know, General Motors is foolish to leave Ernie Breech on the loose. He knows the GM system; he's bright as can be, and some company—Hudson, Nash, Packard—is going to make him an offer. I don't think he'll be tempted by anybody but Chrysler or Ford, but I think he'd be tempted by them.' Within forty-eight hours Henry Ford was calling Ernie Breech and asking if he could come over and see him." (Authors' interviews with Gossett, May 23 and Dec. 5, 1984; Feb. 12 and 27, April 28, July 19 and Aug. 25, 1985.)

p. 176 Breech background: See J. Mel Hickerson, *Ernie Breech: The Story of His Remarkable Career at General Motors, Ford, and TWA* (New York, 1968). Also, authors' interview with Thelma Breech, Feb. 27, 1985.

p. 176 the Sloan faction had been stalemated: Authors' interview with William Breech, son of Ernest Breech, Feb. 6, 1985.

p. 177 "In what capacity?": For the meeting between Henry and Breech, see interviews with Ernest Kanzler and Breech, Accession 975, Ford Archives.

p. 177 "about as good as a small tool shop...": Interview with Ernest Breech, Accession 975, Ford Archives.

p. 177 "I couldn't sleep...": Authors' interview with Thelma Breech.

p. 177 "My lawyer says...": Interview with Ernest Breech, Accession 975, Ford Archives.

p. 178 Davis and Bugas were miffed: Interview with John R. Davis, Accession 975, Ford Archives.

p. 178 "Tex had in mind...": Authors' interviews with Ben Mills, Oct. 17 and 29, Nov. 28, Dec. 10 and 13, 1984.

p. 178 "If you sign it...": Ibid.

p. 178 "Well, I don't know.": Hickerson, pp. 135-36.

p. 179 Breech stopped his Lincoln: Ibid., p. 130.

p. 179 Ozarks saying about a bundle of sticks: Ibid., p. 131.

p. 179 Ford hired GM executives: Authors' interviews with William T. Gossett and Gerald Lynch, Nov. 30, 1984. See also George Koether, "How Henry Ford II Saved the Empire," *Look*, June 30, 1953.

p. 180 "Look, we're rebuilding...": Authors' interview with Alan Gornick, May 30, 1985.

p. 180 "When I was leaving...": Authors' interview with Gerald J. Lynch. ("When I came to Ford, I said to an old-timer there, Scotty Rourke, who was in charge of facility management in the Rouge Division, 'How do you guys adjust to this new crowd? These fellows come in with all these academic credentials, myself included.' He said, 'Listen, I've got a college degree, but for twenty-five years I never told a goddamn soul.' I asked why. He answered, 'I would have been fired.' ")

p. 180 at thirteen he had written an essay: Authors' interview with Lewis Crusoe II, Dec. 3, 1984. Also authors' interview with James Crusoe, Nov. 14, 1984.

p. 180 "He inspired great loyalty...": Authors' interviews with Chase Morsey Jr., Nov. 27, Dec. 3 and 5, 1984; Jan. 17, 1985.

p. 180 "making the pancakes...": Interview with Lewis Crusoe, Accession 975, Ford Archives.

p. 180 "I can try it....": Ibid.

p. 180 "If you want to swim...": Nevins, III, p. 357.

p. 180 "Everything ran together...": Interview with Lewis Crusoe, Accession 975, Ford Archives.

p. 181 "What's this car... ?": Nevins, III, pp. 332ff. Also Reminiscences of V. Y. Tallberg.

p. 181 model would do for the new Mercury: Authors' interviews with James O. Wright.

p. 181 "It looked so real,": Nevins, III, p. 334.

p. 181 "George, who are these men?": Reminiscences of William Mielke.

p. 182 Clara forced him to sit: Reminiscences of Rosa Buhler.

p. 182 "My gracious...": Ibid.

p. 182 Dahlinger drives him around: Reminiscences of Irving Bacon.

p. 182 "Boy, you fellows...": Reminiscences of Floyd Apple.

p. 182 "Henry, *please* speak to me.": Reminiscences of Rosa Buhler. According to Henry Ford II, the first person Clara called after Henry's death was Evangeline Dahlinger.

p. 185 "We talked about everything...": Authors' interview with Josephine Ford, March 3, 1986.

p. 185 she shut one room after another: Reminiscences of Floyd Apple.

p. 185 "You know I can't eat.": Reminiscences of Rosa Buhler.

p. 186 search team headed by Robert Bahmer: Sidney Olson, "The Ford Archives," a publication of Greenfield Village, 1953.

p. 186 "You know, a lot of my grandfather's stuff...": Reminiscences of Floyd Apple.

p. 186 Ford heirs could come with their families: Reminiscences of Rosa Buhler.

p. 187 Benson marriage's rocky start: Authors' interviews with Rosine Supple, Sept. 25, 1985; Ed Stroh, Jan. 23, 1986; Travers Smith, Nov. 12, 1985.

p. 187 "A week from today...": Edie Ford to HF and CBF, 6/17/43, Accession 1, Ford Archives.

p. 187 Benson a little surprised: Interview with Benson Ford, Accession 975, Ford Archives.

p. 187 square-toed army-issue shoes: Authors' interview with Helen Mills.

p. 187 "I got to get out": Authors' interview with Ed Stroh.

p. 187 Benson silent at meetings: Authors' interview with Gerald J. Lynch.

p. 187 "This appointment...": *New York Times*, Jan. 31, 1948.

p. 188 "I'm going to have to learn...": Authors' interviews with Carlton Higbie.

p. 188 He had never seen the tension: Authors' interview with William Clay Ford.

p. 188 "Bill had to cope...": Authors' interview with Josephine Ford.

p. 188 "He's so good-looking.": Authors' interview with Martha Ford, Oct. 10, 1985.

p. 188 "Without anyone knowing...": Robert E. Charm, "William Clay Ford: In the Lion's Den," *Monthly Detroit*, December 1984.

p. 189 Bill and Heftler: Authors' interview with William Clay Ford.

p. 189 "He was an excellent player...": Authors' interview with William Talbert, Nov. 8, 1984.

p. 189 "That's all there was...": Authors' interview with William Clay Ford.

p. 189 "In order to become acquainted...": *Detroit News*, Feb. 13, 1949.

p. 189 "No, you can't win...": Authors' interview with Mel Lindquist.

p. 190 Reuther an unprincipled demagogue: Authors' interview with William Clay Ford.

p. 190 "She told me that Henry...": Ibid.

p. 190 He tried to buy Volkswagen: Nevins, III, p. 392.

p. 190 "She started out being...": Authors' interview with confidential source, July 1 and 15, 1985.

p. 191 "This company is fun!": Authors' interview with E. R. Breech Jr., Feb. 4, 1985.

p. 191 profits were rising: Nevins, III, p. 341.

p. 191 "Well, I'm going to have him five days...": Authors' interviews with Robert S. Dunham.

p. 192 Whiz Kids to be broken up: Interview with Ernest Breech, Accession 975, Ford Archives. Also, "Executive Blue Letter," Sept. 19 and 26, 1946, AR-74-19368:1-4, Ford Industrial Archives.

p. 192 Most of the Whiz Kids bowed: Authors' interviews with Ben Mills.

p. 192 Crusoe and Thornton conversations: Authors' interviews with James O. Wright.

p. 192 Thornton warred with Breech: Authors' interviews with William T. Gossett, Charles Bosworth and Gerald J. Lynch. Also authors' interview with Lowell Kreig, November 1984.

p. 192 Thornton had to pass Breech: Lay, *Someone Has to Make It Happen*, p. 89.

p. 192 "Crusoe should have been smarter...": Authors' interviews with Ben Mills.

p. 192 "I've been here awhile...": Authors' interviews with William T. Gossett.

p. 193 Ernie Breech called me...": Authors' interviews with Robert S. Dunham. (Dunham was present at the party.)

p. 193 "This car is a piece of junk....": Authors' interviews with William T. Gossett.

p. 193 Creation of Ford Division: Authors' interviews with William T. Gossett, Lowell Kreig, Ben Mills, James O. Wright, Chase Morsey.

p. 194 "Well, Lewis...": Interview with Lewis Crusoe, Accession 975, Ford Archives.

p. 194 "mink test": Authors' interviews with Eugene Bordinat, May 22, 1984.

p. 194 Breech took down license numbers: Authors' interview with Robert Kanzler.

p. 194 "guard the independent thinking...": Nevins, III, p. 350.

p. 194   Crusoe was absent: Authors' interviews with James O. Wright. (Wright was assistant general manager of the Ford Division under Crusoe.)

p. 194   "Gee, looks like a guppy's anus...": Authors' interviews with John Najjar.

p. 195   "George, which model do you like?": Authors' interviews with Chalmers Goyert, Nov. 12, 1984.

p. 195   "This is a nickel-and-dime business....": Authors' interviews with Chase Morsey and Eugene Bordinat.

p. 195   Jack Reith: Authors' interviews with Maxine Reith Andraea, Chase Morsey and Ben Mills, supra; authors' interview with Robert J. Eggert.

p. 195   While at college: Authors' interview with Robert Throckmorton, Jan. 14, 1985.

p. 195   "Well, boys, we're going to start...": Authors' interview with Lowell Kreig.

p. 196   "You do it, Chase...": Authors' interview with Emmet Judge, Feb. 26, 1985.

p. 196   Breech and Crusoe: Authors' interviews with James O. Wright. ("Breech saw that the division was working. But Crusoe was very strong-minded, very independent in his actions, and occasionally I got the feeling that Breech felt the Ford Division was running off by itself. I even talked to Crusoe about that. I even suggested he go over and have lunch with the boys in the central office. But to no avail.")

p. 196   Breech had watched Henry tilt: Authors' interviews with William T. Gossett and Gerald J. Lynch.

p. 196   "To be a good product man...": Authors' interviews with Eugene Bordinat, May 22 and 23, Nov. 10 and 21, Dec. 6, 1984, and Nov. 21, 1985.

p. 196   Morsey launched a protest: Authors' interviews with Chase Morsey.

p. 197   Crusoe approached Finance: Authors' interviews with Chase Morsey and James O. Wright; see also David Halberstam, *The Reckoning* (New York, 1986), pp. 236ff.

p. 197   "We are going to have to live in sin...": Nevins, III, p. 351.

p. 197   "That's it!...": Authors' interviews with Chase Morsey.

p. 197   Ford captured 17.6 percent: Nevins, III, p. 352.

p. 197   "How much does that son of a bitch weigh?": Authors' interviews with William T. Gossett.

p. 198   "Their job was getting pictures....": Authors' interviews with Chase Morsey.

p. 198   McNamara tried to kill it: Ibid.

p. 198   fiftieth-anniversary celebration: Nevins, III, pp. 371-74.

p. 199   "Oh, no, Mother wouldn't like this.": Authors' interviews with Win Sears and David Crippen.

p. 199   "I went to the UN....": Authors' interview with Henry Ford II.

p. 199   "What do you think *I* was doing... ?": Authors' interviews with William T. Gossett.

p. 200   He opened a personal office: Authors' interview with Gerald J. Lynch. Lynch reported directly to Henry.

p. 200   "All the Fords, even Dodie...": Authors' interview with Lowell Kreig.

p. 200   "You want me to be frank?": Authors' interview with Gerald J. Lynch.

p. 201   an almost pathological need: Authors' interviews with Harley Copp.

p. 201   "That one...": Authors' interviews with Chalmers Goyert, supra.

p. 201   Reith was likely to be banging on drums: Authors' interview with Robert S. Dunham, supra.

p. 201   Crusoe had called Maxine: Authors' interview with Maxine Reith Andraea.

p. 201   "shameless brown-nosing": Authors' interviews with Ben Mills.

p. 201 "If I could have only one man...": Authors' interview with Emmet Judge, supra.

p. 202 Breech and Ford's troubled French subsidiary: Authors' interviews with William T. Gossett.

p. 202 Breech phone call to Crusoe: Authors' interviews with Ben Mills.

p. 203 "We're just growing customers...": Authors' interviews with Chase Morsey.

p. 203 Davis Committee: Nevins, III, pp. 376ff. Authors' interviews with Emmet Judge and Harley Copp.

p. 204 "Really, how important is this?...": Authors' interviews with Emmet Judge and Lowell Kreig.

p. 204 Carlton Higbie dropped out: Authors' interviews with Carlton Higbie.

p. 204 "You're Benson Ford...": Authors' interview with Bill Stroppe, Jan. 19, 1985.

p. 204 "Ben really worked hard at it....": Authors' interview with William Clay Ford.

p. 205 Bill had been "treading water": Authors' interview with William Clay Ford.

p. 205 But as one of the stylists said: Ed Martin, unpublished article, "Birth of the Continental," Sept. 3, 1951. Copy provided to the authors by John Najjar.

p. 205 "You know, we keep getting letters...": Authors' interview with William Clay Ford.

p. 206 "Bill Ford came to this task...": Authors' interview with John Reinhardt, June 19, 1984.

p. 206 A large and friendly man: Richard Austin Smith, "The Solid Gold Continental," *Fortune*, December 1955.

p. 206 Sometimes he would come into the studio: Authors' interview with John Reinhardt.

p. 206 "I wouldn't give you a dime...": Smith, "The Solid Gold Continental," loc. cit. Authors' interview with William Clay Ford.

p. 206 Bill wrote a letter: Copy of letter, dated Jan. 22, 1953, supplied to authors by William Wallace, administrative assistant to William Ford, along with other documents herein referred to as the Wallace Papers.

p. 207 Breech tried to pull back: Authors' interviews with Lowell Kreig, Harley Copp, John Reinhardt and William Clay Ford, supra. Authors' correspondence with William Clay Ford.

p. 256 Bill's personal style: Authors' interviews with George Haviland, May 22 and Nov. 10, 1984.

p. 256 Davis had to cool his heels: Authors' interviews with Harley Copp.

p. 256 Bill suspected that design elements had been "stolen": Authors' private correspondence with William Clay Ford. Authors' interview with Tom Case, Jan. 14, 1985. (Case was the product planner for the Thunderbird.)

p. 207 "If you see the hood ornament...": Authors' interview with William Clay Ford.

p. 207 "What was that creep doing here?": Authors' interviews with Harley Copp.

p. 208 "She was especially pleased...": Authors' interview with William Clay Ford.

p. 208 Negotiating a public stock offering: Authors' interviews with Alan Gornick and William T. Gossett. See also Nevins, III, p. 423.

p. 209 "If it ain't broke, don't fix it.": Authors' interview with William Clay Ford.

p. 209 "Well, all right, dammit...": Ibid.

p. 209 "Listen, forty percent is better...": Ibid.; authors' interviews with Eugene Bordinat.

p. 209 "If you don't accept...": Authors' interview with William Clay Ford.

p. 210 "We believed we could catch up with GM...": Authors' interviews with William T. Gossett.

p. 210 "I never really visualized...": Authors' interview with Maxine Reith Andraea.

p. 210 "Lewie was sort of running wild....": Authors' interviews with William T. Gossett.

p. 210 Reith was the best man Ford had: Authors' interview with Emmet Judge.

p. 211 "Reith asked me about our plan...": Authors' interviews with Paul F. Lorenz, Feb. 26, 1985, and April 4, 1986.

p. 211 "Jack chose Mercury...": Authors' interviews with Eugene Bordinat.

p. 211 Reith wanted to scrap the Mercury: Authors' interview with Emmet Judge.

p. 211 "Man, you're really smoking opium...": Authors' interviews with Harley Copp.

p. 212 "This is what we've been waiting for....": Authors' interviews with William T. Gossett.

p. 212 "We're going to do it....": Authors' interview with Emmet Judge.

p. 212 a newly created title: Henry Ford II Blue Letter, Jan. 27, 1955, AR-74-19368-1, Ford Industrial Archives.

p. 212 "You can't break into a market...": Authors' interview with Robert S. McNamara.

p. 213 "He was so excited...": Authors' interviews with William T. Gossett.

p. 213 "This could be a great tragedy...": Mel Hickerson, *Ernie Breech*, op cit.

p. 213 "He's out on the lake...": Authors' interviews with Harley Copp.

p. 213 "He thought he was the natural...": Authors' interview with Lowell Kreig.

p. 213 Benson didn't count: Interview with Benson Ford, Accession 975, Ford Archives; authors' interview with William Clay Ford.

p. 213 "It was a fancy-title nonjob...": Authors' interview with William Clay Ford.

p. 214 "This was the worst thing...": Authors' interview with Ed Stroh.

p. 214 "I could fire you...": Authors' interview with Emmet Judge.

p. 214 "Okay, but remember...": Ibid.

p. 214 "Bob didn't want to be part of the E-Car....": Authors' interviews with Chalmers Goyert.

p. 214 A man swept with a telescope: John Brooks, *The Fate of the Edsel and Other Business Ventures* (New York, 1963), p. 249.

p. 215 "The smart car...": Ibid., p. 32.

p. 215 "Let's take another look...": Ibid., p. 35.

p. 215 "Over my dead body.": Gayle Warnock, *The Edsel Affair* (Prowest Publications; Paradise Valley, Arizona, 1980), p. 76.

p. 215 "Henry was so pumped up...": Authors' interview with confidential source, July 7, 1985.

p. 216 the times had soured: After a near-record first quarter, net earnings in the auto industry dropped to less than half the levels of the previous year. (*New York Times*, Oct. 24, 1956.)

p. 216 "Sorry to be late to your funeral.": George Koether, "Bill Ford Builds the Continental," *Look*, Nov. 16, 1954.

p. 216 "Ford's new Continental is selling...": *Business Week*, Nov. 26, 1955.

p. 216 "You know, Harley...": Authors' interviews with Harley Copp.

p. 216 Mills pushed the break-even point farther off: Authors' interviews with William Wallace, John Reinhardt and Harley Copp.

p. 217 "Historically four-door sedans have dominated...": Wallace Papers.

p. 217   "This was a mortal blow...": Authors' interview with William Clay Ford.

p. 217   "I'm not going to go...": Authors' correspondence with Douglas McClure and William Clay Ford. Cf. Ben Mills: "The demise of the Continental Division was related more to the organization of the company which was undertaken under Lew Crusoe and Jack Reith. They broke the car divisions up and made a Lincoln, a Mercury and an Edsel Division. With these divisions we could hardly have a Continental Division, and the Continental, which was never meant to be a volume product, wouldn't have supported the division structure anyway." (Authors' interview.)

p. 217   "They're moving the goalposts...": Authors' correspondence with William Clay Ford; authors' interview with Douglas McClure, June 28 and Nov. 15, 1984.

p. 217   "If you'd just quit listening to goddamn Crusoe...": Authors' interview with William Clay Ford.

p. 218   "Do you see any point... ?": Authors' interviews with William Clay and Martha Ford.

p. 218   "If it were me...": Authors' interviews with Harley Copp.

p. 218   Everyone supported Crusoe: Authors' interviews with William T. Gossett and William Clay Ford.

p. 219   "I hope you heard my no...": Ibid.

p. 219   "Because he doesn't want us to...": Authors' interview with William Clay Ford.

p. 219   "Henry was walking this tightrope...": Authors' interview with confidential source, July 7, 1985.

p. 220   McNamara's moves: Authors' interviews with Paul F. Lorenz, James O. Wright, Harley Copp, Chase Morsey and Tom Case.

p. 220   "I don't want anything to prevent us...": Authors' interview with Tom Case.

p. 220   "In the last few months...": Ben Mills Blue Letter dated Oct. 25, 1956, AR-66-31:7, Ford Industrial Archives.

p. 221   "What's this, Lewie?": Authors' interviews with Harley Copp.

p. 221   "That son of a bitch Ernie Breech...": Authors' interview with Lowell Kreig.

p. 221   Benson realized: Interview with Benson Ford, Accession 975, Ford Archives.

p. 221   He insisted on making all decisions: Authors' interviews with Ben Mills.

p. 221   Mary Creecy noticed: Authors' interview with Mary Creecy.

p. 222   "McNamara *seemed* to be talking...": Authors' interview with Harley Copp.

p. 222   Breech weighed in: Blue letter dated Feb. 5, 1957, AR-65-71:38, Ford Industrial Archives.

p. 222   Reith memo: AR-66-31:7, Ford Industrial Archives.

p. 222   "On and off...": *Consumer Reports*, March 1957.

p. 222   Breech accused Reith of deception: Authors' interviews with Eugene Bordinat.

p. 222   Reith June 4 letter: AR-66-31:7, Ford Industrial Archives.

p. 222   Ben Mills and Reith's IQ: Authors' interviews with Harley Copp.

p. 222   "McNamara wanted to make Reith Say 'yessir'...": Authors' interviews with William T. Gossett.

p. 222   Henry backed McNamara: Ibid.

p. 222   "It's just a wrist-slapping....": Authors' interview with Maxine Reith Andraea.

p. 222   Aug. 30, 1957 memo: Ford Industrial Archives.

p. 223   McNamara insisted: Authors' interview with Paul F. Lorenz. Cf. Gayle Warnock, *The Edsel Affair*, pp. 200, 242-43.

p. 223 "You can't possibly think...": Warnock, p. 91.

p. 223 "With just two months to go...": Authors' interviews with Paul F. Lorenz.

p. 223 "I've got plans...": Warnock, p. 207.

p. 223 One Ford public-relations executive: Brooks, p. 49.

p. 224 "a sinister personality change": Ibid., p. 54.

p. 224 "The amount of shake present...": *Consumer Reports*, January 1958.

p. 224 "The Edsel Show": Warnock, p. 202.

p. 224 McNamara memo: AR-65-71:38, Ford Industrial Archives. The memo was dated Dec. 4, 1957. Cf. also McNamara Executive Communication to Members of the Executive Committee, April 15, 1958, ibid.

p. 225 "They could have made it...": Authors' interviews with Eugene Bordinat.

p. 225 "You're always sensitive...": Authors' interview with William Clay Ford.

p. 225 Reith never recovered: Authors' interview with Robert Throckmorton.

p. 225 "For insurance purposes...": Authors' interview with Helen Mills. Also, authors' interviews with Robert S. Dunham, who investigated the incident for Ford.

p. 225 "When the Edsel went down...": Authors' interview with Robert Throckmorton.

p. 226 "just rotting away": Authors' interview with Bill Stroppe.

p. 226 "He wouldn't make the necessary...": Authors' interviews with William T. Gossett.

p. 226 "I remember the exact moment...": Authors' interview with William Clay Ford.

p. 226 he was transfixed by it: Authors' interviews with Robert S. Dunham.

p. 227 "Suddenly there were 'grades'...": Authors' interview with Alan Gornick.

p. 227 Henry held secret meetings with McNamara: Authors' interviews with Robert S. Dunham.

p. 227 "Mr. Ford recognized...": AR-66-12:9, Ford Industrial Archives.

p. 228 "Well, Mr. Ford...": Authors' interview with Robert Eggert, Dec. 5, 1985.

p. 228 "I am the captain of the ship...": Authors' interviews with Alan Gornick and William T. Gossett.

p. 228 "Bob, a lot of things are changing...": Authors' interviews with Robert S. Dunham.

p. 228 "My name is on the building": Authors' interview with Gerald J. Lynch.

p. 228 "I have stopped recommending our cars...": Authors' interviews with Harley Copp.

p. 229 "Mr. Ford, I'd like to propose...": Ibid.

p. 229 "It's all for you....": Henry Ehrlich, "Charlotte, the Latest Model Ford," *Look*, Aug. 12, 1969.

p. 230 "We didn't see much of my father....": Ibid.

p. 230 Edsel's II's unhappiness: Authors' interview with William Chapin, Oct. 11, 1985.

p. 230 Tension between Anne and Edie: Authors' interviews with Rosine Moore Supple, Sept. 25, 1985, and Gretie Bodell Wheeler, Jan. 1, 1986. p. 284 Anne had become a social arbiter: Authors' interviews with Eleanor Breitmeyer, Aug. 8, 1985, and confidential source, July 1 and Nov. 13, 1984.

p. 231 "It was a good twelve years of Mass....": Ehrlich, "Charlotte," loc. cit.

p. 231 "I am glad...": Margaret Sterne, *The Passionate Eye: The Life of William Valentiner* (Detroit, 1978), p. 369.

p. 231 "I talked it over with Henry...": Authors' interview with Frank Donovan, Sept. 8, 1985.

p. 231 "She had already had children...": Ibid.

p. 231 "Go up and get her out of bed...": Authors' interview with Charles Cudlipp, Sept. 24, 1985.

p. 232 "We were at a restaurant...": Authors' interview with Charlotte "Kitzie" Eaton, Aug. 11, 1985.

p. 232 "Henry! I've got your sock!": Authors' interview with Helen Bogle, Oct. 9, 1985.

p. 232 "He couldn't really show his money...": Authors' interview with Charles Cudlipp, supra.

p. 232 "Here I am...": Authors' interview with Count Rudi Crespi, April 7, 1984.

p. 232 "Henry was entering his forties....": Authors' interview with Taki Theodoracopolous, April 9, 1984.

p. 233 "I'm going to visit Paul Valery.": Ibid.

p. 233 It was a midlife crisis: Authors' interviews with Frank Donovan and confidential source, July 7, 1985.

p. 233 "Where's Arjay?": Authors' interview with Gerald J. Lynch.

p. 233 "This is awful....": Authors' interview with Lowell Kreig.

p. 234 "Henry, now you've come of age....": Authors' interview with Holmes Tuttle, supra.

p. 234 "I've got... good news, Thelma.": Authors' interview with Thelma Breech.

p. 234 McNamara made his own reservations: Authors' interviews with Chalmers Goyert.

p. 234 "No, I'm all right, darling....": Ibid.

p. 234 "It was conceived...": Authors' interviews with Eugene Bordinat.

p. 234 "Bob had a deep desire...": Authors' interviews with Harley Copp.

p. 235 "Okay, then I want him...": Ibid.

p. 235 "he came back horrified...": Authors' interview with Jacques Passino, May 25, 1984.

p. 235 For McNamara it was simple: Authors' interview with Robert S. McNamara.

p. 235 "What they sell in a year...": Warnock, p. 36.

p. 236 "Because Bob insists...": Authors' interviews with Harley Copp.

p. 236 "I'm going to prove to you...": Authors' interview with Tom Case.

p. 236 "He wears granny glasses": Herndon, p. 86.

p. 236 Henry had influential figures try to dissuade him: Authors' interview with James Newmyer. (Newmyer was one of them.)

p. 237 "This may be one of the worst days of my life....": Authors' interview with Charles Cudlipp.

p. 238 McNamara told a colleague: Authors' interviews with Robert S. Dunham.

p. 239 Henry moved his name card: Authors' interview with Cristina Ford, May 5, 1985.

p. 239 Crespi's family asked him to stop seeing her: Authors' interview with Count Rudi Crespi.

p. 239 "I'm going to marry you.": Authors' interview with Cristina Ford.

p. 240 "I'm married to one....": Ibid.

p. 240 "A strike of lightning....": Ibid.

p. 240 "You're emotionally involved": Authors' interview with John Carlisle, Aug. 9, 1985.

p. 240 "John's marriage is in trouble...": Authors' interview with Cristina Ford.

p. 241 "What the hell's going on here?": Authors' interviews with Eugene Bordinat.

p. 241 "I feel like I'm floating...": Authors' interview with Cristina Ford.

p. 241 "Don't give me this shit...": Ibid.

p. 242 "The Second Party of the Century": Authors' interview with Henry Hay, July 14, 1985.

p. 242 "Thank you, Mr. Ford...": Authors' interview with Kitzie Eaton.

p. 242 His wife heard him talking to his lover: Authors' interview with Robert Kanzler.

p. 243 "Henry always come to me...": Authors' interview with Cristina Ford.

p. 243 She bought secondhand dresses: Ibid.

p. 243 He gave her $10,000: Ibid.

p. 243 "Anne left the house cold...": Authors' interview with Robert Kanzler.

p. 243 "Anne was in New York...": Authors' interview with Helen Bogle.

p. 243 Henry said the event had a profound impact on him: Authors' interview with Bonnie Swearingen, June 18, 1985.

p. 244 Revson affair: Authors' interview with Cristina Ford. See also Andrew Tobias, *Fire and Ice: The Story of Charles Revson* (New York, 1976).

p. 244 "Do you really like him?": Authors' interview with Cristina Ford.

p. 245 "I've got the company....": Ibid.

p. 245 "McNamara gave up a bundle of stock options": Considine, *The Fabulous Henry Ford II*, p. 42.

p. 245 "In today's auto sales race": *Business Week*, March 16, 1963.

p. 246 Henry meets Donner: Authors' interview with Henry Ford II.

p. 246 Bugas felt he deserved the top spot: Authors' interviews with Pat Bugas Harris, Feb. 26 and 27 and April 24, 1985, and Ray Stuart, Feb. 27, 1985.

p. 246 "Dykstra couldn't talk....": Authors' interviews with William T. Gossett.

p. 246 Henry tried to recruit "Bunkie" Knudsen: Authors' interview with Semon E. ("Bunkie") Knudsen, June 25, 1984.

p. 247 "This is a camel with three humps...": John S. Bugas memoir, citation, tape copy supplied by Joan Bugas, transcribed by authors.

p. 247 "Lewie Crusoe planted the seed corn...": Authors' interviews with Harley Copp.

p. 247 Iacocca: Lee Iacocca, *Iacocca* (New York, 1984), and David Abodaher, *Iacocca* (New York, 1982). Authors' interviews with David Abodaher, Jacques Passino and Robert S. Dunham.

p. 247 "Mr. Ford called me over...": Herndon, p. 252.

p. 248 "You whore!...": Kirk Cheyfitz and J. Patrick Wright, "The Rise and Fall and Rise of Lee Iacocca," *Monthly Detroit*, February 1979.

p. 248 "With McNamara...": Authors' interview with John Najjar. (Najjar was a Ford stylist.)

p. 248 "You either get into the black...": *Newsweek*, April 20, 1986.

p. 249 One of his first moves: Authors' interview with Jacques Passino. See also Brock Yates, *The Decline and Fall of the American Automobile Industry* (New York, 1983), p. 133.

p. 249 "The Cardinal is a loser....": Iacocca, p. 62.

p. 249 "Lee was the first guy...": Authors' interview with Donald Frey, Nov. 5, 1985.

p. 249 "When Lee had to make an appearance...": Authors' interview with Tom Case.

p. 250 "I remember sitting there and thinking...": Gary Witzenberg, *The Mustang* (Princeton Publishing Company: Princeton, N.J., 1979), p 11.

p. 250 "a poor man's Thunderbird...": *Newsweek*, April 18, 1964; Iacocca, p. 70.

p. 250 "I've got your sporty car.": Authors' interview with Donald Frey.

p. 250 A call came from Charlie Moore: Iacocca, p. 69.

p. 251 "Enough of that shit, Lee....": Authors' interview with Donald Frey.

p. 251 Iacocca got Bob Hefty to invite Jones: Authors' interviews with James C. Jones, June 29, 1984, and Robert Hefty.

p. 251 Jaroff was given a similar promise: Donald MacDonald, *Detroit 1985*, (New York, 1980), p. 186.

p. 251 "the hottest young man...": *Time*, April 17, 1964.

p. 251 "I see this as the start...": Ibid.

p. 252 the Santa Maria: *Newsweek*, April 22, 1963.

p. 252 a German U-boat: Authors' interview with Taki Theodoracopolous.

p. 252 "Well, Mrs. Ford, I see...": Authors' interview with Frank Donovan.

p. 252 "I should have done this earlier": Ibid.

p. 253 she sat chatting with Bugas' wife: Authors' interviews with Pat Bugas Harris.

p. 253 he had asked Bugas to do a background investigation: Authors' interview with Ray Stuart. (A former FBI man, Stuart was Bugas' secretary at Ford until his retirement in 1968.)

p. 253 "It was a strange time...": Authors' interview with a confidential source, July 21, 1985.

p. 253 "What else is there for a girl... ?": Authors' interview with Josephine Ford.

p. 253 Benson and Dealer Policy Board: Authors' interviews with Earl Essye, Feb. 12, 1985, and Walter Adams, Feb. 12, 1985.

p. 254 "They loved him....": Authors' interview with Ed Stroh.

p. 254 "I don't want to make waves....": Ibid.

p. 254 "I'll do it my way.": Authors' interview with Travers Smith.

p. 254 "Aw, tell those guys to go screw themselves.": Authors' interview with Ed Stroh.

p. 254 Ford officials would be called to rescue him: Authors' interviews with Eugene Bordinat and Robert S. Dunham.

p. 254 "She had this pixie cut": Authors' interview with Lynn Maxwell.

p. 255 "Someday you're going to...": Kirk Cheyfitz and Hillel Levin, "Crashing in the Fast Lane," *Metropolitan Detroit*, December 1984 and January 1985.

p. 255 He would always remember the way the servants: Ibid.

p. 255 "Benson could take the punches....": Authors' interview with Ed Stroh.

p. 255 "The boat was the one place...": Ibid.

p. 256 "Where can you always park... ?": Authors' interview with Kirk Cheyfitz.

p. 256 "What I needed most of all...": Authors' interview with William Clay Ford.

p. 256 "I always wanted something...": Authors' interview with George Puscas, Aug. 9, 1985.

p. 256 "I couldn't do a car again....": Authors' interview with Martha Ford.

p. 256 "He drank hot gin...": Authors' interviews with Bill Curran.

p. 257 the company got calls from the police: Authors' interviews with Robert S. Dunham. (Dunham was in charge of executive personnel at Ford.)

p. 257 Henry called Ford executives to take Bill's keys: Authors' interviews with Eugene Bordinat.

p. 257 "The trouble is...": Authors' interviews with Harley Copp.

p. 257 "I got into a situation...": Authors' interviews with Joan Bugas, March 15, April 2 and Aug. 25, 1985.

p. 257 Bugas called J. Edgar Hoover: FBI memo, February 1949, from D. M. Ladd to the Director, in Bennett FBI file, Ford Archives.

p. 257 "I've been meaning to talk to you...": John S. Bugas memoir, supra.

p. 258 Bugas didn't have the right background: Authors' interviews with William T. Gossett.

p. 258 "The Director was telling me...": John Z. De Lorean with Ted Schwartz, *De Lorean* (Grand Rapids, 1985), p. 84.

p. 258 "It was the biggest mistake in my life.": Authors' interview with John Carlisle, supra.

p. 258 During dinner at Les Ambassadeurs: Conversation from John S. Bugas memoir, supra.

p. 259 Miller and Lundy made the case: Ibid.; authors' interview with Arjay Miller, April 1986.

p. 259 "It must come as a surprise...": Bugas memoir, supra.

p. 259 "It's a long way...": Authors' interview with James Newmyer.

p. 260 "...I've never been anyone else.": Authors' interviews with George Haviland.

p. 261 "Garcia": Authors' interview with Cristina Ford.

p. 261 "Henry, let's go.": Ibid.

p. 261 She was an immediate hit: Authors' interview with Helen Bogle, who held the first Grosse Pointe dinner party for Cristina and Henry.

p. 262 Charlotte visited Niarchos: Ehrlich, "Charlotte," loc. cit.

p. 262 "Did you notice how Stavros... ?": Authors' interview with Cristina Ford.

p. 263 "She's the funniest person alive.": Doris Lilly, *Those Fabulous Greeks* (New York, 1970), p. 287.

p. 263 "With Cristina you were just bathed in sunshine....": Authors' interview with Eleanor Breitmeyer, Aug. 8, 1985.

p. 263 "We've been screwed...": Authors' interview with Gerald J. Lynch.

p. 263 He started a Government Affairs Organization: Authors' interview with Patrick J. Hillings, Sept. 23, 1985.

p. 264 "When JFK's bunch went...": Ibid.

p. 264 One amusing moment: Authors' interview with William Clay Ford.

p. 264 Henry's endorsement of LBJ: Authors' interview with Patrick J. Hillings.

p. 264 he brought a Model T: Authors' interview with Bonnie Swearingen, supra.

p. 264 "Washington will be talking...": *Detroit Free Press*, Nov. 27, 1965.

p. 264 "She symbolizes sexiness...": *New York Times*, Dec. 31, 1965.

p. 265 Charlotte and Niarchos: Ehrlich, *Look*, Aug. 12, 1969.

p. 265 "Well,... we'd better talk to Stavros": Lilly, pp. 282ff.

p. 265 "It was Daddy who...": Ibid.

p. 266 "We'd have been much better off...": Authors' interview with Frank Donovan.

p. 267 "Well, it all worked out.": *Time,* Jan. 7, 1966.

p. 267 "This was the year of the Fords.": *New York Times*, Dec. 31, 1965.

p. 268 Details of the 1966 Washington meeting of Ford executives: Authors' interview with James Newmyer.

p. 270 "the most obstinate man...": *New York Times*, Oct. 19, 1969.

p. 270 "We can build a tank....": Ibid.

p. 270 "Henry was, as usual...": Authors' interviews with Bill Curran.

p. 270 Henry and Whitney Young: Herndon, pp. 332ff.

p. 271 "I'm going to make you the white Moses....": Ibid.

p. 272 "Equal employment opportunity requires more...": Ibid., p. 105.

p. 272 "Given the system of values...": William Serrin, "At Ford Everyone Knows Who Is the Boss," *New York Times Magazine*, Oct. 19, 1969.

p. 272 "Henry likes to sit under the fig tree...": Authors' interview with Cristina Ford.

p. 273 "Arjay would announce the end of the world...": Authors' interview with Donald Frey.

p. 274 "That's very interesting...": Authors' interviews with William T. Gossett.

p. 274 "Bunkie" Knudsen: Authors' interview with Semon E. Knudsen.

p. 274 "No, my wife has some people here...": Ibid.

p. 275 Henry summoned him back from South America: Authors' interviews with Robert S. Dunham.

p. 275 "About fifty-six years ago...": *New York Times*, Feb. 7, 1968.

p. 275 "A managerial masterstroke": *Time*, Feb. 16, 1968.

p. 275 "In one deft stroke...": *Fortune*, March 1968.

p. 339 "cruel and unconscionable": Authors' interviews with Robert S. Dunham.

p. 276 circumventing Miller: Authors' interview with Donald Frey.

p. 276 "*I* am the product man...": Authors' interview with Robert Hefty.

p. 276 she posted a friend outside a public lavatory: Ibid.

p. 276 "rub some of that Mustang ointment...": Iacocca, p. 78.

p. 276 "At that point Lee was still...": Authors' interviews with Paul F. Lorenz.

p. 276 The unveiling: Iacocca, p. 81. Also, authors' interviews with Jacques Passino and Leo Arthur Kelmenson, June 5 and Nov. 7, 1984.

p. 277 "That fucking prick!...": Authors' interviews with Robert Hefty, Robert S. Dunham and George Haviland.

p. 277 "Lee makes the decisions...": Authors' interviews with Leo-Arthur Kelmenson.

p. 277 Iacocca's own calculations: Iacocca, p. 86.

p. 277 "To bring in someone over Lee...": Authors' interview with Jacques Passino.

p. 277 "Look, you're still my boy....": Iacocca, p. 87.

p. 277 "The day Bunkie was hired...": Authors' interview with Donald Frey.

p. 278 Pinto battle: Authors' interviews with Harley Copp.

p. 278 Iacocca's guerrilla campaign: Authors' interview with Donald Frey.

p. 278 "Lee did a lot of swimming...": Authors' interviews with William T. Gossett.

p. 278 Iacocca's "red team": Authors' interviews with Paul F. Lorenz.

p. 278 "He was so much younger than I....": Authors' interview with Semon E. Knudsen.

p. 278 "Every time Bunkie screwed up...": Authors' interview with Donald Frey. Also, authors' interviews with Robert S. Dunham.

p. 278 "It was like being the meat...": Authors' interview with Donald Frey.

p. 279 "Man, you got problems...": Ibid.

p. 279 "Lee began to hold counsel...": Authors' interviews with Eugene Bordinat.

p. 279 "it got to be voting time": Authors' interviews with Chalmers Goyert.

p. 279 "Either he goes or we go.": *Business Week*, Sept. 20, 1969.

p. 279 "Bunk, I'm sorry to tell you this...": *Detroit Free Press*, Sept. 14, 1969. Also, authors' interview with Semon E. Knudsen.

p. 279 "Henry Ford once said...": Iacocca, p. 92.

p. 279 "I had no personal conflict with Knudsen.": *Detroit Free Press*, Sept. 14, 1969.

p. 280 A friend who had ordered a plaque: Authors' interviews with Bill Curran.

p. 280 "Take that away and burn it!": Authors' interview with Cristina Ford.

p. 280 "You think I'm bad?...": Ibid.

p. 281 "Without it...": Article by Henry Ford II in *Look*, April 21, 1970.

p. 281 "Before they got married...": Authors' interviews with Pat Bugas Harris.

p. 281 "I think what happened is...": Authors' interview with Helen Bogle.

p. 281 "When he was married to Anne...": Authors' interview with Kitzie Eaton.

p. 281 Cristina was forced to spend time alone: *Detroit Free Press* feature on Cristina, Dec. 6, 1966.

p. 281 Cristina ordered the flowers out: Authors' interview with Bonnie Swearingen.

p. 281 "The whole thing was kind of a disaster...": Authors' interview with Robert Kanzler.

p. 282 "I want to go alone to England...": Authors' interview with Cristina Ford.

p. 282 "The Agnellis were there...": Authors' interview with Helen Bogle.

p. 282 she took off for Mexico: *Detroit Free Press*, Dec. 19, 1970.

p. 283 "My husband is in London...": *Chicago Daily News*, Feb. 28, 1970.

p. 283 Journalists played it up as a triumph: *Detroit Free Press*, May 3, 1970.

p. 283 "While they were cloistered there...": Authors' interviews with Eugene Bordinat.

p. 283 "He was always trying...": Authors' interview with Semon E. Knudsen.

p. 284 "Greeks don't like to see you dead....": Victor Lasky, *Never Complain, Never Explain*, p. 118.

p. 284 "What will I do?": Authors' interview with Josephine Ford.

p. 285 "I'll bet she got a black sweater.": Authors' interview with Henry Hay.

p. 285 "He spends a lot of money...": Authors' interview with confidential source, July 7, 1985.

p. 285 "The adults stood around and got drunk...": Authors' interview with Kitzie Eaton.

p. 285 "She had been so witty...": Ibid.

p. 285 "Waiting for the end.": Authors' interview with confidential source, July 7, 1985.

p. 285 "I'd always thought, Oh, what the hell...": Authors' interview with William Clay Ford.

p. 286 his son Billy answering the door: Authors' interviews with William Clay ("Billy") Ford Jr., April 26 and 29 and Oct. 8, 1985.

p. 286 Bill giving back his executive bonus: Authors' interview with Charles Cudlipp.

p. 286 Bill got a janitor and "Night Train" Lane: Authors' interview with Billy Ford.

p. 286 "You've got the company....": Authors' interview with William Clay Ford.

p. 286 Martha never badgered him: Ibid.

p. 287 "Martha is a strong woman...": Authors' interview with Lynn Maxwell.

p. 287 "Whether Billy is under...": Authors' interview with Martha Ford.

p. 287 "The only way we could talk...": Authors' interview with William Clay Ford.

p. 287 "I've got no use for that group....": *New York Times*, Oct. 19, 1969.

p. 288 "Well, anybody who's against this war...": Authors' interview with William Clay Ford.

p. 288 "Who are you?": Ibid.

p. 288 "I had a wonderful time...": Ibid.

p. 288 Bill had remained her "pride and joy": Authors' interview with Josephine Ford.

p. 290 "In this business...": *Time*, Feb. 16, 1968.

p. 290 "I like it....": *New York Times*, Sept. 23, 1970.

p. 291 for the sixth consecutive year: Ford Annual Report, 1970.

p. 291 "It was a dumb, dumb...": Authors' interview with Henry Ford II, Jan. 28, 1986.

p. 291 "We make as much selling one Mark...": Iacocca, p. 84.

p. 292 bringing wines from France: Authors' interview with James Newmyer.

p. 292 "Yes,... we have done more innovative...": *New York Times*, Oct. 19, 1969.

p. 292 "There was just something...": Authors' interviews with Eugene Bordinat.

p. 292 Henry called Iacocca to his office: Iacocca, p. 92.

p. 292 "Shit, Leo, do you realize... ?": Authors' interviews with Leo-Arthur Kelmenson.

p. 293 "This is a great photo.": Iacocca, p. 100.

p. 293 Max Fisher: Authors' interview with Max Fisher, March 11, 1986. Authors' interview with Joan Bugas. *The Fishers—A Family Portrait* (privately published).

p. 293 Bugas was unable to overcome its anti-Semitism: Authors' interviews with Pat Bugas Harris.

p. 293 they became especially close after 1962: Authors' interview with Max Fisher.

p. 293 "Are you sitting down?...": Ibid.

p. 294 "You're full of shit": Ibid.

p. 294 Details of the trip to Israel: Ibid.

p. 294n "I don't care if you tear the place down.": Authors' interview with Donn Werling.

p. 295 Henry appeared with his own design: Authors' interview with J. L. Hudson Jr., May 31, 1985.

p. 295 "The logo... should be a twisted arm.": *Detroit News*, Oct. 8, 1978.

p. 295 "Henry Ford is synonymous with Detroit....": Lasky, p. 148.

p. 295 "What else can I do?": Authors' interview with Cristina Ford. Also interviews with Dr. Richmond Smith, Stanley Nelson and Carlton Higbie. (Dr. Smith wrote the report on which the hospital's request for a Ford grant was based; Stanley Nelson is administrative head of the Henry Ford Hospital; Carlton Higbie is president of its board.)

p. 296 "How can you do this?...": Authors' interview with Cristina Ford.

p. 296 "Christina, I'll try to talk...": Ibid.

p. 296 this was a "terminal" grant: *New York Times*, Oct. 28, 1973.

p. 297 "No, Mother,... Cristina did it.": Authors' interview with Cristina Ford.

p. 297 "There ought to be something for Benson.": Ibid.

p. 297 "Hurray, hurray, the first of May...": Lasky, p. 153.

p. 297 "There were a lot of business-oriented...": Authors' interview with Billy Chapin.

p. 298 "Hi, Maggie, want to see my cock?": Authors' interviews with confidential source, July 1 and 16, 1984, and Sept. 7, 1985.

p. 298 "Some people think he's a bastard....": Ibid.

p. 298 Cristina and Imelda: Authors' interviews with Taki Theodoracopolous, Bonnie Swearingen and Kathy Ford, Jan. 23, 1986. Also, authors' interviews with confidential source.

p. 299 Henry and Nixon: Authors' interview with Patrick J. Hillings.

p. 299 Imelda at the party: Lasky, p. 122.

p. 299 "His problem is...": Authors' interview with Cristina Ford.

p. 299 "When we met...": Ibid.

p. 299 "*Bambi*, come to bed": Authors' interview with Bonnie Swearingen.

p. 299 "Let's fuck!": Authors' interview with Cristina Ford.

p. 300 Kathy DuRoss: Authors' interview with Kathy Ford, Jan. 23, 1986. Also, see Edward Phelan, "The Real Kathy Ford," *Monthly Detroit*, July 1981.

p. 301 "Kathy fought and scratched through life...": Phelan, "The Real Kathy Ford," loc. cit. Also authors' interview with Walter Shelden.

p. 301 "You're just like my first wife.": Authors' interview with Kathy Ford.

p. 301 "I could kill John. ....": Authors' interview with Cristina Ford.

p. 301 He became more involved in his Wyoming ranch: Authors' interview with Ann Gardner, Feb. 27, 1985. (Ann Gardner was Bugas' secretary after his retirement in April 1968.)

p. 302 Henry and Bugas: Authors' interviews with Joan Bugas, Pat Bugas Harris and John Bugas Jr., Feb. 27, 1985.

p. 302 One day Henry called Bugas: Authors' interviews with Joan Bugas.

p. 302 Henry asked Bugas for his catalogue: Authors' interviews with Kathy Ford and Joan Bugas.

p. 302 Fisher had introduced Bugas to Joan Murphy: Authors' interviews with Joan Murphy Bugas.

p. 302 Joan and Bugas: Ibid.

p. 302 "There is going to be a friend": Ibid.

p. 303 "What the hell are you doing here?": Ibid. Authors' interview with Kathy Ford.

p. 303 "That was Henry....": Ibid.

p. 303 "Well, now Henry has two wives...": Authors' interviews with Joan Bugas.

p. 303 "It's funny you should mention this....": Authors' interview with Bonnie Swearingen.

p. 304 "Look, my life is going ahead....": Authors' interview with Kathy Ford.

p. 305 Detroit auto executives believed: Yates, p. 112.

p. 306 an ad pointing out that "bored people build bad cars": Emma Rothschild, *Paradise Lost* (New York, 1972), pp. 5ff.

p. 306 A Ford "concepts manager": Ibid., p. 19.

p. 306 Ford analysts warned: *New York Times*, Dec. 18, 1973.

p. 306 The actual drop was 75 percent: *New York Times*, March 27, 1974.

p. 307 a move Lorenz regarded as an attempt to "sidesaddle him": Authors' interview with Paul F. Lorenz.

p. 307 "There wasn't any question...": Authors' interview with Leo Arthur Kelmenson.

p. 307 "Henry Ford never had to work...": Iacocca, p. 99.

p. 308 "What the hell was Lee talking about?...": Authors' interviews with Chalmers Goyert.

p. 308 "Who *needs* another Mustang?": Authors' interviews with Eugene Bordinat.

p. 308 He bragged about having "made it": Lasky, pp. 119-20.

p. 308 De Tomaso: Authors' interviews with Eugene Bordinat and George Haviland. See also Wallace Wyss, *De Tomaso Automobiles* (Osceola, Fla., 1981).

p. 309 "Lee was real crazy for anything Italian....": Authors' interviews with Eugene Bordinat.

p. 309 "Iacocca is no dummy....": Authors' interviews with George Haviland.

p. 310 "building a monument to himself": Iacocca, p. 106.

p. 310 The 727 jet: Authors' interviews with Cristina Ford and Eugene Bordinat.

p. 311 "Iacocca makes too many speeches....": Authors' interview with Cristina Ford.

p. 311 "Lee saw it as a golden opportunity": Authors' interviews with Chalmers Goyert.

p. 311 He had respected the experience: Authors' interview with Henry Ford II.

p. 311 "Henry... usurped my power": Ibid, p. 112.

p. 312 "How can the head...": Authors' interviews with Eugene Bordinat.

p. 312 "He's under a lot of pressure....": Iacocca, p. 113.

p. 312 "I'm going to Katmandu.": Authors' interview with Kathy Ford.

p. 313 *I am his wife now*: Ibid.

p. 313 "Go home....": Ibid.

p. 313 Cristina claimed that Kathy was a friend: Authors' interview with Bonnie Swearingen.

p. 313 "I thought I could compartmentalize...": Authors' interview with Henry Ford II.

p. 314 He swore he would never see her again: Authors' interview with Cristina Ford.

p. 314 a sort of Last Supper: Authors' interviews with Joan Bugas.

p. 314 He had started seeing her again: Authors' interview with Kathy Ford.

p. 315 The "Ten Thousand Dollar Screw House": Authors' interview with Kitzie Eaton.

p. 315 "The E. Howard Hunt of Grosse Pointe": Lasky, p. 162.

p. 315 there had been whistle-blowing: Authors' interviews with Harley Copp.

p. 315 Choosing a day when Iacocca was absent: Iacocca, p. 113.

p. 316 Iacocca called Lorenz into his office: Ibid.

p. 316 Lorenz always denied: Authors' interviews with Paul F. Lorenz.

p. 316 Henry began amassing a file: Authors' interviews with Robert S. Dunham.

p. 316 "I've just learned...": Iacocca, p. 114.

p. 316 Henry's investigation was coordinated by Bugas: Authors' interviews with Robert S. Dunham and Ray Stuart.

p. 316 "Aren't you afraid...": Iacocca, p. 117.

p. 317 He had the fantasy that Bill Ford would come to him: Iacocca, p. 120.

p. 317 According to one account...: Lasky, p. 134.

p. 317 "She's a *whore!*": Authors' interview with Cristina Ford.

p. 317 "Yeah, she's a whore....": Ibid.

p. 317 "Anything she said...": Authors' interview with Kitzie Eaton.

p. 318 "Remember, *bambina*, I am the King...": Authors' interview with Cristina Ford.

p. 318 "We were at a dinner party...": Authors' interview with Bobby Kanzler.

p. 318 a secret visit to the cardiologist: Authors' interviews with Joan Bugas and Kathy Ford.

p. 318 he was suddenly stabbed by a pain: Authors' interview with Henry Ford.

p. 318 "I've got to make the biggest decision...": The incident is from the authors' interview with Cristina Ford.

p. 320 Henry in London: Authors' interview with Joan Bugas.

p. 320 "The company has been my mother...": Authors' interview with Kathy Ford.

p. 320 "I did it for my father...": Authors' interviews with Joan Bugas and Kathy Ford.

p. 321 Bugas called his cardiologist: Authors' interview with Joan Bugas.

p. 321 His family did not visit him: Ibid.

p. 321 "I can't believe my son did that....": Authors' interview with Cristina Ford.

p. 322 "*I need to simplify my life.*": Authors' interviews with Joan Bugas, Max Fisher and Kathy Ford.

p. 322 "I've always been envious of GM...": *Fortune*, May 1973.

p. 322 He told them he was confident: Authors' interview with Arjay Miller.

p. 323 "It's just something to think about...": Lasky, p. 159.

p. 323 "We've had a nice oblivion....": Authors' interview with Martha Ford.

p. 323 "Bill did not enjoy...": Authors' interviews with Malcolm Denise, April 21, 1985, and William Clay Ford.

p. 323 "God, I can't believe it....": Authors' interview with Charles Cudlipp.

p. 323 "Bill's a professional dilettante.": Authors' interview with a confidential source, July 7, 1985.

p. 324 "If it meant simply serving as chairman...": *Detroit News*, April 2, 1976.

p. 324 "She was always putting those pills...": Authors' interview with Josephine Ford.

p. 325 He had contempt for Bundy's stewardship: Lally Weymouth, "Tycoon: The Saga of Henry Ford II," *New York Times Magazine*, March 5 and 12, 1978.

p. 325 Henry's resignation: Ibid.

p. 326 "Before the heart attack...": Authors' interview with Ray Stuart.

p. 326 He told the group about his heart: Authors' interview with Arjay Miller.

p. 326 Bill Winn firing: Authors' interviews with Robert S. Dunham and Leo Arthur Kelmenson. See also David Abodhaer, *Iacocca*, p. 189.

p. 327 "Keep that son of a bitch out...": Authors' interviews with Leo Arthur Kelmenson.

p. 327 "Sperlich was a smart-ass....": Authors' interview with John Reinhardt.

p. 327 "I hate that goddamn Sperlich....": Iacocca, p. 122.

p. 327 "Fire him now...": Ibid., p. 123.

p. 327 "If Phil Caldwell were Secretary of State...": Authors' interviews with Joan Bugas.

p. 328 "It was a real crack in the face....": Iacocca, p. 124.

p. 328 "Since 1960 the Ford Division...": Yates, p. 36.

p. 328 the profits of Ford International: Donaldson, Lufkin and Jenrette Research Bulletin, July 1978, Ford Annual Reports, 1972-1978. Authors' interviews with Paul F. Lorenz.

p. 329 "When Henry began to realize...": Iacocca, p. 111.

p. 329 "Henry Ford II is not at this time...": Ibid.

p. 330 Lorenz' bonus: Ibid., p. 114.

p. 331 Cristina abandoned: *Newsweek*, Aug. 22, 1977.

p. 331 "Is Cristina going to be out of town...": Ibid. Also authors' interview with Kathy Ford.

p. 331 They would leave telltale signs: Authors' interview with Cristina Ford.

p. 331 "I would go in there and sit...": Ibid.

p. 332 Pinto trial: See Lee Strobel, *Reckless Homicide* (South Bend, Ind., 1980), p. 22.

p. 332 The author estimated that 180 people could die: Ibid., p. 98.

p. 333 "Iacocca assured Henry Ford...": Authors' interviews with Harley Copp.

p. 333 Roy Cohn suit: New York State Supreme Court index number 71891/78. See also Iacocca, op. cit., and Lasky, op cit. Minutes of annual stockholders' meeting of Ford Motor Co., May 11, 1978, supplied to authors by the company.

p. 333 "I have been criticized...": *New York Times*, May 2, 1978.

p. 334 he had concluded that the suit was a joint production: Authors' interviews with Joan Bugas, Kathy Ford and Walter Hayes, June 19, 1986.

p. 334 Speeches by Henry Ford II, Cohn and Bugas: Minutes of May 11, 1978, stockholders' meeting.

p. 335 The amended suit: New York State Supreme Court, supra.

p. 335 De Tomaso put his holdings behind Cohn: Authors' interviews with Paul F. Lorenz and Walter Hayes.

p. 335 "You know what we're looking down on...": Authors' interviews with George Haviland.

p. 336 "The Iacocca people wanted Bill to do something...": Authors' interviews with Chalmers Goyert.

p. 336 Bill asked several executives what to do: Authors' interviews with Chalmers Goyert and Eugene Bordinat.

p. 336 "Information in that article would have been known to only a few people": Authors' interviews with Paul Lorenz. Also authors' interview with Walter Hayes.

p. 336 "It's him or me....": Authors' interviews with Chalmers Goyert. Also, Iacocca, p. 126.

p. 336 "Well, sometimes you just don't like somebody.": Ibid.

p. 336 "Your timing stinks....": Ibid.

p. 338 "I have no desire to be on the board...": Detroit *News*, July 30, 1970.

p. 338 "Benson kind of...": Authors' interview with Ed Stroh.

p. 338 "Let's go....": Ibid.

p. 339 "What is this, a funeral or a social gathering?": Lasky, p. 185.

p. 339 "Until I was 14...": Ibid, pp. 212ff.

p. 340 "He felt like there was a real barrier....": Cheyfitz and Levin article, supra.

p. 340 Benson, Stroppe and Fuentes: Authors' interview with Bill Stroppe, See also Cheyfitz, and Levin article, supra.

p. 341 "My father was an alcoholic....": Ibid.

p. 342 "I envisaged myself...": Iacocca, p. 142.

p. 342 telling him he found it "shocking": Cheyfitz article, supra.

p. 342 "I've never seen anyone so furious...": Authors' interviews with Joan Bugas.

p. 342 Ford family gathering: Lasky, pp. 7ff. Cheyfitz article, supra. Also, authors' interview with William Ford and William Ford Jr.

p. 343 "Next year, you'll find me in the audience.": Text supplied to authors by Ford Motor Co.

p. 343 Benson and Cohn remarks: Tape of stockholders' meeting supplied by Ford Industrial Archives, transcribed by authors.

p. 343 "You put your money in Chrysler...": Ibid. *New York Times* account, May 21, 1979.

p. 343   "There are no crown princes...": Ibid.

p. 344   "Bill disappointed a lot of people....": Authors' interviews with Chalmers Goyert.

p. 345   "Well that's wonderful....": Authors' interview with William Clay Ford.

p. 345   "I think my brother hates me.": Authors' interviews with Joan Bugas.

p. 346   "She never loved him....": *People*, March 3, 1980.

p. 346   His principal fear was that she would change: Authors' interview with Kathy Ford.

p. 346   "Will you marry me?": Authors' interview with Kathy Ford.

p. 346   "Henry thought I was crazy.": Authors' interview with Kathy Ford.

p. 347   Henry began to talk about his children: Authors' interviews with Joan Bugas.

p. 347   Anne had said: Authors' interview with Kathy Ford.

p. 347   "Please don't let Charlotte and Anne...": Authors' interviews with Joan Bugas.

p. 347   "Call a cab....": Authors' interviews with Kathy Ford and Joan Bugas.

p. 349   "Like maybe after a Thanksgiving dinner...": Authors' interview with Walter Buhl III.

p. 349   Buhl decided it was a triumph not to self-destruct: Ibid.

p. 350   "Ben kept thinking...": Authors' interview with a confidential source, Jan. 27, 1986.

p. 350   "Actually, things worked out for the best...": Authors' interview with William Clay Ford.

p. 350   "I realized that everything I have...": Authors' interview with Billy Ford.

p. 350   "Are you sure that's what you want to do?": Ibid.

p. 351   "It's too big for one man anymore....": Authors' interview with William Clay Ford.

p. 351   "I feel sorry for him....": Ibid.

p. 351   "Edsel says he will never...": *Monthly Detroit*, Feb. 2, 1984.

p. 352   he couldn't keep Iacocca from buying his home: Authors' interview with Robert Kanzler. Also, *Detroit Free Press*, June 15, 1986.

p. 354   "I love this man.": Authors' interview with Frank Denton, May 29, 1985.

p. 354   "I don't care if I ever see that goddamned...": Authors' interviews with Joan Bugas.

p. 354   Arjay Miller always had lunch: Authors' interview with Arjay Miller.

INDEX

first automobile built by, 1-3, 21, 40
grandchildren's relations with, 110-
11, 139-42, 151
Henry II's hatred of, 160, 161, 171,
185, 280
illegitimate son rumors and, *see*
Dahlinger, John
love affairs of, 72-74, 77, 86, 110, 266
mental deterioration of, 136, 145,
146, 168
pacifist views of, 54-58, 59-60, 66
paranoia and ruthlessness of, 59, 61,
74, 79
as representative American, 3, 54,
65, 66, 70-71, 103
rural values of, 84-85, 103, 104
wealth of, 35, 47-48, 51-52, 97
will of, 159, 165-66
Ford, Henry II ("Hank the Deuce"), 111-
12, 127, 156, 355
baptism of, 140
birth of, 64
drinking of, 190, 231, 231-32, 233,
237, 241, 242, 243, 256, 261, 270,
298, 299, 313, 347
excommunication of, 261
as father, 229, 261-62, 265-66, 297,
347
marriages of, *see* Ford, Anne McDonnell; Ford, Cristina Vettore
Austin; Ford, Kathy DuRoss
midlife crisis of, 232-33, 241, 243
outrageous behavior of, 232, 242,
270, 298, 299, 308
in politics, 199, 263-64, 270-72, 275,
288, 299
in World War II, 149-51, 156, 160
Ford, Josephine Ford ("Dodie"), 88, 89,
92, 104, 112, 152-53, 186-87, 200,
209, 253, 284, 288, 330n, 349
alcoholism of, 253, 284, 348
father's relationship with, 111, 137
marriage of, 149
Ford, Kathy DuRoss, 300-04, 312-22,
331, 339, 342, 344, 346, 351, 354
background of, 300
Henry II's affair with, 301-04, 306,
312-15, 317-19, 335
second marriage of, 346-47

Ford, Lynn, 254, 255, 285, 289, 341
Ford, Margaret, 3, 8, 9, 12-15, 16
Ford, Martha Firestone, 188, 189, 230,
256, 286-87, 323, 345, 350
Ford, Mary Litogot O'Hern, 8-11
death of , 11, 12, 13
Henry I influenced by, 9-11
Ford, Muffy, 285-86, 287, 288
Ford, Sheila, 287, 289
Ford, Thomasina, 6
Ford, Walter Buhl ("Wally"), 149, 152-
53, 186, 253, 333
Ford, William (Henry I's brother), 9, 13,
53
Ford, William (Henry I's father), 3, 6-9,
10-12, 43, 49, 84
death of, 33
emigration of, 6-7
Henry I's relationship with, 3, 9, 12,
13, 14, 16, 33, 44
marriage of, 8
Ford, William, Jr. ("Billy"), 285, 287,
340, 350-51
Ford, William, Sr. ("Bill"), 88, 109, 112,
188-90, 225, 233, 253, 285-89, 350,
353-54
alcoholism of, 219, 226, 232, 253,
255-56, 266, 286-87
father's relationship with, 111, 137-
382, 152-53
Henry II and, 216, 218, 286, 287-88,
344-45, 351
Iacocca and, 309-10, 317, 329-30
marriage of, 189
recovery from alcoholism of, 285-86,
287
stock and, 209, 317, 330n
Ford Division 195-96, 201-02, 210, 212,
214, 220, 241
creation of, 193-94
Iacocca in, 247, 249, 250-51
Ford family, 247, 249, 250-51, 276
Henry II's estrangement from, 253-
56, 283-84
Ford Foundation, 208, 208-09, 274, 295-
96, 325
Ford International Division, 190, 226,
257, 259, 291, 307, 328-29, 351